INDIA @100

'*India@100* offers a strategic blueprint for sustained growth by leveraging sound economic policies to enable our nation's rise as a global economic powerhouse and actualize Prime Minister Narendra Modi's vision of *Amrit Kaal*. I hope this book is widely read by those seeking to delve into bold strategies that promise to reshape India's economic landscape.'

—Piyush Goyal
Minister of Commerce and Industry; Consumer Affairs, Food and Public Distribution; and Textiles; and Leader of the House in Rajya Sabha

'*India@100* is a tour de force that brings forth Krishnamurthy V. Subramanian's distinctive courage of conviction and deep understanding of India's economic landscape. With clarity and depth, the book boldly projects India to be an economic powerhouse in 2047 and describes the journey needed to achieve that goal.'

—Ashwini Vaishnaw
Minister for Railways; Communications; and Electronics and Information Technology

'Noted Chicago-school economist, Prof. K Subramanian, uses data and sound economic logic to argue the success of India's ambition to reach a GDP of US$ 55 trillion by 2047 and gladdens the heart of all Indians. The book is a must-read for Indian politicians, bureaucrats, corporate leaders and economic thinkers.'

—N.R. Narayana Murthy
Founder, Infosys

'*India@100* lays out a compelling and comprehensive vision of India for anyone interested in understanding both the challenges as well as the great promise of this vast economy.'

—N. Chandrasekaran
Executive Chairman, Tata Sons

'*India@100* is a bold, audacious book for a $55 trillion economy from the present $3.8 trillion in 24 years. The detailed analysis of how we can get there is fascinating. I congratulate Subbu for ambition and belief in the Indian awakening.'

—Uday Kotak
Founder and Director, Kotak Mahindra Bank

'Big things never happened by thinking small. Prof. Krishnamurthy Subramanian reminds us of that in *India@100*. With so much opportunity ahead, fact-based insights like this book can help those interested in the country's future contribute to the next stage of India's economic journey.'

—Michael Miebach
CEO, Mastercard

'Subbu's intriguing and optimistic projection is based on his economic analysis and stint as an impactful policymaker both in New Delhi and in Washington. Personally, I resonate especially with the thesis that social and economic inclusions are necessary and almost-sufficient conditions for an idyllic future for India.'

—Tarun Khanna
Professor and Director, Lakshmi Mittal and Family
South Asia Institute, Harvard University

INDIA @100

ENVISIONING TOMORROW'S ECONOMIC POWERHOUSE

KRISHNAMURTHY SUBRAMANIAN

RUPA

Published by
Rupa Publications India Pvt. Ltd 2024
7/16, Ansari Road, Daryaganj
New Delhi 110002

Sales centres:
Bengaluru Chennai
Hyderabad Jaipur Kathmandu
Kolkata Mumbai Prayagraj

P-ISBN: 978-93-90260-83-6
E-ISBN: 978-93-90260-61-4

Fourth impression 2024

10 9 8 7 6 5 4

Printed in India

My Appa dear,
Your love is always crystal clear;
You paved my way, though your life was askew,
For you were denied education by poverty's brew.

Through your hardships deep, you forged my fate,
You ensured my comfort, despite your young shoulders bearing elders' weight;
You showed a father's love, one that you never knew,
For you lost your own Appa when you were just a few.

In your heart burnt a patriot's flame,
Burned bright, never tame;
For the nation's pride, I saw you toiling away,
In your difficult roles in Indian Railways, day by day.

Appa, from up in the stars, I know you see,
Satisfied that your hard work's fruits luckily bloomed in me;
With pride and love, I hope you witness how your legacy lives on,
In every step, and in every dawn.

So, stay peaceful and happy, my dear Appa, in celestial space,
As I hold close your sacrifices, your grace;
For your labour, your strife,
Gifted me this blessed life.

CONTENTS

LIST OF ABBREVIATIONS

AA	Account Aggregator
AAI	Airports Authority of India
ABRY	Atmanirbhar Bharat Rozgar Yojana
ACE	Advanced Chemistry Cell
AEA	American Economic Association
AEP	Assembled End Products
AERA	Airports Economic Regulatory Authority
AI	Artificial Intelligence
AIIMS	All India Institute of Medical Sciences
AIoT	Artificial Intelligence of Things
ANBC	Adjusted Net Bank Credit
APMC	Agricultural Produce Marketing Committee
AR	Augmented Reality
ARC	Administrative Reforms Commission
ASI	Annual Survey of Industries
BIFR	Board for Industrial and Financial Reconstruction
BOB	Bank of Baroda
BPCL	Bharat Petroleum Corporation Limited
BPL	Below the Poverty Line
BPO	Business Process Outsourcing
CAB	Current Account Balance
CAD	Current Account Deficit
CAG	Comptroller and Auditor General
CAGR	Compound Annual Growth Rate
CapEx, Capex	Capital Expenditure
CapEx, Revex	Revenue Expenditure
CBI	Central Bureau of Investigation
CBO	Congressional Budget Office

CCI	Competition Commission of India
CCR	Case Clearance Rate
CDRF	Climate Disaster Reserve Fund
CENTA	Centre for Teacher Accreditation
CEPEJ	European Commission for the Efficiency of Justice
CIBIL	Credit Information Bureau (India) Limited
CIL	Coal India Limited
CLV	Customer Lifetime Value
CMIE	Centre for Monitoring Indian Economy
COE	Council of Europe
CPI	Consumer Price Index
CPSE	Central Public Sector Enterprises
CSS	Central Staffing Scheme
CRILC	Central Repository of Information on Large Credits
CVC	Central Vigilance Commission
D&S Court	District & Subordinate Court
DARPG	Department of Administrative Reforms and Public Grievances
DBT	Direct Benefit Transfers
DFI	Doubling Farmers' Income
DOPT	Department of Personnel and Training
DPI	Digital Public Infrastructure
DRT	Debts Recovery Tribunal
ECA	Essential Commodities Act, 1955
ECLGS	Emergency Credit Line Guarantee Scheme
EDGAR	Electronic Data Gathering, Analysis, and Retrieval
EHR	Electronic Health Record
EM-DAT	Emergency Events Database
EME	Emerging Market Economy
e-NAM	e-National Agriculture Market
EoDB	Ease of Doing Business

EPF	Employment Provident Fund
ESRL	Earth System Research Laboratories
EU	European Union
EY	Ernst & Young
FAO	Food and Agriculture Organization
FCI	Food Corporation of India
FDI	Foreign Direct Investment
FEMA	Foreign Exchange Management Act
FERA	Foreign Exchange Regulation Act
FLS	Foundational Learning Study
FPI	Foreign Portfolio Investment
FRBM	Fiscal Responsibility and Budget Management
FRED	Federal Reserve Economic Data
FTA	Free Trade Agreement
FTC	US Federal Trade Commission
FTE	Full-Time Equivalent
FY	Financial Year
GCF	Gross Capital Formation
GCP	Global Carbon Project
GDDP	Gross District Domestic Product
GDIM	Global Database on Intergenerational Mobility
GER	Gross Enrolment Ratio
GFC	Global Financial Crisis
GFCF	Gross Fixed Capital Formation
GHGs	Greenhouse Gases
GIC	General Insurance Corporation of India
GII	Global Innovation Index
GLD	The Great Lockdown
GoI	Government of India
GPF	General Provident Fund
GPS	Global Positioning System

GSDP	Gross State Domestic Product
GST	Goods and Services Tax
GSTN	Goods and Services Tax Network
GVA	Gross Value Added
GVC	Global Value Chain
GW	Gigawatts
HCR	Human Capital and Research
HE	Higher Education
HELP	Hydrocarbon Exploration and Licensing Policy
HP	Hodrick–Prescott
HPCL	Hindustan Petroleum Corporation Limited
I4I	Ideas for India
IAMAI	Internet and Mobile Association of India
IAS	Indian Administrative Service
IBBI	Insolvency and Bankruptcy Board of India
IBC	Insolvency and Bankruptcy Code
IBEF	India Brand Equity Foundation
IBS	Indian Business School
ICT	Information and Communication Technology
IIM	Indian Institute of Management
IIT	Indian Institute of Technology
IMF	International Monetary Fund
IMR	Infant Mortality Rate
IoT	Internet of Things
IP	Intellectual Property
IPCC	Intergovernmental Panel on Climate Change
IPCL	Indian Petrochemicals Corporation Limited
IPR	Intellectual Property Regime
IRDA	Insurance Regulatory and Development Authority
IT	Income Tax
JEC	Joint Economic Committee

JNN	Johnny No Name
KTO	Knowledge and Technology Outputs
LAYS	Learning-Adjusted Years of Schooling
LFPR	Labour Force Participation Rate
LGD	Loss Given Default
LIC	Life Insurance Corporation of India
LiFE	Lifestyle for Environment
LMICs	Low- and Middle-Income Countries
LOOP	Law of One Price
MCA21	Ministry of Corporate Affairs database
MFIL	Modern Foods Industries (India) Ltd
MFI	Microfinance Institution
MHA	Ministry of Home Affairs
MHRD	Ministry of Human Resource Development
mHealth	Mobile Health
MIT	Massachusetts Institute of Technology
ML	Machine Learning
MMR	Maternal Mortality Ratio
MNE	Multinational Enterprise
MoD	Ministry of Defence
MoHPW	Ministry of Health and Family Welfare
MOSPI	Ministry of Statistics and Programme Implementation
MRTP	Monopolies and Restrictive Trade Practices
MRTPC	Monopolies and Restrictive Trade Practices Commission
MSME	Micro, Small and Medium Enterprises
MSP	Minimum Support Price
MUL	Maruti Udyog Limited
NAPCC	National Action Plan on Climate Change
NBFC	Non-Banking Financial Company
NCD	Non-Communicable Diseases

NCEI	National Centers for Environmental Information
NCERT	National Council of Educational Research and Training
NDC	Nationally Determined Contribution
NDEAR	National Digital Education Architecture
NDHM	National Digital Health Mission
NDMA	National Disaster Management Authority
NELP	New Exploration Licensing Policy
NEP	National Education Policy
NHA	National Health Accounts
NHM	National Health Mission
NHP	National Health Policy
NHS	National Health Service
NJDG	National Judicial Data Grid
NLP	Natural Language Processing
NOAA	National Oceanic and Atmospheric Administration
NPA	Non-Performing Assets
NPB	New Private Banks
NPCI	National Payments Corporation of India
NP	Network Products
NRAI	National Restaurant Association of India
NRDC	National Research Development Corporation
NSDP	Net State Domestic Product
NSSO	National Sample Survey Organization
NSE	New Structural Economics
NTC	National Textile Corporation Ltd
NTS-I	National Testing Service-India
NVA	Net Value Added
OCEN	Open Credit Enablement Network
OECD	Organisation for Economic Co-operation and Development
ONGC	Oil and Natural Gas Commission

OOP	Out-of-Pocket (Payments)
OOPE	Out-of-Pocket Expenditure
OPM	Office of Personnel Management
ORF	Observer Research Foundation
P&C	Parts and Components
PD	Possibility of Default
PDS	Public Distribution System
PF	Provident Fund
PIH	Permanent Income Hypothesis
PLI	Production Linked Incentive
PM	Prime Minister
PMJAY	Pradhan Mantri Jan Arogya Yojana
PMJDY	Pradhan Mantri Jan Dhan Yojana
PNB	Punjab National Bank
PPP	Purchasing Power Parity
PSB	Public Sector Bank
PSE	Public Sector Enterprise
PSL	Priority-Sector Lending
QOF	Quality and Outcomes Framework
R&D	Research and Development
RBI	Reserve Bank of India
ROA	Return on Assets
ROC	Registrar of Companies
ROE	Return on Equity
SBI	State Bank of India
SEBI	Securities and Exchange Board of India
SEC	Securities and Exchange Commission
SME	Small and Medium Enterprise
TFP	Total Factor Productivity
TFR	Total Fertility Rate
TPDS	Targeted Public Distribution System

TRAI	Telecom Regulatory Authority of India
TVE	Township and Village Enterprise
UNCTAD	United Nations Conference on Trade and Development
UN-DESA	United Nations Department of Economic and Social Affairs
UNWPP	United Nations World Population Prospects
UPI	Unified Payments Interface
VC	Venture Capital
VR	Virtual Reality
WHO	World Health Organization

PREFACE

Oozing confidence, India@100 can be a $55 trillion economy if India doubles down on the sound economic policies implemented in the last decade to grow at 8 per cent annually. The next two decades present an unparalleled opportunity for India to emerge as a leading economy of that time, a prospect that arises only once in several centuries.

A $55 Trillion Economy in 2047: Audacious or Achievable?

You may question if this estimate is bold and overly ambitious. After all, global consulting firm Ernst & Young (EY) predicts India's GDP to be less than half that size at $26 trillion by 2047.[1] Global investment bank Goldman Sachs forecasts India's GDP to be about $50 trillion three decades later by 2075.[2]

Early contrarian predictions may often be seen as bold. My assessment of a $55 trillion economy in 2047—and not in 2075—stems from the combination of a careful tracking of data, a nuanced understanding of Indian realities and clear thinking using fundamental economic principles. As a researcher, I was taught to follow Sherlock Holmes's credo of: 'Never theorize before you have the data. Invariably you end up twisting facts to suit theories instead of theories to suit facts.' I have also been fortunate enough to gain insight into India by living here. My understanding of the Indian economy combines global comparisons with the rigour honed through decades of academic research. Further, my initial training as an engineer taught me to think clearly by applying fundamental concepts ab initio, free from any preconceived notions.

I have lived through the incredulity that early contrarian predictions often evoke. At the height of Covid-19 in September 2020, when many were

[1]'EY Projects India to Become a US$26 Trillion Economy by 2047 with a Six-Fold Increase in per Capita Income to US$15,000', *EY*, 18 January 2023, http://tinyurl.com/3umjnzsd. Accessed on 21 February 2024.

[2]'How India Could Rise to the World's Second-Biggest Economy', *Goldman Sachs*, 6 July 2023, http://tinyurl.com/mspbzf9j. Accessed on 21 February 2024.

forecasting doom for the Indian economy, my analysis foretold a V-shaped economic recovery for India. The subsequent consistent growth of over 7 per cent has vindicated this prediction.[3] The basis for this prediction was a comprehensive weekly tracking of about 60 high-frequency indicators conducted by my team at the Ministry of Finance. Additionally, in contrast to the commentary claiming structural problems hobbling growth before Covid-19, I strongly believed that structural flaws did not cause the growth slowdown. The decline in the GDP growth before Covid-19 was a result of the overhang of crony lending, leading to the 'dual balance-sheet problem' involving both corporates and banks in India. Thus, I was convinced that the decline in GDP during the pandemic was due to the restrictions on economic activities during the lockdown, rather than any structural problems with the Indian economy.

The assessment of India as a \$55 trillion economy in 2047 appears audacious, but only if we do not pay careful attention to *all* the underlying drivers that contribute to its growth. The predictions by EY and Goldman Sachs may appear reasonable if we assume that the annual depreciation of the rupee/dollar (₹/\$) would follow the historical pattern of nominal depreciation over the last three decades. Yet, a regime change is in the offing for the ₹/\$ due to two seminal macroeconomic changes in India. First, India has implemented the inflation targeting framework, which requires the Reserve Bank of India (RBI) to target inflation of 4 ± 2 per cent. Unlike historical inflation of over 7 per cent, this policy change reduces average inflation by at least 2 per cent when compared to historical average. Conceptually, the nominal depreciation of the ₹/\$ equals the real depreciation plus the difference between the rate of inflation in India and the US. As a lower rate of inflation in India leads to lower nominal depreciation of the currency, this change can reduce the nominal depreciation per annum by at least 2 per cent.

Second, the implementation of several structural reforms after 2014 has resulted in a significant increase in productivity growth in the Indian economy. Data from the Penn World Tables, which economists across the globe use to study the drivers of economic growth, shows that the

[3]'People More Pessimistic than Needed, India Will Have V-Shaped Recovery, Says CEA Subramanian', *Moneycontrol*, 14 May 2020, http://tinyurl.com/rchbt7mh. Accessed on 21 February 2024.

rate of productivity growth, which equalled 1.3 per cent from 2002 to 2013, rose to 2.7 per cent 2014 onwards. This increase can be attributed to the reformist zeal of the Narendra Modi-led government.

Readers may question why the higher rate of productivity growth did not result in higher rate of overall economic growth. It is important to understand that the rate of economic growth is determined not only by the rate of productivity growth, but also by the level of investment in the economy. The decline in investment due to the dual balance sheet problem prevented significant growth despite the increase in productivity. However, the tepid investment environment has changed as the government has taken the lead in making unprecedented investments in digital public infrastructure (DPI) and physical infrastructure. Private investment is joining this phenomenon, as the recent *State of the Economy* report by the Reserve Bank of India indicates double-digit growth in private investment. The higher rate of productivity growth will continue owing to the continued formalization of the economy as well as investments in DPI. In fact, it is not just the formalization that can boost productivity growth, but also the improvement in productivity among firms in the formal sector to match their global peers. The increased rate of investment can combine with greater productivity to deliver real GDP growth of 8 per cent per annum for the next two decades. This substantial growth in real GDP can contribute to a significant increase in real per capita income in India, thereby leading to higher real appreciation of the ₹/$.

Post the liberalization of the Indian economy in 1991, higher rate of growth in India vis-à-vis the US has delivered real appreciation of about 1–1.5 per cent per annum. However, this appreciation has been offset by high difference in inflation between India and the US of about 5 per cent. As a result, nominal depreciation of ₹/$ has been between 3.5 and 4.5 per cent per annum over the last three decades. In contrast, because of the two seminal changes described above, the annual rate of nominal depreciation of the ₹/$ is likely to be about 0.5 per cent per annum if the GDP can grow at 8 per cent annually. Of course, in the scenarios where GDP grows at lower rates if the risks to 8 per cent growth crystallize, the rate of depreciation would be greater resulting in lower size of the economy in 2047.

8 per cent Growth: Ambitious but Achievable

So is 8 per cent growth a done deal? No. In its 75-year history, India has never grown at an average rate of 8 per cent for over two decades. In the last two decades, India has recorded growth of over 7 per cent. Amidst uncertainty about global growth, growing at 8 per cent is, no doubt, ambitious. But India can grow at this rate even in this global environment provided we redouble our focus on sound economic policy that is carefully tailored to suit India's needs.

China, whose GDP per capita in 2007 was about the same level as that of India now, experienced an average growth rate of about 8 per cent since then. It is important to note that China managed to achieve this high rate of growth despite the Global Financial Crisis (GFC) significantly affecting global demand. This was made possible through its policy framework that enabled China to successfully utilize its domestic engines of growth together with exports, allowing the country to detach itself from the global economy and achieve a significantly higher rate of growth. India, with a demographic dividend similar to what China had in previous decades, can grow at similar rates by steadfastly implementing favourable economic policies.

This book provides a comprehensive explanation of the four-pillar economic strategy that India must pursue to achieve the target of 8 per cent growth in the next two decades. This is similar to the approach followed by other developed economies. In the late 1970s, Chinese leader Deng Xiaoping envisioned Four Modernizations—agriculture, industry, defence, and science and technology—that laid the foundation for the country's rapid economic growth and turned it into the powerhouse it is today. Japan's post-War resurrection stemmed from its economic vision, which hinged on four pillars: industrial policy, education, infrastructure and export-oriented growth. This strategic framework propelled Japan into becoming an economic juggernaut, underscoring the transformative power of a well-structured economic vision. Similarly, Germany's famed 'social market economy' relied on a four-pillar approach comprising a balance between a competitive market economy, a strong welfare state, labour market policies and active fiscal policies. This comprehensive strategy laid the groundwork for Germany's economic prowess.

In order to actualize Prime Minister (PM) Narendra Modi's vision of

Atmanirbhar Bharat (self-reliant India), I propose an economic strategy based on four key pillars. These pillars, which provide the essential foundations for prosperous and equitable progress, are shown in Figure 1 below.

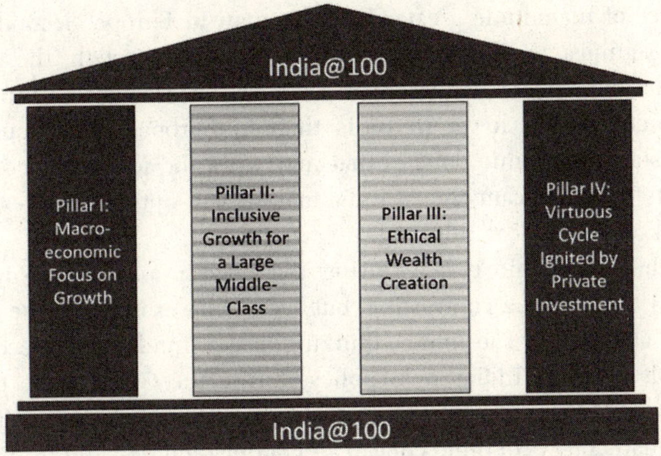

Figure 1: Four Pillars to realize PM Modi's vision of Atmanirbhar Bharat
Source: Author's design

Pitfalls to Progress

Given the unparalleled opportunity that beckons India@100, I cannot emphasize enough the imperative for deep thinking to evolve economic policies that suit the Indian realities, on the one hand, and ab initio thinking using fundamental economic principles, on the other hand. Both these aspects are a sine qua non for India to deliver 8 per cent growth for the next two decades.

Fiscal policy provides a glaring example of the first pitfall that we should avoid. While the thresholds of 3 per cent to GDP fiscal deficit and 66 per cent debt to GDP are bandied around as the Holy Grail for macroeconomic stability and fiscal sustainability, the evidence supporting such thresholds is scant. Indeed, these thresholds were the outcome of a political agreement—the Maastricht Treaty that brought the European nations into a monetary union—that required fiscal coordination for the monetary union. Yet, fiscal rules suggested by committees that have studied the Fiscal Responsibility and Budget Management (FRBM) Act, 2003, have advocated these thresholds without accounting adequately for two salient differences between India and the European Union (EU). First, as highlighted in the *Economic Survey 2020–21*, the need for the sovereign to invest in infrastructure—physical, human and digital—is an order of magnitude greater in India than in Europe. Second, given India's significantly higher potential for economic growth, the risks to debt sustainability engendered by sovereign borrowing to fund such investment are far lower in India than in Europe. Thus, injudicious cut–paste of economic policies that may work for advanced economies presents the significant risk of India making sub-optimal choices due to the lack of deep, clear thinking.

India's economic policy during the once-in-a-century pandemic, Covid-19, provides a contrasting, but successful, example of the second pitfall: abandoning ab initio thinking using fundamental economic principles. Unlike India's own policy during the GFC or the policies implemented by advanced economies during the pandemic, India used the fundamental economic concepts of supply and demand to diagnose the crisis as a twin shock to aggregate demand and aggregate supply. This contrasted with typical textbook theory characterizing an economic crisis as a negative shock to aggregate demand. This thinking helped India implement a judicious mix of supply and demand-side policies to emerge with high growth, moderate inflation, and strong macro fundamentals, despite the Russia–Ukraine war adding to the economic woes posed by the pandemic.

For India to realize the opportunity that only comes once in a few centuries, every Indian must internalize the immortal words of Swami Vivekananda: 'Arise, awake and stop not till the goal is reached.' Only then can India capitalize on the unprecedented opportunity to emerge as a $55 trillion economic powerhouse in its centenary year.

SECTION ONE

THE BIG PICTURE

INDIA STANDS AT THE CUSP of transformation, poised to redefine its global stature as it marches towards its centennial milestone. As the world's largest democracy and the fastest-growing major economy, India's journey towards becoming an economic powerhouse by its 100th year of Independence is both compelling and complex. In the first section, I explore how India's economic landscape will appear in 2047 and lay out the economic roadmap that India must pursue to fulfil its dream of becoming tomorrow's economic powerhouse.

Chapters 1 and 2 provide a panoramic view of India's economic terrain in 2047 by projecting ab initio the potential growth rate of GDP that India can achieve in the coming two-and-a-half decades. These growth rates are then utilized to forecast the trajectory of the rupee/dollar (₹/$) exchange rate, and to estimate the size of the Indian economy in US$ in 2047. Chapter 3 ventures into the need for innovative economic policies, advocating sui generis approaches that are tailored to India's unique context but arrived at through deep and clear thinking that incorporate fundamental economic principles. At the heart of India's quest for economic sovereignty lies the concept of Atmanirbhar Bharat or self-reliant India. In Chapter 4, the focus is on delineating the four pillars that can shape PM Modi's vision of Atmanirbhar Bharat. By elucidating a strategic roadmap using these four pillars, this chapter charts the course for India's sustainable and equitable progress. In the final chapter, the spotlight is on overcoming the middle-income trap, a challenge faced by many emerging economies. Drawing lessons from global experiences and domestic imperatives, this chapter unpacks the drivers of the middle-income trap and prescribes strategies to transcend it.

1

TOMORROW'S ECONOMIC POWERHOUSE

India@100's Economic Landscape

It is the 15th of August 2047. As I look through my 75-year-old eyes that day, I see the sky painted in vibrant shades of saffron, white and green. I am captivated by a mesmerizing display created by artificial intelligence (AI), which showcases the Ashoka Chakra spinning rapidly and expanding from a small, delicate one *anna* to a larger circumference that resembles the celestial ring of the rupee symbol. I reflect on my father's discussions about the one anna—a unit of currency worth one-sixteenth of a rupee used mostly in British India—and wonder: back in 1991, while reading about economic liberalization in the reading room of Hall-2 at the Indian Institute of Technology (IIT) Kanpur, did I even imagine that the rupee would have this aura to it in 2047?

In a pace not befitting a 75-year-old's knees, I step out to soak in the celebratory atmosphere. The streets are adorned with colourful decorations, and the air is filled with the sound of joyous celebrations. Youngsters, dressed in traditional attire, eagerly await the PM's address. Prior to its commencement, virtual fireworks fill the sky with intricate designs and shapes that represent India's rich culture and history. The streets are lined with AI-generated holographic displays, showcasing India's journey from 1947 to India@100. Throughout this year-long celebration, citizens have tuned in to virtual reality shows that transported them through pivotal moments in India's history. This unique experience has allowed them to witness first-hand the struggles and triumphs that have shaped the nation's journey towards this significant milestone. As my 75-year-old memory sometimes orphans me, I ask a child: what is the occasion for this revelry? He responds, 'Oh! It is 15 August 2047! Don't you want to celebrate our nation's 100th birthday?'

No doubt, this imagery of our Independence Day in 2047 is soaked in optimism. But does reason back this optimism? How would India's economy look in 2047? What would be the size of our economy? Of course, it is impossible to predict the future with certainty. However, based on current progress and the economic vision for India, I describe, in this chapter, my projection for the Indian economy in 2047.

To estimate the size of the Indian economy in 2047, I analyse rupee/dollar (₹/$) depreciation over various 25-year periods in the past using the concept of relative purchasing power parity (PPP) and the Balassa–Samuelson effect. After finding that the framework effectively explains out-of-sample the nominal depreciation over various 25-year periods in the past, I use it to project the value of ₹/$ in 2047. The projections, of course, must be taken with the caveat that they cannot incorporate unanticipated events such as pandemics or wars that can change the course of economies in completely unanticipated ways.

The next two decades present an unparalleled opportunity for India to emerge as a leading global economy, a prospect that arises only once in several centuries. If India redoubles its commitment to the sound economic policies implemented in the last decade, aiming for an annual growth rate of 8 per cent, India@100 could potentially achieve a $55 trillion economy! Scepticism may arise regarding the boldness of this estimate as the global consulting firm Ernst & Young (EY) predicts India's GDP to be less than half that size at $26 trillion by 2047,[1] while the global investment bank Goldman Sachs forecasts India's GDP to be about $50 trillion by 2075.[2]

The assessment of India as a $55 trillion economy in 2047 appears audacious, but it only holds true if we pay careful attention to *all* the underlying drivers that contribute to its growth. The GDP growth measured in US$ equals the nominal GDP growth measured in ₹ minus (or plus) the depreciation (or appreciation) of the ₹ with respect to the $. As depreciation corresponds to the value of the ₹ reducing with respect to the $, depreciation subtracts from GDP growth as measured in $. Conversely, as appreciation corresponds to the value of the ₹ increasing with respect to the $, appreciation adds to GDP growth as measured in $. Therefore, GDP growth (in $) = Real GDP growth (in ₹) + Inflation in India – Rate of Depreciation of ₹ with respect to the $.

If we assume real GDP growth to be 7 per cent, inflation to be 5 per cent and the rate of depreciation of the ₹ with respect to the $ to be

[1]Ernst & Young LLP, *India@100: Realizing the Potential of a US$26 Trillion Economy*, 2023, http://tinyurl.com/42zdb5ky. Accessed on 30 January 2024.

[2]'The Global Economy in 2075: Growth Slows as Asia Rises', *Goldman Sachs*, 8 December 2022, http://tinyurl.com/22busc3e. Accessed on 30 January 2024.

3 per cent—which approximates the historical rate of depreciation over the last three decades—then the rate of GDP growth as measured in $ equals 9 (7+5–3) per cent. To understand the EY estimate of $26 trillion by 2047, we can use the rule of 70, which provides a simple rule to calculate the number of years required for a sum of money to double in value. At 9 per cent rate of growth, the number of years equals 70/9 = 8 years. Over the 24-year period from 2023 to 2047, the GDP in $ terms would thus double thrice, or equivalently eight times (2×2×2=8). As the GDP in 2023 was approximately $3.25 trillion, it would increase from $3.25 trillion in 2023 to equal $3.25×8 = $26 trillion in 2047. Thus, the EY prediction appears reasonable if we assume that the annual depreciation of the ₹/$ would follow the historical pattern of nominal depreciation of 3 per cent over the last three decades.

Yet, a regime change is in the offing for the ₹/$ due to two seminal macroeconomic changes in India. First, India has implemented the inflation targeting framework, which requires the Reserve Bank of India (RBI) to target inflation of 4 ± 2 per cent. Unlike historical inflation of over 7 per cent, this policy change reduces average inflation by at least 2 per cent when compared to the historical average. In fact, after the inflation targeting framework was introduced in 2016, the average inflation over 2016 to 2023 equals precisely 5 per cent. Conceptually, the nominal depreciation of the ₹/$ equals the real depreciation plus the difference between the rate of inflation in India and the US. As a higher rate of inflation in India leads to greater nominal depreciation of the currency, this change can reduce the nominal depreciation per annum by at least 2 per cent.

Second, as you will read in detail in Chapter 2, the implementation of several structural reforms after 2014 has resulted in a significant increase in productivity growth in the Indian economy. Data from the Penn World Tables, which economists across the globe use to study the drivers of economic growth, show that the rate of productivity growth, which equalled 1.3 per cent from 2002 to 2013, rose to 2.7 per cent from 2014.[3] This increase can be attributed to the reforms implemented by the Narendra Modi-led government.

---

[3]Feenstra, Robert C., Robert Inklaar and Marcel P. Timmer, 'The Next Generation of the Penn World Table', *American Economic Review*, Vol. 105, No. 10, 2015, pp. 3150–82, www.ggdc.net/pwt. Accessed on 8 April 2024.

Readers may question why the higher rate of productivity growth did not result in higher rate of overall economic growth. It is important to understand that the rate of economic growth is determined not only by the rate of productivity growth but also by the level of investment in the economy. The decline in investment due to the dual balance-sheet problem prevented significant growth despite the increase in productivity. However, the tepid investment environment has changed, as the government has taken a lead in making unprecedented investments in DPI and physical infrastructure. The higher rate of productivity growth will continue owing to the continued formalization of the economy as well as investments in DPI. In fact, it is not just the formalization that can boost productivity growth, but also the improvement in productivity among firms in the formal sector to match their global peers. The increased rate of investment can combine with greater productivity to deliver real GDP growth of 8 per cent per annum for the next two decades. This substantial growth in real GDP can contribute to a significant increase in real per capita income in India, thereby leading to higher real appreciation of the ₹/$. Because of the two seminal changes—lower inflation and higher growth rate in GDP per capita described above—the annual rate of nominal depreciation of the ₹/$ is likely to be about 0.5 per cent per annum if the GDP can grow at 8 per cent annually.

Using the lower rate of depreciation and 8 per cent real GDP growth, we can recalculate the GDP in $ in 2047. The rate of GDP growth in $ now equals 12.5 (8+5–0.5) per cent. Using the rule of 70, this implies doubling in less than six years as 70/12.5=5.6=6. Thus, over the 24-year period from 2023 to 2047, the GDP in $ terms would double four times, or equivalently 16 times (2×2×2×2=16). So, the GDP would increase from $3.25 trillion in 2023 to equal $3.25×16=$52 trillion in 2047. As the doubling would occur every 5.6 (not six) years, the actual estimate would be higher at $55 trillion in 2047.

The above estimations clearly demonstrate that the difference in the EY prediction of $26 trillion by 2047 and my estimate of $55 trillion by 2047 stems primarily from the difference in the rate of depreciation for the ₹/$. While the EY and Goldman Sachs predictions do not seem to account for the regime changes that are likely to deliver significantly lower level of depreciation of the ₹/$, my estimates account for this important difference.

Conceptual Description of the Framework

Conceptually, noting that a negative value for depreciation implies appreciation, we can write:

Nominal Depreciation of ₹/$ = Real Depreciation of
₹/$ + (US inflation − Indian inflation)

While depreciation of ₹/$ in the short term depends upon several factors, research in international economics shows that the real depreciation over long horizons such as a few decades depends primarily on the difference in productivity in the tradeable sector between India and the US.

Box 1: Testing the Conceptual Framework for Predicting INR–USD Movement over 25-Year Periods

The well-known theory of PPP posits the idea that a (foreign) exchange rate equalizes prices of identical goods (or baskets of goods) in different countries. Economists think about PPP as the application of the Law of One Price (LOOP). Intuitively, the law makes sense because, if after adjusting for transaction costs, the price of a tradeable good is different in two geographies, then market participants will utilize this opportunity to profit. As 'buy low, sell high' represents the maxim for making such profits, the buying of the good in the lower price geography will raise its price, while the (simultaneous) selling of the good in the higher price geography for making profits will lower its price. This process will continue till the price equalizes between the two geographies, thereby establishing the LOOP. In other words, profits from deviations in the LOOP represent 'off-equilibrium' phenomena that lead to the equilibrium of the LOOP. Applied to the context of exchange rates, if a change in the exchange rate gives rise to a price discrepancy internationally, this will soon lead to arbitrage and, thereby, to an adjustment in prices or the exchange rate or both.

As PPP rarely holds in absolute terms across countries, economists generally examine if relative PPP exists among countries. Relative PPP captures the *change* in the price index domestically vis-à-vis the change in the price index for the foreign country but converted into local currency. For the ₹/$ exchange rate, therefore, we analyse the change in the consumer price index (CPI) for India (denominated in ₹) and the change in the CPI for the US (converted into ₹).

Figure 1 shows this relationship for relative PPP. The top panel shows this relationship for the entire time-period from 1990 to 2022, while the middle panel shows the relationship for 1993 to 2007, thereby excluding the years just after liberalization and the two years during the GFC 2008 and 2009 as potential outliers when the relationship may be less likely to hold. The bottom panel shows the relationship from 2010 to 2022. We find that the relationship has become much tighter 2010 onwards with the R^2 equalling over 99 per cent. The relationship was less tight—but still very significant with an R^2 of over 95 per cent—during the previous periods as well. Thus, we can conclude that relative PPP prevails robustly between India and the US over the last three decades.

Sample period: 1990–2022

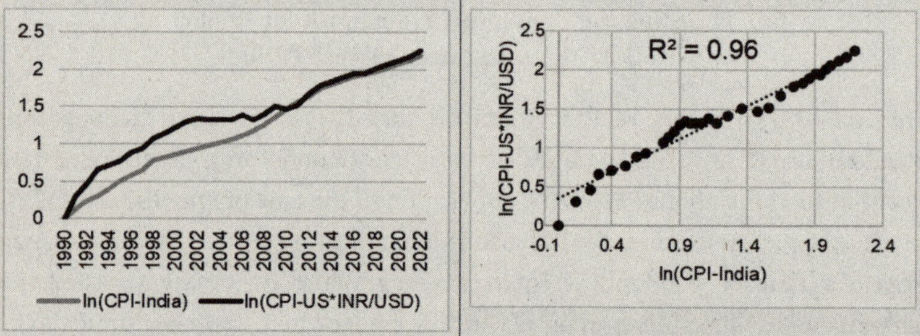

Sample period: 1993–2007

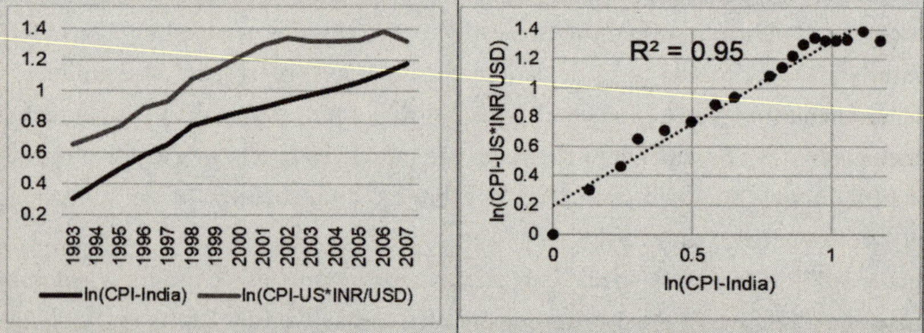

Sample period: 2010–22

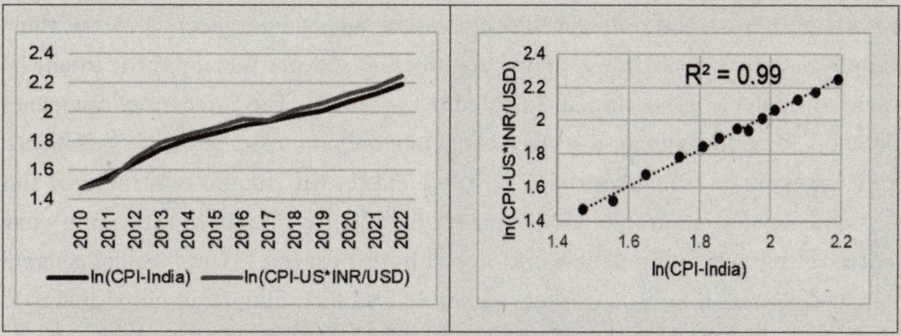

Figure 1: Relative PPP for India and the US (1990–2022)
Source: The World Bank; IMF; author's calculations

The economy of every country comprises tradeable sectors and non-tradeable sectors. Tradeable sectors denote those sectors of the economy that produce goods or services that can be imported and exported via international trade, and include industries that produce mobile phones, computers, toys and clothes, among others. Non-tradeable sectors include industries producing goods or mainly services that cannot be traded. For example, let's say you are interested in getting an Ayurvedic massage. If the masseuse in Hyderabad quotes ₹5,000 per massage session, you cannot bargain with him by saying that the masseuse in Guntur charges only ₹1,000 per massage. This is because the masseuse in Guntur cannot provide the massage service in Hyderabad. Similarly, it is impossible to have your hair styled by a barber in Guntur while being located in Hyderabad. Likewise, you cannot engage in sightseeing in Shimla or explore the temples in Varanasi from the comfort of your home in Hyderabad. None of these services can be traded, and, as a result, potential opportunities for profiting from differences in prices across geographies do not exist in these sectors. Therefore, in the context of PPP, international price discrepancies can continue to exist.

To examine the currency appreciation and depreciation, it is important to incorporate changes in relative productivity of the tradeable sectors vis-à-vis the non-tradeable sectors in India and the US. Suppose a country experiences productivity growth in its traded goods sector. So, firms operating in this sector will demand more labour. Over long horizons, such as a 25-year period, the long-run supply of labour will also increase in the tradeable sectors when productivity increases. As an example, consider the increase in productivity in software services in India in the 1990s (from zero as this sector did not exist before the 1990s). Not only did the demand for software engineers increase, their supply also grew over time as many engineering colleges increased the intake in their computer engineering and related departments. The increase in aggregate demand for and aggregate supply of labour will increase both the workforce and wages in tradeable sectors. These two effects will combine to increase the demand for non-tradeable goods and services. For example, as more well-paid software engineers joined the workforce in India post the 1990s, they collectively demanded more domestic workers and drivers while indulging in more domestic tourism and wanting fancier haircuts and more massages.

In general, productivity in the non-traded sectors lags behind productivity in the traded sectors. This is because firms in the traded sectors face competition from international firms. If domestic firms do not keep pace with international firms in increasing their productivity, they will go out of business. Therefore, the need for firms in the traded sectors to match global productivity is much higher. As the productivity in the non-tradeable sectors lags behind that in the traded sectors, the increase in the demand for goods and services offered by firms in the non-traded sectors increases more than its supply, thereby pushing up prices in the non-traded sectors.

As the price level in a country equals the weighted average of the prices in all sectors of the economy, the domestic price level is given by the weighted average of the prices in the traded and non-traded sectors, with the weights being the relative contribution of the sectors in the economy. Therefore, higher productivity in the tradeable sector in the domestic economy leads to higher overall prices in the domestic economy. As real appreciation of the ₹ with respect to the $ corresponds to the increase in the cost of living in India relative to the US, provided the nominal exchange rate for the ₹/$ is the same, an increase in productivity in the tradeable sector in India will lead to a real (not nominal) appreciation of the ₹ versus the $. This is the essence of the Balassa–Samuelson effect.

Improvements in productivity usually manifest slowly over a long time. Therefore, we expect such effects to manifest primarily in the medium to long term. As we have seen, changes in productivity increase wages and, therefore, the per capita income and price levels are higher in countries where the per capita income is higher.

Figure 2 displays a plot of this relationship, labelled the Penn–Balassa–Samuelson effect, where we can see that the relationship holds strongly in the

India–US context. Note that the CPI for India in $ is arrived at by dividing the CPI indexed in ₹ by the nominal exchange rate.

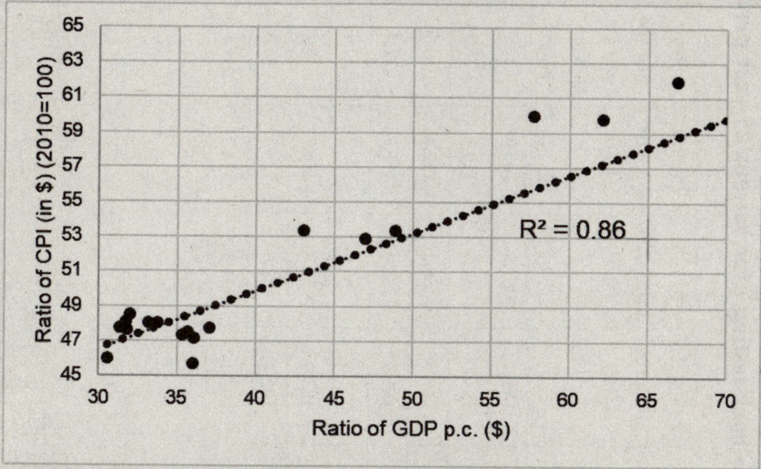

Figure 2: Penn–Balassa–Samuelson effect for India–US

Source: The World Bank; IMF; author's calculations

Back-Testing the Change in ₹/$ Over Various 25-Year Periods

We use the framework described above in the box to back-test the currency depreciation for the ₹/$ over various 25-year periods. The basic data that we employ, obtained from the World Bank and International Monetary Fund (IMF), is displayed in Table 1.

The key takeaway from this table is that even though real appreciation of ₹/$ over different 25-year periods has been between 1.2 and 1.5 per cent, owing to the productivity differentials, the very high difference in inflation between India and the US of about 5 per cent has ensured that the nominal depreciation of ₹/$ is in the range of 3.0–4.5 per cent.

Using this basic data, the predicted and actual depreciations are displayed in Table 2.

As Figure 1 clearly shows, the predicted and actual depreciations of various 25-year periods in the past are very close to each other.

Table 1

Data for per capita (p.c.) GDP, CPI indices and ₹/$ used for back-testing over various 25-year periods

Time Period	*GDP p.c. (PPP$) India (Start)*	*GDP p.c. (PPP$) India (End)*	*GDP p.c. (PPP$) US (Start)*	*GDP p.c. (PPP$) US (End)*	*GDP p.c. ($) India (Start)*	*CPI India 2010=100 (Start)*	*CPI India 2010=100 (End)*	*CPI India 2010=100 (Start)*	*CPI US 2010=100 (End)*	*₹/$ Average over the Year (Start)*	*₹/$ Average over the Year (End)*
1991–2015	1,232.0	5,412.3	24,342.3	56,762.7	303.9	26.1	146.8	62.5	108.7	22.7	64.2
1992–2016	1,301.8	5,778.3	25,419.0	57,866.7	317.6	29.2	154.1	64.3	110.1	25.9	67.2
1993–2017	1,367.7	6,112.1	26,387.3	59,907.8	301.5	31.1	159.2	66.2	112.4	30.5	65.1
1994–2018	1,460.1	6,590.9	27,694.9	62,823.3	346.2	34.2	165.5	68.0	115.2	31.4	68.4
1995–2019	1,572.0	6,897.8	28,690.9	65,120.4	373.6	37.7	171.6	69.9	117.2	32.4	70.4
1996–2020	1,688.4	6,517.8	29,967.7	63,528.6	399.6	41.1	183.0	71.9	118.7	35.4	74.1
1997–2021	1,753.1	7,368.0	31,459.1	70,219.5	414.9	44.1	192.4	73.6	124.3	36.3	73.9
1998–2022	1,847.3	8,400.4	32,853.7	76,329.6	412.5	49.9	205.3	74.8	134.2	41.3	78.6

Source: The World Bank; IMF; author's calculations

Table 2

Predicted and actual depreciations for per capita (p.c.) GDP, CPI indices and ₹/$ used for back-testing over various 25-year periods

Time Period	*India GDP p.c. Growth Using PPP$*	*US GDP p.c. Growth Using PPP$*	*India Inflation*	*US Inflation*	*Real Appreciation*	*Predicted Nominal Depreciation*	*Actual Nominal Depreciation*
1991–2015	6.36%	3.59%	7.46%	2.34%	1.25%	3.87%	4.42%
1992–2016	6.41%	3.49%	7.17%	2.26%	1.33%	3.58%	4.05%
1993–2017	6.44%	3.48%	7.05%	2.23%	1.45%	3.37%	3.21%
1994–2018	6.48%	3.47%	6.78%	2.22%	1.41%	3.15%	3.30%
1995–2019	6.36%	3.47%	6.51%	2.18%	1.37%	2.97%	3.28%
1996–2020	5.79%	3.18%	6.42%	2.11%	1.26%	3.05%	3.12%
1997–2021	6.16%	3.40%	6.33%	2.21%	1.32%	2.80%	3.01%
1998–2022	6.51%	3.57%	6.07%	2.47%	1.47%	2.13%	2.72%

Source: The World Bank; IMF; author's calculations

This evidence supporting the conceptual framework is crucial for our estimation of the ₹/$ in 2047. This is because a large literature in international economics examines if the Balassa–Samuelson framework works in explaining the movement of currencies in the long run. Numerous studies in the literature indicate that the framework is effective, whereas several other studies present evidence suggesting the framework's ineffectiveness. Apart from the evidence for 25-year periods shown here, I have examined whether this framework works in explaining the movement of the ₹/$ over shorter periods of 10, 15 and 20 years. I find that as the time-period increases, the explanatory power increases significantly. Therefore, we can reassure ourselves that the framework effectively explains the movement of the ₹/$, which is critical for us to use the framework for prediction. Using the time-series of various 25-year periods in the past, we crucially note here that the actual and predicted depreciations have been declining over time.

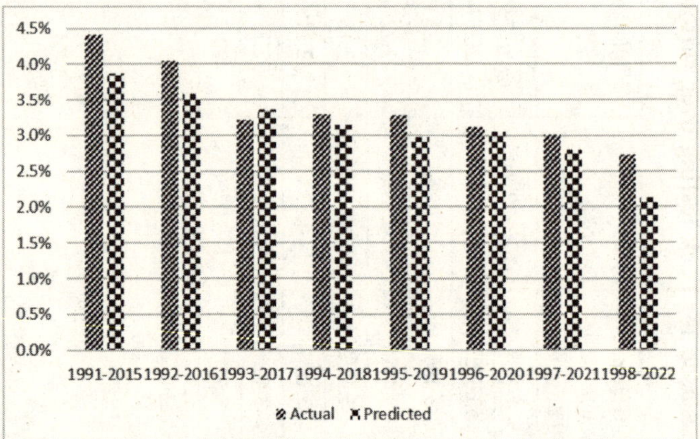

Figure 3: Actual and predicted depreciations of ₹/$ over various 25-year periods

Source: The World Bank; IMF; author's calculations

What Is the Likely Level of ₹/$ in 2047?

Having seen that the Balassa–Samuelson framework employed here has been very precise in predicting the actual change in the level of the ₹/$ over various 25-year periods, we use this framework to predict the likely levels for ₹/$ in 2047.

We use the average level of the ₹/$ in 2023 for projecting the ₹/$ for a 25-year period to 2047. As a result, we use a more depreciated value of 82.6 for the ₹/$ for our projections. This is because the $ appreciates in the short term against other currencies when economic uncertainty increases. This happens due to the combination of (i) 'home bias', which is the phenomenon of investors preferring to keep their investments in home countries during times of greater uncertainty; and (ii) 'flight to safety', where investors prefer investing in safe assets during times of greater uncertainty. The home bias and the flight to safety phenomena favour the US because a large proportion of global investors are American, thereby creating a favourable home bias, and the continued perception of US Treasury and Agency Securities being safe assets. In the medium to long term, however, home bias and flight to safety phenomena do not matter as these are primarily short-term phenomena that do not affect the ₹/$ in a long period of 25 years. Therefore, the more depreciated value of the ₹/$ used for projections represents a conservative assumption for projecting the ₹/$ level for 2047.

The growth rates assumed for per capita GDP for 2022–47 are projected using two sources. First, I take the GDP growth rates for India that are estimated in Chapter 2. A question that would arise is: can India grow at an average rate of 6.1 per cent, 7.1 per cent and 8 per cent over the next 23 years? Would the law of diminishing returns not set in and slow growth? I consider this facet specifically in Chapter 5 on the middle-income trap. It is important to note here that China, whose GDP per capita in 2007 was about $2,600, which is similar to India's GDP per capita in 2023, grew on average at 7.7 per cent over the span of 15 years from 2007 to 2022. Given India's comparable demographic dividend now, India can achieve similar growth rates. Second, unlike the advanced economies where diminishing returns set in because growth stemmed only from productivity improvements within the formal sector, about half of India's economy is still informal. Formalization of this informal economy can provide growth through improvements in productivity. Third, even within the formal economy, India's productivity is still a fraction of that of advanced economies.

I project the growth rate for the Indian population to be 0.5 per cent based on the demographic projections till 2041 provided in Chapter 7 of the *Economic Survey 2018–19*.[4] These population projections were based on a rigorous analysis of the total fertility rate (TFR) at the state level. By examining whether the TFR is above or below the replacement level, the population growth in each state is projected. Population growth at the national level is aggregated using these state-level projections. This Survey found the population growth rates in India to be 1.77 per cent per annum during 2001–11 and 1.12 per cent per annum during 2011–21. Using its analysis, the Survey projected growth rates of 0.72 per cent per annum during 2021–31 and 0.46 per cent per annum during 2031–41. As the growth rate in every decade has been 63–64 per cent of the growth rate in the previous decade, I project the growth rate to be 0.63 × 0.46 per cent = 0.29 per cent in 2041–51. The weighted average of these decadal growth rates provides a cumulative annual growth rate of 0.5 per cent from 2022 to 2047. The growth rate estimated by United Nations Development Programme (UNDP) World Population Prospects 2022 is similar.[5]

I assume the GDP growth for the US to be at 1.8 per cent as assessed by policymakers at the Federal Reserve, inflation at 2 per cent and population growth at 0.5 per cent.[6] Given the high level of debt in the US, which, as projected by the Congressional Budget Office (CBO), is expected to balloon in the coming years,[7] inflation in the US could very likely be higher than 2 per cent. Yet, to be conservative in my projections, I assume the US inflation to be 2 per cent.

India's inflation is assumed to be 5 per cent. As the inflation targeting regime requires inflation to be within 4 ± 2 per cent, assuming inflation to be 5 per cent is conservative. The fifth column in Table 3 shows the projections for the level of the ₹/$ in 2047 under various scenarios.

---

[4]Ministry of Finance, GoI, *Economic Survey 2018–19: Volume 1*, July 2019, http://tinyurl.com/5ccw6unz. Accessed on 14 February 2024.

[5]United Nations Department of Economic and Social Affairs, *World Population Prospects 2022*, http://tinyurl.com/s98pbzsj. Accessed on 30 January 2024.

[6]Schneider, Howard, 'Fed's Long-Term GDP Outlook Is Dismal; The Economy Hasn't Got the Message Yet', *Reuters*, 21 August 2023, https://tinyurl.com/3pdk8e92. Accessed on 8 April 2024.

[7]'CBO's February 2024 Budget and Economic Outlook', *Committee for a Responsible Federal Budget*, 7 February 2024, https://tinyurl.com/yzhunukv. Accessed on 8 April 2024.

Table 3
India's GDP per capita (p.c.) in 2047 in US$

	India GDP Growth p.c.	*Real Appreciation p.a.*	*Nominal Depreciation p.a.*	*$/₹ in 2050*	*India GDP in 2047*	*India GDP p.c. in 2047*
Pessimistic	5.60%	1.52%	1.48%	117.4	29.0	20,043.3
Realistic	6.60%	2.06%	0.94%	103.2	40.9	28,531.6
Optimistic	7.50%	2.55%	0.45%	92.0	55.6	39,143.9

Source: GDP growth estimates from Chapter 2; population growth estimates from *Economic Survey 2018–19* and author's calculations

Note: GDP per capita growth = GDP growth rate – population growth rate

The key takeaway is that the average 3.5–4.5 per cent level of annual depreciation of the rupee in 1990–2020 will most certainly be a thing of the past. This high level of depreciation stemmed from real appreciation of ₹/$ over different 25-year periods of about 0.8–1 per cent being offset by the very high difference in inflation between India and the US of about 4–5 per cent. As is shown in Chapter 2, the growth of productivity, as measured by the growth of total factor productivity (TFP), has more than doubled 2014 onwards when compared to its growth till 2013. This reflects the several reforms that have been undertaken post 2014.

Going forward, therefore, I expect that the higher differences in productivity between India and the US will manifest as higher real appreciation of the ₹/$ of 1.8–3.4 per cent. With a much lower inflation differential of about 3–4 per cent and higher real appreciation, over the next 25 years, annual depreciation will be less than 1 per cent per annum in most scenarios. Even in the pessimistic scenario, where growth in GDP per capita during 2022–31 is 5.6 per cent and commensurate thereafter, annual depreciation will be 1.15 per cent—only slightly higher than 1 per cent per annum. Thus, a regime change for ₹/$ is brewing.

The Size of the Indian Economy in 2047

Using the ₹/$ projected in 2047, I forecast the size of India's economy in 2047. India's GDP of ₹272.4 lakh crore, or ₹272.4 trillion, as estimated by Ministry of Statistics and Programme Implementation (MOSPI) for financial year (FY) 2023 is used for this purpose.[8] The sixth column in Table 3 displays these projections. In the pessimistic scenario, where growth in GDP per capita equals 5.6 per cent, India's GDP would grow to $29.0 trillion. In the baseline scenario, where growth in GDP per capita equals 6.6 per cent, India's GDP would grow to $40.9 trillion. In the optimistic scenario, where growth in GDP per capita equals 7.5 per cent, India's GDP would grow to $55.6 trillion.

Table 3 shows the predicted GDP per capita. In the pessimistic, realistic, and optimistic scenarios, India's GDP per capita would grow to $20,043, $28,532, and $39,144, respectively.

Risk Factors

While the realistic scenarios projected above are predicated on current policies, the optimistic scenario of 8 per cent growth in GDP requires doubling down on salutary economic policies. But risks to the realistic and optimistic scenarios loom large, including an inward turn by Western countries that undermines trade, capital flows and technology; AI and cyber risks; geopolitical aggression; and climate shocks.

Given the natural tendency to not foresee regime changes and, thereby, (linearly) extrapolate from existing regimes, EY predicts India's GDP to be $26 trillion by 2047, while Goldman Sachs predicts India's GDP to be slightly above $50 trillion by 2075. The key differences in their predictions vis-à-vis mine are:

(i) the endogenous modelling of the ₹/$ depreciation rather than an exogenous (linear) extrapolation of past phenomena of depreciation in ₹–$; and
(ii) ab initio modelling of growth rates for India's GDP, as explained in the next chapter.

---

[8]National Statistical Office, Ministry Of Statistics and Programme Implementation, GoI, *Press Note On Provisional Estimates Of National Income 2022–23 and Quarterly Estimates Of Gross Domestic Product For The Fourth Quarter (Q4) of 2022–23*, 31 May 2023, https://tinyurl.com/2bxav8at. Accessed on 8 April 2024.

Given the different scenarios presented, the primary challenge for India to become a $55 trillion economy by 2047 is consistently growing at 8 per cent annually in real terms. Ensuring a good policy mix that delivers this growth, thus, remains the most critical risk factor in achieving this goal.

◆

What does a $55 trillion economy in 2047 mean for the common citizen? First, the substantial increase in GDP per capita—even in terms of the US dollar—will mean that the purchasing power of common Indians will increase substantially. Apart from being able to afford many more domestically produced goods and services, Indian middle-class citizens would also be able to afford several foreign-produced goods. Second, the quality of living would be substantially higher with a large section of the population affording both domestic and foreign goods and services. Third, the diffidence that pervaded the Indian psyche, which possibly led to the worship of Western ideas and cultural notions at the cost of deeper Indian ones, would become a thing of the past as India rubs shoulders with the largest economies. For example, derisive labels such as 'Hindu rate of growth' would gain little traction. Last, but perhaps the most important, by occupying its deserved place as an economic leader in the comity of nations, India would do justice to the civilization that has offered so many profound ideas to mankind.

2

UNLEASHING ECONOMIC POTENTIAL

Projecting Future Growth Rates

Once upon a time, there lived a king who was a great chess enthusiast. He had a habit of inviting his visitors to a game of chess. One day, he extended this invitation to a wise sage and proposed a wager: if the sage emerged victorious in their match, he would be granted any desired reward by the king. The sage modestly asked for just a few grains of rice in the following manner: 'Put one single grain of rice on the first chess square, then double it on every consecutive square thereafter.' The arrogant king, surprised by the sage's demand for an apparently inconsequential reward, gladly accepted. After he lost the game of chess to the sage, the king ordered a bag of rice to be brought to the chess board. The king's courtiers then started to place rice grains as promised. They started with one grain on the first square, then doubled the amount to two grains on the second square, and continued this pattern, doubling the number of grains on each subsequent square. As this process went along, the king quickly realized that he would be unable to fulfil his promise. On the twentieth square, the king needed about one million grains of rice. By the fortieth square, this had increased to about a trillion grains of rice. Finally, on the sixty-fourth square, the king needed to place more than 210 billion tons of rice. However, giving such a huge quantity of rice to the sage would have impoverished his kingdom. Realizing the king's discomfiture, the wise sage pardoned the king while admonishing him for his arrogance.

This story reveals the tremendous power of compounding. Let us understand this power in the context of economic growth. If India grows its GDP per capita at 5 per cent per annum, its GDP per capita will multiply 3.2 times from 2023 to 2047. If the country grows its GDP per capita at 8 per cent per annum, the GDP per capita will multiply 6.3 times from 2023 to 2047. A 3 per cent increase in growth almost doubles the growth of GDP per capita. And if India is fortunate enough to grow its GDP per capita at 10 per cent per annum, its will multiply 9.8 times from 2023 to 2047. This arithmetic begs the question: what is India's GDP growth likely to be in the coming two-and-a-half decades?

To answer this question, I estimate the potential GDP growth for India using three different, yet complementary, approaches. In the first approach, I estimate growth in value added at the sectoral level by projecting the growth rate of investment and the growth of productivity in the sector. Growth in value added for the Indian economy is then estimated by aggregating the growth rates at the sectoral level. Adding the growth in net taxes, which equals taxes minus subsidies, delivers the potential growth rate of GDP for the economy. This approach, advocated by Dr C. Rangarajan, former governor of the RBI, is called the 'disaggregated approach'.

In the second approach, growth is estimated directly for the entire economy by modelling the economy as a homogeneous aggregate. In this approach, which was postulated by Nobel Laureate Robert Solow and is called the 'aggregated approach', rates of growth of productivity, capital and labour are estimated to arrive at the potential growth rate for the economy. Finally, I employ various statistical methods that track the historical trend for GDP growth to estimate potential GDP growth using a third method. These methods complement each other as the disadvantages in any one method is overcome by the absence of the same disadvantages in the other two methods.

In the baseline scenario, I assume no change in the growth rates of investment and productivity vis-à-vis the median obtained over the last two decades. Thus, in the baseline scenario, I assume that the growth rates for investment and productivity would remain equal to the middle observation when the growth rates obtained in the past two decades are arranged in an order. I obtain potential GDP growth rate of 7.1 per cent using the aggregated approach and 7.7 per cent using the disaggregated approach. In the pessimistic scenario, where I replace the median values with the fortieth percentiles, potential growth equals 6.1 per cent using both approaches. In the optimistic scenario, where I replace the median values with the sixtieth percentiles, potential growth rate is estimated to be 8 per cent using the aggregate approach and 9.4 per cent using the disaggregated approach. The pure statistical trend estimations from historical data deliver potential growth rates ranging from 7.1 to 7.5 per cent.

Disaggregated Structural Estimation

I used the disaggregated approach advocated by RBI Governor C. Rangarajan as the first to estimate potential GDP growth for India. He proposed this methodology to capture the multifaceted influences on potential growth rate of output in the Indian economy. Boxes 1 and 2 describe the conceptual methodology and the assumptions employed to estimate GDP growth using this approach. For the estimation, I disaggregate the economy into eight sectors: (i) agriculture, forestry and fishing ('Agri' hereafter), (ii) mining and quarrying ('Mining' hereafter), (iii) manufacturing ('Mfg' hereafter), (iv) electricity, gas, water supply and other utility services ('Elec' hereafter), (v) construction ('Constrn' hereafter), (vi) trade, hotels, transport, storage and communications ('Trade' hereafter), (vii) financial, real estate and professional services ('FinServ' hereafter), and (viii) public administration, defence and other services ('PubAd' hereafter).

Box 1: Technical Description of the Estimation Methodology and Assumptions

Let the proportion of total investment in sector i parameter be given by α_i Thus, investment in sector i is given by $I_i = \alpha_i * I$, where I denotes the aggregate investment in the Indian economy and by definition, $\sum_{i=1}^{8} \alpha_i = I$. Then the growth in real value added in the economy is given by:

$$g_{GVA} = \frac{1}{GVA_{-i}} \sum_{i=1}^{8} \Delta y_i = \frac{1}{GVA_{-i}} \sum_{i=1}^{8} IOCR_i * \alpha_i * \frac{I}{PI} \quad (1)$$

where $IOCR_i$ denotes the incremental output-capital ratio in sector i, GVA_{-1} denotes gross value added (GVA) at constant prices in the previous year and PI denotes the price deflator for investment. Thus I/PI denotes the investment at constant prices for the economy. Here,

$$IOCR_i = \Delta GVA_i / (I * \alpha_i) \quad (2)$$

GVA growth is translated into GDP growth by adjusting for product taxes net of product subsidies. Using β to denote the buoyancy of real net indirect taxes with respect to real GVA, GDP growth is linked to GVA growth using this buoyancy:

$$g_{GDP} = \frac{g_{GVA} \cdot (GVA_{-1} + \beta * NPT_{-1})}{GDP_{-1}}, \text{ where } \beta = \left(\frac{\Delta NPT}{NPT_{-1}}\right) \Big/ \left(\frac{\Delta GVA}{GVA_{-1}}\right) \quad (3)$$

So, the estimation of GDP growth requires the following variables to be projected:

(i) **Growth rate of real investment, I/PI, in the economy:** I consider four different scenarios for this variable. In the pessimistic scenario, I take the growth rate to be the fortieth percentile of the rate of growth that has been obtained over the last two decades. In the baseline, I take the growth rate to be the median value while in the optimistic scenario, I assume it to be the sixtieth percentile. The baseline growth rate of investment equals 8.7 per cent, which is similar to the average growth in real investment rate of 8.5 per cent for 2023–24 to 2028–29 estimated for the World Economic Outlook (April 2023) by the IMF.

(ii) **Measure of productivity ($IOCR_i$) for each sector i:** As with growth rate of investment, productivity is assumed to be fortieth percentile, median and sixtieth percentile in the pessimistic, baseline and optimistic scenarios.

(iii) **The share in investment of sector i (α_i):** As the share of investment of various sectors has been quite stable over the last two decades, this is assumed to equal the median share over last two decades for each sector.

(iv) **The buoyancy of real net indirect taxes with respect to real GVA (β):** Tax buoyancy is assumed to be constant at 1.2. Tax buoyancy over the last decade has been much higher in India with the mean and the median being 1.8 and 1.6, respectively, which reflects the significant formalization of the economy over the last several years. As this trend of formalization will continue, a tax buoyancy of 1.2 is, therefore, conservative.

(v) **Inflation rate for computing price deflator for investment (PI)**: This deflator is assumed to be 4 per cent. This is reasonable as the median and average for inflation in the price deflator for gross capital formation (GCF) over the last two decades equals 3.7 per cent and 4.2 per cent respectively. Also, inflation targeting regime requires headline inflation to be 4 per cent ± 2 per cent.

As Table 1 shows, the baseline GDP growth rate, which assumes median levels for the rate of growth of investment and productivity, equals 7.7 per cent. We note that this growth rate assumes no major reforms or major change in the global economic prospects as the median is computed over two decades that includes the decline in economic prospects due to the

GFC. In contrast to the baseline, growth rate is estimated at 6.1 per cent in the pessimistic scenario and 9.4 per cent in the optimistic scenario.

Table 1
Projected growth rates for GDP for India using the disaggregated structural approach

Scenario	*Growth Rate of Real Investment*		*Productivity (IOCR) Assumption*	*Estimated Growth Rate of GDP*
	Assumption	*Value*		
Optimistic	60th percentile	11.2%	60th percentile for each sector	9.4%
Baseline	Median	8.7%	Median for each sector	7.7%
Pessimistic	40th percentile	7.0%	40th percentile for each sector	6.1%

Source: Author's calculations

Box 2: Conceptual Description of the Disaggregated Approach Used Here

The disaggregated approach incorporates the possibility that: (i) prices of investment goods vary across sectors, (ii) investment varies across sectors depending on the demand conditions in the sector, and (iii) productivity varies across sectors. Moreover, the distributions of weights across sectors are derived organically in the disaggregated approach by using the sectoral-level investment and measures of productivity calculated through IOCRs; as the name suggests, the IOCR captures the ratio of output generated to capital invested for incremental investments made in the sector. The disaggregated approach also incorporates the resilience of net product taxes with respect to GVA.

My approach differs from Rangarajan's in one salient aspect. He and his co-author follow the theory postulated by the celebrated economists Roy Harrod and Evsey Domar, called the Harrod–Domar model. This model states that economic growth depends on the amount of capital that is available for investment. In particular, the Harrod–Domar model assumes that the rate of capital accumulation is proportional to the rate of savings in the economy. Therefore, Rangarajan and his co-author model investment as directly proportional to the savings in the economy, which is comprised of domestic and foreign savings. In contrast, I assume that the investment in the economy is primarily driven by demand conditions in the economy. In other words, higher the expected demand in the economy, greater the investment irrespective of savings. Thus, my modelling approach assumes that savings do not really constrain investment in an economy, especially in an increasingly open economy like India.

First and foremost, in my book with Professor K. Vaidyanathan, *Money: A Zero-Sum Game*, I show that banks are money-creators in the economy. Loans provided by banks create deposits and not vice-versa as postulated by the extant theory of financial intermediation. As investment in an economy like India depends critically on bank financing for investment, and bank financing depends primarily on demand, savings are not the constraint on investment.[9] Indeed, as shown in the charts here, the correlation between investment and savings does not suggest that savings drive investment. Other recent research also lends solid support to this crucial assumption. Growth dynamics in Asia show that savings follow when incomes grow in an economy.[10] As incomes grow as part of the virtuous cycle driven by investment, investment primarily responds to anticipated consumption in the economy.

Moreover, Figure 1 provides suggestive evidence that investment is a catalyst for savings in the economy and not vice-versa. First, we observe that the correlation of change in savings with future change in investment decreases secularly with increase in lags. If savings this year were causing investment in subsequent years, then the correlation should increase with increase in lags, as savings accumulating over years would enable investment. However, we do not observe that. In contrast, change in investment correlates strongly with future

[9]Some would contend that the current slowdown in China may be indicative of the fact that savings indeed constrain investment. However, China's savings rate has continued to be very high at 45.9 per cent of GDP in 2021. Yet, growth has become anaemic due to (lack of) demand, structural headwinds from worsening demographics, and bad assets in the real estate and banking sector. Thus, the recent Chinese experience serves to buttress rather than invalidate the case for savings being an outcome rather than the driver of economic prospects.

[10]From 1960 to 2011 for non-OECD countries, Sandri (2014) shows that growth spurts cause a steeply increasing savings rate. Carroll and Weil (1994), Bosworth and Chodorow-Reich (2007) show for Asia that savings rises with the proportion of the working population. Curtis, Lugauer and Mark (2011) find that jobs that pay meaningful wages drive savings rate in the economy. Lee, Mason and Miller (2000) and Bloom et al. (2007) show that savings increases as average life expectancy increases in a country.

change in savings, with the correlation increasing from a lag of one year to a lag of five years and then declining thereafter. Thus, the change in investment over a five-year period correlates with future changes in savings over the next five-year period, thereby suggesting that investment is likely to be causing savings and not vice-versa. This suggestive evidence of investment causing savings is consistent with the virtuous cycle originating from investment and driving economic growth—thereby savings—in the Indian economy.

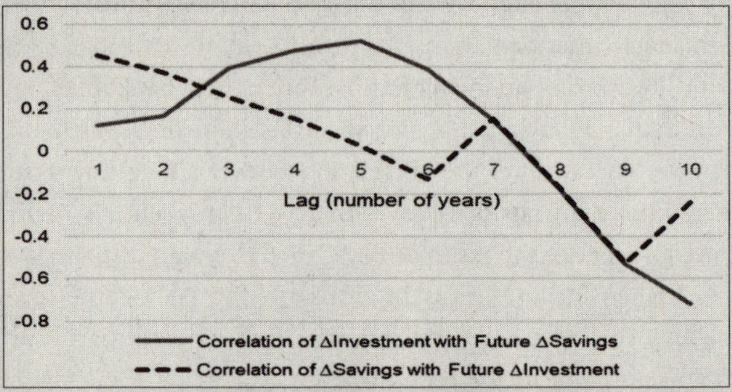

Figure 1: Correlation of change in investment with future change in savings and vice-versa for different lags

Source: Economic surveys and author's calculations

It is important to note that labour availability is not a limiting factor, given the robust expansion of the working-age population in the Indian context. As shown in the *Economic Survey 2018–19*, India has already entered the demographic phase in which a large share of its population is of working age.[11] Moreover, India will remain in this 'demographic dividend' zone for over two decades. This Survey, in fact, highlighted that the working-age population (20–59 years), which comprised 50.5 per cent of the overall population in 2011, will increase to about 60 per cent in 2041. Furthermore, as the growth estimation using the aggregated Solow model shows, capital and total factor productivity (TFP) drive potential growth far more than labour in India. Therefore, the modelling of growth using investment and productivity is particularly suited to the Indian situation.

[11]Ministry of Finance, GoI, *Economic Survey 2018–19: Volume 1*, July 2019, http://tinyurl.com/5ccw6unz. Accessed on 1 February 2024.

Estimates from the Aggregated Solow Model

The aggregate model postulated by Robert Solow represents the traditional workhorse for estimating potential growth. Unlike the disaggregated approach employed above, this model adopts a one-size-fits-all approach that treats the economy as one homogeneous entity across all the sectors of the economy. I complement the above estimates using this approach as well. Box 3 describes conceptually the methodology underlying the aggregate approach.

I obtain the data from the Penn World Table, version 10.0, for the two-decade period of 2000–2019.[12] As before, I end the time period in 2019 to avoid the period of Covid-19.

I note that given the significant reforms that have been implemented in India from 2014, productivity has improved post 2014. Figure 2 plots the level of TFP against time for 2002–19, 2002–13 and 2014–19. We clearly see that the slope of the trend line for the 2014–19 sub-period is higher than the earlier 2002–13 sub-period. This is also reflected in the average TFP from 2014–19 being 2.7 per cent or more than double the average of 1.3 per cent from 2002–13.

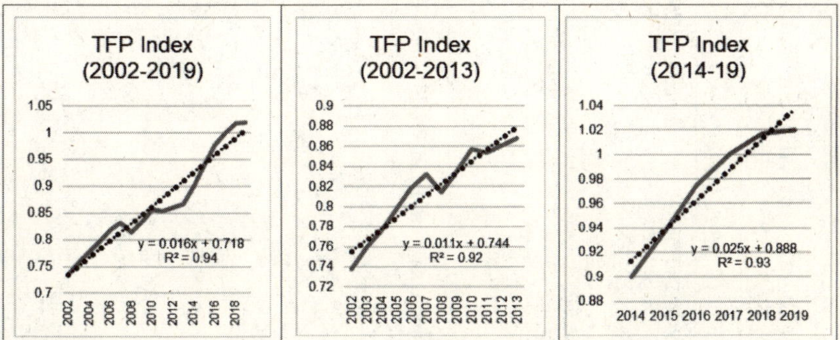

Avg growth rate of TFP: 1.8%	*Avg growth rate of TFP: 1.3%*	*Avg growth rate of TFP: 2.7%*

Figure 2: TFP for India over 2002–19 and sub-periods 2002–13 and 2014–19

Source: Penn World Table, version 10.0; author's calculations

[12]'Penn World Table Version 10.0', *Groningen Growth and Development Centre*, University of Groningen, http://tinyurl.com/a4ksucmw. Accessed on 1 February 2024.

Table 2

Projected growth rates for GDP for India using the aggregated structural approach (in %)

Scenario	*Assumption*	*Assumed Value for Growth in:*					*Estimated GDP Growth*
		TFP	*Human Capital*	*Employment*	*Average Hours*	*Capital Services*	
Optimistic	60th percentile	2.6%	1.1%	0.9%	0.1%	8.8%	8.0%
Baseline	Median	2.4%	1.1%	0.9%	0.1%	7.2%	7.1%
Pessimistic	40th percentile	1.7%	1.1%	0.7%	0.1%	7.0%	6.1%

Source: Author's calculations using data from Penn World Tables

In Table 2, the baseline growth rate I obtain using the aggregated model equals 7.1 per cent, while the optimistic and pessimistic scenarios yield estimates of 8.0 per cent and 6.1 per cent, respectively.

Sceptics will wonder if the values of TFP growth of 2.4 per cent and 2.6 per cent in the baseline and optimistic scenarios are attainable for India in the future. China had a decade where TFP growth was above 2 per cent. As some of the TFP growth stems from implementing the best practices in advanced economies—including process innovation—this high TFP growth can certainly continue in India. This is especially true given the reform path that India has pursued, investments in DPI and physical infrastructure, and the ongoing formalization of the economy.

Box 3: Conceptual Description of the Aggregated Approach

The Solow model forecasts potential growth using estimates of growth in labour, capital and TFP. A production function, like the Cobb–Douglas model, is used for the purpose:

$$Y = AK^{\alpha}L^{1-\alpha}$$

where K denotes capital, L labour and A the TFP. Labour incorporates the quantity of labour input augmented by the quality of labour as captured by an index of human capital. The quantity of labour input itself is defined as working hours per person times persons employed. For capital, I use 'capital services' to adjust the aggregate capital stock to capture its real productive impact.

The growth estimates obtained using the disaggregated approach are at least as much as those provided by the aggregated model. Specifically, the baseline estimate in the latter equals 7.1 per cent, which is lower than the baseline estimates of 7.7 per cent in the former. Similarly, the growth rate estimated in the optimistic scenario is also lower at 8 per cent in the aggregated model as against 9.4 per cent in the disaggregated approach. In the pessimistic scenario, the estimates are identical at 6.1 per cent. To understand why, let me examine the concerns raised by Dale Jorgenson, who did similar work in the US. In a research study published in 1991, he writes:

> The concept of an aggregate production function is highly problematical, requiring very stringent assumptions on production patterns at the level of individual sectors of the economy. Intuitively speaking, the technology of each sector must contain a replica of the aggregate production function[...]

> In technical jargon the existence of an aggregate production function requires that the technology of each sector is separable in value added and that value added is a function of capital and labour inputs and the level of technology. Moreover, the sectoral value-added functions must be identical for all sectors, while the functions relating labor and capital inputs to their components must also be identical for all sectors. Finally, each component of these input aggregates must receive the same price in all sectors.[13]

Jorgenson finds for the US that for the period 1947–85, the rate of aggregate productivity growth is lower than the weighted sum of sectoral productivity growth rates. He finds that the reallocations of value added, capital input and labour input across sectors explain why growth estimated in aggregate is lower than the disaggregated growth rate. The same reasons manifest in the Indian setting as well with the aggregate model per force requiring that the production function be the same across all sectors. In contrast, disaggregation allows for the production functions, and thereby investment rates and productivities, to be different across the various sectors.

Historical Estimation

Finally, I complement the two approaches with estimation of potential growth based *purely* on historical data, which employs a variety of statistical methods. As this estimate is predominantly retrospective in nature, it offers a complementary estimate to those obtained above. Since this book does not go into detail about these methods, I recommend that readers who are interested in learning more refer to the extensive body of economic literature on this subject. I use quarterly data from the first quarter of 1999–2000 to the last quarter of 2018–19 for this estimation exercise.

As seen in Table 3, the approaches using historical data deliver growth estimates in the range of 7.1–7.5 per cent.

[13]Jorgenson, Dale W., 'Productivity and Economic Growth', *Fifty Years of Economic Measurement: The Jubilee of the Conference on Research in Income and Wealth,* Ernst R. Berndt and Jack E. Triplett (eds), University of Chicago Press, Chicago, 1991, pp. 19, 24, http://tinyurl.com/2spm24wa. Accessed on 1 February 2024.

Table 3
Summary of estimated potential growth rates using purely historical data from 1999–2000 to 2018–19

Method	*Average Potential Growth (%) (1999–2001 Q1–2018–19 Q4)*
Linear trend	7.50
Quadratic trend	7.50
Cubic trend	7.40
Fractional polynomial	7.45
HP filter	7.32
Christiano Fitzgerald	7.11
Beveridge Nelson	7.21
Kalman filter	7.53
Composite estimate	7.38

Source: Author's calculations

The *Economic Survey 2015–16* estimated India's potential growth to be in the range of 8 to 10 per cent up to 2029–30. Here, I estimate India's potential growth rate to be between 6.1 and 9.4 per cent using three different but complementary approaches. In the baseline scenario, potential growth rate can be expected to be over 7 per cent. A question that may arise is: can GDP growth continue to be over 7 per cent from now till India turns 100?

There are multiple factors that support this possibility. First, consider China whose GDP per capita in 2007 was about $2,600, which is similar to India's GDP per capita in 2023. Over the span of 16 years, from 2007 to 2022, China's average GDP growth has been 7.7 per cent. Given India's comparable demographic dividend to that which China experienced in the past few decades, it has the potential to achieve similar growth rates, provided there is a supportive economic policy in place. Second, about half of India's economy is still informal. Formalization of this informal economy can provide growth through improvements in productivity. Third, even within the formal economy, India's productivity is still a fraction of that of advanced economies. Finally, India's demographics offer the advantage of a large workforce, which could turn this possibility into a reality provided the policies that we describe later are implemented to empower the workforce.

3

FOUR PILLARS OF PROGRESS

Shaping Atmanirbhar Bharat @100

In the late 1970s, China's supreme leader Deng Xiaoping envisioned 'Four Modernizations' as a strategic plan for China's economic development. Agriculture, industry, defence, and science and technology represented the four pillars that laid the foundation for China's rapid economic growth and turned it into the powerhouse it is today. Japan's post-War resurrection stemmed from its economic vision, which hinged on four pillars: industrial policy, education, infrastructure and export-oriented growth. This strategic framework propelled Japan into becoming an economic juggernaut, underscoring the transformative power of a well-structured economic vision. Similarly, Germany's famed 'social market economy' relied on a four-pillar approach comprising a balance between a competitive market economy, a strong welfare state, labour market policies, and active fiscal policies. This comprehensive strategy laid the groundwork for Germany's economic prowess.

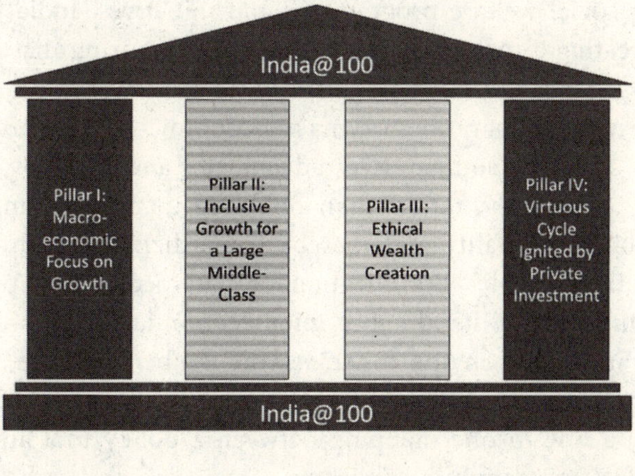

Figure 1: The Four Pillars to realize PM Modi's vision of Atmanirbhar Bharat

Source: Author's design

To realize PM Narendra Modi's vision of Atmanirbhar Bharat, I propose an economic strategy grounded on four essential pillars. These pillars, which represent the essential foundations for prosperous and equitable progress, are shown in Figure 1.

Economic Development for All

The first two pillars specify objectives at the macroeconomic and microeconomic levels: to complement a laser-like focus on economic growth at the macroeconomic level with socio-economic inclusion at the microeconomic level. This will ensure that the benefits of economic growth are equitably shared among citizens. The macroeconomic focus on growth will uplift the lives of millions directly as the high rates of economic growth in India since 1991 and in China since the 1970s have demonstrably achieved. Simultaneously, high rates of growth will help to generate the resources that can be utilized for welfare programmes to double down on the economic development of the poor and vulnerable.

The microeconomic focus on socio-economic inclusion will help to not only reduce inequality, but also enhance aggregate demand in the economy. This pillar recognizes the importance of inclusivity in economic development. It aims to reduce income inequality and provide equal opportunities for all citizens, especially marginalized groups. By promoting social welfare programmes and initiatives, India is working towards creating a more equitable society and ensuring that all citizens have access to necessities and opportunities to thrive.

The explicit separation of macroeconomic and microeconomic objectives enables comparative advantage, and thereby enhances efficiency. Specifically, rather than hobbling macroeconomic policies with reducing inequality and thereby jeopardizing growth prospects, the separation enables optimization of macroeconomic policies for growth on the one hand, and microeconomic policies for socio-economic inclusion on the other. As the Tinbergen Rule, advocated by the recipient of the first Nobel Prize in Economics, Jan Tinbergen, postulates, a one-to-one mapping between a policy tool and a policy objective fosters economic efficiency.

A Seminal Turn Embracing Ethical Wealth Creation

Prime Minister Modi's reply on the Motion of Thanks to the President's Address during the Budget Session of Parliament on 10 February 2021 highlighted a seminal turn in India's economic history as he underlined the importance of 'wealth creation' and the role of the private sector.[14] Acknowledging this pivotal moment, on 11 February, *The Hindu Businessline* titled its lead editorial 'Watershed Moment' and wrote:

> On the floor of the Lok Sabha, he [the PM] made two major points: One, the country needs wealth creators or producers in the first place for that wealth to be distributed, and that they should not be unfairly attacked; and, two, the idea of the government running public enterprises has outlived its time and that the bureaucracy in any case should not be running them. Scarcely ever has any senior politician, let alone a prime minister, spoken with such candour in Parliament in recent years.[15]

The third pillar—focus on ethical wealth creation—reflects this shift in the thinking of new India, which views wealth and wealth creation, acquired ethically, as a boon and not a bane. This is a significant break from the muddled narratives of the past that viewed profit as a dirty word. This change towards embracing wealth creation is a durable one because our policy now recognizes that ethical wealth creation has been part of India's DNA for millennia. The idea of ethical wealth creation as a noble human pursuit is rooted in India's old and rich tradition ranging from Kautilya's *Arthashastra* to Thiruvalluvar's *Thirukural*. The primacy of wealth creation in India's DNA is reinforced by the fact that the common person writes 'शुभ लाभ' (*shubh-labh*; generate profit by doing good) at the altar in his home. Given the demonstrated economic benefits that India reaped from pursuing wealth creation by enabling economic freedom—both historically and post the 1991 economic reforms—India's conviction towards embracing wealth creation by enabling economic freedom is solid.

---

[14]*Prime Minister Narendra Modi: Reply on Motion of Thanks to the President's Address (10-02-2021)*, Parliament Digital Library, 10 February 2021, http://tinyurl.com/3bkj6639. Accessed on 9 January 2024.

[15]'Watershed Moment', *The Hindu BusinessLine*, 11 February 2021, http://tinyurl.com/5ffchwtw. Accessed on 9 January 2024.

To enable the process of wealth creation, the government is not only enabling and empowering the private sector, but is also assuming the responsibility of investing in physical and digital infrastructure. The policy of enabling the private sector in areas where there are no market failures allows two fundamental drivers of economic policy—incentives and information—to work for the economy rather than against it. As the private sector usually under-provides on public goods or indulges in monopoly pricing when it does create them, the government has taken on the task of creating both the soft and hard infrastructure as public goods so that access to the same is universal. Thus, to return back to India's DNA of treating ethical wealth creation as a boon, the government is now focussing on doing what it should do and relinquishing activities that are better done by the private sector.

The Nehruvian socialist era saw the State playing the twin roles of a mass employer of citizens and a mass producer of goods. To drive India@100 to peak economic heights, India must boldly jettison anachronistic ideologies about the large and pervasive role of the State as the provider of employment and producer of goods. In many spheres of the economy, controls still proliferate thereby inhibiting both growth and citizens' welfare. Reforms to dismantle them are being undertaken to not only enhance growth but also enable citizens' ease of living. India needs to take these reforms to their logical conclusion.

From a provider of employment through its public sector enterprises (PSEs), the State needs to transform fully into a catalyst for employment. Given the uncertain global environment, demand-side shocks remain inevitable. Most government-run businesses often struggle to maintain the agility and dynamism required to thrive in such an environment. Moreover, data, analytics and technology are increasingly assuming significance as the fourth factor of production and are ushering in the fourth Industrial Revolution. State-owned enterprises lack the nimbleness in business practices or the adaptability in technology to keep pace with the changes in this factor of production. Further, lifelong job security, which derived from the State's role as the primary employer, is an anachronism in a fast-evolving economy where the churn among businesses, let alone employees, is at a historical high. The State can no longer play the role of mass employer. Instead, the State will act as a catalyser of employment so that firms find the talent they need and workers find the rewarding employment they seek.

Similarly, the State will no longer play the role of mass producer in India. Although exceptions exist, the average public sector entity is less profitable, grows slower, and is less productive than the average private sector entity. To achieve the goal of becoming a global economic powerhouse by 2047, India must grow at 8 per cent annually in real terms or 13 per cent in nominal terms. India cannot grow at 13 per cent when India's PSEs grow at barely 5 per cent on average. It is simple arithmetic! A country cannot grow at 13 per cent unless its businesses grow at that rate. Each PSE that lags its private counterparts in innovation and growth is depressing the growth of the economy. India's policy has, therefore, recognized that the only way to unleash growth is for the government to open up the closed sectors. Except for some strategically critical sectors, where the State's role cannot be ceded to the private sector, the government needs to get out of business to enable better business. There is no dearth of private players in India, nor is there any dearth of finance or technology, to prevent the private sector from taking on the State's role in managing businesses.

Virtuous Cycle for Economic Development

The fourth pillar, a 'virtuous cycle' driven by private investment, adds substance to the macroeconomic model for high growth. This virtuous cycle has at its centre public expenditure on physical and digital infrastructure to 'crowd in' private investment as well as supply-side reforms that will help remove various frictions on the supply side of the economy, thereby accelerating private investment.

The virtuous cycle originating from private investment is crucial for sustained economic growth in India. Investment leads to productivity gains and creation of jobs, both of which increase disposable income in the economy and thereby foster consumption. Thus, in the first-round effects embedded in the virtuous cycle, private investment is most crucial for enhancing consumption. In the second-round effects embedded in the virtuous cycle, anticipated increases in consumption spur further investment by the private sector. The virtuous cycle delivers explosive growth as consumption and investment feed each other symbiotically.

This virtuous cycle model for economic development is an

adaptation of the 'multiplier-accelerator' model developed by Nobel laureates Paul Samuelson and John Hicks. Though they developed the model to analyse business cycles, Jay Wright Forrester, a pioneering Massachusetts Institute of Technology (MIT) professor in the fields of computer engineering, management theory, and systems design, viewed this model as better fitted to study long-run economic development. In a research paper titled 'Economic Theory for the New Millennium' in 2003, Forrester wrote:

> The usual economic literature presents economics as a science, with economists trying to emulate the hard sciences such as physics. Those attempts to force economics into the mold of a science have not been satisfying. As a result of trying to pose as a science, the field of economics has become substantially detached from real-world behavior, and has tended toward a closed theoretical discipline disconnected from the world it tries to explain. Instead of being a science, I suggest that economics should become a systems profession. As a systems profession, economics would be parallel to management, engineering, and medicine, each of which is based on underlying sciences. An economics systems profession would be based on underlying sciences such as psychology, decision-making, and nonlinear feedback dynamics. As a systems profession, economics would then reach beyond its basic sciences to understand and redesign economic systems.
>
> Academic economics has evolved away from real economic behavior over the last fifty years. *In the beginning, economics started from direct observation and theorizing about business activity, but since, in its effort to appear as a science, economics has drifted toward a conceptual structure that is narrow, is based on unrealistic assumptions, emphasizes equilibrium conditions, and is committed to mostly linear mathematical methods.*[16]

As an engineer-turned-economist, I have found Forrester's 'systems design' approach to macroeconomics to be far more persuasive than the traditional macroeconomic theories relying on the elusive concept of

---

[16]Forrester, Jay W., 'Economic Theory for the New Millennium', *System Dynamics Review*, Vol. 29, No. 1, 2003, pp. 26–41.

equilibrium. Therefore, as envisioned and outlined in the *Economic Survey 2018–19*, the conception of macroeconomic growth as a virtuous cycle, which incorporates feedback effects among consumption, investment, employment and growth, explains the real-world economy much better than academic economic models.

The virtuous cycle originating from private investment relies on public capex, especially in physical and digital infrastructure, and reforms to alleviate supply-side frictions. India's model, with its emphasis on public capital expenditure (capex) during economic downturns, differs significantly from the Keynesian prescription of government spending via revenue expenditure (revex) or doles during economic downturns. This emphasis on public capex is necessary in India today as research shows that an increase in revex by ₹100 only adds ₹98–99 to the economy, while increase in capex by ₹100 adds ₹245 to the economy in the same year and ₹480 over the next several years.

Supply-side reforms are pivotal in pushing India's production frontier by boosting productivity and attracting private investment. These include, inter alia, financial sector reforms to enhance access to capital, labour market reforms to reduce the frictions due to stringent and complex labour laws, and expanding the definition of small and medium enterprises (SMEs) to avoid dwarfism among them, stemming from the nature of taxpayer incentives provided to small firms. Such structural reforms are geared towards bolstering 'ease of doing business' and bringing down 'cost of doing business'—two non-negotiables in enhancing global competitiveness and tapping the entrepreneurial energies of both young and seasoned businesspersons.

Intellectual Underpinning of the Economic Strategy

The intellectual underpinning for the economic strategy articulated here stems from New Structural Economics (NSE).[17] Former World Bank Chief Economist Justin Yifu Lin coined this term by studying carefully the economic growth models of several developing economies—both successful ones in Asia and the unsuccessful ones in Latin America and Africa.

---

[17]Lin, Justin Yifu, 'New Structural Economics: The Third Generation of Development Economics', GEGI Working Paper 027, Global Development Policy Center, January 2019, http://tinyurl.com/2yvubzx6. Accessed on 19 February 2024.

Two features of NSE align harmoniously with the framework developed here. First, it emphasizes the coordinated role of the market as well as the state in fostering economic progress. It advocates competitive markets as a sine qua non for the following reason: In order for firms to prioritize profits and spontaneously enter industries and choose technologies that align with the economy's comparative advantage, the price system must reflect the relative scarcity of factors in the country's endowment. This only happens in an economy with competitive markets. Therefore, a competitive market should be the economy's fundamental mechanism for resource allocation at each level of its development.

While market mechanisms are fundamental for resource allocation, the dynamic nature of economic processes demands continuous industrial upgrading. Aligning industrial upgrading with changes in comparative advantage ensures competitiveness in domestic and global markets. As economies progress, the indivisibility of capital equipment necessitates an increase in the scale of production. This requires corresponding improvements in power, transportation and financial structures. Advancing up the industrial ladder brings about changes in technology, capital requirements and market size. Coordinated improvements in education, finance, legal institutions and infrastructure are vital for smooth industrial and technological upgrading. Government intervention is essential to actively support these processes and effectively coordinate, as individual firms or industries cannot efficiently internalize these changes. Successful industrial upgrading requires the government to also develop soft and hard infrastructure. Examples of hard infrastructure are highways, port facilities, airports, telecommunication systems, electricity grids and other public utilities. Soft infrastructure consists of institutions, regulations, social capital, value systems and other socio-economic arrangements.

The synchronous role of competitive markets and the government in the economic model advocated by NSE resonates with the economic model advocated in this book. Here the first pillar—macroeconomic focus on growth—and the second pillar—social and economic inclusion—bring into spotlight the role of the government in achieving these twin objectives. At the same time, the third pillar—ethical wealth creation—and the fourth pillar—virtuous cycle driven by private investment—

emphasize the role of the private sector and a competitive market. The ethical dimension in wealth creation also brings up the role of the government in developing the soft infrastructure referred to above to ensure that wealth is not created unethically.

Second, NSE highlights the need for a developing country's model for economic progress being tailored to the economic conditions peculiar to the country. This idea is consistent with the emphasis on *sui generis* economic policies tailored to India as advocated in Chapter 3. While India can benefit from adopting certain positive aspects of economic development of rich countries, it may not be wise to simply imitate them due to the unique challenges faced by developing economies.

Historical Role of Government Policy in Advancing Economic Progress

As the economic strategy proposed here advocates a key role for the government, I now explain using historical episodes the crucial role that government policy has played has played in enabling economic progress. Nobel Laureate Eric Maskin, in an article in 2021 titled 'Government and Economics: An Emerging Field of Study', describes the crucial role that government policy—especially industrial policy—played in the economic progress of many of the developed nations.[18] By examining the policies followed during five different high-growth episodes—the US post the Civil War, Germany and Japan in the nineteenth century, South Korea from the 1960s and China from late 1970s—the study throws essential light on the importance of government policy in supporting the development of competitive markets domestically.

Table 1 shows the key elements of government policy during these historical growth episodes.

---

[18]Li, David Daokui, and Eric S. Maskin, 'Government and Economics: An Emerging Field of Study', *Journal of Government and Economics,* Vol. 1, Spring 2021. http://tinyurl.com/yckx9ukf. Accessed on 19 February 2024.

Table 1
Key elements of government policy during five historical growth episodes

	US (post Civil War)	*Germany (19th Century)*	*Japan (19th Century)*	*South Korea (1960–90)*	*China (1978–2018)*
Industrial policy including protection for domestic industry till they can compete	✓	✓	✓	✓	✓
Infrastructure investment	✓	✓	✓	✓	✓
Investment in education	✓	✓	✓	✓	✓
Enabling financing for private investment	✓	✓	✓	✓	✓
Promoting exports	✓	✓	✓	✓	✓
Enabling technological innovation	✓	✓			

Source: Author's compilation using Li and Maskin (2021)

I now highlight some of the specific policies that were pursued.

Industrial Policy Including Protection for Domestic Industry

- **US post the Civil War:** In contrast to its open policy on foreign investment, the US government protected its growing industries by maintaining high tariffs on foreign goods. In the early 1900s, when protectionist tariffs were no longer needed, the government lowered tariff rates dramatically. In 1934, the US Congress passed the Reciprocal Tariff Act to promote trade liberalization. Since then, the US generally has maintained a policy of free trade, with low tariff rates. The McKinley Tariff Act of 1890 substantially raised the duty on imported tinplate to encourage the entry and growth of domestic producers. The Act also contained an unusual provision in which the tariff would be completely eliminated in six years if, by that time, domestic production did not amount to at least one-third of imports.[19] The tariff succeeded in promoting domestic production leading to a rapid expansion in output. Consequently, by about 1910, the price of US tinplate fell below those produced in the UK.

- **Germany (19th century):** The German government first vigorously supported its infant industries through trade protectionism. In 1879, in order to protect infant industries, the German parliament Reichstag raised tariffs to 18 per cent on pig iron and 15–30 per cent on textiles and raised them twice more in the following years. As a result, Germany was able to balance its trade and protect its domestic industries. With the help of trade protectionism, the country developed strong, competitive industrial sectors. Once this advantage was firmly established, German industries were re-exposed to foreign competition, as the country returned to free trade in the 1890s.
- **Japan (19th century):** In sectors where private enterprises were weak, the Japanese government provided support until they could stand on their own. The case of Mitsubishi is a good illustration. Between 1875 and 1876, the government supplied over 30 ships for Mitsubishi to use free of charge and provided a shipping subsidy of 2,50,000 Japanese yen (J¥ or JPY) to help Mitsubishi cut its prices and compete with the Pacific Mail Steamship Company, its US-based competitor. The government imposed cumbersome boarding procedures on Japanese passengers taking foreign ships, thus inducing them to choose domestic options. The government also provided special convenience and low freight rates for Mitsubishi's goods, while enacting tariffs and transportation barriers against British goods.
- **South Korea (1960–90):** The South Korean government enabled growth of its domestic industry through tax reductions for these industries and protectionist import tariff rates. During this period, the iron and steel industry grew by 246 per cent, the machinery industry by 300 per cent, the electronics industry by 338 per cent, the shipbuilding industry by 211 per cent, and the petrochemical industry by 311 per cent. The government built industrial parks and sold them directly to large enterprises.

---

[19]Irwin, Douglas A., 'Historical Aspects of US Trade Policy', *The Reporter*, 6 January 2006, http://tinyurl.com/mrynrtcj. Accessed on 19 February 2024.

South Korea's original comparative advantage was cheap and diligent labour. It was, therefore, reasonable for it to initially engage in sectors like textiles, garments, footwear and simple electronics. As the domestic wage rate rose and more capital was accumulated, South Korea moved into more capital-intensive sectors such as steel or petrochemicals. The Electronics Promotion Law in 1969 recognized electronics as a 'strategic export industry'.[20]

- **China (1978–2018):** Local governments set up industrial parks in which necessities, such as electricity, steam power, water, roads and waste collection, were pre-established. As of 2017, there were more than 5,000 industrial parks in China, all competing with one another to provide the most enticing incentives to attract new enterprises. For example, in 2019, the municipal government of Shanghai wooed Tesla with free land and tax breaks. As a result, Tesla began production in 2020 after only one year of investment! The Chinese government also deliberately induced the exit of many enterprises during episodes of excess production capacity by offering a significant subsidy to enterprises willing to exit.

Enabling Investment in Infrastructure

- **US post the Civil War:** In the Pacific Railway Act of 1862, the federal government authorized two companies to construct the Pacific Railroad and granted them the land to do so. State and local governments invested on a huge scale in other infrastructure projects, including roads, waterworks, schools, hospitals and recreational parks.
- **Germany (19th century):** Up till 1850, funds of the German government provided over 73 per cent of railway finance in the German states.
- **Japan (19th century):** The Japanese government during this period made significant investment to rapidly construct railroads.
- **South Korea (1960–90):** During the 1960s, the lion's share of public funds went to fund infrastructure including highways, port facilities, electricity, irrigation, transportation, communication, etc.

---

[20]Kim, Kwan S., 'The Korean Miracle (1962-1980) Revisited: Myths and Realities In Strategy and Development', *Kellogg Institute*, November 1991, http://tinyurl.com/mr2hcufc; Accessed on 19 February 2024.

The government and public enterprises accounted for close to 40 per cent of the total domestic investment in the period between 1963 and 1979.

- **China (1978–2018):** The Chinese government invested in infrastructure for electricity generation, highways and railroads and telecommunications.

Facilitating Investment in Education

- **US post the Civil War:** The Morrill Act of 1862 expanded tertiary education in agricultural modernization. Federal and local governments granted over 17 million acres of land to be sold to raise money for the establishment of land-grant colleges, which specialized in agriculture, engineering, and the sciences. Most of these colleges gradually became state universities that grew to offer a full spectrum of educational opportunities and made higher education available to ordinary people.
- **Germany (19th century):** By the end of the 1840s, 82 per cent of school-aged children were enrolled in school. By the end of the 1860s, the enrolment rate stood at 97.5 per cent. The German government also worked to enhance secondary education, which greatly improved the quality of the German labour force. In order to strengthen the technical education of young workers and apprentices, the government set up many technical schools, vocational schools, amateur technical night schools and Sunday schools.
- **Japan (19th century):** National compulsory education of four years, which was increased to six years in 1907, was promulgated in 1872.
- **South Korea (1960–90):** To build human capital, the government established many universities and colleges including Korea Electronics Technology Institute, Korea Advanced Institute of Science and Technology and Electronic Industries Association of Korea for research, adaptation and development.
- **China (1978–2018):** Primary education was made free and compulsory. The government introduced a law that made it illegal for any organization or individual to employ youth before they completed their nine years of schooling. The same law also authorized students whose families had financial difficulties to receive subsidies. The Ministry of Education was abolished and the State Education

Commission was established. The new Commission had a higher status than the old Ministry and was put in charge of all educational organizations (except the military). This reform decentralized power by empowering local authorities to run and financially support primary education. Notably, significant advancements were made in the training of a large number of qualified teachers. A national system of teacher qualification regulations was set up in 2001 to certify qualified teachers. According to new regulations, only those with teaching certificates could teach.

Assisting Financing for Private Investment

- **US post the Civil War:** The federal and state governments provided about $350 million in railroad construction subsidies between 1862 and 1873. Public services like schools and parks were recognized as special types of governmental institutions with debt-financing powers. Thus, these public services were able to raise their own debt independent of government.
- **Germany (19th century):** German universal banks made possible the rapid accumulation of capital on a scale vast enough to finance the building of transportation and communication infrastructure. These banks provided initial capital for new industrial ventures and helped guide them through their early years of growth. They were represented on supervisory boards. The German system of investment finance enabled the universal banks to deal with the problems of asymmetric information, which were inevitable when investment had to be financed by external sources of funds.
- **Japan (19th century):** The government provided Mitsubishi with preferential loans of J¥8,00,000, which ultimately pushed Pacific Mail Steamship Company out of the Yokohama–Shanghai route. Nippon Railway, Japan's first private railway company, was founded in 1881 with the direct support of the government, which raised J¥20 million for railway construction. The Japanese government raised the funds necessary for this accomplishment by issuing public debt and reforming. In 1870, J¥4.88 million was raised in Britain to build the Tokyo–Yokohama line, the first modern railway of Japan. In 1878, J¥12.5 million in public debt was issued expressly to finance construction of railways, mines, ports, and roads. The National Bank

Act established four national banks in Tokyo, Yokohama, Osaka and Niigata. Then, in August 1876, Japan revised its national banking regulations to support privately-owned commercial banks.

- **South Korea (1960–90):** To accomplish the ambitious goal of rapid industrialization and export growth, the government first nationalized privately-owned commercial banks and took control of the credit supply. The idea was to funnel investment into key industrial firms, which remained in private hands and continued to compete in the free market. The national pension service and the Korea Development Bank provided low interest loans for key industries.
- **China (1978–2018):** The central government recapitalized government-owned banks and invited foreign banks, such as the Bank of America, to become strategic investors. As a result, these banks were significantly modernized and were able to issue tradable shares, and eventually became highly profitable.

Promoting Exports

- **US post the Civil War:** The US's export of manufactures surged during this period. Manufactured goods jumped from 20 per cent of US exports in 1890 to 35 per cent by 1900 and nearly 50 per cent by 1913.
- **Germany (19th century):** From 1890 to 1913, Germany's share in world exports increased from 17.2 per cent to 26.6 per cent. German exports tripled during this period.
- **South Korea (1960–90):** At first, South Korea focussed on cultivating labour-intensive light industries and handicraft exports. Later, it gradually turned to heavy and high-tech industries. Along the way, multiple policies were used to support exports. Financial support was provided through export promotion funds, foreign exchange loans, tax breaks and tariff reductions for export industries importing raw materials from overseas. In addition, the government lowered shipping and transportation fees for exporting firms and encouraged exporting industries to form export associations. The export manufacturer could obtain subsidized loans from institutions such as the Korea Development Bank, the Export-Import Bank, the Technology Finance Corporation and the National Investment Fund. A series of legislations and regulations, such as the Tax Incentives

Law, the Government Budget and Accounting Law and the Tariff Law, provided various forms of tax relief and tariff reductions for imported inputs to the manufacturer.

Fostering Technological Innovation

- **US post the Civil War:** The US government established the world's first modern patent system. The government gave ownership rights to innovators, thus encouraging innovation and promoting the creation of new technologies.
- **Germany (19th century):** The German government actively promoted scientific research. It established a series of scientific research institutions. It also invested in national research institutes and helped universities and enterprises set up research centres, institutes and laboratories. A series of new inventions, such as generators, gas engine, electrical furnaces and automobiles, were born out of these scientific research institutions. The German government also passed the patent law of 1879 and revised it in 1895. By the late nineteenth century, Germany had become the world leader in the production of acids, alkalis, dyes and other chemicals. The electrical industry provides a particularly vivid example: in the 22 years from 1891 to 1913, the total output of Germany's electrical industry increased by 28×. By 1913, German electrical products accounted for 34 per cent of global production of similar products.

Discovering Self-Serving Postulates of Economic History

Maskin's study highlights that many of the self-styled economic postulates for economic progress—as captured in the Washington Consensus—were developed *after* these countries had developed their economies.[21] Before attaining economic advancement, advanced economies adopted the same 'insular' policies that they advocate developing economies to shun now, including tariff and non-tariff trade barriers, supporting their domestic nascent industry, etc. In fact, even now, when these advanced economies face economic difficulties in some areas, they resort to the same insular

[21]The Washington Consensus, coined by British economist John Williamson in 1989, refers to a set of free-market economic policies supported by prominent financial institutions such as the IMF, the World Bank and the US Treasury.

policies they adopted when their domestic industries were weak. The trade war between the US and China following the hollowing out of the manufacturing sector in the US is a good case in point.

As advocated in Chapter 3, India needs to carefully assess the economic postulates before applying them, by incorporating the differences between India and the advanced economies. Incorporating the following two tenets is important for India to achieve the Goldilocks balance.[22] First, economic trade-offs remain very similar across countries. However, and this is the crucial second point, the policy that resolves the trade-off may not be the same for India as it is for the advanced economies as the economic conditions are quite different. In order to understand the right learnings from the policies followed by the advanced economies, India needs to study carefully through apples-to-apples comparisons. Specifically, Indian policymakers need to study the policies that the advanced economies implemented when they faced economic conditions similar to that of India today, not the policies that the advanced economies implement now when their economic conditions are starkly different from that of India.

Importance of Job Creation in the Economic Strategy

As explained above, enabling market forces represents a key element of economic strategy. However, many opine that the market may be broadly efficient, but it can be quite unfair too. While the invisible hand of the market effectively allocates resources where they are most productive, creates new technologies and fuels entrepreneurship, it also, in the process, rewards success, while leaving behind those that are unsuccessful and unskilled. This view suggests the necessity of redistributive policies that aim to share the gains of economic prosperity equitably and invest in enhancing the skills of the less fortunate. Supporters of the efficient-but-unfair market hypothesis propose an even greater level of redistribution, similar to the socialist paradigm that India followed until 1991. The problem with this view is that no society has achieved shared prosperity

[22]Goldilocks rate/balance is characterized by an economy that is neither too heated (inflationary) nor is it in a recessionary state, i.e., the currency is not too strong or weak in global markets.

by just redistributing income from the rich to the less fortunate. Rather, shared prosperity results from the ability of societies to forge 'inclusive markets' that devise a level-playing field for people and provide conditions for broadly shared growth.

Good jobs—those that provide not only a wage consistent with a 'middle class' living standard but also some stability and protection against harsh and dangerous working conditions and excessive power of employers—play a crucial role in generating such shared prosperity. A bountiful supply of good jobs is the best way to generate shared prosperity. When the economy has a shortage of work or many jobs pay a pittance, a natural inequality emerges between those that are able or fortunate enough to get good jobs and the rest. Once it takes root, this inequality is very hard to undo, with or without enthusiastic fiscal redistribution. Furthermore, when good jobs are scarce, civic engagement becomes more difficult, and political participation, if any, becomes more likely to be underpinned by grievances and economic hardships, opening the door to both populism and patronage politics.

In contrast, a plentiful supply of high-wage jobs is often self-reinforcing. When high-wage jobs are available in manufacturing and services, workers are less willing to take up a job that pays much less, putting upward pressure on the pay of low-wage workers. This wage pressure both improves the pay of these jobs and makes them less attractive for firms (compared to high-wage jobs). Higher wages may also encourage firms to invest in technologies and training to support good jobs. This is because once firms are weaned off low-wage jobs, they will have an incentive to invest more in the general and specific human capital of their employees. This is because when firms must pay higher wages, their incentives to increase worker productivity are greater. Higher wages may also trigger more innovation that aims to partially substitute for labour, while still increasing economy-wide productivity.

The creation of high-wage jobs does more than ensure shared prosperity; good jobs are also necessary for society to enable a meaningful, fulfilling life for its citizens. It is unlikely that individuals can find a similar meaning or purpose from pure redistribution, no matter the scale. Most individuals define their worth largely through their jobs and form their social networks and support groups during their careers. Therefore, good jobs are the essential ingredient to fulfilling the objective embodied in the second pillar—social and economic inclusion.

◆

The transformative change in India's economic thinking articulated in this chapter will provide impetus to inclusive economic growth via job creation in the organized sectors. As economic growth stems from the combination of investment and productivity growth in the economy, the four-pillar approach will enhance both. The twin effects will lead to real growth of 7–8 per cent in the next two decades.

4

BEYOND COPY–PASTE

Sui Generis Policies for India's Centennial

During the GFC, India achieved the dubious distinction of becoming a Fragile Five economy by imitating the economic policies of advanced economies. Subsequently, in contrast to such copy–paste, India thought for herself ab initio and implemented sui generis policy fit for the country. The outcome now is starkly different too: instead of being one of the Fragile Five, India has become a top five economy with GDP growth greater than 7 per cent and strong macro-fundamentals. This chapter explains the sui generis economic policy that India pursued during Covid-19 as an example of the ab initio thinking that India needs to become a global economic titan.

When the world was reeling with the once-in-a-lifetime crisis caused by the pandemic in 2020, there was no playbook available to governments, economists and policymakers around the world. India's policy response to Covid-19 drew on key lessons learnt from the Spanish Flu pandemic a century back in 1918 and India's economic policy response to the 2007–08 GFC. As the economic survey of the GoI for the financial year 2020–21 highlighted:

> Faced with unprecedented uncertainty at the onset of the pandemic, India focused on saving lives and livelihoods by its willingness to take short-term pain for long-term gain. India's response stemmed from the humane principle advocated eloquently in the Mahabharata that 'saving a life that is in jeopardy is the origin of dharma.' Therefore, India recognized that while GDP growth will recover from the temporary shock caused by the pandemic, human lives that are lost cannot be brought back. The response drew on epidemiological and economic research, especially those pertaining to the Spanish Flu, which highlighted that an early, intense lockdown provided a win-win strategy to save lives and preserve livelihoods via economic recovery in the medium to

> long term. The strategy was also motivated by the Nobel-Prize winning research in Hansen & Sargent (2001) that recommends a policy focused on minimizing losses in a worst-case scenario when uncertainty is very high. Faced with an unprecedented pandemic and the resultant uncertainty, loss of scores of human lives captured thus the worst-case scenario.[23]

India entered the once-in-a-century pandemic with an economy that was slowing down due to a myriad of financial sector problems. With a sovereign credit rating that was just one notch above non-investment grade, the downgrades in India's ratings outlook created the material risk of India being relegated to a non-investment grade rating, thereby triggering capital flight. This risk would materialize if India did not manage the balance between growth, on the one hand, and fiscal spending and possible inflation, on the other hand, during Covid-19. Despite entering the pandemic with such difficult prior conditions, India has managed to emerge as the fastest-growing large economy in the world, registering a robust recovery with strong macroeconomic fundamentals. This is reflected in relatively low inflation, fiscal deficit and debt-to-GDP ratio that is under control and on a downward trajectory; an external sector that is robust despite the double whammy of the Russia–Ukraine war following the pandemic; investment inflows—both foreign direct investment (FDI) and foreign portfolio investment (FPI)—that have touched unprecedented highs; and currency depreciation that is one of the lowest among all major currencies.

This economic performance stands in stark contrast to India's shambolic economic performance following the GFC, when the triple blow of very high inflation, high fiscal deficit and high current account deficit (CAD) culminated in India becoming part of the Fragile Five economies. As *Economic Survey 2020–21* highlighted, India's economic policy during Covid-19 represented a 'sui generis case in strategic policymaking amidst a once-in-a-century pandemic'.[24] More specifically, it says:

[23]Ministry of Finance, GoI, *Economic Survey 2020–21: Volume 1*, January 2021, p. 1, https://tinyurl.com/mwkb3psz. Accessed on 22 November 2023.
[24]Ibid. 2.

> On the economic policy front, India recognized that, *unlike previous crises, the Covid-19 pandemic affects both demand and supply.* Furthermore, given disruptions in the labour markets that can affect disposable income and firms suffering financial distress, the loss of productive capacity due to hysteresis could not be ruled out. Therefore, a slew of structural reforms was announced; together, these would help to expand supply significantly in the medium to long term. On the demand side, at the onset of the pandemic, India's policies focused purely on necessities. This was optimal given the uncertainty and the resultant precautionary motives to save as well as the economic restrictions during the lockdown. After all, pushing down on the accelerator while the brakes are clamped only wastes fuel. During the unlock phase, demand-side measures have been announced in a calibrated manner. A public investment program centred around the National Infrastructure Pipeline is likely to accelerate this demand push and further the recovery. The upturn in the economy while avoiding a second wave of infections makes India a sui generis case in strategic policymaking amidst a once-in-a-century pandemic.[25]

Now, a couple of years post the pandemic, we have a good vantage point to examine India's economic policy and derive lessons that can be useful elsewhere. As Figure 1 shows, India's GDP growth post Covid-19 has not been completely fuelled by fiscal stimulus, unlike the case for most other countries which resulted in excessive inflation. India's balance of supply-side and demand-side policy measures ensured real growth, whereas other countries that indulged in demand-side stimulus alone were left with short-term growth fuelled by runaway inflation.

[25]Ibid. Author's italicization.

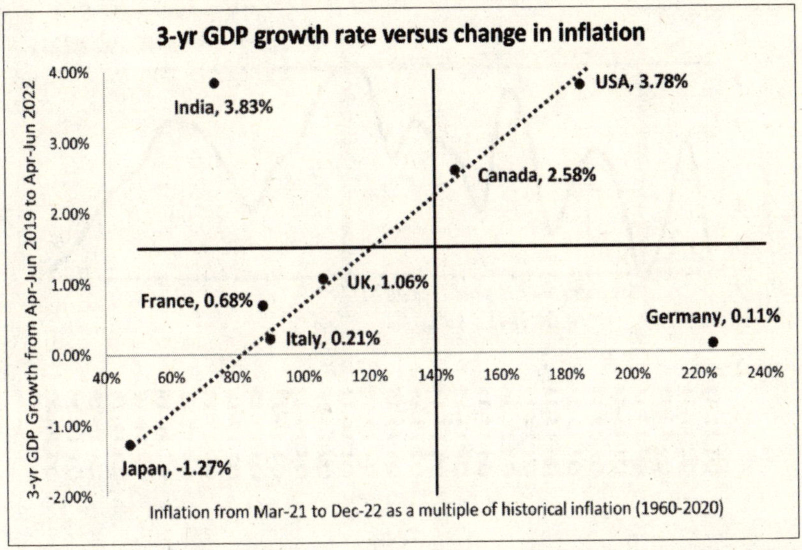

Figure 1: Three-year GDP growth during Covid-19 versus change in inflation for large economies

Source: IMF and individual country statistics

Pre-Covid Economic Situation

Growth Slowdown from Q4 of 2017–18

India entered Covid-19 with a growth slowdown due to the overhang caused by financial sector problems that, in turn, had stemmed from crony bank lending till 2013. Comprehensive evidence for this is provided in Volume 2 of *Economic Survey 2019–20.*[26] In assessing the economy before Covid-19, *Economic Survey 2019–20* analysed the slowdown in GDP growth starting from the fourth quarter (Q4) of the fiscal year 2017–18; Figure 9 from the first chapter of this Survey that has been reproduced as Figure 2 shows this continuous decline in GDP.

[26]Ministry of Finance, GoI, *Economic Survey 2019–20: Volume 2*, January 2020, pp. 20–7, https://tinyurl.com/5yx738a3. Accessed on 23 November 2023.

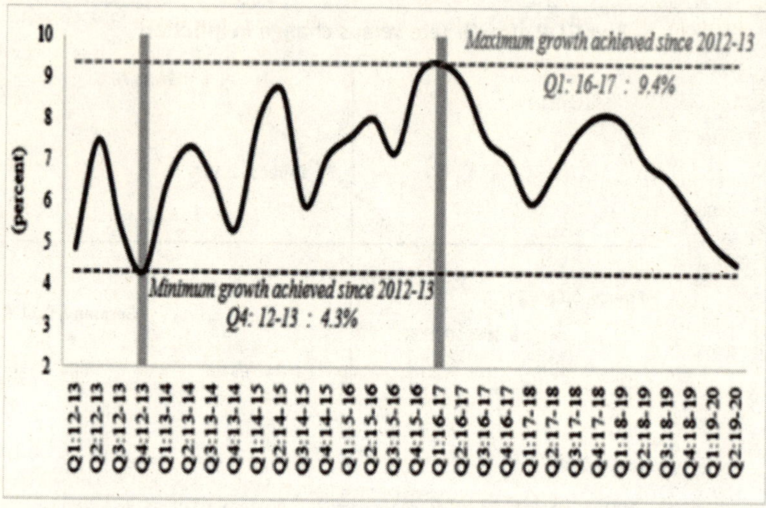

Figure 2: Quarterly growth rate of India's GDP before Covid-19
Source: Economic Survey 2020–21

Given the lags in the effect of economic policy and the dynamic interdependencies between investment, consumption and GDP growth in any economy, *Economic Survey 2018–19* introduced the idea of 'virtuous cycle', wherein an increase in the rate of fixed investment accelerates the growth of GDP that in turn induces a higher growth in consumption. Higher growth of consumption improves the investment outlook, which results in a still higher growth of fixed investment; this further accelerates the growth of GDP, inducing an even higher growth of consumption.[27]

By using this framework to analyse the growth decline before Covid-19, *Economic Survey 2019–20* explains:

> The Indian economy, since 2011–12, has been under the influence of slowing cycle of growth. The fixed investment rate has started declining sharply since 2011–12 and subsequently plateaued from 2016–17 onwards. Given the lagged impact of the investment rate on GDP growth shown in Figure 24 [Figure 4 here] (with the effect being most pronounced after four years), the deceleration in

[27]Ministry of Finance, GoI, *Economic Survey 2018–19: Volume 1*, July 2019, p. 1, https://tinyurl.com/5ccw6unz. Accessed on 23 November 2023.

growth since 2017–18 is consistent with the framework described here (Figure 26) [Figure 3 here].[28]

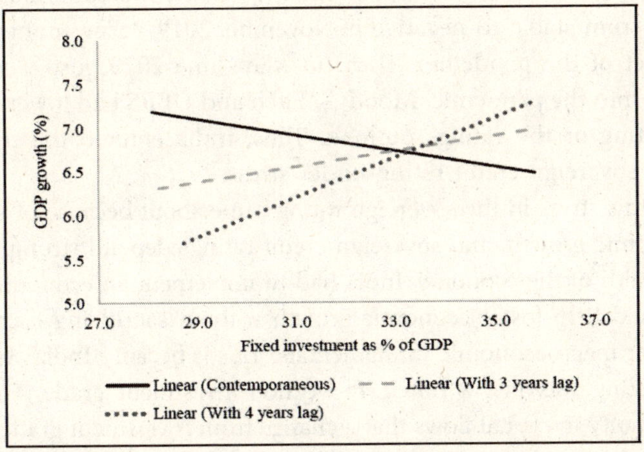

Figure 3: Lagged effect of investment on growth (2004–2019)
Source: Economic Survey 2019–20

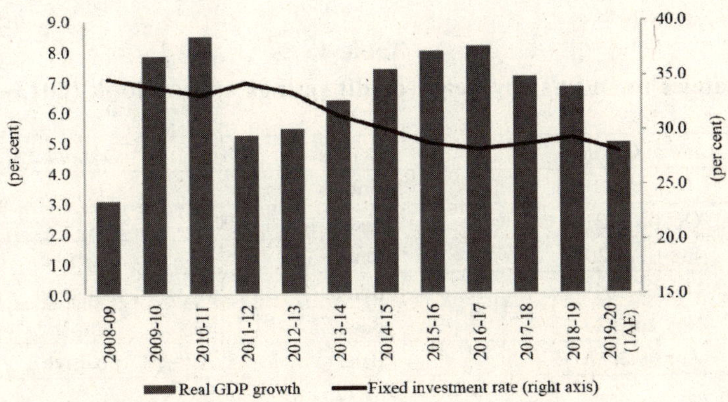

Figure 4: Real GDP growth and investment—annual movement
Source: Economic Survey 2019–20

[28]Ministry of Finance, GoI, *Economic Survey 2019–20: Volume 2*, January 2020, pp. 20–6, https://tinyurl.com/5yx738a3. Accessed on 23 November 2023.

Sovereign Credit Rating under Stress

The slowdown in growth, in turn, brought India's sovereign credit rating under stress. As Table 1 shows, Moody's had lowered India's ratings outlook from 'stable' to 'negative' in November 2019—a few months before the onset of the pandemic. Then, in May–June 2020, just a couple of months into the pandemic, Moody's, Fitch and DBRS had lowered either their rating or the ratings outlook. Thus, India entered the pandemic with its sovereign credit rating under stress.

As this stress in the sovereign rating came about because of a decline in economic growth, and sovereign credit ratings depend strongly on the fiscal health of the economy, India had to implement an economic policy that would help foster economic growth without sacrificing fiscal health and other macroeconomic fundamentals. This is because India's sovereign credit rating was just a notch above non-investment grade. Given the discontinuity in capital flows that a change from investment grade to non-investment grade or vice-versa brings, as highlighted in the third chapter of first volume of the *Economic Survey 2020–21*, India faced the distinct possibility of capital flight if India's sovereign credit rating was lowered because of a decline in economic growth or macroeconomic instability.[29]

Table 1

Changes in India's sovereign credit ratings and outlook (2013–23)

Date of Change	*Rating*	*Outlook*
	Moody's	
Oct 05 2021	Baa3	stable
Jun 01 2020	Baa3	negative
Nov 07 2019	Baa2	negative
Nov 16 2017	Baa2	stable
Apr 09 2015	Baa3	positive

[29]It is pertinent to note here that *Economic Survey* 2020–21 (Chapter 3, Volume 1) acknowledged that India's economic fundamentals did not get reflected in its sovereign credit rating. Markets factored this in fully, as none of the equity, fixed income or foreign exchange markets reacted much to a change in India's sovereign credit rating, except when this change involved the discontinuity of a change from investment grade to non-investment grade or vice-versa.

Date of Change	*Rating*	*Outlook*
	S&P	
Sep 26 2014	BBB-	stable
	Fitch	
Jun 10 2022	BBB-	stable
Jun 18 2020	BBB-	negative
Jun 12 2013	BBB-	stable
Jun 18 2012	BBB-	negative
	DBRS	
May 19 2021	BBB (low)	stable
May 21 2020	BBB	negative
Nov 05 2015	BBB	stable
Nov 05 2014	BBB (low)	positive
Sep 30 2013	BBB (low)	stable

Source: Bloomberg

Note: Highlighted cells show the downgrades in ratings outlook

The Thinking behind Sui Generis Economic Policy

India's response to Covid-19 was meticulous and rooted in first principles. The following section highlights the key principles that guided India's economic policy.

Core Principles of India's Policy Response

- **Principle #1** *(Impact of macro policy on economic outcomes is felt with a lag)*: Figure 5 illustrates the lag between investment and GDP growth. While the contemporaneous correlation of fixed investment as a percentage of GDP and GDP growth is negative, the correlations with a three-year and a four-year lag are positive. In fact, investment in year *t* correlates the highest with GDP growth in year (*t*+4), i.e., four years later. Given these lags in the effect of economic policy and the dynamic interdependencies between investment, consumption and GDP growth in any economy, *Economic Survey 2018–19* introduced the idea of 'virtuous cycle' mentioned earlier.

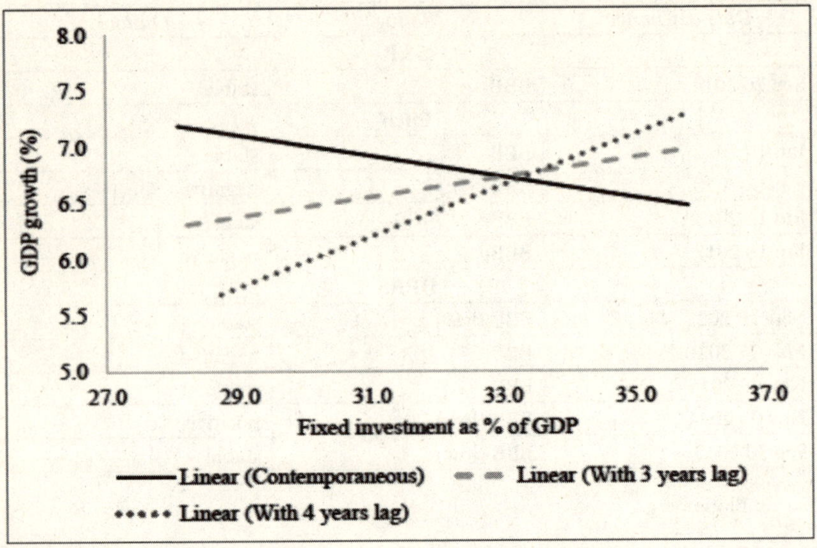

Figure 5: GDP growth (%) vs fixed investment as % of GDP

Source: Economic Survey 2020–21, Chapter 1, Volume 1

- **Principle #2** (*Macro policy that only increases demand delivers short-term growth along with high inflation in the long term. In contrast, macro policy that increases both demand and supply delivers long term growth without high inflation*): To understand the impact of Covid-19 on GDP and prices, start by considering, as a benchmark, the case of no policy intervention (Figure 6). Define Q_0 and Q_1 as the quantity, or GDP in our case, before and after Covid-19, and P_0 and P_1 as the prices, or the level of the consumer price index (CPI) in our case. Thus, the difference between Q_0 and Q_1 captures the change in GDP, while the difference between P_0 and P_1 captures change in CPI or inflation. When there is no intervention, GDP drops considerably (Q_0 to Q_1, where $Q_1 << Q_0$) but inflation does not rise ($P_1 \approx P_0$), as both supply and demand fall.

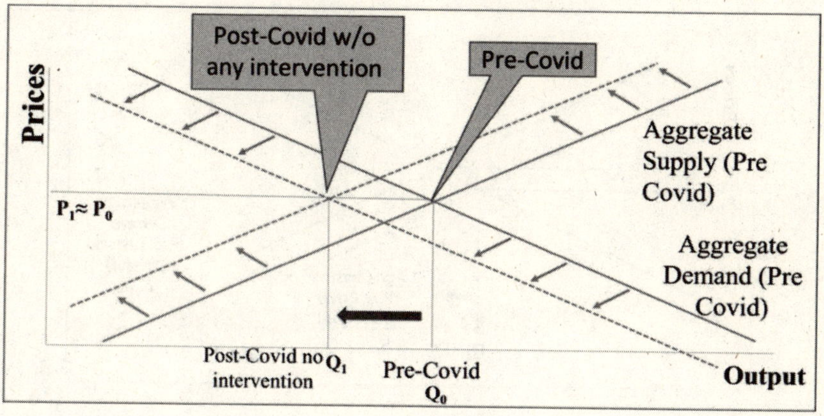

Figure 6: Absent any intervention, both supply and demand fall. So, GDP falls precipitously, but inflation is unaffected

Source: Author's design

Using this benchmark, consider two alternate policy stances.

First, when only aggregate demand is raised in the economy without any change in aggregate supply, the GDP growth obtained is not sustainable in the long run. Moreover, even this short-term growth comes with inflation (Figure 7). The boost to growth that results from the demand-side push ($Q_3>Q_2$) does not get sustained in the long term because an increase in inflation due to the demand-side push, as reflected in $P_3>P_2$, necessitates monetary policy tightening. The tightening eventually serves to reduce demand and thereby rob growth of any momentum. Therefore, growth is obtained only in the short term but with inflation.

Second, when aggregate demand and aggregate supply are both increased in the economy, the growth that results is stronger ($Q_4>Q_3>Q_2$) and gets sustained over the long term. Moreover, inflation is not high as the effect of the increase in demand is offset by the increase in supply (Figure 8). In the absence of high inflation ($P_4 \approx P_2$), monetary policy can remain more accommodative and thereby not impact private investment adversely.

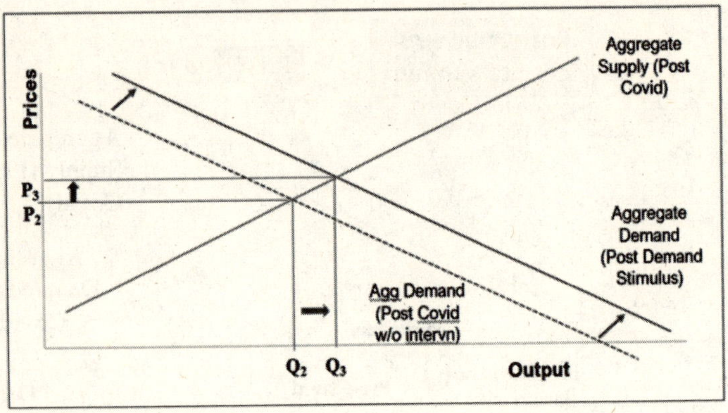

Figure 7: Only demand stimulus => demand ↑ but supply ↔. So, ↓ in GDP is lower, but inflation ↑ sharply

Source: Author's design

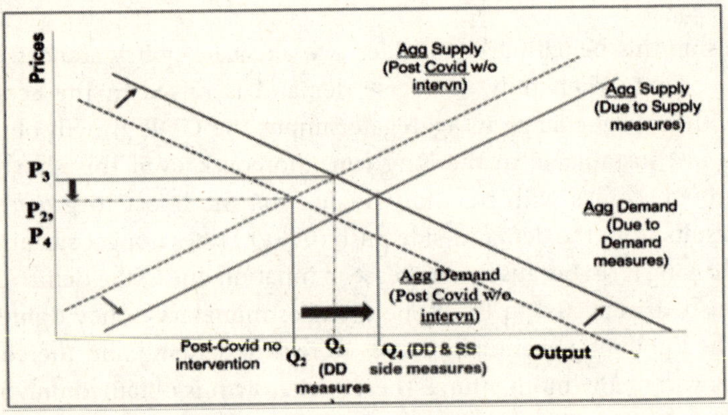

Figure 8: Demand + supply measures => both demand and supply ↑. So, ↓ in GDP is much lower, and ↑ in inflation is lower

Source: Author's design

- **Principle #3** *(Capex increases both demand and supply, while revex only increases demand)*: Revex only puts money in the hands of people in the short term. There is no increase in supply as no assets are built in this process. In contrast, capex creates assets, thereby increasing the aggregate supply in the economy. On the demand side, capex increases construction activity significantly, which creates jobs both in the informal and formal sectors. Construction activity also has linkages to several sectors such as steel, cement, etc. As the demand increases in these sectors, more people are hired and jobs get created in these sectors as well.

As the Permanent Income Hypothesis or PIH (Friedman 1957) posits, aggregate demand increases in a sustained manner only when a person is assured of income over a few years. A job provides this assurance of income over a few years. Subsidies never provide this assurance because the person remains uncertain when the subsidy, especially those announced during crises, will be withdrawn. So, even on aggregate demand, capex create sustained aggregate demand while revex only create it ephemerally. Goyal and Sharma (2018) provide evidence consistent with this principle.

- **Principle #4** *(Capex 'crowds in' private investment, while revex 'crowds out' private investment)*: As mentioned earlier, capex significantly increases construction activity, especially in sectors such as steel, cement, etc. To supply the necessary cement, steel, etc., required for construction, private firms invest as well. Moreover, as savings increase in the economy when GDP growth goes up, the pool of savings available to the private and public sector increase with capex. Thus, capex 'crowds in' private investment. However, as GDP growth does not increase much with revex, the pool of savings does not change much with revex. Therefore, revex 'crowds out' private investment as the government borrows more but the pool of savings does not increase.
- **Principle #5** *(Increase in only revex is myopic policymaking while increase in capex is farsighted policymaking)*: Bose and Bhanumurthy (2013) show in the Indian context that when government increases revex by ₹100, only ₹98–99 gets added to the economy because of deadweight costs of ₹1–2. So, there is no multiplier effect of increases in revex. In contrast, when government increases capex by ₹100, ₹245 gets added to the economy in the same year and ₹480 gets added in aggregate over the next several years. So, the multiplier effect of increase in capex is not only strong in the year in which it occurs, but also over the next few years. Goyal and Sharma (2018) show that the multiplier for capex in India is 2.4–6.5 times the multiplier for revex. Moreover, consistent with capex enhancing aggregate supply,

Goyal and Sharma (2018) find that, over the long term, capex also reduces inflation more than revex.

- **Principle #6** (*As private investment always collapses during economic crises, to keep the investment rate from falling precipitously, thereby impacting growth, government should increase its capex*): External shocks created by economic crises create tremendous uncertainty. The impact of such uncertainty is always disproportionately more on private investment than on any other aspect of GDP. This is because investment is lumpy, irreversible and has a longer horizon than consumption, exports or imports. Therefore, private firms never invest during periods of extreme uncertainty, unless the government takes steps through public investment and capex to provide the assurance that the government is committed to certainty in capex through a public capex programme.

Covid-19 vs GFC: Decoding India's Brilliant Macroeconomic Performance

In this section, I demonstrate that adhering to the principles described above led to superior macroeconomic performance during Covid-19 when compared to that during the GFC.

Table 2 shows that India's macroeconomic performance was excellent during Covid-19 vis-à-vis the shambolic performance during GFC. We have omitted for brevity the metrics for two more periods—2021–22 and 2020–22—as they correspond to the Russia–Ukraine war. However, the contrast to India's poor performance during GFC despite the double whammy of Covid-19 and the war remains salient.

The table clearly shows the triple whammy of high inflation, high fiscal deficit and high current account deficit (CAD) during the GFC, leading India directly into the Fragile Five group. In contrast, during Covid-19 and its aftermath, India's GDP exceeded that of its colonial master, the UK, to become the fifth largest economy in the world, or part of Fab-5. On each of the three key macroeconomic indicators—inflation, fiscal deficit and CAD—India's performance during Covid-19 and the war has been robust.

Table 2
Macroeconomic fundamentals more resilient in once-in-a-century Covid-19 crisis than in GFC (2008)

Indicators	*2009–10 (GFC)*	*2020–21 (Covid-19)*
Three key macro-indicators (inflation, fiscal deficit and CAD):		
CPI inflation (%)	11.5	5.6
Fiscal deficit (% of GDP) for India as a multiple of that for peer economies*	3.3	1.4
Current account balance (CAB) as % of GDP	-4.8	0.9
Nature of government expenditure and related outcomes:		
ΔRevex as % of GDP (central govt)	27	5.9
ΔCapex as % of GDP (central govt)	-4.8	13.1
ΔGross fixed capital formation (GFCF) as % of GDP	-4.5	2.2
Δ10-year government bond yields	4.0	0.9
External sector:		
₹Depreciation (%)	56	5.5
External debt as % of GDP	20.7	21.1
Forex reserves ($ billion)	252	579
Foreign investment into India:		
FDI ($ billion)	8.3	80.1
FPI ($ billion)	–9.9	36.2

Source: Economic surveys of GoI, RBI annual reports, IMF database, World Bank's National Accounts data and World Development Indicators database

*Emerging & developing Asia as defined in World Economic Outlook

While revex increased significantly (27 per cent) and capex decreased by 4.8 per cent during the GFC, revex has increased much less (5.9 per cent) than the increase in capex during Covid-19 (13.1 per cent). This is reflected in the GFCF declining sharply during the GFC (–4.5 per cent), while it has increased by 2.2 per cent during Covid-19. The increase in revex during the GFC is also reflected in the 10-year bond yields increasing by 4 per cent during the GFC, while the increase during Covid-19 and the war has been very marginal at 0.9 per cent.

On the external sector, rupee has depreciated by 5 per cent in 2020–22 as against a massive 56 per cent depreciation in 2009–10. A 10× FDI investment during Covid-19 and the war as compared to the amounts during the GFC, overall FPI inflows of $20.1 billion during Covid-19 and the war as compared to a net outflow of $9.9 billion during the GFC, and forex reserves that are 3× that during the GFC, underline the strength of the Indian economy during the pandemic and the war when compared to the GFC.

Finally, as captured in Figure 9, India's external debt performance was much better post Covid-19, as captured by the Great Lockdown (GLD), than during the GFC.

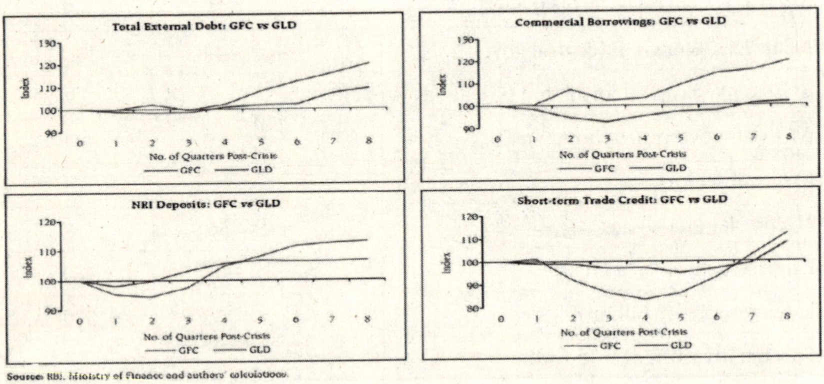

Figure 9: Performance of India's external debt: GFC vs GLD

Source: RBI; Ministry of Finance; author's calculations

Supply-Side Measures during Covid-19

Capex Especially Focussed on Infrastructure Creation

Figure 10 shows that capex in absolute numbers and capex as a percentage of total expenditure have increased significantly post Covid-19.

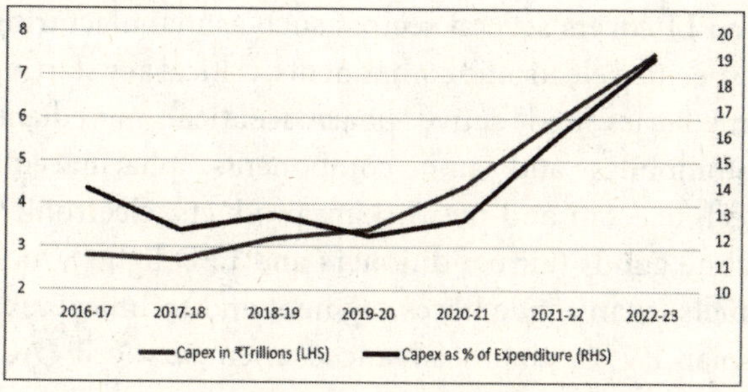

Figure 10: Capex—the cornerstone of India's post-Covid-19 fiscal policy
Source: Economic surveys and MOSPI

Evidence of the positive effects of public capex is already visible. The ratio of GFCF to GDP reached 31.2 per cent in fourth quarter (Q4) of the fiscal year 2020–21, among the highest in over 26 quarters (Figure 11). This created positive effects on construction, which grew at 14.5 per cent; private consumption, which grew at 2.7 per cent after falling for three consecutive quarters; and contact-intensive sectors that contracted by only 2.3 per cent after large declines in previous quarters.

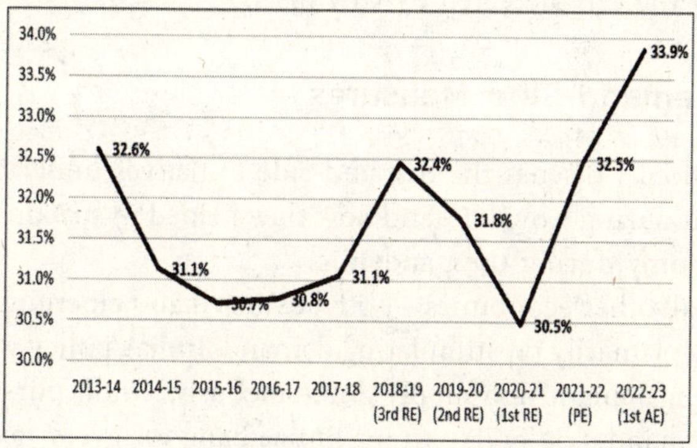

Figure 11: GFCF as a percent of GDP (in constant prices)
Source: Economic surveys and MOSPI

Production-Linked Incentives

To shore up supply during a time of extreme uncertainty, India offered producers incentives through the Production Linked Incentive (PLI) scheme. The PLI covers several sectors such as manufacturing of mobile phones and specified electronic components, critical key starting materials/drug intermediaries and active pharmaceutical ingredients, medical devices, automobiles and auto components, pharmaceutical drugs, specialty steel, telecom and networking products, electronic/technology products, white goods (air conditioners and LED lights), food products, textile products (man-made fibres segment and technical textiles), high-efficiency solar PV modules, advanced chemistry cell (ACC) battery, drones and drone components.

Structural Reforms

Indian policymakers also recognized that the supply shock induced by the lockdown would disrupt the productive capacity of the economy. This capacity would have needed to be strengthened to meet the pent-up demand once it resumed—any mismatch would have led to macroeconomic instabilities. India initiated a slew of supply-side structural reforms across sectors to lend flexibility and resilience to supply chains as a part of the Atmanirbhar Bharat Abhiyaan. India is the only country to have undertaken structural reforms on the supply side during the crisis created by Covid-19.

India's Demand-Side Measures

In this section, I discuss the demand-side initiatives undertaken by the government during Covid-19 and how they helped in sustaining demand in the economy during the pandemic.

While all other economies—both advanced and emerging—focussed their policy primarily on stimulating demand, India's policy was focussed on enhancing demand and supply simultaneously.[30] India pursued a three-pronged demand-side policy to maximize bang for every taxpayer buck spent during Covid-19.

1. India undertook in-kind transfers of cereals and pulses to 800 million citizens through its public distribution system (PDS). These did not impose additional fiscal costs as they tapped into

[30]@SubramanianKri, X (formerly Twitter), 30 July 2022, 8.30 a.m. http://tinyurl.com/3c5e7zuz. Accessed on 20 December 2023.

existing reserves created from its food procurement policy.

2. India recognized that the financial sector not only possesses granular information on borrowers, which the sovereign can never rival, but also employs financial leverage. So, India provided sovereign loan guarantees for lending to SMEs by banks and the urban poor by microfinance institutions (MFIs). Kapoor and Dasher (2023) estimate the impact of the sovereign loan guarantees for lending to SMEs to be about 4.9–5.4 per cent of GDP. In other words, if this programme had not been implemented, GDP of that magnitude may have been lost during the pandemic. A State Bank of India (SBI) research report estimated that almost 1.35 million micro, small and medium enterprises (MSMEs) accounts were saved due to Emergency Credit Line Guarantee Scheme (ECLGS).[31] Almost 93.7 per cent of such accounts are in the micro and small category. In absolute terms, MSME loan accounts worth ₹1.8 trillion were saved from slipping into the category of non-performing assets (NPAs) during the period. This is equivalent to 14 per cent of the outstanding MSME credit being saved from becoming NPAs. If these units had turned non-performing, 15 million workers would have become unemployed. In effect, the ECLGS saved the livelihood of 60 million families (assuming four family members per worker including herself). The trading sector (including small *kirana* or mom-and-pop shops) benefitted the most, followed by food processing, textiles and commercial real estate.
3. Government undertook direct benefit transfers (DBT) to the vulnerable by leveraging the digital identity of Aadhaar and over 400 million Pradhan Mantri Jan-Dhan Yojana (PMJDY) bank accounts created for the poor post 2014.
4. The government initiated a programme to incentivize employers to bring back employees who had lost their jobs during the Covid-19-induced lockdowns.

---

[31]'The ECLGS that Saved 13.5 Lakh MSME Units, 1.5 Crore Jobs & 14% of Outstanding MSME Loans Turning into NPA', *SBI Research*, 6 January 2022, https://tinyurl.com/yc462wy9. Accessed on 23 November 2023.

◆

India's sui generis economic policy during Covid-19 represents a good example of a policy that was conceptualized by employing ab initio thinking tailored to India's economic realities rather than a copy-paste of policies implemented by the advanced economies. The contrast to economic policy implemented during the GFC—which was a copy-paste of the policy implemented by advanced economies without accounting for Indian realities—provides an important lesson for India. India must seek inspiration from the sui generis economic policy during Covid-19 to conceptualize and implement economic policies that are optimally tailored for India. Such careful thinking of economic policy is essential for India to become an economic titan by the time India turns 100.

5

THE MIDDLE-INCOME TRAP IS NOT DESTINY

How to Break Free from It

A conversation on life's eternal question—the struggle between destiny and the power of one's effort to overcome destiny—ensues right at the beginning of Vasistha's Yoga. This timeless classic captures the spiritual essence extracted from a conversation between Lord Rama and his guru, Vasistha Muni, who was one of the *saptarishi*s or seven great saints, in the Vedic tradition. In this conversation, which appears in the second chapter appropriately titled 'Self Effort', Vasistha Muni explains the power of self-effort in overcoming destiny by asserting that 'there is no power greater than right action in the present moment!'[32]

As the country marches towards India@100, India's policymakers should regularly revisit and remind themselves, as well as India's perennial pessimists, of this wisdom shared in Vasistha's Yoga. Our perennial pessimists will exert significant effort to convince others that India is destined to remain trapped in the middle-income trap. The middle-income trap refers to the challenge that countries face in registering high rates of growth once they become middle-income countries. This phenomenon has plagued many developing countries—especially those in Latin America—in the past. Inspired by Vasistha Muni's exhortation to Lord Rama about the power of self-effort to burn destiny, in this chapter, I argue that India is well-equipped to avoid obstacles in its growth odyssey to India@100.

[32]Rajendran, Abhilash, 'Valuable Lessons From Lord Ram Sage Vasishta Conversation'; *Hindu Blog*, 15 April 2019, http://tinyurl.com/ytwwr9m2, Accessed on 19 February 2024.

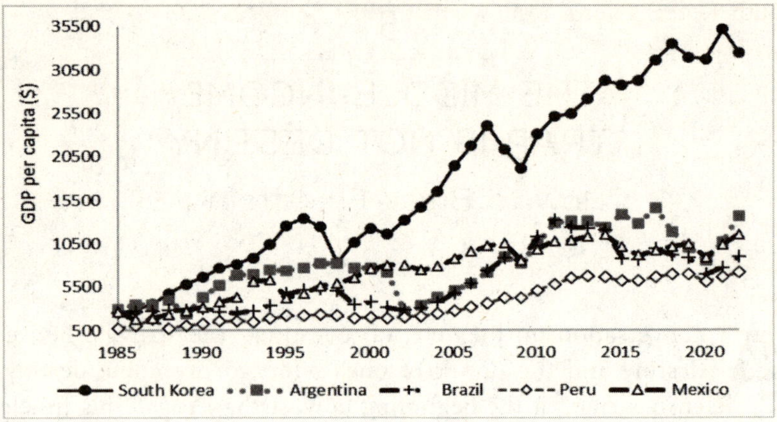

Figure 1: GDP per capita of Latin American economies vis-à-vis South Korea

Source: Federal Reserve Economic Data (FRED) and author's calculations

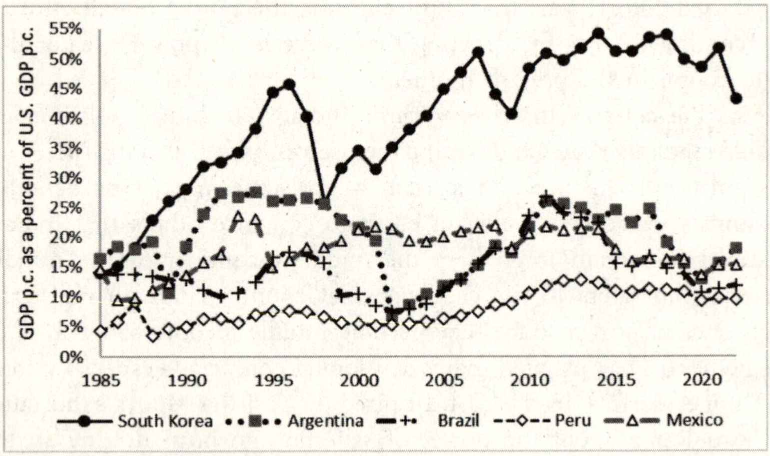

Figure 2: GDP per capita of Latin American economies vis-à-vis South Korea (as a per cent of US GDP per capita)

Source: FRED and author's calculations

Figures 1 and 2 demonstrate the middle-income trap. Figure 1 shows that the GDP per capita in the Latin American countries—Argentina, Brazil, Peru and Mexico—has grown at a much lower rate when compared to

South Korea. Figure 2 shows that while South Korea's GDP per capita increased significantly when compared to the GDP per capita of the US, the GDP per capita of the Latin American economies has remained stagnant when compared to the GDP per capita of the US.

Figure 3 shows the GDP per capita of Latin American economies over a longer horizon—from 1950 to 2010. It is clear here that the GDP per capita in these countries either remained stagnant relative to that of the US, as in the case of Brazil, Mexico and Peru, or declined sharply as seen in the case of Argentina. In fact, Argentina's average per capita GDP growth rate stood at a mere 1.1 per cent during the period 1950–2010 at constant dollar prices.

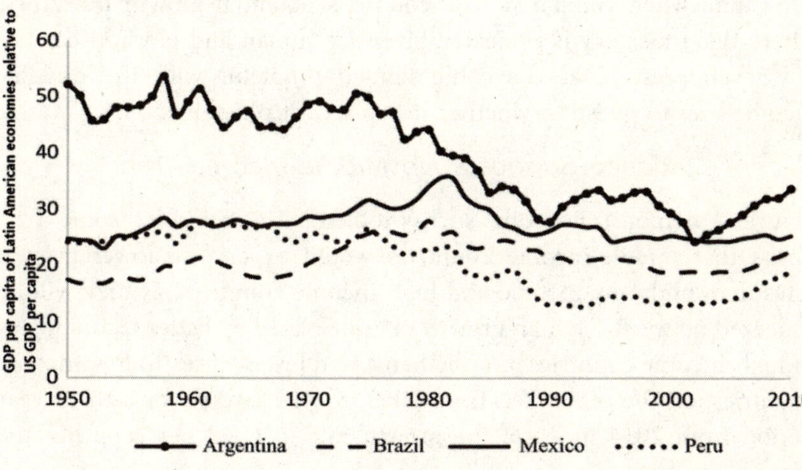

Figure 3: GDP per capita of Latin American economies relative to US GDP per capita (%)
Source: Zhou and Hu (2020)

Understanding the Middle-Income Trap

Gill and Kharas (2015) proposed that the middle-income trap arises when rapidly growing countries, experiencing rising wages, struggle to sustain an economy based on labour-intensive manufacturing and export-led growth. Although the term 'middle-income trap' remains ambiguous and is interpreted in multiple ways, there are two broad ways in which the term is defined in the economics literature: (i) absolute convergence, which captures convergence to the GDP per capita of high-income countries in absolute levels; and (ii) relative convergence, which captures convergence in relative terms, i.e., when compared to the GDP per capita of high-income countries. While absolute convergence was defined by Barry Eichengreen and colleagues, relative convergence is attributed to Shekhar Aiyar and others.

Using absolute convergence, the middle-income trap is identified as two key stages of slowdown manifesting at GDP per capita levels of \$10,000–\$11,000 and \$15,000–\$16,000, where the GDP per capita of the country is measured using PPP prices in 2005 dollars. Using relative convergence, the middle-income trap is identified as slowdowns in GDP per capita when compared to a country's potential growth trajectory, where this trajectory is projected given its human and physical capital.

Several researchers have highlighted problems with the middle-income trap to question whether it is a robust phenomenon.

Recent Evidence Suggests No Middle-Income Trap

Figure 4 demonstrates one such problem. The middle-income trap posits that middle-income countries would experience lower growth rates than both low-income and high-income countries, as they will be squeezed between the high growth rates delivered by better technologies in high-income countries, on one hand, and lower wages in low-income countries, on the other. Yet, from 2005 to 2022, except for a three-year period from 2014 to 2016, the growth rate in GDP per capita of the

Table 1

Percentage of countries in different income groups in 2000 transitioning to other income groups in 2015

Income Group in 2000	*Income Group in 2015*			
	Low Income %	*Lower Middle-Income %*	*Upper Middle-Income %*	*High Income %*
Low income	47.6	47.6	4.8	0.0
Lower middle-income	0.0	37.7	58.5	3.8
Upper middle-income	0.0	0.0	51.4	48.6
High income	0.0	0.0	0.0	100.0

Source: Engel and Taglioni (2017)

upper middle-income countries was consistently higher than all countries in other groups. In fact, the growth rate in GDP per capita of the lower middle-income countries was only slightly lower than that of the upper middle-income countries. Collectively, the middle-income countries grew at significantly higher growth rates than both the low-income and the high-income countries.

Rich economies need advanced technologies and skills to offset high wages. Low-income countries need low wages to offset low levels of technology and skill. Thus, it is not obvious that middle-income countries cannot compete with both sets of countries by combining middling wages with middling levels of skill, technology and productivity. The evidence in Figure 4 seems to support the thesis that the middle-income countries can indeed compete successfully with both low-income and high-income countries.

Table 1 shows that about half of the countries (48.6 per cent) that were in the upper middle-income group in 2000 successfully transitioned to high-income status by 2015. These countries, thus, did not remain trapped in the middle-income status. Even more importantly, 3.8 per cent of countries that were in the lower middle-income group in 2000 successfully transitioned to high-income status by 2015. Thus,

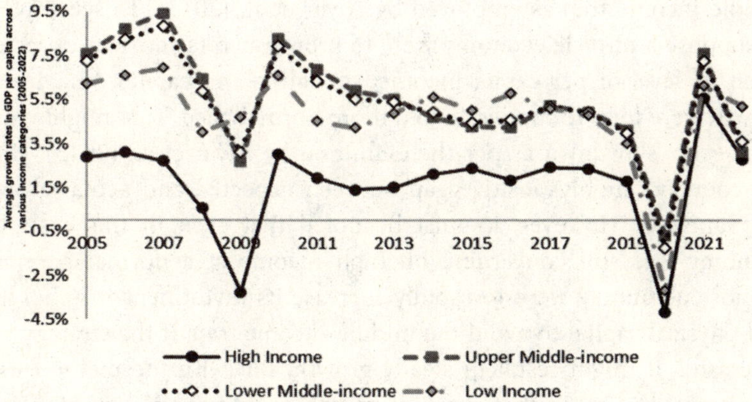

Figure 4: Average growth rates in GDP per capita across various income categories (2005–2022)

Source: World Bank data and author's calculations

more than half of the countries that enjoyed middle-income status in 2000 transitioned to high-income status by 2015. The higher growth rates of middle-income countries shown in Figure 4 and the successful transition of middle-income countries to high-income status from 2000 to 2015 calls into question the robustness of the phenomenon of the middle-income trap.

Conceptual Problems with the Phenomenon

With the absolute convergence definition of middle-income trap—countries with GDP per capita over $10,000 experiencing slowdowns in their growth—the statistical problem is that middle-income countries are only as vulnerable to such setbacks as poor countries. As slowdowns among poorer economies are at least as prevalent as among middle-income ones, this could be the result of global economic factors that may have little to do with the middle-income trap.

While middle-income countries do slow down more often than rich countries, this is partly because rich economies rarely grow fast enough to experience the kind of slowdowns that middle-income countries do. Nor is such a slowdown sufficient to trap an economy. Hong Kong, Singapore, South Korea and Taiwan have all endured at least one slowdown, and none of them is trapped in middle income.

Similar problems bedevil the relative convergence definition of the middle-income trap as employed by Aiyar et al. (2013). To see why, let us suppose a miracle economy were to grow much faster than expected, given its level of per capita income, schooling and capital. Imagine its growth were then to moderate to a more normal pace. That might count as a severe slowdown as per the definition by Aiyar et al. (2013), since the country's highly positive gap between expected and actual growth has vanished. However, it must be noted that even in this case, the economy was still converging on high income at a normal pace. Or suppose a country were to rapidly increase its investment in schooling and physical capital to avoid the middle-income trap. If the strategy was successful, it might result in steady growth. But with the method used by Aiyar et al. (2013), that constant growth could nonetheless count as a severe slowdown because, other things being equal, their model expects improved education and deeper capital to raise the pace of growth, not merely shore it up.

Recent research finds no evidence for unusual stagnation at any particular middle-income level. As seen in Table 1, while the transition from middle to high income is certainly challenging, it is no more challenging than the transition from low income to middle income.

Range for Middle-Income Countries Too Broad

More importantly, the thresholds for countries being classified as middle-income are both idiosyncratic and too broad. They include any country with a GDP per capita between 5.2 per cent and 42.75 per cent of the US, with GDP per capita measured at PPP. By its definition, a country with a GDP of just $590 per person (at 1990 prices) counted as middle income in 1960. That includes countries like China in the middle of its Great Famine. At the other extreme, a country with a GDP per person of $13,300 in 2008 also counted as middle income. This upper threshold for 2008 is more than 20 times higher than the lower one for 1960. No wonder so many countries remained stuck between them.

Root Causes of Middle-Income Trap

Several factors contribute to the challenges faced by middle-income countries in sustaining economic growth. First, sectors that enable a country to rise to middle income may become the albatross around their neck when the country attempts to rise to upper income. So, the development of specific sectors that the government supported for rise to middle-income status can create powerful interest groups that resist the weaning away of such policy support. These groups may resist the elimination of subsidies and protections, hindering the process of transformation of the country from middle income to high income. Additionally, economic transformation can be costly, especially if emerging manufacturing sectors in lower-income countries initially rely on imported intermediate goods without becoming internationally competitive.

Second, many countries achieve middle-income status by relying on traditional industrial policy tools like subsidies and neglecting efforts to promote knowledge and innovation. Third, institutions may not keep pace with increasingly complex economies, leading to corruption challenges and poor accountability in many middle-income countries.

Lessons from Argentina and South Africa

Argentina and South Africa exemplify the middle-income trap, having undergone similar transformation processes. Both countries implemented policies from the 1950s to 1970s, incurring costs to foster diverse domestic manufacturing activities, including steel, aluminium and car manufacturing. They also developed typical middle-income manufacturing sectors like textiles, garments and plastics, while concurrently raising productivity levels in traditional sectors like agriculture.

However, recent productivity growth in both nations has been sluggish, primarily concentrated within specific sectors. The productive structure in both nations features highly productive, competitive firms in specific sectors alongside sectors with extremely low productivity. The productivity growth did not move across sectors. Both governments made a critical error by neglecting active policies for the reconfiguration of their productive sectors and the skills of their workforce, particularly in the shift from domestic to export-oriented industries.

Broader Findings from Cross-Country Studies

Eichengreen et al. (2011, 2013) analysed countries in the middle-income trap and showed that total factor productivity (TFP) explains 85 per cent of the stagnation of economic growth in these. Kim (2023) analysed necessary and sufficient conditions for escaping the middle-income trap. He found that productivity improvements as measured using TFP are necessary for this. When productivity improvements are accompanied by improvements in rule of law and reduction in corruption, this combination provides a sufficient condition for escaping the middle-income trap. Eichengreen et al. (2013) found that growth slowdowns were more likely in economies with high old-age dependency ratios, high investment rates and undervalued real exchange rates. Bulman and others (2014) found that escapees from the middle-income trap had higher TFP growth, faster transformations toward industry, better macroeconomic management and consistently more export orientation. Furthermore, countries with high secondary and tertiary education and with a larger share of high-tech products in exports are less likely to fall into the trap.

Does India Risk Falling into the Middle-Income Trap?

The evidence in this chapter shows that the middle-income trap is not a robust empirical or conceptual phenomenon. If the phenomenon itself is not very robust, the possibility of India falling into the middle-income trap becomes a moot point.

Nevertheless, an analysis of the factors that can help a country avoid the middle-income trap provides considerable assurance that India should be able to continue to grow at steady rates till 2047 without encountering obstacles caused by the middle-income trap. First, the preponderance of evidence suggests that productivity improvements are critical to avoiding the middle-income trap. As shown in Chapter 2, average TFP growth rate from 2014–19 in India has been 2.7 per cent, which is more than double the average growth rate of 1.3 per cent from 2002–13. The higher TFP growth rates from 2014 are consistent with increase in productivity due to the several reforms launched post 2014. The five-year compound annual growth rates (CAGR) for TFP growth in India in 2019 was 2.5 per cent, the four-year CAGR was 2.2 per cent, and the seven-year CAGR was 2.5 per cent. The emphasis on formalization of the economy and the development of DPI will continue to further productivity improvements in India. Thus, the productivity improvements driven by reforms suggest that the necessary condition for avoiding the middle-income trap is being fulfilled in the Indian scenario.

Areas Requiring Policy Emphasis for India to Avoid Middle-Income Trap

The analysis of factors that can contribute to a country remaining in or escaping the middle-income trap leads to specific recommendations about the areas that require policy emphasis:

1. Growth from middle income to high income would require weaning away government support to the sectors that helped India rise to middle-income status. These groups will resist the elimination of subsidies and protections provided as part of the growth to middle-income status, thereby hindering the process of transformation of the country from middle income to high

income. So, as India's GDP per capita grows, industrial policies need to alter their focus away from sectors that supported growth to middle income, to sectors that will help India transition to high income. Therefore, it is crucial for all forms of industrial policy support to include 'sunset clauses' with clear end dates, making it clear to all stakeholders that the support is not intended to be permanent.

2. As foreign competition is vital both for continued productivity growth in domestic firms and for stimulating innovation, India needs to set a timeline for removal of trade protections to domestic firms. Additionally, economic transformation can be costly, especially if emerging sectors rely only on importing intermediate goods without becoming internationally competitive. As was explained in Chapter 3 of the *Economic Survey 2018–19*, government protection must be directed towards children, not dwarfs in the economy.[33] Therefore, trade policy needs to set the expectation for staged removal of protection. Otherwise, trade policy would perversely be incentivizing the sustenance of dwarfs in the economy, thereby hampering growth in domestic productivity.
3. Consistently greater orientation towards exports and participation in global value chains (GVCs) enable countries to escape the middle-income trap. Therefore, India needs to enhance its export penetration and participation in GVCs.
4. Faster transformation toward industry remains an important factor in avoiding the middle-income trap. Therefore, India cannot escape investing in its manufacturing capabilities.
5. Along with productivity enhancement, improvements in the rule of law and reduction in corruption provide sufficient conditions for escaping middle-income trap. Therefore, reforming the bureaucracy, the judicial system and bureaucratic processes are critical.
6. Countries with high levels of secondary and tertiary education

[33]'Nourishing Dwarfs to Become Giants: Reorienting Policies for MSME Growth', *Economic Survey 2018–19: Volume 1*, July 2019, http://tinyurl.com/5ccw6unz. Accessed on 11 January 2024.

> and with a larger share of high-tech products in exports are less likely to fall into the trap. They need to invest in transforming their education systems in a way that will equip the labour force to continuously adapt. Therefore, investments in education and healthcare to enhance the quality of our human capital are essential.

While it is unlikely that India will encounter the obstacles faced by countries like Argentina and South Africa that have been stuck in the middle-income trap, India must ensure focus on the above policy areas to ensure that even remote possibilities of being in the middle-income trap are eliminated.

SECTION TWO

THE FIRST PILLAR
MACROECONOMIC FOCUS ON GROWTH AND GROWTH ALONE

INDIA HAS THE POTENTIAL TO grow at 8 per cent annually for the next two decades. Policymakers need to recognize that 6 or 7 per cent growth is not ambitious enough, considering the favourable demographics and the considerable potential for productivity growth within the formal sector as well as through formalization of the informal sector. As we explore ways to generate annual GDP growth of 8 per cent for the economy, Chapters 6 to 10 serve as guiding beacons.

Continuing with the idea exposited in Chapter 3 of India pursuing a sui generis economic path that suits the Indian realities, it is crucial for the country to achieve a good balance between economic growth and redistribution. Following the GFC, inequality has become a contentious issue in the advanced economies. A large section of the Indian intelligentsia, especially those that draw inspiration from issues capturing the imagination in the West, would inevitably urge India to imitate the West in placing a similar emphasis on redistributive policies. Policymakers need to avoid the pitfall of bringing a Western prism to this important issue. Chapter 6 examines the growth versus inequality debate in the Indian context by distinguishing it from the Western context to argue that macroeconomic policies in India must remain focussed on growth and growth alone.

To enable this growth, fiscal policy—which corresponds to the sovereign's strategy to raise resources, including borrowing, to invest in the welfare of citizens—needs to be an enabler rather than a spoiler. Here again, as argued in Chapter 3, India needs to think differently from the advanced economies to implement sui generis policies that enable the sovereign to create digital, physical and human capital.

While corruption at the highest levels in the central government has not been a concern during the last decade, the same cannot be assured at other levels of government. Chapters 8 to 10 bring the focus on the need to reform two critical pillars—the judiciary and the bureaucracy—in reducing corruption and enabling governance that can foster a salutary economic environment for rapid economic progress. By elucidating the imperatives for enhancing judicial efficacy, Chapter 8 underscores the pivotal role of legal reforms in fostering an enabling environment for economic prosperity.

The bureaucratic machinery forms the sinews of governance, channelling policy imperatives into actionable outcomes. Yet, bureaucratic inertia and inefficiency frequently frustrate the realization of India's socio-economic goals. Chapter 9 advocates for a comprehensive overhaul of the bureaucracy to make them comparably efficient with the top economies of the world. This chapter urges the imperative for India to have a bureaucracy that befits its economic status as one of the world's top economies. Continuing in this spirit, Chapter 10 delves into the process reforms that are essential to foster administrative innovation and streamlining of bureaucratic processes. It is crucial to note that each of these reforms—the judiciary and the bureaucracy—will reinforce the impact of the other in enabling ease of doing business, on the one hand, and rule of law, on the other hand.

India's policymakers and its citizens must have a sense of urgency in striving for 8 per cent growth so that we can deliver on the opportunity that comes once in a few centuries.

6

INEQUALITY AND GROWTH

Conflict or Convergence?

Do you remember the popular television serial *Malgudi Days*? In one of the episodes, Swami—the main character—comes home to his mother crying, 'Amma, I am not going to study Mathematics anymore!' When his surprised mother enquires why, Swami explains, 'I got 100/100 in my exam. But the headmaster took 20 marks from me and gave to Shankar who got only 60 marks saying that he would like both our marks to be equal at 80.' Meanwhile, Shankar runs to his mother elated, saying, 'Amma, I do not need to study Mathematics anymore! The headmaster gave Swami's 20 marks to me. As I will anyway get 20 marks from Swami, I will pass easily. So, I don't need to study Mathematics.' This episode illustrates the trade-offs inherent to growth and inequality. While we all desire an equitable society, excessive redistribution can dull incentives.

Inequality is an often-repeated concern expressed with capitalism and wealth creation. In the *Arthashastra*, which advocated private enterprise and capitalism for economic progress, Kautilya addresses the problem of inequality by positing, '[The King] shall maintain, at state expense, children, the old, the destitute, those suffering from adversity, childless women and the children of destitute women.'[34] In advanced economies, higher inequality leads to adverse socio-economic outcomes but income per capita, a measure that reflects the impact of economic growth, has little impact (Wilkinson and Pickett 2009, Atkinson 2014, Piketty 2020). Some commentaries, especially in advanced economies post the GFC, argue that inequality is no accident but an essential feature of capitalism. They thus highlight a potential conflict between economic growth and inequality.[35]

---

[34]Sihag, Balbir S., 'Kautilya on Public Goods and Taxation', *History of Political Economy*, Vol. 37, No. 4, 2005, https://tinyurl.com/yyxx5hv7. Accessed on 27 November 2023.

[35]See Wilkinson and Pickett (2009) and Piketty (2013) among others for the research on inequality, mostly focussed on advanced economies.

The significant reduction in poverty that high economic growth has delivered in India and China presents the most striking challenge to this notion of conflict between economic growth and inequality. Could the fact that both the absolute levels of poverty and the rates of economic growth are low in advanced economies generate this conflict? If so, could it be that a developing economy such as India can avoid this conflict because of the potential for high levels of economic growth on the one hand and the significant scope for poverty reduction on the other?

This question remains important for India as choices in economic policy always present inherent trade-offs. Resolving these trade-offs in a manner that suits the specific economic context of the day is, therefore, critical in order to determine clear policy objectives. The advanced economies may choose to focus on alleviating inequality given their stage of development, their potential rate of economic growth, and the absolute levels of poverty that they face. Thus, they may resolve the trade-off between growth and inequality by leaning towards alleviating inequality. However, despite facing the same trade-off, the policy objective of focussing on inequality may not apply in the Indian context given the differences in the stage of development, India's higher potential rate of economic growth, and the higher absolute levels of poverty. Given these motivations, we examine if inequality and growth conflict or converge in the Indian context in an effort to identify the correct policy objective for India.

By examining the correlation of inequality and per capita income with a range of socio-economic indicators, I highlight that in India both economic growth and inequality have similar relationships with socio-economic indicators. Thus, unlike in advanced economies, in India, economic growth and inequality converge in terms of their effects on socio-economic indicators. Furthermore, this chapter finds that economic growth has a far greater impact on poverty alleviation than on inequality. Therefore, given India's stage of development, she must continue to focus on economic growth to lift the poor out of poverty by expanding the overall pie. Note that this policy focus does not imply that redistributive objectives are unimportant, but that redistribution is only feasible in a developing economy if the size of the economic pie grows. In sum, for a developing country such as India, where the growth potential is high and the scope for poverty reduction is also significant, the focus must continue on growing the size of the economic pie rapidly at least for the foreseeable future.

Growth, Inequality and Socio-Economic Outcomes: India vs Advanced Economies

This section examines whether the findings in advanced economies about the conflict between economic growth and inequality extend to India. For this purpose, Figures 1 to 7 simultaneously display the correlation of socio-economic outcomes with inequality and income per capita across advanced economies and Indian states. In each figure, the top panel displays these correlations for the Indian states, while the bottom panel displays the same for the advanced economies. The chart on the left displays the correlation with inequality, while the chart on the right displays the same with income per capita.

These figures clearly demonstrate, across a range of socio-economic outcomes, the stark contrast between India and the advanced economies in the correlation of socio-economic outcomes with inequality and income per capita. Across Indian states, it is observed that both inequality and income per capita correlate similarly with socio-economic outcomes. In these figures, inequality across Indian states is measured as the Gini coefficient of consumption.

As the Gini coefficient is used extensively to measure inequality, we must understand it conceptually. Think about a hypothetical society where every individual or household consumes the exact same amount. In this hypothetical society, inequality in consumption is zero. In contrast, if one household consumes everything that is produced in a society and no other household gets to consume anything whatsoever, then this hypothetical society has the highest level of inequality, i.e., 100 per cent. The Gini coefficient of consumption mirrors this concept by measuring the extent to which the distribution of consumption expenditure among individuals or households within an economy deviates from perfectly equal distribution. A Gini index of 0 represents perfect equality, while an index of 100 implies perfect inequality. Similarly, the Gini coefficient of income estimates inequality in income, while the Gini coefficient of wealth estimates inequality in wealth. As the *Economic Survey 2020–21* demonstrated, the findings remain robust to using other measures of inequality.

Figure 1 shows clearly that the index of health outcomes correlates positively with both inequality and income per capita across Indian states. However, across the advanced economies, inequality correlates negatively with the index of health and social outcomes, while income per capita correlates positively. Thus, while the conflict between growth and inequality is clearly seen across the advanced economies, inequality and growth converge in their effects on health among Indian states. Figures 2 to 5 show the same result using the index of education, life expectancy, infant mortality and crime, respectively. It is evident from Figure 6 that neither inequality nor income per capita among Indian states correlate strongly with drug usage; however, inequality correlates strongly with drug usage in the advanced economies. On mental health, Figure 7 shows that the effects of inequality and income per capita remain similar across Indian states and advanced economies.

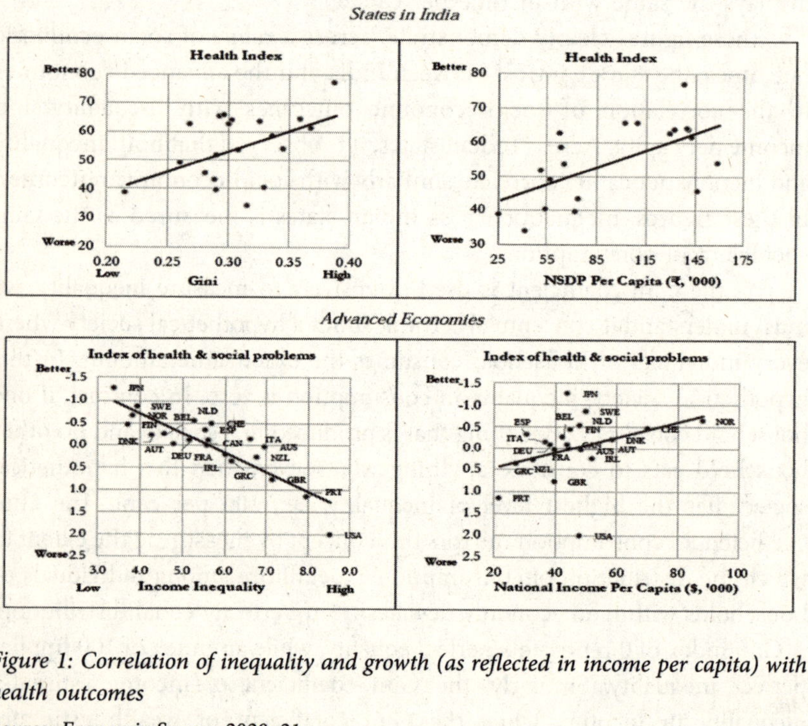

Figure 1: Correlation of inequality and growth (as reflected in income per capita) with health outcomes

Source: Economic Survey 2020–21

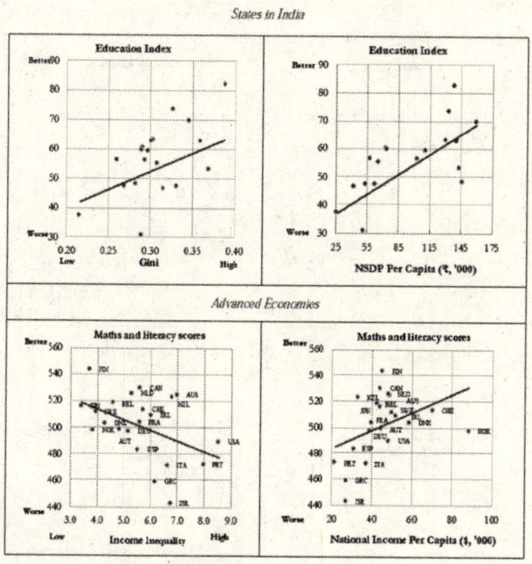

Figure 2: Correlation of inequality and growth (as reflected in income per capita) with education outcomes

Source: Economic Survey 2020–21

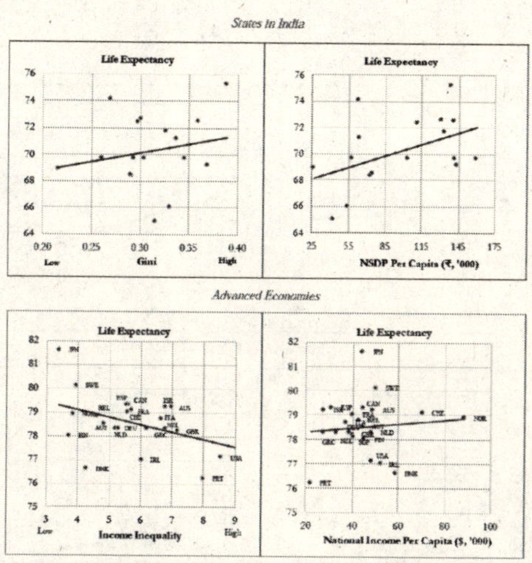

Figure 3: Correlation of inequality and growth (as reflected in income per capita) with life expectancy

Source: Economic Survey 2020–21

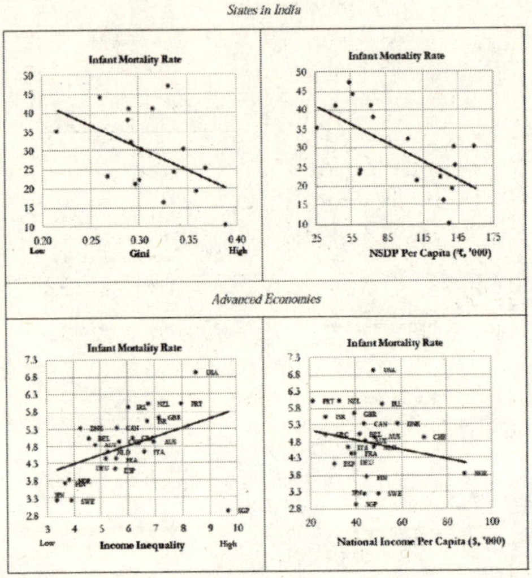

Figure 4: Correlation of inequality and growth (as reflected in income per capita) with infant mortality

Source: Economic Survey 2020–21

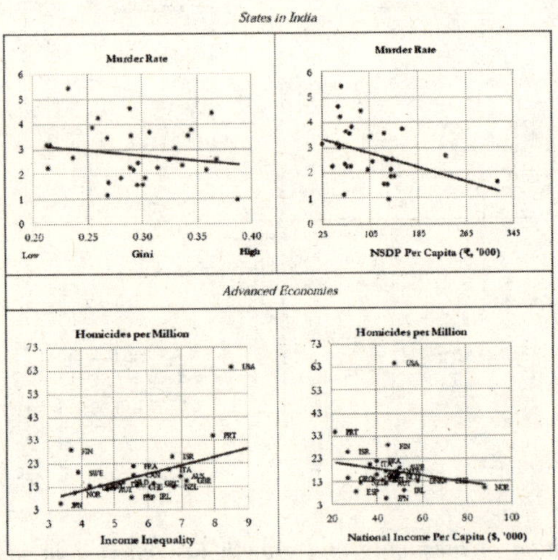

Figure 5: Correlation of inequality and growth (as reflected in income per capita) with crimes

Source: Economic Survey 2020–21

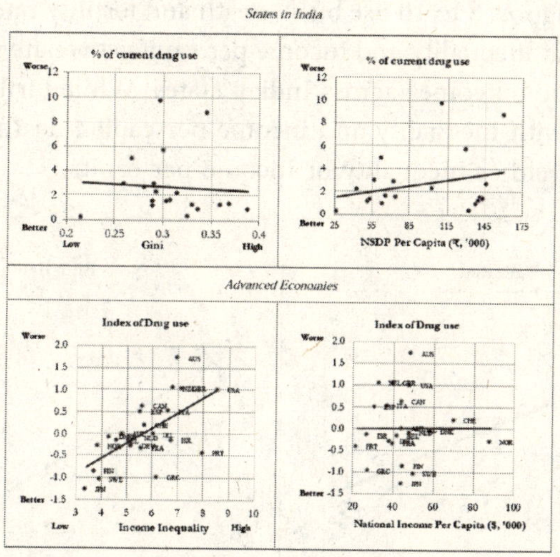

Figure 6: Correlation of inequality and growth (as reflected in income per capita) with drug usage

Source: Economic Survey 2020–21

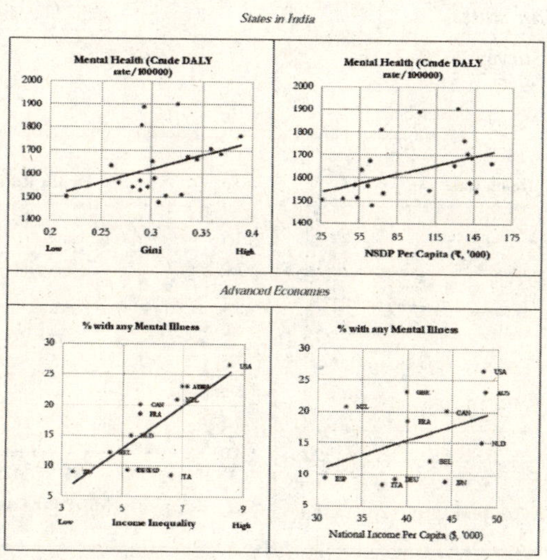

Figure 7: Correlation of inequality and growth (as reflected in income per capita) with mental health outcomes

Source: Economic Survey 2020–21

In addition, Figures 8 to 10 use birth, death and fertility rates to augment the finding that inequality and income per capita correlate similarly with socio-economic outcomes across Indian states. While birth and fertility rates decline with inequality and income per capita, death rates do not correlate with either inequality or income per capita.

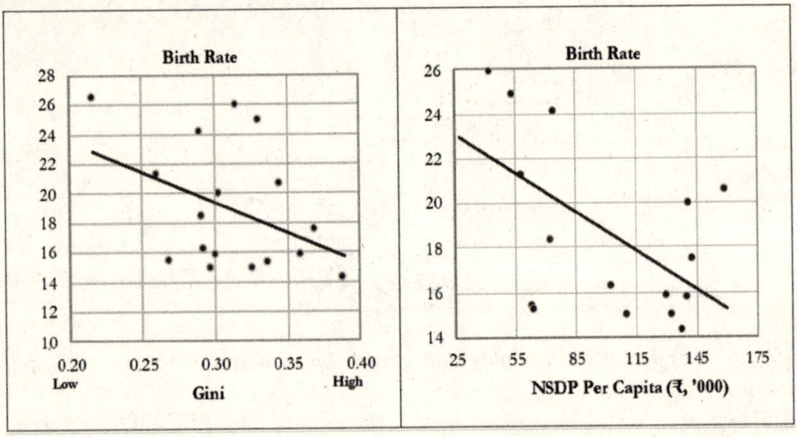

Figure 8: Correlation of inequality and growth (as reflected in income per capita) with birth rate in Indian states

Source: Economic Survey 2020–21

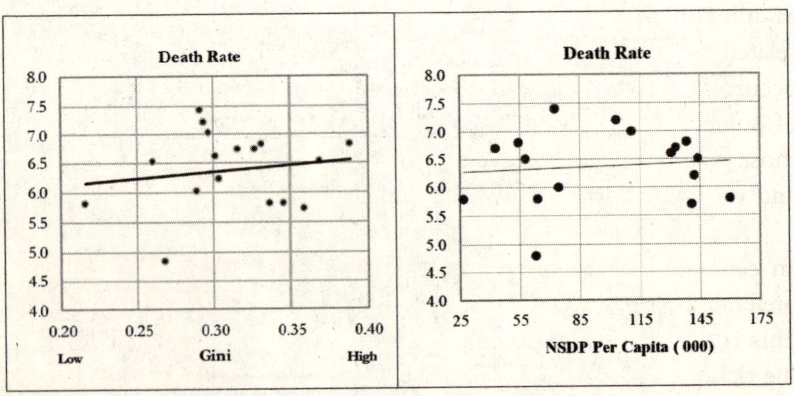

Figure 9: Correlation of inequality and growth (as reflected in income per capita) with death rate in Indian states

Source: Economic Survey 2020–21

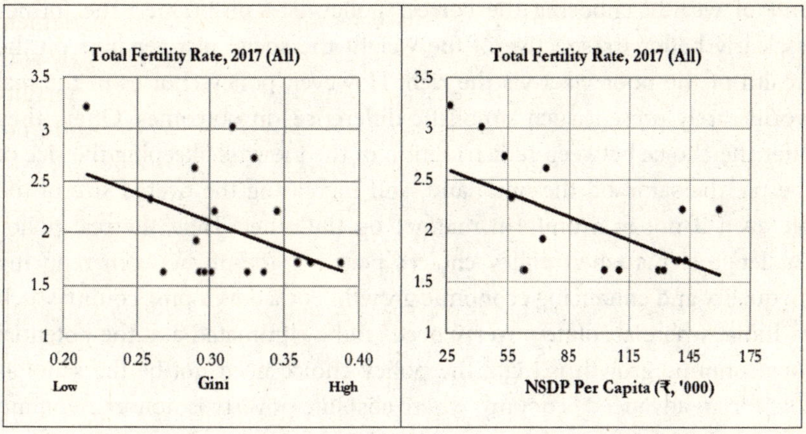

Figure 10: Correlation of inequality and growth (as reflected in income per capita) with total fertility rate in Indian states

Source: Economic Survey 2020–21

Is Perfect Equality Optimal?

Having established that inequality and income per capita do not diverge in their relationship with socio-economic outcomes in India, it is now worth asking: is perfect equality optimal? In most cases, inequality of opportunity is much more objectionable than inequality of outcomes, as individuals' opportunities are influenced by endowments that are related to their parents and other adults, peers and a variety of chance occurrences throughout their lifetimes. Note that perfect equalization of outcomes *ex-post*, i.e., after the efforts have been exerted to obtain those outcomes, can reduce individuals' incentives for work, innovation and wealth creation.

A benevolent social planner seeks to maximize aggregate welfare—an economy in which each individual possesses two units of wealth is preferable to one in which each individual possesses only one unit of wealth. This is true even if the planner assigns greater weight to the poor than the rich, i.e., the planner's social welfare function depends on not just the size of the pie but also how it is distributed. When a policy choice in the real world offers the outcome of everyone possessing two units of wealth, while another policy choice offers the outcome of everyone possessing one unit of wealth, choosing the correct policy is a no-brainer: the former is clearly better irrespective of the weight the social planner puts on the wealth of the poor vis-à-vis the rich. However, policy choices in the real world rarely present such simplistic differences in outcomes. Often, they offer the choice between redistribution of the pie while keeping the size of the pie the same on the one hand, and increasing the overall size of the pie even if not in a uniform manner on the other. Thus, the real policy challenge stems when policy choices pose a trade-off between reducing inequality and enhancing economic growth. For a developing country such as India, where absolute poverty needs to be eliminated and the potential for economic growth is high, the policy choice need not be the same as that for an advanced economy, where absolute poverty is non-existent and the potential for economic growth is not high.

Inequality or Poverty?

Inequality needs to be distinguished from poverty. Inequality refers to the degree of dispersion in the distribution of assets, income or consumption. Poverty refers to the assets, income or consumption of those at the bottom of the distribution. Poverty could be conceptualized in relative terms or in absolute terms. People feel themselves to be poor and think others to be poor if they have substantially less than what is commonplace among others in their society. Poverty, in this view, is relative deprivation (Brady 2003, Iceland 2003). If poverty is conceptualized in relative terms, there is no need to distinguish it from inequality. A relative measure of poverty is indeed a measure of inequality.

On the other hand, if poverty is conceptualized in an absolute sense, i.e., focussing on the absolute levels of assets, income or consumption of those at the low end of the distribution, then increases in inequality may be accompanied by reduction in poverty. Feldstein (1999) disagrees with the common assertion of the popular press and academic discussions that regards inequality and not poverty as the problem. He postulates that policy should aim at addressing poverty rather than inequality. He explains with an example of a magic bird providing $1,000 to each subscriber of *The Public Interest* (the journal in which Feldstein's article was published). He says that everyone would see it as a good thing. However, since each subscriber had greater average income, it would result in greater inequality in the nation. Feldstein finds it inaccurate to contemplate the $1,000 bonanza as morally suspect.

The Feldstein-type challenge is consistent with a variety of other views about distributive justice. Perhaps the best known is that of John Rawls (1971). Rawls argues that the most reasonable way to decide upon a fair distributive principle is to imagine making that decision while being aware of the fact that you will be born into the world without any knowledge about your assets and characteristics—intelligence, personality traits, parents, neighbourhood, gender, skin colour, etc. Rawls refers to this hypothetical scenario as the 'original position'. He suggests that in such a situation a rational person will choose a distributive principle in which any increase in inequality will increase the income of those at the bottom.

In Feldstein's example, according to the Rawlsian criterion, the $1,000 windfall given to the well-to-do would only be justifiable if it was accompanied by some increase for those at the low end. Rawls's distributive principle is a 'maximin' one—whatever distribution maximizes the income of the poorest (and provides basic liberties) is to be preferred.

Experimental evidence suggests that the maximin principle is not how people in the original position would choose. In experiments in which five or so participants are placed in a situation approximating Rawls's original position, most participants do not choose based on this distributive principle. Instead, they choose a principle in which the average income is maximized with a floor under the incomes of those at the bottom (Frohlich, Oppenheimer and Eavey 1987). In this view, as long as the poor have 'adequate' incomes, an increase in the incomes of the rich need not benefit the poor to be considered just. The results of such experiments suggest that (absolute) poverty should be of greater concern than inequality.

Of course, it is possible that if the incomes of the rich pull too far away from the rest of the society, growing frustration may lead to rising crime, withdrawal from civic engagement and loss of social cohesion (Krugman 2002). In this context, the evidence provided above against the conflict between inequality and income per capita among Indian states suggests that at the level of development that India is currently in, the focus on poverty alleviation through growth must be central to India's economic strategy.

Relative Impact of Economic Growth and Inequality on Poverty

Given the earlier discussion, which highlights that poverty alleviation through growth must remain the economic focus for India, this section examines whether income per capita or inequality has a greater impact on poverty in the country. The correlations between income and poverty, and inequality and poverty in Indian states are estimated. To analyse the relationship between income and poverty, per capita Net State Domestic Product (NSDP) and the official head count ratio are plotted (Figure 11). The data for four years (1993, 1999, 2004 and 2011) suggests an overall strong negative relationship, implying that the states with greater income or high per capita NSDP experienced low rates of poverty, and vice versa. However, such a strong relationship is absent between inequality and poverty. As illustrated in Figure 12, there does not exist any correlation between inequality and poverty among Indian states, leading to an ambiguous conclusion.

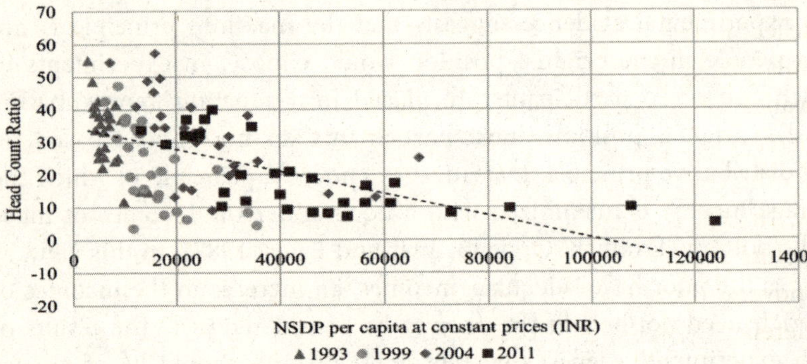

Figure 11: Relationship between income (NSDP per capita at constant prices, non-spliced series [INR]) and poverty (head count ratio) in Indian states

Source: Economic Survey 2020–21

India has had a history of copying ideas from the Western world without adequate reflection on whether the idea is suitable to India's DNA or not. The socialist model of economy—when India had prospered historically by enabling private enterprise instead of shunning it—is one such example

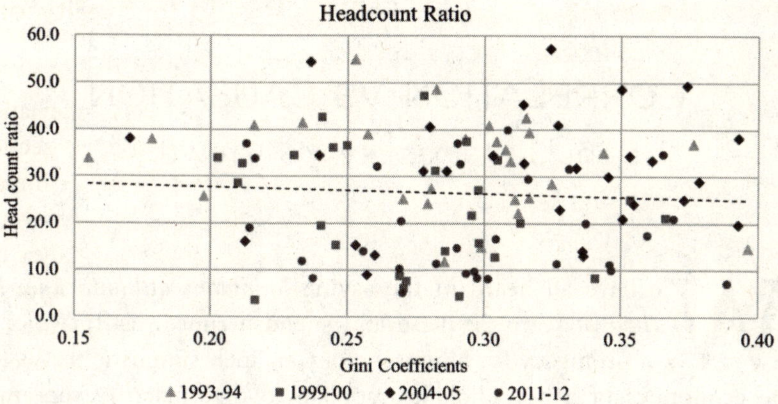

Figure 12: Relationship between inequality (Gini based on consumption) and poverty (head count ratio) in Indian states
Source: Economic Survey 2020–21

of mindless copy–paste that India has paid for dearly. To become the global economic titan by the time India turns 100, we must shun such intellectual laziness. The debate on inequality represents a banana peel similar to socialism that we must avoid slipping on. This is because the advanced economies are at a very different stage of development—a stage where, on the one hand, the number of absolute poor is low, while on the other, the potential for growth to lift millions out of poverty is also low. In contrast, India is a developing economy where the number of absolute poor is high. High rate of economic growth can lift millions out of poverty in India given its stage of development. Therefore, given these differences, this chapter showed that while inequality leads to adverse socio-economic outcomes in advanced economies, that is not the case in India. In our case, while inequality has very little correlation with socio-economic outcomes, poverty does. Therefore, till India becomes 100 years old, with respect to policies that present a trade-off between inequality and economic growth, she must choose policies that enhance economic growth.

7

CORRELATION VS CAUSATION

Debt Sustainability via Growth?

We have all heard of the saying '*aamdani atthanni kharcha rupaiya* (earn 50 paise and spend a rupee)' as the maxim of profligacy for a household. Can such simplistic truths for the economics of a household extrapolate to the (macro) economics of a country? Specifically, does a household have the responsibility of creating (infrastructure) assets that other households will benefit from using? No! But a sovereign must. Is a rich household obligated to take care of poor ones? No! But a sovereign must. Not surprisingly, the fiscal responsibilities of a sovereign have been written about in India's epics. Mahakavi Kalidasa's *Raghuvansham* captures the salutary role of fiscal policy beautifully through this couplet:

प्रजानामेवभूत्यर्थ सताभ्योबलिमग्रहीत्।
सहस्रगुणमुत्स्रष्टुमादत्तेहिरसंरवि: ।।1-18।।

[The state collects tax for the greater welfare of its
citizens in the same way as the sun evaporates water, only to
return it manifold in the form of rain.] (Chapter 1, Verse 18)[36]

The key question that arises with respect to India's fiscal policy is: does growth lead to debt sustainability? Or does fiscal austerity foster growth? This kind of confusion about the direction of causality—from growth to debt sustainability or vice versa—is typical of several macroeconomic phenomena, where natural experiments to identify causality are uncommon. Though the direction of causality is quite hard to nail in the real world, understanding it is extremely critical for India. India has significant requirements for the government to allocate funds for building physical and digital infrastructure as well as the improvement of human

[36]*Economic Survey 2020–21*, Vol. 1, GoI, Ministry of Finance, January 2021, p. 43, https://tinyurl.com/35ap4azk. Accessed on 19 December 2023.

capital through investments in healthcare and education. Therefore, while India cannot afford to use fiscal policy to spend unwisely on revex such as salaries, subsidies and freebies, she certainly needs to employ fiscal policy to build public goods.

Thus, as exhorted by Mahakavi Kalidasa, fiscal policy in India needs to use the tax collected to return it manifold by building physical and digital infrastructure as well as human capital.

Fiscal Policy Tailored for India

Pre-Covid-19 Cut-Paste from Advanced Economies

As argued in Chapter 2, India needs to be careful to not copy–paste the fiscal policy from advanced countries, where the sovereign does not have much need for building infrastructure as is in India. In the past, India has made this mistake. For instance, the Fiscal Responsibility and Budget Management (FRBM) Act, 2003—which was suspended during the time of Covid-19—mandated India to keep its fiscal deficit below 3 per cent of GDP and for the debt-to-GDP ratio to be below 67 per cent. These fiscal rules represent a classic example of cut–paste from Europe. The Maastricht Treaty, which was the political document that brought Europe together as a single monetary unit and created the European Monetary Union, specified these thresholds for the European nations to follow. This was required in order to coordinate their fiscal policy, thereby making the monetary union meaningful. Indian policymakers imitated this policy without accounting for substantial differences between India and the European nations.

Serving India's Infrastructural Needs

As mentioned above, India's needs to build infrastructure and other public goods are hugely different from Europe. The potential for high growth to enable debt sustainability is non-existent in the European context. Blunt fiscal rules like these do not make a distinction between revex and capex. By mixing apples and oranges, specifically revex and capex in this case, they restrict important capex by the sovereign that is crucial for promoting economic growth and attracting private investment. As a result, the capex becomes self-financing over time and provides benefits to the economy. This distinction is crucial to make because, unlike capex, revex does not have these beneficial characteristics associated with it.

Avoid Conceptual Schizophrenia

Above all, fiscal policy in India needs to be aware of the conceptual schizophrenia that predominates this area of macroeconomics. To comprehend this conceptual nuance, it is crucial to understand the difference between 'stock variables' and 'flow variables'. Think about water flowing into a tank. The level of water in the tank corresponds to the stock of water in the tank, while the amount of water flowing into the tank per day represents the flow of water into the tank. If one wants to understand whether the water in the tank is sustainable for the village, two measures can be used. First, 'flow' measures such as ratio of the amount of water required per day to the amount of water flowing into the tank per day. Second, the ratio of stock of water in the tank to the stock of water required for the village over a week, month or any other duration. If either of these ratios becomes less than 100 per cent, then the water in the tank may not be sustainable. For instance, if the ratio of amount of water required per day to the amount of water flowing into the tank per day is greater than 100 per cent, then water will deplete quickly, imperilling sustainability.

Normally, ratios employed to assess sustainability use either flow variables both in the numerator and the denominator or stock variables. The actual ratios are then compared with respect to desirable thresholds to assess sustainability. Take corporate finance, where the ratio of total debt to assets or the interest coverage ratio, which equals the ratio of interest payments to earnings, are used to assess the debt situation of a firm. In the former, both total debt and assets are stock variables, while in the latter, both interest payments to be made and earnings generated in a year or in a quarter are flow variables. By employing both, these ratios do not mix apples with oranges.

On the other hand, in macroeconomics relating to fiscal policy, the ratio debt-to-GDP has a stock variable—debt in the numerator—and a flow variable—GDP—in the denominator, as GDP measures the value of economic activities undertaken in a year. Thus, this ratio mixes up apples and oranges. When the ratio solely uses either flow or stock variables, the threshold of 100 per cent assumes economic importance. This is because this threshold conveys that liabilities are greater than assets when both numerator and denominator use stock variables and that cash outflows are greater than inflows when they use flow variables. However, this threshold does not have much economic meaning in the debt-to-GDP ratio. This is because the entire stock of debt of a country is not required to be paid in the same year. In fact, the total stock of debt gets paid over several years, and the GDP generated in *each* of these years—and not just the GDP generated in the current year—is utilized by the country to repay the cumulative debt. Therefore, 100 per cent or, for that matter, 200 per cent or 50 per cent have very less economic meaning in the case of the debt-to-GDP ratio when compared to the interest coverage ratio or the debt-to-assets ratio of a firm.

In fact, academic and policy research *does not provide any consensual inference on the optimal level of debt for a country*. Some studies argue that there is a threshold effect where growth outcomes worsen in advanced economies—not necessarily in emerging economies—when debt exceeds 90 per cent of GDP.[37] Others dispute the notion that there is any clear threshold even for advanced economies—let alone for emerging ones. These studies, in fact, point out that the direction of causality runs the other way around: it is weak growth that causes the debt-to-GDP ratio to blow up rather than high debt causing weak growth.[38] Researchers from the IMF write in an article titled 'Debt and Growth: Is There a Magic Threshold?' that 'there appears to be no clear point above which a nation's debt dramatically compromises medium-term growth.'[39]

[37]See Reinhart, Carmen M., and Kenneth S. Rogoff, 'Growth in a Time of Debt', *American Economic Review*, Vol. 100, No. 2, pp. 573–8; Reinhart, Carmen M., Vincent R. Reinhart, and Kenneth S. Rogoff, 'Public Debt Overhangs: Advanced-Economy Episodes since 1800', *Journal of Economic Perspectives*, Vol. 26, No. 3, 2010, pp. 69–86.

[38]Herndon, Thomas, Michael Ash, and Robert Pollin, 'Does High Public Debt Consistently Stifle Economic Growth? A Critique of Reinhart and Rogoff', Working Paper No. 322, 2013, Political Economy Research Institute, University of Massachusetts; Panizza, Ugo, and Andrea F. Presbitero, 'Public Debt and Economic Growth: Is There a Causal Effect?', Working Paper No. 65, 2012, Money and Finance Research Group, Ancona, Italy.

[39]Pescatori, Andrea, Damiano Sandri, and John Simon, 'Debt and Growth: Is There a Magic Threshold?', IMF Working Paper # 2014/034, 2014.

Growth Leads to Debt Sustainability, Not Vice Versa

In the specific context of growth and debt sustainability, the conceptual confusion for emerging economies also stems from the fact that academic and policy literature in macroeconomics focusses primarily on advanced economies, where the direction of causality has been harder to pin down, as the possibility of the phenomenon of 'growing out of debt' is lower when compared to India. This phenomenon essentially captures the fact that the debt-to-GDP ratio, which is the primary measure used to assess the extent of debt in a country, decreases faster when the GDP growth rate is higher. Thus, countries with high GDP growth rates—like India—can decrease their debt-to-GDP ratios faster than countries with low GDP growth rates, like the advanced economies. Indeed, as the *Economic Survey 2020–21* showed, growth causes debt to become sustainable in countries with higher growth rates. However, such clarity about the causal direction is not witnessed in countries with lower growth rates.

In this section, I highlight the empirical relationship between debt-to-GDP ratios and GDP growth for India.

Disentangling the Direction of Causality for India

Does higher growth lead to lower debt-to-GDP or lower debt-to-GDP cause higher growth? Conceptually, causality could flow in either direction. The argument supporting higher debt-to-GDP leading to lower growth is as follows: higher levels of public debt-to-GDP are accompanied by more taxes in the future to pay for the debt. This, in turn, leads to lower lifetime wealth, which may decrease consumption and savings, eventually resulting in lower aggregate demand and growth rates. If higher public debt (i.e., lower public savings) is not accompanied by an increase in private savings, it may also lead to lower total savings in the economy. This may put upward pressure on the interest rates, resulting in crowding out of investment and thus negatively impacting growth rates. On the other hand, higher GDP growth leads to lower public debt-to-GDP ratios through the increase in the denominator, i.e., GDP.

Evidence over the last two-and-a-half decades demonstrates clearly that in India, higher GDP growth causes the ratio of debt-to-GDP to decline but not vice versa. An examination of the contemporaneous correlation between real GDP growth and ratio of general government debt-to-GDP—though clearly negative and statistically significant as seen in Figure 1—does not provide clarity about the direction of causation. Inferring the direction of causation that manifests in India is important. This is because the negative contemporaneous correlation seen in Figure 1 can be incorrectly interpreted as: higher debt causes the GDP growth rate to decline. However, the correlation can equally imply that the direction of causation is exactly the opposite—higher GDP growth rate causes the debt as a percentage of GDP to decline.

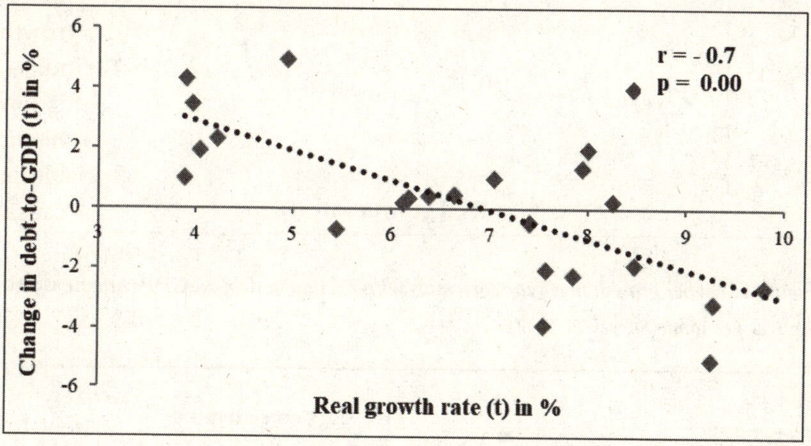

Figure 1: GDP growth in one year correlates with decline in general government debt in the same year

Source: Economic Survey 2020–21

To infer the direction of causation, we examine the differences in their lagged correlations. Figure 2 demonstrates the lagged relationship between real GDP growth rates and change in general government debt-to-GDP levels over the last 25 years. Over the last two-and-a-half decades, real GDP growth rates and one-year-ahead change in general government debt-to-GDP levels show a significant negative correlation. However, as seen in Figure 3, during the same time period, the correlation between change in general government debt-to-GDP levels and one-year-ahead growth rates turns out to be statistically indistinguishable from 0. The evidence, therefore, shows the direction of causality between the two variables: higher growth leads to lower public debt in India, but not vice versa.

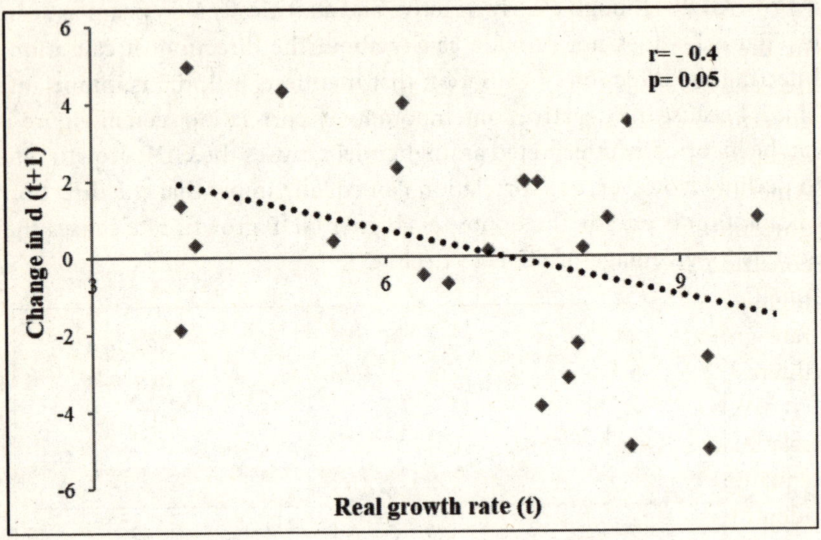

Figure 2: Higher growth in a year correlates with decline in debt-to-GDP ratio next year

Source: Economic Survey 2020–21

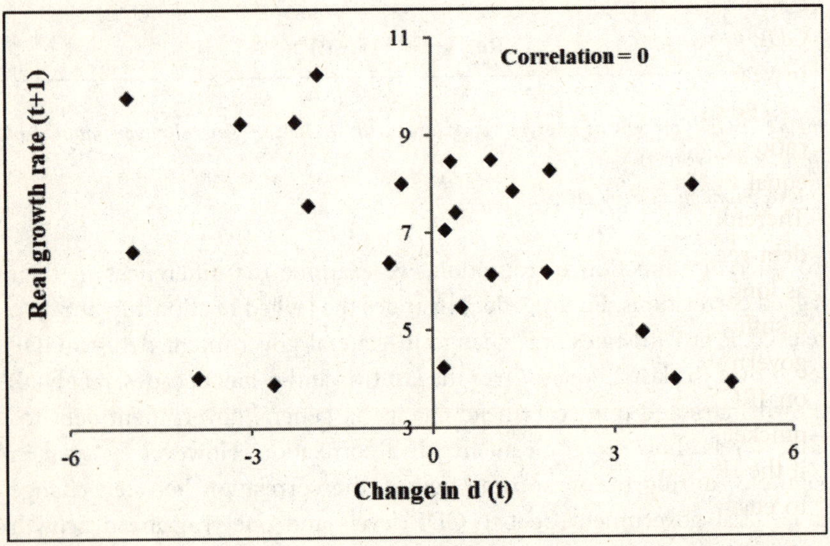

Figure 3: Change in debt-to-GDP ratio in a year does not correlate with GDP growth next year

Source: Economic Survey 2020–21

Why Does Higher Growth Lead to Lower Debt-to-GDP?

In the Indian context, growth leads to debt sustainability but not necessarily vice versa because the interest rate on debt paid by the Indian government has been less than India's growth rate by norm, not by exception. As Blanchard explains in his 2019 presidential address at the American Economic Association (AEA): 'If the interest rate paid by the government is less than the growth rate, then the intertemporal budget constraint facing the government no longer binds.'[40] This phenomenon highlights that debt sustainability depends on what is called the interest rate growth rate differential (IRGD), i.e., the difference between the interest rate and the growth rate in an economy.

We start by understanding the conceptual underpinnings of the relationship between public debt and growth, as seen in the simple equation for debt dynamics discussed in *Economic Survey 2020–21*. This identity for debt dynamics is given by:

$$\Delta d_t = (r_t - g_t)\, d_{t-1}/(1 + g_t) - pb_t$$

where Δd_t denotes change in general government debt-to-GDP in year t, r_t denotes the nominal interest rate paid in year t, g_t denotes the nominal GDP growth in year t, d_{t-1} denotes the general government debt-to-GDP in year (t–1) and pb_t denotes the primary balance-to-GDP in year t.

From the above equation, it becomes clear that the debt-to-GDP ratio remains stable over time (i.e., $d_t = d_{t-1}$) if the primary deficit is equal to. When g>r, this threshold level of primary deficit is positive. Therefore, as long as the primary deficit remains below this threshold, debt remains sustainable. Along these lines, De Luca (2012) shows that as long as primary deficit is a constant fraction of GDP, r-g still remains a sufficient statistic for debt sustainability. Thus, the ease with which a government can reduce its debt-to-GDP ratio (d_t) depends primarily on IRGD, which equals r-g. More negative the IRGD, the easier (and quicker) it is for the government to ensure debt sustainability. Conversely, if the IRGD is positive, the harder (and slower) it is for the government to ensure debt sustainability. A negative IRGD thus creates an enabling

[40]Blanchard, Olivier, 'Public Debt and Low Interest Rates', *The Peterson Institute for International Economics*, 4 January 2019, https://tinyurl.com/22fmw7dk. Accessed on 19 December 2023.

environment for debt sustainability.

Intuitively, when nominal growth rate exceeds the nominal interest rate for the foreseeable future, debt sustainability is obtained, as explained in Figure 4 below. Here, we take the nominal growth rate and the nominal interest rate as their historical estimates for the last 25 years—8.8 per cent and 12.8 per cent, respectively. As the government's investment of a ₹100 produces ₹112.8 while the principal and interest repayment equal ₹108.8, ₹4 can be added to the economy after the loan of ₹100 is rolled over to the next period. Of course, this rollover of the debt that yields debt sustainability can only manifest if nominal growth rate exceeds the nominal interest rate. If the inequality reverses, then rollover of debt does not become automatic, thereby jeopardizing debt sustainability.

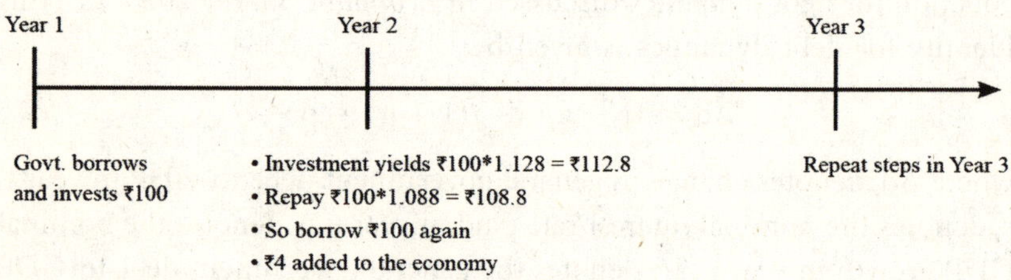

Figure 4: Obtaining debt sustainability

This inequality has thus led to a negative IRGD for most of the last three decades, which, in turn, has caused debt levels to decline. Figure 5 shows the strong correlation observed between IRGD and change in general government debt. Since this inequality reduces the fiscal costs of a debt rollover (Blanchard 2019), it expands the scope for fiscal policy to:

(i) cater to slowdowns in aggregate demand, and
(ii) thereby enable growth to foster debt sustainability.

A closer look at the trends in interest rates and growth rates in India in Figure 6 highlights a perceptibly higher variability in the growth rates relative to interest rates over the past two-and-a-half decades. This implies that changes in IRGD are mostly attributable to changes in growth rates rather than the changes in interest rates. Thus, it is higher growth that provides the key to sustainability of debt for India.

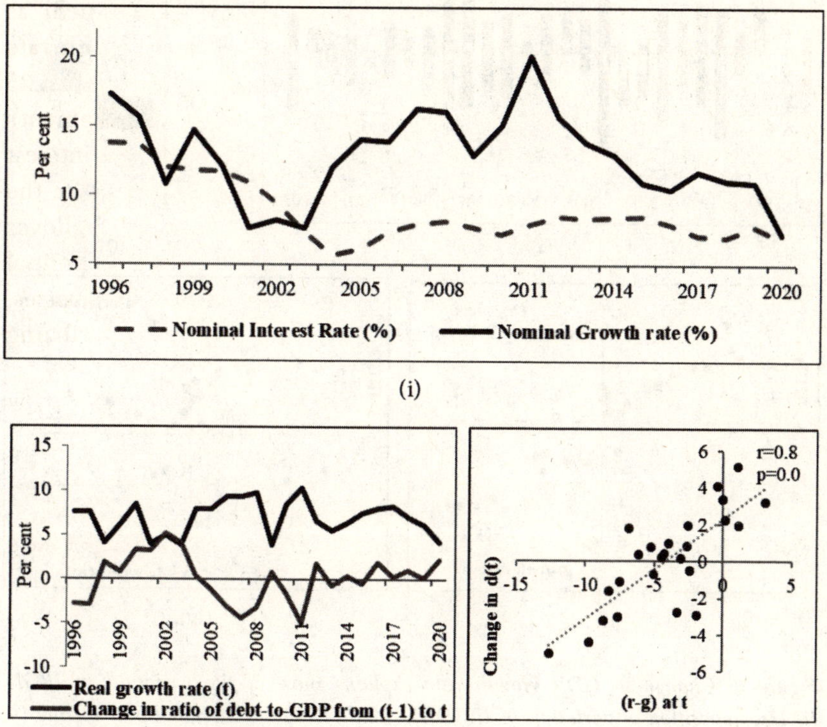

Figure 5: During the last 25 years, nominal growth rate higher than nominal interest rate is a norm, except for a short period during the Asian Financial Crisis. (i) Trends in nominal growth rate and nominal interest rate; (ii) trends in real growth rate (g) and change in debt-to-GDP ratio (d); (iii) strong correlation between (r-g) and change in debt to GDP ratio.

Source: Economic Survey 2020–21

Note: d(t) is general government debt as a per cent of GDP at time period (t); years represented in the figures are FY ending; nominal interest rate is the weighted average interest rate on central government securities; real interest rate is calculated using the nominal interest rate and GDP deflator.

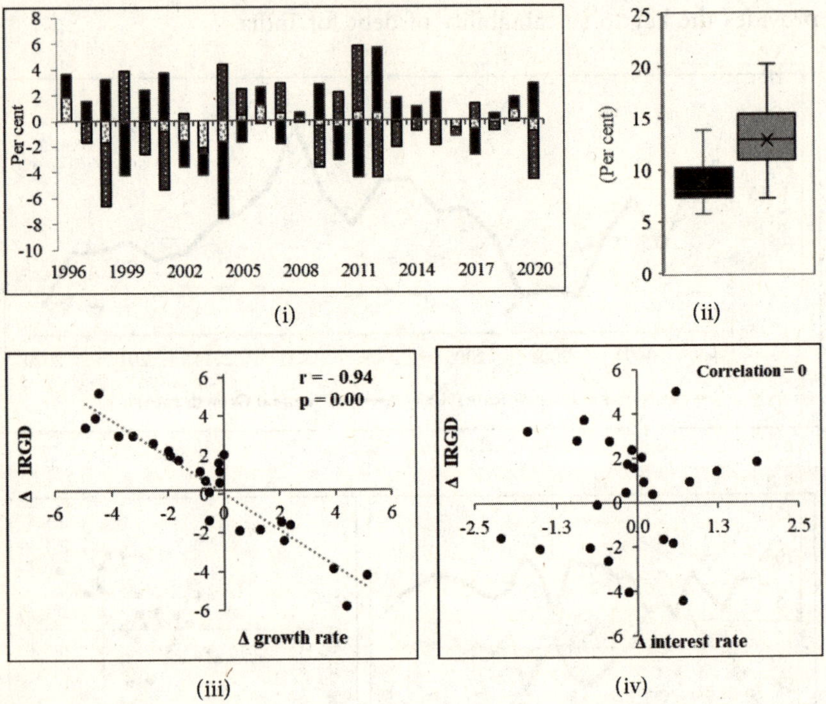

Figure 6: Change in GDP growth rate explains most of the variation in IRGD. (i) Decomposition of variation in IRGD (in solid black) into nominal growth rate (in grey dots) and nominal interest rate (in white dots); (ii) variation in nominal growth and interest rates; (iii) strong correlation between variation in growth rate and variation in IRGD; (iv) no correlation between variation in interest rate and variation in IRGD.

Source: Economic Survey 2020–21

Direction of Causality in Other Economies

Is India an outlier, where higher growth rates lead to lower public debt but not vice versa?

On examining the trends in IRGD and change in debt-to-GDP ratio for low-growth economies like the US and UK in Figure 7, no correlation is observed between the two variables. This indicates lack of evidence for direction of causality from real growth rate to government debt-to-GDP for these countries.

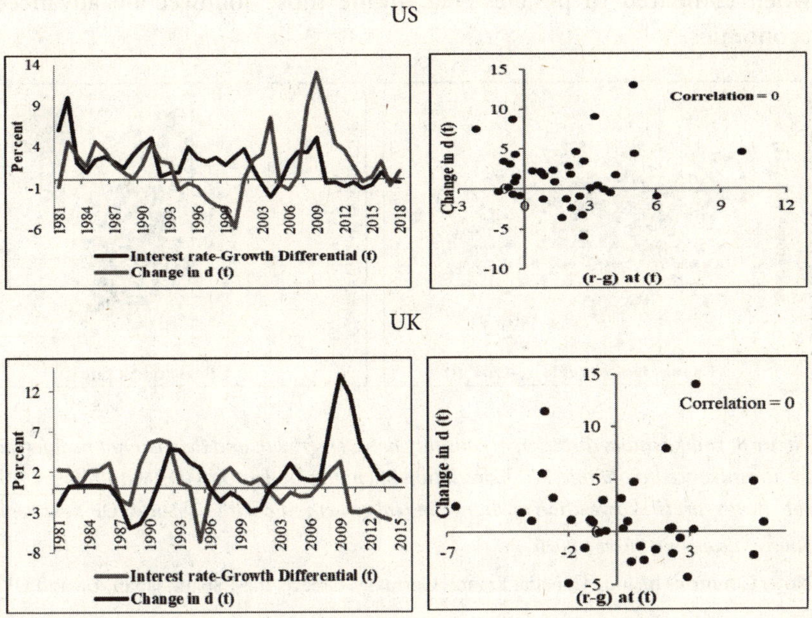

Figure 7: No correlation between IRGD and change in debt-to-GDP ratio for US and UK. (i) Trends in IRGD and change in debt-to-GDP ratio and subsequent correlation for the US; (ii) trends in IRGD and change in debt-to-GDP ratio and subsequent correlation for the UK.

Source: Economic Survey 2020–21

Figure 8 shows the same time–series correlations as estimated for India above for the advanced economies—Canada, France, Germany, Greece, Italy, Spain, Japan, US and UK. These correlations are estimated by pooling the data for these countries over the last four decades. The correlation between real GDP growth rates and one-year-ahead change in general government debt-to-GDP levels is significantly negative. Similarly, the correlation between change in general government debt-to-GDP levels and one-year-ahead growth rates is also negative and statistically significant. Thus, unlike in the case of India, the time–series correlations do not suggest the direction of causality, as both sets of correlations are statistically significant. This difference is extremely important to highlight because the implications for fiscal policy—especially during the Covid-19 crisis—are starkly different for India when compared to policies that mimic those followed by advanced economies.

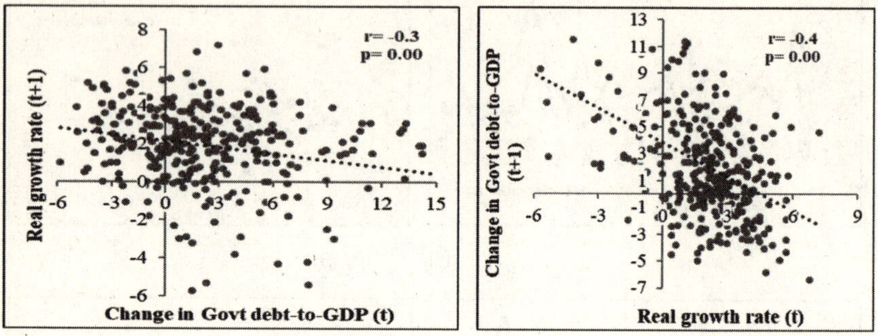

Figure 8: Unlike India, direction of causality between growth and debt cannot be inferred for the advanced economies. (i) Correlation of change in debt-to-GDP with real growth rate next year; (ii) correlation of change in real growth rate with debt-to-GDP next year.

Source: Economic Survey 2020–21

Note: Countries include Canada, France, Germany, Greece, Italy, Spain, Japan, US and UK.

The evidence that the magnitude of GDP growth affects the direction of causality from growth to debt sustainability is buttressed by the proof of this causal relationship for all high-growth emerging market economies (EMEs) put together, which include India, China, Indonesia, Malaysia, Thailand, the Philippines, Vietnam and Türkiye. Figure 9 shows that higher growth leads to lower debt-to-GDP ratios over the period 1980 to 2018 but not vice versa. This may be inferred from the statistically significant negative correlation observed between real growth rate and one-year-ahead change in general government debt-to-GDP, and statistically insignificant correlation between change in debt-to-GDP and one-year-ahead real growth rate.

Thus, the evidence clearly points out that for countries growing their GDP at high rates, growth leads to lowering of their public debt as measured by their debt-to-GDP ratios but not vice versa. In contrast, when the GDP growth rate is low, no such causal relationship manifests between growth and public debt.

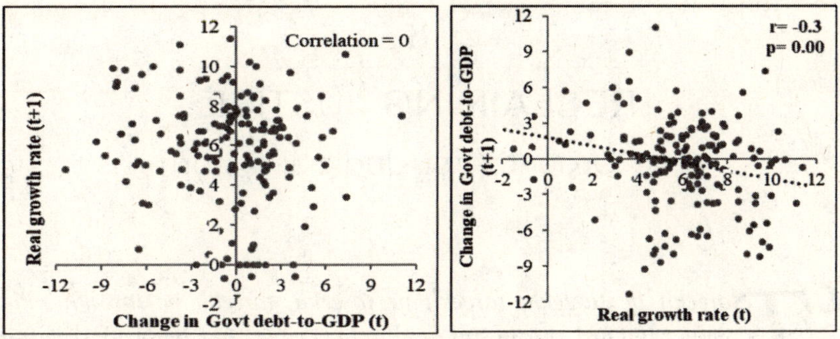

Figure 9: Direction of causality: Growth to debt in high-growth EMEs. (i) Correlation of change in debt-to-GDP with real growth rate next year; (ii) correlation of change in real growth rate with debt-to-GDP next year.

Source: Economic Survey 2020–21

Note: Countries include India, China, Indonesia, Malaysia, Thailand, the Philippines, Vietnam, Türkiye.

◆

Given India's high growth potential, the IRGD is expected to be significantly negative in the foreseeable future. Therefore, a fiscal policy that provides an impetus to growth will lead to lower, not higher, debt-to-GDP ratios. While acknowledging the counterargument from critics that governments may have a natural proclivity to spend, this chapter exhorts the government to borrow to fund investments in digital, physical and human capital, where human capital encompasses investments in healthcare and education.

8

RECLAIMING JUSTICE

The Urgency for Judicial Reform

'*Tareekh pe tareekh, tareekh pe tareekh, tareekh pe tareekh milti gayi, My Lord, par insaaf nahi mila* (Dates after dates, dates after dates, dates after dates; all one gets is dates, My Lord, but not justice).' Many of us remember actor Sunny Deol from the 1993 film *Damini* thundering these dialogues in the courtroom in exasperation because justice delayed is justice denied after all. Three decades have passed since that iconic scene. Yet, the Indian justice system continues to infuriate with over five crore pending cases. Five years after the issue was covered in the *Economic Survey 2018–19*, the number of pending cases has increased from 3.5 crore to over 5 crore—a 43 per cent jump! Justice continues to be delayed and thereby denied to the common citizen.

Economic activity is affected by the long shadow of delays and pendency across the legal landscape. Contract enforcement remains the single biggest constraint to improving the ease of doing business (EoDB) in India. Given the possible benefits of improvement in contract enforcement for the economy, this may be the best investment that the economy can make.

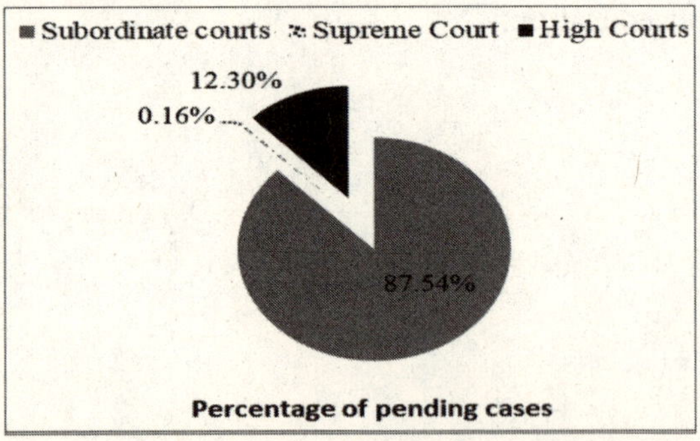

Figure 1: Distribution of pending cases among different levels of courts

Source: Supreme Court of India; National Judicial Data Grid (NJDG), 2023

Given that District and Subordinate (D&S) courts account for 87.5 per cent of pending cases (Figure 1), I focus on this segment and evaluate its performance on parameters such as disposal time, pendency time, case types and case clearance rate. I further analyse the requirement of additional judges across various level of courts to achieve 100 per cent clearance rate to eliminate the stock of pendency in the next 10 years.

Pendency

The pendency of a case on a given date is the time since the date of filing. The distribution of pending cases, age-wise, as on 16 December 2023 is shown in Figure 2. It reveals that the distribution of pendency of both civil and criminal cases is more or less the same. About 60 per cent of all cases are pending for more than one year. Figure 3 shows the large inter-state variation in average pendency of cases in D&S courts. It reveals that Odisha, Bihar, West Bengal, Uttar Pradesh and Gujarat have higher average pendency for both civil and criminal cases as compared to the national averages, whereas Punjab and Delhi have the least average pendency of cases.

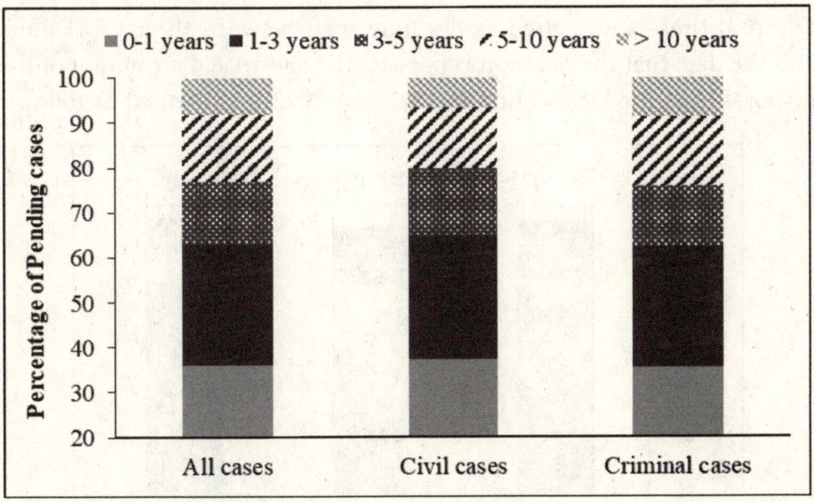

Figure 2: Distribution of pending cases (age-wise) in D&S courts

Source: NJDG, as on 16 December 2023

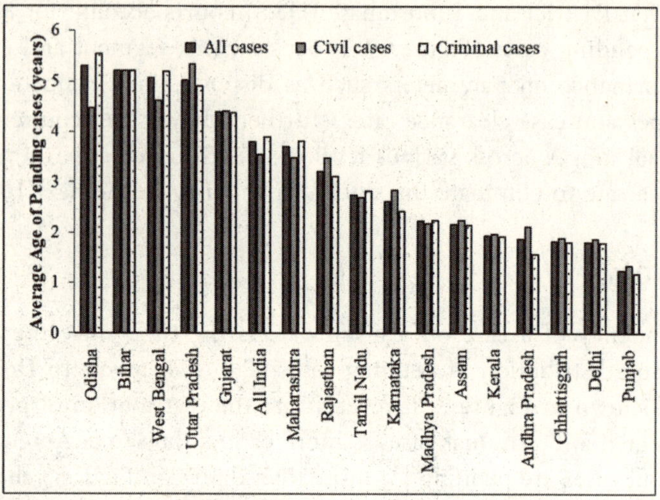

Figure 3: State-wise average pendency in D&S courts

Source: NJDG, as on 16 December 2023

Disposal

Disposal time is measured as the time span between the date of filing and the date that the decision is passed. The age-wise distribution of the disposal time for D&S courts for the year 2023 is presented as follows:

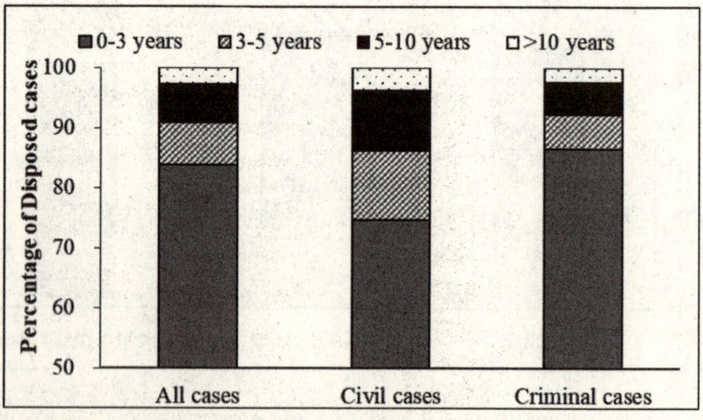

Figure 4: Distribution of disposed cases in D&S courts in 2023

Source: NJDG, 2023

Figure 4 reveals that over 65 per cent of civil cases and around 90 per cent of criminal cases are disposed within three years. Further, the distribution of state-wise disposal rate is presented below. Figure 5 reveals that Odisha, Bihar, West Bengal, Uttar Pradesh and Gujarat have higher average disposal time than the national average for both civil and criminal cases. Further, Punjab and Delhi have the lowest average disposal time. These trends are consistent with the distribution of state-wise average pendency age. Again, the states in eastern India perform the worst in time taken for disposal.

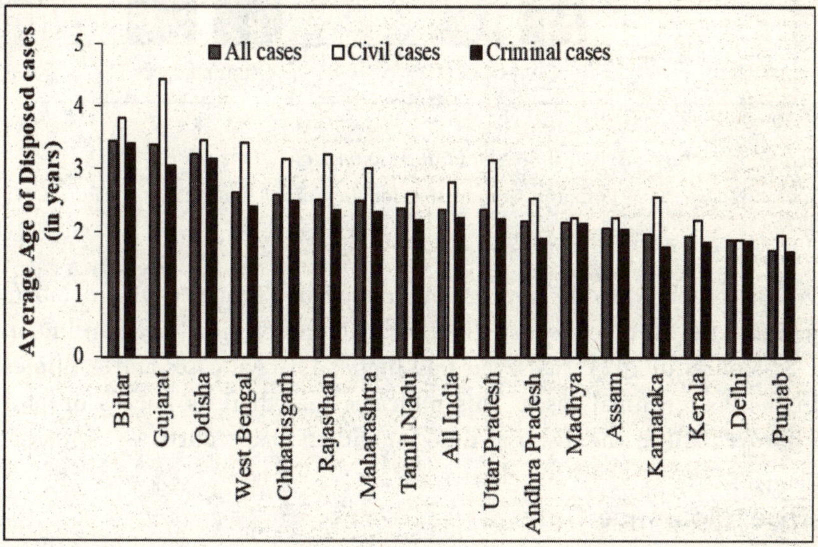

Figure 5: State-wise average disposal time in D&S courts in 2023

Source: NJDG, 2023

Comparison to Global Peers

How do Indian courts perform compared to global peers? International comparison of disposal rates is presented in Figure 6.

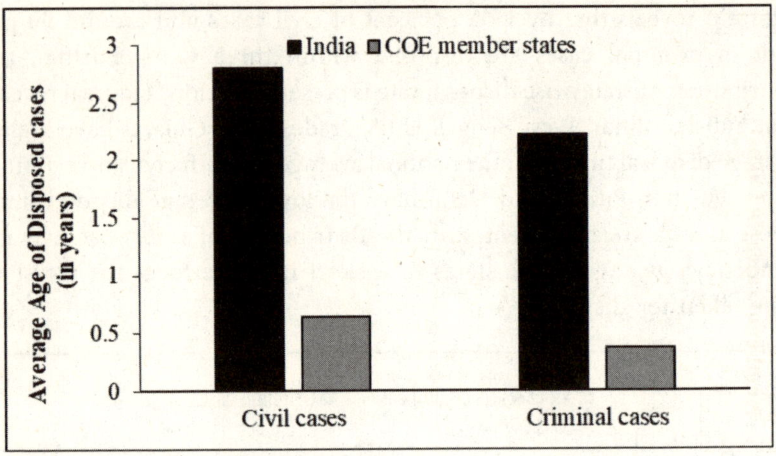

Figure 6: Average disposal time—India and Council of Europe (CoE)

Source: NJDG, 2023; European Commission for the Efficiency of Justice (CEPEJ), CoE, 2022

When compared to the average of Council of Europe (COE) members in 2022, the average disposal time for civil and criminal cases in Indian D&S courts in 2023 was seven-fold higher for civil cases and 4.4 times higher for criminal cases. This indicates that there is huge scope for improvement in the disposal time for Indian D&S courts.

Case Clearance Rate

The case clearance rate (CCR) is the ratio of the number of cases disposed of in a given year to the number of cases instituted in that year, expressed as a percentage. It may be noted that the cases disposed of need not have been filed in the same year, as some proportion of them will typically be backlog from previous years. Clearance rate is mainly used to understand the efficiency of the system in proportion to the inflow of cases.

Figure 7 shows the relationship between the institution and disposal of cases, and CCR at an all-India level. While the number of cases instituted each year in D&S courts has gone up, so has the number of disposals. However, the gap between institution and disposals allows cases to accumulate, which results in an increase in pendency. This is

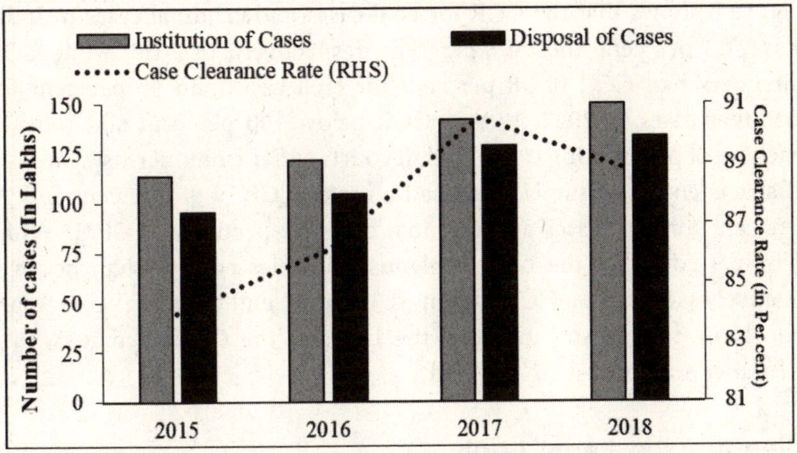

Figure 7. Institution of cases, disposal of cases and CCR in D&S courts
Source: NJDG, 2023

because the CCR remains structurally below 100 per cent. After declining to 62.2 per cent in 2020 and 81 per cent in 2021 due to Covid-19, an encouraging sign was that the CCR had increased from 88.9 per cent in 2019 to 91.8 per cent in 2023. The international comparison of CCR is presented in Figure 8:

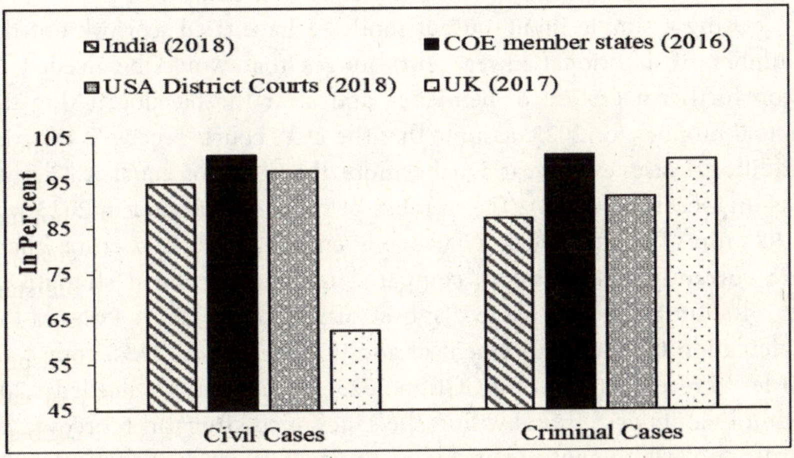

Figure 8: International comparison of CCR
Source: NJDG; CEPEJ; US Courts; UK Parliament research briefing, 2022

Figure 8 shows that the CCR for civil cases and criminal cases in India was 97.2 per cent and 90.7 per cent, respectively, in 2023, while COE members had CCR of 98 per cent for civil cases and 95 per cent for criminal cases in 2022. With a CCR below 100 per cent and a heavy backlog of pre-existing cases, Indian courts suffer from increasing delays. Districts courts in the US also had a better CCR of 98 per cent and 92 per cent for civil cases and criminal cases, respectively, in 2021. While criminal courts in the UK's England and Wales court system perform relatively well, with a CCR of almost 100 per cent, their civil courts fare poorly in comparison to India, the US, and the COE average, with a clearance rate of just 62 per cent.

Clearing the Legal Logjam

There are two key issues at hand that need to be dealt with in order to make the judiciary more efficient. First is to achieve a 100 per cent clearance rate so that there is no accumulation of pending cases. Second is to remove the backlog of cases already present in the system. The following analysis is done to solve both these issues by using the concept of an input–output matrix of cases at different court levels. While it is recognized that the disposal rate can be increased, for the purpose of this analysis, productivity is assumed to be constant.

Using a simple input–output model, I have tried to work out the number of additional lower court judges that would be needed to stop further accretion of pendency and clear the backlog. Using the actual number for 2023, assume that the D&S courts receive 2.15 crore additional cases every year. Furthermore, their backlog equals 4.32 crore (as on December 2022). The number of cases disposed of in 2023 was 1.98 crore. Thus, the closing balance in end-2023 was 4.37 crore. There are currently 19,858 judges compared to the sanctioned strength of 25,246. On average, a judge disposes of 997 cases. Chart 1 shows the calculation for the requirement of additional judges in D&S courts. In order to reach 100 per cent CCR in 2023, the D&S courts needed 1,705 additional judges. This is within the sanctioned strength! Moreover, in order to clear the entire backlog in the next 10 years, a further 4,503 judges are needed. Adding the number of judges required to ensure 100 per cent CCR and to eliminate the backlog in 10 years, the total

Chart 1: Additional judges required in D&S courts

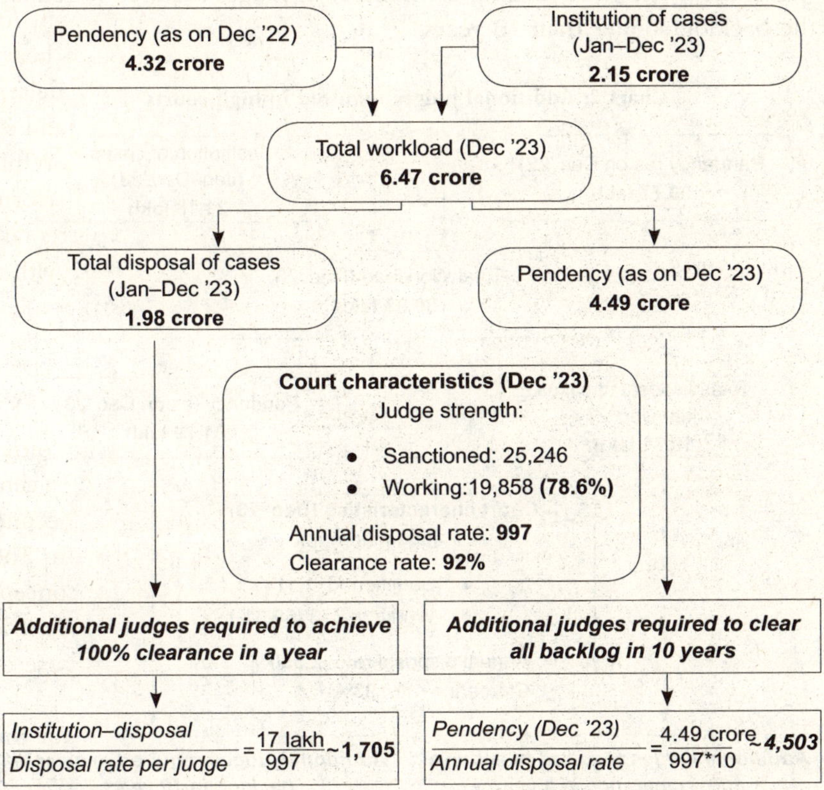

Source: Court News, Supreme Court; NJDG, 2023; author's calculations

number of additional judges required is 1,705 + 4,503 = 6,208. As the current difference between the sanctioned and working number of judges in D&S courts is 5,388 (25,246 – 19,858), just filling up the sanctioned strength can help reduce the backlog significantly in 10 years. Also, the sanctioned strength in D&S courts has been increased from 22,750 in 2018 to 25,246. Therefore, the difference between the number required (6,208) and the current sanctioned that have not been filled (5,388), which equals only 820, can be easily sanctioned. Admittedly, these are no more than a rough calculation, but it shows that we are not dealing with astronomical numbers even if we make no improvements in efficiency. Of course, improvements in efficiency will certainly help in reducing the number of judges required to reduce the backlog sooner than 10 years.

Chart 2: Additional judges required in high courts

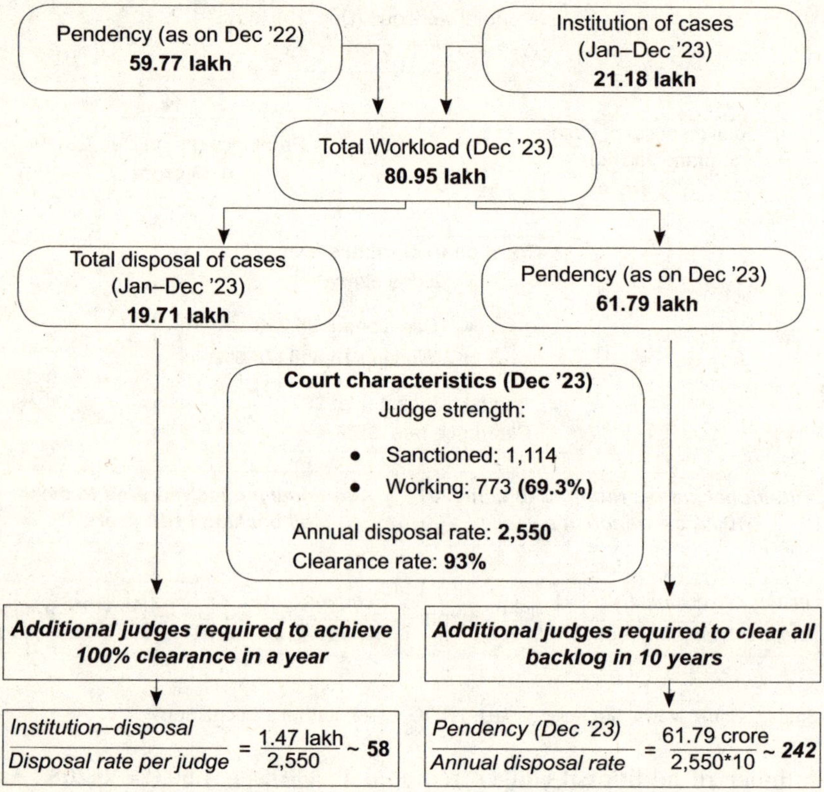

Source: Supreme Court Annual Report, 2023; author's calculations

Applying the same framework to higher courts, the numbers are even smaller (note that the data sets here are from July–June). As of December 2023, High Court judges were working at 69.3 per cent of their sanctioned strength. With a CCR of 93 per cent, each judge achieved an average disposal rate of 2,550 cases per year. This is an exceptionally good disposal rate. The backlog of cases as on December 2022 was 59.77 lakh. In order to reach 100 per cent CCR, they need just 58 additional judges. To clear the backlog in the next 10 years, High Courts need 242 additional judges. Adding the number of judges required to ensure 100 per cent CCR and to eliminate the backlog in 10 years, the total number of additional judges required in High Courts is 58 + 242 = 300. As the current difference between the sanctioned and working number of judges in D&S courts is 341 (1,114–773), just filling up to the sanctioned strength can help to reduce the backlog completely in 10 years.

Chart 3: Additional judges required in Supreme Court

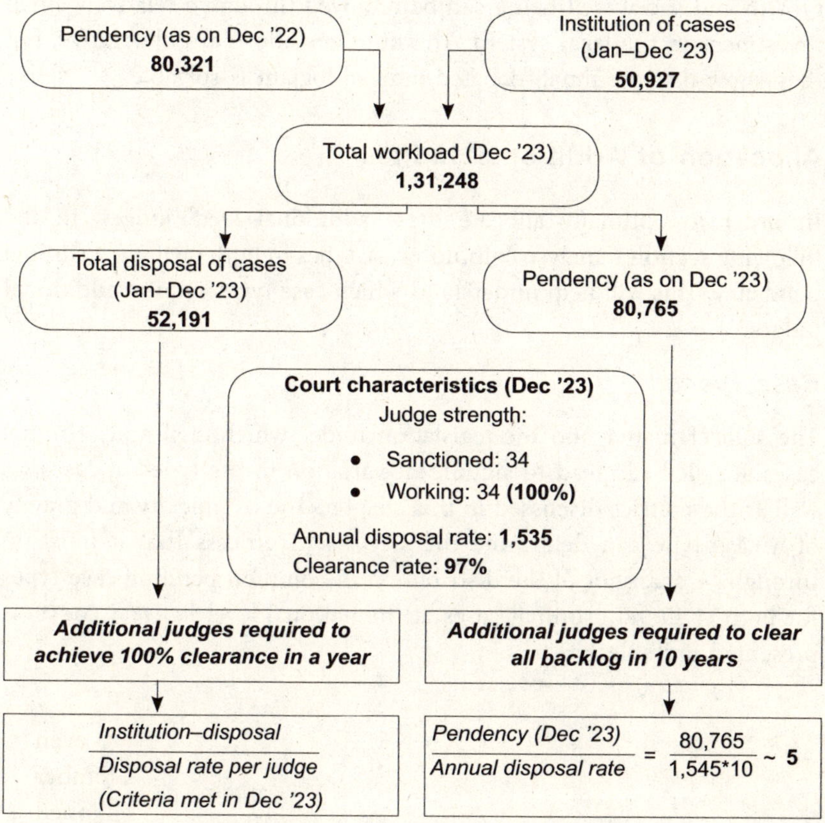

Source: Supreme Court Annual Report, 2023; author's calculations

As of December 2023, Supreme Court judges were working at 100 per cent of their sanctioned strength. With a high of 97 per cent, each judge disposes 1,535 cases per year on average. The backlog of cases as on December 2022 was 80,321. As the CCR in Supreme Court was more than 100 per cent, no additional judges are required to reach 100 per cent CCR. To clear the backlog in the next 10 years, additional five judges are required. To clear the accumulated cases, the Supreme Court needs to increase its sanctioned strength by five and continue working at its new full strength.

The main point of my analysis is that a major hurdle to economic growth and social well-being can be removed through a relatively small investment in the legal system. The numbers above are illustrative, but they show that the much-debated judicial logjam is solvable.

Allocation of Additional Judges

In order to optimally allocate these additional D&S judges, in the following section I analyse common case types in both civil and criminal pendency. This will help understand which case types require additional judges.

Case Types

The subject matter and the legislation under which civil and criminal cases are filed can lead to significant variation in the types of cases, as well as the metrics discussed in this chapter. The complexity and gravity of a case type can determine the stages and process that it must go through. A snapshot of the distribution of common pending case types for both civil and criminal cases at the national level in D&S courts is presented in Table 1.

Table 1
Common case types' weight in total pendency

Common Case Types		*% in Total Pendency (as on 16 Dec 2023)*
A. Civil cases		
Civil Original Suits	Civil Suit	12.5
	Motor Vehicle	1.9
	Marriage Petition	1.4
	Land Reference	0.3
	Other Civil	2.0
Total Civil Original Suits		18.2
Civil Applications		1.5
Civil Executions		3.3
Civil Appeals		1.1
Total Civil Suits		**24.9**
B. Criminal cases		
Criminal Original Suits	Warrants/Summons	61.3
	Sessions Cases	5.6
	Other Criminal	1.2
Total Criminal Original Suits		**68.0**
Criminal Applications	Bail Applications	0.5
	Misc. Applications	5.1
Total Criminal Applications		**5.6**
Criminal Appeal		**0.9**
Total Criminal Suits		**75.1**

Source: NJDG, 2023

Table 1 reveals that as on 16 December 2023, civil cases contribute only a quarter of total pendency while criminal cases contribute the remaining three-quarter in D&S courts. Further, warrants/summons account for over 60 per cent of the backlog. Therefore, focussing on clearing the backlog in warrants/summons will significantly reduce the total backlog in the D&S courts. I have calculated the case type-wise clearance rate in D&S courts for 2023 so as to understand which of these cases have a tendency to have backlogs. This is presented in Table 2.

Table 2

Case type institution, disposal and CCR for D&S courts in 2023

Common Case Types	*Institution (in lakh)*	*Disposal (in lakh)*	*CCR (%)*
A. Civil cases (Overall)	**34.7**	**33.7**	**97.2**
Civil Original Suits	**24.5**	**23.6**	**95.9**
Civil Suit	13.2	12.4	94.0
MACP	3.5	3.5	99.7
Marriage Petition	4.0	3.9	97.7
Land Reference	0.2	0.3	130.6
Civil Applications	**3.7**	**3.5**	**96.1**
Civil Executions	**4.8**	**5.1**	**105.4**
Civil Appeals	**1.4**	**1.4**	**96.5**
B. Criminal cases (Overall)	**180.5**	**163.8**	**90.7**
Criminal Original Suits	**119.4**	**105.4**	**88.3**
Warrants/ Summons	113.3	100.7	88.8
Sessions Cases	8.6	7.5	86.6
Criminal Applications	**54.2**	**53.0**	**97.8**
Misc. Criminal Applications	37.7	36.8	97.7
Bail Applications	19.6	19.4	99.1
Criminal Appeals	**5.2**	**5.1**	**97.6**

Source: NJDG, 2019

Table 2 reveals that the average CCR for all civil and criminal cases in D&S courts for 2023 was 97.2 per cent and 90.7 per cent, respectively. This means that not only the backlog of criminal cases is three times higher than civil cases, criminal case type also has a lower CCR. Thus, the situation for criminal cases is distinctly worsening. The problem is especially acute for criminal original suits such as warrants/summons. These contribute over 60 per cent of the total pendency as of 16 December 2023. This implies that the additional judges need to specialize in warrants/summons so as to speed up the disposal of such cases. Lastly, it may be noted that 'civil execution' and 'land reference' case types have done quite well, maintaining a CCR of 105.4 and 130.6 per cent, respectively, in 2023. These areas merely need to maintain the current pace.

Priority to States

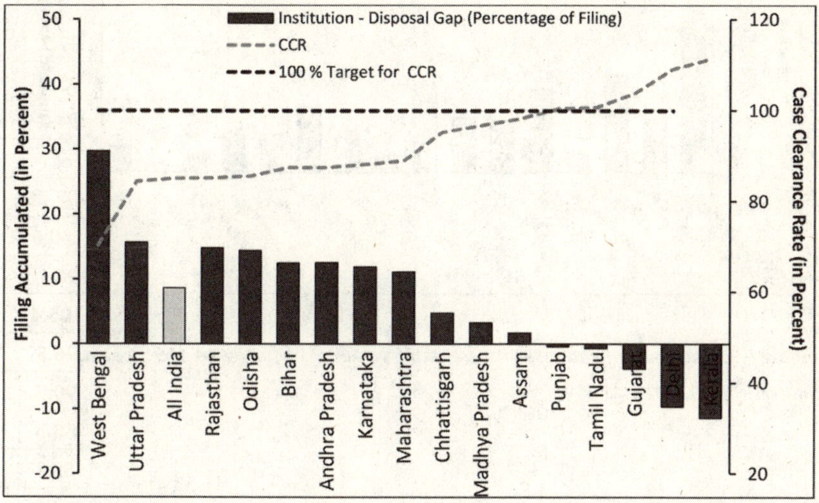

Figure 9: State-wise institution–disposal gap and CCR in D&S courts in 2023
Source: NJDG, 2023

Figure 9 shows that Kerala, Delhi, Gujarat, Tamil Nadu and Punjab have clearance rates of above 100 per cent in 2023. These states have achieved a level of efficiency where they are not only able to cope with fresh filings but can also address backlog from previous years. In contrast, West Bengal is the worst with about 30 per cent of the cases filed accumulating in the state in 2023. Uttar Pradesh, Rajasthan, Odisha, Bihar, Andhra Pradesh, Karnataka and Maharashtra each have accumulated about 10% of the cases filed in the state in 2023.

There is a great amount of variation in the extent to which the subordinate judiciary in each state is capable of dealing with the inflow of new cases. There are, therefore, huge gaps between the demand for courts and the current capacity of the subordinate courts in many states—possibly a key factor in the development inequalities between states.

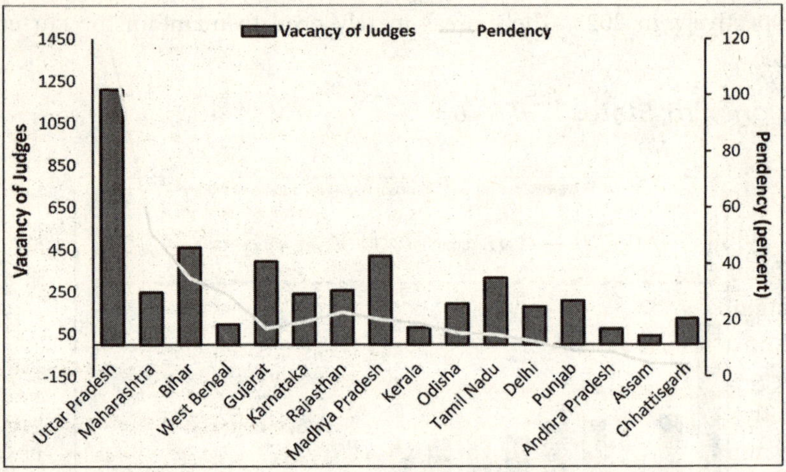

Figure 10: State-wise pendency of cases and vacancy of judges in D&S courts
Source: NJDG, 2023

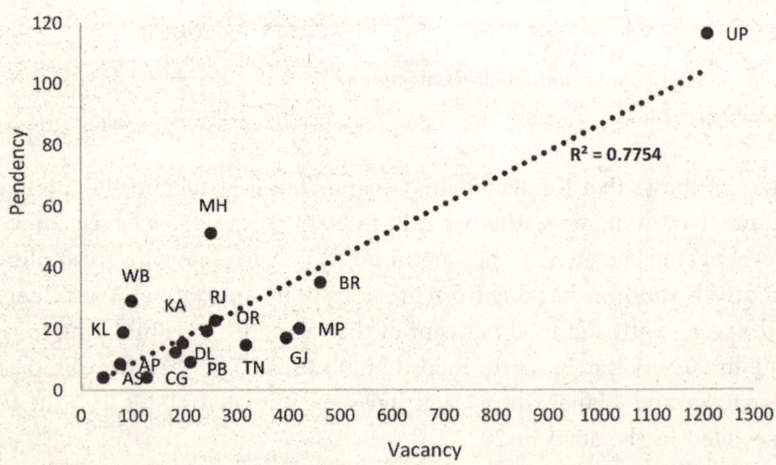

Figure 11: Strong correlation between pendency of cases and vacancy of judges in D&S
Source: NJDG, 2023

Figure 10 and 11 together reveal that there is a strong correlation between vacancy and pendency. As the pendency is especially high for Uttar Pradesh, Madhya Pradesh and Gujarat, the focus should be on filling vacancies in D&S courts in these states.

◆

Reducing the judicial backlog and achieving 100 per cent clearance rate for cases represents the best investment that India can make in improving EoDB in India. Much of the problem is concentrated in the district and subordinate courts. Contrary to conventional belief, however, the problem is not insurmountable and can be solved with relatively simple solutions. A case clearance rate of 100 per cent (i.e., zero accumulation) can be achieved with the addition of merely 1,705 judges in the lower courts and 58 in High Courts even without efficiency gains. This is already within sanctioned strength and only needs filling vacancies. The numbers needed to clear the backlog over 10 years is also quite manageable. Given the potential economic and social multipliers of a well-functioning legal system, the judiciary and the governments—especially in the states, given the backlog in lower courts—need to work together. The economic rewards that India will reap in its pursuit of economic prosperity will be humongous.

9

REVITALIZING THE STEEL FRAME

Why Bureaucratic Reform Is an Essential Prerequisite

In September 2020, the United Kingdom (UK) appointed a 41-year-old civil servant, Simon Case, as its cabinet secretary. Having previously served as Downing Street permanent secretary to the then PM Boris Johnson, Case was not parachuted from outside but grew to occupy the highest position in the UK's bureaucracy from within. Contrast this with the Indian bureaucracy: even the brightest, most motivated, incorruptible 41-year-old Indian Administrative Service (IAS) officer would be about two decades away from holding that post. While some may dismiss the UK example as irrelevant in the current Indian context, it can serve as an aspirational polestar as India@100 prepares for its amrit kaal.

Since Independence, more than 45 committees and commissions have made scores of recommendations to reform the Indian bureaucracy. Today, our colonial ruler—whom we overtook to become the fifth largest economy—has a truly modern bureaucracy with market competitiveness in remuneration, open market recruitment through applications for each position, and flexible arrangements for retirement savings, among several other improvements over its earlier tenured civil service system. In contrast, India's tenured civil service system remains anachronistic by broadly retaining the characteristics inherited at the time of Independence.

Of course, the Indian bureaucracy provides some stellar examples both for individuals and their accomplishments. Over the years, many outstanding civil servants have delivered yeoman service to the nation. I had the privilege to know and work with some during my stint in the GoI. However, we must recognize that outliers in any field can beat even severe odds because of the personal characteristics that make them the outlier in the first place. As there is always wide variation in the quality of individuals in any system, comparisons between two systems must always be undertaken by comparing the average in one system with the average in another.

I show in this chapter that while most large economies have reformed their bureaucracy since the 1980s, India has been a laggard in this important area of reform. As governments have come and gone over the seven decades since Independence, reforming our bureaucracy must now be undertaken in earnest if India must fulfil its aspirations of becoming a global economic powerhouse. After all, post Covid-19, the global economy has entered a multi-shock environment that is characterized by elevated economic and geopolitical uncertainty. Optimal policy formulation in this uncertain environment needs highly specialized expertise. India cannot hope to become a global economic powerhouse without bringing about the necessary changes to equip its bureaucracy with the specialized expertise in policy making and policy implementation.

Global Trends in Administrative Reforms

In most countries, significant civil service reforms have been undertaken since the 1970s. Table 1 provides a decadal overview of these reforms across a cross-section of countries that includes advanced economies and emerging ones.

Table 1
A decadal overview of civil service reforms

Reform Type	*1971–80*	*1981–90*	*1991–2000*	*2001–10*	*2011–20*
Training/ Competency Management	Singapore Malaysia		Singapore South Korea	Germany Canada Singapore Brazil Japan	Mexico Japan
Recruitment	Pakistan	China Australia Japan	Argentina	Canada Australia India France	France Japan Switzerland India
Rationalization/ Decentralization/ Privatization/ Streamlining	Sri Lanka The Philippines Pakistan Nepal Thailand USA Australia UK	France USA UK China Malaysia Australia	Argentina Sri Lanka Malaysia Italy Nepal Singapore South Korea Switzerland	Indonesia Italy France Japan Russia Thailand Australia Vietnam	Germany New Zealand UK

Reform Type	*1971–80*	*1981–90*	*1991–2000*	*2001–10*	*2011–20*
		The Philippines Sri Lanka Bhutan Canada Türkiye	New Zealand South Africa Brazil Thailand Vietnam Bhutan	The Philippines Sri Lanka UK Germany Mexico Bhutan Bangladesh The Netherlands Italy Russia	
Performance Appraisal/ Incentives		USA Australia China Singapore	Malaysia Singapore Australia Canada China Malaysia Argentina Sri Lanka South Korea Mexico Nepal Russia UK	Malaysia Vietnam Mexico Russia Singapore Bhutan France Australia Italy	Brazil India New Zealand Russia South Africa Myanmar
Senior Executive Management, Senior Executive Service (SES)	USA	Australia Japan	Argentina Australia The Netherlands Italy Singapore	Australia South Korea Italy France	
Diversity and Inclusivity			Australia		Australia South Korea Japan France
E-Government and Data		Singapore			

Source: Compiled from country-specific studies

Based on a cross-country study of key reforms of civil services, particularly after 1980, such reforms have been grouped under four categories in Table 2:

Table 2

Major types of civil service reforms

A. Management reforms	*B. Performance management systems for senior bureaucrats*	*C. Training and capacity building reforms*	*D. Diversity and inclusivity in representation*
Recruitment reforms A1. Entry into civil service through a competitive examination that provides for entry into a specific group of the public service A2. Any recent reforms towards reduction of seniority-based pay increments (pay advancement according to years of experience) **Pay reforms** A3. Performance-related pay in country's central government A4. Pay in government indexed to economic variables **Accountability reforms** A5. Existence of general accountability framework for civil servants in which the management of human resources is one of the core strategic parts **Mobility in civil service** A6. Existence of specific programmes to encourage mobility in civil services	**Identification of senior civil servants** B1. Frameworks for identification of senior civil servants **Performance management regime** B2. Performance management regime for senior civil servants	**Overhaul of training** C1. Civil service-wide training strategy and/ or action plan C2. Existence of organizational and individual civil servant learning plans C3. Structured online course development C4. Executive leadership training and coaching C5. Information technology/digital skills training C6. Coaching and mentoring	**Representation of women** D1. Women's share in employment, public sector employment, parliament and ministerial positions **Inclusivity in recruitment process** D2. Laws or policies for enhancing inclusivity in recruitment process

A. Management reforms	*B. Performance management systems for senior bureaucrats*	*C. Training and capacity building reforms*	*D. Diversity and inclusivity in representation*
A7. If yes, are these programmes targeted to all civil servants? A8. These programmes enable mobility within the civil service (exchanges between ministries) A9. These programmes enable civil servant placements in the private/not-for-profit sector A10. These programmes enable private/not-for-profit sector employee placements in the civil service **E-governance reforms** A11. Measures to enhance e-governance **Rationalization reforms** A12. Streamlining of staff and restructuring of departments A13. Privatization of departments A14. New public management			

Source: Compiled from country-specific studies

i. Type A including recruitment, pay, accountability and rationalization
ii. Type B relating to identification and performance assessment of senior bureaucrats
iii. Type C pertaining to training and capacity building
iv. Type D focussing on diversity and inclusivity in the bureaucracy

Table 3 compares India vis-à-vis China and the advanced economies on some of the major characteristics of the bureaucracy. We note that, except for Australia, every other major economy has the feature of guaranteed tenure in service. Similarly, on merit-based recruitment at entry level and on age restrictions pertaining to entry into and exit from the bureaucracy, the Indian bureaucracy resembles those of the other major economies.

However, on several key characteristics that potentially impact the efficiency of the bureaucracy, the Indian system does not match the features prevailing in most major economies. These include:

i. remuneration that is competitive with relevant public/private sector peers;
ii. term limits and/or fixed term periods for senior executive positions;
iii. retirement/pension systems that allow mobility between public and private sector without cost;
iv. lateral entry and open market-based hiring for recruitment;
v. special programmes for laterally hired senior executives; and
vi. accountability mechanisms like monitoring of effort and performance-linked pay incentives.

Table 4 examines in detail the key differences by expanding the sample of countries and the granularity with which each feature of the bureaucracy in India is compared with that of the other countries.

Table 3

Cross-country comparison: India, China and advanced economies

	India	Australia	UK	USA	New Zealand	China	Japan	France	Germany	Canada	Italy
Characteristics where India is similar to other major economies											
Merit-based recruitment at entry level with open competition (through competitive exam or open market, as opposed to patronage-heavy discretionary hiring)	☑	☑	☑	☑	☑	☒	☒	☒	☑	☒	☑
Lack of or weak age restrictions (no or low minimum age of entry, no or high maximum retirement age, etc.)	☑	☑	☑	☑	☑	☒	☑	☑	☒	☑	☑
Guaranteed tenure in service (minimum or lifetime tenure)	☑	☒	☑	☑	☑	☑	☑	☑	☑	☑	☑
Characteristics where India is *not* similar to other major economies											
Merit-based selection/empanelment for senior posts (based strictly on performance appraisal, qualifications and domain experience as opposed to seniority)	☑	☑	☑	☑	☑	☒	☒	☒	☒	☑	☑
High horizontal mobility for civil servants between departments/ministries	☑	☑	☒	☑	☒	☒	☑	☑	☑	☒	☑
Market-competitive remuneration (seen through consistent pay upgrade or private/public-sector earnings comparisons)	☒	☑	☒	☑	☒	☑	☑	☒	☒	☑	☒

Term limits and/or fixed term periods for senior executive positions	☒*	☑	☒	☑	☑	N/A	N/A	☒	☒	☑	☑
Retirement/pension systems that allow mobility between public and private sector without cost	☒	☑	☒	☒	☑	☒	☒	☒	☑	☒	☑
Lateral entry/open-market hiring for recruitment	☒	☑	☑	☑	☑	☒	☑	☑	☒	☑	☑
SES (special programmes for laterally hired senior executives)	☒	☑	☒	☑	☒	☒	☑	☑	☑	☒	☑
Accountability mechanisms like monitoring of effort, performance-linked pay incentives, etc.	☒	☑	☑	☑	☑	☑	☒	☒	☑	☑	☑

Source: Compiled from country-specific studies

Note: *Except for home secretary and defence secretary

Table 4

Cross-country comparison: India, OECD and Southeast Asian countries

R	Yes	India is assessed as Yes if there is substantial reform for the specific characteristic
Q	No	India is assessed as No if there is no or only sporadic reform for the specific characteristic

4.1. Type A Reforms: Recruitment, pay and accountability-related

Country	*Does one become a civil servant through a competitive examination that provides for entry into a specific group of the public service?*	*Is seniority-based pay advancement (pay advancement according to years of experience) still in place?*	*If yes, have there been recent reforms where seniority-based pay increments have been reduced in overall compensation?*	*Is performance-related pay in use in the country's central government?*	*Is pay in government indexed to economic variables?*	*In the government, is there the equivalent of a general accountability framework which defines main managerial standards and targets for which managers are held accountable?*
India	☑	☑	☒	☒	☑	☒
Advanced economies						
Australia	Depends on the post	☒	N/A	☑	☒	☒
Belgium	☑	☑	☒	☒	☑	☑
Canada	☑	☒	N/A	☑	☒	☑
Denmark	☑	☑	☑	☑	☑	☒
Finland	☑	☒	N/A	☑	☒	☒
France	☑	☑	☒	☑	☑	☑
Germany	☑	☑	☑	☑	☒	☒
Israel	Depends on the post	☑	☒	☑	☒	☑

Italy	☑	☒	N/A	☑	☑	☑
Japan	☑	☒	N/A	☑	☒	☑
Korea	☑	☑	☑	☑	☒	☒
The Netherlands	☑	☑	☒	☑	☒	☑
New Zealand	Depends on the post	☑	☑	☑	☒	☒
Norway	☑	☑	☒	☑	☒	☒
Portugal	☑	☒	N/A	☑	☒	☑
Singapore	☑	☑	☑	☑	☒	☒
Spain	☑	☑	☒	☑	☒	☑
Sweden	☑	☒	N/A	☑	☒	☑
Switzerland	☑	☑	Q	☑	☑	☑
UK	Depends on the post	☑	☑	☑	☒	☑
USA	☑	☑	☒	☑	☑	☑
Emerging market economies						
Chile	☑	☑	☒	☑	☒	☑
Indonesia	☑	☑	☑	☑	☑	☑
Malaysia	☑	☑	☒	☑	☑	☑
Mexico	☑	☒	N/A	☒	☑	☒
The Philippines	☑	☑	R	☑	☒	☑
Thailand	☑	☒	N/A	☑	☒	☑
Türkiye	☑	☑	R	☒	☑	☑

Source: Department of Administrative Reforms and Public Grievances (DARPG), GoI; Department of Personnel and Training (DOPT), GoI; Organisation for Economic Co-operation and Development (OECD); World Bank, country-specific studies

4.2. Type A reforms: Mobility in civil services

Country	*Are there specific programmes to encourage mobility in the civil service?*	*If yes, are these programmes targeted to all civil servants?*	*Do these programmes enable mobility within the civil service (exchanges between ministries)?*	*Do these programmes enable civil servants' placements in the private/not-for-profit sector?*	*Do these programmes enable private/not-for-profit sector employee placements in the civil service?*
India	☑	☑	☑	☒	☒*
Advanced economies					
Australia	☑	☑	☑	☑	☒
Belgium	☑	☑	☑	☒	☒
Canada	☑	☒	☑	☑	☑
Denmark	☒	N/A			
Finland	☒	N/A			
France	☒	N/A			
Germany	☑	☑	☑	☒	☒
Israel	☑	☑	☑	☒	☒
Italy	☑	☑	☑	☒	☒
Japan	☒	N/A			
Korea	☑	☑	☑	☒	☒
The Netherlands	☑	☑	☑	☑	☑
New Zealand	☑	☒	☑	☒	☒
Norway	☒	N/A			
Portugal	☒	N/A			
Singapore	☑	☑	☑	☑	☑

Spain	☒	N/A			
Sweden	☒	N/A			
Switzerland	☒	N/A			
UK	☑	☒	☑	☑	☑
USA	☑	☑	☑	☒	☒
Emerging market economies					
Chile	☒	N/A			
Indonesia	☑	☒	☑	☒	☒
Malaysia	☑	☑	☑	☑	☒
Mexico	☑	☑	☑	☑	☑
The Philippines	☑	☒	☑	⑤	⑤
Thailand	☑	☒	☑	☒	☒
Türkiye	☒	N/A			

Source: DARPG; DOPT; OECD; World Bank, country-specific studies

Note: *Indian Civil Service provides for deputation to the posts under Central Staffing Scheme (CSS). Policy for lateral entry in bureaucracy introduced in July 2019 decided, in principle, to appoint outside experts to 10 positions of joint secretary in identified ministries/departments, out of approximately 391 joint secretary positions to GoI (7th Central Pay Commission [CPC] 2015). However, we consider it a sporadic reform of limited scope and therefore, India is marked No (Q) for the mobility reform characteristic (i.e., do these programmes enable private/not-for-profit sector employee placements in the civil service?).

4.3. Type B reforms: Identification of senior civil servants irrespective of existence of an official 'senior management'

Country	*Is there a specific mechanism to identify senior civil servants early on in their careers and then manage as a group throughout their careers?*	*Are senior civil servants identified through career progression within the public service only?*	*Are senior management positions open to external recruitment (outside of public service)?*	*Is there any programme to recruit and develop young candidates (civil servants/ graduates from universities/ external candidates) for senior management positions?*	*Is there a centrally defined skills profile for senior managers?*	*What is the average length of apex-level civil servants' tenure in a particular position?*
India	☒	☑	☒	☒	☒	1–2 yrs
Advanced economies						
Australia	☒	☒	☑	☒	☑	5.7 yrs
Belgium	☒	☒	☑	☒	☑	6 yrs
Canada	☑	☑	☒	☒	☑	2–3 yrs
Denmark	☒	☒	☒	☑	☑	NA
Finland	☒	☒	☑	☒	☑	Fixed term (5 yrs) with no limits on renewals
France	☑	☑	☒	☑	☑	3–4 yrs
Germany	☒	☑	☒	☒	☑	4–5 yrs
Israel	☒	☑	☑	☑	☑	6–8 yrs
Italy	☑	☑	☒	☑	☒	3–4 yrs
Japan	☒	☑	☒	☒	☑	2–3 yrs

Korea	☑	☒	☑	☑	☑	2–3 yrs
The Netherlands	☒	☒	☑	☑	☑	5–7 yrs
New Zealand	☒	☒	☑	☒	☑	8 yrs
Norway	☒	☑	☑	☒	☒	N/A
Portugal	☒	☒	☑	☒	☑	5 yrs with possible renewals
Singapore	☒	☑	☒	☑	☑	4–5 yrs
Spain	☒	☑	☒	☒	☒	3–4 yrs
Sweden	☒	☒	☑	☒	☒	6 yrs renewable for 3 more yrs
Switzerland	☒	☒	☑	☒	☑	N/A
UK	☒	☒	☑	☑	☑	2–3 yrs
USA	☒	☑	☑	☑	☑	4–5 yrs
Emerging market economies						
Chile	☒	☒	☑	☒	☑	2–3 yrs
Indonesia	☒	☒	☑	☒	☑	4–5 yrs
Malaysia	☑	☑	☒	☑	☑	3–4 yrs
Mexico	☒	☒	☑	☒	☒	<2 yrs
The Philippines	☒	☑	☑	☑	☑	>5 yrs
Thailand	☒	☑	☒	☒	☑	3–4 yrs
Türkiye	☒	☒	☑	☑	☑	2–3 yrs

Source: DARPG; DOPT; OECD; World Bank, country-specific studies

4.4. Type B reforms: Performance-management systems for senior bureaucrats

Country	*Is there a well-established performance-management regime?*	*Are they subject to fixed-term appointments?*	*Does the performance-management regime for senior managers include any of the following features?*			
			Is there a formal performance agreement with the minister?	*Is there a formal performance agreement with administrative head of civil service?*	*Is performance assessed on outcomes?*	*Dismissal for bad performance*
India	☒*	N/A	☑	☒	☑	☑***
Advanced economies						
Australia	☑	☑	☒	☑	☑	☑
Belgium	☑	☑	☑	☒	☑	☑
Canada	☑	☒	☒	☒	☑	☑
Denmark	☑	☑	☒	☑	☒	☒
Finland	☑	☑	☒	☒	☑	☑
France	☑	☑	☑	☒	☑	☒
Germany	☑	☒	☒	☒	☑	☑
Israel	☑	☑	☒	☒	☑	☑
Italy	☑	☑	☑	☒	☒	☑
Japan	☑	☑	☒	☒	☒	☒
Korea	☑	☑	☑	☒	☑	☑
The Netherlands	☒	☑	☑	☑	☒	☒
New Zealand	☑	☑	☒	☑	☒	☒
Norway	☑	☑	☑	☑	☒	☒

Portugal	☑	☑	☑	☒	☑	☑
Singapore	☑	☒	☒	☒	☒	☑
Spain	☑	☒	☑	☒	☒	☑
Sweden	☑	☑	☑	☒	☒	☒
Switzerland	☒	☒	☑	☒	☒	☒
UK	☑	☑	☒	☑	☑	☑
USA	☑	☑	☒	☑	☑	☑
Emerging market economies						
Chile	☑	☑	☒	☒	☒	☑
Indonesia	☑	☑	☒	☒	☑	☑
Malaysia	☑	☒	☒	☒	☑	☒
Mexico	☒	☑	☒	☒	☑	☑
The Philippines	☑	☒	☒	☒	☒	☑
Thailand	☑	☑	☒	☒	☑	☒
Türkiye	☒	☑	☒	☒	☒	☒
Vietnam	☑	☒	☒	☒	☒	☒

Source: DARPG; DOPT; OECD; World Bank, country-specific studies

Note: *The government's Result Framework Document (RFD) is a system for monitoring and evaluating the performance of government departments and ministries introduced in 2009–10. However, since there is no specific and separate evaluation procedure for senior civil servants, India is marked no (Q). **In April 2015, the central government introduced the 360-degree appraisal procedure for the empanelment of civil servants for central government posts. However, we assess it as a reform that has not yet been implemented completely, and therefore, India is marked no (Q). ***Periodic review of central government employees for strengthening of administration under Fundamental Rule (FR) (560)1(l) and Rule 48 of CCS (Pension) Rules, 1972, August 2020.

4.5. Type C reforms: Training and capacity building

	Planning learning and training			*Are the following one of the most important current priorities in the area of training and competence development of civil servants?*			
Country	*Is there a civil service-wide training strategy and/or action plan*	*Does each organization within the central public administration produce an organizational learning plan?*	*Are civil servants required to develop individual learning plans?*	*Online course development (e-learning, m-learning, blended learning)*	*Executive leadership training and coaching*	*IT/digital skills training*	*Coaching and mentoring*
India	☑	☒	☒	☑	☒	☑	☒
Advanced economies							
Australia	☑	☑	☑	☒	☑	☑	☒
Belgium	☑	☒	☑	☑	☑	☒	☑
Canada	☑	☒	☑	☑	☑	☒	☒
Denmark	☒	☒	☑	☑	☑	☑	☒
Finland	☒	☑	☑	☑	☑	☑	☒
France	☑	☑	☒	☑	☑	☑	☑
Germany	☒	☑	☒	☒	☑	☑	☑
Israel	☑	☑	☒	☑	☑	☒	☒
Italy	☑	☒	☒	☑	☒	☑	☒

Japan	☑	☑	☒	☒	☒	☒	☑
Korea	☑	☑	☑	☑	☑	☑	☑
The Netherlands	☒	☒	☒	☑	☒	☑	☒
New Zealand	☒	☑	☑	☒	☑	☒	☒
Norway	☒	☒	☑	☑	☒	☑	☒
Portugal	☑	☑	☑	☒	☑	☑	☒
Spain	☑	☑	☒	☑	☑	☑	☒
Sweden	☒	☑	☑	☑	☑	☑	☒
Switzerland	☑	☒	☒	☑	☑	☑	☒
UK	☑	☑	☑	☒	☑	☒	☒
USA	☒	☑	☒	☒	☑	☒	☑
Emerging economies							
Chile	☒	☑	☒	☑	☑	☒	☒
Mexico	☑	☒	☒	☑	☑	☒	☒
Türkiye	☒	☑	☒	☑	☑	☑	☑

Source: DARPG; DOPT; OECD; World Bank, country-specific studies

Specialized Expertise: A Sine Qua Non

The IAS is situated at the nerve centre of the bureaucracy. Therefore, the lion's share of the discussion on reforming the Indian bureaucracy must focus on the IAS, which is inherently an institution that promotes general rather than specialized skills. An IAS officer can be expected to work in ministries as disparate as finance, commerce, home, health, defence, agriculture, law, sports, culture or minority affairs. The expertise required in the Ministry of Defence (MoD) is so different from that required in the Ministry of Health and Family Welfare (MoHFW).

For instance, bureaucrats working in the Ministry of Finance must inter alia possess expertise in one or more areas of economics such as macroeconomic policy, fiscal policy, monetary policy, financial and capital markets, centre–state financial relations, trade and foreign investment policy, privatization, and disinvestment policy. Each of these areas requires highly specialized skills encompassing several sub-areas of research in economics. Similarly, bureaucrats working in the ministry of commerce or ministry of defence require specialized skills.

The specialists in international trade that man the (equivalent of) ministries of commerce in advanced economies bring their specialized expertise to the negotiating table when India is negotiating free trade agreements (FTAs) with these nations. India, on the other hand, gets represented mostly by generalists from the bureaucracy. This battle at the negotiating table of FTAs is like Bill Gates facing up to the world chess champion, Magnus Carlsen, in a game of chess in 2014. Gates, while a highly intelligent and accomplished individual, is a generalist in the game of chess, while the world chess champion is clearly a specialist. No wonder, Carlsen made mincemeat of Gates by checkmating him in just 80 seconds!

Yet, this phenomenon of Gates expecting Carlsen to adhere to policies related to chess created and implemented by Gates is common in India. The armed forces for whom bureaucrats in the MoD enact policies or the doctors who must comply with the policies made by bureaucrats in the MoHWF spend a lifetime acquiring expertise in their area of specialization. Can the bureaucrat possess more expertise in defence than a brigadier or a colonel when he works in the MoD and simultaneously possess more expertise than the doctors at the All India Institute of Medical Sciences (AIIMS) when he works in the MoHFW? No! Of course not. Because the pool of extremely talented individuals that join the IAS is similar to those that occupy the top echelons of the armed forces or the medical community. Similarly, the chairpersons of the public-sector banks, who have spent a lifetime learning and doing banking, must listen to the diktats from the secretary in the department of financial services who is unlikely to have a fraction of their expertise.

Given the fact that the IAS officer can expect to be frequently rotated across several disparate departments requiring very different skills and expertise, it is rational for the IAS officer to not see much value in specializing in any particular area. Thus, the incentives for specialization are minimal within the IAS. In addition, the internal culture within the bureaucracy is not friendly to the acquisition of specialized skills. Youngsters within the service who decide to go on leave to acquire professional degrees in various areas of specialization do not necessarily get posted in the ministries that utilize their specialized expertise. Moreover, it is not unheard of for youngsters who have pursued professional degrees to be told by their superiors upon return that they should not harbour any illusion that they can perform tasks that their counterparts who did not acquire such specialized knowledge cannot perform.

This emphasis on general skills in the bureaucracy made sense when the economy was relatively small and the task of policymaking and policy administration was simple. But today, when India is the fifth largest economy poised for unprecedented growth, the stakes from policymaking are incredibly high; both the benefits from good policies following from specialized expertise and costs stemming from the absence of the same have multiplied when compared to the time when the Indian bureaucracy was conceptualized as a general service.

Specialization in the bureaucracy, therefore, is a sine qua non if India must realistically aspire to be a global economic titan.

Outliers Are Misleading as Averages Characterize a System

The media, common folks, and bureaucrats themselves often provide anecdotal examples to claim that specialization is neither necessary nor sufficient. Examples of outstanding bureaucrats who have served in a role with great distinction are used to compare with specialists who have occupied the same role. It is important to be careful when using such anecdotal examples to build arguments for or against specialization. As there is always wide variation in the quality of generalists as also in the quality of specialists, comparisons between a system comprising specialists with one comprising generalists must be undertaken by comparing their averages, not selected outliers.

Risk Aversion and Indecision

While the lack of specialization in the bureaucracy can contribute to risk aversion, the carrots and sticks in the bureaucratic system—or their absence—foster significant risk aversion. Risk aversion can stem from rational self-preservation that any individual would indulge in because he/she remains vulnerable to significant personal losses. The behavioural economics framework provided by Kahneman and Tversky (1979) explains that risk-aversion stems from the extremely high personal costs that bureaucrats have to bear for even well-intentioned decisions that may *ex-post* go wrong only because of the inherent uncertainty that impacts outcomes (Box 1).

Box 1: Behavioural Economics Explains Bureaucratic Risk Aversion

Imagine a bureaucrat who is designing a new contract for employees in a public-sector factory. The introduction of the contract, the bureaucrat's economic advisors say, could result in two equally likely scenarios: in the first scenario, workers respond to incentives in the contract, and production increases by 20 per cent; in the second, the workers protest, causing unrest, and production decreases by 2 per cent. Since both events occur with the same probability, it would seem logical for the bureaucrat to propose the contract to the workers. However, most bureaucrats would choose not to do so, preferring to be risk-averse in the face of even mild downsides to their actions. What does this tell us about the bureaucrat's decision-making process?

The following plots a 'value function', i.e., a curve that plots the value to the bureaucrat (y axis) of a gain or loss in production (x axis) due to the introduction of the contract. For the same loss or gain x, the value of the gains is smaller than the value of the losses. As the curve becomes steeper in losses, the bureaucrat grows more and more unwilling to endure even the smallest of losses.

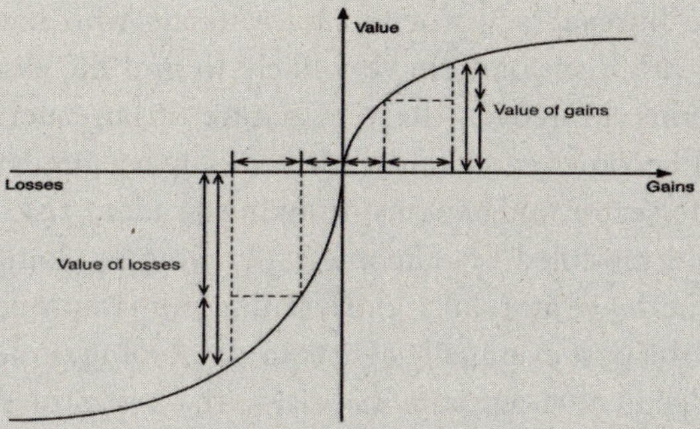

Figure 1: Prospect theory—loss aversion

Behavioural economics, especially 'prospect theory', which explains why individuals display loss aversion, provides important clues. In classical expected utility theory, expected utility equals 0.5×0.2 − 0.5×0.02 = 0.09. This positive utility suggests that the bureaucrat would propose this contract. However, under prospect theory, individuals display loss aversion, i.e., the aggravation one experiences with a loss is greater than the pleasure experienced by a gain. In particular, the 'value function' is an S-shaped curve as shown in Figure 1. Formally, the 'value function' is concave in gains and convex in losses. Thus, a bureaucrat prefers to avoid a loss of x per cent in production than increase the production by the very same x per cent.

We can now understand the causes for bureaucratic risk aversion: as the curve becomes flatter in gains and steeper in losses, the bureaucrat becomes more sensitive to the tiniest of losses.

The Curse of the Four Cs

Bureaucrats often cite the fear of the four Cs—the three investigating agencies Central Bureau of Investigation (CBI), the Central Vigilance Commission (CVC), the Comptroller and Auditor General (CAG), and the Courts—in fostering paralysis in decision making. The fear of the four Cs leads to a fundamental and deep irony. Skills in decision-making are probably the most critical in the bureaucracy, yet, those brave bureaucrats who take the most far-reaching decisions are more likely to find themselves targeted by the four Cs than those who refuse to take any important decision. As a result, a perverse belief pervades the bureaucracy wherein bureaucrats who have not 'soiled their hands with decisions' are very likely to find the easiest path into senior positions. Moreover, the very nature of bureaucratic decision-making then becomes mechanistic, driven only by stipulated processes. In the private sector, judgements in taking prudent risks are acquired over time and modified by outcomes. 'Learning by doing' is a part of gathering experience and skills, and learning from improper judgements exercised in the past eventually assists in developing professionals with excellent judgement about potential risks. The best professionals in the private sector use discretion innovatively and thereby often deviate from established procedures. In the private sector, deviation from procedure does not imply culpability. In contrast, in the bureaucracy, when the outcome of a decision turns out *ex-post* to be unfavourable, culpability is often presumed if there are deviations in procedure. Furthermore, there is no assurance on when a case, once initiated, would be closed if the enforcement authority were to conclude that the officer is not culpable. Cases drag on for years, with permanent damage to careers exacerbating the uncertainty and anxiety about whether and when an officer would face criminal action in courts. Where cases against an officer commence just before he/she retires, it becomes part of the officer's retirement traumatic reality. The most damaging aspect of this phenomenon is that the genuinely corrupt get away because they have invested their decades of experience in the bureaucracy to learn how to cover their tracks and thereby escape getting caught. In contrast, the honest and sincere bureaucrats who take difficult decisions in the interest of the nation get caught and become 'collateral damage' because they have invested their decades of experience in how to make better decisions, not caring as much as the corrupt about covering their tracks.

No Tolerance for Failure of Government Officials

Policymaking by our bureaucrats and public-sector officials involves a lot of peril. Yet, these are rarely even acknowledged, let alone celebrated. Would we be celebrating the Chandrayaan-3 success if the culture at ISRO abhorred risk-taking and instead encouraged sitting on the fence? Of course not! In an uncertain world, policymaking can throw up adverse outcomes even when policy is conceptualized and implemented with the best judgement and thought. If you have to spend your post-retirement life running from pillar to post because a decision you took in your best judgement went kaput, will you take the risk? Many will not; only a few exceptional ones will! And yet, one of the cardinal principles in economics is that decent returns cannot be generated without assuming well-managed risk; zero risk cannot deliver decent returns. Yet, because failure from policymaking is unceremoniously orphaned, our government and public-sector officials suffer huge personal losses if the risks they take end up delivering unfavourable outcomes *ex-post*. To create a system where failure in policymaking is not orphaned, the system of investigation and prosecution needs to recognize hindsight bias. Officials must make decisions with the information available at that time. Over time, of course more information becomes available. However, such information was not available to the official while making the decision. Investigating as if the official must have foreseen that information creates huge hindsight bias and scares off risk-taking.

Recommendations for Reform

Advanced countries and China have implemented significant reforms in their bureaucracy by implementing ideas from agency theory, public choice, knowledge management, innovation, human resource management and organizational behaviour. These reforms have helped these countries align their bureaucracy with the goals of political leaders by rewarding expertise and leadership in their bureaucracy. Such reforms have helped these countries overcome problems that are common across all bureaucracies—be it in advanced economies or in emerging ones. Thus, such reforms have helped to transform their public servants into active agents of positive change.

To become a global economic powerhouse, India must transform its bureaucrats into motivated agents of change. For this purpose, India needs to implement some key reforms in its bureaucracy.

Open Competition for Senior Positions

As argued earlier, specialization in the bureaucracy is not just desirable but a sine qua non.

Table 3 shows that except for Germany, all the advanced economies allow for open competition for senior positions in the bureaucracy. This ensures that appointments to such critical positions of policymaking and implementation are based strictly on performance appraisal, qualifications and domain experience as opposed to seniority.

In India too, both the first Administrative Reforms Commission (ARC), constituted in 1966, and the second ARC, constituted in 2005, recommended greater competition for senior positions in the bureaucracy even though there were some differences in their specific recommendations. The second ARC made the case for greater competition for positions at the joint secretary level and above, in both central and state governments. It also recommended opening additional secretary positions to qualified individuals from the private sector.

Competitive pressure is as much essential to promoting excellence in the top bureaucracy as elsewhere. Without competition from specialists, the incentives for the bureaucracy to alter its approach will never surface. As incentives for specialization are severely lacking in the current system, the most critical reform of the bureaucracy is to enable specialization via open competition for all senior positions. The usual, risk-averse approach of slowly building a specialized bureaucracy through many incremental steps will take too long. By that time, the horse representing India becoming a global economic powerhouse would already have bolted. So, incrementalism in this most critical change—creating a specialized bureaucracy—will not work.

The discontinuous reform that India needs is the conversion of all posts of joint secretary and above positions at the centre and states into fixed five-year-term positions with salaries and contractual obligations resembling the private sector. As Table 3 shows, in several advanced economies, including Australia, the US, New Zealand, Canada and Italy, senior positions in the bureaucracy are all for a fixed term. In the Indian case, these term positions for all posts of joint secretary and above would coincide with the term of the ministerial cabinet in the centre and the states.

The senior positions must be opened to both insiders and outsiders based on a set of pre-specified criteria. This change is necessary to attract talented outsiders in the academic, business and financial fields to compete with the best bureaucrats for the top policymaking positions in the government. This will make it necessary for the most talented officers within the bureaucracy to compete for these top posts with the best and the brightest in the country. As IAS officers are indeed extremely bright and motivated individuals, in just a few years, their incentives for specialization would alter dramatically.

Such reform cannot be piecemeal where a few posts are subject to this change. In March 2019, such a piecemeal approach was tried with nine joint secretaries being recruited from the private sector. As outsiders are not familiar with the internal workings of the bureaucracy and have not had the opportunity to build networks that are so essential for effective functioning, it is relatively easy for the bureaucratic system to isolate such outsiders and ensure that such experiments fail. These failures can then be pointed out as examples to deter further attempts at reform.

Reform Pension Plan to Enable Mobility to and from the Private Sector

If open competition, as advocated above, must become a reality, it cannot and should not be implemented without giving bureaucrats the opportunity to go work in the private sector or the not-for-profit sector and then come back into the government. As a professional who worked in the private sector and has also worked in the government, I realize that both the private sector and the bureaucracy can benefit from commingling with each other where bureaucrats get to work on deputation in private sector firms and professionals from the private sector get to work in government. This can enable a healthy appreciation of each other's relative strengths and motivations. For instance, in government, the stereotypical caricature of the private sector can sometimes be of mercenaries who only care about money. This is despite the fact that a bulk of people working in the private sector derive a lot of meaning in what they do and hardly care about money more than it being a means to afford some comforts. Similarly, people in the private sector caricature bureaucrats as indolent and incompetent, when the reality is that many bureaucrats are incredibly driven by the spirit of service to the nation and are extremely capable as well. Commingling of bureaucrats with the private sector—not just in periodic meetings but as colleagues—can help break down such mounds of misperception. Moreover, if folks from the private sector can get to experience the joy of contributing to the nation by holding senior bureaucratic positions, it is only fair that bureaucrats also get to legally and legitimately experience the freedom of choice and joys of receiving handsome compensation by working in the private sector.

A key stumbling block to such mobility is the pension system for bureaucrats. Government officials in India become eligible for pensions only after completing 20 years of service. The government then pays a portion of their last salary as a pension for life, along with a lump-sum gratuity. Officials also contribute 6 per cent of their salary to a mandatory general provident fund (GPF); the amount in the GPF can be used for emergencies leading up to retirement.

However, a major problem with this system is its inflexibility. It hinders the movement of talented professionals between the public and private sectors. For example, bureaucrats who want to work in the private sector must wait 20 years before taking voluntary retirement. Moreover, they cannot return to public service if they resign earlier, and leaving before 20 years means losing significant pecuniary benefits. India needs to change the pension system for bureaucrats. Similar to how individuals can easily transfer their pension plans when transitioning between private sector companies, government officials must also be able to transfer their retirement plans to the private sector and vice versa when moving to and from the private sector.

Tables 3 and 4 show that most advanced economies and several EMEs provide the necessary flexibility in their retirement/pension systems to enable mobility of their bureaucrats. India needs to do the same.

Pay for Senior Positions Comparable to the Private Sector

In addition to enabling mobility of bureaucrats to and from the private sector, compensation for positions of joint secretary and above needs to be comparable to similar senior management positions in the private sector. As shown in Table 4, all advanced economies except Belgium and five out of seven EMEs have already implemented this aspect in the bureaucracy. India needs to follow suit: while bureaucrats are not motivated only by money, they do also expect fair recognition and support for the work they do. Pay parity with the private sector should apply *only* to positions of joint secretary and above. It is important to avoid across-the-board salary hikes, i.e., for positions below that of joint secretary.

Performance Contracts

Tables 3 and 4 show that most advanced economies and several EMEs have implemented accountability mechanisms like monitoring of effort, performance-linked pay incentives, etc., within their bureaucracies. These typically included clear flagging of periodic goals and commitments, building high frequency administrative data, live evaluation of performance vis-à-vis goals, higher delegation and autonomy in exchange for tracking of performance indicators, a focus on objective performance appraisal and merit for postings and promotions.

Separate Policy Formulation and Policy Implementation

Apart from the above reforms, the bureaucracy needs to be separated into (i) the small core of civil servants involved in policymaking and ministerial support; and (ii) the vast majority of civil servants who are involved in service delivery or executive functions of state and central governments. The ultimate goal is that within a few years, most of the latter group will be transferred to semi-autonomous executive agencies, headed by chief executives who have set performance targets and are given certain financial and managerial freedoms. This will result in a reduced core of policymakers and a large number of independent agencies carrying out the rest of the work of implementation of policy.

In the US, strategic and operational objectives and targets for an agency can be directly cascaded down to a senior civil servant. Thus, for a head of department in the Office of Personnel Management (OPM), targets outlined in the OPM strategic plan are reiterated. The strategic plan translates the mission (outcome objective) of OPM into various concrete outputs and targets, for which a senior civil servant is then made responsible.

'Qualified Immunity' to Reduce Risk Aversion

A cardinal principle of natural justice is that even if a thousand guilty go unpunished, even one innocent should not get unjustly punished. To action this cardinal principle for government officials, many advanced economies have enacted the concept of qualified immunity. This concept is commonly applied for civil lawsuits brought against government officials. For qualified immunity to apply, the government official must show that their actions were reasonable considering the legal rules that were clearly established at the time of the conduct. Crucially, if the official's actions were objectively reasonable, even if mistaken, they may be shielded from personal liability.

The concept of qualified immunity balances two competing but important interests—'the need to hold public officials accountable when they exercise power irresponsibly and the need to shield officials from harassment, distraction, and liability when they perform their duties reasonably.'[41] The immunity's broad protection is intended for 'all but the plainly incompetent or those who knowingly violate the law' and to give government officials 'breathing room' to make reasonable mistakes of fact and law.[42] Qualified immunity, when applied, provides immunity not only from civil damages but also from having to defend against litigation altogether. Jurisprudence has set forth a two-part analysis when determining whether an official is entitled to qualified immunity:

i. whether the facts alleged by the plaintiff amount to a constitutional violation;
ii. if so, whether the constitutional right was 'clearly established' at the time of the misconduct; and
iii. whether the conduct was 'objectively reasonable' considering clearly established law.

All these conditions must be met for a lawsuit against a government official to proceed. Conversely, if either condition is absent, then the official is immune from lawsuit.

In criminal cases, the standard of proof required for a conviction must be even stronger in the form of demonstrated self-benefit, monetary or in any other form. If there is no demonstrable evidence of self-benefit, first information reports (FIRs) and charge sheets should not be allowed to be filed. The present process adopted is to scrutinize all cases where the *ex-post* outcome was undesirable and to identify procedural lapses as the basis for action without necessarily obtaining evidence of self-benefit.

---

[41]'Policing the Police: Qualified Immunity and Considerations for Congress', *Congressional Research Service*, 10 June 2020, http://tinyurl.com/5aydzfxp. Accessed on 18 January 2024.

[42]Ibid.

Thus, the present process of subjecting every major decision to scrutiny based on fidelity to procedure creates tremendous risk aversion among bureaucrats. The intention is not to understate the problem of corruption in bureaucracy—which is a major public policy concern—but instead to suggest that the instruments for identifying and tackling it need to differ, because the burden of evidence needs to be more demanding. If the enforcement agencies are unable to demonstrate self-benefit, but nevertheless bring accusations of corruption against government officials, it is the enforcement process that requires an upgrade and would need to subject itself to a higher standard of professional scrutiny.

◆

Along with the reform of the judiciary to deliver timely justice to our citizens, reforming the bureaucracy represent the two most important reforms that India must undertake to realize its ambitions of becoming a global economic powerhouse.

10

EFFICIENCY REDEFINED

Paradigm Shifts in Bureaucratic Processes

Do you remember the Indian television sitcom *Office Office*, where the protagonist Mussadi Lal is shown running from pillar to post to obtain permission for routine, daily activities? The show represents a comic take on how a common person gets mired in the web of endless bureaucratic formalities and delays to undertake even routine activities. Our bureaucracy does a phenomenal job in delivering mission-critical endeavours such as the national elections or the Kumbh Mela or responding to crises. However, it is the routine, daily tasks where significant improvement is needed, as Mussadi Lal finds out often.

Notwithstanding the significant improvements in EoDB, India continues to trail in parameters such as ease of starting business, registering property, paying taxes and enforcing contracts. International comparisons show that the problems of India's administrative processes stem more from over-regulation rather than lack of compliance with processes or regulatory standards. The problem of over-regulation and opacity in Indian administrative processes flows from the emphasis on having complete regulations that account for every possible outcome. This is due to the inadequate appreciation of the difference between 'regulation' and 'supervision' on the one hand, and the inevitability of incomplete regulations on the other. Real-world regulation is inevitably incomplete because of the combination of:

i. bounded rationality due to 'unknown unknowns',
ii. complexity involved in framing 'complete' contracts across all possible contingencies, and
iii. the difficulty for a third party to verify decisions.

This makes some discretion unavoidable in decision-making. Evidence shows that over-regulation, not simpler regulation, leads to opaque decision-making. The problem is that policymakers, by default, tend to favour prescriptive regulation over supervision. Unlike supervision, regulation can be easily measured. After all, regulations provide criteria or checklists, making it easier for regulators to follow and reduce their accountability later on. In contrast, it is difficult to quantify the amount and quality of supervision.

The optimal solution is to have simple regulations combined with a transparent decision-making process. Having provided the government decision-maker with discretion, it is important then to balance it with three things: improved transparency, stronger systems of *ex-ante* accountability and *ex-post* resolution mechanisms. Moreover, a holistic assessment and a sustained effort to ease business regulations require a nuts-and-bolts approach of feedback loops, monitoring and continuous adjustment.

Global Comparisons in EoDB

Setting up a business in India takes an average of 18 days today, down from 30 days in 2009. On the other hand, New Zealand has a seamless process of business incorporation, which takes place through a single window with one agency. It takes just half a day with a single form and minimal cost to set up a business in that country. Although India has significantly reduced the time and cost of starting a business, a lot more needs to be done. To register one's property in India, it takes nine procedures, at least 49 days, and 7.4–8.1 per cent of the property value. Meanwhile, New Zealand has only two procedures and a minimal cost of 0.1 per cent of the property value. In the case of 'paying taxes' parameter, though the number of payments per year has significantly reduced in India from 59 to 12 over the last decade, time spent on this activity has not reduced much. While India takes 250–254 hours per year to pay taxes, New Zealand spends just 140 hours a year. 'Enforcing contracts' is one parameter in which India's performance has been very poor over the years. While India takes 1,445 days to resolve an average dispute, New Zealand takes approximately one-seventh of it, i.e., 216 days.

When compared to the performance of India's peer nations, namely, China, Brazil and Indonesia, on the same parameters, it can be seen that China fares much better than India on virtually all parameters (Table 1). The comparisons with the others are not so one-sided. While an entrepreneur has to go through 10 procedures to set up a business in both India and Brazil, on an average, India takes four days less to do so. Indonesia requires one extra process to open a business, although it takes four days less there than in India to do so. In fact, countries like Pakistan, Türkiye and Sri Lanka (ranked 72, 77 and 85, respectively, in the 'starting a business' parameter) have a less cumbersome process to start a business than India. Similarly, while both Brazil and India have nine procedures to register one's property, it takes less time to do so in Brazil (40.5 days) than in India (49–68 days). Indonesia, on the other hand, has only six procedures and takes a month's time to register property. In case of 'paying taxes', although Indonesia (26) has more than double the number of payments per year than India (10–12), its citizens spend far less time in paying them than in India. Brazil seems to fare particularly poor in this segment.

India's performance in contract enforcement is poor even when compared to her peer nations. While it takes approximately four years to enforce a contract in India, Brazil and Indonesia spend 2.5 and 1.1 years, respectively, to do so. With a rank of 163 out of 190 nations in the 'enforcing contracts' segment, only a few countries like Afghanistan, Mozambique and Zimbabwe perform worse than India.

Table 1
India vs peers on EoDB

	India	*China*	*Brazil*	*Indonesia*
Starting a business				
Number of procedures	10	4	10	11
Time (number of days)	17/18	9	21.5	13
Cost (% of income per capita)	5.3/9.3	1.4	5.1	5.7
Registering your property				
Number of procedures	9	4	9	6
Time (number of days)	49/68	9	40.5	31
Cost (% of property value)	8.1/7.4	4.6	3.6	8.3
Paying taxes				
Number of payments	10/12	7	9	26
Time (hours per year)	250/254	138	1,501	191
Total tax payable (% of gross profits)	49.7	62.6	65.7	30.1

	India	*China*	*Brazil*	*Indonesia*
Enforcing contracts				
Time (number of days)	1,445	485	911	403
Cost (% of debt)	31	15.1	24	70.3
Overall doing business rank	**63**	**31**	**124**	**73**

Source: Doing Business Report, 2020, cited in *Economic Survey 2019–20*

Compliance Requirements in Manufacturing

A major challenge most companies face is the complex architecture of the Indian governance framework, including the density of legislation and statutory compliance requirements. Manufacturing units have to conform with 6,796 compliance items, which is a tedious and time-consuming task. It must be noted that this is not a comprehensive list and not every rule applies to every manufacturer. It is just an illustration of the bewilderingly wide range of rules that the sector faces.

Regulatory Hurdles in Opening a Restaurant

The service sector too faces many regulatory hurdles even for routine businesses. The bars and restaurants sector is an important source of employment and growth everywhere in the world. It is also a business that, by its nature, faces a high frequency of starting new businesses and shutting old ones. The *Economic Survey 2019–20* showed that the number of licenses required to open a restaurant in India are significantly more than elsewhere. While China and Singapore require only four licenses, India requires several more mandatory licenses and approvals (see Table 2). According to the National Restaurant Association of India (NRAI), a total of 36 approvals are required to open a restaurant in Bengaluru, while Delhi requires 26 and Mumbai 22. Moreover, Delhi and Kolkata also require an 'eating house' license provided by the police. The number of documents needed to obtain this license from the Delhi Police is 45—far more than the number of documents required for a license to procure new arms and major fireworks—19 and 12, respectively.[43]

[43]Ibid. 134–5.

Moreover, in India, the list of licenses and permissions can only be obtained from a government portal or information centre. On the other hand, in New Zealand, the website of Auckland Council, which is operated by a private third-party agency, has all detailed guides and stepwise procedures about permissions, fees and timelines to open a restaurant. The website is also equipped with ready-to-use business plan templates and comprehensive information on different businesses irrespective of the scale of business. The contrast reflects a difference in approach—government control versus curation/partnership.

Table 2
Licenses required to open a restaurant

Country	*Market Size (US$ billion)*	*No. of Licenses*
India	61	12–17
Singapore	8.3	4
China	815	4

Source: Economic Survey 2019–20

Construction Permits

With respect to permits required for construction, it takes almost four months to get all the permits in Delhi. In comparison, in Hong Kong, which tops the World Bank rankings for ease of obtaining construction permits, it takes just over two months to obtain a construction permit. Moreover, it takes 35 days to get water and sewer connection in Delhi.

Trading across Borders

The 'trading across borders' indicator records the time and cost associated with the logistical process of exporting and importing goods. Globally, transportation by ports is most favoured, followed by railways and then roads; whereas in India, it is the opposite. Italy tops the EoDB rankings in trading across borders. While border and documentary compliance for exports and imports takes 60 and 88 hours, respectively, in India, these procedures take only one hour each in Italy. Moreover, the cost of compliance is zero in Italy. In India, it costs $260 and $360 for exports and imports, respectively. Almost 70 per cent of the delays (both in exports and imports) occur on account of port or border handling processes, which essentially pertain to procedural complexities (number and multiplicity of procedures required for trade), multiple documentations, and involvement of multiple agencies for approvals and clearances. Time delays and procedural inefficiencies end up increasing the cost of trade. While the government has already reduced procedural and documentation requirements considerably, increasing digitalization and seamlessly integrating multiple agencies onto a single digital platform can further reduce these procedural inefficiencies significantly and improve user experience substantially.

The Problem of Regulatory Effectiveness

It is often believed that India's regulatory problems are due to the lack of regulatory standards and poor compliance with processes. International comparisons, however, show that India ranks better than its peers on having regulatory standards in place and compliance with processes. The real issue seems to be effectiveness of regulations impacted by undue delays, rent seeking, complex regulations and quality of regulation.

The *WJP Rule of Law Index* published by the World Justice Project provides cross-country comparison on various aspects of regulatory enforcement.[44] In 2023, India's rank was 54 out of 142 countries in the category of 'due process is respected in administrative proceedings' (proxy for following due process). In contrast, in the category 'government regulations are effectively enforced' (proxy for regulatory quality/effectiveness), the country's rank is 120 (Table 1). India stands at ninetieth rank in 'administrative proceedings are conducted without unreasonable delay' (proxy for timeliness) and 123rd in 'government regulations are applied and enforced without improper influence' (proxy for rent seeking).

This shows that, contrary to popular belief, India is relatively good at complying with processes, but lags in regulatory effectiveness.

[44]'Regulatory Enforcement', *WJP Rule of Law Index*, World Justice Project, https://tinyurl.com/tz2wnkpd. Accessed on 27 November 2023.

Table 3

India's rank in various categories of regulatory enforcement

	2023
Regulatory enforcement overall rank	83
Government regulations are effectively enforced	120
Government regulations are applied and enforced without improper influence	123
Administrative proceedings are conducted without unreasonable delay	90
Due process is respected in administrative proceedings	54
Number of countries	142

Source: Economic Survey 2020–21

The index shows that the UK, US, Singapore and Canada are placed much better than India in case of both, following due process and regulatory effectiveness. However, the gap between India and these countries is much wider in regulatory effectiveness than in due processes being followed. Similarly, India is placed better than other BRICS countries (barring South Africa) in terms of respecting due process, but fares worse than them in the effectiveness of those standards (Table 4).

Table 4

Comparison of regulatory standards and regulatory enforcement in 2023

Rank	*US*	*UK*	*Singapore*	*Canada*	*Brazil*	*Russia*	*China*	*South Africa*	*India*
Regulatory enforcement	22	18	5	12	76	92	74	60	83
Government regulations are effectively enforced	26	16	5	12	70	57	62	107	120

Government regulations are applied and enforced without improper influence	21	8	9	5	67	92	73	80	123
Administrative proceedings are conducted without unreasonable delay	30	17	1	21	139	34	27	61	90
Due process is respected in administrative proceedings	20	11	7	3	73	113	107	41	54

Source: Economic Survey 2020–21

The same conclusion can be derived from various World Bank studies. Its regulatory quality index shows that despite improvements in India's regulatory quality since 2013 (Figure 1), it is still much lower than UK, US, Singapore, Japan, etc. (Figure 2). Similarly, the World Bank's EoDB report (2020) shows that despite making huge strides in the overall EoDB rank, India still lags behind in the sub-categories 'starting a business' and 'registering property', where the country's ranks are 136 and 154, respectively. The report points out that this is due to the high number of procedures required to legally start and formally operate a company as well as the time and cost consumed to complete each procedure.

As the *Economic Survey 2020–21* showed, the time taken from the point of decision of closure to the company actually getting struck off from the Registrar of Companies (ROC) is 1,570 days (i.e., 4.3 years), even if all paperwork is in place and the company is not involved in any litigation or dispute. This is the best possible case of a routine activity. Interestingly, out of the total time taken, about 1,035 days are taken for clearances by the income tax (IT), provident fund (PF) and goods and services tax (GST) departments, and in taking back security refunds from various departments. In contrast, voluntary liquidation takes about 12 months in Singapore, 12–24 months in Germany, and 15 months in the UK. In Germany, for very large and active companies, it takes two to four years. Given the likelihood of disputes and litigation, for the comparable large cases it may take up to a decade in India.

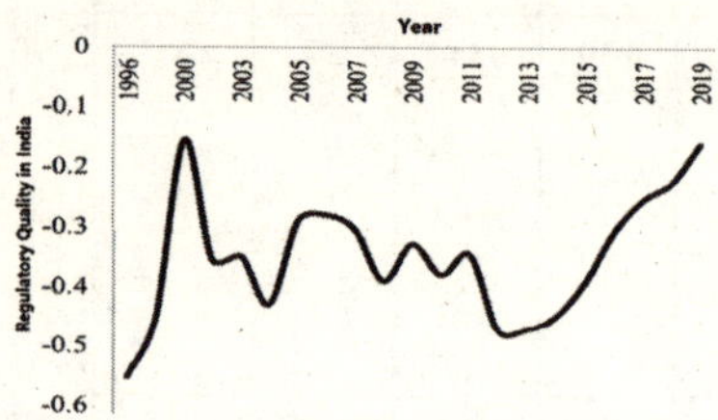

Figure 1: Regulatory quality in India

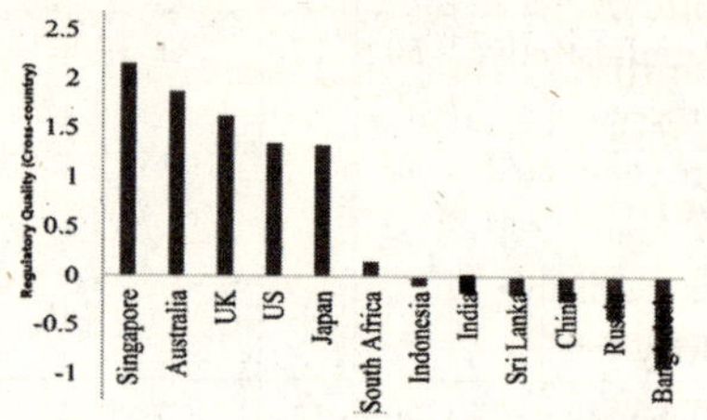

Figure 2: Cross-country comparison of regulatory quality (as of 2019)

Source: Economic Survey 2020–21

Note: In Figures 1 and 2, higher number indicates improvement (unlike in other rankings).

The Inevitability of Incomplete Regulations

The problem of over-regulation stems from not recognizing the inevitability of incomplete contracts and regulations in a world of uncertainty. Real-world contracts are inherently incomplete because of three key reasons that reinforce one another's influence. First, as Herbert A. Simon has highlighted in his Nobel prize-winning work, humans are boundedly rational because the future comprises 'unknown unknowns'.[45] Note that radical uncertainty of 'unknown unknowns' is fundamentally different from the notion of risk as defined by Frank Knight. Second, as another Nobel prize-winning work on incomplete contracts by Oliver Hart highlights, complexity in framing contracts arises from the difficulties involved in anticipating and specifying all obligations for all parties in full, across all possible contingencies. In fact, with radical uncertainty, it is impossible to know the possible characteristics of all the future states of the world. Therefore, writing complete contracts that

[45]Ministry of Finance, GoI, *Economic Survey 2020–21*, Volume 1, January 2021, p. 184, https://tinyurl.com/44a5n22t. Accessed on 27 November 2023.

will efficiently fit every future situation is inherently impossible in the real world. Finally, because of these two features, a third party may be able to observe outcomes *ex-post*, but cannot verify *ex-ante* decisions unambiguously.

Incomplete regulations become inevitable when the reality of incomplete contracts is acknowledged. In theory, regulators and policymakers can choose to invest entirely in the drafting process by identifying every possible state of the world that might materialize and by specifying an appropriate solution to each state. But, in reality, they confront a vexing problem: the future is unknown and unknowable. As a result, when faced with uncertainty, it simply costs too much to foresee and then describe appropriately the contractual outcomes for all (or even most) of the conceivable states of the world. Thus, the reality of incomplete contracts leads to the inevitability of incomplete regulation. This makes some discretion unavoidable.

In a complex and uncertain world, moreover, the actual outcomes or situations do not fit in the neat boxes assumed in the regulation; hence, the supervisor has to exercise some judgement. There is a widespread belief, however, that ever more detailed regulations reduce discretion. On the contrary, complex rules and regulations create more discretion because of the multiple ways in which they can be interpreted. This is made worse by the opacity of increasingly complex rules, which makes it difficult for a third party to monitor how the discretion was exercised. Black (2001) argues that 'discretion and rules are not in a zero-sum relationship such that the more rules there are the less the discretion there is and visa-versa [sic].'[46] In short, a complex, uncertain world makes discretion inevitable where over-regulation, not simpler regulation, leads to excessive and opaque discretion.

In their book *Regulating Aged Care: Ritualism and the New Pyramid*, Braithwaite, Makkai and Braithwaite (2007) study the healthcare sector in the US and provide evidence that is consistent with the above thesis. The book focusses on the impact of regulating care for the elderly. It was argued that inspectors manning the aged care homes had a lot of discretion. To change this scenario and reduce their discretion, the inspectors were provided with detailed protocols to audit. These standards were further

[46]Ibid. 185.

broken into sub-standards and had reached over 500 standards at the federal level. By 1986, the federal standards were complemented by some standards that were specific to each state. For instance, the Illinois code for nursing included over 5,000 care regulations. Consistent with the bounded rationality posited above, the authors found that inspectors could not cope up with the rise in the number of standards. Most of these standards were completely forgotten and only about 10 per cent of the standards were repeatedly used to make norms. The study noted that the results depended on the background of inspectors, such that, 'If you've got a nurse, it will be nursing deficiencies in the survey report; if a pharmacist, you'll get pharmacy deficiencies; a lawyer, patient rights, etc.'[47]

The complex set of rules, in fact, gave more discretion to the inspector. Owing to the complex and large number of standards that needed to be examined, idiosyncratic factors associated with the narrow expertise of the inspector caused particular standards to be checked in some homes, while neglecting them in others. Thus, over-regulation caused endemic unreliability and defeated the whole purpose of having detailed regulations. The timelines associated with closing down a clean company with no litigation/dispute, described above, represent an example of this problem.

Similarly, as shown in the *Economic Survey 2020–21*, an increase in the number of regulations, which is proxied by the increase in the de jure days to get the permit, correlates positively with the variation in the actual number of days taken. As variation against the de jure norm proxies the discretion exercised across the various applications from firms, this shows that more the number of regulations, higher the discretion in implementing them in the case of award of construction permits. Thus, the evidence is consistent with the thesis that discretion increases with the number of regulations.

Solving for Discretion

From the above discussion, it is clear that there is no substitute for active supervision and discretion. Specifically, *ex-ante* regulation cannot substitute *ex-post* supervision; in fact, more *ex-ante* regulation only serves to dilute the quality of *ex-post* supervision by fostering opaque discretion.

---

[47]Ibid.

So, how can supervisors be kept accountable while giving them discretion? We explore three possible ways:

a. **Strengthen *ex-ante* accountability:** The property rights literature based on incomplete contracts argues for the strengthening of governance in institutions by vesting more power in boards and then holding them accountable *ex-ante*. Instead of relying too much on *ex-post* audits, which anyway suffer from hindsight bias, *ex-ante* accountability needs to be entrusted with the boards of institutions. In most common law countries, there is a case law-derived doctrine of business judgement rule. The rule states that boards are presumed to act in good faith and protect companies from frivolous lawsuits by assuming that, unless proved otherwise, management is acting in the interests of shareholders. It exists in India as well, however not exactly codified in the same language. But there is a great deal of apprehension that it is not taken into account in audits and post-facto investigations.
b. **Bring transparency in the decision-making process:** The second way towards effective supervision is to incorporate transparency into the decision-making process. Transparency, apart from having intrinsic value, is appreciated because it promotes trust in public institutions and makes the market efficient. The discretion in the system needs to be balanced with transparency in decision-making.
c. **Build resilient *ex-post* resolution mechanisms:** When outcomes are uncertain, it is important to have a resilient *ex-post* resolution mechanism. Despite having all regulations in place and best efforts to deal with effective supervision *ex-ante*, devising a robust *ex-post* resolution mechanism is imperative. Grossman and Hart's (1986) work on 'incomplete contracts' demonstrates that the contracts are contingent on future states, and it is not possible to write complete contracts and, by extension, regulations, for every future state. Thus, adding *ex-ante* complexity to contracts and regulations or risk analysis cannot resolve this issue.

◆

When compared to advanced economies, India suffers significantly from over-regulation. If India has to become the global economic titan by 2047, we must tackle head-on this problem, which adds to the difficulties in doing business and engenders corruption. To overcome this problem of over-regulation and opacity in Indian administrative processes, policymakers must recognize that real-world regulation is inevitably incomplete. As a result, allowing some discretion in decision-making is unavoidable. India must diligently simplify its regulations on one hand and enhance transparency in its decision-making processes and build systems for *ex-ante* accountability and efficient *ex-post* resolution on the other. This process of streamlining of the regulatory and supervisory apparatus is a sine qua non for India to occupy its place as the global economic titan.

SECTION THREE

THE SECOND PILLAR
SOCIAL AND ECONOMIC INCLUSION

WHILE 'GARIBI HATAO' *(REMOVE POVERTY) has been part of the political rhetoric in India, genuine quest for social and economic inclusion of all citizens has rarely been seen as a strategic imperative. The last decade has heralded a seminal change in this direction, as the Modi government has shown that implementing sound economic policies to uplift the poor can be politically advantageous as well. Over the last decade, when the Modi government has been in power, poverty has declined drastically while inequality has declined in both rural and urban areas.*[48] *By utilizing technology to reduce pilferage and improve targeting of welfare spending, the government has developed a prototype for 'good economics equals good politics', which promises to bring about significant social and economic inclusion.*

Employment lies at the heart of inclusive growth, serving as a conduit for economic empowerment and social mobility. Given India's socialist past and the continued influence of leftist ideologies in economic discourse, large sections of the commentariat still paint entrepreneurs and businessmen with a broad brush of 'necessary evil'. It is important to dispel such notions and recognize that entrepreneurs and businesses contribute tremendously to Indian society by creating meaningful jobs. One high-quality job that an entrepreneur creates positively impacts four or five lives by bringing them all into the social and economic mainstream. At the same time, we must understand that only a productive firm continues to grow and thereby keeps creating jobs. In contrast, those firms that continue to remain small despite ageing—the economic dwarfs—consume costly resources, but do not give back enough to our society by creating adequate jobs. Our policy must not only foster entrepreneurs to create wealth—an aspect that I cover in Chapter 20 in the next section—but also encourage children that become corporate giants rather than dwarfs. Chapter 11 covers this critical aspect of job creation by encouraging firm growth. Chapter 12 continues this theme by underlining the need for 'Assemble in India' to precede '(Fully) Make in India' to utilize our comparative advantage—our demographics.

Through the leapfrogging that India has undertaken in creating digital infrastructure as a public good, India has taken an unparalleled step for socio-economic inclusion of all its citizens; after all, public goods are available for use by one and all. Chapter 13 details the policy steps to reap fully the dividend from DPI. Climate change poses an

---

[48]Bhalla, Surjit S., and Karan Bhasin, 'India Eliminates Extreme Poverty', *Brookings*, 1 March 2024, https://tinyurl.com/26vm67up. Accessed on 5 March 2024.

existential threat to humanity, yet its impacts and consequences are unevenly distributed across the global landscape. Chapter 14 shines a spotlight on the unfair climate divide, dissecting the asymmetries that characterize climate action and climate justice. For genuine socio-economic inclusion, India must approach agriculture with the exclusive focus of benefiting the small farmer. Chapter 15 champions the cause of agrarian revitalization, foregrounding the pivotal role of small farmers as the vanguards of agricultural reform. Chapter 16 combines the data and insights from the Thalinomics and Bare Necessities indices with the behavioural economics of nudge to chart out a path for reducing poverty and enhancing the livelihoods of the poor and vulnerable.

In the last decade, India's economic policy has shifted from 'of the elite, for the elite and by the elite' to 'of the people, for the people and by the people.' In order to achieve its goal of becoming an economic powerhouse by 2047, socio-economic inclusion of all Indian people is as strong an imperative as robust economic growth.

11

EMPOWERMENT THROUGH EMPLOYMENT

Good Jobs to Transform Lives

In the early 1980s, when Infosys was created, a close relative of mine also founded their own firm. Starting with seven founders, Infosys today employs more than 3,20,000 employees. In contrast, the firm created by my relative never went beyond 20 employees. Since its humble beginnings with an initial investment of ₹10,000, Infosys has emerged as a symbol of wealth creation with a market capitalization equalling almost ₹7 trillion now. A similar investment that was made by my relative is worth less than ₹10 million today. These contrasting outcomes teach us a key lesson that I explain in this chapter: jobs are created by small firms that grow to become giant firms. Small firms that remain small and never grow beyond their small size despite ageing—the dwarfs—do not create jobs in the economy.[49] The contrasting examples also highlight the importance of entrepreneurs generating wealth in order to create jobs in the economy.

Given India's socialist past, some of us perceive wealth creators and the act of wealth creation as evil. Have you ever wondered who provides more jobs and thereby helps to sustain the livelihoods of families—the wealthy or the poor person? Let me explain using a personal example. During my teens, we had employed a domestic worker solely for dishwashing duties. She worked for 10 households, including ours. Thus, 10 lower middle-class families collectively provided employment for one domestic worker; put differently, each lower middle-class family created *one-tenth* of a worker's job. In contrast, the wealthy jeweller in our town employed at least 100 people, both within his business and his

[49]In this chapter, the term 'dwarfs' for firms that remain small despite being old is contrasted to 'infants' for firms that are small because they are young. This usage is purely for firms and has no correlation with such usage for individuals and is, therefore, not intended to harm any sensibilities, whatsoever.

home. Each of these jobs created by the wealthy jeweller offered salaries at least 10 times higher than the domestic worker's wages. Thus, when accounting for both the quantity and quality of jobs together, the rich jeweller contributed 10,000× more than each lower middle-class family.

The key takeaway from this chapter is understanding that individuals who generate wealth in an economy do so by productively undertaking economic activities. Additionally, they make a valuable contribution to society by creating job opportunities.

This idea is important because job creation in large numbers remains an urgent imperative to provide financial and social inclusion for our young population. After all, a well-paying job provides these benefits to not only the individual, but also to his/her entire family. As estimated by the *Economic Survey 2018–19*, the working-age population will grow by roughly 9.7 million per year in this decade and over 4 million per year in the 2030s.[50] If we assume that the labour force participation rate (LFPR) would remain at about 60 per cent in the next two decades, about 5.5–6 million jobs will have to be created annually this decade and about 2.4–2.5 million annually in the 2030s. Micro, small and medium enterprises that experience growth not only generate increased profits for their promoters, but also contribute towards job creation and productivity in the economy. It is imperative that our policies focus on enabling the growth of MSMEs by unshackling them.

The Bane of Dwarfism and Its Impact

It is astonishing to observe the significant impact of the curse of dwarfs on the Indian economy, hindering both job creation and productivity. For the purposes of the analysis in this section, I categorize firms employing less than 100 workers as small and firms employing 100 or more workers as relatively large. Though a firm with 100 workers is definitely not large on a global scale, as I show, firms employing 100 workers are relatively large in the Indian context. Firms that are both small and older than 10 years are categorized as dwarfs as these firms have continued to be stunted in their growth despite surviving for more than 10 years.

---

[50]Ministry of Finance, GoI, *Economic Survey 2018–19: Volume 1*, July 2019, http://tinyurl.com/5ccw6unz. Accessed on 5 February 2024.

Figure 1 shows the share of small and large firms in the total number of firms, and in terms of employment and net value added (NVA). This analysis has been conducted using firm-level data from the *Annual Survey of Industries (ASI) 2019–20*, which is the latest available survey.[51] Figure 1 shows that while small firms (firms that have less than 99 employees) account for over 83 per cent of all firms in India by number, their share in employment is only 21.5 per cent. In fact, their share in NVA is a mere 12.4 per cent despite them accounting for almost 83 per cent of the landscape of firms. In contrast, large firms (firms that have more than 99 employees) account for only 16.8 per cent of firms by number, but contribute 78.5 per cent of employment and 87.6 per cent of the NVA.

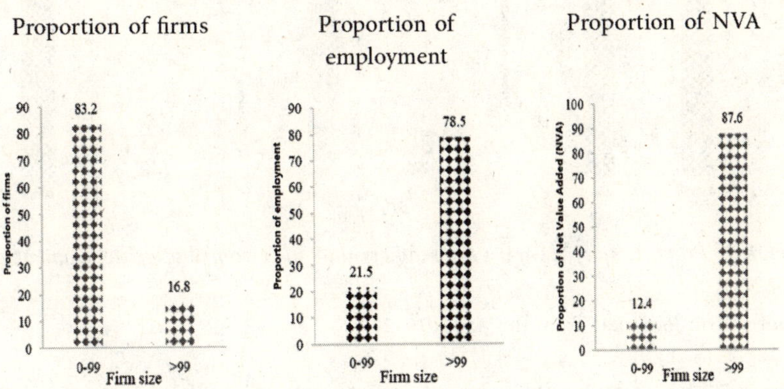

Figure 1: Proportion of small and large firms and their contribution to employment and NVA

Source: Firm-level data from the *ASI 2019–20*

Figure 2 shows the share of dwarfs versus other firms in the number of firms, employment and NVA. We see that while dwarfs account for 58 per cent of all firms in India by number, their share in employment is only 14.8 per cent. In fact, their share in NVA is incredibly low at a mere 6.3 per cent despite them accounting for 58 per cent of the landscape of firms. In contrast, the firms that are not dwarfs account for 42 per cent

[51]Ministry of Statistics and Programme Implementation, GoI, *Annual Survey of Industries 2019–2020*, http://tinyurl.com/2s4dxb7u. Accessed on 5 February 2024.

of firms by number but contribute 85.2 per cent of employment and 93.7 per cent of the NVA.

Thus, dwarfs remain the lowest per capita contributors to employment and productivity in the economy. In contrast, firms that are able to grow over time to become large are the biggest per capita contributors to employment and productivity in the economy.

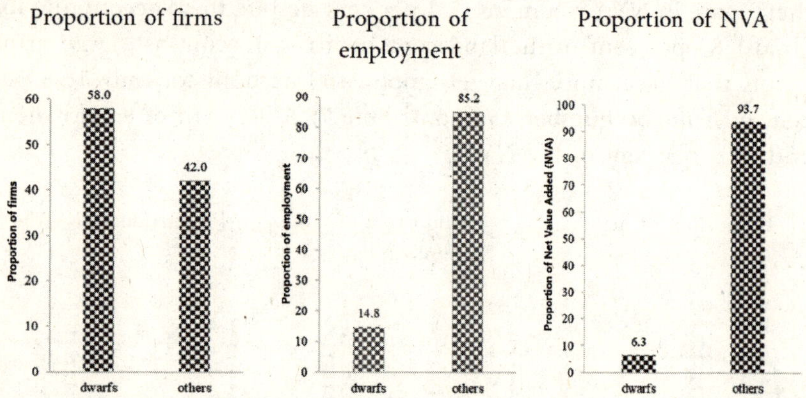

Figure 2: Proportion of dwarfs versus others and their contribution to employment and NVA

Source: Firm-level data from the *ASI 2019–20*

These findings dispel the common notion that small firms generate the most employment. Small firms may generate a higher number of new jobs. However, they destroy as many jobs as well. Thus, higher levels of job creation in small firms coexist with job destruction, thereby leading to lower levels of net job creation.

What is the impact of the size distribution of firms on jobs and productivity? Figure 3 compares growth of employment and productivity with firm age in three countries: US, Mexico and India. The comparison is done using both organized and unorganized manufacturing firms. For India, the data include both from the *ASI* and the surveys of unorganized manufacturing organized by the National Sample Survey Organization (NSSO). The left and right panels use the size and productivity as of age five or younger as the base for comparison. The average number of employees in established 40-year-old enterprises in the US is more than seven times higher compared to when the company was first established. In contrast, the average number of employees in 40-year-old firms in India is only 40 per cent higher than the initial employment level. Thus, the average 40-year-old firm in the US creates employment opportunities that are five times (7/1.4) greater than those generated by an average Indian firm of the same age. Even Mexico does far better on this score than India. The average employment level in 40-year-old firms in Mexico is twice as high as when the business is initially established. Thus, once they survive for 40 years, the average 40-year-old firm in Mexico generates 40 per cent more (2/1.4) employment than the average 40-year-old Indian firm.

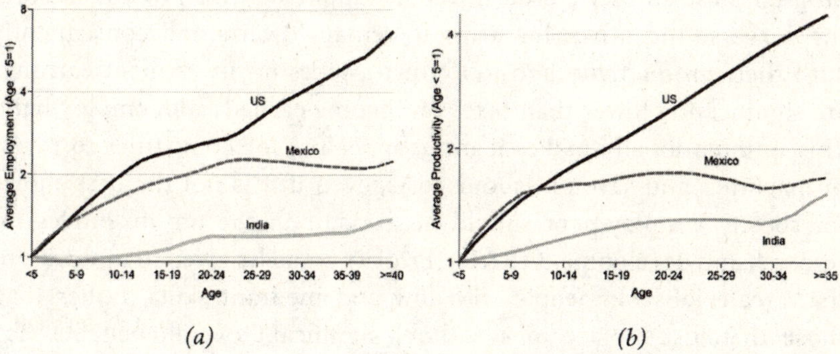

Figure 3: Growth of employment and productivity with firm age in three countries: US, Mexico and India. (a) Change in employment with firm age; (b) change in productivity with firm age

Source: Hsieh and Klenow (2014)

A similar narrative emerges in terms of productivity. The impact of ageing firms on productivity can also be observed when comparing these three countries. The average productivity level for 40-year-old enterprises in the US was more than four times higher than that of a newly established enterprise. In contrast, the average productivity level for 40-year-old firms in India was only 60 per cent higher than that of newly set-up enterprises. This means that after surviving for forty years, the average 40-year-old firm in the US is 2.5 times (= 4/1.6) more productive than the average 40-year-old Indian firm. Mexico does far better than India in this aspect as well. The average productivity level of 40-year-old firms in Mexico is 1.7 times higher than that of newly established enterprises.

Thus, the comparison with other countries highlights that both employment creation and productivity do not grow adequately as firms age in India.

Role of Government Policy in Fostering Job Creation

Good jobs do not just appear magically; they depend on companies being more productive and successful businesses growing. In particular, creating good jobs consistently over a period of time requires labour productivity to grow in the economy. However, government programmes can play a crucial role in supporting this process. Besides the perverse incentives for firms to remain dwarfs and consequently curb their productivity and job growth, taxes on investment earnings are significantly lower than taxes on income earned from employment. This unintentionally makes it more appealing for companies to invest in machines and save on labour costs, even if it is not the best choice for society. Employment should be a factor in the tax incentives for research and development (R&D). Priority could be given to innovations that create jobs for people with low and medium skills, rather than those that just replace jobs without significant overall benefits. Tax incentives for R&D should be staggered based on the actual number of jobs created using the investment in innovation.

The way in which private companies are encouraged to innovate can often be hostile to job creation. Research shows that venture capital (VC) tends to invest in areas where profits come quickly. This means that some valuable innovations with longer-term benefits for society—like enhancing the productivity of labour and thereby adding to job creation—may get overlooked. Moreover, there are two approaches to bridging the divide between skills and technology: improving education to meet the needs of new technologies and directing innovation towards utilizing existing skill sets. The second approach does not get much attention but is worth considering. Government policy should be focussed on directing technology in a way that aligns with the current workforce's skills, in addition to equipping the workforce with the necessary capabilities to adapt to emerging technologies.

Post-War Job Creation in Western Europe and North America

During the post-War era, scores of high-paying jobs were created in Western Europe and North America; such job creation led to the rise of a burgeoning middle class. The primary contributor to such job creation was the increase in labour productivity, which fuelled labour demand. This increase in labour productivity was fostered by high-quality education. Of course, firms would not have been willing to hire millions of well-paid workers if these workers lacked useful skills. The US federal government supported university education through GI Bill grants, Pell Grants and generous research support.[52] Moreover, local governments increased spending on primary and secondary education.

Evidence from the Atmanirbhar Bharat Rozgar Yojana

The Atmanirbhar Bharat Rozgar Yojana (ABRY) was implemented in October 2020 with the aim of stimulating job preservation during Covid-19. The scheme incentivized new hiring, including for those who had lost their jobs due to the pandemic. Under this scheme, the government covered both the employee and employer contributions to the Employment Provident Fund (EPF), which accounted for 24 per cent of wages, for all new hires in firms with up to 1,000 employees. In the case of firms with more than 1,000 employees, the employee's EPF contributions for all new hires, which amounted to 12 percent of wages, were covered.

Data from the Ministry of Labour and Employment of the GoI reveals that over 6 million employees were hired under this scheme by over 1,50,000 firms. Two lakh establishments specializing in expert services, textiles and trading-commercial sectors emerged as the top three contributors to employment recovery and growth.

---

[52]The GI Bill is a federal effort to provide financial and social benefits to World War II veterans after they have returned home. Federal Pell Grants usually are awarded only to undergraduate students who display exceptional financial need and have not earned a bachelor's, graduate or professional degree.

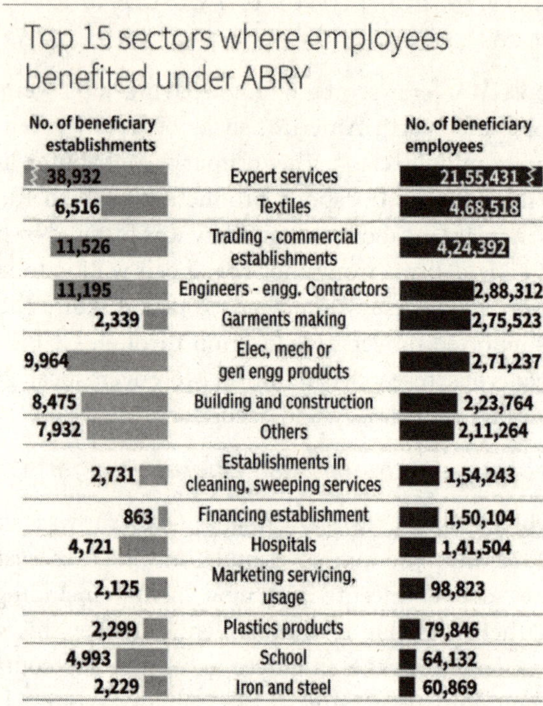

Figure 4: Beneficiaries of ABRY
Source: The Hindu Businessline[53]

Manufacturing Jobs in the Age of AI

Remember the film *Naya Daur*, in which the competition between a horse carriage and an automobile—competition between capital and labour—forms the central part of the story? This movie from the 1950s starring thespian Dilip Kumar reminds us that automation technologies have been around for a long time. It is crucial to remember this when rationally analysing the fear about job losses in manufacturing due to automation and AI.

[53]Jadhav, Radheshyam, 'How Atmanirbhar Bharat Rozgar Yojana Helped Foster Employment During the Pandemic', *The Hindu Businessline*, 6 January 2024, http://tinyurl.com/5bkwvkue. Accessed on 15 February 2024.

Of the 270 occupations in the 1950 US census, 232 of them (86 per cent) still exist today; 37 of them disappeared because of changes in consumer demand or technological obsolescence. Only one occupation disappeared purely due to automation: elevator operators. However, some commentators argue that this time things will be different, especially because of advances in AI.

In this context, it is useful to recall the story of automation at Tesla. In 2016, Elon Musk announced that Tesla's Model 3 would be built in a new, fully automated car factory with robots operating beyond human speed, raw materials coming in at one end and finished cars rolling out the other.[54] By mid-2018, the automation was not working as expected, and Tesla was driven close to financial collapse.[55] Tesla then launched a new assembly line full of human workers. Learning from this experience, Musk admitted that people are way better at dealing with unexpected circumstances than robots. He conceded on X (formerly Twitter) that excessive automation at Tesla was a mistake and that humans are underrated.[56]

This experience reveals important lessons. First, it highlights how production techniques relying on human labour can still dominate automation in situations where uncertainty cannot be fully addressed and all tasks cannot be standardized. For instance, many of us can relate to the frustration experienced when an AI-powered automated voice fails to resolve our customer service issue as effectively as a human customer service representative. Second, it is indicative of the excessive faith many business leaders often place on new technologies. Third, it reminds us that technology adoption is a choice that businesses must make. They are presented with a range of options about the types of innovations to use and deploy. These choices have significant implications for the workforce, and occasionally even for society at large. However, these implications are not typically internalized during the decision-making process.

---

[54]Rodrik, Dani, and Stefanie Stantcheva, 'Fixing Capitalism's Good Jobs Problem', *Oxford Review of Economic Policy*, Vol. 37, No. 4, 2021, http://tinyurl.com/5exbdbbf. Accessed on 5 February 2024.

[55]Ibid.

[56]Aiello, Chloe, 'Elon Musk Admits Humans Are Sometimes Superior to Robots, in a Tweet about Tesla Delays', *CNBC*, 13 April 2018, http://tinyurl.com/vynkdbt4. Accessed on 5 February 2024.

If we look at forecast studies that predict the impact of automation on employment in the future, the first and foremost aspect to note is the significant disparity in estimates. The range spans from a mere 9 per cent of American workers being at risk, all the way up to a staggering 47 per cent of workers in the US facing potential job loss over the next two decades. A McKinsey study estimates that 60 per cent of all occupations in the world contain at least 30 per cent technically automatable activities.[57] Manufacturing is categorized as the top three automatable activities, particularly low-skilled manufacturing in the Global South. Crucially, the study highlights that automation will lead to restructuring of the labour force rather than large-scale unemployment. In developing countries, the World Bank estimates that two-thirds of all jobs are susceptible to automation.[58] However, like the McKinsey study, this study also cautions against equating automatability with unemployment.

The fear of automation and AI leading to drastic changes in employment in India are exaggerated. For example, during the Industrial Revolution, machines automated over 90 per cent of human work in the textile industry. However, prices in the industry rapidly decreased due to productivity growth and an increase in demand for clothes, which in turn increased demand for weavers in factories. A recent study of the South African apparel industry showed that most firms that implemented new automation technologies increased employment levels, largely because these technologies increased the firm's productivity.[59] While some industries have experienced short-term spikes in unemployment following technology shocks, research shows that mid-term and long-term effects on employment have generally been positive.

Further, there are many barriers that prevent the adoption of automation technologies in labour-intensive industries within India

---

[57]McKinsey Global Institute, *A Future That Works: Automation, Employment and Productivity*, January 2017, http://tinyurl.com/53pk7evz. Accessed on 5 February 2024.

[58]World Bank Group, *Digital Dividends: World Development Report 2016*, http://tinyurl.com/3ey3y7sn. Accessed on 5 February 2024.

[59]Hauge, Jostein, and Christian Parschau, 'Is Automation Stealing Manufacturing Jobs? Evidence from South Africa's Apparel Industry', *LSE Blogs*, 29 May 2020, http://tinyurl.com/36nn5mzm. Accessed on 5 February 2024.

and the Global South. A technology that is technically feasible is not always also economically profitable, especially in countries with low labour costs relative to capital. A report by United Nations Conference on Trade and Development (UNCTAD) identifies many industries that display automation potential from a technical standpoint but not from an economic standpoint.[60] The report particularly highlights the textile and food industry because automation technology cannot compete with the low cost of labour in these industries.

The concept of reshoring, in which advanced economies withdraw previously offshored production owing to the availability of new automation technologies within their own countries, presents an additional concern for employment in labour-intensive industries. Research, however, shows that when reshoring does occur, it is on a small scale, smaller than the new offshoring activity.

Consistent with these arguments, economists at MIT David Autor and Daron Acemoglu reckon that the concerns about automation and AI displacing human work are overblown.[61] For instance, Acemoglu avers, 'The rate of job loss from automation or this particular branch of automation, robotization, is relatively small over the last 20 years or so, perhaps less than half a percentage point of the population (the working-age population). So, we're not talking about huge numbers.'[62] They find that even with tremendous acceleration in the adoption of robots, the impact on employment would be only a few percentage points in the advanced economies in the next several decades.

Policies to Foster Job Creation

The evidence provided in the previous sections highlights that dwarfs have low productivity and low value added. In contrast, infant and large firms together account for a significant part of employment generation

---

[60]UNCTAD, *Trade and Development Report 2017: Beyond Austerity: Towards A Global New Deal*, http://tinyurl.com/ythm7atm. Accessed on 5 February 2024.

[61]Autor, David, 'Will Automation Take Away All Our Jobs?' *Ideas.Ted.Com*, 29 March 2017, http://tinyurl.com/yf3wck3j. Accessed on 15 February 2024.

[62]Pethokoukis, James, 'Will Technology Enable Workers or Replace Them? A Long-Read Q&A with Daron Acemoglu', *AEIdeas*, 2 October 2017, http://tinyurl.com/47w44xye. Accessed on 15 February 2024.

and productivity in the economy. Therefore, while dwarfs consume vital resources that could possibly be given to infant firms, they contribute much less to creation of jobs and economic growth as compared to infant firms. This necessitates recalibration of policy towards supporting infant firms as detailed below.

Incentivizing Infant Firms rather than Small Firms

Incentives need to be shifted away from dwarfs to infants. When such incentives are provided to firms irrespective of their age, these can create 'perverse' incentives for firms to stay small. Such perverse incentives would not exist if age is the criterion. Misuse of the age-based criterion can be easily prevented by using Aadhaar-related data to track any misuse that may occur. If, for instance, a promoter starts a new firm, takes advantage of the age-based incentive for a period of 10 years and then shuts down the firm in order to start another one to continue benefitting from the age-based benefits through this new firm, the promoter's Aadhaar can alert authorities regarding this misuse. Once small firms know that they would receive no benefits from continuing to remain small despite ageing, their natural incentives to grow would get activated. This will generate economic growth and employment.

Re-orienting Priority-Sector Lending

As per extant policy, certain targets have been prescribed for banks for lending to the MSME sector that exacerbates perverse incentives to firms to remain small. As per priority-sector lending (PSL) guidelines, 7.5 per cent of adjusted net bank credit (ANBC) or credit equivalent amount of off-balance sheet exposure, whichever is higher, is applicable to micro enterprises. Under the MSME's PSL targets, it is necessary to prioritize start-ups and infants in high employment elastic sectors. This would direct credit flow towards sectors that have the potential to generate employment opportunities in the economy.

Table 1 shows the high employment elastic sub-sectors and their employment elasticity.

Table 1
Employment elasticity across various sectors

Subsector	*Employment Elasticity*
Rubber and plastic products	0.85
Electrical and optical equipment	0.48
Transport equipment	0.27
Electricity, gas and water supply	0.22
Machinery	0.15
Basic metals and fabricated metal products	0.10
Chemicals and chemical products	0.07
Textiles, textile products, leather and footwear	0.02
Other non-metallic mineral products	0.02
Wood and products of wood	0.01

Source: Economic Survey 2019–20

Sunset Clause for Incentives

Every incentive for fostering growth should have a 'sunset' clause, say, for a period of five to seven years after which the firm should be able to sustain itself. The policy focus would thereby remain on infant firms.

Focus on High Employment Elastic Sectors

The manufacture of furniture, leather and leather products, apparel, motor vehicles and trailers, rubber and plastic products, computers, electronics and optical products are the sub-sectors that exhibit highest employment elasticities. We must focus on such high employment elastic sectors in order to increase the employment intensity of economic growth.

Focus on Service Sectors with High Spillover Effects

As the recent experiences with Varanasi and Ayodhya illustrate, developing key tourist centres will have ripple effects on job creation in areas such as guided tours and safaris, hotels, catering and housekeeping businesses, shops at tourist spots, etc. It is possible to identify 10 tourism attractions in each of the larger 20 states and five spots in the nine smaller states.

Developing road and air connections to these tourist destinations could boost economic activity along the entire route and simultaneously reduce the migration of rural workers, who constitute a major proportion of the total labour force.

◆

India@100 cannot become an inclusive and progressive nation without creating quality employment opportunities. These jobs not only ensure shared prosperity but also provide a sense of fulfilment to citizens.

12

RUN AFTER LEARNING TO WALK

Assemble and Make in India for the World

When Maruti Udyog Ltd (MUL) started assembling cars in the early 1980s, it employed 883 employees.[63] Over decades, as Maruti progressively integrated operations backward by manufacturing all parts and components indigenously, the Indian automobile industry grew tremendously. Today, the industry employs about two crore employees across the entire value chain. Thus, starting from the modest assembly operations, employment in this industry has grown by 50,000 times in five decades. The industry accounts for about half of India's manufacturing GDP and over 7 per cent of its overall GDP.

More recently, a similar phenomenon is playing out in electronics manufacturing. Following the 'make in India' push by the government, production of mobile phones has gone up from 6 crore in 2015 to 31 crore in 2022, which translates into an annual growth rate of 26 per cent. In this process, as shown in Figure 1, the imports of mobile phones have declined sharply from about $7.5 billion in 2014–15, when the Make in India initiative was launched, to less than $4 billion in 2016–17. Once sub-component manufacturing took off in 2017, imports have further reduced to less than $200 million in 2021–22. In the process, value addition has grown from just 2 per cent in 2014, when only assembly was being done, to about 15 per cent in 2022 with indigenous manufacture of sub-components contributing to the higher value addition.

[63]Satia, J.K., and P.S. Thomas, 'Maruti Udyog Limited', *Vikalpa: The Journal for Decision Makers*, Vol. 14, No.3, July–September 1989, http://tinyurl.com/32r734ft. Accessed on 8 January 2024.

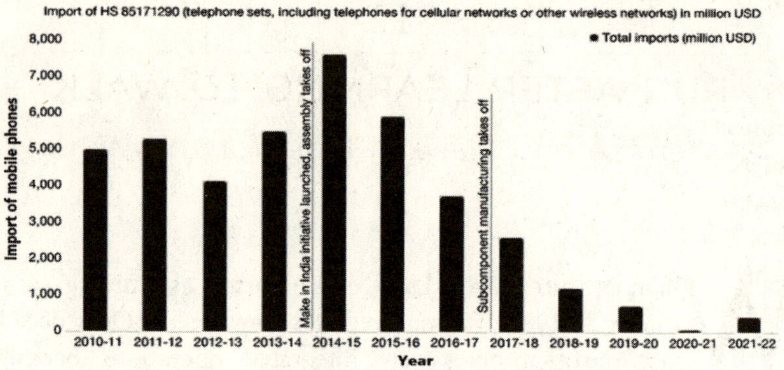

Figure 1: Decline in imports of mobile phones from 2014–15

Source: PWC Report 'India Calling: Decoding the Country's Electronics Manufacturing Journey and the Way Forward', 2023

The two case studies of automobiles and mobile phones clearly illustrate 'learning to walk'—or low-value-added assembly operations, before 'running'—or full-fledged end-to-end manufacturing, capturing the value addition completely. By integrating 'Assemble in India for the world' into Make in India, India can create eight crore jobs by 2030.

Growth in exports provides a much-needed pathway for job creation in India. For instance, in the five-year period 2001–06, labour-intensive exports enabled China to create 70 million jobs for workers with primary education. In India, increased exports explain the conversion of about 8,00,000 jobs from informal to formal between 1999 and 2011, representing 0.8 per cent of the labour force (Artuc et al. 2019). The China+1 strategy of multinational firms presents India with an unprecedented opportunity to chart a similar export trajectory as that pursued by China and create unparalleled job opportunities for its youth. As no other country can match China in the abundance of its labour, we must grab the space that is being vacated in labour-intensive sectors.

India's Export Underperformance vis-à-vis China

To understand the export strategy that India needs to pursue, we must examine the reasons for India's underperformance in exports vis-à-vis China.

Lack of Specialization

Is India's lacklustre export performance caused by a lack of diversification in its export basket or is it because of a lack of specialization? We examine this question by decomposing India's and China's share of world exports of manufactured products into the effects of diversification versus concentration (see Figure 2). It can be seen that Panel (a), which depicts the world market shares of the two countries, is a mirror image of Panel (b), which shows the contribution of specialization. Thus, the China–India gap in world market share is almost fully driven by the effect of specialization. On the other hand, India is clearly catching up with China in terms of diversification across products and markets (Panel [b]). Overall, high diversification combined with low specialization implies that India is spreading its exports thinly over many products and partners, leading to its lacklustre performance compared to China.

The specialization effect itself is further decomposed into quantity and price effects. Figure 3 shows that the China–India gap with respect to specialization has been fully driven by the quantity effect. Thus, China has exploited economies of scale to lower the average costs of its

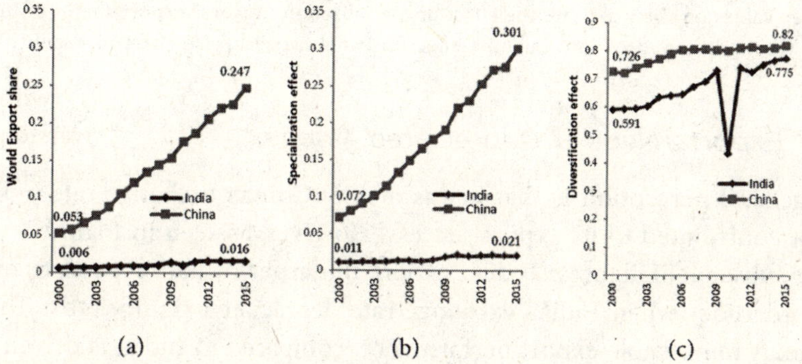

Figure 2: Decomposition of world export market shares of manufactured products into specialization and diversification effects: India and China, 2000–15: (a) world export share, (b) specialization effect, (c) diversification effect

Source: Economic Survey 2019–20

Note: Values on the y axis are the world export shares of India and China in Panel (a), these shares decomposed into effect of specialization in Panel (b) and effect of diversification in Panel (c).

manufacturing products to compete effectively in global markets. The bottom line is that if India wants to become a major exporter, it should specialize more in the areas of its comparative advantage and achieve significant quantity expansion.

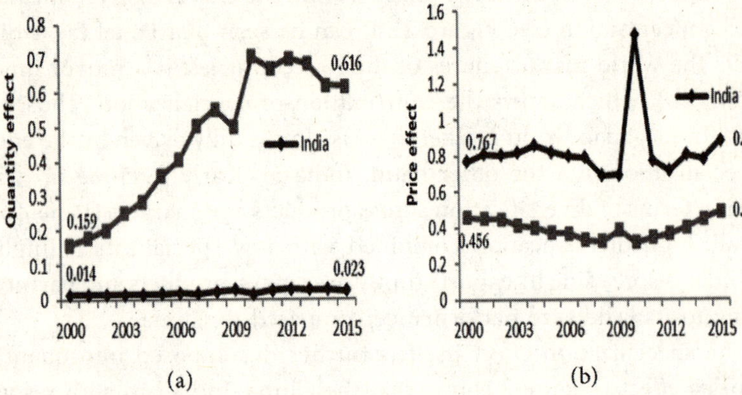

Figure 3: Decomposition of specialization effect of manufactured goods into quantity and price effects: India and China, 2000–15: (a) quantity effect, (b) price effect

Source: Economic Survey 2019–20

Note: Values on the y axis are the effect of specialization in world export shares of India and China decomposed into quantity effect in Panel (a) and price effect in Panel (b).

Do Exports Need a Depreciated Rupee?

A general perception is that it was mainly China's exchange rate policy that contributed to its export success. However, as seen in Figure 2 and the subsequent figures, India's export underperformance persists over two decades when India's exchange rate depreciated significantly. Thus, China's remarkable export performance, compared to India, is driven by a high degree of specialization in labour-intensive production activities and large scale in the chosen sectors of specialization.

Potential Gains in Employment and GDP

India has huge potential to emerge as a major hub for final assembly in a range of products, referred to as network products (NPs) that are manufactured as part of GVCs. Global value chains are controlled by leading multinational enterprises (MNEs), such as Apple, Samsung, Sony, etc., within 'producer-driven' networks. In general, these products are not produced from start to finish within a given country; instead, countries specialize in particular tasks or stages of the goods' production sequence. Within the production network, each country specializes in a particular fragment of the production process; this specialization is based on the country's comparative advantage. Labour-abundant countries, like China, specialize in low-skilled, labour-intensive stages of production such as assembly, while richer countries specialize in capital- and skill-intensive stages such as R&D. Thus, the lead firms retain skill- and knowledge-intensive stages of production in high-income headquarters (e.g., the US, European Union [EU] and Japan), but locate assembly-related activities in low-wage countries (e.g., China and Vietnam).

A higher level of participation in GVCs implies that for any given country, the share of foreign value added in gross exports is higher than when most inputs are sourced locally. However, owing to scale and productivity effects of selling in the world markets, participation in GVCs can lead to higher absolute levels of domestic value added and domestic job creation. Figure 4 illustrates the conceptual framework explaining this phenomenon. The scale effect creates millions of jobs and is therefore particularly suited for implementation in a labour-intensive economy such as India.

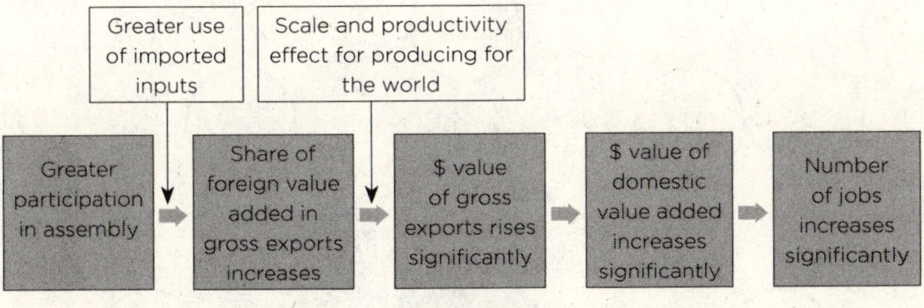

Figure 4: Gains from assembling in India as part of Make in India

Source: Economic Survey 2019–20

Focussing on NP can create significant gains both in employment creation and GDP growth. The *Economic Survey 2019–20* estimated that the total number of jobs resulting from participating in GVCs, which includes direct employment in the NP sector and through backward linkages to the NP sectors, will go up from about 4.4 million in 2020 to 25.5 million in 2030. Thus, based on the first-order effects, over 20 million jobs can be created during the next 10 years. Accounting for the second-order effect of increased consumption by workers, the *Economic Survey 2019–20* estimated that it is possible to generate an additional 82.2 million jobs by 2030. Further, the total domestic value added is likely to increase from $168 billion in 2020 to $1,134.3 billion by 2030.

Research shows that GVC participation helps countries escape the middle-income trap. Participation in GVCs lead to higher output, productivity and value added through five main transmission channels:

i. backward and forward links in the supply chain of NPs;
ii. higher competition among domestic firms to do business as part of GVCs, which enables productivity improvements;
iii. technology spillovers into domestic firms;
iv. increase in the size of domestic firms as they grow to achieve the minimum scale required to reduce their average costs; and
v. labour market effects, including the demand for skilled workers and their training.

As shown in Figure 5, these individual effects interact and thereby reinforce each other.

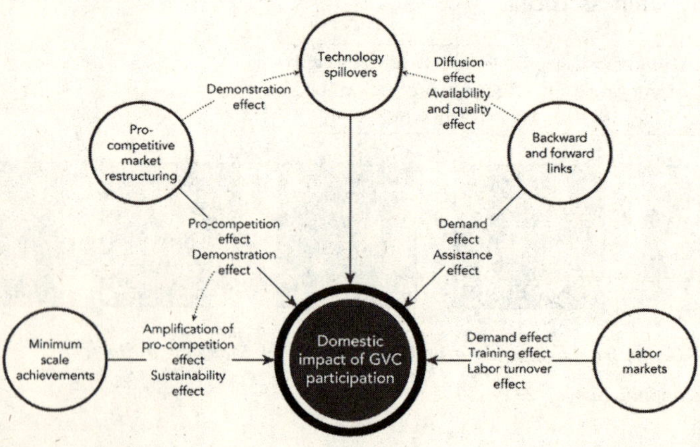

Figure 5: Gains from participating in GVCs

Source: Taglioni and Winkler (2016)

As shown in Figure 6, overall integration into GVCs increases a country's domestic value added. In fact, integration into GVCs as a seller correlates even more strongly with increase in GDP per capita when a country that is low-income or low middle-income sells into GVCs than buys from GVCs. The key takeaway from India's perspective is that integration into GVCs as a seller correlates positively with increase in GDP per capita at all levels of income.

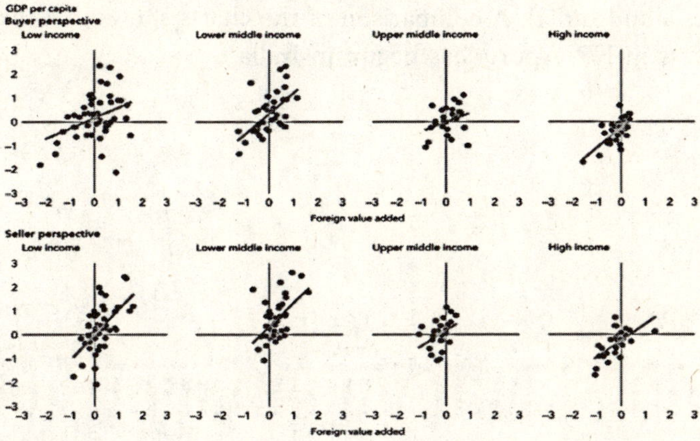

Figure 6: Growth of GVC integration and growth in GDP per capita by income categories
Source: Boffa et al. (2016)

The Wild Geese Flying Model: Assembly before End-To-End Production

It is important to understand the sequencing adopted by countries that became powerhouses of manufacturing exports by entrenching themselves deeply in NPs. The pattern of entry, rise, survival and relative decline of countries in the export market for NPs has consistently followed the 'wild geese flying model', in which a leading nation like Japan is compared to a 'lead goose', providing capital, technology and managerial know-how to 'follower geese' countries in East and Southeast Asia. This model is characterized by two key features. First, the sequence of the country increasing the value added in manufacturing proceeds as imports for assembly, domestic production of parts and components, and finally exports. Second, the sequence with respect to the sophistication of products proceeds from consumer goods to capital goods and from crude and simple articles to complex and refined articles.

The export market participation of several of the Asian countries over the years indeed depicts the wild geese flying pattern (see Figure 7). Panel (a) in the figure depicts the pattern for the early entrants (Japan, Singapore, Korea, Malaysia and the Philippines). Panel (b) shows the pattern for the late entrants (China, Thailand and Vietnam) and laggards (Indonesia and India). A comparison of the charts shows that the take-off process in NP exports has begun in India.

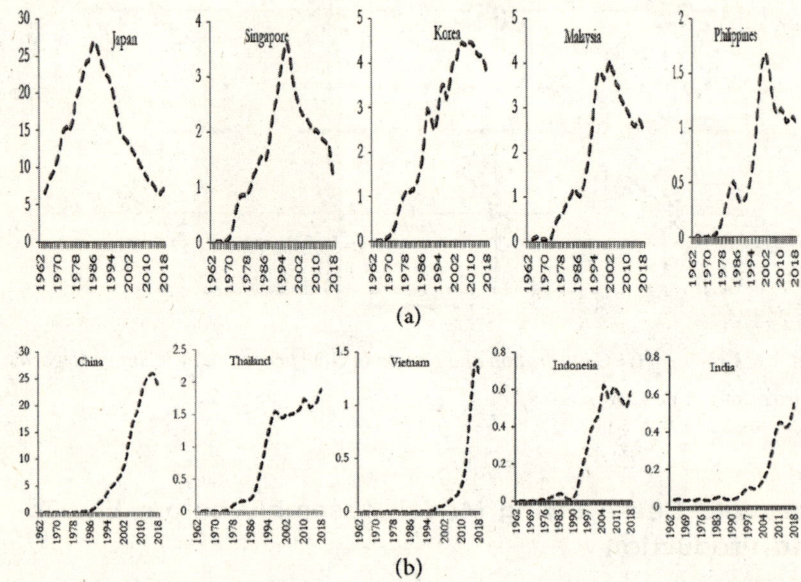

Figure 7: Wild geese flying pattern of exports in network products: (a) early entrants, (b) late entrants and laggards

Source: Economic Survey 2019–20

Note: Values on the y axis are three-year moving averages of the world export shares of the respective country.

Larger countries like Japan and China, which have survived in the market for longer periods of time, took off with an expansion of assembled end products (AEP), while parts and components (P&C) followed suit

(Figure 8). Japan's descent on the inverted V-path also began with AEP in 1985, followed by P&C circa 1993. China seems to have reached the inflection point of the inverted V-curve for AEP circa 2015, while its world market share in P&C continue to increase. The most recent entrants, Thailand and Vietnam, have taken off with an expansion of AEP exports while P&C is following suit. For India, P&C has recorded some growth in recent years, while AEP, with exceptions such as passenger cars and telecom handsets, has declined.

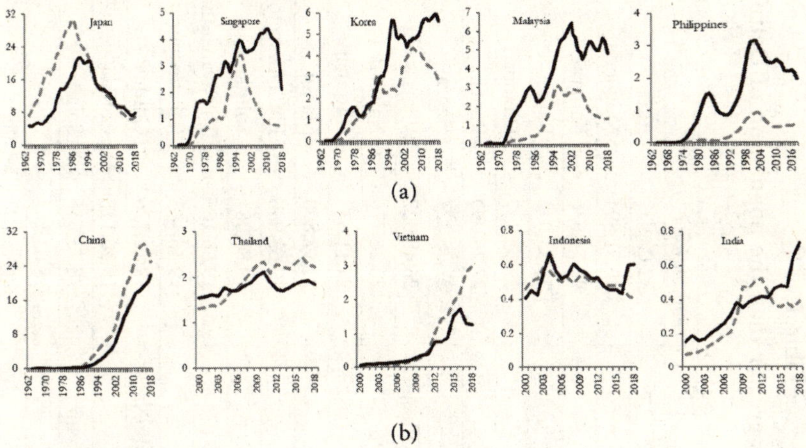

Figure 8: Wild geese flying pattern of NP exports—AEP versus P&C: (a) early entrants, (b) late entrants and laggards

Source: Economic Survey 2019–20

Note: Values on the y axis are three-year moving averages of the world export shares of the respective country.

Will India Remain Competitive in Wages?

A key concern with respect to India utilizing its competitive advantage in labour to participate in GVCs is: will economic development, which will increase the per capita income, and thereby wages, render India uncompetitive? Here, India must utilize the fact that per capita incomes, and therefore wages, land costs and cost of living are in general significantly lower in Tier-2 cities than in Tier-1 cities. Post Covid-19, the acceptance and use of digital technologies for communication have increased significantly.

Table 1

Population of all Tier-2 cities greater than the population of Detroit (USA)

City	*Population (2024)*	*City*	*Population (2024)*	*City*	*Popluation (2024)*
Jaipur	76,85,041	Kanpur	32,03,932	Agra	18,37,197
Patna	72,07,001	Tumakuru	30,51,894	Nalgonda	17,54,687
Nashik	67,88,138	Surguja	29,74,636	Kangra	16,50,512
Purbi Champaran	62,94,664	Jabalpur	28,83,033	Rajkot	14,98,723
Muzaffarpur	59,26,431	Sagar	27,83,747	Dhanbad	14,13,101
Madhubani	55,39,221	Bhopal	27,75,090	Ranchi	13,04,858
Belgaum	54,44,990	Amritsar	27,38,227	Haora	11,90,599
Raipur	51,22,511	Medchal-Malkajgiri	26,45,527	Vijayawada	11,21,451
Kanchipuram	46,38,372	Gurdaspur	25,26,776	Nainital	11,07,342
Vellore	45,66,538	Jalandhar	24,11,633	Guwahati	11,04,401
Tiruvallur	43,24,973	Haridwar	21,92,890	Mandi	10,92,756
Jodhpur	42,76,374	Faridabad	20,63,096	Bhubaneswar	9,46,381
Alwar	42,61,313	Hissar	19,88,081	Shimla	8,89,713
Durg	42,14,951	Dehradun	19,68,165	Thiruvananthapuram	7,72,472
Ludhiana	38,46,514	Vadodara	19,46,155	Jamshedpur	7,67,486
Nagaur	38,36,320	Udham Singh Nagar	19,12,726	Guntur	7,02,028
Indore	38,35,046	Ghaziabad	19,10,118	Cuttack	6,84,693
Mysuru	34,18,884	Visakhapatnam	18,73,636	Solan	6,34,290
Bilaspur	33,57,504	Bhiwani	18,63,267		

Source: Indiacensus.net

Therefore, manufacturing activities could be moved to Tier-2 cities even while management functions continue to operate out of nearby Tier-1 cities. As Table 1 shows, several of the Tier-2 cities in India have populations of over a million. As a comparison, the city of Detroit in the US, which has been a huge hub for automobile manufacturing, has a population of about 6,00,000. Thus, each of the Tier-2 cities shown in Table 1 has a population that is greater than that of Detroit.

However, the current per capita income in Tier-2 cities is between $1,500 and $2,000. As Figure 9 shows, salaries of production workers in India in 2022 are about five times lower than those in China. Using the salaries in China in 2022 of $15,000 as the level where the competitiveness from lower wages disappears, we can clearly estimate that wage levels for manufacturing workers in Tier-2 cities will reach such uncompetitive levels only by 2047 (see Table 2). Till 2040, the possibility of manufacturing wages reaching such uncompetitive levels is ruled out. Therefore, manufacturing in Tier-2 cities can remain competitive from the perspective of wages for the large part of India's journey till 2047.

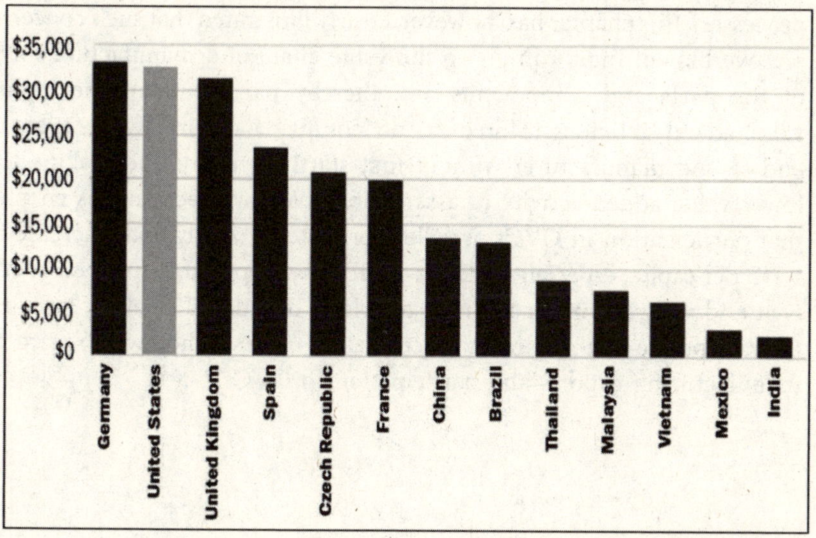

Figure 9: Average salaries of production workers/machine operators in 2022

Source: Reshoring Institute 2022. Data collected from Indeed.com, Glassdoor.com, Salaryexplorer.com, Salary.com, Payscale.com

Table 2
Projected per capita (p.c.) income in Tier-2 cities in 2030, 2035, 2040 and 2047

Growth rate of GDP p.c.	*Income p.c. in Tier-2 cities (in 2022 $)*			
	2030	*2035*	*2040*	*2047*
5.60%	3123	4392	6177	11037
6.60%	3452	5216	7882	14999
7.50%	3779	6090	9815	19756

Source: Author's calculations

◆

An often-repeated argument against labour-intensive manufacturing, which caters to India's comparative advantage of being a labour-intensive economy, is that participation in assembly operations would ensure that India remains perpetually stuck at the lower end of the production processes. This chapter has, however, clearly illustrated that such concerns are overblown. India can go up the value chain and manufacture some of the parts and components and thereby participate in the higher value-added activities. Moreover, no country has directly become an end-to-end manufacturer without first starting out by undertaking the lower value-added activity of assembling. We have seen in this chapter that participation in GVCs as seller correlates strongly with increase in GDP per capita, especially at levels of GDP per capita that India currently is at and will remain for the next couple of decades. Therefore, learning to walk before running must be critical to India's policy with regard to manufacturing exports and participation in GVCs.

13

DIGITAL BRIDGES

Leveraging Digital Public Infrastructure for Inclusive Growth

Just outside the Indian School of Business (ISB) campus in Hyderabad, a vendor makes delicious coffee and tea in a small, informal set-up. Before I moved to Delhi to work with the GoI, this vendor would accept payments only in cash. He devoted considerable time to finding change to give back to customers who paid ₹100 or ₹50 for a ₹10 coffee or tea. However, when I returned to Hyderabad three years later, I noticed an important change. This vendor was now taking digital payments primarily using Google Pay and Paytm. Since I could converse with him in Telugu, we engaged in a discussion about how his business had changed because of the use of digital payment. The first thing he mentioned was that he does not have to spend time searching for cash to give back to the customer. As he prepares a fresh cup of coffee or tea for the next customer, the individual he just served takes out his/her phone to settle the payment. The speaker device chimes in, notifying everyone that a payment of ₹10 had been successfully made. As a result, he was able to serve his customers without having to make them wait, which also meant that he was serving more customers now by shifting to digital payment. Thus, his productivity and his business had both improved. The other important change happened in the supply chain of this informal set-up. Three years back, the supplier of milk would deliver milk in the morning and come back late evening to collect his payment. Now, the coffee vendor paid the milk supplier digitally, thereby eliminating the need for the supplier's second trip in the evening. This simple example illustrates the enormous transformation that is happening in Indian business, especially in the small and micro firms in the informal sector.

By creating the digital infrastructure as a public good, India is generating enormous opportunities for equitable development.

Typically, due to the significant externalities involved in public goods, the private sector is reluctant to build them, since they are unable to accurately reflect the external effects in their pricing strategies. Even when the private sector provides for or builds such digital goods, these lead to monopolies due to the significant entry barriers created by the upfront investment. As monopolies charge prices that are significantly higher than socially optimal, access becomes restricted, with the poor and the less privileged getting deprived of access to such public goods. Therefore, left to the private sector, such digital infrastructure either does not get created or when it does, the access to the same is not universal. However, by creating the digital infrastructure as public goods, the government has ensured that access to it can be universal. Therefore, in this chapter, I highlight the enormous potential for equitable development that DPI can generate across several sectors of the economy.

Envisioning Tomorrow's Techno Indian

Imagine a common Indian—Raju—in his 60s living the transformative impact of India's DPI in 2040 in Almora, Uttarakhand. In the morning, Raju converses with his daughter Anita, residing in Bengaluru, via a video call. During this call, she shares her frustration in explaining the nuances of a particular technology to her boss John sitting in the San Francisco office of her firm.

Raju reminisces how his father could not provide him access to quality education due to geographical and financial constraints. He feels happy that despite living in Almora, he was able to provide Anita a high-quality education with the help of digital technology and online learning platforms. In his generation, only his peers residing in big cities like Delhi, Mumbai, Bengaluru and Hyderabad could receive such high-quality education. It was because of the quality of her education that Anita was able to secure a well-paying job with a multinational company in Bengaluru.

Raju feels gratified that Anita's high-quality education has not only provided financial stability to their family but also opened up new opportunities for future generations in his family. Seeing his grandson Nishant describe enthusiastically the possibility of life on Mars within a metaverse education world—a platform for education through virtual reality—makes him aware of how India's digital infrastructure has helped shape the learning experiences of the younger generation.

During the video call, Raju mentions that he has been experiencing some pain in his knees over the last few days. Following Anita's insistence, Raju opens an app on his smartphone where he books an appointment with an orthopaedic in Delhi. Through a virtual appointment facilitated by the app, Raju gains timely medical advice. Raju remembers how he could not provide such high-quality healthcare to his father as his remote location made it difficult for him to access proper medical care. However, now the use of digital technology has not only improved his health but also saved him time and money that he would have otherwise spent on travelling to Delhi.

While speaking to the doctor, Raju gets a notification on his phone alerting him to a potential pest infestation in his crop field. He immediately opens his Agri app to speak to a representative from his agriculture advice firm. He is reminded of the times when his father—also a farmer—used to suffer losses due to pest infestations, which his father had no way of predicting or preventing. However, with the use of AI-enabled apps and drones, he is now able to receive real-time information about his crops and take immediate action to protect them. This has not only increased his crop yield but also reduced his dependence on expensive pesticides.

Though this story may seem like science fiction à la Isaac Asimov, India's path-breaking efforts in creating DPI that is accessible to common Indians make this scenario a real possibility. The story illustrates the transformation that can be brought in the lives of common citizens via education, healthcare and agriculture, to name a few. India's DPI can not only provide common Indians like Raju with new opportunities, it can also empower them to overcome the challenges they face due to their economic status or geographical barriers.

The Promise of India's Digital Economy

India has witnessed a significant digital transformation since the launch of PMJDY in 2014, setting a world record for opening about 1.8 crore bank accounts in one week.[64] The triple combination of Jan Dhan, Aadhaar and Mobile, also known as the JAM trinity, has enhanced transparency of DBTs and helped in the timely delivery of financial benefits. A McKinsey survey from March 2019 indicates that small businesses in India lead in accepting digital payments, with 94 per cent of small firms accepting card payments compared to 79 per cent of large firms.

The e-commerce industry report of India Brand Equity Foundation (IBEF) estimates that India is the second-largest online shopping market globally, with around 350 million contributing to a robust $148 billion digital commerce market, leading a tech revolution from a cash-dependent economy to a digital payments powerhouse. India boasts of over 800 million Internet subscribers, 80 per cent financial account penetration and the world's largest instant transfer system, the Unified Payments Interface or the UPI. With a youthful population, by 2030, one in every five consumers under 30 is projected to be from India, and the middle class could double to 800 million people.[65]

The government use of Aadhaar for digital services has positioned India as a global leader in technology-based social inclusion. Digital services show an eightfold surge in average monthly mobile data usage from 2018 to 2022. As per the RBI and the National Payments Corporation of India (NPCI), digital payments in India grew by 550 per cent from 2017 to 2023, reaching 134 billion transactions valued at over $4 trillion. According to the Ministry of Finance, UPI represents 62 per cent of all digital transactions in 2022–23 and is the world's largest instant transfer system.[66]

Major marketplaces like Amazon and Flipkart have embraced UPI, and the government's push for accessibility is seen in UPI 123PAY for

---

[64]Ministry of Finance, GoI, 'Pradhan Mantri Jan Dhan Yojana (PMJDY), Launched by the Prime Minister Shri Narendra Modi on 28th August, 2014, Celebrates its First Anniversary', *Press Information Bureau*, 28 August 2015, http://tinyurl.com/2thxmy7j. Accessed on 22 January 2024.

[65]'E-commerce Industry in India', *India Brand Equity Foundation*, http://tinyurl.com/u3wa2p87. Accessed on 15 February 2024.

[66]Ministry of Finance, GoI, 'UPI Transactions Grew from ₹1 lakh Crore in FY 2017-18 to ₹139 Lakh Crore in FY 2022-23 in Value, at a CAGR of 168%', *Press Information Bureau*, 18 December 2023, http://tinyurl.com/mvjxh4k7. Accessed on 15 February 2024.

feature phones. RuPay, launched by the NPCI, accounts for $10 billion in digital commerce. As per the e-commerce industry report of IBEF, India's digital commerce market is projected to reach $200 billion by 2026, with online retail growing at a 27 per cent CAGR until 2026.[67]

Beyond e-commerce, India's online travel market is set to reach $31 billion by 2025, as estimated by EaseMyTrip.[68] The video streaming market, valued at $3.8 billion, is expected to double by 2027, and the online gaming industry reported a 34 per cent sales increase in 2022, reaching $1.6 billion.[69]

Figures 1–7 depict the evolution of various features of India's digital economy.

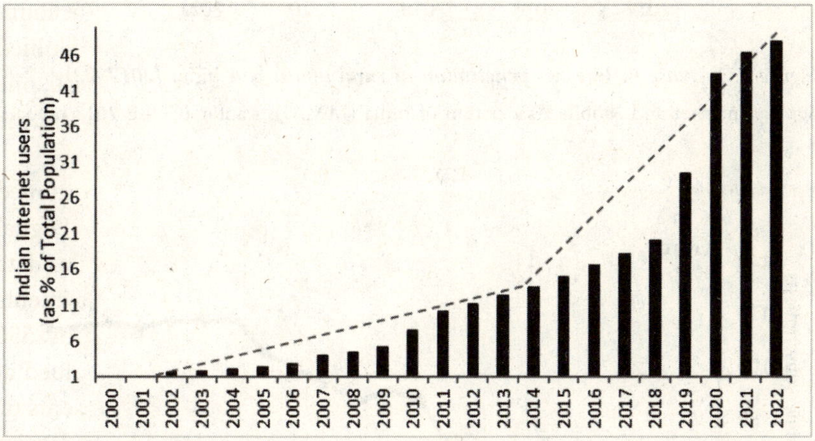

Figure 1: Growth of Internet users in India (2000–22) as % of total population
Source: The World Bank

[67]'E-commerce Industry in India', *India Brand Equity Foundation*, http://tinyurl.com/u3wa2p87. Accessed on 15 February 2024.
[68]EaseMyTrip, *From Humble Beginnings to Global Prominence: 2021-22 Annual Report*, http://tinyurl.com/3fhu2t49. Accessed on 15 February 2024.
[69]'Media and Entertainment Industry', *India Brand Equity Foundation,* http://tinyurl.com/mr4ab6xw. Accessed on 15 February 2024.

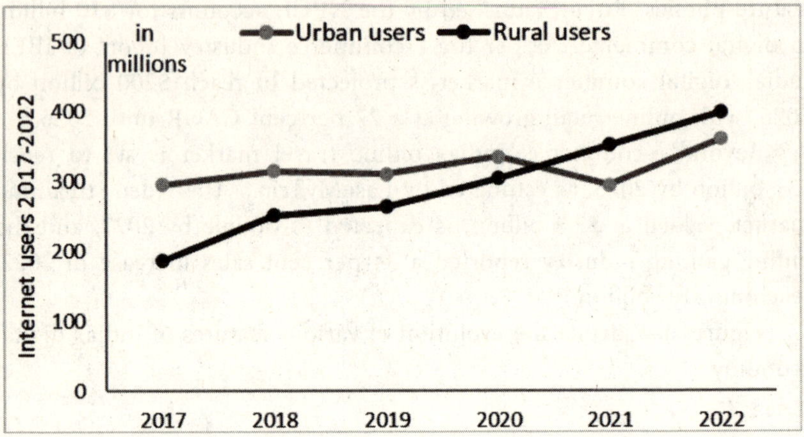

Figure 2: Increase in Internet penetration in rural and urban India (2017–22)

Source: Internet and Mobile Association of India (IAMAI); Kantar ICUBE 2018 report

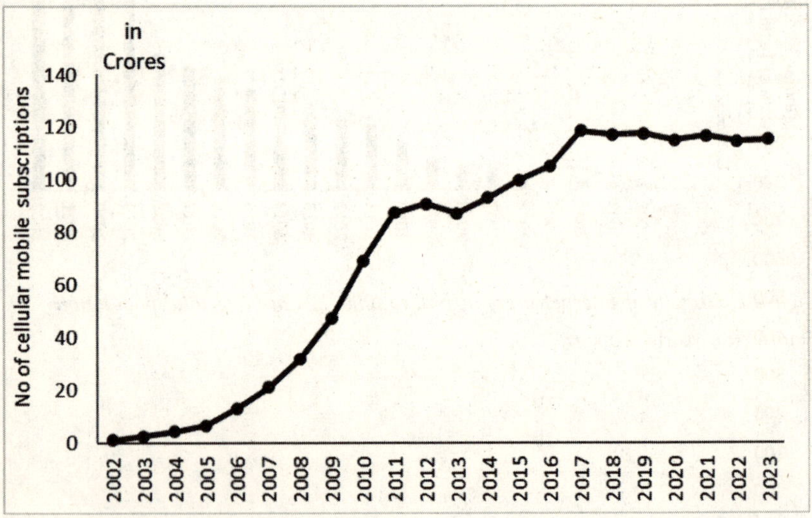

Figure 3: Growth of cellular mobile subscriptions in India (2002–23)

Source: Telecom Regulatory Authority of India (TRAI)

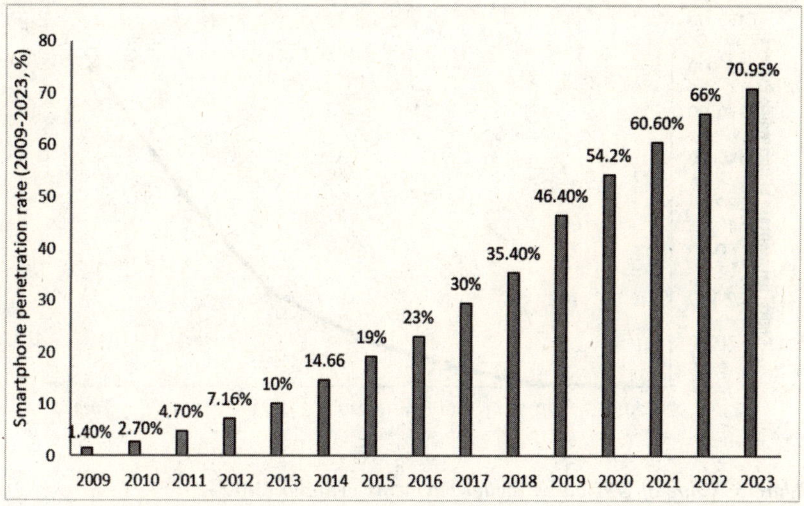

Figure 4: Smartphone penetration rate in India (2009–23)

Source: Statista Survey, 2009–23

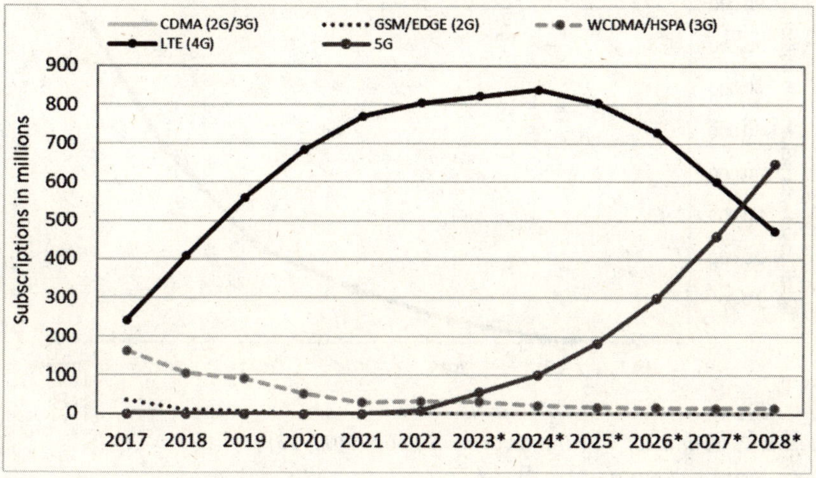

Figure 5: Smartphone subscriptions by technology in India (2017–22); forecasts till 2028

Source: Ericsson survey, 2017–2022, with forecasts from 2023 to 2028

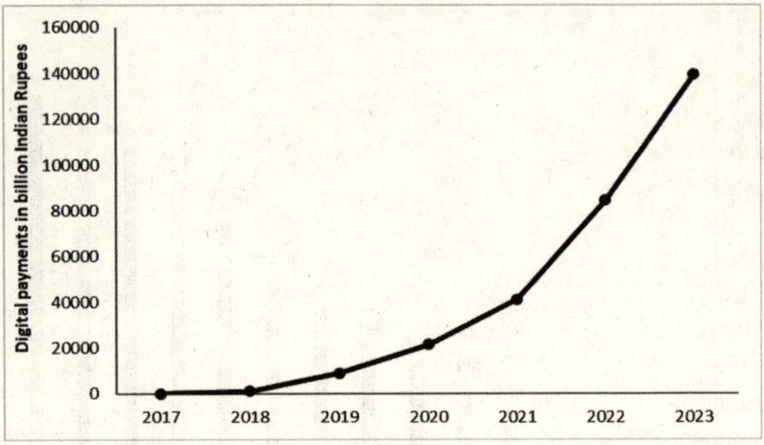

Figure 6: Value of UPI-based digital payments in India (2017–23)
Source: RBI and NPCI

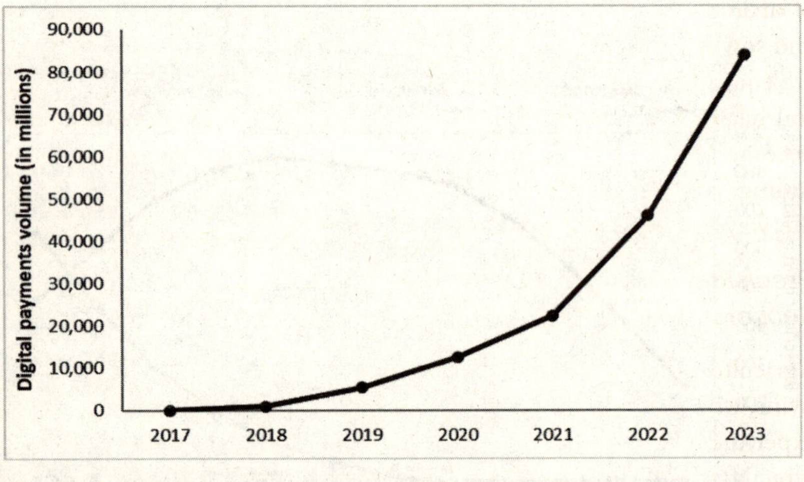

Figure 7: Volume of UPI transactions in India (2017–23)
Source: RBI and NPCI

Benefits of Wrapping DPI onto Agriculture

Digital technology can transform India's agriculture ecosystem in several ways. Online bank accounts can provide the income and spending data that farmers need to qualify for cheaper credit from banks. Digital land-registry records could make crop insurance available to more farmers. Precision agriculture—delivering real-time data to farmers' mobile phones to help them optimize fertilizer, pesticide and other inputs—can increase yields. After harvest, farmers could use variants of online marketplaces for agricultural produce to transact with a larger pool of potential buyers. One such platform, the government's e-National Agriculture Market (e-NAM), is available in several states and shows potential to increase prices realized by farmers.

Transforming Agriculture through Artificial Intelligence of Things

Agriculture can undergo a profound transformation with the integration of artificial intelligence of things (AIoT) technologies. Seed selection and sowing processes are no longer conventional tasks; instead, farmers are equipped with real-time monitoring capabilities for resource usage, soil health and pest developments. Leveraging big data analysis, AIoT becomes the driving force behind optimal crop selection and harvest timing, contributing significantly to overall crop success while paving the way for sustainable agricultural practices.

Precision Farming Unleashed with Digital Twins and Smart Sensors

Agriculture can be improved by deploying smart sensors and digital twins, which is a digital copy of the real-world object that enables virtual experimentation to gain insights into the real-world object without directly affecting it. Digital twins help us in understanding, predicting and improving the performance of the real-world object by leveraging digital technology and data. These technologies can enable precision agriculture, providing farmers with a vivid 3D digital representation of their entire farm. Within these digital landscapes, agronomic models and decision-making algorithms can guide farmers to make informed decisions about crop selection, output, water use and fertilizer access throughout the entire production value chain.

Revolutionizing Post-Harvest and Distribution through AI Analytics

Propelled by AI analytics and linked sensors, real-time intelligence on the movement of agricultural products through value chains can be delivered, effectively addressing supply chain challenges through the implementation of blockchain technology. Digital traceability, certification technology and the seamless integration of machine learning (ML) algorithms with blockchain empower farmers to predict and schedule client orders, offering customers the option of annual purchases for a steady supply of farm products.

Empowering Transparency in Market Linkage and Digital Mandis

The fusion of digital *mandi*s with blockchain and AI technologies elevates transparency in the supply chain, particularly benefitting underserved rural areas. Market linkages empower farmers with essential information about market prices, weather forecasts and pest outbreaks, effectively reducing risks and enhancing overall income. This transparency not only facilitates better access to services, but also ensures decentralized data exchanges and operational transparency through smart contracts, ultimately empowering farmers to make well-informed decisions.

Digital Water Management and Conservation

Digital infrastructure can facilitate smart water management systems to address the growing water scarcity exacerbated by climate change. Evidence from water conservation projects utilizing sensors and Internet of things (IoT) devices indicates that digital technologies can optimize water usage, minimize wastage and ensure access to clean water for vulnerable communities. By integrating digital water management solutions into India's DPI, the country can enhance water efficiency, mitigate the impact of droughts and improve water access for the poor. This evidence-driven strategy aligns with sustainable water practices crucial for climate-resilient communities.

Climate Information Services for Farmers

Providing climate information services through digital platforms can empower farmers to make informed decisions based on weather forecasts and climate patterns, ultimately improving crop yields and livelihoods. Evidence from successful implementations suggests that delivering real-time climate information to farmers enhances their ability to adapt agricultural practices to changing conditions.

Benefits of Wrapping DPI onto Healthcare

India's DPI can usher in a new era of possibilities in healthcare. The convergence of multiple technologies, such as AI, natural language processing (NLP) and robotics, as well as innovative collaborations among diverse stakeholders across the healthcare ecosystem can fundamentally change a patient's journey, resulting in drastically improved health outcomes and a much-enriched patient experience.

Towards More Personalized Healthcare Services

The integration of modern technologies, such as NLP, will enable patients to make better choices by becoming better informed and exhibiting a preference for paths that offer seamless, transparent and frictionless care. Natural language processing can enable barriers in local language to be surmounted, thereby enabling the poor and vulnerable to access doctors that do not speak their local language. Technologies such as sensors, genetic analysis and AI will enhance the early detection of diseases and risk factors, and promote preventive care.

A Transition of Care Delivery: From Hospitals to Home

Telemedicine, remote patient monitoring, home-based healthcare delivery and mobile health apps have been growing at a CAGR of more than 30 per cent since the outbreak of Covid-19. These will continue to gain traction, improving access to healthcare services, particularly in rural and historically underserved areas. Telemedicine facilitates doctor–patient consultations through digital voice or video links, enabling doctors to reach more patients and mitigating the shortage of doctors in rural areas. In trials and pilots, telemedicine has demonstrated a remarkable reduction in consultation costs. If telemedicine were to replace even one-third of in-person outpatient consultations, India could significantly increase care for underserved populations in remote areas. The advent of IoT devices and robotics will further augment the shift of healthcare delivery from hospital to non-hospital settings, such as homes. In a decade, most patient healthcare tasks in India can be performed remotely using telehealth technology rather than a traditional clinical environment; at-home advanced healthcare services may in fact become the accepted norm.

Less Dependence on Hospitals and Doctors

India's DPI enables the creation of digital health records, ensuring that individuals have a comprehensive and accessible medical history. Evidence from initiatives like the National Digital Health Mission (NDHM) indicates that the standardization and interoperability of health records enhance the quality of care by enabling seamless information sharing among healthcare providers.

Aggregating individual patients' comprehensive medical histories into electronic health records (EHRs) empowers healthcare providers to make more accurate diagnoses and reduce the risk of medical errors. Stripped of patient-identifying information, EHRs could further minimize administrative costs and contribute valuable data for medical research. Some hospitals in India are already embracing evidence-based care, utilizing digital platforms to provide doctors and nurses with access to the latest research, complementing their clinical expertise. The Manipal Hospitals chain, for instance, employs IBM Watson for Oncology, a cognitive computing platform, to analyse cancer patients' records and present oncologists with a spectrum of potential diagnoses and personalized treatment options.

The collection of massive amounts of data will aid in the development of algorithms that will help develop AI- and NLP-based decision support tools for physicians. Such tools will reduce physicians' workload and mitigate doctor shortages by supporting their diagnostic tasks with evidence-based recommendations. This will enable patients to receive more prompt, accurate and personalized diagnoses and prescription recommendations remotely.

Wearable devices, another facet of India's digital landscape, have the potential to revolutionize preventive healthcare. Evidence from the global adoption of wearable technology in monitoring health parameters suggests that these devices can play a crucial role in preventing and managing chronic diseases. By encouraging the use of affordable wearable devices and integrating them into healthcare initiatives, India can shift the focus towards preventive care, reducing the burden on the healthcare system and improving health outcomes for the poor and vulnerable.

The proliferation of smartphones, a result of increased digital penetration, opens avenues for mobile health (mHealth) applications that can cater to the specific needs of the poor and vulnerable. Evidence suggests that mHealth applications can provide information, support and even diagnostic services, bringing healthcare closer to individuals who might otherwise face barriers to access. By promoting the development and use of mHealth applications, India can empower the underserved with valuable healthcare resources at their fingertips.

Revolutionize Surgery and Reduce Training Time

Advancements in highly sensitive miniaturized sensors and robotics, combined with ML and AI methodologies, will simplify even the most complex surgeries and significantly reduce the time required to train doctors, mitigate patient risk and improve surgical outcomes.

Benefits of Wrapping DPI onto Education

Digital infrastructure, a cornerstone of India's DPI, plays a pivotal role in expanding access to education. Evidence from initiatives like the National Digital Education Architecture (NDEAR) indicates that digital platforms and inclusive learning management systems can democratize education, ensuring that even the poor have access to quality learning resources. By fostering the development of inclusive learning platforms, India can provide equal educational opportunities to the poor and vulnerable.

Virtual Reality and Augmented Reality

The widespread integration of virtual reality (VR) and augmented reality (AR) in education has revolutionized the traditional learning experience. These immersive technologies transport students to simulated environments, enabling experiential and interactive learning. From virtual field trips to complex scientific simulations, VR and AR enhance understanding by providing dynamic 3D perspectives that traditional methods cannot replicate.

Microlearning and Nano Learning

The advent of microlearning and nano learning modules addresses the evolving needs of modern learners. These bite-sized, easily digestible pieces of information cater to short attention spans and enable a continuous learning culture. By breaking down complex concepts into manageable segments, microlearning ensures that students can absorb and retain information more effectively, promoting a more efficient and flexible educational experience.

Collaborative and Team-Based Learning Approach

Digital platforms facilitate collaborative and team-based learning, encouraging students to engage in interactive discussions, joint projects and shared knowledge creation. This approach not only enhances critical thinking and problem-solving skills but also nurtures effective communication and collaboration, thus preparing students for a collaborative work environment in their future careers.

Holistic Approach to Cognitive, Emotional and Social Skills

Digital technology in education is adopting a holistic approach, emphasizing the development of cognitive, emotional and social skills. Beyond academic knowledge, educators recognize the importance of nurturing emotional intelligence, critical thinking and social awareness. This holistic perspective aims to equip students with a well-rounded skill set essential for success in both personal and professional spheres.

Mobile Learning and Learning Analytics

Mobile learning has transformed education, offering flexibility and accessibility. Students can access educational content anytime, anywhere, using their mobile devices. Learning analytics complement this by providing data-driven insights into student performance and engagement. Educators use this information to tailor teaching strategies, ensuring a personalized learning experience that meets individual needs.

Gamification of Learning

The incorporation of gamification techniques into educational platforms introduces an element of fun and competition. By transforming the process of learning into a game-like experience, students are motivated to actively participate, complete challenges and achieve milestones. Gamification not only enhances engagement but also fosters a sense of accomplishment, making the learning process more enjoyable and rewarding.

Algorithms and ML for Hyper-Personalized Learning Experiences

Machine learning algorithms are deployed to deliver hyper-personalized learning experiences. These technologies analyse individual learning patterns, preferences and performance data to tailor content, pacing and assessments to each student's unique needs. The result is an adaptive and responsive educational ecosystem that maximizes the effectiveness of the learning journey. Evidence from adaptive learning platforms suggests that tailoring educational content to individual needs and learning styles improves comprehension and retention, benefiting students with diverse learning abilities, including those from underprivileged backgrounds.

Online Educational Resources and e-Libraries

The proliferation of online educational resources within India's DPI framework enhances the availability of learning materials. Evidence suggests that the digitization of textbooks, creation of e-libraries and development of open educational resources contribute significantly to resource accessibility for the economically marginalized. By expanding the digitization of educational content, India can ensure that the poor have access to a wealth of learning materials, reducing the burden of acquiring expensive textbooks.

Equitable Credit Creation Using Account Aggregator and Open Credit Enablement Network

The Account Aggregator (AA) framework is a significant component of India's DPI aimed at transforming the financial data ecosystem. The key aspects are as follows:

i. User consent: AAs facilitate the secure sharing of financial data with user consent. Individuals have control over their financial information and can selectively share it with financial institutions, enabling a more informed and personalized financial experience.
ii. Centralized platform: AAs act as intermediaries, providing a centralized technology platform that connects various financial information providers, such as banks, mutual funds, insurance companies, etc. This consolidation allows users to access their financial data from different sources in one place.
iii. Streamline credit decisions: The AA framework streamlines the credit-decision process. With user consent, lenders can access a comprehensive view of an individual's financial data, leading to more accurate and efficient credit assessments. This benefits both borrowers and lenders in the credit ecosystem.
iv. Encourage innovation: AAs encourage innovation by fostering the integration of financial technology or FinTech services. Startups and financial institutions can leverage the AA framework to create new and innovative financial products and services that rely on access to individual financial data.
v. Data privacy and security: AAs ensure secure data exchange through standardized protocols and encryption. This prioritizes user privacy and protects sensitive financial information, adhering to regulatory standards for data security.
vi. Financial inclusion: AAs contribute to financial inclusion by providing a more comprehensive and accessible financial profile. This is particularly beneficial for individuals with limited credit history, enabling them to access a broader range of financial services.
vii. Regulatory oversight: The AA framework operates within a robust regulatory framework set by the RBI and other financial regulators. This ensures that data sharing is governed by strict guidelines, fostering trust among users and financial institutions.

Using the AA framework, the Open Credit Enablement Network (OCEN) has been launched as a set of protocols and standards to enable credit providers to access and analyse the financial data shared through the AA framework. The network enables formal credit flow to the most vulnerable segments, especially particularly small businesses. It also helps financial institutions to reach large segments easily by lowering their distribution costs.

The FinTech space in India has started utilizing the AA framework to become one of the fastest growing FinTech markets with more than 2,100 FinTechs. By incorporating OCEN and leveraging the existing digital ecosystem, these platforms become ideal for channelling credit to the underserved through innovative embedded finance solutions. Small and medium-sized firms have also rapidly adopted FinTech solutions whether for credit, payments, accounting, or tax filing.

Carebnb Using Digital Technologies

India should invest heavily in the care sector, focussing on childcare and eldercare centres, as it can offer solutions for women seeking to pursue careers while creating millions of new jobs. Professionalizing the sector, implementing industry-wide accredited training and setting professional standards are essential for building trust and transforming the caregiving market. However, as the adoption of childcare services in India is low due to the guilt associated with outsourcing care, technology can play a crucial role in addressing this concern.

Start-Ups for Elderly and Child Care

Technology-driven platforms like Bumo and Bambino aim to make hiring caregivers as convenient as hailing an Uber. Startups like MyVillage use technology to match parents with caregivers and handle administrative tasks, transforming the day-care industry. Childcare tech entrepreneurs offer home-based caregivers assistance with tasks like payroll, marketing, billing and scheduling. They provide curricula, training webinars, mentorship and search portals to match parents and local providers.

Smart Cameras and Monitoring Systems

Smart cameras and monitoring systems installed in care facilities and homes can enable the parent or family member to observe the caregiver's interactions with children or seniors at random. These systems may include features such as video streaming, recording and remote access, allowing family members or supervisors to monitor care activities. Global Positioning System (GPS) tracking devices are often used in elder care to monitor the movements and whereabouts of seniors. This ensures that caregivers can locate seniors in case of emergencies and provides family members peace of mind regarding their loved ones' safety.

Time and Attendance Tracking Systems

Caregivers may use electronic time and attendance tracking systems, often integrated with biometric or electronic identification methods, to record their work hours accurately. This helps ensure that caregivers are present during scheduled hours and provides a transparent record of their activities. In some cases, biometric monitoring systems may be used to track caregivers' physical presence and activities during their shifts. This technology aims to ensure that caregivers adhere to their responsibilities and duties.

Electronic Medication Dispensers, Smart Sensors and Wearables

For elder care, electronic medication dispensers with monitoring capabilities can track whether seniors are taking their medications as prescribed. These devices often send alerts to caregivers or family members if doses are missed. Sensors placed in the living environment or wearable devices can monitor the daily activities and health metrics of seniors. This includes detecting movements, sleep patterns and vital signs, providing valuable data to assess the well-being of the elderly.

Digital Communication Platforms

Caregivers and family members may use digital communication platforms to share updates, photos and other information. These platforms allow for real-time communication and contribute to the overall transparency of care provision.

Electronic Care-Planning Software

Caregivers can use electronic care-planning software to document and track the care provided to individuals. This includes logging activities,

Table 1

Illustration of market failure perspective to evolve technological solutions

Problem	*What is the 'market failure'?*	*Tech-based solution*	*Examples*
Skilling	Information asymmetry and externalities create a gap between the skills demanded by the job market and those possessed by the workforce.	Develop online skill assessment and training platforms that identify the skills in demand and provide personalized training.	Coursera, Udacity, upGrad, Simplilearn
Adequate credit to SMEs, MSMEs and poor individuals	Information asymmetry and collateral constraints make it challenging for lenders to assess the creditworthiness of small businesses and individuals.	See heading 'Equitable Credit Creation Using AA and OCEN'.	Lendingkart, Capital Float, Kiva
Agriculture productivity	Information asymmetry, lack of access to markets and externalities in agriculture impede efficient resource allocation and productivity.	See heading 'Benefits of Wrapping DPI onto Agriculture'	AgroStar, Farmcrowdy, WeFarm
Pollution	Negative externalities from pollution are often not internalized by polluters, leading to inefficient resource use.	Implement smart-city technologies, IoT-based pollution monitoring and emissions trading systems.	Chakr Innovation measures air pollution by capturing and converting it into ink and paint. Globally, cities like Singapore utilize smart-city technologies and congestion pricing, with companies like Plume Labs providing air quality data to the public through mobile apps.

Source: Author's design

meals, medication administration and other relevant information, creating a comprehensive record. Caregivers may use digital checklists and reporting tools to document daily tasks and activities. Supervisors or family members can review these digital reports to assess whether proper care procedures are being followed.

A 'Market Failure' Prism for Tech-Based Solutions

In the previous sections, I have outlined technological solutions to the important problems that India faces. In general, many of India's problems can benefit when they are analysed from a 'market failure' perspective, i.e., why is it that a market-based solution has not evolved for the problem? Such an analysis can help to evolve technological solutions that address the identified market failures. Table 1 illustrates this using some examples.

India has become the undisputed leader in developing DPI that can be availed by every Indian. Instead of the private sector developing this infrastructure, which would have restricted access, the sovereign has created this infrastructure to ensure that every Indian has access to it. This positions India uniquely to benefit from this critical infrastructure in multiple areas that can help the poor and the vulnerable gain economic and social mobility: education, healthcare, agriculture, elderly and child care that can in turn further participation of females in the labour force, as well as credit provision for the hitherto unbanked. Fully utilizing the public digital infrastructure will, therefore, be a critical component of India@100's odyssey to inclusive and sustained economic progress.

14

THE UNFAIR CLIMATE DIVIDE

Wealthy Nations' Actions, Developing Economies' Burden

On 5 December 2023, following news reports of the devastating floods in Chennai, as I checked the well-being of my close relatives, the following WhatsApp conversation with my cousin left me very worried.

Kumar, thaks for checking. It is devastating. Worse than 2015 6.55 am

Water everywhere 6.55 am

Mobile network is on and off 6.55 am

We are struggling for basic necessities 6.57 am

If my cousin living in one of the posh townships in Chennai was facing such difficulties, I shuddered at the thought of the plight of the poor and vulnerable in Chennai and Tamil Nadu. In the past five years, Chennai had experienced devastation of varying magnitudes: in 2015 from the devastating floods, 2016 from Cyclone Vardah, 2021 from floods again, 2022 from Cyclone Mandous and 2023 from Cyclone Michaung. With 1,000 mm of rainfall in just four weeks in 2023, these rains were the worst since the 2015 floods when it poured for 22 out of 30 days in December, setting a record of 1,049 mm. Even three days after Cyclone Michaung had moved away, parts of Chennai still did not have power or mobile signals, and water lay stagnant inside and outside homes.

The disquieting reality that such chaos and human suffering reveals is symptomatic of climate change. However, the narrative on climate change—one that you will rarely hear from writers based in advanced economies—is one of profound injustice. It is a tale where the cumulative actions of the affluent nations are inscribed in the very fabric of our planet, yet it is the developing ones like India that bear the burden. This chapter delves into the history of degradation of our planet: the wealthy nations, who have cumulatively emitted the most greenhouse gases (GHGs), continue to be shielded from the true cost of their actions, while developing ones like India shoulder the consequences. The chapter, therefore, underscores the urgency for transformative policies, international cooperation and a recalibration of responsibilities.

Natural Disasters and Their Macroeconomic Impact in India

As Figure 1 shows, the frequency and intensity of natural disasters, proxied using the human lives that are impacted and the total damages caused, have increased sharply in India.

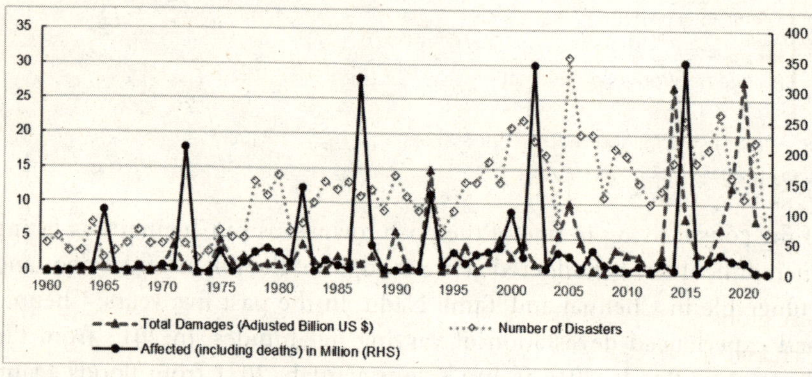

Figure 1: Trends in damages from natural disasters for India (1960–2022)

Source: Author's calculations using data from EM-DAT, The International Disaster Database

As seen in Figure 2, during 2000–22, India experienced 383 disasters that claimed 88,000 lives and affected 1.11 billion people. The resulting cumulative economic loss amounted to $136 billion. Compared to the previous two decades (1980–99), the number of disasters and economic losses increased by 72 per cent and 177 per cent, respectively, during the last three decades (2000–22).

While the average impact of each natural disaster on number of deaths and total affected has decreased significantly in India over the last two decades when compared to the previous three decades, the economic impact per disaster has increased significantly. The number of deaths per disaster decreased from 367 in 1980–99 to 230 in 2000–22; total affected people also recorded a decline from 4.07 million to 2.9 million per disaster. However, the economic losses per disaster grew sharply, indicating a growth of 61 per cent from 0.22 billion in 1990–99 to 0.36 billion in 2000–22.

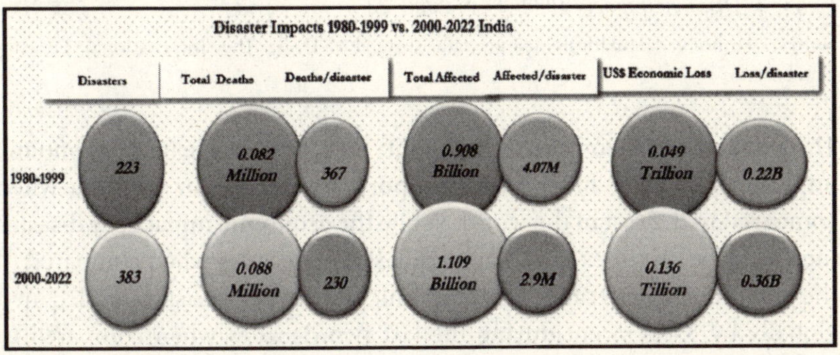

Figure 2: Impact of disasters in India: 1980–99 versus 2000–22

Source: Author's calculations using data from EM-DAT, The International Disaster Database

A global comparison can help to highlight how the risks from climate change have impacted India differentially. Globally, 9,399 disasters were recorded during the period 2000–22, claiming 1.39 million lives and affecting 4.37 billion. In total, these disasters resulted in economic losses of $3.59 trillion. These statistics illustrate a sharp rise as compared to the figures of the previous 20 years, i.e., 1980–99. The number of disasters and economic losses rose by 123 per cent and 50 per cent, respectively, during the last two decades (2000–22) when compared to the previous two decades (1980–99).

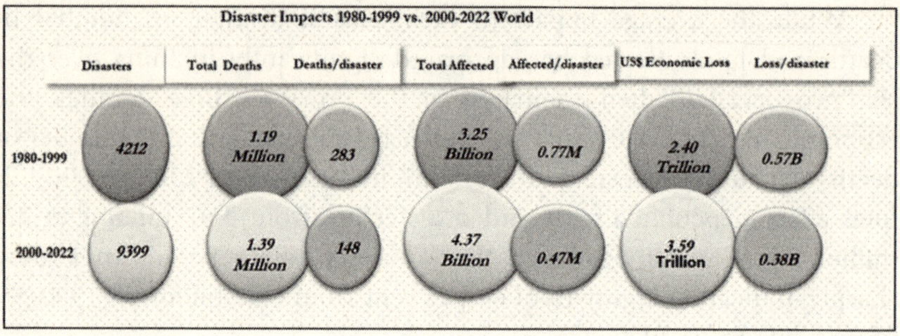

Figure 3: Disaster impacts 1980–99 vs 2000–22 in the world

Source: Author's calculations using data from EM-DAT, The International Disaster Database

The global comparison clearly highlights that the increase in the economic impact per disaster has been disproportionately greater in India when compared to the rest of the world. While the economic impact per disaster increased by 1.6 times in India in the last two decades when compared to the previous three decades, the economic impact per disaster has declined globally by 33 per cent during the last two decades when compared to the previous three decades.

Disasters and Climate Change: An Innate Connection

In recent years, climate change has contributed to the notable rise in the frequency and intensity of natural disasters. The Intergovernmental Panel on Climate Change (IPCC) in 2014 postulated three reasons for disasters caused by climate change. First, GHG emissions alter atmospheric GHG concentrations, thereby impacting temperature and precipitation levels. Starting from 1983, the three decades were the warmest in the past 1,400 years in areas of northern Greenland, alongside shrinking of worldwide glaciers and loss of mass of Antarctic ice sheets. These have led to rising sea levels, earth's warming atmosphere and oceans, and diminishing snow and ice. Second, these changes in turn affect the frequency and intensity of climate-related hazards. Third, this frequency then impacts the risk of natural disasters.

Innumerable studies have been conducted to establish the linkages between human-induced climate change and severe climatic events.

Anderson and Bausch (2006) forecast that a doubling of atmospheric CO_2 concentrations will result in a tripling of the number of Category 5 storms. Grinsted (2013) predicts that for every 1°C rise in global temperature, there will be a two to seven times increase in the frequency

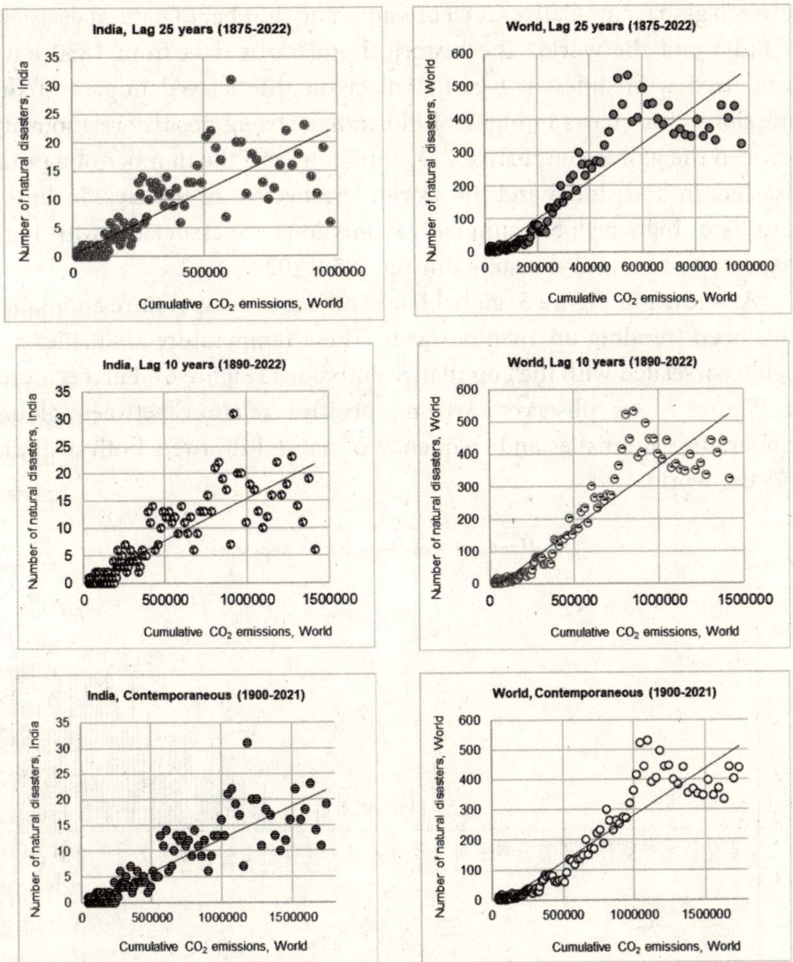

Figure 4: Correlation between global cumulative CO_2 emissions and natural disasters in India and world (1850–2022) with different lags

Source: Emissions data from Our World in Data based on Global Carbon Project (GCP); United Nations World Population Prospects (UNWPP); and disasters data from EM-DAT: The International Disaster Database of disasters similar to the magnitude of Hurricane Katrina. Webster et al. (2005) analyse global hurricane data to predict doubling of the frequency of Category 4–5 hurricanes, from 50 every five years in 1970 to approximately 90 every five years in 2000s.

Here, I establish a similar relationship by studying the correlations between global cumulative CO_2 emissions and number of natural disasters in India and the world. The historical emissions data from 1850 have been used with different lags to reflect on the delayed impact of the emissions. The charts in Figure 4 illustrate a strong positive relationship between the global cumulative CO_2 emissions and the number of natural disasters in both India and the world, irrespective of the lags. In India, periods of higher global cumulative emissions are associated with high frequency of natural disasters during 1850–2022.

As shown in Figure 5, global land and ocean temperature anomalies have been trending up 1880 onwards. These temperature anomalies are highly correlated with the cumulative emissions (Figure 6). Furthermore, in Figure 7, we observe a strong positive relation between global temperature anomalies and frequency of natural disasters both in India and the world.

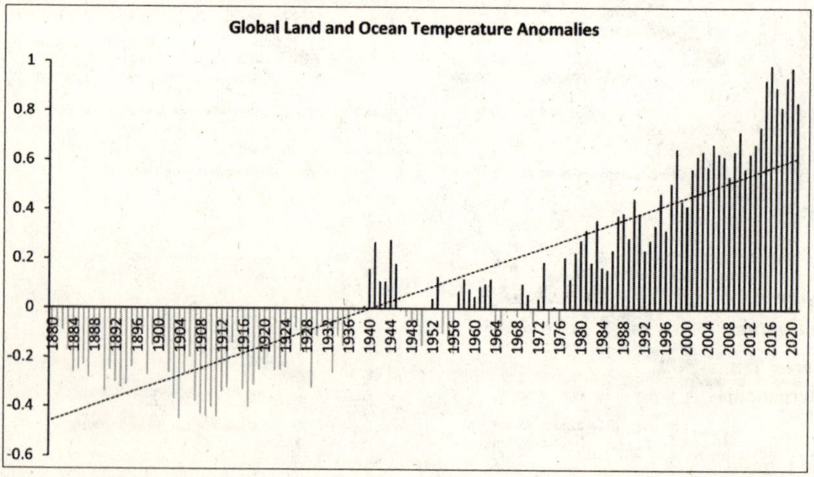

Figure 5: Global land and ocean temperature anomalies (1880–2021)

Source: National Oceanic and Atmospheric Administration (NOAA); Earth System Research Laboratories (ESRL)

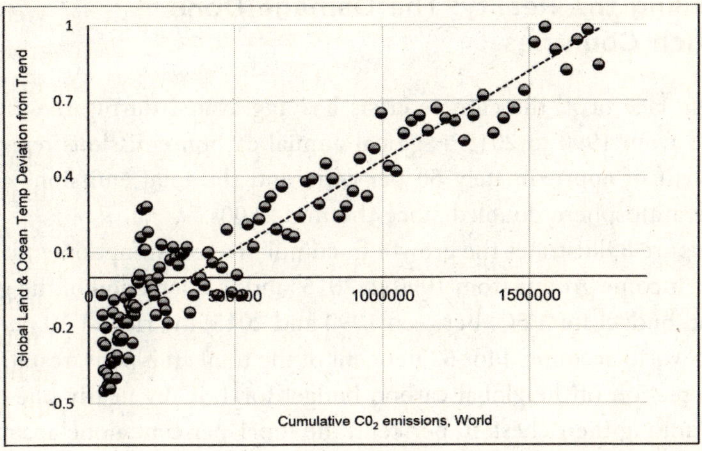

Figure 6: Correlations between global cumulative CO_2 emissions and global land and ocean temperature deviation from trend (1900–2022)

Source: Temperature anomalies data from National Centers for Environmental Information (NCEI); emissions data from Our World in Data based on GCP; UNWPP

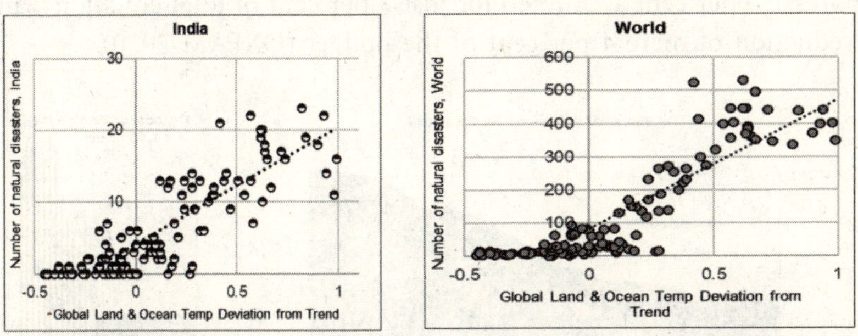

Figure 7: Correlations between global land and ocean temperature deviation from trend and natural disasters in India and the world

Source: Temperature anomalies data from NCEI and disasters data from EM-DAT: The International Disaster Database

As I have already established, the advanced economies, particularly the rich in those economies, are responsible for majority of the cumulative emissions. I now reveal suggestive evidence in the following section that India is suffering immensely due to the climate-change sins committed by the developed economies.

Unveiling the Reality: The Damage Done by Rich Countries

On the face of it, the climate crisis has aggravated during the 25-year period from 1990 to 2015 as global annual carbon emissions registered a growth of approximately 60 per cent, and the total emissions added to the atmosphere doubled since the mid-1800s.

Figure 8 illustrates the growth in cumulative consumption emissions across income groups from 1990 to 2015, and the depletion of the global carbon budget for 1.5C. Between 1990 and 2015, the richest 10 per cent in the world accounted for 52 per cent of the total emissions, resulting in the depletion of the global carbon budget for 1.5C by nearly one-third. Even among the richest 10 per cent, the top 1 per cent alone accounted for over 15 per cent of the total emissions, reducing 9 per cent of the carbon budget. Thus, the richest 1 per cent reduced the carbon budget by more than twice that of the poorest 50 per cent in the world. The middle 40 per cent of the world population accounted for 41 per cent of the total emissions, and 25 per cent of the carbon budget, while the poorest 50 per cent accounted for just 7 per cent of total emissions, and a reduction of mere 4 per cent of the budget (OXFAM 2020).

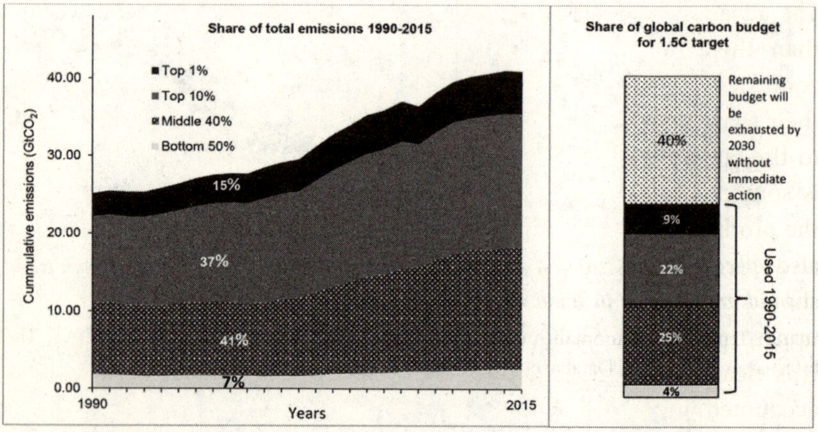

Figure 8: Share of total emissions from 1990 to 2015 and use of the global carbon budget for 1.5C linked to consumption by different global income groups

Source: Emissions Inequality Dashboard, Stockholm Environment Institute (SEI)

Figure 9, which illustrates the consumption emissions for each ventile (income) class, shows in an even more striking manner that the disproportionate impact of the world's richest people on climate change is indisputable.

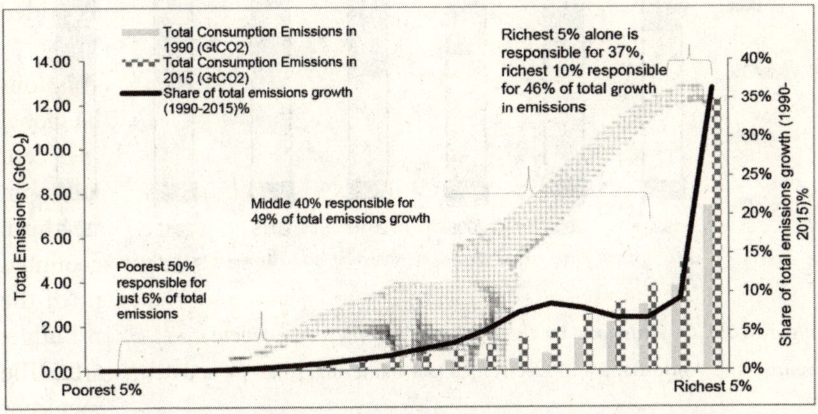

Figure 9: The 'dinosaur graph' of unequal carbon emissions growth, 1990–2015
Source: Emissions Inequality Dashboard, SEI

The advanced nations have contributed far more to the stock of GHGs than their poorer counterparts. Figure 10 shows that high-income countries contributed about half of all emissions till 2005. Although their share has reduced to 33.5 per cent as of 2019, this is primarily due to the fact that a significant portion of consumption in these countries is sourced from upper middle-income countries. Thus, by outsourcing the production of goods consumed by high-income countries, they have also effectively transferred a portion of their GHG emissions. So, we should examine the cumulation of emissions by the high-income and the upper middle-income countries to understand the unfair climate divide. It is clear that even in 2019, 82.5 per cent of cumulative emissions are accounted for by this group of countries.

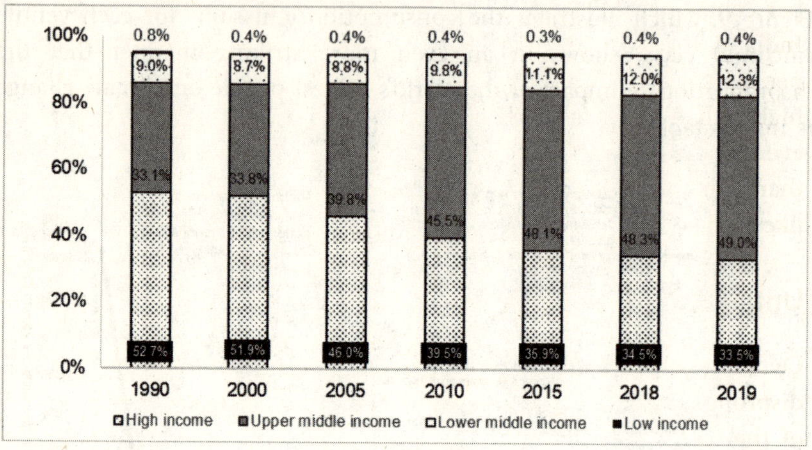

Figure 10: CO_2 emissions by the level of economic development

Source: The World Bank and Electronic Data Gathering, Analysis, and Retrieval (EDGAR)

Similarly, average per capita emissions by level of development clearly illustrate that the historic trend of emissions for high-income countries has been far greater than developing countries. Canada (15.69 per cent), United States (15.52 per cent), South Korea (13.56 per cent), Russia (12.54

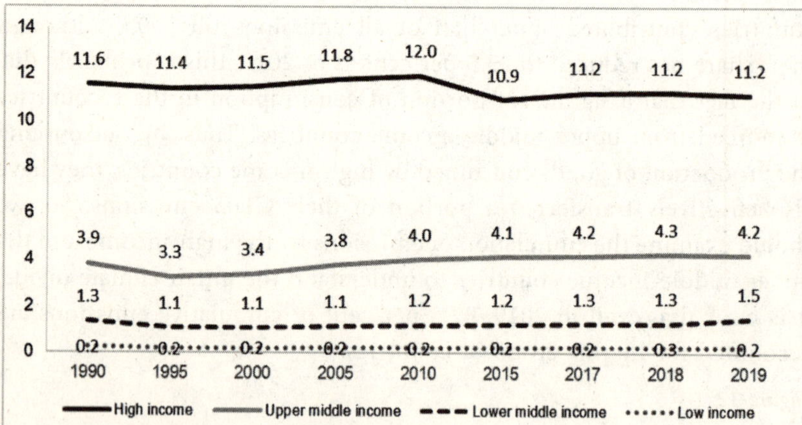

Figure 11: Per capita CO_2 emissions by the level of development

Source: The World Bank and EDGAR

per cent), Japan (9.09 per cent) and China (8.12 per cent) far outpace India (1.9 per cent) in per capita CO_2 emissions. Figure 11 shows that per capita emissions by high-income countries are an order of magnitude higher than those by lower middle-income countries like India. In fact, even in upper middle-income countries, per capita emissions are more than three times higher than those in lower middle-income countries like India.

Unfair Burden on the Poor

Over the last two decades, the impact of climate-induced disasters is disproportionately borne by the Asian continent. Eighty-three per cent of the total affected and 58 per cent of the total deaths from natural disasters are borne by the Asian continent, as 39 per cent of the natural disasters—the maximum for any continent—occur here. This results in 41 per cent of the global economic loss from natural disasters manifesting in Asia (Figures 12–14).

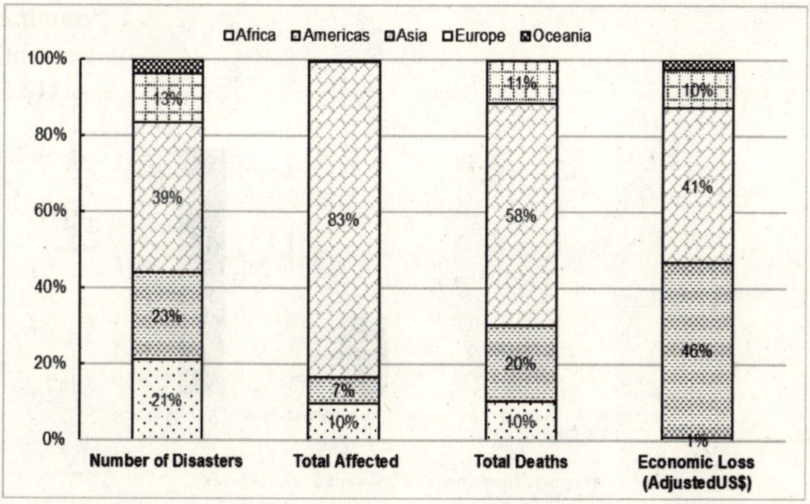

Figure 12: Disaster impacts across different regions of the world groups, 2000–22

Source: Author's calculations using data from EM-DAT, The International Disaster Database

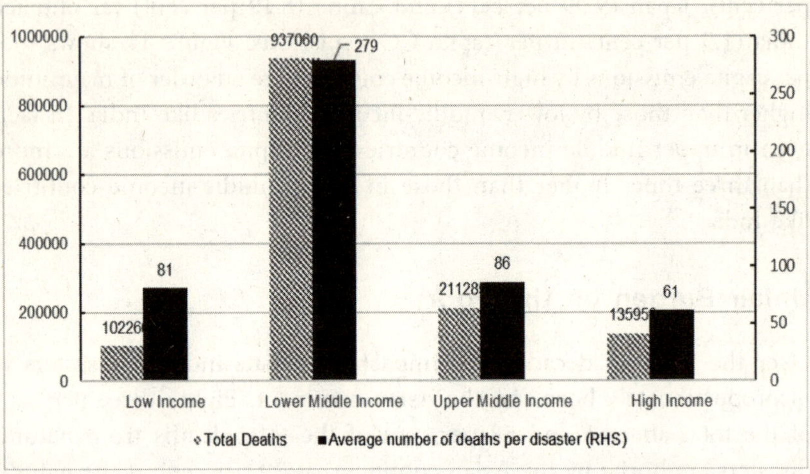

Figure 13: Total numbers of deaths compared to the average number of deaths per disaster by income group (2000–12)

Source: Author's calculations using data from EM-DAT, The International Disaster Database

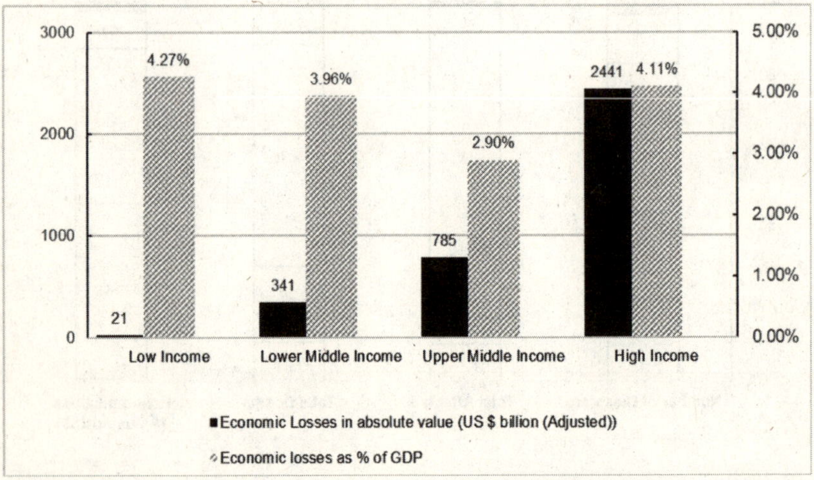

Figure 14: Economic losses in absolute value (US$) compared to losses as percentage of GDP by income group

Source: Author's calculations using data from EM-DAT, The International Disaster Database

Developed nations are better endowed and equipped to absorb the economic concussions of natural disasters because of better disaster-resilient infrastructure, disaster risk financing mechanisms, effective pre-disaster preparedness, public policy and proactive private support for disaster risk reduction. These capacities allow them to be more resilient and less vulnerable towards the adverse consequences of natural disasters. Largely, these capacities are either absent or limited in developing nations.

In contrast, climate change poses a double whammy for lower middle-income countries like India. Being in Asia, they bear the brunt of the disasters caused by climate change. But, more importantly, even within India, it is the poor who suffer the maximum damage from such disasters (Figure 15).

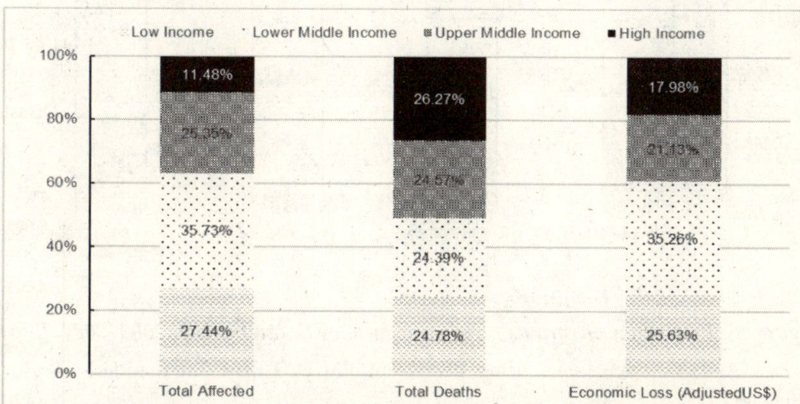

Figure 15: Disaster impact across different income groups, India 2000–2022

Source: Author's calculations using data from EM-DAT, The International Disaster Database

Impact by Type of Disasters

In India, hydrological disasters account for the bulk of disaster events (60 per cent) and economic losses (62 per cent), making them the costliest disasters (Figure 16). While the climatological disasters account for the highest percentage of people affected (62 per cent), geophysical disasters account for the maximum deaths (44 per cent), making them the most fatal. The high incidence of hydrological disasters is attributed to the retreat of Himalayan glaciers due to global warming. For example, the East Rathong glacier retreated by about 15 m per year during 1962–2011, while the Gangotri glacier retreated by about 20 m per year during 1965–2006. There has also been a reduction in the net area of Indian glaciers over the past four to five decades. For example, the East Rathong glacier in the eastern Himalayas lost 15 per cent of the total glacierized area during 1962–2011 (Agrawal 2013).

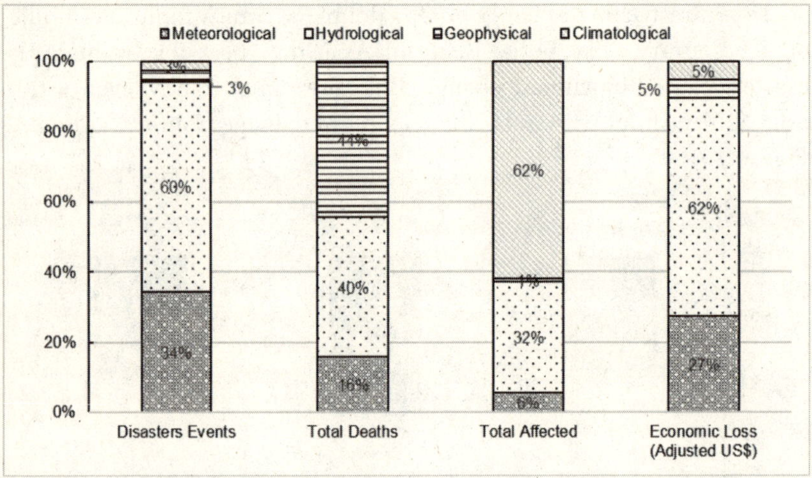

Figure 16: Proportion of various types of impacts by disaster group, 2000–2022, India

Source: Author's calculations using data from EM-DAT, The International Disaster Database

Among all the natural disasters in India, floods account for the maximum number of disaster events (49.3 per cent) and are the costliest, accounting for 62.3 per cent of the total economic losses (Figure 17). However, the most fatal disaster is earthquake accounting for 43.2 per cent of mortalities. Droughts affect the maximum percentage of people (62 per cent).

Droughts and floods account for the maximum share of climate-induced disasters both in India and the world, with droughts accounting for a much greater proportion in India than the world (Figure 18). Earthquakes were the deadliest form of natural disasters, accounting

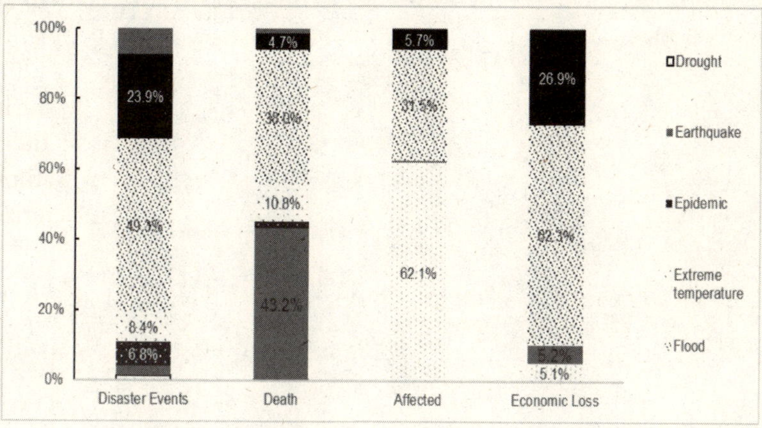

Figure 17: Disaster impact by category, India (2000–2022)
Source: Author's calculations using data from EM-DAT, The International Disaster Database

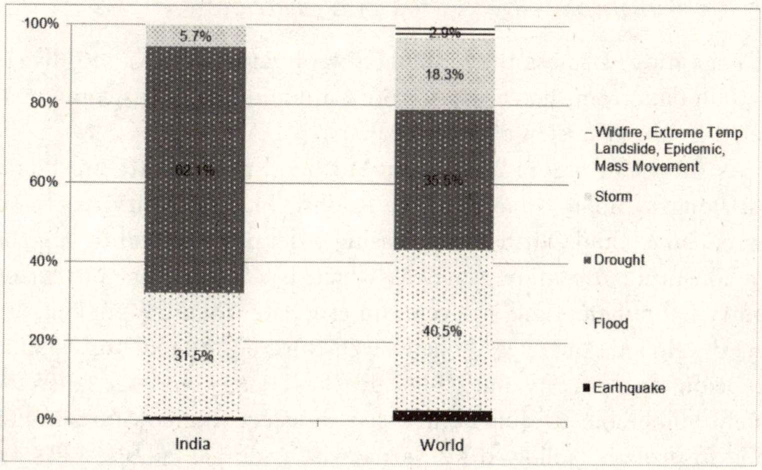

Figure 18: Percentage affected by disaster type, 2000–22
Source: Author's calculations using data from EM-DAT, The International Disaster Database

for 52 per cent and 43 per cent of the total deaths in the world and India, respectively (Figure 19). Floods accounted for 38 per cent of the total deaths in India, but only 8.8 per cent in the world.

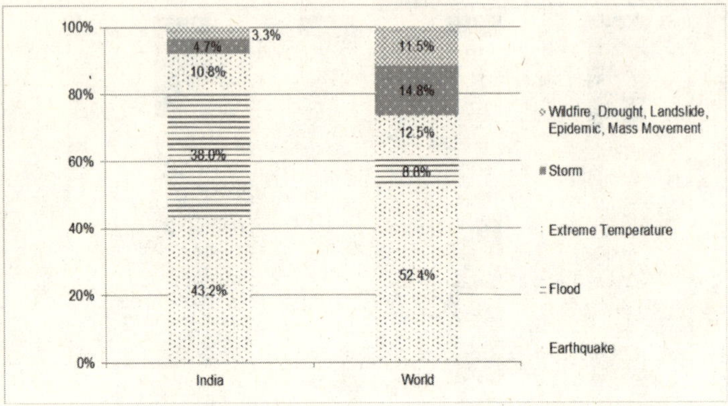

Figure 19: Percentage deaths by disaster type, 2000–2022

Source: Author's calculations using data from EM-DAT, The International Disaster Database

Variation in Impact by States and Districts

In this section, I assess the vulnerability of various states and districts based on data from the Disaster Score Card and its various components created by the Ministry of Home Affairs (MHA), GoI.

As shown in Figure 20, the top ten flood-prone states are Punjab, West Bengal, Bihar, Uttar Pradesh, Andhra Pradesh, Haryana, Kerala, Assam, Gujarat and Odisha in decreasing order of vulnerability. Together, they constitute 700 million people, which is ~51 per cent of the total country's population and is several times greater than the population of some developed countries altogether. Of this 700 million, 163.8 million live below the poverty line (BPL) in these states and are, therefore, acutely vulnerable to climate-induced disasters. Maharashtra is most prone to drought, followed by Karnataka, Andhra Pradesh, Rajasthan, Jharkhand and Telangana, in that order. Maharashtra, Gujarat, Assam, Madhya Pradesh, Karnataka, Chhattisgarh, Bihar, West Bengal, Haryana and Rajasthan are the most vulnerable to climate-induced shocks to agriculture and livestock production. In terms of food security, climate change may lead to loss of 4–5 million tons in wheat production with every rise of 1°C temperature throughout the growing period even after considering carbon fertilization. This translates to about 3.5–4.5 per cent of the current wheat production. Losses for other crops are still uncertain but are expected to be smaller, especially for kharif crops (*Press Information Bureau* 2016–17).

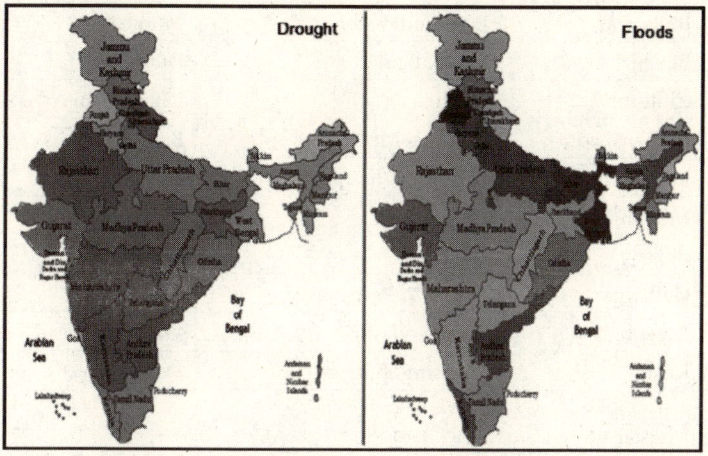

Figure 20: Geographical analysis of disasters and indexes

Source: Disaster Score Card, MHA, GoI; author's calculations

The 20 districts that are most vulnerable to natural disasters, such as drought, cyclones and floods, are shown in Table 1.

Table 1
Exposure of Indian districts to natural disasters (drought, cyclones, floods) in India, 2021

#	*Drought-exposed*	*Cyclone-exposed*	*Flood-exposed*
1	Rajkot	Nayagarh	Darbhanga
2	Anantapur	Puri	Madhubani
3	Aurangabad	Khordha	Samastipur
4	Barmer	Chennai	Nayagarh
5	Churu	Baleswar	Puri
6	Jaisalmer	Bhadrak	Chennai
7	Jodhpur	Cuttack	West Tripura
8	Nagaur	Gajapati	Dhemaji
9	Ahmednagar	Ganjam	Dhubri

#	*Drought-exposed*	*Cyclone-exposed*	*Flood-exposed*
10	Ajmer	Sri Potti Sriramulu Nellore	Khordha
11	Bhilwara	East Godavari	Mumbai
12	Bijapur	Srikakulam	Dibrugarh
13	Chittoor	Krishna	Lakhimpur
14	Osmanabad	Paschim Medinipur	Barpeta
15	Rajsamand	Guntur	Golaghat
16	Udaipur	Imphal East	Nagaon
17	Bidar	Jamnagar	Sheohar
18	Gulbarga	North 24 Parganas	Sitamarhi
19	Jalgaon	West Godavari	West Godavari
20	Kolar	Jagatsinghpur	Darrang

Source: Disaster Score Card, MHA, GoI

Health Impacts of Climate Change

Burgess et al. (2017) estimate that the death rate due to extreme hot weather (above 95°F or 35°C) in India (0.74 per cent) is much higher than the US (0.03 per cent). Hot weather notably impacts mortality in rural India and not in urban India. However, mortality responses are similar in urban areas of both countries despite huge disparities in incomes.

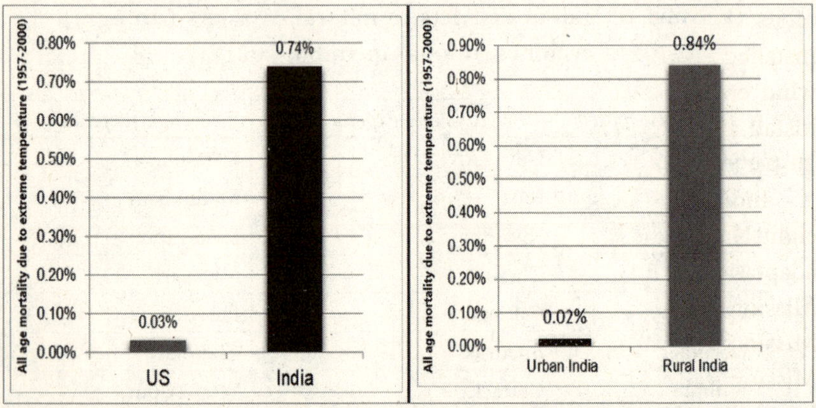

Figure 21: All age mortality due to extreme temperature (1957–2000)

Source: Burgess et al. (2017)

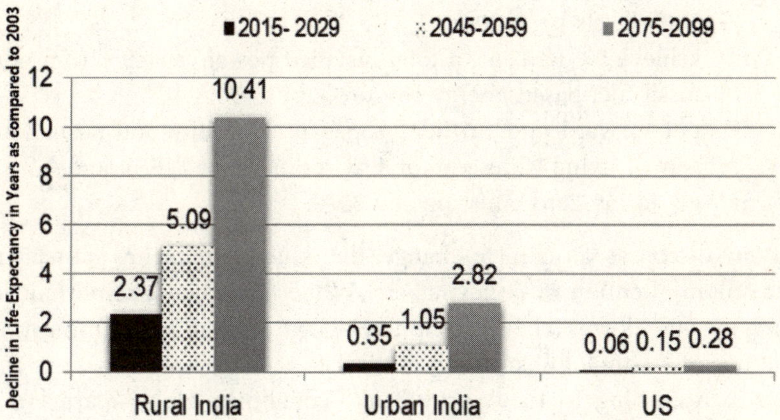

Figure 22: Decline in life expectancy in years as compared to 2003

Source: Burgess et al. (2017)

Policy Suggestions

As a highly populous, tropical, developing country, India faces a bigger challenge in coping with the consequences of climate change and climate justice than most countries. As per the report of the National Research Development Corporation (NRDC), India is on track to meet its Paris Agreement targets—to reduce emissions by 33 per cent to 35 per cent of its GDP by 2030 from 2005 levels, and to achieve 40 per cent of installed power capacity from non-fossil fuels by 2030. With solar and wind energy at the heart of India's climate goals, the country aims to install an ambitious 175 gigawatts (GW) of renewable energy by 2022, 20 per cent more than India's current electricity grid capacity.

India's National Action Plan on Climate Change (NAPCC) comprises eight National Missions focussing on different aspects of development, adaptation, mitigation and sustainability. It includes the National Solar Mission, National Mission for Enhanced Energy Efficiency, National Mission on Sustainable Habitat, National Water Mission, National Mission for Sustaining the Himalayan Ecosystem, National Mission for a Green India, National Mission for Sustainable Agriculture, and National Mission on Strategic Knowledge for Climate Change. As part of its nationally determined contributions (NDCs), India has committed to:

i. lower the emissions intensity of its GDP by 45 per cent from 2005 levels by 2030;
ii. achieve 50 per cent of total installed power capacity from non-fossil fuel-based energy resources by 2030;
iii. put forward and further propagate a healthy and sustainable way of living (Lifestyle for Environment, or LiFE); and
iv. get to net zero emissions by 2070.

In any discourse on climate change, the issue of financing gathers the maximum attention of policymakers. While financing is important for carrying out reforms relating to climate change adaptation and mitigation, the use of technology is equally critical to tackling the climate-related issues. According to the World Bank, 'containing global warming to 1.5 degrees is technically feasible with existing low-carbon technology—but only if it is deployed on a massive scale to developing countries.'[70] Achieving the climate-related target, therefore, requires not only a rapid and systemic transformation of the carbon-intensive energy sector—starting with energy conservation and efficiency and the progressive phasing out of fossil fuels with gradual shift to renewable energy—but also large-scale deployment and transfer of low-carbon technologies from high-income countries to low-income countries.

As was the case with waivers demanded by developing countries on intellectual property protections for Covid-19 vaccines, thus far, developed countries seem unwilling to find ways to provide a waiver on technologies that are vital to dealing with the climate crisis. Therefore, India must endeavour to implement a favourable intellectual property regime (IPR) so that technology transfer on climate-related innovations can be facilitated to developing and low-income economies. Private financing for climate change mitigation and adaptation cannot happen without supportive IPR for technology transfer of climate-change innovations to developing economies. Availability of adequate technology will also help developing countries attract private financing for climate-related projects by instilling confidence among investors about the effectiveness of policy measures.

India's domestic climate policy must be combative as well as

[70]'Technology Transfer and Innovation for Low-Carbon Development', *The World Bank*, 30 March 2020, http://tinyurl.com/59u4nme5. Accessed on 10 January 2024.

preventive. The following combative measures must be implemented. First, future finance commissions should allocate funds for combating climate-related disasters to states that have high vulnerability to climate-related disasters, for (i) building facilities for evacuation and rehabilitation in these states; and (ii) creating a 'climate disaster reserve fund' (CDRF) in these states. The funds provided by the finance commission must be allocated only for creating facilities for evacuation and rehabilitation to mitigate fatalities in the districts that are most vulnerable to climate-related disasters. The CDRF funds can be utilized by the states only when a climate-related emergency is declared in the state by the National Disaster Management Authority (NDMA).

Second, states must also invest in warning and forecasting systems that allow for timely measures and contain disaster impacts. Development of disaster-resilient infrastructures, such as construction and maintenance of river embankments, canals, roads and bridges, and construction of flood shelters in low-lying districts, must also be a priority. Third, massive community awareness and engagement plans must be implemented regarding alternative sources of energy, impacts of deforestation and overgrazing as well as 'to-do' and 'not-to-do' in an event. These measures can also help limit the impacts of a catastrophic event, especially in areas with low literacy on the subject.

Climate change disproportionately impacts the poor in a society, worsening inequality. Given India's large population still living in poverty and dependent on agriculture, the country is highly vulnerable to climate change-induced mishaps. As climate change is primarily created by the excesses of the rich nations, India needs to continue highlighting that for the world to succeed in combating climate change, developed economies need to properly respect the principles of equity and common—but differentiated—responsibilities, and respective capabilities. This should consequently reflect in commitments that are accompanied by climate financing and technology transfer for climate-related innovations.

15

AGRARIAN RENAISSANCE

Small Farmers—the 'Labharthi' of Agricultural Reforms

Let me present three narratives that illustrate the challenges faced by Indian agriculture.

Narrative #1: Unravelling the Widespread Pernicious Effects of MSP

Let us assume that the publisher of this book—Rupa Publications—demands that the book be necessarily purchased by the government for at least ₹1,000 a copy. What would happen if the government was to announce a minimum support price (MSP) of ₹1,000 a copy and create a procurement infrastructure for acquiring these books? You may find these fictional questions ludicrous, but this apocryphal narrative has important ramifications for India's agriculture sector. If this procurement infrastructure is established primarily in one state and solely for English-language books, what would be the outcome?

Currently, there is a wide array of book producers and publishers encompassing various regional languages apart from English. Remember that every business involved in production, whether it is of books, rice, wheat or vegetables, carries a certain amount of risk in exchange for the potential reward. A producer, therefore, rationally weighs the risk with the expected reward to make her production decision. After all, in any well-governed sector, the price of a product is determined by the balance between its demand and supply. When these factors fluctuate, the price also changes, thereby posing a risk for the producer. Taking risks and experiencing either profits or losses is and must be the reality of doing business in any well-regulated sector. But if the government assures at least ₹1,000 a copy for English-language books, its producer faces no risk on the selling price. Such producers will then make riskless profits. Who would pay for this largesse? It is us the taxpayers. Remember, even for the government, money doesn't appear magically. This MSP policy will only benefit English-language publishers, while leaving us, the general public, in financial hardship.

What could possibly be the next disaster? Every regional-language publisher will shift to producing books in English. After all, there is riskless profit to be made. Imagine the quality of the English books produced by individuals who lack expertise in the language. Specialization, whether it pertains to English books, regional books, rice, wheat or vegetables, allows for the development of expertise in that particular field. As every publisher is involved in producing English books, the publishing industry will lose its diversity and, with it, the expertise that comes from specialization in diverse languages.

Next, with everyone switching to producing books in the English language, the government will have to create a 'Publisher Corporation of India' to procure and store these English books. This is because there will be a greater supply of English books than the demand for them. These books will be stored under plinths, left in the open air to rot and for rats to feast on. As most books—with the exception of some classics—tend to depreciate in value over time, they would be sold to the *raddiwala* (scrap dealer) at throwaway prices. The scrap dealer industry will boom because of this policy. Unfortunately, this policy places an additional burden on honest taxpayers, who end up bearing the cost of inefficiencies once again.

Next, readers will be deprived of all books in regional languages as only English books will be sold. Although there may still be a few publishers producing regional books, the supply of these books will decrease significantly. As a result, their prices will skyrocket. Over time, these high prices will lead to complacency among regional-language publishers, causing them to inflate their costs and become inefficient. This inefficiency will attract Chinese or Vietnamese producers, who will produce regional books more efficiently and export them to India at lower prices. In response, the trader lobby of regional books will advocate for protectionism and demand higher tariffs to stop imports and safeguard jobs in the regional language publishing industry. Unfortunately, this protectionism will come at a cost for regional-book readers—the consumers—who will be forced to pay much higher prices due to the inefficiencies of the protected publishers.

Though the above narrative using books is apocryphal, Table 1 demonstrates that these important lessons apply to agriculture as well, since the farmer too is a producer who takes risks and rewards into account.

Table 1
Lessons for agriculture in India

#	*In the Apocryphal Story*	*Equivalent Effect in Agriculture*
1	English-book publishers—a producer—getting MSP	Farmer—also a producer of crops—getting MSP primarily for rice and wheat
2	If the government procures English books in a state, publishers can sell their books at MSP in that state. So, MSP matters in that state.	The government procures rice and wheat primarily in a select few states, with Punjab being the most dominant. So, farmers can sell rice and wheat at MSP in select states. So, MSP matters most for farmers in Punjab, who are the most vocal about it.
3	With MSP, the English-book producers face minimal risk and high returns. As a result, they make huge profits and become rich at the expense of taxpayers like you and me.	With MSP, farmers in Punjab and Haryana, who produce rice and wheat, face minimal risk and high returns. As a result, they make huge profits and become rich at the expense of taxpayers. In Punjab, more than 95 per cent of paddy growers benefit from MSP, whereas in UP only 3.6 per cent of farmers benefit.[73] The Dalwai Committee on Doubling Farmers' Income (DFI) noted that the government's market interventions like procurement of food grains including wheat and rice have mostly helped large farmers.[74]

[71]Shankaran, Sanjiv, 'An Overview of the Things Agitating the Farmers', *The Times of India*, 3 December 2020, http://tinyurl.com/jezdu98z. Accessed on 13 February 2024.
[72]Committee on Doubling Farmers' Income, Ministry of Agriculture & Farmers' Welfare, *DFI Report Volume XIII: Structural Reforms and Governance Framework, 2018*, http://tinyurl.com/3w756y43. Accessed on 13 February 2024.

#	*In the Apocryphal Story*	*Equivalent Effect in Agriculture*
4	If the government does not procure English books, MSP is irrelevant.	As the government does not have good procurement infrastructure for other agricultural commodities apart from rice and wheat, MSP does not matter much for other agricultural commodities. Even for rice and wheat, the government does not have good procurement infrastructure outside Punjab, Haryana and Andhra Pradesh. So, MSP does not matter even for rice and wheat outside these states.
5	Publishers who cannot avail MSP remain poor compared to producers that can avail this benefit.	Farmers outside Punjab and Haryana cannot avail MSP due to the lack of procurement infrastructure. They remain quite poor compared to farmers in Punjab and Haryana who can avail MSP.
6	No risk, but significant reward in producing English books results in excess production of English books, surpassing demand. As a result, this excess production has to be stored.	Excess production of rice and wheat must be stored by the Food Corporation of India (FCI). Of course, here there's an important difference. Food stocks are important for the country while stocks of books are not critical. Yet, the parallel is vital as the stocks of rice and wheat exceed the necessary amount for ensuring food security.
7	Every regional-language publisher shifts to producing English books. After all, there is riskless profits to be made. The publishing industry loses its diversity.	Most farmers in Punjab and Haryana produce rice and wheat due to the riskless profits associated with these crops. Diversity in agricultural production disappears. As rice consumes significant water, the already depleted water table in Punjab diminishes further. Consequently, when Punjab exports rice, India effectively exports a substantial amount of its limited water resources, putting it at a disadvantage compared to other countries.

#	*In the Apocryphal Story*	*Equivalent Effect in Agriculture*
8	Specialization results in expertise, whereas a decline in diversity and specialization leads to a decrease in the quality of English-language books published by a non-specialized publisher.	Quality of rice and wheat produced by farmers who do not specialize in it is low. Nutrition obtained from rice and wheat suffers as quality decreases.
9	As all diversity disappears, prices of regional-language books go up as demand is much greater than production.	As diversity in agricultural production has disappeared with rice and wheat being produced most, prices of edible oils and pulses have increased significantly as demand for these is much greater than production.
10	As English-language books are primarily produced, regional-language books must be imported.	As rice and wheat are produced in excess, edible oils and pulses, whose demand is much greater than production, are imported in large numbers. A supply-side shock such as the Ukraine war, which affected global supply of sunflower oil, raises prices of sunflower oil and contributes to food inflation. When Indonesia or Malaysia imposes export restrictions on palm oil, oil prices increase, thereby resulting in food inflation.

Source: Author's compilation

Each of the effects in agriculture that are described above has been shown in extensive research conducted by economists such as Bharat Ramaswami, Ashok Gulati and others. Here, I provide evidence on a select few phenomena. Figure 1 shows the dominance of procurement of wheat and rice from a select few states, especially Punjab.

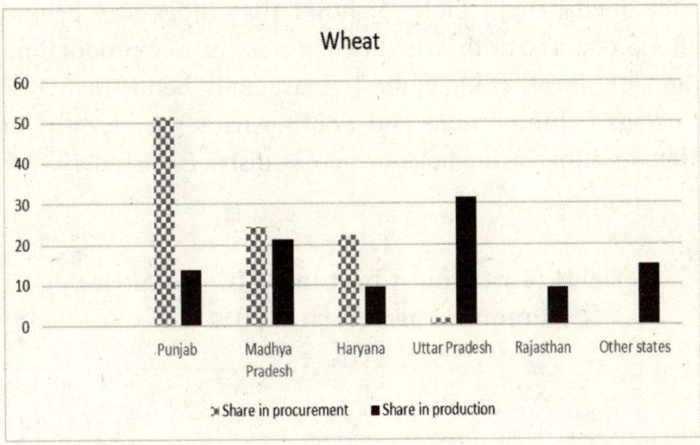

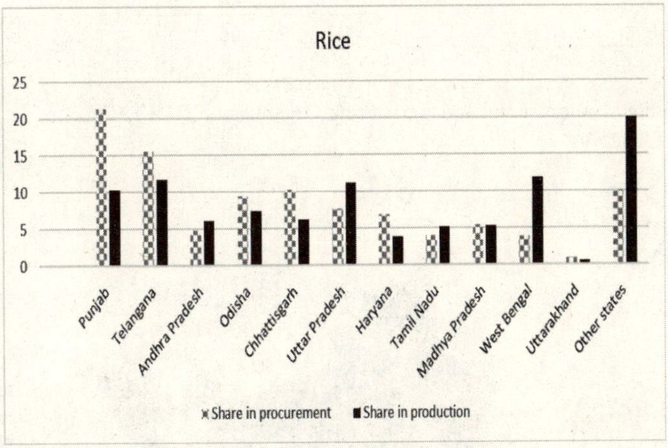

Figure 1: Dominance of procurement of wheat and rice in Punjab and a select few states

Source: MOSPI; various economic surveys

The inefficiency of land usage for agriculture is ably demonstrated by professors at Indian Institute of Management (IIM) Bangalore.[73] They calculated this inefficiency in a district or state as the percentage difference between actual and optimal land usage—the higher this difference, the

[73]Dasgupta, Kunal, and Rahul Rao, 'Land Misallocation and Industrial Development', IIM Bangalore Research Paper No. 668, 2002, http://tinyurl.com/2p8xhxhk. Accessed on 13 February 2024.

greater the inefficiency. Table 2 shows that India lags behind every other BRICS country in the yield per hectare in rice production. In the production of wheat, while India is marginally better than Brazil and Russia, it lags behind China and South Africa significantly. Figure 2 shows the variation in inefficiency across districts in India.

Table 2
Yields of rice and wheat in BRICS countries, in tonnes per hectare (2014–18)

	Rice	*Wheat*
India	2.5	3.1
China	5.3	5.4
Brazil	4.6	2.4
South Africa	4.6	3.4
Russia	2.6	2.7

Source: United Nations Food and Agriculture Organization (UN FAO), cited in Dasgupta and Rao (2022)

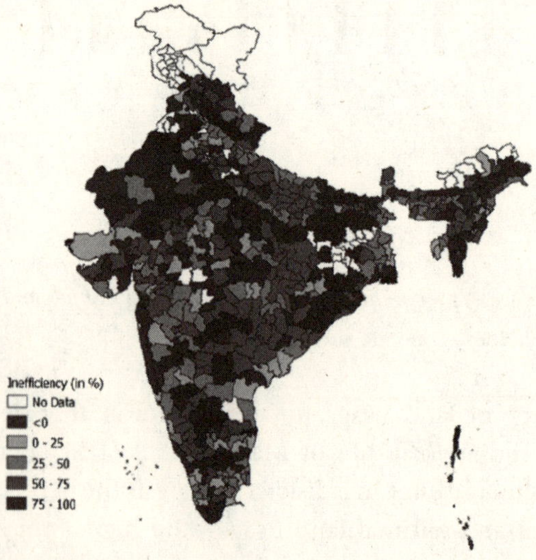

Figure 2: Inefficiency in agricultural production across districts in India

Source: Dasgupta and Rao (2022)

Figure 3 shows the significant economic costs of storing food grains with the FCI. Using the 523.35 lakh metric tonnes that the FCI has stored, including 280 lakh metric tonnes of wheat and 243 lakh metric tonnes of rice, the economic loss due to storage works out to over ₹1,50,000 crore.

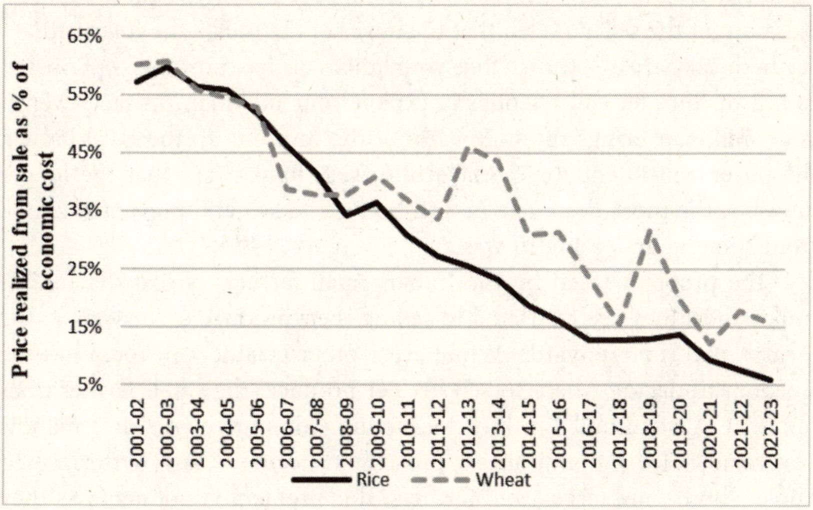

Figure 3: Steady increase in economic losses from stored rice and wheat
Source: FCI annual reports

Narrative #2: The APMC Act and the Abysmal State of Small Farmers

Consider the example of a milkman who delivers milk to you every day. Imagine a law is enacted that stipulates that the milkman can only sell his milk to an intermediary at the nearest bazaar. He is prohibited from selling milk directly to you or any other producer who intends to use the milk for making ice cream or sweets. What will happen then? The local bazaar where the milkman is compelled to sell his milk will now become a local monopoly for milk, since the middleman in that local bazaar knows that the milkman has no other option but to sell his product there.

John Nash, Nobel Prize-winning economist—and the main protagonist of the 2001 film *A Beautiful Mind*—showed in his research that the value that a seller gets in his relationship with the buyer depends upon whether the seller has an alternative option.[74] If a seller can credibly threaten to sell his produce to buyer B instead of buyer A, it forces buyer A to bargain with the seller, thereby providing him a higher price. However, if the seller has no alternative, the buyer exploits his monopoly power to squeeze the last paisa out of the seller. Given that the buyer of the milk—the intermediary in the local bazaar—knows that your milkman has no other option but to sell to him, he will relentlessly exploit your milkman. In fact, even if your milkman brings the milk early in the morning to the local bazaar, the buyer will intentionally make him wait, fully aware that the longer he waits, the more desperate he will become to sell and prevent the milk from spoiling and going to waste.

The problem faced by the Indian small farmers is like that of the milkman as they are restricted to selling their produce exclusively at the local *mandi* (market yard). While every other producer in India has the freedom to decide where to sell his/her produce, the small farmer does not. The Agricultural Produce Marketing Committee (APMC) mandis have enabled local monopolies to prosper at enormous costs to the farmer. For medium- and large-sized farmers, this problem is not acute as they have the option to either store their produce until the excessive supply during harvest season subsides or sell their produce in another mandi by greasing the right palms. The buyer in the mandi, therefore, realizes that the threat of losing business from the medium- and large-sized farmers is a credible one. So, these medium- and large-sized farmers do not get adversely affected by the APMC laws. In contrast, as the small farmer does not have the wherewithal to store his produce and cannot sell his produce anywhere else but at the local mandi, he is left to the (non-existent) mercy of the intermediaries.

Research by professors at IIM Ahmedabad provides forceful evidence of this phenomenon.[75] As seen in Figure 4, the marginal farmer receives

---

[74]Subramanian, Krishnamurthy, 'Why Are Farm Bills Opposed? Hostility Is Based on a Discredited Economic Model That Upholds Vested Interests', *The Times of India*, 5 October 2020, http://tinyurl.com/bdzef2a7. Accessed on 13 February 2024.

[75]Sharma, Vijay Paul, and Harsh Wardhan, *Assessment of Marketed and Marketable Surplus of Major Foodgrains in India*, Centre for Management in Agriculture, Indian Institute of Management, 2015, http://tinyurl.com/39sh746c. Accessed on 13 February 2024.

an abysmal 2.7 per cent of the marketing surplus in wheat, while the medium- and large-sized farmers receive 30 per cent of the same surplus. Thus, the seller and the middlemen together corner 97.3 per cent of the surplus when they buy from the marginal farmer. Such cornering is greater in wheat than in rice. This difference is important because wheat is primarily produced in the states with dominant mandis—Punjab and Haryana—while rice is produced significantly in Andhra Pradesh where mandis are not as dominant as those in Punjab and Haryana. Can there be better proof of the unfair exploitation of the small farmer in the current set-up?

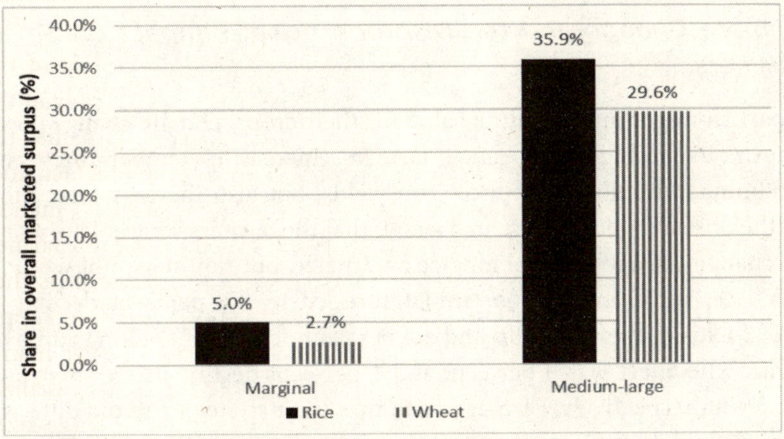

Figure 4: Small/marginal farmers get exploited by the APMC Act

Source: Sharma (2016)

In the Ideas for India (I4I) blog, economist Dilip Mookherjee writes about the absence of markets in Indian agriculture. He says:

> As numerous researchers have documented, agricultural marketing arrangements in the country are caught in a time-warp, resembling those in the Middle Ages or sub-Saharan Africa. Large parts of the country still rely on the traditional arrangement of a long vertical chain of intermediary middlemen who earn hefty margins. Farmers sell to local middlemen (kachha arhatiyas, phorias, village banias) who re-sell to (or are commission agents of) wholesale traders, who in turn sell in large mandis to wholesale buyers and retailers[…] The

> APMCs severely limit the set of buyers that can participate in the auctions, besides prohibiting direct sales by farmers. The auctions are conducted in a perfunctory manner; there is much evidence of collusion among the buyers that is not prevented and perhaps even facilitated by the state-appointed overseer[…] *There are long queues of farmers waiting to sell with their produce wilting in the hot sun, with limited ability to take their produce elsewhere*[…] The net result: farmers realise low prices for their produce[…] *If there were a way for[…]farmers to sell directly to wholesale buyers, the price they receive would double or more.*[76]

Climate Change and the Disproportionate Impact on Small Farmers

Apart from getting very little value for their crops, climate change poses enormous problems for small farmers. Increasing temperatures and declining precipitation reduce crop yields, but also increase dispersion of the observed yields. Research shows that the farmers were able to adapt to changes in temperature for rice and maize, but not in case of wheat.[77] For rice, a 1°C increase in temperature led to a 6 per cent decline in crop yields in the short run and a 4 per cent decline in the long run. For maize, the effect was 9 per cent and 1 per cent decline in the short and long run, respectively. Farmers customize their strategies across different regions and crops. For example, heat-prone districts would naturally fare better with higher temperatures compared to districts in colder regions.

Crucially, the impacts are higher at the lower end of the productivity distribution but are lower at the higher end. A 1°C increase in temperature lowers rice and wheat productivity by 23 per cent and 9 per cent, respectively, for the smallest farmers (in the first quantile), but the damage is only 6 per cent and 5 per cent for the largest farmers (in

---

[76]Mookherjee, Dilip, 'Moving Past the Mandis: A Revolution Waiting to Happen', *Ideas for India*, 20 January 2016, http://tinyurl.com/36yjw4tp. Accessed on 15 February 2024. Author's italicization.

[77]Kumar, Surender, and Madhu Khanna, 'Distributional Heterogeneity in Climate Change Impacts and Adaptation: Evidence from Indian Agriculture', *Agricultural Economics*, Vol. 54, No. 2, 2023, pp. 147–60, http://tinyurl.com/3ud677mf. Accessed on 13 February 2024.

the ninth quantile), respectively. A 100-mm decrease in precipitation reduces rice yields by 2.4 per cent on average, but rice productivity decreases by 3.5 per cent for the smallest farmers as compared to only about 1 per cent for the largest farmers. Less productive regions benefit more from the increase in precipitations relative to high productive regions, consistent with the fact that high productive regions have better irrigation facilities.

Narrative #3: Stalling of Reforms in Agriculture

Remember the time when you had to travel in an unreserved compartment of a train. If you recall, the unreserved compartment gets chock-a-block right at the originating station itself. While many others also want to travel to their destination despite not having a reservation, those individuals who managed to board the unreserved compartment at the first station do not let anyone else enjoy the 'privilege' of reaching their destination. Those travelling in the unreserved compartment are, of course, common folk who will question being called 'privileged.' They would emphasize that their condition is worse than those travelling in the reserved compartments. However, the comparison to those travelling in the reserved compartment obfuscates the real issue. The apples-to-apples comparison should be between those who could not secure a reservation—the minority who are fortunate enough to reach their destination versus the majority who wish to but cannot. This story is critical to understand the political economy of reforms in general, but agricultural reforms in particular. Any structural reform pits two sets of stakeholders against each other—the vocal minority that opposes the reform versus a silent majority that will benefit from the reform. Having benefited from the status quo, the vocal minority is richer and therefore knows how to have its voice heard in the corridors of power. In contrast, the silent majority, which has remained impoverished due to the status quo, struggles to have its voice heard. Unlike the vocal minority, the silent majority does not have the financial cushion to leave its daily work to raise its voice. Finally, the vocal minority clearly knows its costs from reform. In contrast, the silent majority remain uncertain of the benefits till such benefits manifest. The resultant asymmetry in information and voice skews the odds in favour of the vocal minority and, thereby, fosters populism and can stymie reform. We citizens must, therefore, take care to understand this political economy of reform.

Given this political economy, compared to the reforms undertaken in 1991, implementing agricultural reforms is more challenging. Reform of the product markets, i.e., markets where various producers sell their goods and services, creates competition between domestic capitalists and foreign capitalists. As capitalists rarely evoke emotion in a democracy, demagogues find it difficult to frame their 'common man' rhetoric against such reform. In contrast, the 'common man' rhetoric can be easily framed using the rich farmer from, let's say, Punjab, even though he may be significantly richer than the crores of farmers in the remaining 28 states.

In the context of agricultural reforms, we all must think carefully using the simile of the unreserved compartment. Research by the Observer Research Foundation (ORF) shows that the farm protests by the farmers from Punjab, Haryana and parts of Uttar Pradesh stem neither from overall unemployment or youth unemployment. In fact, the report finds that farmers from these regions offer the greatest resistance to reforms despite having the least number of farmers in the country.[78] The rich farmer from these regions represents the more privileged traveller, who got into the unreserved compartment at the first station and stops millions of others from getting in after him. The rich farmer is thus blocking the potential benefits that can accrue to his less privileged brethren in the other states. Therefore, the rhetoric of farm bills being against the common man is vacuous.

We citizens must discern the deception by individuals who oppose reform as they draw their political clientele from the more privileged vocal minority that benefits from status quo. The common man that they espouse is, in fact, privileged and has a substantial voice in the corridors of power. In contrast, those advocating for reform appeal to the millions of underprivileged people who form the silent majority—the 'genuine common man'. It is imperative for us to see through this deception and recognize that those opposing reform are actually championing the cause of the privileged, while those supporting reform are genuinely fighting for the rights of the underprivileged.

[78]'The Puzzle of Farmers Protest', *Observer Research Foundation,* 11 March 2022, http://tinyurl.com/2ye6b9r3. Accessed on 15 February 2024.

Finally, we citizens must also appreciate that reformers are driven by their conviction to take risk. As the reformers cater to the underprivileged, who do not have a voice at the time the reform is announced, the reformers take political risk. In a democracy such as ours, therefore, we must value reformers just as we value entrepreneurs. Only then can India@100 progress to provide benefits to one and all.

Almost Non-Existent Markets

Economists think about the LOOP as a reliable symptom of an integrated, robust market. Intuitively, the law makes sense because, if after adjusting for tariffs, taxes and transportation costs, the price of a tradeable good is different in two geographies, then market participants will utilize this opportunity to profit. As 'buy low, sell high' represents the maxim for making such profits, purchasing the good in geographies where it is priced lower will raise its price. Simultaneously, selling the good in the higher price geographies for making profits will lower its price. This process should continue till the price equalizes between the two geographies, thereby establishing the LOOP. Conversely, if prices across two geographies do not converge to the same price after adjusting for tariffs, taxes and transportation costs, then the markets are segmented or not integrated with each other.

To test for segmentation in agricultural markets in India, I, therefore, examine the range of dispersion in prices across different states and agricultural commodities. As explained above, integrated markets would imply low dispersion in prices while high dispersion in prices suggests segmentation in markets. Figure 5 presents box plots of absolute price deviation of different crops from the weighted average price of the crop in the state for each state.[79] For these box plots, the data used is based

[79]To understand a box plot, imagine representing the data of ages of all the people attending a wedding. The box plot shows us the 'middle-aged' guests—the ones in the box—where most of the group falls. The line in the box is like the 'average' age of the group. The whiskers show us how spread-out the ages are, and any guests who are really young or really old might be considered outliers. So, with a box plot, we can quickly see how the ages are distributed and if there are any standout ages in the group. Similarly, using the box plot we can see how dispersed the prices of a crop is within a state.

on monthly quantity arrivals and prices of a crop across different mandis located across different districts of a state. This data is obtained from Centre for Monitoring Indian Economy (CMIE) because its data on agricultural prices is reliable.

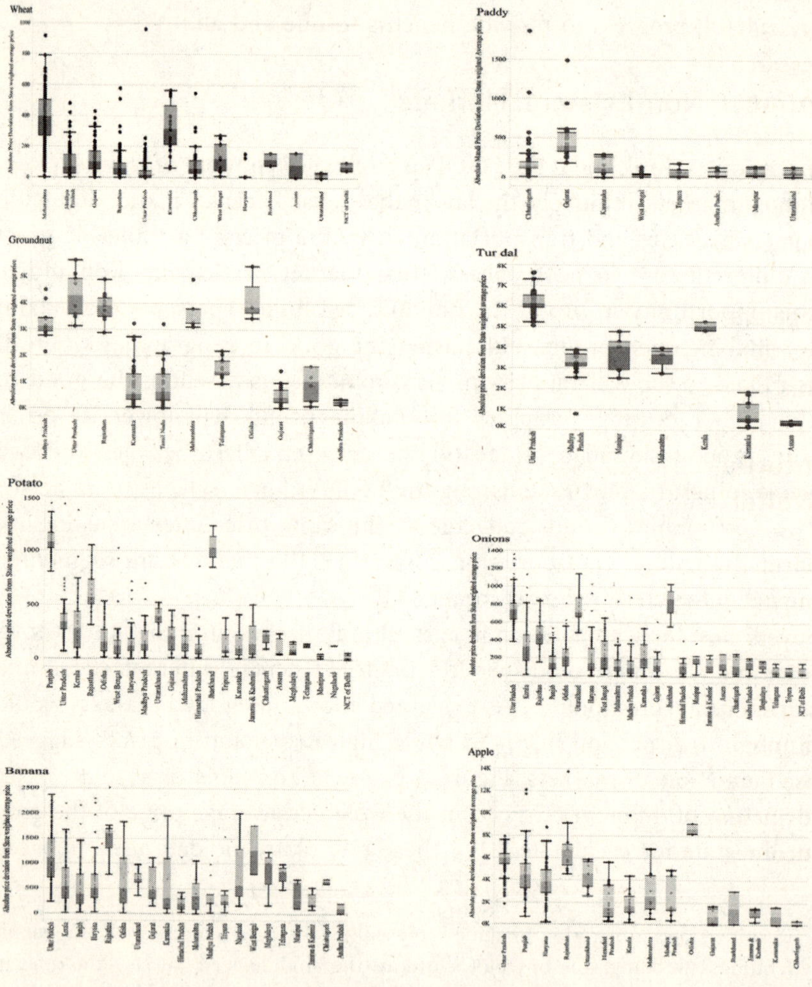

Figure 5: Evidence of agricultural markets being segmented across various states and agricultural commodities

Source: CMIE and author's calculations

Figure 5 shows significant dispersion in the prices of rice, wheat, groundnut, tur dal, potato, onion, banana and apple, thereby covering a range of food items spanning cereals, oil seeds, pulses, vegetables and fruits. The dispersion is not only across states but also significant within states. As explained above, this dispersion is symptomatic of the agricultural markets not being integrated even within a state. As recent research explains, a key reason contributing to the low prices received by farmers—as shown in Figure 1—is the considerable market power wielded by intermediaries.[80] The source of this market power exercised by the intermediaries is the limited ability of farmers to arbitrage between different intermediaries. The inability to arbitrage itself stems from the APMC Act, which require that the first sale and purchase of agricultural produce take place in government-regulated mandis within the state. This regulation of cross-state trade has led to segmented and less competitive markets. The dispersion in prices shown in Figure 5 clearly demonstrates this phenomenon.

Integrate Agricultural Markets for Small Farmers' Welfare

Given the above discussion, integrating agricultural markets is particularly important for the welfare of small and marginal farmers. When many buyers bid for a farmer's produce, the farmer is likely to get a higher price. As shown in Figure 6, enabling competition for the farmer's produce can substantially increase the price paid to farmers, especially the small farmers. Furthermore, once farmers get better prices, they can afford to use better inputs like seeds, fertilizers, pesticides, etc., which contribute to increased agricultural output leading to a further increase in their incomes.

---

[80]Chatterjee, Shoumitro, 'Market Power and Spatial Competition in Rural India', *The Quarterly Journal of Economics*, Vol. 138, No. 3, 2023, pp. 1649–711, http://tinyurl.com/2y433b8d. Accessed on 13 February 2024.

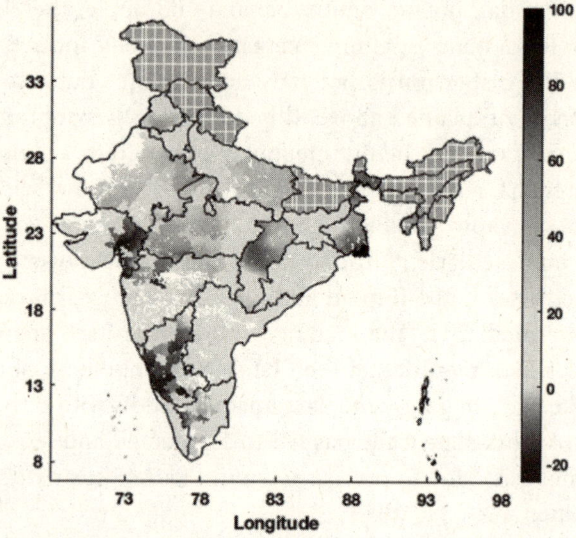

Figure 6: Potential increase in prices available to farmers from enabling competition for the farmer's produce

Source: Chatterjee (2023)

The Dalwai Committee Report in 2018 highlights the critical role of enabling markets for small and marginal farmers: 'The small & marginal farmers, with uneconomical sized marketable lots, find it difficult to aggregate their produce and move to these APMCs to participate in the auction system for suitable price discovery. They, therefore, use local agents and traders, who relieve small farmers of their produce at locally determined prices.'[81] India has only 8,900 markets regulated through various government agencies for selling of farmers' produces. Each village has a market within a radius of 12 km (Gulati et al. 2018). According to the Dalwai Committee, 40 per cent of fruits and vegetables, which are produced primarily by small farmers, do not get sold because the farmer cannot access a market to sell these. Therefore, integrating markets and bringing them to the small/marginal farmer is imperative.

[81]Committee on Doubling Farmers' Income, Ministry of Agriculture & Farmers' Welfare, *DFI Report Volume XIII: Structural Reforms and Governance Framework*, 2018, http://tinyurl.com/3w756y43. Accessed on 13 February 2024.

Steps to Enhance the Power of e-NAM

While National Agriculture Market (e-NAM) has been launched to integrate agricultural markets in India, there are two key aspects that need to be enabled to empower e-NAM fully. First, barrier-free movement of agricultural produce needs to be enabled across state borders. Second, a uniform set of rules and taxes on agricultural trade need to be created across the country. Research shows that farmers can gain substantially more from simultaneous reduction of transport costs and elimination of inter-state border restrictions to trade than if these two policy changes were enacted alone.[82] Crucially, these gains occur in locations where the middlemen exercise greater power thereby depriving small farmers of their fair share of value. To enable barrier-free movement of agricultural produce, both institutional reforms and creation of infrastructure for high-quality assaying are essential. In contrast, institutional reform can enable uniform set of rules and taxes on agricultural trade.

Institutional reform: Institutional reform that establishes a legal framework and shapes the context and actors in agricultural market is a necessary condition. For e-NAM, the need of the hour is a roadmap to ensure that a new legal framework is in place that supports a new architecture for agricultural transactions across the country. Failure to institute legal reform across the states limits the idea of a seamless, unified national market. In this scenario, the state with the most restrictive APMC Act would determine the extent of the reforms. A precondition for unification is a regulatory framework that can settle disputes across states and one that keeps the implementation agency distinct from the regulatory agency.

Infrastructure for high-quality assaying using AI/ML technologies: A key factor deterring cross-mandi bidding is quality assessment. On the one hand, it seems traders would much rather rely on commission agents to assess the quality of produce than on assaying. Further, officials in several mandis mention that although voluntary assaying is available, traders typically prefer visual inspection and trusted commission

---

[82]Chatterjee, Shoumitro, 'Market Power and Spatial Competition in Rural India', *The Quarterly Journal of Economics*, Vol. 138, No. 3, 2023, pp. 1649–711, http://tinyurl.com/s8y4nzfm. Accessed on 13 February 2024.

agents to do this. Without a credible assaying mechanism, traders are, therefore, unlikely to bid on the electronic platform in distant mandis. Where facilities do exist, they seemed inadequate for the task at hand. On assaying, agri-tech startups that use AI tools to assess quality can offer an important solution. Artificial intelligence-based tools can use computer vision and deep learning to build a platform for grading and quality monitoring of agricultural commodities. Image-based solutions can be delivered through a smartphone app, which helps in bringing transparency and standardization to quality assessment and reducing value risk and wastage in agriculture supply chains. These solutions can reduce the testing time for assessing quality and provide reliability. They also allow real-time data sharing across multiple locations and screens and remove subjectivity.

Need for Mandi Reform

Advocates of APMCs point out the dangers associated with unfettered market competition that may arise if the restrictions on trade, which form the basis of the APMC Act, are eliminated. However, this fear is misplaced for several reasons. First, as shown in Figure 4, the status quo provides small and marginal farmers a miniscule share of 2.7–5 per cent of the overall surplus. Therefore, the dangers of unfettered market competition are unfounded because such competition will provide small farmers with at least as much share of the surplus as they currently receive. Second, the majority of farmers will persist in producing generic agricultural goods and vending them through local intermediaries, who will continue to distribute them within mandis. Transactional hurdles will continue to exist when numerous small-scale farmers interact directly with agribusiness purchasers located far away. Consequently, should agribusinesses aim to procure generic goods on a large scale, they will need to engage existing supply chain intermediaries, mirroring the experiences of numerous other developing nations. Third, direct trading between farmers and agribusinesses empowers developing countries to access GVCs built on advanced technology across various domains: from seeds and production methods to transportation and storage infrastructure, as well as national and global marketing strategies. Lastly, even in affluent countries, the significance of scale economies in retail cannot be understated, leading to consolidation as these chains expand backwards. However, in India, the likelihood of the organized sector monopolizing food retail seems dubious. Although the organized sector enjoys a significant presence in milk sales, accounting for about 20 per cent or less of the market share, this presence diminishes substantially outside major metropolitan areas. The aggregation of produce presents a formidable challenge, making it difficult for the organized sector to compete with traditional chains in sectors such as fruits, vegetables, or grains. In contrast, reforming the mandis will facilitate established agri-businesses to invest more in supply chains. With more reliable supplies, they can emerge as significant players in agricultural exports. Moreover, the removal of monopolies grants farmer organizations greater autonomy in forging partnerships.

The infrastructure of mandis is an essential enabling factor and, in this context, includes both the physical and financial aspects that support market transactions. To enhance this infrastructure, it is necessary to establish a comprehensive set of grades and standards for various products. Additionally, there is a need to invest in assaying facilities that are quick, cost-effective and credible. Currently, these facilities are lacking in many mandis. As per a 2019 report of the Parliament's Standing Committee on Agriculture, Animal Husbandry and Food Processing, only 22 per cent mandis have grading facilities, 50 per cent have weighing facilities, 30 per cent have drying facilities, 7 per cent have banking facilities, and 15 per cent of the produce goes into cold storage facilities.[83]

Empowering the Small Farmer as the Labharthi of Reforms

Apart from integrating markets, other agricultural reforms need to be prioritized with the explicit focus on the small farmer as the *labharthi* (beneficiary) of these reforms. Rhetoric aside, the small farmer has been the biggest loser from the status quo and can be the biggest beneficiary of agricultural reforms. According to the Dalwai Committee on Doubling of Farmers' Income, the average annual earnings of a small and marginal

[83]Standing Committee on Agriculture (2018–2019), Ministry of Agriculture and Farmers' Welfare, *Agriculture Marketing And Role of Weekly Gramin Haat*, 2019, http://tinyurl.com/upf9yrj8. Accessed on 14 February 2024.

farmer household were less than ₹80,000 in 2015–16, while that of large farmers was more than ₹6,00,000 in 2015–16, i.e., seven-and-a-half times more.[84] Thus, *85 per cent of farmer households earn 9 per cent of total income, while the rest earn 91 per cent.* This statistic highlights the plight of small and marginal farmers in India.

As PM Modi has repeatedly emphasized, bringing welfare benefits to the poor and the underprivileged can not only be economically beneficial but also provide significant political dividends. The political messaging regarding agricultural reforms should make the distinction between the large, rich farmer and the small, poor farmer. Not only does the large, rich farmer earn almost riskless profits because of the MSP policies, but also these profits are completely tax-free as agricultural income is not taxed. Therefore, the political messaging must highlight the large, rich farmers as a stumbling block to improving the economic and societal status of the small, poor farmers.

Reforms in Three Areas

Drawing on research by Professor Ashok Gulati and others, I outline three other areas for agricultural reforms besides integrating markets. First, the focus of agricultural policies must shift from production per se to farmers' livelihoods. This will help to bring the focus on the precarious livelihoods of the small, poor farmers. Second, policies to improve the allocation and efficiency of land and water are essential if these critical resources are to be conserved. Third, reforms are needed to help farmers cope with the growing risks of weather and price volatility. On both the second and third reform areas, as explained earlier, the small farmer remains the most vulnerable. The specific reform steps that must be taken are as follows.

To begin with, the priority should be to reduce cereal procurement while ensuring that the hike in MSP for rice and wheat remains below the inflation rate and in line with international prices. Second, foster the development of robust markets for less water-intensive crops such as pulses and oilseeds by removing constraints on stocking, trading

---

[84]Committee on Doubling Farmers' Income, Ministry of Agriculture & Farmers' Welfare, *DFI Report Volume XIII: Structural Reforms and Governance Framework*, 2018, http://tinyurl.com/3w756y43. Accessed on 13 February 2024.

and exports. This measure will also contribute positively to addressing water scarcity issues, particularly in regions like north-western and southern India. Third, introduce income transfer schemes for farmers alongside reductions in subsidies for power, water and fertilizer, which currently distort incentives and impede progress. This approach will yield significant environmental benefits and enhance natural resource management. Additionally, maintain the real prices of subsidized grains under the National Food Security Act, 2013, linking them to MSP to encourage the production and consumption of non-cereal crops. Fourth, abolish outdated legislation, such as the Essential Commodities Act, 1955, which was formulated decades ago, to address conditions of scarcity that are no longer prevalent. India now faces more challenges related to surplus rather than scarcity. Fifth, discontinue support for rehabilitating inefficient urea plants and devise a plan for phasing out the most inefficient facilities. The gains resulting from inefficiencies in fertilizer production primarily benefit large corporations than small farmers. Finally, incentivize the enactment of state laws that facilitate easy leasing or renting of agricultural land. Additionally, relax restrictions on land conversion for alternative uses. Currently, these restrictions depress the value of agricultural land and pose obstacles to transitioning out of agriculture. These measures should be viewed as a comprehensive package, as their collective implementation will have a more substantial impact than isolated measures.

Insuring Prosperity: Why Small Farmers Need Insurance

Three different research studies examine the downside risks faced by Indian farmers from three different perspectives, revealing that mitigating these downside risks lead to enhanced productivity by crowding in other productive investments. In line with my initial expectations when the PM-KISAN scheme was launched in 2019, recent research by Professor Pulak Ghosh and Nishant Vats showed that this scheme reduces downside risks and enables productive investments.[85] They find that ₹1 of guaranteed

[85]Pattanayak, Banikinkar, 'PM-Kisan Scheme to Drastically Cut Farmers' Vulnerability: CEA Krishnamurthy Subramanian', *Financial Express*, 18 February 2019, http://tinyurl.com/3p55ebkm. Accessed on 14 February 2024; 'PM-KISAN to Provide Multiple Benefits to Farmers: CEA', *Economic Times*, 17 February 2019,

income to small and marginal farmers each year increases their income by an additional ₹1.7. Similarly, research published in the *American Economic Review* in 2016 shows that a new rice variety that reduces downside risk increase productivity by crowding in investment.[86] Finally, improving storage infrastructure not only enhances productivity but also minimizes downside risks for small farmers by reducing their potential wastage. Moreover, it prevents distress sale of their produce to intermediaries in the local mandi. Collectively, all these research studies highlight the critical need to provide insurance coverage to small and marginal farmers.[87]

◆

In conclusion, the politics of agricultural reforms needs to bring the small farmer as the primary labharthi—the central beneficiary of agricultural reforms in India. Enabling market mechanisms can lead to increased efficiency, productivity and sustainability for the small farmer. This approach will not only promote economic resilience in agriculture but also foster social inclusivity and rural development. However, realizing this vision requires concerted efforts from policymakers and all stakeholders to address the systemic barriers that impede the welfare of the small farmer in India.

---

http://tinyurl.com/cpkmh7b3. Accessed on 14 February 2024; Ghosh, Pulak, and Nishant Vats, 'Safety Nets, Credit, and Investment: Evidence from a Guaranteed Income Program', *SSRN*, http://tinyurl.com/y9pj9bw8. Accessed on 15 February 2024.

[86]Emerick, Kyle, et al., 'Technological Innovations, Downside Risk, and the Modernization of Agriculture', *American Economic Review*, Vol. 106, No. 6, 2016, http://tinyurl.com/bdem5ske. Accessed on 14 February 2024.

[87]Chatterjee, Somdeep, 'Storage Infrastructure and Agricultural Yield: Evidence from a Capital Investment Subsidy Scheme', *Economics*, Vol. 12, No. 1, 2018, http://tinyurl.com/5emz49cz. Accessed on 14 February 2024.

16

MANIFESTING DREAMS FROM DATA

Data-Driven Nudge Using Thalinomics, the Bare Necessities Index and Behavioural Economics

Do you remember the angry young man of Bollywood, Amitabh Bachchan, thundering in the 1989 film *Main Azaad Hoon*, '*Chalis baras mein aap ek insaan ko ek gilas pani nahin de sakte, toh aap kya kar sakte hain*? (In 40 years, you were unable to give a person a glass of water, then what credibility do you possess to accomplish anything at all?)' Bollywood's rhetoric, which often mirrors socio-economic issues in the country, has focussed on the basic necessities of food, clothing and shelter in movies such as *Roti Kapada Aur Makaan*.

The idea that economic development can be viewed as a process of providing the 'bare necessities of life' to citizens has been around in India since Pitambar Pant advocated the idea of 'minimum needs' in the 1950s.[88] A family's ability to access bare necessities—such as food, housing, water, sanitation, electricity and clean cooking fuel—has therefore been regarded as an important barometer of economic development in academic and policymaking circles. The three Economic Surveys of the GoI that I had the privilege of authoring attempted to quantify these basic necessities using data-driven indices so that such indices can be employed for targeted policymaking.

The concept of 'Thalinomics', which was discussed in *Economic Survey 2019–20*, has gained significant popularity possibly because it relates to a plate of food or *thali*, which each one of us encounters every day.[89] While popular media called it India's Big Mac Index,[90] this

[88]Ministry of Finance, GoI, *Economic Survey 2020–21: Volume 1*, January 2021, p. 1, https://tinyurl.com/mwkb3psz. Accessed on 22 November 2023.

[89]Ministry of Finance, GoI, *Economic Survey 2019–20: Volume 1*, January 2020, p. 1, https://tinyurl.com/3jru7c4r. Accessed on 22 November 2023.

[90]Jayaram, Anup, 'Economic Survey 2020: The Thali, India's Own Big Mac Index', *Business Today*, 31 January 2020, https://tinyurl.com/2j2v9h8e. Accessed on 8 April 2024.

comparison misses the crucial difference in the underlying intent behind the conceptualization of Thalinomics. The Big Mac Index corresponds to the price of the McDonald's burger, which is unhealthy, processed food. In contrast, the Thalinomics corresponds to wholesome, nutritious food as is in the Indian thali. Therefore, as an index, it captures the price of wholesome, nutritious food. By adopting their own versions of Thalinomics instead of relying on the Big Mac Index, countries will have the ability to track the price of wholesome, nutritious food and can thereby encourage their citizens to pursue healthier eating habits.

As nutritious food, drinking water, sanitation, hygiene and housing conditions capture some of the basic needs that affect the lives of common citizens, *Economic Survey 2020–21* extended the idea underlying Thalinomics to construct the Bare Necessities Index for both rural and urban areas.[91] This index captures 26 different indicators spanning five dimensions of basic necessities: access to water, quality of housing, quality of sanitation, micro-environment and other facilities. In this chapter, I examine the various policy measures that can be taken to provide access to both by using the Thalinomics and the Bare Necessities indices for policymaking.

Imagining Myriad Uses of Data-Driven Welfare

For weeks, Priya, a single mother of two young children in Mumbai, had been struggling to make ends meet. Despite working long hours as a domestic worker, her meagre income barely covered the cost of rent, let alone the bare necessities of food, clothing and education for her family. As Priya navigated her way through the crowded market, she found herself lost in thought. Clutching a crumpled piece of paper in her hand, she scanned the stalls, her heart sinking with each passing moment. With a heavy sigh, she reluctantly handed over the few rupees she had left, knowing all too well that it wouldn't be enough to adequately feed her starving children for more than a single day.

But then, a subtle nudge intervened. A nearby Anganwadi worker, armed with a tablet displaying information about government subsidies

[91]Ministry of Finance, GoI, *Economic Survey 2020–21: Volume 1*, January 2021, p. 1, https://tinyurl.com/mwkb3psz. Accessed on 22 November 2023.

for nutritious food items, approached Priya with a warm smile. She gently guided Priya towards the healthier options, explaining how the existing food subsidies that the government provides could make these items more affordable for her family. Priya, initially hesitant, found herself drawn to the idea of providing her children with healthier meals, especially when she realized that these options were financially within her reach.

In the days that followed, Priya started introducing healthier food options into her family's meals. She was guided by the subtle nudges and the valuable information she learnt from Thalinomics, which was shared in Marathi. She discovered that small changes in her purchasing habits could have a big impact on her family's health and well-being. Priya did not realize that more help was on its way as Anganwadi workers equipped with tablets and smartphones fanned out across the city, conducting surveys and collecting data on households like Priya's.

Through the power of data analytics and machine learning, policymakers were able to analyse vast troves of data. This included Thalinomics insights into the cost of nutritious meals and the Bare Necessities Index's assessment of the affordability of essential goods and services. This data-intensive approach allowed them to identify patterns, trends and areas of need with unprecedented accuracy. Armed with this insight, they could tailor welfare programmes to target the most vulnerable populations and provide assistance where it was needed most.

Policymakers were also able to implement additional nudges to further support families like Priya's. They redesigned the layout of local markets to prominently display healthier options, making them more visible and appealing to shoppers. They also introduced educational campaigns that employed behavioural nudges, such as leveraging social norms and peer comparisons, to promote healthier eating habits within the community. For Priya and countless others like her, this data-intensive approach to welfare programmes proved to be a lifeline in their darkest hour.

As a result, Priya and many others like her found themselves on a path towards improved health and socio-economic well-being. By combining insights from Thalinomics, the Bare Necessities Index, and the principles of behavioural economics, policymakers were able to empower individuals like Priya to make positive choices for themselves and their families, ultimately leading to better outcomes for all.

Utilizing Thalinomics and the Bare Necessities Index

In this section, I present some ideas to utilize Thalinomics and the Bare Necessities Index more effectively.

Incorporate into Strategies for Poverty Alleviation

As access to nutritious food and other bare necessities have a substantial impact on the lives of all citizens, Thalinomics and the Bare Necessities Index can be integrated into poverty alleviation strategies. This would help to ensure that poverty lines are not only based on income but also on the ability to afford a basic nutritious diet and other basic necessities as captured by the Bare Necessities Index. By accounting for the affordability of essential goods and services such as food, shelter, healthcare and education, policymakers can establish poverty thresholds that better capture the lived experiences of low-income individuals and families.

Thalinomics can be applied as a tool for assessing food security at both national and subnational levels. By analyzing the affordability of a standard plate of food across different regions, policymakers can identify areas with higher food insecurity and target interventions accordingly.

Findings from Thalinomics can be employed to inform nutrition education programmes aimed at improving dietary habits and promoting the consumption of balanced meals. Understanding the cost of nutritious food can help tailor messaging and interventions to make healthy eating more accessible and affordable for all.

The Bare Necessities Index can be applied as a metric for monitoring economic progress and evaluating the effectiveness of poverty reduction efforts over time. By tracking changes in the affordability of bare necessities, policymakers can assess whether socio-economic policies are effectively improving living standards and reducing deprivation among vulnerable populations.

The Bare Necessities Index can be utilized to target social welfare programmes and subsidies more effectively towards those in need. By identifying specific items or services that low-income households find disproportionately difficult to afford, policymakers can design targeted interventions to alleviate financial strain and promote social inclusion.

Findings from the Bare Necessities Index can also be incorporated into education policy reform to address barriers to educational access and attainment. By assessing the affordability of school fees, supplies and other educational expenses, policymakers can develop initiatives to ensure equitable access to quality education for all children, regardless of socio-economic background.

The Bare Necessities Index can be leveraged to inform disaster response and resilience planning by identifying vulnerable populations at risk of deprivation during crises. By understanding the affordability of bare necessities in disaster-prone areas, policymakers can develop targeted interventions to support affected communities and enhance their resilience to future shocks.

Integration into Healthcare Policy

Policymakers can collaborate with healthcare experts to incorporate Thalinomics data into strategies aimed at addressing diet-related health issues such as malnutrition, obesity and non-communicable diseases. By understanding the affordability of nutritious meals, policymakers can design interventions to promote healthier eating habits among populations. Similarly, the Bare Necessities Index can be used to assess healthcare access and equity by examining the affordability of essential healthcare services and medications. Policymakers can identify barriers to healthcare access faced by marginalized populations and implement strategies to improve affordability, reduce disparities and enhance health outcomes.

Urban Planning and Development

Data and findings from Thalinomics can be incorporated into urban planning and development initiatives to ensure access to affordable and nutritious food for residents of urban areas. This can involve zoning policies to encourage the establishment of grocery stores and markets in underserved neighbourhoods, as well as initiatives to promote urban agriculture and community gardens.

The Bare Necessities Index data can be integrated into the development of housing policies to ensure access to affordable and adequate housing for all. By analysing housing affordability relative to other bare necessities, policymakers can identify gaps in housing provision and implement measures to address housing insecurity and homelessness.

Development Projects for the Global South

Principles from Thalinomics can be applied in international development projects in the Global South aimed at improving food security and nutrition in low- and middle-income countries (LMICs). By assessing the affordability of local staple foods, policymakers and organizations can design interventions that are culturally appropriate and economically feasible. Similarly, principles from the Bare Necessities Index can be employed in the allocation of international aid and development assistance to prioritize investments in essential goods and services that are critical for human well-being. By focussing on addressing deprivation in areas such as food security, healthcare and education, policymakers can maximize the impact of aid efforts in improving socio-economic conditions in low-income countries.

Overall, by integrating Thalinomics and the Bare Necessities Index into various policy domains and initiatives, policymakers can better address the complex challenges of food affordability, nutrition and health. Policymakers can apply these indices into policy formulation, implementation and evaluation processes to target resources better, address inequities and improve the well-being of populations by ensuring access to essential goods and services for all.

Nudge towards Desirable Behaviour

Decisions made by real people often deviate from those by impractical robots theorized in classical economics. Drawing on the psychology of human behaviour, behavioural economics provides insights to 'nudge' people towards desirable behaviour. First, a key principle of behavioural economics is that while people's behaviour is influenced significantly by social norms, understanding the drivers of these social norms can enable change. In India, where social and religious norms play such a dominant role in influencing behaviour, behavioural economics can therefore provide a valuable instrument for change. So, beneficial social norms can be furthered by drawing attention to positive influencers, especially friends/neighbours that represent role models with which people can identify. Second, as people are given to tremendous inertia when making a choice, they prefer sticking to the default option. By the nearly costless act of changing the default to overcome this inertia, desired behaviour can be encouraged without affecting people's choices. Third, as people find it difficult to sustain good habits, repeated reinforcements and reminders of successful past actions can help sustain changed behaviour.

Behavioural Insights in Food Subsidy Programmes

Insights from behavioural economics can be employed to design food subsidy programmes that nudge individuals towards healthier food choices. For example, instead of providing generic subsidies, they could be tailored to incentivize the purchase of nutritious food items identified through analysis of Thalinomics data. Additionally, policymakers can implement behavioural interventions such as labelling healthy options more prominently or offering discounts on healthier alternatives to encourage healthier eating habits.

Default Options for Enrolment in Essential Services

Policymakers can leverage nudges to increase enrolment in essential services such as availing nutritious food items from the PDS, as well as essential healthcare and education. For instance, default enrolment options can be applied in social welfare programmes identified through the Bare Necessities Index to ensure that eligible individuals are automatically enrolled unless they actively opt out. This approach can reduce barriers to access and increase participation among the vulnerable population.

Simplified Decision-Making Processes

Policymakers should look to simplify decision-making processes related to accessing bare necessities and nutritious food by applying principles of behavioural economics. Application procedures for social assistance programmes and for availing nutritious food from the PDS need to be streamlined based on insights from the Bare Necessities Index, making it easier for individuals to navigate bureaucratic hurdles and access the support they need.

Behavioural Messaging to Promote Investment in Nutrition

Behavioural messaging campaigns can be developed to promote nutritious eating regimens and ensuring universal access to the bare necessities among low-income households. Insights from Thalinomics can be utilized to tailor messages that highlight the long-term benefits of investing in nutritious food and essential goods. Behavioural nudges such as social norms or peer comparisons can be employed to encourage nutritious eating regimens savings and universal access to the bare necessities.

Choice Architecture for Healthier Lifestyles

Policymakers must think about redesigning choice architecture in public spaces to promote healthier lifestyles and nutritious eating habits among vulnerable populations. Insights from Thalinomics can be incorporated to influence the availability and affordability of nutritious food options in community settings. Nudges such as placement strategies or portion control can be employed to encourage healthier food choices and discourage unhealthy behaviours.

Incentive Structures for Positive Behaviour Change

Incentive structures can be developed by leveraging behavioural economics principles to motivate positive behaviour change among the poor and vulnerable. For example, implement conditional cash transfer programmes linked to specific health or education outcomes identified through the Bare Necessities Index and to nutritious eating using Thalinomics. Designing rewards systems that provide immediate benefits or feedback to reinforce desired behaviours as well as encouraging sustained engagement can be beneficial in improving health outcomes among the poor and the vulnerable.

Peer Influence and Social Networks

Policymakers must aim to harness the power of peer influence and social networks to promote socio-economic empowerment among marginalized communities. For this purpose, policy should create support networks or peer mentorship programmes that leverage social connections to disseminate information about available resources and opportunities identified through Thalinomics and the Bare Necessities Index. Similarly, policy can be used to encourage collective action and mutual support to overcome barriers and achieve shared goals.

◆

By harnessing the power of data analytics, innovative indices and behavioural economics principles, policymakers can address the complex socio-economic challenges faced by the poor and vulnerable. Through initiatives such as Thalinomics and the Bare Necessities Index, coupled with nudges and behavioural interventions, India can pave the way for inclusive growth, empowering poor and vulnerable individuals to realize their dreams and contribute to the nation's prosperity. As India strives towards its centennial milestone, these data-driven approaches hold the promise of a more equitable and prosperous future for all, embodying the vision of India@100 as a beacon of progress and opportunity on the global stage.

SECTION FOUR

THE THIRD PILLAR
ETHICAL WEALTH CREATION

INDIA'S ECONOMIC PROSPERITY TILL THE eighteenth century and her economic progress post liberalization in 1991 clearly demonstrate that the secret to sustained prosperity lies in enabling private enterprise in sectors where government has no business to be in business. Yet, despite PM Modi speaking about the importance of wealth creation and the need to respect wealth creators from the ramparts of the Red Fort on 15 August 2019, two historical challenges stemming from India's socialist past still hinder the acceptance of private enterprise.

First, several privileged sections benefitted from the socialist system by wielding enormous power as arbiters of national resources, be it in issuing a license or in hiring people in public sector firms. Through the enormous power that these sections wielded, they became the 'mai baap'*—or paternalistic patrons—of the common citizen. Since the common citizen's interactions with the government occurred primarily through such patrons, it led the citizen to perceive the government as his/her mai baap, responsible for taking care of and providing for all his/her activities from cradle to grave. As a result, the emphasis on individual initiative, energy and drive, which are fundamental to the belief in private enterprise, reduced.*

While liberalization removed these shackles, several sections that continue to derive such benefits still oppose the move towards private enterprise. For example, privatization of public-sector firms faces opposition from such vested interests even when such attempts are made, that too in non-strategic sectors where government has no business being involved. Weaning sections with vested interests away from excessive power and privilege—albeit in the national interest—represents a key political challenge. Reforms to enable markets and private enterprise to function smoothly, thereby fostering genuine competition across various sectors, remain critical to wealth creation in the economy.

Second, given the power that the bureaucrats and politicians possessed as the arbiter of national resources in the socialist era, undertaking business often required keeping the bosses in power happy. This created the need for businessmen to develop and nurture 'government connections'. Such norms then encouraged cronyism that led to wealth creation often being viewed with the suspicion of being unethical. The second challenge, therefore, is to enable the rule of law and the power of the state to facilitate ethical wealth creation.

Given these twin challenges, this section builds on the role of the judiciary and the bureaucracy in promoting EoDB, on the one hand, and rule of law, on the other hand, in enabling ethical wealth creation. While enabling EoDB is necessary for wealth creation, ensuring rule of law is imperative to make wealth creation ethical. Chapter 17 explores the need for marrying the invisible hand of markets with the guiding hand of ethics for India to generate equitable and sustained prosperity. Excessive government intervention in economic affairs can impede the natural mechanisms of wealth creation and innovation. Chapter 18 champions the cause of economic liberation, advocating for the minimization of needless government intervention. By fostering an environment conducive to free markets, competition and entrepreneurship, this chapter underscores the importance of unleashing the creative energies of individuals and businesses in driving economic growth and prosperity.

The process of creative destruction lies at the heart of dynamic economic growth, as obsolete industries give way to innovative ventures and technologies. Chapter 19 heralds the transformative power of creative destruction. By embracing change, disruption and innovation, this chapter charts a course towards unlocking new avenues of wealth creation and prosperity.

Entrepreneurship serves as the engine of economic dynamism, driving innovation, job creation and wealth generation. Chapter 20 celebrates the spirit of entrepreneurship, advocating for policies and initiatives that empower individuals to seize opportunities and pursue their entrepreneurial dreams.

Innovation lies at the heart of sustained economic progress, catalysing breakthroughs that reshape industries, create new markets and drive productivity gains. Chapter 21 outlines the policy approach that India needs to cultivate a culture of innovation and creativity.

India cannot grow at 8 per cent consistently if our state-owned enterprises continue to grow anaemically. Chapter 22 advocates for the harnessing of private prowess in driving economic growth through privatization. By transferring ownership and management of public assets to the private sector, this chapter seeks to unlock value, foster competition and stimulate investment, thereby catalysing economic dynamism and prosperity.

17

RESPONSIBLE PROSPERITY

The Invisible Hand of Markets Wedded to the Hand of Ethics

Do you know that for more than three-fourths of known economic history, India has been a dominant economic power globally? This dominance manifested as the economy relied on the energy brought by private enterprise driven by the invisible hand of the market married to the hand of ethics. Specifically, the invisible hand of markets, as reflected in the openness in economic transactions, was combined with the hand of ethics that fostered intrinsic motivation by appealing to ethical and philosophical dimensions.

Contemporary evidence following the liberalization of the economy supports both pillars of the economic model advocated in India's traditional thinking. The exponential rise in India's GDP and GDP per capita post liberalization coincided with wealth generation in the stock market. Similarly, the evidence across various sectors of the economy illustrates the enormous benefits that accrue from enabling the invisible hand of the market.

The events in India's financial sector during 2011–13 and the economic consequences that followed from the same illustrate the need for the hand of ethics to support the invisible hand. In fact, following the GFC, an emerging branch of economics literature now recognizes the need for the hand of trust to complement the invisible hand. India's economic aspirations depend critically on strengthening the invisible hand of markets and the hand of ethics that can support markets.

Importance of Wealth Creation

India has historically been a major wealth creator and a significant contributor to the world's GDP, as shown in Figure 1 and as highlighted by Angus Maddison in his book, *Contours of the World Economy 1–2030 AD: Essays in Macro-Economic History*.[92]

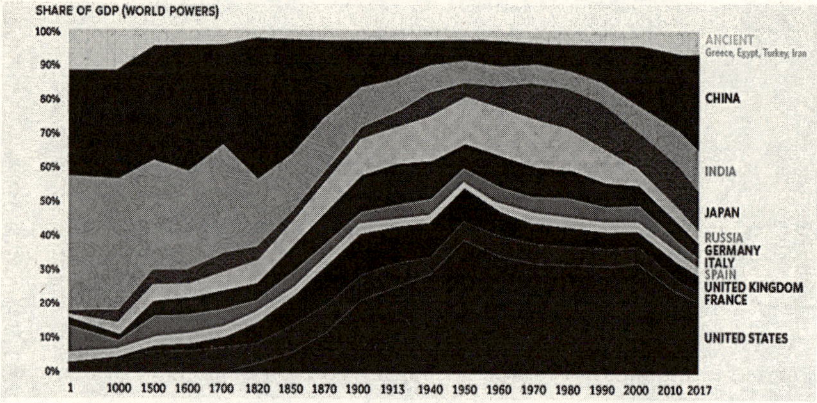

Figure 1: Global contribution to world's GDP by major economies from AD 1 to AD 2017

Source: Maddison (2007)

Note: X axis of graph has non-linear scale, especially for AD 1–1500, which underestimates the dominance of India.

Economic dominance over such long periods manifests by design, not by mere chance. In this context, the *Economic Survey 2019–20* notes that our age-old traditions have always commended wealth creation. While Kautilya's *Arthashastra* is given as a canonical example, wealth creation as a worthy human pursuit is recognized by other traditional literature as well. *Thirukural*, a treatise on enriching human life written in the form of couplets by Tamil saint and philosopher Thiruvalluvar, asserts in verses 753 of chapter 76:

Wealth, the lamp unfailing, speeds to every land,
Dispersing darkness at its lord's command.[93]

In verse 759 of the same chapter, which forms the second part of *Thirukural* called 'Porul Paal' or the essence of material wealth, Thiruvalluvar declares:

---

[92]Maddison, Angus, *Contours of the World Economy 1-2030 AD: Essays in Macro-Economic History*, Oxford University Press, 2007.

[93]Ministry of Finance, GoI, *Economic Survey 2019–20, Volume 1*, January 2020, p. 1, http://tinyurl.com/3jru7c4r. Accessed on 14 December 2023.

'Make money—there is no weapon sharper than it to sever the pride of your foes.'[94] Needless to say, *Thirukural* advocates wealth creation through ethical means. Verse 754 in the same chapter avows: '(Wealth) yields righteousness and joy, the wealth acquired capably without causing any harm.'[95]

Despite such a 'rich' tradition of emphasizing wealth creation, India deviated from this model for several decades after Independence. However, India has returned to these roots post the economic liberalization in 1991. The exponential rise in India's GDP and GDP per capita as seen in Figure 2 post liberalization coincides with wealth generation in the stock market that we demonstrate in Chapter 18.

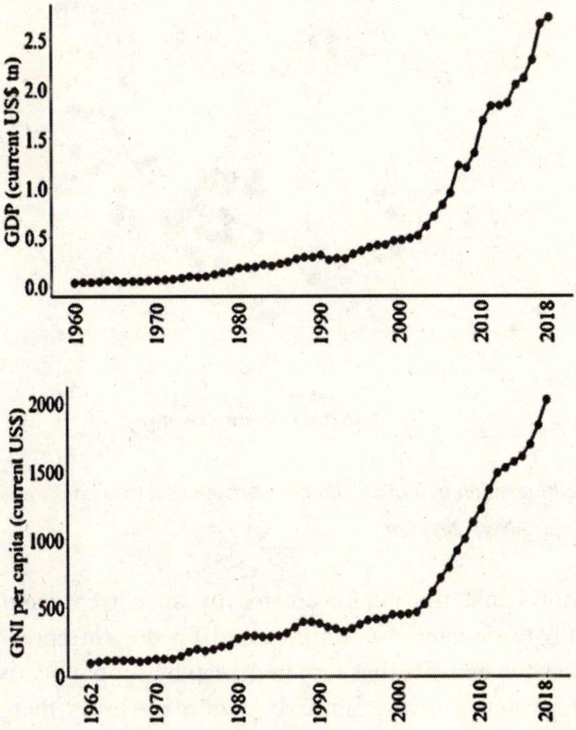

Figure 2: India's GDP and GDP per capita

Source: Economic Surveys

[94]Ibid.

[95]Ibid.

In order to understand the benefits of wealth creation in today's milieu, we collate the companies created by the top 100 wealthy entrepreneurs in the country as estimated by *Forbes* in March 2019. After excluding those with tainted wealth by applying several filters, we correlate the increase in the entrepreneur's wealth over a decade before the pandemic (31 March 2009 to 31 March 2019) with the benefits that accrued to several other stakeholders including employees, suppliers, government, etc. Figure 3 shows that the wealth created by an entrepreneur correlates strongly with benefits that accrue to the employees working in the entrepreneur's firms.

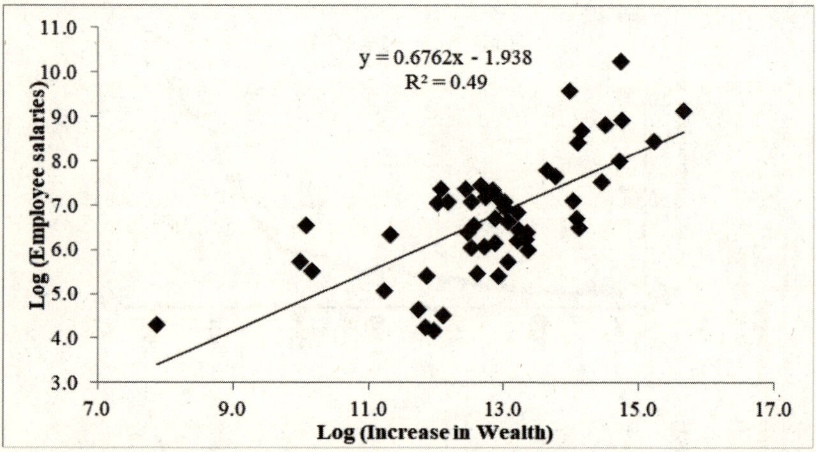

Figure 3: Wealth creation by Indian entrepreneurs and salaries paid to their employees
Source: Economic Survey 2019–20

Figure 4 shows that the wealth created by an entrepreneur correlates strongly with raw material costs incurred by the entrepreneur's firms, which proxies the benefits that suppliers reap by supplying raw materials to the entrepreneur's firms. Similarly, Figure 5 shows that the wealth created by an entrepreneur correlates strongly with the capital expenditure made by the entrepreneur's firms, which proxies the benefits that manufacturers of capital equipment reap by supplying such equipment to the entrepreneur's firms.

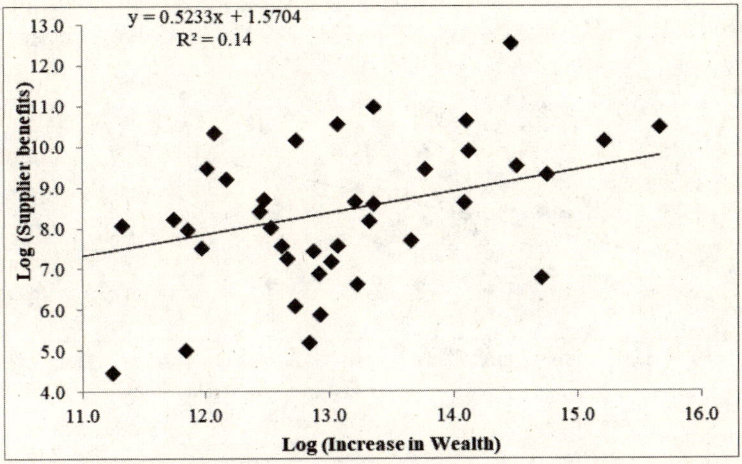

Figure 4: Wealth creation by Indian entrepreneurs and benefits reaped by their suppliers

Source: Economic Survey 2019–20

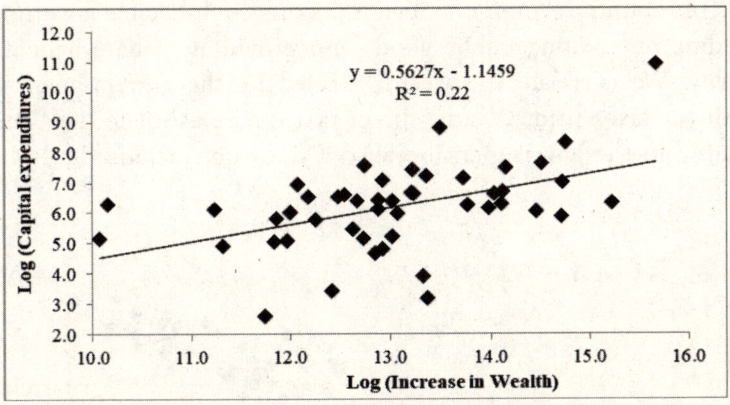

Figure 5: Wealth creation by Indian entrepreneurs and their capital expenditures

Source: Economic Survey 2019–20

Revenues earned in foreign exchange play a crucial role in maintaining macroeconomic stability as they allow the country to pay for its imports and control the CAD within manageable levels. Figure 6 shows that wealth creation by entrepreneurs correlates strongly with the foreign exchange revenues earned by the entrepreneurs' firms.

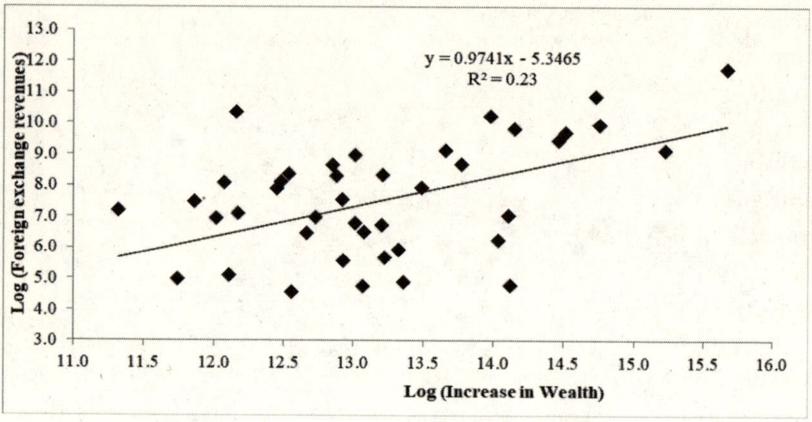

Figure 6: Wealth creation by Indian entrepreneurs and their foreign exchange revenues
Source: Economic Survey 2019–20

Finally, Figure 7 shows that the wealth created by an entrepreneur helps the country's common citizens. Tax revenues enable government spending on creating public goods and providing welfare benefits to citizens. We correlate the wealth created by the entrepreneur with the direct taxes paid. Clearly, direct taxes underestimate the benefits accruing to the government because it does not include the indirect

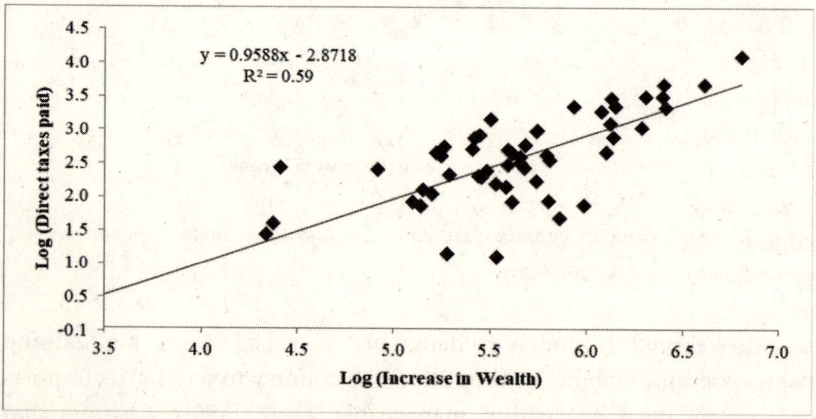

Figure 7: Wealth creation by Indian entrepreneurs and direct tax paid by them
Source: Economic Survey 2019–20

taxes paid by the entrepreneur's firms and the direct taxes paid by the employees or the suppliers. Yet, as a proxy for the benefits accruing to the citizens through spending of tax revenues by the government, this figure captures the benefits derived by the country's common citizens. Therefore, the strong correlation between wealth creation by entrepreneurs and the taxes paid represents another important benefit to society from wealth creation.

Wealth Creation through the Invisible Hand of Markets

Wealth creation happens in an economy when the right policy choices are pursued. For instance, wealth creation and economic development in several advanced economies have been guided by Adam Smith's philosophy of the invisible hand. Despite the dalliance with socialism—four decades is but an ephemeral period in a history of millennia—India has embraced the market model that represents our traditional legacy. However, scepticism about the benefits accruing from a market economy still persists. This is not an accident as our tryst with socialism for several decades makes most Indians believe that Indian economic thought conflicts with an economic model relying on the invisible hand of the market economy. However, this belief is far from the truth.

In fact, our traditional economic thinking has always emphasized enabling markets and eliminating obstacles to economic activity. As far as 2 BCE, Kautilya, postulating on the role of prices in an economy, averred, 'The root of wealth is economic activity and lack of it brings material distress. In the absence of fruitful economic activity, both current prosperity and future growth are in danger of destruction. A king can achieve the desired objectives and abundance of riches by undertaking productive economic activity.'[96] Kautilya advocated economic freedom by asking the king to 'remove all obstructions to economic activity'.[97]

Historically, a stakeholder model existed in India, as is discernible in *Arthashastra*, in which entrepreneurs, workers and consumers share prosperity. Trade and openness in economic transactions were commended. For instance, Book II of the *Arthashastra*, Chapter XVI, specifies the duties

---

[96]Ibid. 1.19.

[97]Ibid.

of the king's superintendent of commerce as: The superintendent shall show favour to those who import foreign merchandise: mariners and merchants who import foreign merchandise shall be favoured with the remission of the trade taxes, so that they may derive some profit.'[98]

Arthashastra as a treatise on economic policy was deeply influential in the functioning of the economy until the twelfth century. As a result, during much of India's economic dominance, the economy relied more on the invisible hand of the market than on the visible hand of the state.

As wealth creation happens by design, one of the key pillars for India@100 is wealth creation and the policy choices that enable the same. At its core, policies seek to maximize social welfare under a set of resource constraints. Resource constraints force policymakers to focus on efficiency—more output to be produced from given resources, such as land, human resources and capital, or the same output for less resource use.

The evidence since 1991 shows that enabling the invisible hand of markets has a huge impact in enhancing wealth both in aggregate and within sectors. Indeed, the evidence presented below shows clearly that sectors that were liberalized grew significantly faster than those that remained closed. This is not surprising as the market economy is based on the principle that optimal allocation of resources occurs when citizens are able to exercise free choice in the products or services they want.

Figure 8 shows how credit in the banking sector expanded at much higher rates after the sector was opened up for competition through licenses granted to private sector banks. As competition expanded the banking choices available to citizens, the sector experienced strong growth. Figure 9 shows a similar effect in the mutual funds sector following important changes in February 2003 that led to opening of the sector. The then government-owned mutual fund Unit Trust of India (UTI) was broken up by repealing the UTI Act, 1963. Furthermore, the UTI Mutual Fund was set up as a private sector entity sponsored by SBI, Punjab National Bank (PNB), Bank of Baroda (BOB) and Life Insurance Corporation of India (LIC).

[98]Kautilya, *Arthashastra*, R. Shamasastry (trans.), Parimal Publications Pvt Ltd, 1956, http://tinyurl.com/25fw46xm. Accessed on 14 December 2023.

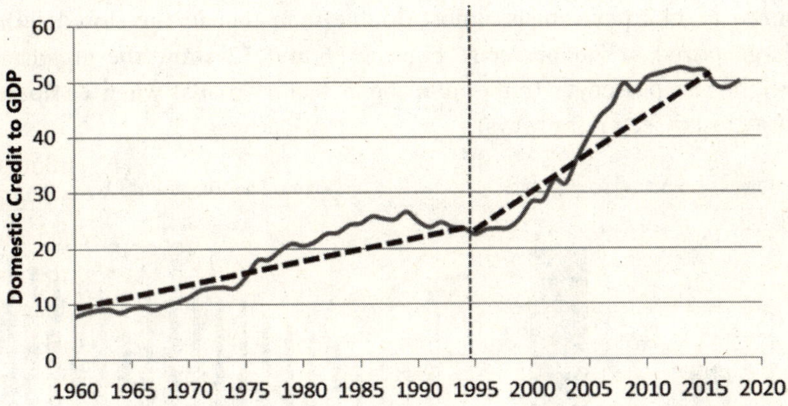

Figure 8: Increase in domestic credit to GDP after entry of private sector banks
Source: Economic Survey 2019–20

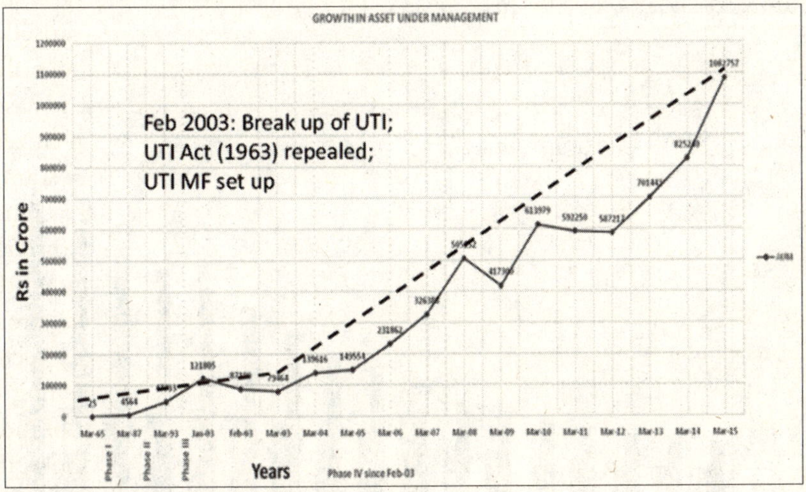

Figure 9: Growth in mutual funds sector after opening up in 2003
Source: Economic Survey 2019–20

In Figures 10–13, we examine growth in an open sector, which is defined as one where citizens can choose among many different producers, vis-à-vis a closed sector, where the citizen cannot exercise this choice. Figure 10 shows that the growth in cargo volumes in an open sector (small ports) at 14.2 per cent is almost double than that in the closed sector (large ports) at 7.8 per cent. Figures 11 and 12 show the growth in freight and passenger traffic in an open sector (roads) when compared to a closed sector (railways).

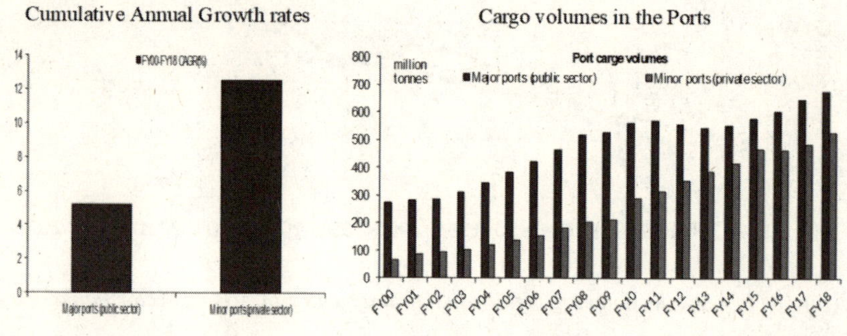

Figure 10: Growth in the ports sector—open (minor ports) versus closed (major ports)
Source: Economic Survey 2019–20

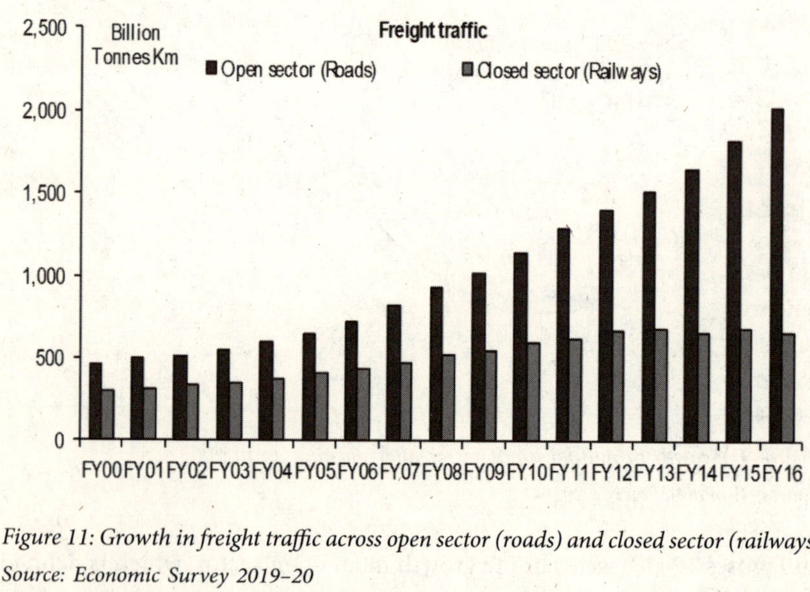

Figure 11: Growth in freight traffic across open sector (roads) and closed sector (railways)
Source: Economic Survey 2019–20

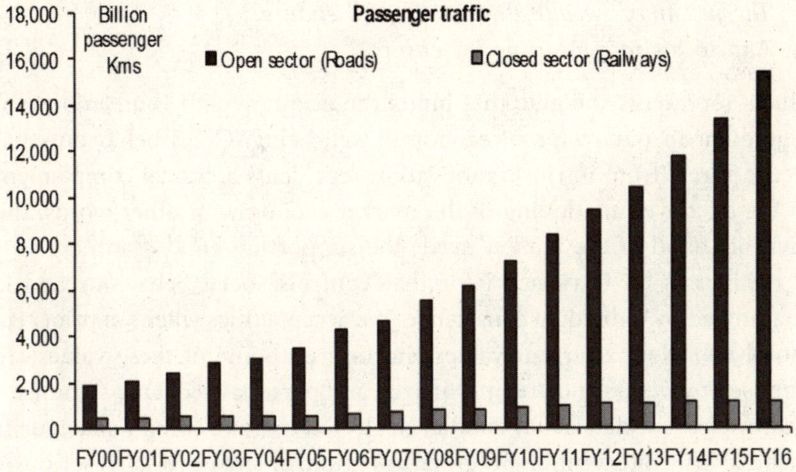

Figure 12: Growth in passenger traffic across open sector (roads) and closed sector (railways)

Source: Economic Survey 2019–20

Across Figures 11–12, we see that growth has been significantly greater in the open sector than in the closed sector. Figures 8–12 thus highlight the positive impact of enabling economic choice for citizens in the economy.

Enabling the Hand of Ethics

Think about a river that is well-banked. Water in such a river flows synchronously irrigating fields to create prosperity. The same river with its banks broken can create enormous destruction, as the water runs helter-skelter flooding fields instead of irrigating them. Ethics in an economy represent the banks that enable the river of market transactions to create prosperity. Without ethics, the same economy resembles an unbanked river creating destruction in its wake.

Recognizing the seminal importance of ethics in an economy, as Thiruvalluvar mentions clearly, our tradition celebrates wealth that is created ethically, not wealth that is accumulated by *any* means.

The just man's wealth unwasting shall endure,
And to his race a lasting joy ensure.[99]

Ethics represents the glue that binds the economy and is an important ingredient in our recipe of economic well-being. Good behaviour that stems purely from intrinsic motivation represents a crucial complement to the effective functioning of the market economy. In other words, the invisible hand of the market needs the supporting hand of ethics.

Ethics is an intrinsic factor that controls social behaviour and is guaranteed by individual conscience. We accept ethics when we prioritize moral behaviour over our values and desires. Some of these values are imposed by others and are internalized and personalized. One significant and unpleasant detail that is often neglected in controlling behaviour is that extrinsic intervention programmes (punishment or reward) seriously damage or eradicate intrinsic motivation. There is ample psychological proof for this. For instance, children who receive prizes for studying will stop it when they are not rewarded anymore. This implies that rewarding has, in some cases, reverse effects and weakens intrinsic desire for an action, such that the individual abandons the action when he feels he will not be rewarded. However, external interventions are not all negative. Studies show that laws and rules help internalize positive behaviours and reinforce ethics under certain circumstances. When the logic behind the rules is explained, justified, taught and enculturated, self-control is strengthened among people and they automatically perform the action, even when the external force is removed. Once ethics is internalized, extrinsic forces can be applied with care to guide and reinforce intrinsic incentives but not turn them into external obligations.

The following measures must be considered by policymakers to promote ethical behaviour in the Indian economy:

Decentralized Communication to Strengthen Intrinsic Motivation

An important initiative is the decentralization of the means of communication used to strengthen intrinsic motivation. When respected

---

[99]*Thirukural,* Chapter 12, Verse 112, cited in Ministry of Finance, GoI, *Economic Survey 2019–20,* Volume 1, January 2020, p. 21, http://tinyurl.com/3jru7c4r. Accessed on 14 December 2023.

local community leaders who are trustworthy are tasked with creating trust and promoting ethical behaviour, they have better impact than, say, government officials, who have economic incentives to be part of such campaigns. Corporate leaders who are iconic and highly respected should be encouraged to mentor other leaders in small groups in their own local business communities. For instance, a business person in Bengaluru or Vadodara should mentor other business persons in his/her city's local business communities to foster ethical behaviour. It should be made evident that these are not networking events, and there may not be any economic gains from such mentoring for either the mentor or the mentees. Besides, iconic corporate leaders in a particular business should avoid mentoring businessmen in the same business as they might be competitors and the mentoring activity may be perceived to have economic implications for both the mentee and the mentor.

Reducing Information Asymmetry

An important factor that increases the potential for opportunism in any economic exchange is information asymmetry. Such opportunism can be remedied increasingly through standardizing enforcement systems and public databases. For instance, in the case of wilful defaults pre 2014, inability to access relevant borrower data was a key driver of information asymmetry. This aspect of access of credit information for corporate borrowers has improved considerably in recent years. It can be argued that if the economy had the data infrastructure, such as the Central Repository of Information on Large Credits (CRILC) during the pre-2014 credit boom, the extent of systemic NPAs may have been lower. This information would have alerted lenders to limit exposures to corporates who have been tagged as NPA by another bank or Non-Banking Financial Company (NBFC). This information availability would have reduced NPAs in the entire banking system considerably because when a borrower defaults with one lender, other lenders can contractually tag their loan too as a default and therefore recall the loan. This is possible because all corporate loan documents have cross-default clauses. This would have limited incremental exposure of other banks that were not aware that at least one other financial institution had tagged a loan as an NPA. Such public databases remove information asymmetry considerably.

Figure 13 shows that the information sharing among lenders on NPAs was minimal in 2014. While this information sharing was better among public sector banks (PSBs) than new private banks (NPBs), about a quarter of accounts that were declared as NPAs by other banks were classified as NPA in the bank's account. This proportion has increased dramatically to reach 95 per cent in just a few years. This has decreased the potential for opportunism and should enable greater trust in lending activities of financial institutions.

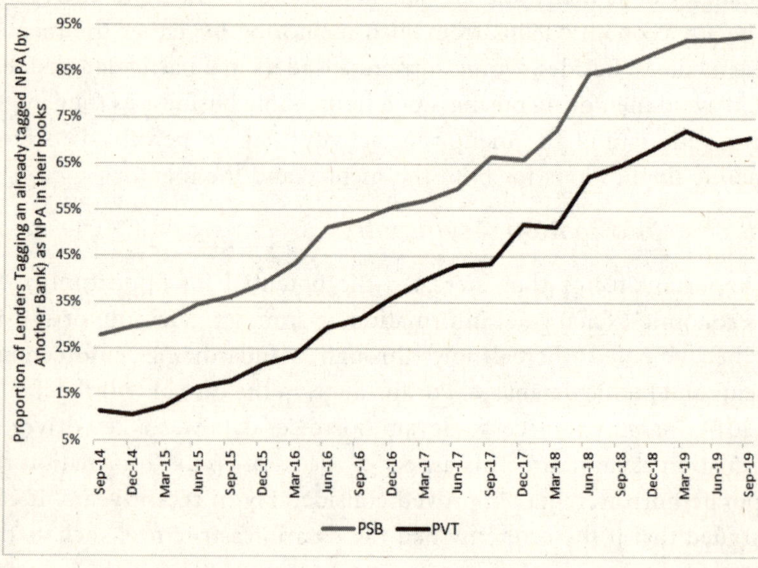

Figure 13: Proportion of lenders tagging an already tagged NPA (by another bank) as NPA in their books

Source: TransUnion CIBIL

Enhancing Quality of Supervision

The government needs to support the moral hand by being a good referee of the economy. The referee's job is to not only report but also detect opportunistic behaviour if people are not playing by the rules. Like wilful defaults, malpractices, such as financial misreporting and market manipulation, need to be detected early because these are termites that eat away investor's faith in financial markets, diminish portfolio investments and crowd out important national investments. They scare away scrupulous and law-abiding market participants and drive away investments and therefore jobs in the economy. To fittingly celebrate wealth creators who make wealth ethically, it is of utmost importance that our financial markets are fair and transparent. In this, the state's role as a competent referee cannot be overemphasized.

The US Federal Trade Commission (FTC) has one employee for every two listed firms, while the Competition Commission of India (CCI) has one employee for every 38 listed firms. The US Securities and Exchange Commission (SEC) has almost one employee for each listed company. In contrast, Securities and Exchange Board of India (SEBI) has one employee for six listed companies. In fact, in key divisions such as corporate finance, SEC has more than 15 times as many employees as SEBI. This resource deficit needs to be reduced to strengthen the government's role as a referee to ensure fair play for all wealth creators.

The SEC and FTC extensively use AI and ML to track and flag market malpractices, while none of our regulators do so. As a result of the limited resources at the regulators' disposal, supervision of the market economy suffers badly, thereby encouraging market malpractices. The Indian economy cannot achieve its ambitious goals if it is plagued by market malpractices and suboptimal supervision. Therefore, significant enhancement in the quantity and quality of manpower in our regulators (CCI, RBI, SEBI, Insolvency and Bankruptcy Board of India [IBBI]) together with significant investments in technology and analytics need to be made. This would enhance the effectiveness of the moral hand in supporting the invisible hand for greater wealth creation.

18

LIBERATING THE ECONOMY

Minimizing Needless Government Intervention

Do you complain about the high prices of Uber rides during peak time? But when selling your car second-hand to someone else, will you complain about the high price of the car? Of course, not! As a buyer, you always probably prefer lower prices for just about everything. But as a seller, you always wish for higher prices. Prices are a fact of life, and so is complaining about them: too high when you are a buyer and too low when you are a seller! However, to an economist, prices are the key to widespread prosperity. Prices contain vital information: they show us how scarce resources are. The Uber ride costs more during peak hours as cabs for hire are more scarce. The higher price reflects that several office goers are demanding an Uber ride back home. Entrepreneurs and innovators rely on prices to decide what to make and how to make it.

But not all prices are meaningful. Too often, the government interferes to set prices: it sets the prices at which farmers can sell their rice and wheat through MSP ostensibly to support farmers. To provide food to vulnerable sections of the society, the government sets extremely low prices for rice, wheat and other food items to be sold via the PDS. Such interventions by the government may be well intentioned, but they distort the economy by reducing the valuable information that prices convey, thereby enhancing poverty in the economy instead of mitigating it.

The economy looks chaotic. Every day, billions of people independently make trillions of decisions. From what food to buy to which car to sell at what price, consumers and producers are making countless purchases and sales. The trillions of decisions made by producers and consumers independently result in chaos and also widespread prosperity, owing to the beauty of the market as a means to coordinate via its invisible hand. When governments neglect the crucial role of prices and markets by intervening excessively, they undermine economic freedom, resulting in a decrease in prosperity.

Need to Enhance Economic Freedom for Wealth Creation

The *Economic Survey 2019–20* showed several instances of the government intervening too much in the Indian economy. For India to be an extremely prosperous economy by 2047, this phenomenon must reduce.

Economic freedom enhances wealth creation by enabling efficient allocation of entrepreneurial resources and energy to productive activities, thereby promoting economic dynamism.

While there is a case for government intervention when markets do not function properly, excessive intervention, especially when markets can do the job of enhancing citizens' welfare perfectly well, stifles economic freedom. Government can affect markets either through direct participation (as a market maker or as a buyer or supplier of goods and services) or through indirect participation in private markets (for example, through regulation, taxation, subsidy or other influence). Any government intervention of the first kind, however, affects the dynamic interaction of supply and demand in markets and, thereby, determination of 'equilibrium' market prices. When the price is too high, there is an excessive amount of the product for sale compared to what people want. When the price is too low, it causes consumers to want more of the product than producers have available. In both cases, serious welfare loss results because not enough of the product is sold. The wasted chance to create both producer and consumer welfare from such sales leads to 'deadweight loss'—income that is lost forever. In addition to creating deadweight loss, an artificially high price transfers profits from consumers to producers and creates opportunities for rent seeking. On the other hand, an artificially low price leads to transfer of profits from producers to consumers, which results in low incentive to invest further and exacerbates the scarcity of the product.

As we illustrate in this chapter, the Indian economy is replete with examples where the government intervenes even if there is no risk of market failure, and in fact, in some instances its intervention has created market failures. This may be partly due to the legacy of post-Independence economic policies that the country followed. However, as the role of markets has been recognized globally, it is only natural that markets are allowed to work to enable quick wealth creation and thereby economic growth.

Legislative Change to Reduce Government Interventions

In several spheres of the economy, India has traversed the transition from a command-and-control economy to a market-driven economy. Table 1 illustrates this across several areas. Specifically, industrial deregulation, privatizations of several state-owned enterprises and reduced controls on international trade and investment stand out in this context.

Table 1
Traversing the 'full circle'—from 'control' to 'market'

Act	*Market Distortion Created*	*Transformation towards Developing a Market Economy*
Capital Issues (Control) Act, 1947	The government decided which company could raise how much capital. Control over the amount as well as pricing of shares led to ineffective valuation of capital.	Repealed and replaced by the SEBI Act, 1992, as a regulator of the capital markets. SEBI steered the capital markets to ensure price discovery, governance of securities, allowing efficient mobilization and allocation of capital, protecting the interest of investors and enabling enormous wealth creation (as detailed in Chapter 1).
Oil and Natural Gas Commission (ONGC) Act, 1959	ONGC was created with the mandate to plan, promote, organize and implement programmes for the development of petroleum resources—a government monopoly in this sector.	On 4 September 1993, the Act was repealed and ONGC was converted into a company. The evolution of hydrocarbons policy went through different stages—from state monopoly in 1948, to the beginning of deregulation in 1991 through nomination, to competitive bidding and profit sharing under New Exploration Licensing Policy (NELP), 1997, to gas pricing guidelines in 2014, to Discovered Small Fields Policy in 2015 and, finally, to a uniform licence for exploration and production of all forms of hydrocarbon and revenue sharing under the Hydrocarbon Exploration and Licensing Policy (HELP) in 2016.

Act	*Market Distortion Created*	*Transformation towards Developing a Market Economy*
The Banking Companies (Acquisition and Transfer of Undertakings) Act of 1970 and State Bank of India Act, 1955	To provide for the acquisition and transfer of the undertakings of certain banking companies, 27 nationalized banks were created. Private-sector banks were allowed only after 1994.	Merger of banks announced aimed at reducing PSBs from 27 to 12. Further, attempts to create a level-playing field between private-sector banks and PSBs were put in place.
The Monopolies and Restrictive Trade Practices (MRTP) Act, 1969	The Monopolies and Restrictive Trade Practices Commission (MRTPC) was constituted to prevent concentration of economic power, control of monopolies, prohibition of monopolistic practices and prohibition of restrictive and unfair trade practices. This restricted the growth of companies, which did not grow to achieve a global scale. It also led to the proliferation of small companies.	Repealed to give way to The Competition Act in 2002. The Competition Act aims to 'promote and sustain competition in markets, protect interests of consumers, ensure freedom of trade carried on by various market participants, and prohibit abuse of dominant position'. The focus has shifted from 'prevention of dominance' to 'regulating abuse of dominance'.

Act	*Market Distortion Created*	*Transformation towards Developing a Market Economy*
The Coking Coal Mines (Nationalization) Act, 1972, and The Coal Mines (Nationalization) Act, 1973	The government took over the management of coking and non-coking coal mines, as the energy sector became a crucial sector.	Repealed in 2018. Private firms were permitted to enter the commercial coal mining industry. The mines were to be auctioned to the firm offering the highest per tonne price. The move broke the monopoly of Coal India Limited (CIL) over commercial mining.
Nationalization of Life Insurance, 1956, and The General Insurance Business (Nationalization) Act, 1972	Acquisition and transfer of shares of Indian insurance companies and undertakings of other existing insurers to create LIC and General Insurance Corporation of India (GIC) led to cheap mobilization of resources for investment in sectors decided by the government.	Amended various times. The Insurance Regulatory and Development Authority (IRDA) Act, 1999, enacted to open the insurance sector. This was a journey from nationalization to creation of a monopoly and finally to opening up to private competition.
Foreign Exchange Regulation Act (FERA), 1973	Imposed restriction on foreign equity in companies to 40 per cent, and permission was needed from the RBI to operate, if their shareholding was higher. This restricted access to foreign capital and technology.	Repealed and replaced by Foreign Exchange Management Act (FEMA), 1999, to facilitate external trade and payments. Under FERA, everything was prohibited unless special permissions were received, while under FEMA, everything was permitted unless specifically restricted or regulated to enable development of the forex market.

Act	*Market Distortion Created*	*Transformation towards Developing a Market Economy*
Maruti Limited (Acquisition and Transfer of Undertakings) Act, 1980	The purpose was to modernize the automobile industry and ensure higher production of motor vehicles.	On 14 May 2007, the government exited the company through a two-stage process: a rights issue of ₹400 crore, followed by the sale of its existing shares through a public issue.
Air Corporations Act, 1953	The nationalization of nine airlines to form Air India and Indian Airlines was intended to provide safe, efficient, adequate, economical and properly coordinated air transport services, whether domestic, international, or both. A market-driven, services-oriented, consumer-centric business was nationalized.	Replaced by The Air Corporations (Transfer of Undertakings and Repeal) Act, 1994, wherein private operators were allowed to provide air transport services. The Airports Authority of India (Amendment) Act of 2003 introduced the term 'private airport' and authorized Airports Authority of India (AAI) to transfer operations and management of its existing airports by way of long-term lease to private players. The Airports Economic Regulatory Authority (AERA) of India Act, 2008, was enacted to regulate tariff and other charges and to monitor performance standards.
The Urban Land (Ceiling and Regulation) Act, 1976	Imposition of a ceiling on acquisition of vacant land in urban agglomerations to prevent the concentration of urban land in the hands of a few and bring equity to subserve the common good.	Repealed in 1999.

Act	*Market Distortion Created*	*Transformation towards Developing a Market Economy*
	This led to distortion of land markets in urban areas, a rise in slums, creation of artificial land scarcity and skyrocketing land prices.	
The Sick Industrial Companies (Special Provisions) Act (SICA), 1985	Timely detection of sick and potentially sick companies and speedy determination of preventive, ameliorative, remedial and other measures by the Board for Industrial and Financial Reconstruction (BIFR). It put in place a debtor-friendly regime, in which defaulting borrowers could delay resolution for long periods of time and strip assets of value.	The Act was repealed on 1 January 2004, and the BIFR was dissolved on 1 December 2016 to give way to the Insolvency and Bankruptcy Code (IBC), 2016.

Yet, several areas of unnecessary and inefficient government intervention still remain. Table 2 summarizes some key Acts as low-hanging fruits to begin with, which have outlived their use and need to be repealed by one 'stroke-of-the-pen'—as was done post 1990s—or amended to enable the functioning of competitive markets.

Table 2
Need to complete the transformation: Acts which need to be repealed/amended

Act	*Market Distortion Created*	*Need for Repeal/Amendment*
The Factories Act, 1948	Regulates occupational safety and health in factories and docks. Gives prosecutor powers to a 'chief inspector'—raises cost of such entitlements and may nudge capital away from labour.	Now subsumed by the Occupational Safety, Health and Working Conditions Code passed by Parliament in 2020.
The Essential Commodities Act (ECA), 1955, and the Prevention of Blackmarketing and Maintenance of Supplies of Essential Commodities Act, 1980	Enables the government to regulate the production, supply and distribution of 'essential' commodities such as drugs, oils, kerosene, coal, iron, steel and pulses. It imposes stock limits, which discourages large-scale private investments in agricultural markets.	These Acts owe their origin to times of shortage and inefficient linking of markets. With enhanced production and integration of markets, these Acts have become an instrument of coercion and inhibit proper functioning of markets of these essential commodities.
Food Corporation of India (FCI) Act, 1964	The FCI was created for purchase, storage, transport, distribution and sale of food grains and other foodstuff to safeguard the interests of farmers, maintain buffer stocks for food security and make grains accessible at reasonable prices to the weaker and vulnerable through the PDS.	With a comfortable production scenario for food grains, the role of the FCI, with a total storage capacity of more than 80 million tonnes, must be re-examined. Procurement operations of wheat, paddy and rice need to be given to states. The FCI should primarily focus on creating competition in every segment of the foodgrain supply chain—from procurement to stocking to movement and finally distribution in the targeted public distribution system (TPDS). This would reduce costs and plug leakages in the food management system.

Act	*Market Distortion Created*	*Need for Repeal/Amendment*
The Sick Textile Undertakings (Nationalization) Act, 1974	To acquire sick textile units, reorganize and rehabilitate them. Sick textile mills—103 in number—were nationalized and transferred to the National Textile Corporation Limited (NTC). The Act was amended in 1995 to allow the NTC to transfer, mortgage or dispose of land, plant, machinery or other assets for the better management, modernization, restructuring or revival of a sick textile undertaking.	Land of textile units has been monetized to create offices and residential buildings in Mumbai's Lower Parel area. However, the nationalization of these mills failed to achieve the desired objectives of rehabilitating or reorganizing them and failed to deliver yarn, cloth, fair prices or jobs. This Act, therefore, needs to be repealed and the NTC should be divested.
Recovery of Debts Due to Banks and Financial Institutions Act, 1993	Led to establishment of Debts Recovery Tribunals (DRTs) for 'expeditious adjudication and recovery of debts due to banks and financial institutions.'[100] However, there are huge delays due to insufficient number of presiding officers, recoveries taking two years instead of the recommended statutory six months, lack of sufficient judicial experience of recovery officers, and inconsistency of the decision-making process between tribunals.	With the IBC now firmly in place to fix the problem of NPAs, the DRTs can be phased out or integrated with the IBC.
The Right to Fair Compensation and Transparency in Land Acquisition, Rehabilitation and Resettlement Act, 2013	Regulates land acquisition with 80 per cent of the land to be acquired through negotiations, with the government stepping in only for the balance 20 per cent; for PPP projects, it is 70 per cent.	This tilts the balance in favour of land owners who need to be made an equal partner in the development of land and share the benefits and costs with the developer/acquirer.

[100]'Debts Recovery Tribunals/Debts Recovery Appellate Tribunals', *Department of Financial Services*, Ministry of Finance, https://tinyurl.com/5yjbb3p4. Accessed on 30 November 2023.

Review and Reduce Needless Government Intervention

Competitive markets are effective in allocating resources in an economy. However, while the ideal of a completely efficient market is rare, the costs of government intervention may outweigh the benefits when 'market failures'—a term that economists use to denote situations where markets may not work very well in allocating resources—are not severe. Of course, governments play a crucial role by intervening in situations where 'market failures' are acute (see Figure 2 for a summary).

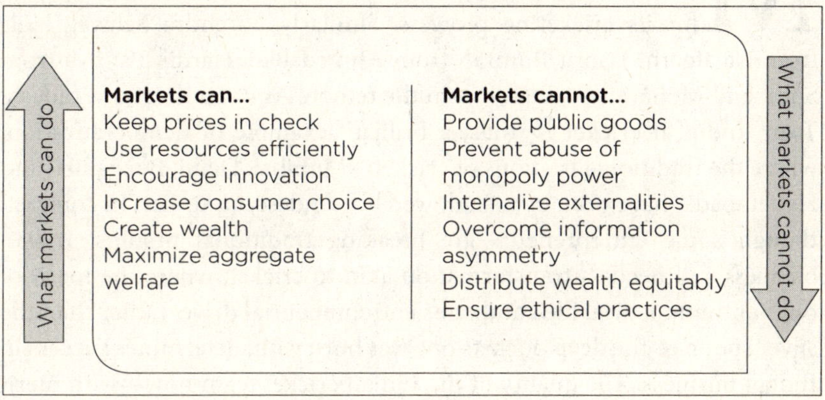

Figure 2: Strengths and weaknesses of markets

Source: Economic Survey 2019–20

◆

In several areas of the Indian economy, the government needlessly intervenes and undermines markets. Note that the case being made here is not that there should be no government intervention. Instead, it is critical for policy to recognize that such intervention makes economic sense only if market failures are severe. Thus, the interventions that were apt in a different economic setting, possibly because the market failures were severe then, may have lost their relevance in a transformed economy where the market failures are not severe. Eliminating such instances of needless government intervention will allow for competitive markets, thereby spurring investments and economic growth.

19

REVOLUTIONIZING SUCCESS

Creative Destruction for Wealth Creation

Mahendra Singh Dhoni became a cricket star purely on merit. He comes from Jharkhand, a state not known traditionally for its cricketing prowess. Similarly, Virendra Sehwag hails from Najafgarh, Jasprit Bumrah from Ahmedabad, Hardik Pandya from Surat and Mohammed Shami from the remote Amroha in Uttar Pradesh. Team India in cricket is, thus, a brilliant example of democratization, where the traditional bastions of cricket—Mumbai, Delhi, Bengaluru and Hyderabad—have been overshadowed by nondescript towns. In contrast, though some entrepreneurs are breaking traditional moulds, Indian business still needs a transformation akin to cricket, where the merit of one's entrepreneurial idea and one's entrepreneurial drive, rather than the silver spoon or the deep pockets one was born with, determines success in Indian business. The quality of the Indian cricket team now—with merit determining success in cricket—when compared to its quality earlier clearly demonstrates the phenomenal transformation that an emphasis on merit will bring to the Indian economy.

Therefore, India's economic aspirations when it turns 100 depend critically on promoting a 'pro-business' policy that unleashes the power of competitive markets to generate wealth on one hand, and steering away from a 'pro-cronyism' policy that may favour specific private interests, especially powerful incumbents, on the other. Economic events since 1991 provide powerful evidence supporting this crucial distinction. Viewed from the lens of the stock market, which captures the pulse of any economy, creative destruction has increased significantly after reform. Before liberalization, a Sensex firm was expected to stay in it for 60 years, which has decreased to only 12 years after liberalization. Every five years, one-third of Sensex firms are churned out, reflecting the continuous influx of new firms, products and technologies into the economy.

Despite impressive progress in enabling competitive markets, pro-crony policies have, in the past, destroyed value in the economy. It is, therefore, critical that India continues to implement policies that foster competition in the economy and keep incumbents on their toes by encouraging creative destruction in the economy.

Pro-business, Creative Destruction and Wealth Creation

The economic liberalization of 1991 led to the emergence of competitive markets. It unleashed the forces of creative destruction, thus generating benefits that we still witness today. Using the lens of equity markets as captured in the S&P BSE Sensex, we can clearly see an increase in market dynamism in the pro-business India of the post-liberalization period. Figure 1 reveals that, after the market reforms of 1991, Sensex has not only grown but has grown at an accelerating pace. While crossing the first incremental 5,000 points took more than 13 years and was achieved in 1999, the time taken to achieve each incremental milestone has substantially reduced over the years.

Broadly, the growth of the Sensex, as seen in the figure, can be divided into three phases after 1999. Phase I from 1999 to 2007 saw acceleration in the growth of the Sensex, with each successive 5,000-point mark taking lesser and lesser time to achieve. Phase II from 2007 to 2014 saw a slowdown in the index's growth. This phase coincides with the global slowdown in 2008 among other unfavourable events. Phase III began in 2014 and saw a revival in response to structural reforms and improvement in global liquidity. Strikingly, in this phase, the Sensex jumped from the 30,000 to the 40,000 mark in just two years, from the 40,000 to the 50,000 mark in less than two years and from the 50,000 to 60,000 mark in just seven months. Overall, in Phase III, the Sensex has jumped from 25,000 in June 2014 to 65,000 in July 2023, which is 2.6 times, or more than double, in nine years. As the cumulative abnormal growth rates shown in the chart depict clearly, the acceleration in the Sensex was not due to the base effect. In fact, the higher acceleration stemmed from a higher CAGR.

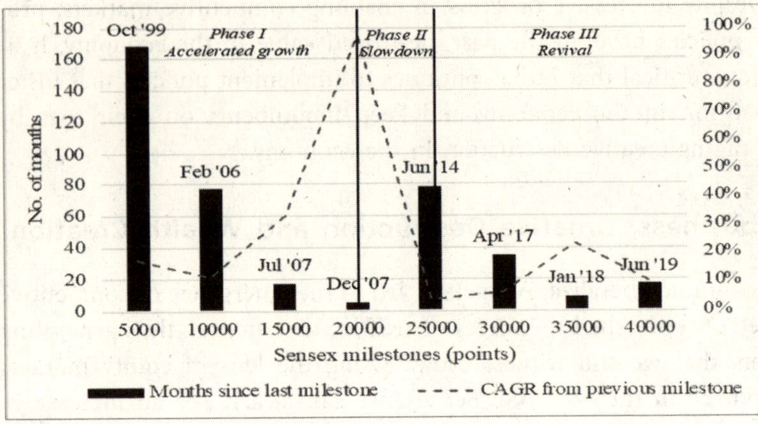

Figure 1: Sensex—incremental months taken to cross each 5,000-point milestone

Source: BSE

Note: Time to cross each milestone is defined as the time elapsed between the first time the Sensex closed at the previous milestone and the first time it closed at the present milestone. Note that milestones are based on closing prices. The CAGR is computed over the period from the previous milestone to the current one. Time elapsed is recorded as number of calendar days and converted to months assuming 30 days a month.

The relationship between pro-business policy and creative destruction is mirrored in the composition of the Sensex over the years.[101] For the first 10 years, since the Sensex's inception in 1986, the firms that constituted the index barely changed. As Figure 2 shows, nearly all the firms that constituted the index during its inception were retained for the majority of the next decade. On the other hand, the constituents of the Sensex of 1997 were steadily churned out over the next decade, resulting in only half of those firms being listed on the Sensex of 2006.

[101]Data gathered from BSE and Bloomberg. Full market capitalization is used rather than free-float capitalization for comparability over time, as free-float methodology was initiated only in 2003. Sensex constituents and market capitalization data were obtained from BSE for 1985–2000. Data is available from BSE on the following dates of observation: December 1991, June 1992, June 1993, November 1994, March 1995, March 1996, March 1997, June 1998, March 1999, March 2000. Data for subsequent years obtained from Bloomberg with September of each corresponding year as the month of observation, basis the latest available data as of this writing (data for 2019 is as of 3 September 2019).

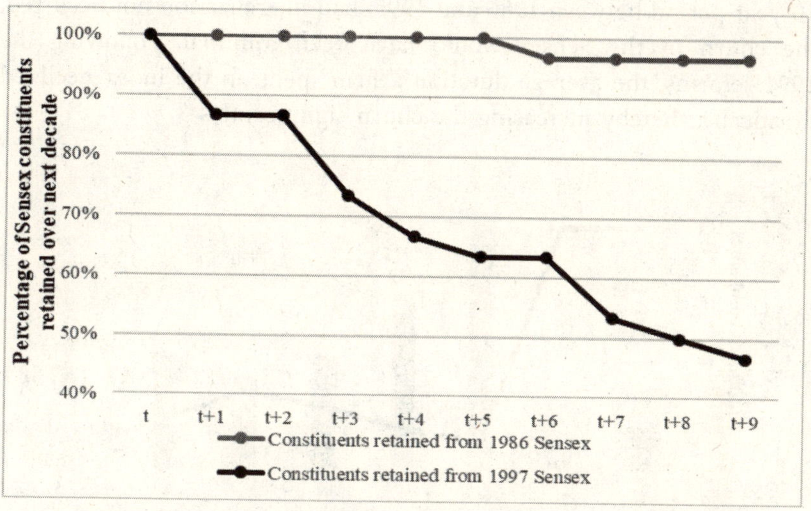

Figure 2: Percentage of Sensex constituents retained over next decade

Source: Bloomberg, BSE

Note: Due to slight discrepancy in the month of observation before and after 2001 (due to distinct data sources), consider individual annual churn rates for 2000–02 as approximate; however, the aggregated churn over these years is accurate.

The lack of dynamism in the constitution of the index in its initial years was largely representative of the lack of dynamism in the economy in general. However, the years following the 1991 liberalization saw the rapid emergence of new firms, new ideas, new technologies and new operating processes, causing a steep revision of the Sensex in 1996. After 1996, the Sensex underwent more frequent revisions, owing to the more dynamic nature of the now substantially more competitive Indian market.

Figure 3 shows the number of firms that exited the Sensex in each five-year period following 1986. Pro-business policy, i.e., liberalization, caused a spike in the number of firms churned in the years that immediately followed it, but the churn rate did not decline to pre-liberalization levels in later years. Ten firms were churned out in the five years from 2006 to 2010, eight in 2011–15, and ten in 2016–19. Put differently, every five years, roughly one-third of the firms in the index are replaced.

The figure also indicates the average duration a Sensex constituent remains on the index. Given that only five firms exited the index in the

10-year period between 1986 and 1995, had liberalization not occurred, the churn in the Sensex would have been minimal. Following the 1991 reforms, the average duration a firm spent on the index declined drastically, thereby increasing the churn significantly.

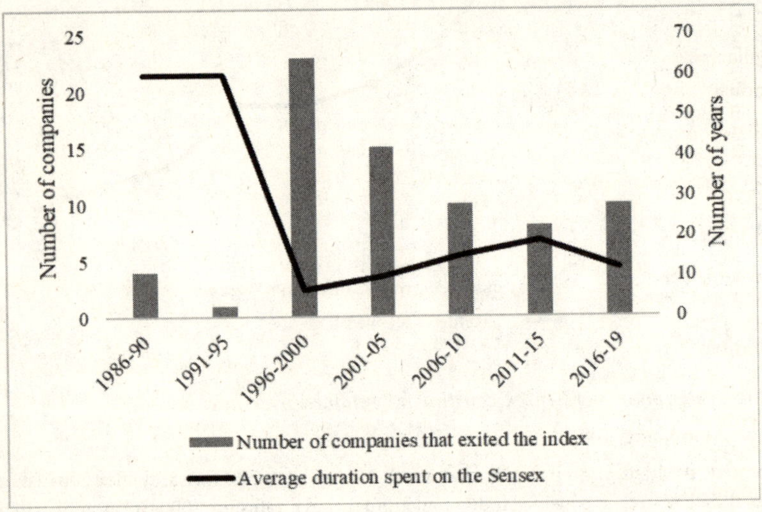

Figure 3: Increasing churn in the Sensex

Source: Bloomberg, BSE

Note: Average time spent on the Sensex is calculated as the reciprocal of the churn rate in that period. Because of the very low churn in the first two periods, the total churn rate during 1986–95 is used to infer the time spent on the Sensex for these two periods.

A pertinent question that arises at this stage is whether the churn, illustrated earlier, was beneficial to the economy. A monopolist taking the place of another identical monopolist is hardly beneficial. However, in the Indian case, the Sensex does represent a process of creative destruction rather than spurious dynamism. The firms that displaced the incumbents on the Sensex brought with them new ideas, technologies and processes. For an illustration, consider Table 1 that depicts the major Sensex revision of 1996 following market reforms. New sectors like banks and financials entered the index for the first time, eroding the predominance of the manufacturing sector, placing the services sector on the map for the first time and reflecting the far-reaching changes that the economy was witnessing in the wake of liberalization.

Table 1
Revision of the constituents of the Sensex index in 1996

Exit		*Replacement*	
Firm	*Industry*	*Firm*	*Industry (New Highlighted)*
Ballarpur Industries	Materials	Arvind Mills	Consumer durables and apparel
Bharat Forge	Materials	Bajaj Auto	Automobiles and Components
GSFC	Materials	Ambuja Cements	Materials
Indian Organic	Materials	ICICI	Diversified financials
Mukand Iron	Materials	MTNL	Telecommunication services
Bombay Dyeing	Consumer durables and apparel	BHEL	Capital goods
Century Textiles	Consumer durables and apparel	Colgate	Household & personal products
Indian Rayon	Consumer durables and apparel	IDBI	Diversified financials
Philips	Consumer durables and apparel	Ranbaxy Labs	Pharma, biotech and life sciences
Voltas	Consumer durables and apparel	Tata Chemicals	Materials
Ceat	Automobiles and components	BSES	Utilities
Hindustan Motors	Automobiles and components	HPCL	Energy
Premier Auto	Automobiles and components	SBI	Banks
Kirloskar Cummins	Capital goods	IPCL	Materials
Siemens	Pharma, biotech and life sciences	SAIL	Materials

Source: BSE, Bloomberg

Note: Highlighted cells represent new sectors that entered the index for the first time.

Figure 4 depicts the size of various sectors in the Sensex by market capitalization over time. Financials and IT, which were virtually non-existent in the Sensex of the early 1990s, are responsible for more than 50 per cent of its market share today. It is, therefore, incontrovertible that the churn in the Sensex represents a very real process of creative destruction that brought altogether new technologies, products and services to consumers.

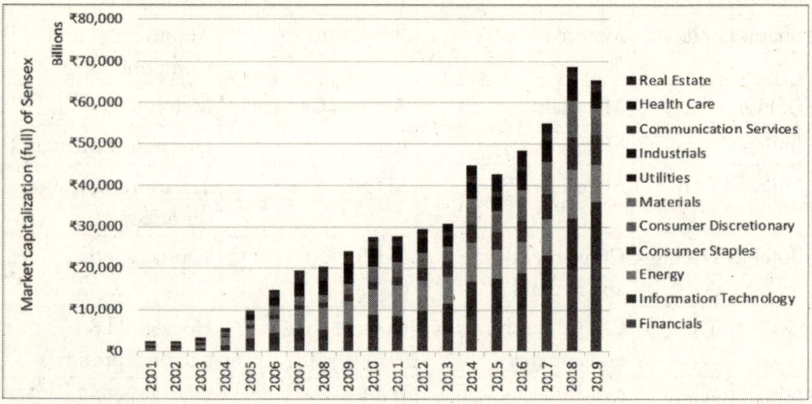

Figure 4: New sectors emerged in the Sensex following liberalization
Source: Bloomberg, BSE

The diversity of sectors in the Sensex steadily increased over time following market reforms, as shown in Figure 5. The initial Sensex of 1986 was dominated by the materials and consumer discretionary sectors, accounting for two-thirds of the firms on the Sensex. Sectors like financials, telecommunications and IT were non-existent on the index then. With the entry of these new sectors, today's Sensex is far less concentrated than the Sensex of the 1980s and 1990s and mirrors the far lower sectoral concentration of the economy as a whole.

Today's Sensex is not only composed of a larger number of sectors but also is far more democratic in terms of the size of companies. In 1991, the largest firm on the index was roughly 100 times the smallest in terms of market capitalization. Ten years later, the ratio declined to roughly 75. In 2018, the ratio was only 12. The benefit of liberalizing markets does not end with a one-time drop in the ratio and continues

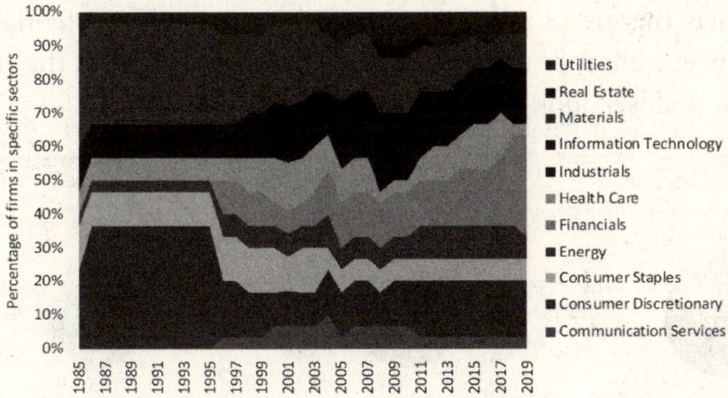

Figure 5: Sectoral concentration of the Sensex decreased post liberalization as new sectors emerged

Source: Bloomberg, BSE

to be felt even today, as indicated by the decreasing trend in the ratio in Figure 6. Similarly, while the largest firm of 1991 constituted around 20 per cent of the market capitalization of the Sensex, the largest firm of 2019 contributed only 13 per cent.

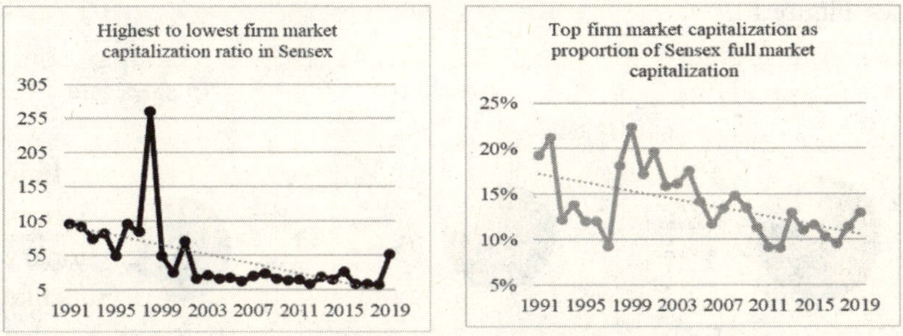

Figure 6: Decreasing size concentration of firms in the Sensex

Source: Bloomberg, BSE

Note: See earlier footnote about the dates on which market capitalization for each corresponding year is observed. Data for 2019 is as of 3 September 2019.

The forces of creative destruction following economic liberalization have led to the rise of new sectors such as financials and IT. The share of these sectors in the total market capitalization has increased over the years, so much so that these sectors dominate the Sensex today (see Figure 7). At first glance, this trend indicates a cause for concern: a potential case of more concentration or a reversal in creative destruction in the economy. However, a closer look reveals otherwise.

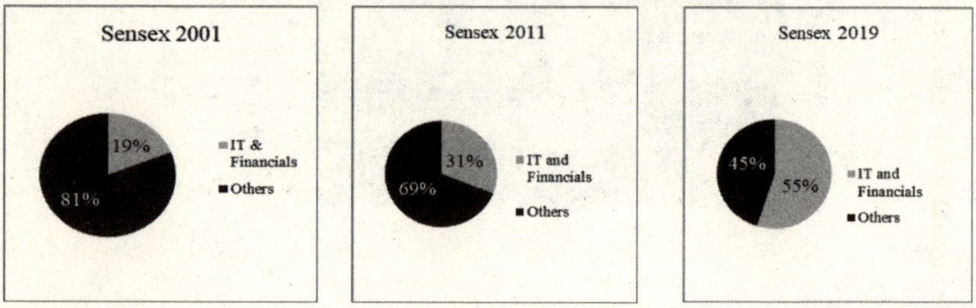

Figure 7: Increasing share of IT and financials sector in total market capitalization of Sensex

Source: Bloomberg, BSE

First, the rising share in market capitalization has been achieved by an increase in the number of companies rather than an expansion in the size of incumbents, suggesting greater competition within these sectors (see Figure 8).

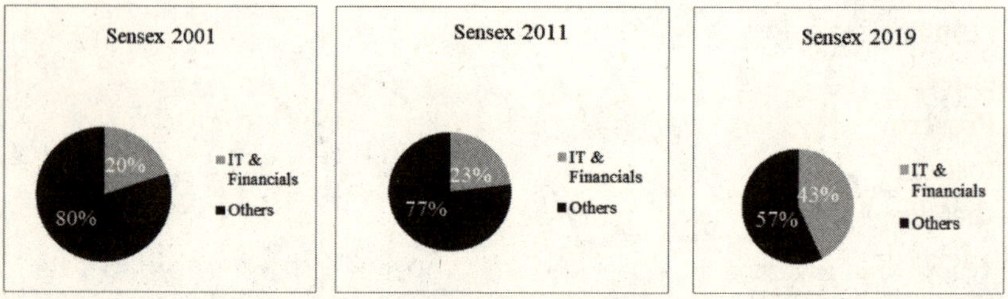

Figure 8: Increasing share of IT and financials sector (by count) in the Sensex

Source: Bloomberg, BSE

Second, using the Herfindahl–Hirschman Index to analyse degree of competition within the two sectors reveals an overall decline in concentration in both sectors. However, the IT sector has recently begun to show a slight increasing trend in the Herfindahl index, indicating that there is room to increase competition in the sector (see Figure 9).

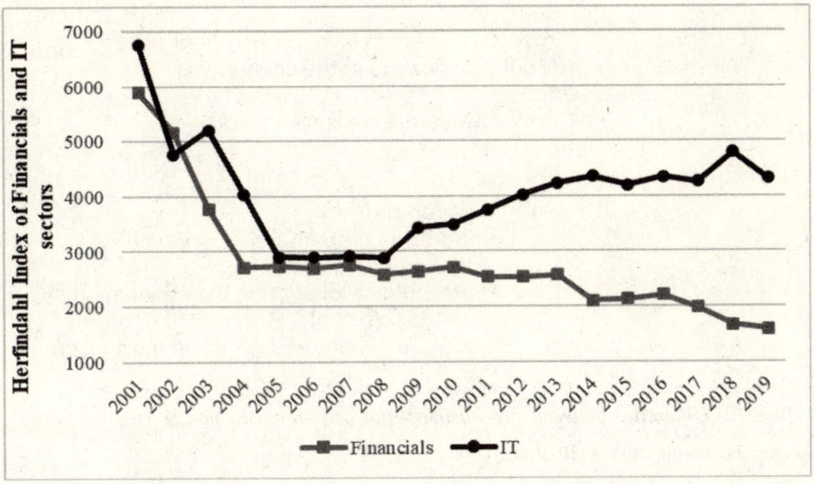

Figure 9: Herfindahl–Hirschman Index of financials and IT sectors

Source: Bloomberg, BSE

'There is a common misconception that people who are in favour of a free market are also in favour of everything that big business does. Nothing could be further from the truth,' wrote Milton Friedman (1999).[102] A policy stance in favour of competitive markets and free enterprise, or pro-business, is often confused with a pro-cronyism stance. Pro-cronyism policy supports incumbent firms but does not necessarily foster competitive markets (see Figure 10). On the other hand, policy that fosters competitive markets (hereafter pro-business policy) creates a level-playing field for businesses to compete. It unleashes the powerful forces of creative destruction that create wealth.

Austrian economist and creator of the term 'creative destruction', Joseph Schumpeter, described it as a 'process of industrial mutation that incessantly revolutionizes the economic structure from within, incessantly destroying the old one, incessantly creating a new one.'[103]

[102]Ministry of Finance, GoI, *Economic Survey 2019–20 Volume I*, January 2020, p. 51, https://tinyurl.com/3jru7c4r, Accessed on 7 December 2023.
[103]Ibid.

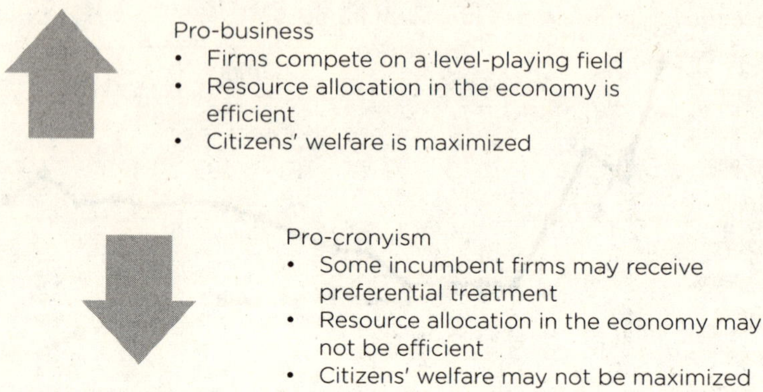

Figure 10: Difference between pro-business and pro-cronyism policy

Source: Economic Survey 2019–20

◆

Creative destruction brings new innovations into the market that serve people better than the old technologies they displace. It brings new firms into the markets, which compete with existing firms and lower prices for consumers. It brings dynamism to the marketplace that keeps firms on their toes and encourages them to continuously seek innovative ways to cater to customers' needs. It has only one pre-requisite—a pro-business policy stance that fosters competitive, unfettered markets.

When creative destruction is fostered, sectors, as a whole, will always outperform individual companies within the sector in creating wealth and maximizing welfare. Therein lies the motivation for India to pursue pro-business growth, rather than pro-crony growth.

Policy Suggestions

While pro-business policies increase competition, correct market failures and enforce business accountability, pro-cronyism policies hurt markets. Such policies may promote narrow business interests and may impact social welfare negatively, as the objectives of crony businesses may conflict with greater economic good. For example, crony businesses may lobby the government to limit competition in their industry, restrict imports of competing goods, or reduce regulatory oversight. These initiatives enhance the lobbying group's income but undermine markets and reduce aggregate welfare.

Pro-business policies—for example, those that make it easy to start a business, register property, enforce contracts, obtain credit, bid for natural resources, get permits and resolve insolvency—help firms to function effectively and, thereby, enable competitive markets. Making it easy to do business in a jurisdiction furthers the eventual goal of maximizing social welfare. Reforms aimed in this direction must continue. However, catering to the needs of crony businesses alone without regard for other businesses and the remaining stakeholders in the economy may end up benefitting the preferentially treated firms at the expense of other firms, market efficiency and social welfare.

A pro-cronyism economy is an outcome of specific environmental conditions that make the state vulnerable to capture. Tackling those contributing conditions can help curb the phenomenon. Here, I outline a few broad measures to keep cronyism under check and steer the economy towards a more pro-business policy paradigm.

1. **Require firms to be transparent about their political connections:** Sunlight is said to be the best of disinfectants. Firms may be asked to disclose whether directors, key management personnel or their relatives occupy public office. The disclosure may be required as part of the firm's annual financial filings. It is, of course, possible that firms are connected to politicians in indirect ways, as blood relations are a rather small subset of the many types of relationships that could exist between businesses and politicians. For example, a firm's promoters may have contributed funds to the politician's election campaign or may have professional relationships with the politician's business interests. To ensure transparency about all such relationships, the law may mandate the disclosure of a broad range of such relationships for the benefit of the firm's investors and lenders.
2. **Limit concentration of ownership of assets in the economy:** Incumbent rent-seeking firms may have a strong incentive to oppose pro-business policies as such policies increase competition and limit the potential to extract rents. The larger and more powerful the firm, the greater the political influence it can wield and the stronger the

opposition may be to reform. Therefore, the state may take steps to prevent the formation of monopolies and deter the excessive accumulation of capital in the hands of a small number of players. The state should also ease barriers to entry so that there is a steady influx of new entrants into the market; such entry continually challenges the incumbents.

3. **Transparent and fair mechanisms for resource allocation:** India's transition from a discretionary coal block allocation mechanism to an auction-based one serves as an excellent example of eliminating the need for interaction between the state and firms in an area where such interaction is unnecessary and where an efficient market-based alternative mechanism was readily available. This is an important insight because pro-cronyism prevails predominantly in industries that require heavy state involvement. When the state is actively involved in awarding approvals, permits, licenses, tax breaks or other resources necessary for firms to function, an opportunity may naturally develop for the politician to distribute largesse to crony firms. Using pro-business mechanisms such as a transparent auction as well as deregulation and liberalization can enable a more level-playing field for all firms to compete.
4. **Educate citizens on the importance of competitive markets**: In general, the beneficiaries of rent-seeking—generally a small group of politically influential businesses—are able to organize themselves, lobby for their cause and fight any reform that hurts their interests. In contrast, the citizens who end up funding crony firms' rents are scattered across the country and unable to mobilize as easily. Moreover, the benefit to any one citizen from curbing the activities of a given rent extractor is too miniscule to spur drastic action. However, the election mechanism gives citizens an easy and costless way to enforce their preferences. Hence, it is important to maintain broad support from the electorate for competitive markets. The electorate can discipline the state in moving away from pro-cronyism and towards pro-business reform if it is able to appreciate the benefits of competitive markets. Therefore, it is essential to educate citizens on the importance of competitive markets and the distinction between pro-business and pro-cronyism.

It is possible to have competitive markets and generate the efficiency and welfare gains they bring without the spectre of cronyism. We must remember that opposition to pro-crony policies does not equate to opposition to pro-business policies; as this chapter demonstrates, there is a sea of difference between the two, and India must become sensitive to this difference.

20

CARPE DIEM

Empowering Entrepreneurs to Ignite Opportunity

Do you remember Anushka Sharma as Shruti Kakkar in the 2010 Bollywood film *Band Baaja Baaraat*? Shruti Kakkar saying '*Main India ki best wedding planner banugi* (I will become the best wedding planner in India)' captures the entrepreneurial aspirations of young Indians. The 'Startup India' campaign by the GoI recognizes entrepreneurship as an increasingly important strategy to fuel productivity growth and wealth creation in India. This campaign has helped India create the third largest startup ecosystem in the world.

Given this initiative, I examine the content and drivers of entrepreneurial activity at the bottom of the administrative pyramid—over 500 districts in India. The analysis employs comprehensive data from the Ministry of Corporate Affairs database (MCA21) on new firm creation in the formal sector across all these districts.

First, the World Bank's Entrepreneurship Database reveals that new firm creation has gone up dramatically in India since 2014. While the number of new firms in the formal sector grew at a cumulative CAGR of 4.3 per cent from 2006 to 2014, the growth rate from 2014 to 2020 has been 12.5 per cent. As a result, from about 70,000 new firms created in 2014, the number has more than doubled to 1,42,000 new firms being created in 2020. Second, reflecting India's new economic structure, i.e., comparative advantage in the services sector, new firm creation in this sector is significantly higher than that in manufacturing, infrastructure or agriculture. Third, grassroots entrepreneurship correlates very positively with GDP, as a 10 per cent increase in registration of new firms in a district yields a 1.8 per cent increase in the district's GDP. Thus, entrepreneurship at the bottom of the administrative pyramid—a district—has a significant impact on wealth creation at the grassroots level. This impact of entrepreneurial activity on the district's GDP is maximal for the manufacturing and services sectors. Fourth, birth of new firms is very heterogeneous across Indian districts and sectors. Moreover, it is dispersed across India and is not restricted to just a few cities. Fifth, literacy and education in the district foster local entrepreneurship significantly. For instance, the eastern part of India has the lowest literacy rate of about 59.6 per cent according to the census of 2011. This is also the region in which new firm formation is the lowest. In fact, the impact of literacy on entrepreneurship is most pronounced when it is above 70 per cent. Sixth, the level of local education and the quality of physical infrastructure in the district influence new firm creation significantly. Finally, policies that facilitate ease of doing business and flexible labour regulations foster the creation of new firms, especially in the manufacturing sector. As the manufacturing sector has the greatest potential to create jobs for our youth, enhancing ease of doing business and implementing flexible labour laws can create the maximum jobs in districts and thereby in the states. Literacy, education and physical infrastructure are the other policy levers that district and state administrations must focus on in order to foster entrepreneurship and, thereby, job and wealth creation.

District-Level Entrepreneurship and Its Impact on the Economy

Entrepreneurship represents a key focus area for many policymakers, given its role in economic development and subsequent employment growth. Entrepreneurs are seen as agents of change that accelerate innovation in the economy. Figure 1 uses the World Bank's EoDB Entrepreneurship Database together with data from the US Census Bureau to compare the total number of new firms in India with that in a diverse cross-section of countries in Asia, Europe and North America. The chart clearly establishes that India has the third largest entrepreneurship ecosystem in the world.

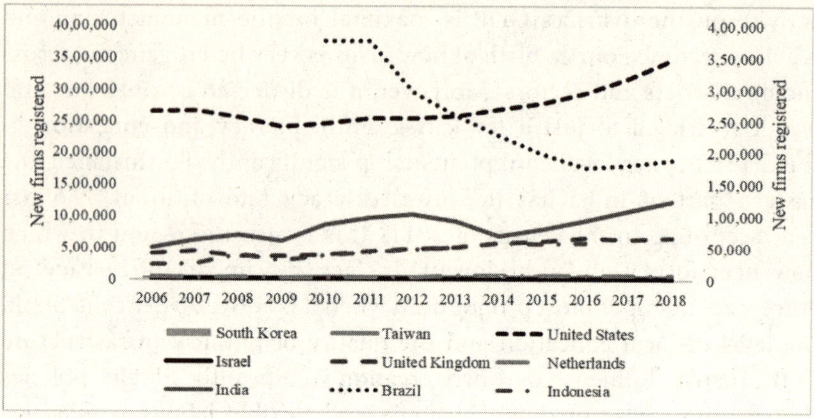

Figure 1: Comparison of entrepreneurial activity (new firms) across countries

Source: The World Bank 's EoDB Entrepreneurship Database; Business Formation Statistics (BFS) of the US Census Bureau

Note: Secondary axis for India, Brazil and Indonesia

On a per capita basis, India has low rates of entrepreneurship in the formal economy. Between 2006 and 2016, the mean (median) number of new firms registered per year per 1,000 workers was 0.10 (0.11). In contrast, the mean (median) entrepreneurial intensity for the UK and the US was 12.22 (11.84) and 12.12 (11.81), respectively. In general, the entrepreneurial intensity is significantly higher for developed economies. It is also growing across all countries, except Brazil, which has seen a significant decline from 2010 to 2018. It is important to note that, in contrast to the other countries, a large number of India's enterprises operate in the informal economy, which is not captured in these data. Notwithstanding the relatively lower rates of entrepreneurial intensity, Figure 2a emphasizes significant growth in the birth of new firms over time. Figure 2b shows that this growth is particularly pronounced in the services sector. This fact reflects India's new economic structure, i.e., comparative advantage in the services sector.

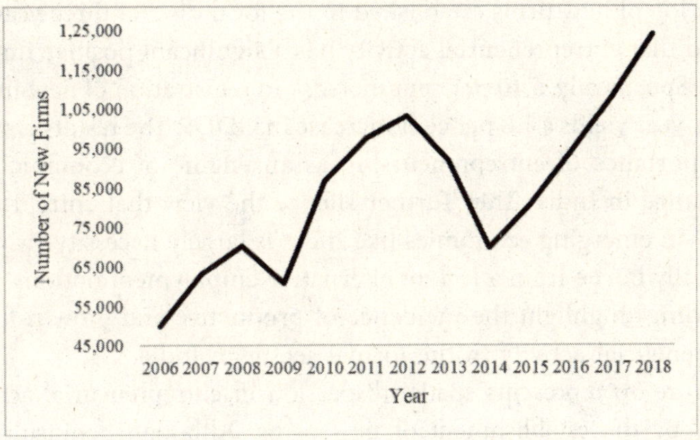

Figure 2a: Growth in new firms over time
Source: The World Bank 's EoDB Entrepreneurship Database

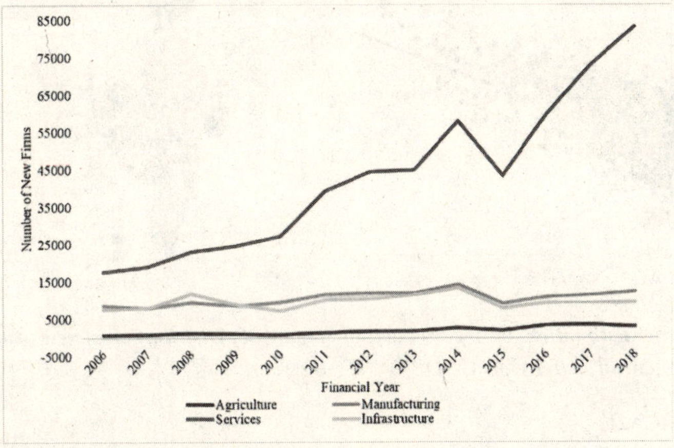

Figure 2b: Growth in new firms across sectors over time
Source: MCA21

Entrepreneurship and GDP

We next relate entrepreneurial activity to economic growth.

Figure 3a presents the scatter plot and trend line for the regression of the natural log of gross district domestic product (GDDP) on the natural log of new firms established in the focal district three years back. We find that entrepreneurial activity has a significant positive impact on GDDP. Specifically, a 10 per cent increase in registration of new firms per district-year yields a 1.8 per cent increase in GDDP. The results emphasize the importance of entrepreneurship as an engine of economic growth and change in India. They further silence the view that entrepreneurial activity in emerging economies like India is largely necessity-driven and is typically borne from a lack of alternative employment options. Rather, the findings highlight the incidence of productive and growth-focussed entrepreneurial activity in the formal sector in India.

Figure 3b represents spatial dispersion in entrepreneurial activity as defined by the establishment of new firms. Although peninsular states are home to the majority of new firms, we find that entrepreneurship is dispersed across India and is not restricted just to a few metropolitan cities.

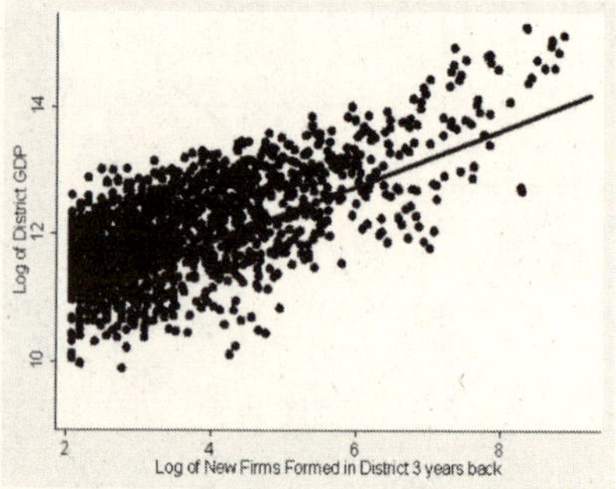

Figure 3a: Estimation of the impact of entrepreneurial activity on GDDP

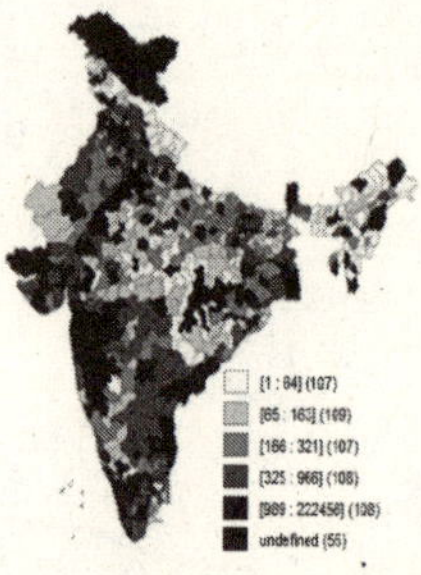

Figure 3b: Distribution of new firms across districts

Source: MCA21

Spatial Heterogeneity in Entrepreneurial Activity and Impact

Figure 4a, which shows the coefficient plot for the estimation of impact of entrepreneurial activity by sector, highlights that the impact of new firm entry is greatest in the manufacturing and services sectors. The findings emphasize the fundamental role that entrepreneurship can play in India's economic growth in the decades ahead. Movement of labour from other unproductive sectors and subsistence entrepreneurship into entrepreneurship in formal manufacturing and services can help close India's productivity gaps. To the extent that the manufacturing and services sectors are underdeveloped relative to economies of similar size, greater entrepreneurial activity will help close such gaps.

Figure 4b presents the growth in entrepreneurial activity over time for each of four regions in India. We find that all regions demonstrate strong growth in entrepreneurial activity over time, with the exception of the eastern states. Irrespective of the level of entrepreneurial activity, all regions demonstrate a strong relationship between entrepreneurship and GDDP, signifying the pervasive benefits of entrepreneurship.

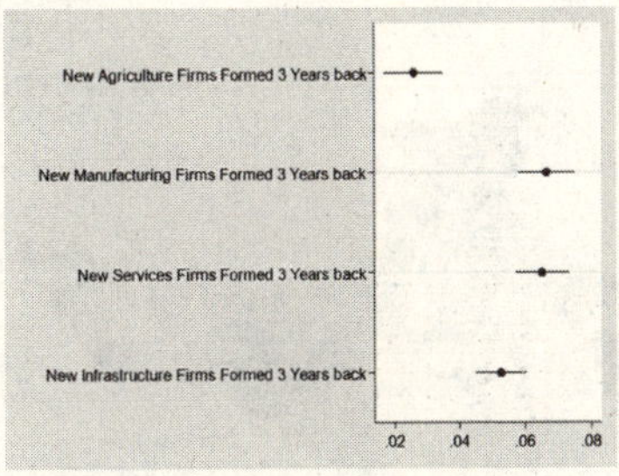

Figure 4a: Effect size—differences in the impact of entrepreneurial activity by sector

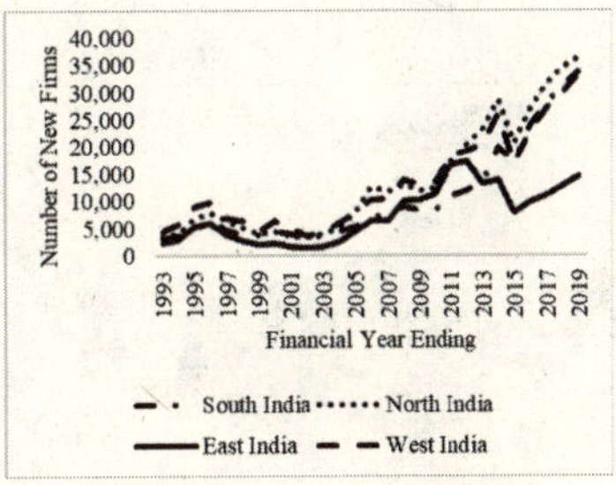

Figure 4b: Growth in new firms across regions over time

Source: MCA21

Next, an index of entrepreneurial activity for each district–sector is created to throw light on how the entrepreneurial capabilities for that sector are distributed across districts. For any specific sector, this index is estimated as a district's share of new firms in that sector, divided by that district's share of all new firms across all sectors. For example, a district responsible for 20 per cent of new firms in the agricultural sector, but only 10 per cent of all new firms, scores 2 on an index of relative entrepreneurial activity in agriculture, suggesting relative strength in that sector. Figures 5a–5d show the relative distribution of the index across districts for agriculture, manufacturing, services and infrastructure, respectively.

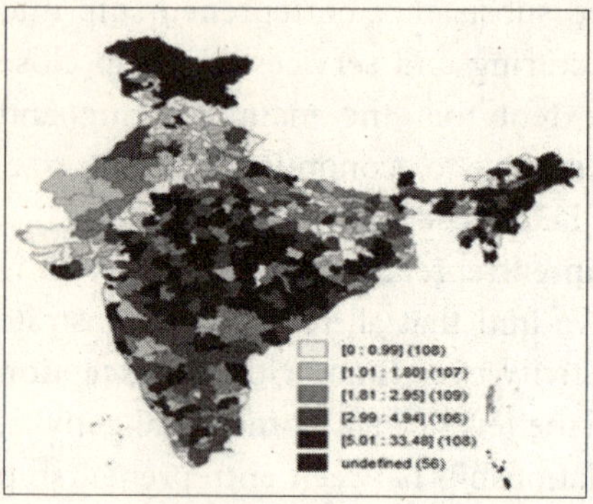

Figure 5a: Relative entrepreneurial capability of districts in agricultural sector

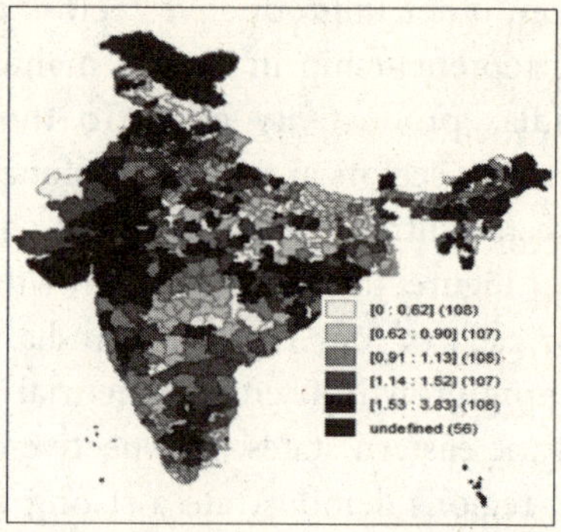

Figure 5b: Relative entrepreneurial capability of districts in manufacturing sector

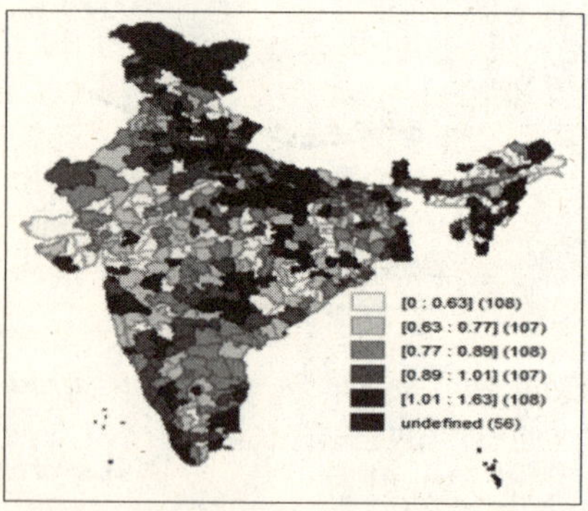

Figure 5c: Relative entrepreneurial capability of districts in services sector

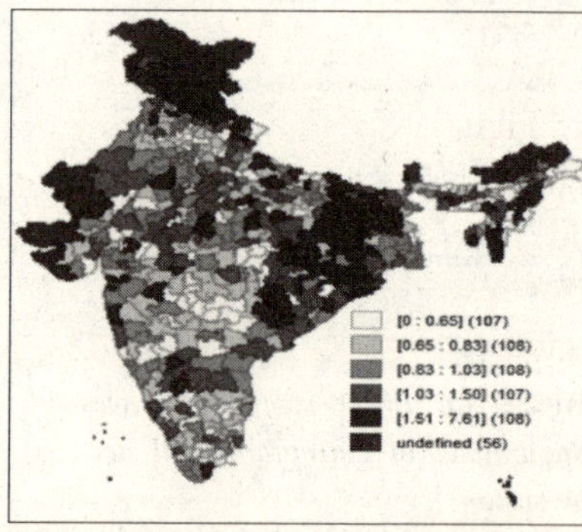

Figure 5d: Relative entrepreneurial capability of districts in infrastructure sector

Source: MCA21

Figure 5a suggests that relative to entrepreneurial capabilities in manufacturing, services and infrastructure, entrepreneurial capabilities in the agriculture sector are not geographically localized and seem to be distributed evenly across most districts in India. States in the highest quintile of relative entrepreneurial activity in the agriculture sector are Manipur, Meghalaya, Madhya Pradesh, Assam, Tripura and Odisha. Establishments in Northeast India are more likely to be private enterprises in the food business such as organic farms and tea plantations, while a majority of the establishments in Madhya Pradesh and Odisha are farmer producer companies, designed as hybrids between cooperative societies and private limited companies that organize farmers into a collective to improve their bargaining strength in markets.

Figure 5b suggests that entrepreneurial activity in the manufacturing sector is highest in the states of Gujarat, Meghalaya, Punjab, Rajasthan and the union territory of Puducherry. Within Gujarat, the most entrepreneurially active districts in this sector are Surendranagar, Rajkot, Bhavnagar and Surat. Establishments in these regions are focussed on manufacturing of textiles, chemicals, metals, plastics and pharmaceuticals. The nature of establishments in each of these regions attests to agglomeration economies documented by prior research in the Indian manufacturing sector (Ghani et al. 2011). That is, incumbent industrial structures for input and output markets and specialized labour in a region are strongly linked to higher entrepreneurial activity in that industry–region.

Figure 5c suggests that entrepreneurial activity in the services sector is highest in the regions of Delhi, Mizoram, Uttar Pradesh, Kerala, Andaman and Nicobar Islands, and Haryana. Consistent with observations of prior research (Ghani et al. 2011), the nature of establishments in these regions is not reflective of agglomeration economies and spans diverse industries such as trading, financial services, tourism and hospitality services, retailing, and even religious groups and missions.

Figure 5d suggests that entrepreneurial activity in the infrastructure sector is highest in the regions of Jharkhand, Arunachal Pradesh, Himachal Pradesh, Mizoram, Jammu and Kashmir, and Bihar, some of which are characterized by poor levels of extant infrastructure. Not surprisingly, new firms in these states are largely engaged in construction, logistics and transport, utilities generation, transmission and distribution, alternative energy distribution, and infratech.

Policy Implications for Fast-Tracking Entrepreneurship and Wealth Creation

Despite being the third largest ecosystem for entrepreneurship in the world, India appears to have lower rates of formal entrepreneurship on a per capita basis when compared to other countries. Consistent with the prevailing wisdom, we find a significant association between the count of new firms born in a district and the GDDP of that district. This contribution of entrepreneurial activity to GDDP is strongest for the manufacturing and services sectors. Further, significant heterogeneity in entrepreneurial activity across districts demonstrates the critical role played by social and physical infrastructure in determining such heterogeneity.

The analysis in this chapter, therefore, suggests the following policy implications. First, measures to increase literacy levels rapidly through the establishment of more schools and colleges will spur entrepreneurship and consequently local wealth creation. Following the successful contribution of privatization of engineering colleges to India's software exports (Arora and Badge 2006), governments could also explore the privatization of education to augment education capacity at all levels of education.

Second, better connectivity of villages through tar roads will likely improve access to local markets and improve entrepreneurial activity. Hence, investments in infrastructure must be focussed on increasing entrepreneurial activity.

Third, as EoDB is affected both by central and state legislation, state-level policies must focus on fostering ease of doing business and enabling flexible labour regulations to foster entrepreneurial activity at the district level.

◆

The pace of entrepreneurship represents a critical barometer of the vibrancy of an economy because entrepreneurship challenges incumbents and thereby enhances competition in the economy. Without the competition provided by new entrepreneurs, incumbents would remain complacent, thereby depriving consumers of better products and services. While India has made rapid strides in creating the third largest entrepreneurship ecosystem in the world, to achieve its status as the economic titan, we should aspire to create the largest entrepreneurship ecosystem in the world.

21

INNOVATION FORGE

Cultivating Creativity for Future Breakthroughs

A bamboo plant has to be nurtured for three years as it remains below the ground for that period before the mother plant starts producing multiple shoots. The ground where it has been planted must be watered and fertilized every day. After three years, once the bamboo plant breaks through the ground, new shoots grow to their full height of 70–90 ft in just two months and last for seven to ten years. In contrast, small herbs sprout very fast but live only for one season and reach an average height of only 2–3 ft. Nourishing innovation is similar to nourishing the bamboo plant. It requires long-term vision to nurture the project by pouring cash in for several years till the innovation 'sprouts' and produces tall, long-lasting returns. Indian firms need to develop the vision to nurture bamboo plants for the nation to become a global economic titan by 2047.

India ranked among the top 40 innovating countries in 2023, improving its position from 81 in 2015. India ranks first in Central and South Asia and among the lower middle-income group of economies. Among the seven pillars of the Global Innovation Index (GII), India ranks 22nd in knowledge and technology outputs; 20th in market sophistication; 57th in business sophistication; 48th in human capital and research (HCR); 56th in institutions; 49th in creative outputs; and 84th in infrastructure. Among sub-pillars, India ranks 29th in knowledge diffusion and 9th in trade, diversification and market scale. Among parameters, India ranks first in domestic market scale (in terms of PPP); fifth in information and communication technology (ICT) services exports; 42nd in government's online services; and 43rd in growth rate of labour productivity.[104]

---

[104]Dutta, Soumitra, et al., *Global Innovation Index 2023*: *Innovation in the Face of Uncertainty*, 16th Edition, World Intellectual Property Organization, p. 132, http://tinyurl.com/88kraju7. Accessed on 21 December 2023.

Among innovation inputs, India ranks 11th in the number of science and engineering graduates; 49th in expenditure on education as a percentage of GDP; 81st in the number of researchers; 54th in gross expenditure on R&D as a percentage of GDP; 22nd in QS university rankings; 101st in ICT access; 9th in finance for startups and scale-ups; sixth in VC financing received as a percentage of GDP; 10th in domestic industry diversification; and 99th in knowledge-intensive employment. Among innovation outputs, India ranks 28th in patents by origin; 20th in citable documents; 9th in unicorn valuation; 56th in software spending; 35th in high-tech manufacturing; 45th in intellectual property (IP) receipts; 46th in production and export complexity; 41st in high-tech exports; 8th in intangible-asset intensity; 31st in global brand value; 18th in cultural and creative services exports; 49th in national feature films per million; and 36th in mobile app creation.[105]

The business sector in India contributes much less to gross expenditure on R&D (about 37 per cent) when compared to businesses in each of the top 10 economies (> 60 per cent in each case). The government does a disproportionate amount of heavy lifting on R&D by contributing 56 per cent of the expenditure, which is three times the average contributed by governments in the top 10 economies. Yet, India's R&D expenditure at 0.65 per cent of GDP is much lower than that of the top 10 economies (2.5–3 per cent of GDP) primarily because of the disproportionately lower contribution from the business sector. Indian residents contribute only 36 per cent of patents filed in India as compared to 89 per cent in China. Indian firms also perform below expectation on innovation for their level of access to equity finance, which is most crucial for innovation.

Indian firms must significantly ramp up investment in R&D if India is to achieve its aspiration to emerge as the third largest economy in terms of GDP (current US$). Mere reliance on '*jugaad* innovation' risks missing the crucial opportunity to innovate its way into the future. India must also focus on strengthening institutions and business sophistication to improve its performance on innovation outputs. The time to innovate is now. Innovation is a necessity for India and no longer a luxury.

[105]Ibid.

Why Innovation Matters

A vast body of literature in economics extols the role of innovation and technological progress in growth and development. The positive correlation between past innovation performance and current GDP per capita can be examined empirically. Figure 1 shows the positive correlation between past innovation performance (in 2019 and in 2017) with GDP per capita in PPP terms (2022) across countries. It is clear that India has performed below expectation for its past innovation performance in terms of recent GDP per capita.

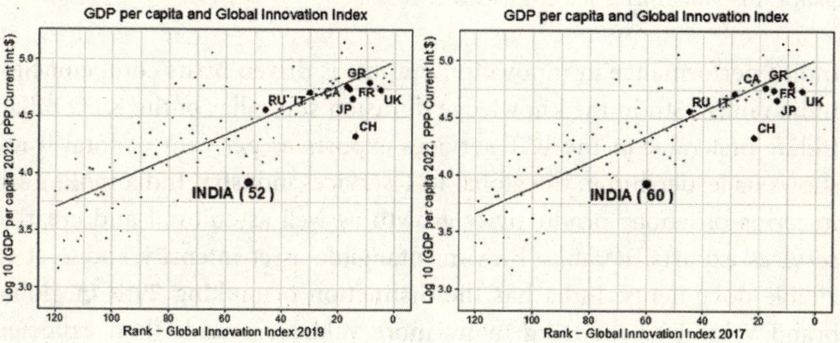

Figure 1: Positive correlation between GDP per capita (2022) and past innovation. (a) Innovation (2019), (b) Innovation (2017)

Source: The World Bank and GII database

India's Performance on Innovation

In 2022, India entered the top 45 innovating countries for the first time since the inception of the GII in 2007, ranking 40th among 132 countries in terms of its innovation performance. India ranks 39th and 42nd on the output and input sub-indices, respectively. Along with three other economies—Vietnam, Republic of Moldova and Kenya—India has the rare distinction of being an innovation achiever for 12 consecutive years.

Figure 2 shows India's performance on the GII 2022 (rank) across the seven pillars. India performed best on the market sophistication pillar (rank 19) followed by knowledge and technology outputs (KTO) pillar (rank 34). India performed lowest on the infrastructure pillar (rank 78).

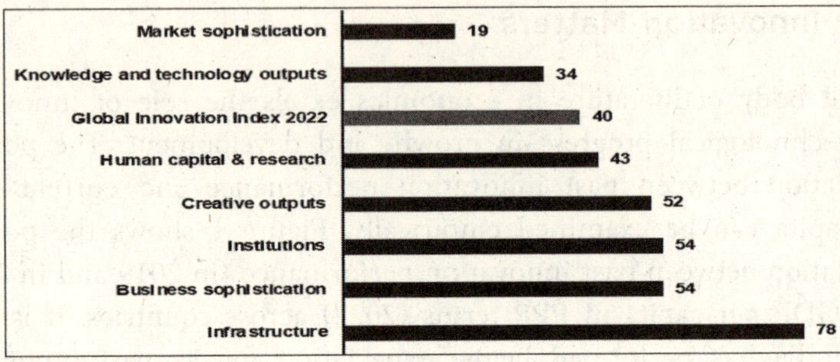

Figure 2: India's performance on pillars of the GII 2022 (rank)
Source: The World Bank and GII database, 2022

India's performance in innovation outputs is driven by its competencies. India ranks 15th in the knowledge diffusion sub-pillar of the KTO pillar. India's first rank in the ICT services exports as per cent of total trade shows its leadership in the global ICT services industry. India ranks 12th in terms of labour productivity growth as well as cultural and creative services exports. It ranks 14th in intangible asset intensity and 21st in citable documents. India has the distinction of ranking 29th in global brand value by producing many more valuable brands than expected for its income level.[106]

India has performed impressively in innovation inputs such as domestic market scale (1st rank) facilitating its overall 9th rank in the trade, diversification, and market scale sub-pillar. Other leading innovation inputs for India include the 6th rank for VC received as a percentage of GDP; 8th rank in finance for startups and scaleups; 11th rank in science and engineering graduates; 12th rank in entrepreneurship policies and culture; 14th rank in domestic industry diversification; 16th rank in global corporate R&D investors; and 19th rank in market capitalization as a percentage of GDP.[107]

Figure 3 takes a closer look at India's performance on the GII and its sub-indices vis-à-vis the country's own level of development (per

[106]Dutta, Soumitra, et al., *Global Innovation Index 2022: What Is the Future of Innovation-Driven Growth?*, World Intellectual Property Organization, p. 142, http://tinyurl.com/36jk2e6p. Accessed on 21 December 2023.
[107]Ibid.

capita GDP). India performs above expectation on the GII as well as the innovation output and innovation input sub-indices.

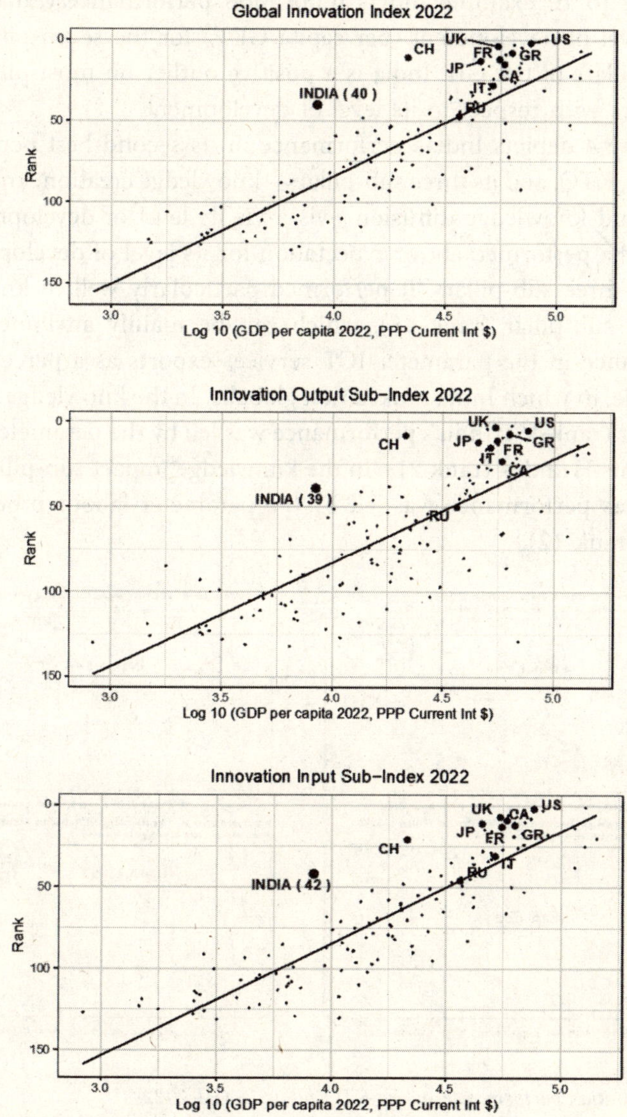

Figure 3: Innovation and level of development

Source: The World Bank and GII database

India's Innovation Performance vis-à-vis Its Level of Development

Figures 4 to 10 examine India's innovation performance (rank) vis-à-vis its level of development (per capita GDP) for the seven pillars and 21 sub-pillars of the GII. India is a positive outlier on most pillars and sub-pillars with respect to its level of development.

Figure 4 depicts India's performance in its second-best performing pillar, i.e., KTO, and its three sub-pillars—knowledge creation, knowledge impact and knowledge diffusion—vis-à-vis its level of development. In 2022, India performed above expectation for its level of development in all these three sub-pillars. It performed particularly well in knowledge diffusion sub-pillar (rank 15), which can be mainly attributed to its performance in the parameter ICT services exports as a percentage of total trade, in which India ranked first globally. In the knowledge creation sub-pillar (rank 46), India's performance was led by the parameter citable documents H-index (rank 21). In the knowledge impact sub-pillar (rank 56), India's performance was led by the parameter labour productivity growth (rank 12).

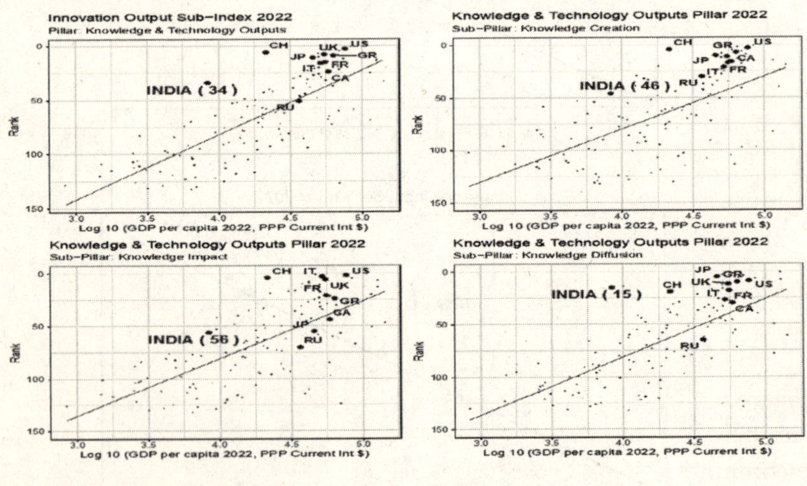

Figure 4: India's performance in the KTO pillar in GII 2022

Source: The World Bank and GII database

Figure 5 shows India's performance in the creative outputs pillar and its three sub-pillars—intangible assets, creative goods and services, and online creativity vis-à-vis its level of development. In 2022, India performed above expectation for its level of development in all sub-pillars of the creative outputs pillar. It performed better in intangible assets (rank 40) pillar and creative goods and services (rank 61) than online creativity (rank 66). The performance in intangible assets sub-pillar was led by the parameter intangible asset intensity, top 15 (rank 14), and global brand value, top 5,000 as a percentage of GDP (rank 29). Performance in creative goods and services sub-pillar was led by the parameters cultural and creative services exports as a percentage of total trade (rank 12).

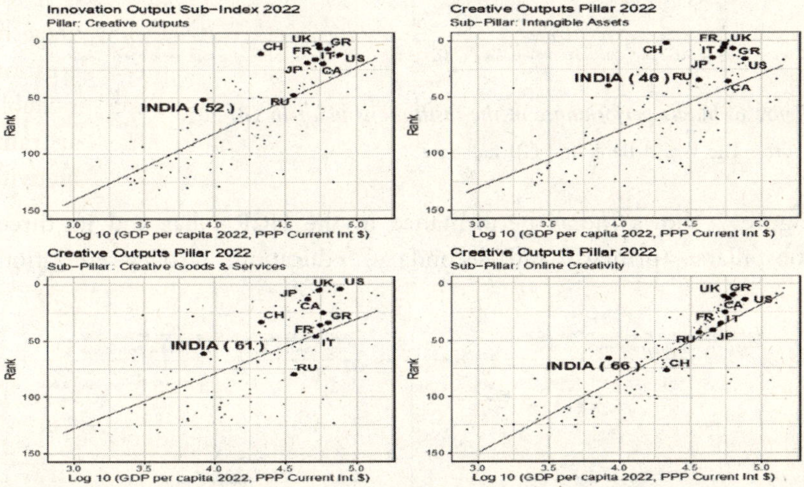

Figure 5: India's performance in the creative outputs pillar in GII 2022

Source: The World Bank and GII database

Figure 6 shows India's performance in the institutions pillar and its three sub-pillars—political environment, regulatory environment and business environment—vis-à-vis its level of development. India performed above expectation for its level of development in all three sub-pillars. It performed better in business environment (rank 40) and political environment (rank 64) than in regulatory environment (rank 67), taking its overall institutions ranking to 54.

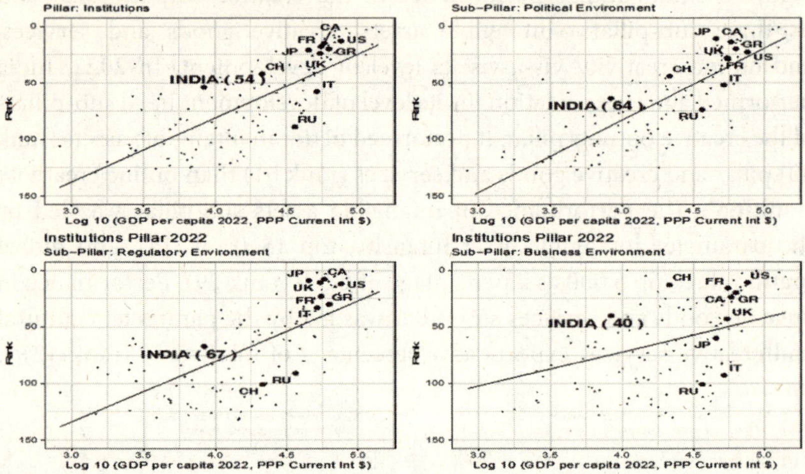

Figure 6: India's performance in the institutions pillar in GII 2022

Source: The World Bank and GII database

Figure 7 shows India's performance in the HCR pillar and its three sub-pillars—(primary and secondary) education, tertiary education

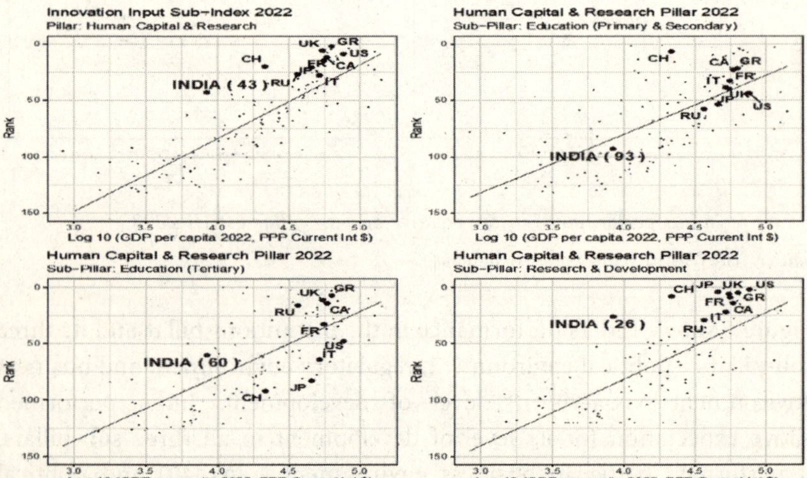

Figure 7. India's performance in the HCR pillar in GII 2022

Source: The World Bank and GII database

and R&D—vis-à-vis its level of development. India performed above expectation in two sub-pillars (tertiary education and R&D), performing particularly well in R&D (rank 26). It performed below expectation for its level of development in the (primary and secondary) education sub-pillar (rank 93), which is mainly attributed to India's poor performance in pupil–teacher ratio in secondary education (rank 95).

Figure 8 shows India's performance in the infrastructure pillar and its three sub-pillars—ICT, general infrastructure (consisting of electricity, logistics and GCF) and ecological sustainability—vis-à-vis its level of development. India performed above expectation in two sub-pillars of the infrastructure pillar in 2022 and performed well in the general infrastructure sub-pillar (rank 50). Its performance in this sub-pillar was led by the parameter GCF as a percentage of GDP (rank 25). India's performance in the ICT sub-pillar was led by the government's online service (rank 24) and e-participation (rank 29) but dragged down by ICT access (rank 99) and ICT use (rank 97). India performed below expectation for its income level in the ecological sustainability sub-pillar (rank 115), which can be mainly attributed to the parameter environmental performance (rank 130).

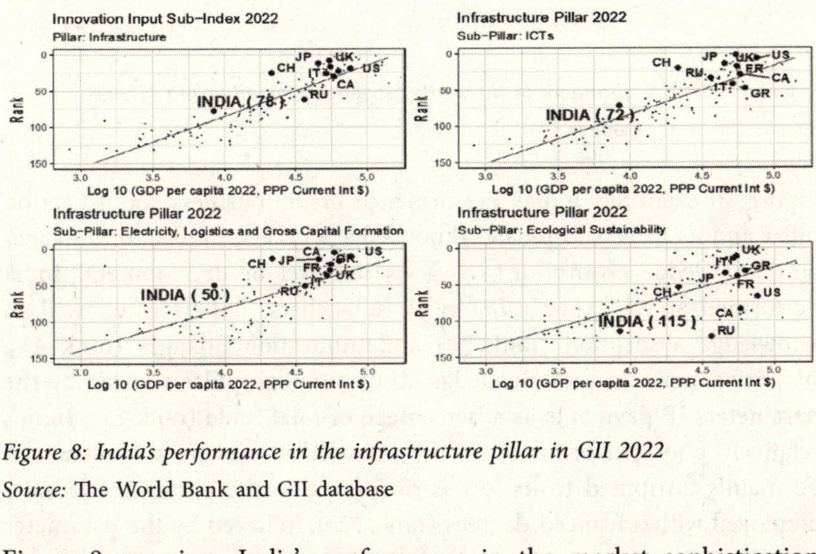

Figure 8: India's performance in the infrastructure pillar in GII 2022

Source: The World Bank and GII database

Figure 9 examines India's performance in the market sophistication pillar (rank 19) and its three sub-pillars—credit, investment, and trade, diversification and market scale—vis-à-vis its level of development. India performed significantly above expectation in all sub-pillars. It performed particularly well in investment (rank 17) and trade, diversification and market scale (rank 9). While India performed higher than expected given its level of development on credit (rank 68), this is one area where significant improvement can happen in the coming years given the leapfrogging that India is now undergoing through its DPI and financial inclusion.

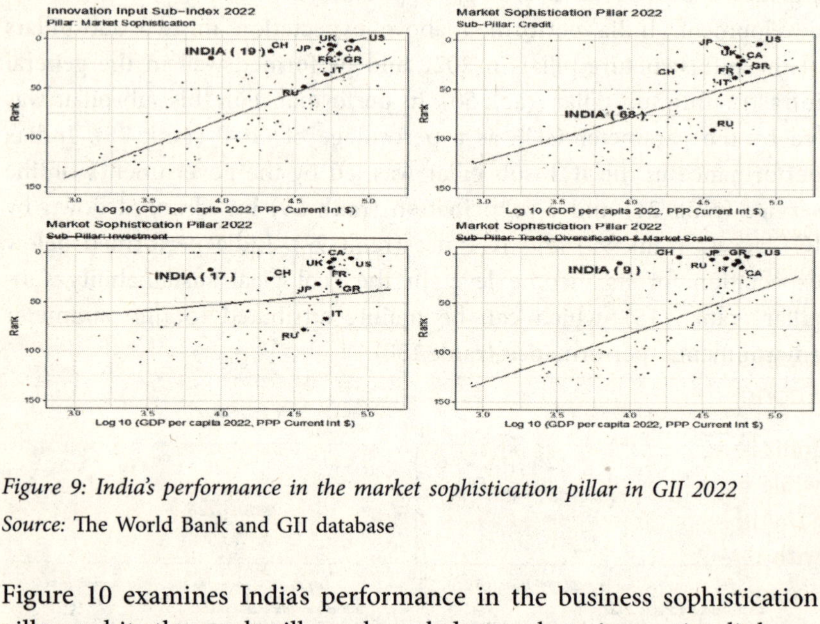

Figure 9: India's performance in the market sophistication pillar in GII 2022
Source: The World Bank and GII database

Figure 10 examines India's performance in the business sophistication pillar and its three sub-pillars—knowledge workers, innovation linkages and knowledge absorption—vis-à-vis its level of development. India performed above expectation in all sub-pillars. It performed well in knowledge absorption (rank 38) and innovation linkages (rank 43). Its performance in the knowledge absorption sub-pillar was led by the parameters IP payments as a percentage of total trade (rank 27). India's relatively poor performance in the knowledge workers sub-pillar can be mainly attributed to its low performance in the parameter females employed with advanced degrees (rank 103), followed by the parameter knowledge-intensive employment (rank 86).

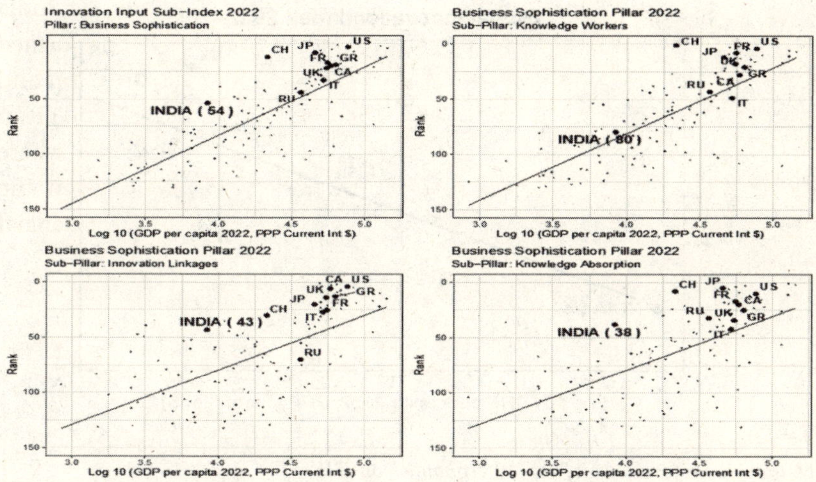

Figure 10: India's performance in the business sophistication pillar in GII 2022
Source: The World Bank and GII database

India's Innovation Performance vis-à-vis the Top 10 Economies

India is currently the fifth largest economy in terms of GDP (current US$), while it is the third largest in terms of GDP (PPP current international $). Although India has performed above expectation on innovation with respect to its level of development, it lags behind most other large economies (top 10 in terms of GDP current US$) on most indicators of innovation.

Figure 11 shows GII performance of the 10 largest economies (measured using GDP current US$; hereafter simply '10 largest economies' or 'top 10 economies'). Although India performs in line with its level of development, it ranks second lowest, after Russia, on the overall GII. Countries such as China and the UK rank much higher than expected for their level of development.

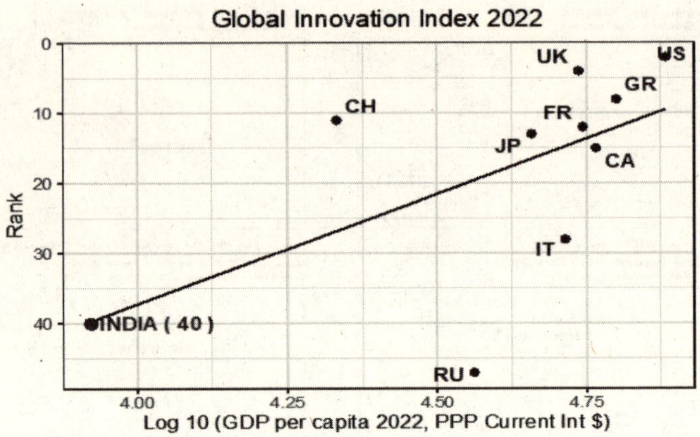

Figure 11: Performance of top 10 economies on GII

Source: The World Bank and GII database

This trend continues in innovation outputs and innovation inputs. Performance on innovation outputs of the 10 largest economies may be seen in Figure 12. Although India performs as per expectations for its level of development, it is ranked second lowest, after Russia, on innovation outputs. Figure 13 shows performance on innovation inputs of the 10 largest economies. India performs in line with its level of development but ranks second lowest, after Russia, on innovation inputs among the top 10 economies.

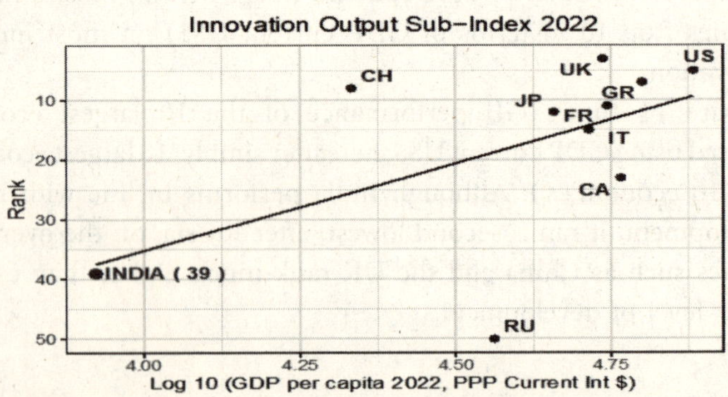

Figure 12: Performance of top 10 economies on innovation output sub-index

Source: The World Bank and GII database

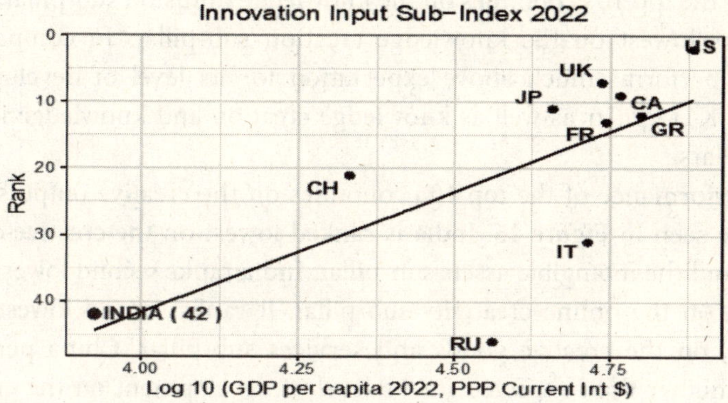

Figure 13: Performance of top 10 economies on innovation input sub-index

Source: The World Bank and GII database

Figure 14 compares India's performance in its second highest-ranked pillar—KTO—with respect to the other largest economies. India performs in line with expectation for its level of development on this pillar and particularly well on the knowledge diffusion sub-pillar. India ranks fifth

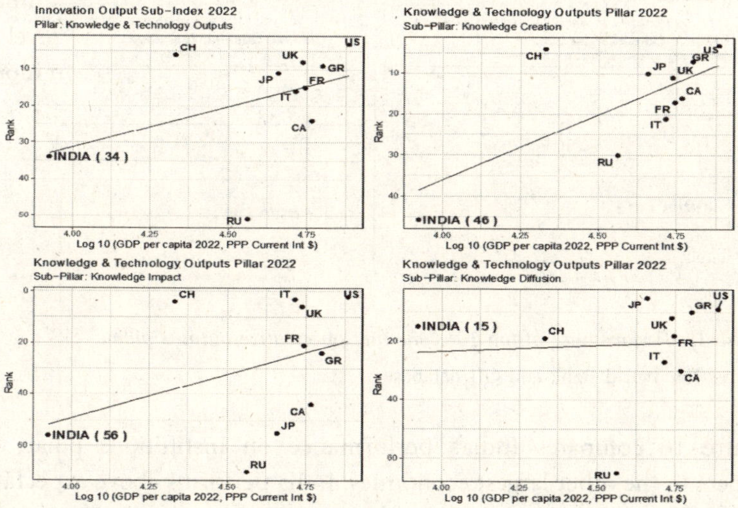

Figure 14: Performance of top 10 economies on KTO pillar

Source: The World Bank and GII database

among the top 10 economies on the knowledge diffusion sub-pillar, while it ranks lowest on the knowledge creation sub-pillar. In comparison, China performs much above expectation for its level of development on the KTO pillar as well as knowledge creation and knowledge impact sub-pillars.

Performance of the top 10 economies on the creative outputs pillar may be seen in Figure 15. India is ranked lowest on the creative output pillar and the intangible assets sub-pillar. India ranks second lowest, after China, on the online creativity sub-pillar. It ranks second lowest, after Russia, on the creative goods and services sub-pillar. China performs much higher than expected for its level of development on the creative outputs pillar and the intangible assets and creative goods and services sub-pillars.

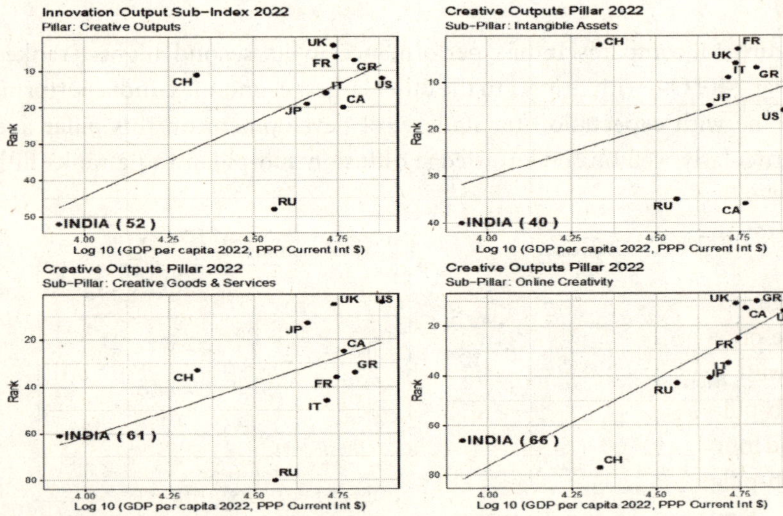

Figure 15: Performance of top 10 economies on creative outputs pillar

Source: The World Bank and GII database

Figure 16 compares India's performance on institutions pillar with respect to the other largest economies. India performs above expectation for its level of development on the institutions pillar and each of its sub-pillars. However, India ranks third lowest, after Russia and Italy, on the institutions pillar. It ranks third lowest on regulatory environment sub-pillar after China and Russia. India ranks second lowest, after Russia, on political environment sub-pillar.

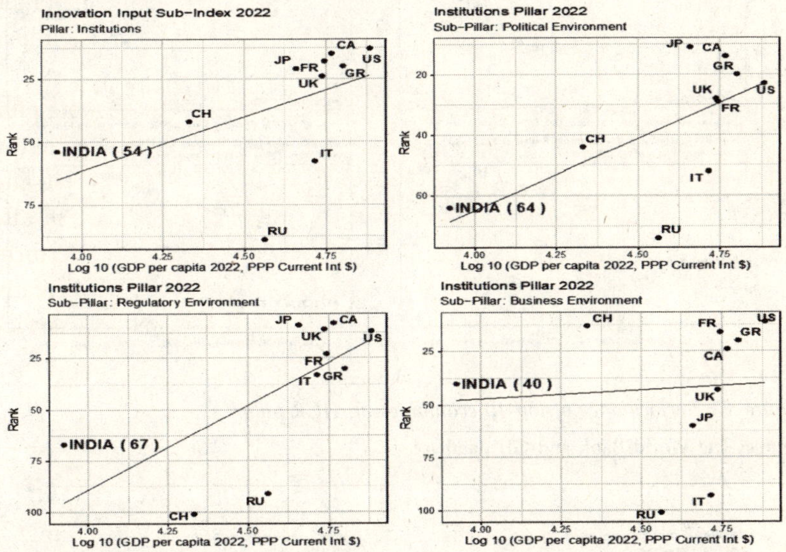

Figure 16: Performance of top 10 economies on institutions pillar
Source: The World Bank and GII database

Figure 17 compares India's performance on the HCR pillar with those of the other largest economies. Among the top 10 economies, India ranks lowest on the HCR pillar and the (primary and secondary) education sub-pillars. India ranks second lowest, after Russia, on R&D sub-pillar and fourth lowest—after China, Japan and Italy—on the tertiary education sub-pillar.

Figure 18 compares India's performance on infrastructure pillar with respect to the other largest economies. India ranks lowest on the infrastructure pillar and the ICT sub-pillars among the top 10 economies. India ranks second lowest, after Russia, on the ecological sustainability and general infrastructure sub-pillars.

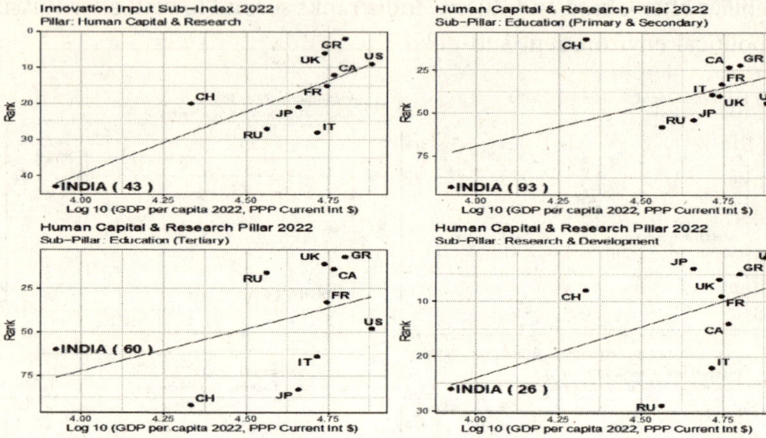

Figure 17: Performance of top 10 economies on HCR pillar

Source: The World Bank and GII database

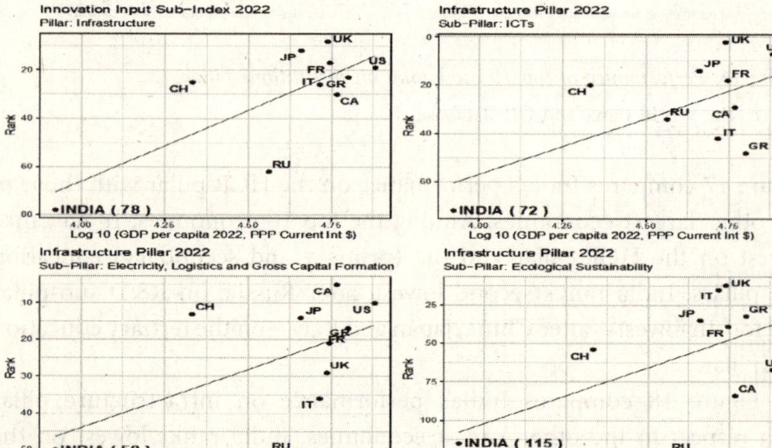

Figure 18: Performance of top 10 economies on infrastructure pillar

Source: The World Bank and GII database

Figure 19 compares India's performance on its best performing pillar—market sophistication—with those of the other largest economies. India performs above expectation for its level of development on the market sophistication pillar and investment sub-pillar. India ranks fifth highest on the investment sub-pillar among the top 10 economies. However, India ranks third lowest, after Russia and Italy, on the market sophistication pillar and above Italy and Canada in the trade, diversification and market scale sub-pillar. It ranks second lowest, after Russia, on the credit sub-pillar.

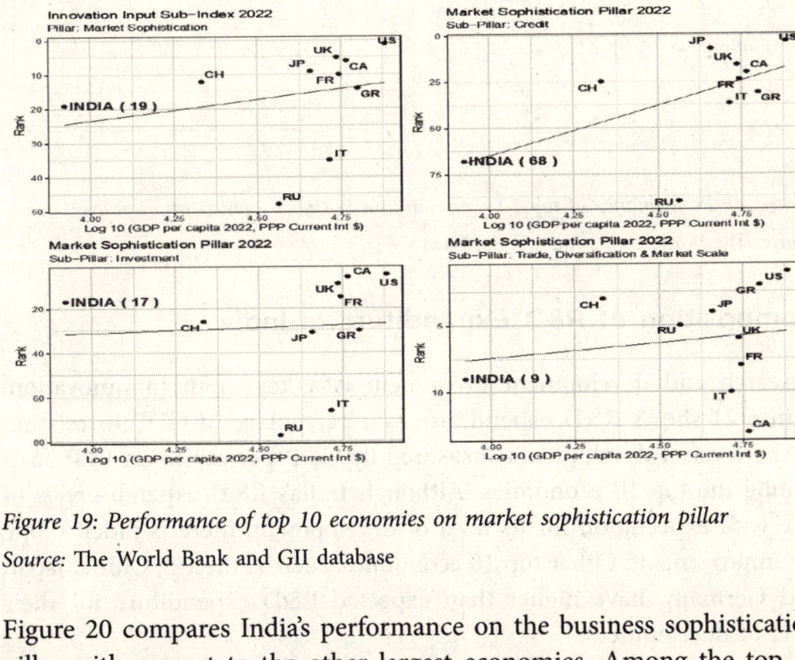

Figure 19: Performance of top 10 economies on market sophistication pillar
Source: The World Bank and GII database

Figure 20 compares India's performance on the business sophistication pillar with respect to the other largest economies. Among the top 10 economies, India ranks lowest on the business sophistication pillar and knowledge workers sub-pillar. It ranks second lowest, after Italy, on knowledge absorption sub-pillar. India ranks second lowest, after Russia, on the innovation linkages sub-pillar.

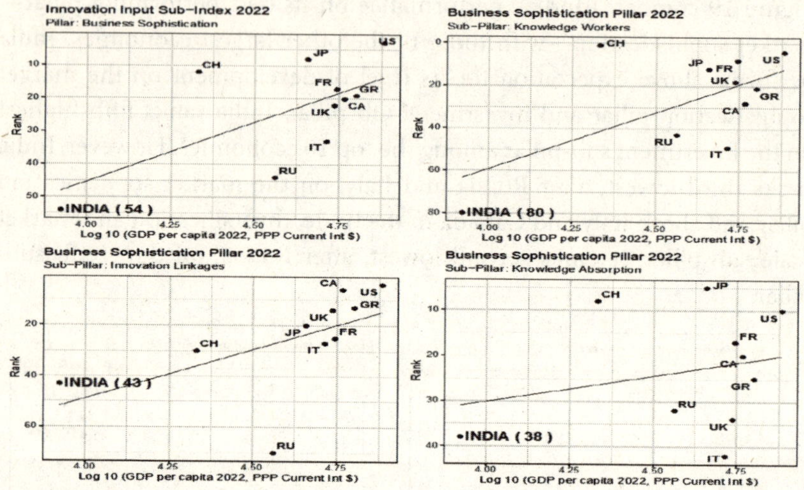

Figure 20: Performance of top 10 economies on business sophistication pillar
Source: The World Bank and GII database

Composition of R&D Expenditure in India

Research and development investment is a key input in innovation. Figure 21 shows R&D expenditure as a percentage of GDP in relation to the level of development measured by GDP per capita on PPP basis among the top 10 economies. Although India's R&D expenditure is in line with expectation for its level of development, there is much scope for improvement. Other top 10 economies, such as the US, China, Japan and Germany, have higher than expected R&D expenditure for their level of development.

Moreover, the contribution of India's business sector to R&D expenditure as a percentage of GDP is lower than expected for its level of development and is the lowest among the top 10 economies. The business sector's R&D expenditure in the US, China, Japan and Germany is much higher, as expected for their level of development. The combined R&D expenditure of India's government sector and the higher education sector as a percentage of GDP is higher than expected for its level of development, but continues to be low as compared to the top 10 economies—it is the second lowest after UK.

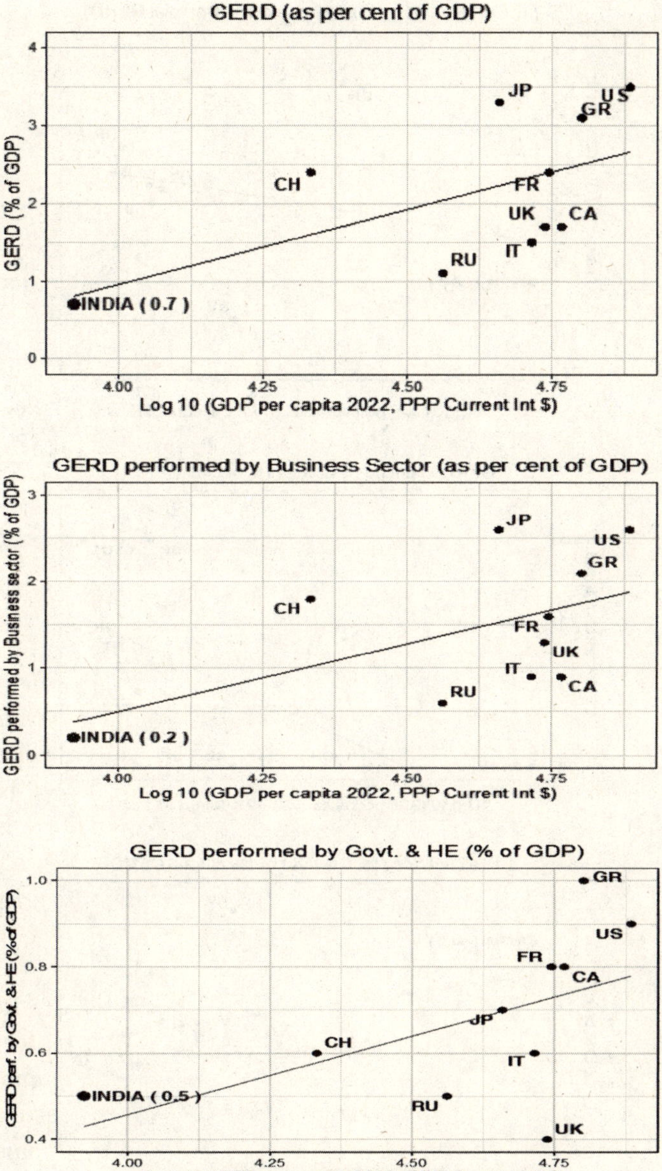

Figure 21: Total R&D expenditure and sector-wise contributions to GDP

Source: The World Bank and GII database. Government and HE values calculated as residual.

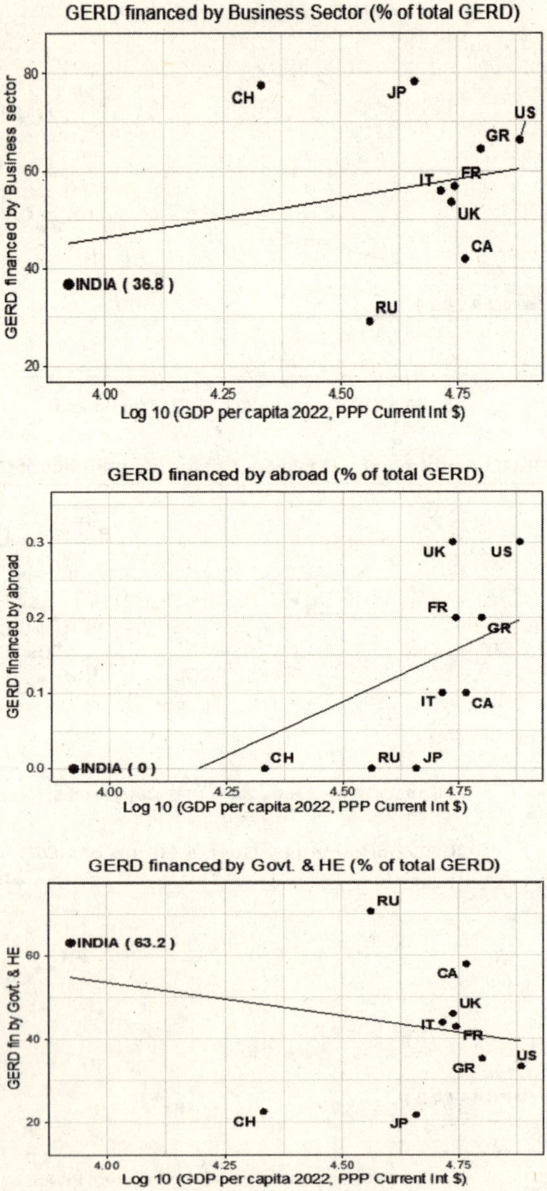

Figure 22: Sector-wise contributions to total R&D expenditure

Source: The World Bank and GII database. Government and HE values calculated as residual

Figure 22 shows the positive correlation between the level of development and the business sector's participation in total R&D expenditure, while the residual government and HE sector's participation in R&D expenditure is negatively correlated with development. In India, the government and the HE sector contribute 63.2 per cent of R&D expenditure, which is the second highest after Russia. Yet, India's R&D expenditure is much lower than other top 10 economies because its business sector contributes a much smaller per cent to total R&D expenditure (about 37 per cent) than the business sector in other top 10 economies (58 per cent on average).

Figure 23 presents the total full-time equivalent (FTE) researchers per million population in relation to the level of development. Among the top 10 economies, India's performance is in line with expectation for its level of development. However, it has the lowest number of researchers per million population among the top 10 economies, making it an area warranting attention. Other large economies, such as Japan, Germany and France have higher than expected R&D manpower for their level of development.

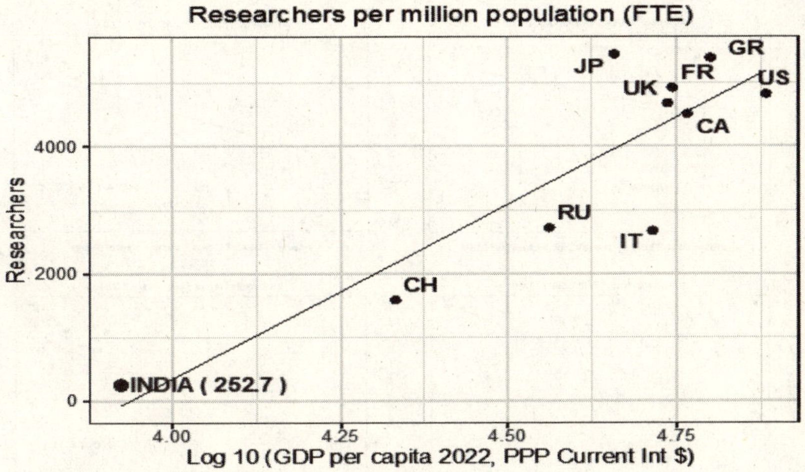

Figure 23: R&D personnel and researchers

Source: The World Bank and GII database

Indian Innovation: Affected by Access to Finance?

Figure 24 examines the performance of top 10 economies on innovation with respect to availability of equity finance—market capitalization of listed domestic companies (as a percentage of GDP) as well as VC availability rank. India and Russia rank much below expectation for their level of equity market development in the overall GII, innovation outputs and innovation inputs among the top 10 largest economies. Given that most of these large economies are more innovative than India and equity market development facilitates greater high-technology innovation, this

A) Equity Capital (Market Capitalization) *B) Equity Capital (VC)*

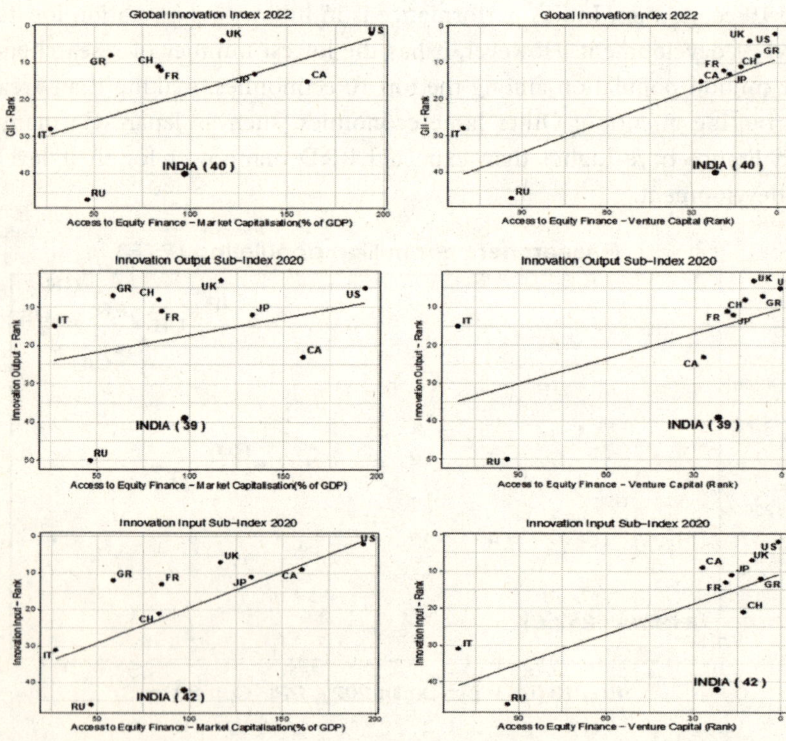

Figure 24: Innovation and access to equity finance

Source: The World Bank and GII database

Note: Venture capital (VC) ranks are from 2019. Market capitalization data for France are from 2018, UK and Italy are from 2014, and rest are from 2020.

potentially indicates that innovation in India needs to become more high-tech-intensive.

Figure 25 shows the performance of top 10 economies on innovation with respect to availability of debt finance in the form of domestic credit to the private sector by banks (per cent of GDP). India and Russia rank much below expectation for their level of debt market development in

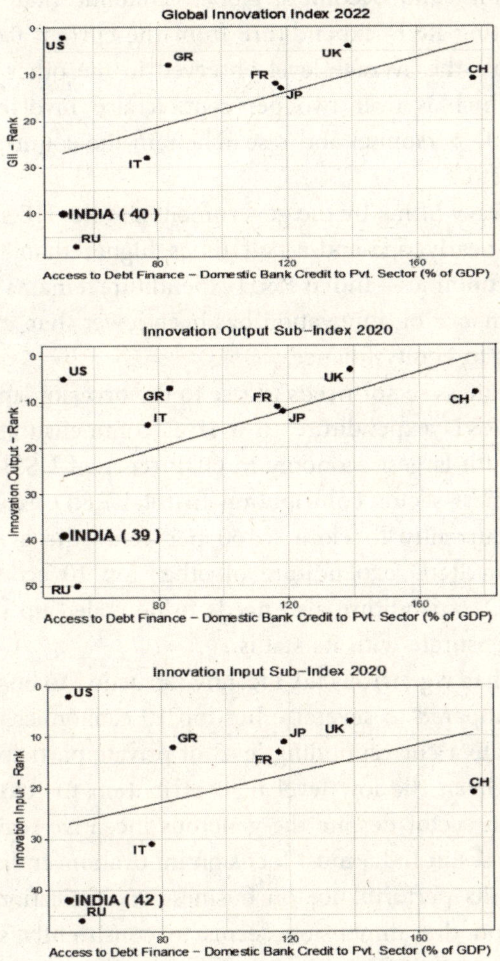

Figure 25: Innovation and access to debt finance

Source: The World Bank and GII database

Note: Debt finance data pertain to 2020.

the overall GII, innovation outputs and innovation inputs amongst the top 10 largest economies.

Policy Implications

India needs greater thrust on innovation to catapult itself to a higher growth trajectory and become a global economic titan by 2047. This requires boosting R&D expenditure from the current 0.65 per cent of GDP to at least the average level observed in the other top 10 largest economies, which is over two per cent. It also involves significantly scaling up R&D personnel and researchers in the country, especially in the private sector.

Despite heavy lifting by the government and the HE sectors in R&D expenditure—nearly one-and-a-half times higher than the average of other top 10 economies—India's R&D expenditure remains low. Moreover, India's performance on innovation has been lower than expected for its level of access to equity finance.

India's business sector needs to rise to the occasion and significantly ramp up its R&D expenditure to a level commensurate with India's status as the fifth largest economy in GDP (current US$). This requires boosting business-sector contribution to total R&D expenditure from 37 per cent currently to close to 60 per cent—the average business contribution in R&D expenditure of other top 10 economies. India's aggregate R&D expenditure also needs to be scaled up significantly to a level commensurate with its status.

India has had a generous tax incentive structure to boost R&D in the country as compared to several other top 10 economies. However, this did not generate a corresponding level of private participation in R&D expenditure. Given the low level of contribution to R&D expenditure by the business sector despite the generous incentive regime prevailing earlier, businesses in India must focus on innovation. India should focus on improving its performance on business sophistication since higher performance on this dimension seems to consistently suggest higher innovation outputs performance.

22

PRIVATE PROWESS

Wealth Creation through Privatization

Think of a parent who has two children. The first one holds expertise in doing business, while the second is proficient in social service. The parent must decide how to distribute his wealth between the two such that both the children are well-off. After thinking a lot, the parent decides to give all his wealth to the first child who has expertise in business under one condition—that he would share his profit with the sibling. In this scenario, both children will be better off. Applying the same logic, disinvestment is beneficial for both the government and the PSEs.

As argued in this part of the book, wealth creation, and thereby economic progress, has been fostered by private enterprise. This has been the case historically as well as after India's economic liberalization in 1991. Historically, the fostering role of private enterprise in the market economy is captured in Kautilya's *Arthashastra*. Contemporary evidence following liberalization of the economy supports the salutary role of private enterprise in enabling wealth creation; sectors that were liberalized grew significantly faster than those that remained closed. Consistent with the wealth created by private enterprise, PSEs that were privatized have, on an average, performed better post privatization than their peers in terms of their net worth, net profit, return on assets (ROA), return on equity (ROE), gross revenue, net profit margin, sales growth and gross profit per employee. More importantly, the ROA and net profit margin turned around from negative to positive, surpassing that of the peer firms, which indicates that privatized enterprises have been able to generate more wealth from the same resources. This improved performance holds true for each PSE taken individually too. Thus, privatization clearly unlocks the potential of PSEs to create wealth. For India to fructify its economic aspirations, aggressive privatization of PSEs becomes a sine qua non.

Wealth Creation from Privatization

In November 2019, strategic disinvestment of the government's shareholding of 53.29 per cent in Bharat Petroleum Corporation Limited (BPCL) was approved by the GoI. Figure 1 shows the share price of BPCL when compared to its peer Hindustan Petroleum Corporation Limited (HPCL). We focus on the difference in BPCL and HPCL prices from September 2019 when the news of BPCL's privatization first appeared.[108] The comparison of BPCL with HPCL ensures that the effect of any broad movements in the stock market or in the oil industry is netted out. We note in Figure 1 that the stock prices of HPCL and BPCL moved synchronously till September. However, the divergence in their stock prices started post the announcement of BPCL's disinvestment. The increase in the stock price of BPCL when compared to the change in the price of HPCL over the same period translates into an increase in the value of shareholders' equity of BPCL of around ₹33,000 crore. As there was no reported change in the values of other stakeholders, including employees and lenders, during this time, the ₹33,000 crore increase translates into an unambiguous increase in the BPCL's overall firm value, and thereby an increase in national wealth by the same amount.

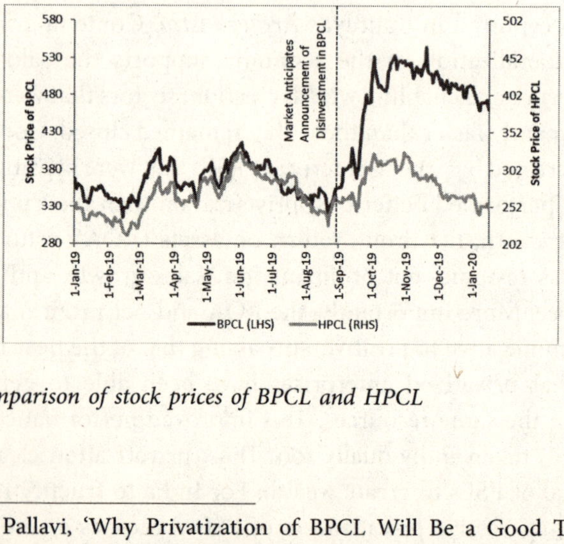

Figure 1: Comparison of stock prices of BPCL and HPCL
Source: BSE

[108]Pengonda, Pallavi, 'Why Privatization of BPCL Will Be a Good Thing for All Stakeholders', *Mint*, 13 September 2019, https://tinyurl.com/3ubf9ftx. Accessed on 5 December 2023.

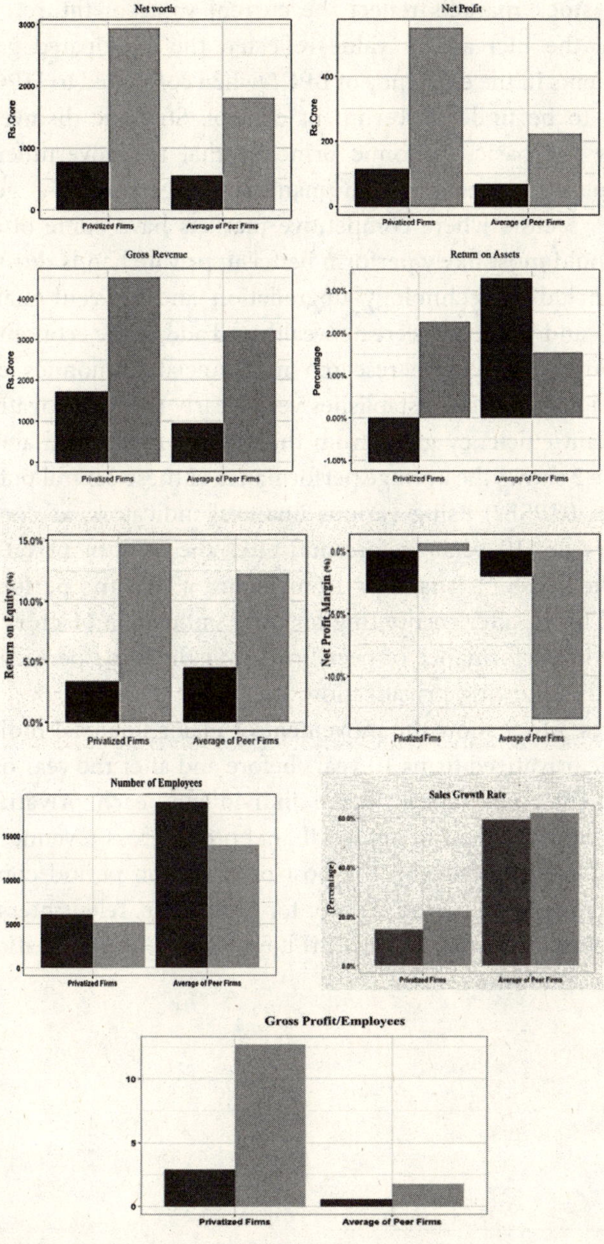

Figure 2. Comparison of financial indicators of privatized firms vis-à-vis peers

Source: Economic Survey 2019–20

Since stock markets reflect the current value of future cash flows of a firm, the increase in value reflected the anticipated gains from improvements in the efficiency of BPCL when compared to HPCL, which continues to be under government control. Strategic disinvestment is guided by the basic economic principle that the government should discontinue its engagement in manufacturing/producing goods and services in sectors where competitive markets have come of age. Such entities would most likely perform better in private hands due to various factors—including technology upgradation and efficient management practices—and would thus create wealth and add to the economic growth of the country. Extensive research in financial economics conducted across various countries establishes very clearly that privatization brings in significant efficiency gains from the sources mentioned above.

Figure 2 shows the average performance of these central public sector enterprises (CPSEs) using various financial indicators, as compared to their peers for 10 years before and after the year of privatization of the specific CPSE.[109] It is clear from Figure 2 that the performance of privatized firms, after accounting for other influencing factors using the difference in performance of peer firms over the same period, improves significantly following privatization.

Figures 3 to 9 show the movement of major financial indicators for each of the privatized firms 10 years before and after the year of strategic disinvestment/privatization. Taken individually, each privatized CPSE witnessed improvement in net worth, net profit, gross revenue, net profit margin and sales growth in the post-privatization period compared to the pre-privatization period (except for Hindustan Teleprinters, Modern Foods Industries [India] Ltd. [MFIL], and Tata Communications in the case of few indicators).

[109]Given data limitations, the financial data of MFIL and Indian Petrochemicals Corporation Limited (IPCL) have been taken for less than 10 years after their disinvestment.

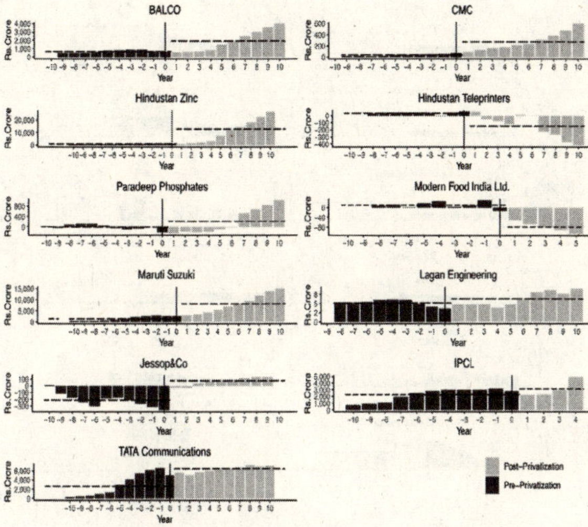

Figure 3: Net worth of privatized firms

Source: Economic Survey 2019–20

Note: '0' denotes the year of privatization.

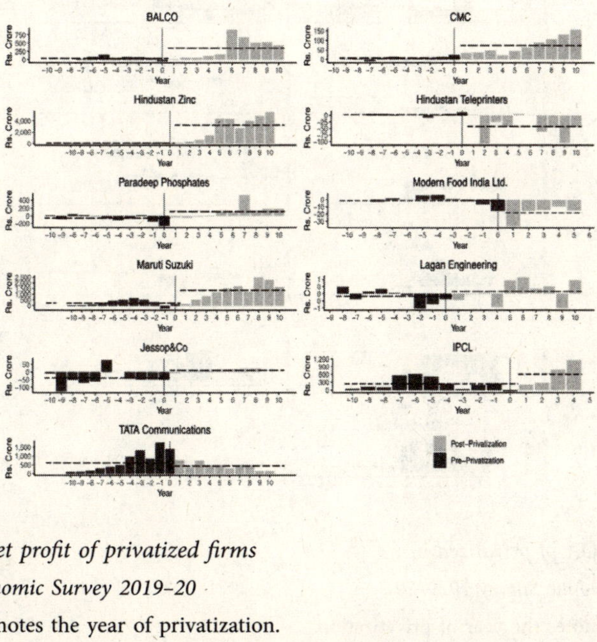

Figure 4: Net profit of privatized firms

Source: Economic Survey 2019–20

Note: '0' denotes the year of privatization.

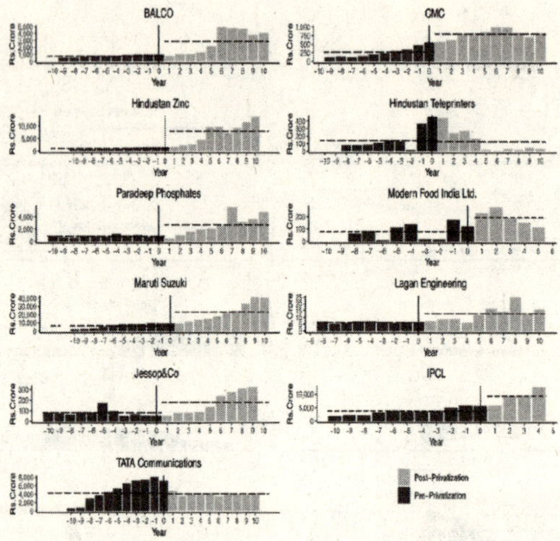

Figure 5: Gross revenue of privatized firms

Source: Economic Survey 2019–20

Note: '0' denotes the year of privatization.

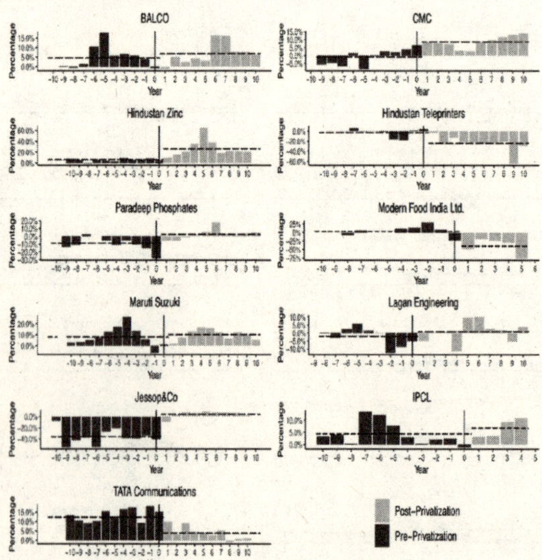

Figure 6: ROA of privatized firms

Source: Economic Survey 2019–20

Note: '0' denotes the year of privatization.

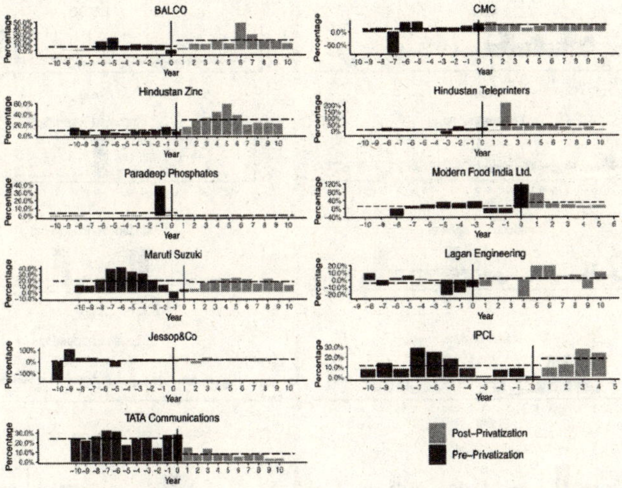

Figure 7: ROE of privatized firms

Source: Economic Survey 2019–20

Note: '0' denotes the year of privatization.

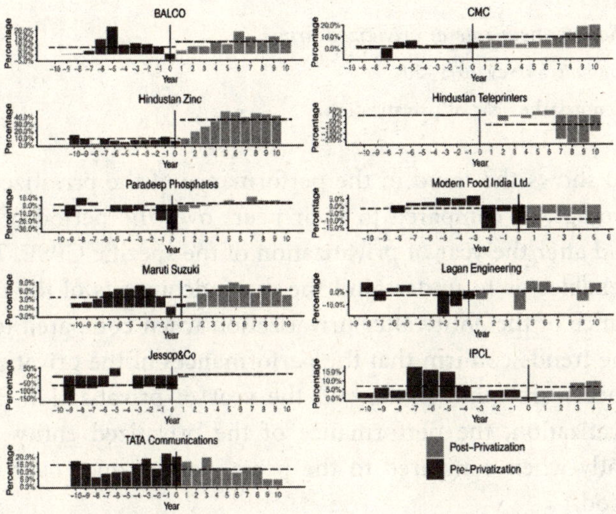

Figure 8: Net profit margin of privatized firms

Source: Economic Survey 2019–20

Note: '0' denotes the year of privatization.

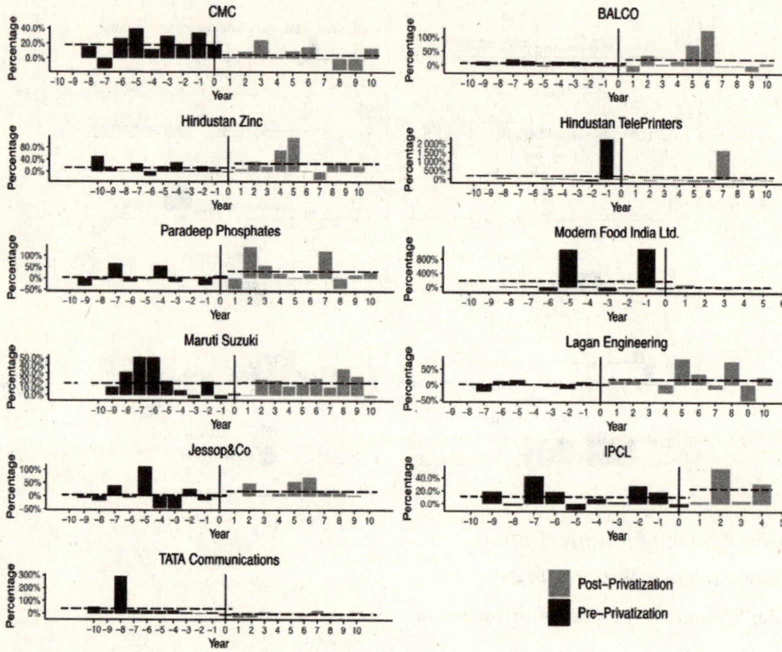

Figure 9: Sales growth rate of privatized firms

Source: Economic Survey 2019–20

Note: '0' denotes the year of privatization.

Figure 10 shows the trend in the performance of the privatized CPSEs, on an average, as compared to their peers over the period of 10 years before and after the year of privatization of the specific CPSE. The trend thereby enables us to understand the dynamic aspects of the change in performance of the entity after privatization when compared to its peer firms. The trends confirm that the performances of the privatized CPSE and its peers are quite similar till the year of privatization. However, post privatization, the performance of the privatized entity improves significantly when compared to the peers' performance over the same time period.

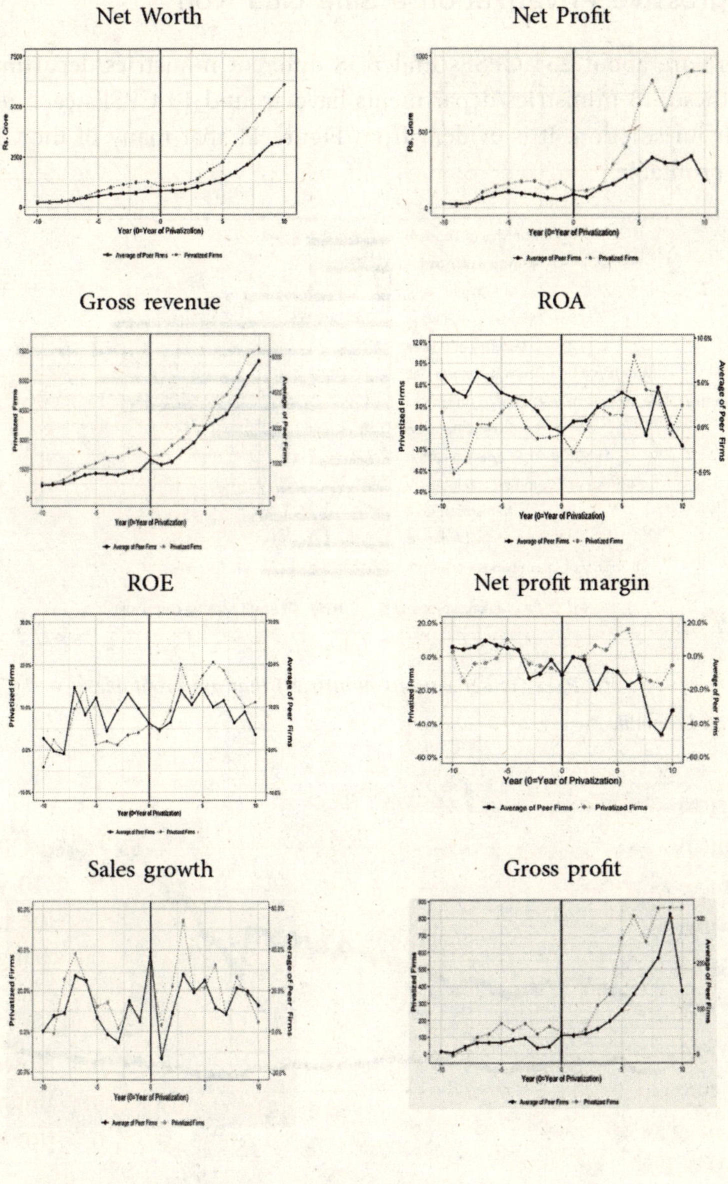

Figure 10: Trend in performance of privatized firms vs peers

Source: Economic Survey 2019–20

Note: '0' denotes the year of privatization.

Aggressive Privatization a Sine Qua Non

There are about 264 CPSEs under 38 different ministries/departments. Of these, 13 ministries/departments have around 10 CPSEs each under their jurisdiction. It is evident from Figure 11 that many of the CPSEs are profitable.

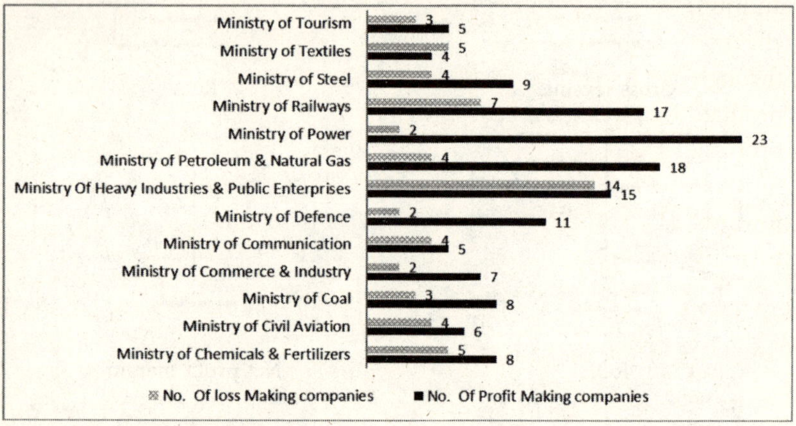

Figure 11: No. of CPSEs (under various ministries) that are profitable
Source: Economic Survey 2019–20

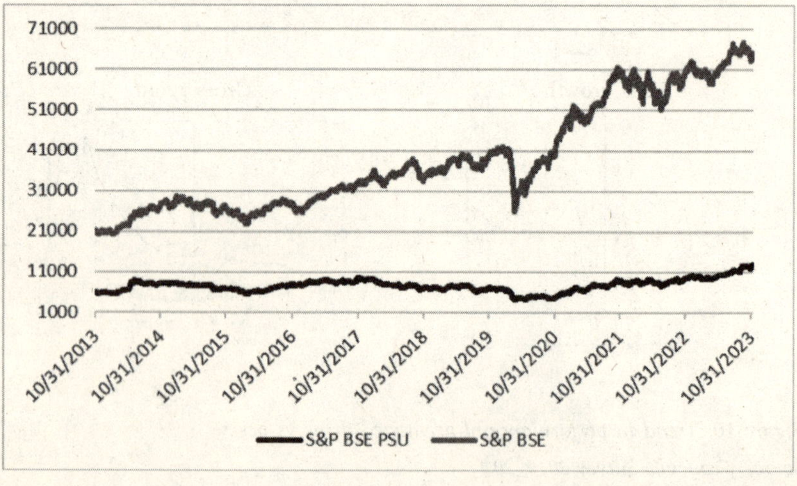

Figure 12: Poor performance of the BSE PSU Index when compared to the BSE SENSEX

However, as shown in Figure 12, CPSEs have generally underperformed in the market, as is evident from the significantly lower average return of the BSE PSU Index as against the return of BSE SENSEX during the period 2014–23.

The analysis in this chapter clearly affirms that privatization demonstrably improves the firm's performance and overall productivity and unlocks its potential to create wealth. This would have a multiplier effect on other sectors of the economy. Aggressive privatization, preferably through the route of strategic sale, should be utilized to bring in higher profitability, promote efficiency, increase competitiveness, and promote professionalism in management of CPSEs. The focus of privatization needs to be to exit from non-strategic business and should be directed towards optimizing economic potential of these CPSEs. This would, in turn, unlock capital for use elsewhere, especially in public infrastructure.

SECTION FIVE

THE FOURTH PILLAR
VIRTUOUS CYCLE IGNITED BY PRIVATE INVESTMENT

WHEN ONE ANALYSES EVERY COUNTRY that has grown at 5 per cent or more for at least a decade following World War II, one common theme that emerges is the key role of private investment in enabling such growth. The virtuous cycle triggered by private investment has served as a catalyst for consumption, job creation and overall economic expansion in these countries. After presenting evidence of this phenomenon in the first chapter, the remaining chapters in this section study how to enable such private investment.

In Chapter 11, we learnt about the importance of high-quality jobs for achieving socio-economic inclusion. To create jobs for all of India's youth, not just those that are born with privilege and/or to well-educated parents, growing the manufacturing sector is an absolute necessity. Chapter 24 delves into the debate that has perennially played out in India ever since the services sector gained prominence: should India focus on growing its manufacturing base or remain focussed only on services? This chapter provides compelling evidence that the manufacturing sector is special for job creation as it not only supports jobs on its own, but also fosters job creation in allied service sectors.

Some commentators claim that India has permanently missed the bus of industrialization. However, such commentators rarely acknowledge that this lack of industrialization is primarily self-inflicted because Indian policymakers—till the launch of the 'Make in India' campaign by the Modi government—never made a serious attempt to reform the factor markets that determine the cost of production for a manufacturing firm. While India opened its product markets to competition in 1991, the markets for factor inputs such as land, labour, power, transportation and capital have remained a relic of the socialist era. These markets suffer from lack of open competition and are hindered by archaic laws, rendering them ineffective and inefficient. As a result, Indian manufacturing firms faced exorbitantly higher costs of production when compared to their Chinese, Vietnamese or Thai peers. For socially and economically inclusive growth via meaningful job creation, Chapter 24 establishes that manufacturing is a sine qua non. The chapter identifies the policy failures that have hobbled manufacturing and describes the investments and reforms that are required to enable growth of manufacturing and thereby socio-economic inclusion of our masses.

A robust financial sector serves as the lifeblood of economic activity, channelling savings into productive investments and facilitating capital formation. Chapter 25 advocates for the strengthening of India's financial infrastructure as a critical enabler of private investment. Human capital lies at the heart of economic development, underpinning productivity, innovation and societal well-being. Chapters 26 and 27 examine the two critical elements of human capital creation: robust healthcare and catalytic education.

As the Indian economy will invariably experience peaks and troughs in its journey to becoming an economic powerhouse by its centennial year, policymakers must remember that the slowing down of the virtuous cycle during troughs will decelerate growth, while the ramp-up in the pace of the virtuous cycle during peaks will deliver growth accelerations. Through highs and lows, therefore, policymakers need to keep a continuous eye on the main trigger for the virtuous cycle—private investment. Doing so is likely to ensure that the promise that India@100 *offers will indeed crystallize.*

23

PRIVATE INVESTMENT

Primary Driver of Consumption, Jobs and Growth

Do you know the key economic ingredient behind every country that has grown at more than 5 per cent per annum for at least a decade—not just a few years—post World War II? As highlighted by the *Economic Survey 2018–19*, such high growth over long time-periods manifested through a 'virtuous cycle' ignited by private investment. Similarly, for India to become a global economic titan by 2047, she needs to sustain a real GDP growth rate of 8 per cent. Such growth can only be sustained by a 'virtuous cycle' where private investment fosters economic growth and creates good jobs. The resulting growth in income accelerates consumption and increases savings. Anticipating such consumption, firms invest further with savings being supported by a favourable demographic phase. Exports also form an integral part of the growth model as increase in private investment enhances productivity to increase the attractiveness of Indian products and services in the global markets.

What are the ingredients of a model that can generate real annual growth of 8 per cent for India? To understand this key question, we examine the drivers of economic growth followed by countries across the globe. In recent times, China's economic development stands out for its explosive growth over a long period of four decades. Post-War economic expansion in Britain and Western Europe led to high growth rates of their economies. Japan grew at an average rate of around 10 per cent from 1950 to 1973, thereby matching the Chinese growth in speed though not in its duration. Post World War II, Hong Kong, Singapore, South Korea and Taiwan successfully maintained a rapid growth rate of more than 7 per cent until the 1980s.

Challenging Traditional Views

Overwhelming evidence across the globe, especially from China and East Asia in recent times, suggests that high growth rates have only been sustained by a growth model driven by a virtuous cycle of savings, investment and exports, propelled and supported by a favourable demographic phase. As I explain in detail below, investment, especially private investment, is the 'key driver' that drives demand, creates capacity, increases labour productivity, introduces new technology, allows creative destruction, and generates jobs.

In outlining a growth model for India that simultaneously enhances productivity, creates jobs and fosters domestic demand and exports, we view the economy as being in either a virtuous or a vicious cycle, and thus never in equilibrium. When the economy is in a virtuous cycle, investment, productivity growth, job creation, demand and exports feed into one another and enable 'animal spirits' in the economy to thrive. In contrast, when the economy is in a vicious cycle, a moderation in these variables leads to one dampening the other, thereby diminishing the animal spirits in the economy. This framework, specifically tailored to India by learning from the East Asian economies and China, in either a virtuous or a vicious cycle—with investment as the key driver of this cycle—stems from two key departures from the traditional, Anglo-Saxon view of the economy.

First, economies are intricately interwoven systems that can be neither meaningfully viewed in silos nor analysed without accounting for dynamic effects over time. Moreover, economies may rarely be in a state of equilibrium. While writing about economic theories following the GFC, Rodrik (2018) laments:

> Why do we focus so much on the perfectly rational individual even though real people do not seem to behave quite that way? Shouldn't we be paying a wee bit more attention to disequilibrium, in addition to equilibrium? Why do our models exclude social and institutional features without which markets could not work? Why do we emphasize math so much and disregard things that cannot be easily quantified?[110]

---

[110]Ministry of Finance, GoI, *Economic Survey 2018–19*, Volume 1, July 2019,

The meltdown of economic activity following the GFC highlighted that economies may be in a vicious cycle. Therefore, as highlighted by Romer (2015), Ramos (2017) and Rodrik (2018), economic thinkers now recognize the need for economics to embrace learnings from other fields. They acknowledge that the concept of treating an economy as always being in equilibrium may force-fit the 'standard' framework to an ever-changing world. Instead, thinking about economies as being in the constant disequilibrium of virtuous or vicious cycles provides a more apt framework for the current times. Therefore, when the economy is viewed thus, proper sequencing of policy levers assumes importance, especially because of the presence of complementarities between different elements of an economy.

The traditional view, which has come under significant challenge following the GFC, considers the concept of equilibrium as a key tenet for the macroeconomy. In contrast, by imbibing some of the new learnings from the economics literature following the GFC, we view the economy as being in a constant state of disequilibrium as captured by a virtuous or a vicious cycle.

Second, the traditional view often attempts to solve job creation, demand, exports and economic growth as separate problems. In contrast, as I show below, these macroeconomic phenomena exhibit significant complementarities. Moreover, at the macroeconomic level, each one of these variables represents both a cause and an effect. Take investments, for example. Greater private and public investment can foster job creation and thereby aggregate demand in the economy. However, greater job creation and consumption, in turn, foster greater private investment to cater to this demand for consumption. Thus, investment acts as the effect in this instance. In reality, these macroeconomic cause-and-effect phenomena manifest through leads and lags in the economy, with investment this year fostering job creation and aggregate demand in the next few years, on the one hand, and job creation and aggregate demand this year, in turn, fostering private investment in subsequent years, on the other hand. Given these deep interlinkages, it is critical to understand and carefully analyse the key driver that creates the domino effect to accelerate the virtuous cycle and enable the growth in each of the other macro phenomena. When viewed

---

pp. 10–11, https://tinyurl.com/5ccw6unz. Accessed on 8 December 2023.

in this manner, the triggering macroeconomic key driver that can create a self-sustaining virtuous cycle in India becomes critical. By accounting for the dynamic cause-and-effect phenomena among all the macroeconomic variables of interest, we posit that private investment is the key driver of the virtuous cycle. This investment includes private investment and government investments in infrastructure, as such investment crowds in private investment (Chakrabarti, Subramanian and Sesha 2017).

Figure 1 shows how the share of GCF, savings and exports in GDP evolved for China as a function of the log of GDP per capita from 1980 to 2016. Crucially, we note that all the three macro-variables increased as the country became richer. Thus, as the economy started doing better, as measured by the rising GDP per capita, China's savings, investment and exports increased further. Figure 2 shows the same relationships for GCF and savings for four countries in East Asia (Thailand, Indonesia, Malaysia and Korean Republic), which witnessed high growth before the 1997 Asian Financial Crisis. The time period employed in these charts is 1980–95, i.e., before the Asian Financial Crisis. Figure 3 shows this relationship for exports, where we observe that except for South Korea, exports as a proportion of GDP increased as the countries became richer. The inference that we made using China, thus, remains unchanged by examining Figures 2 and 3.

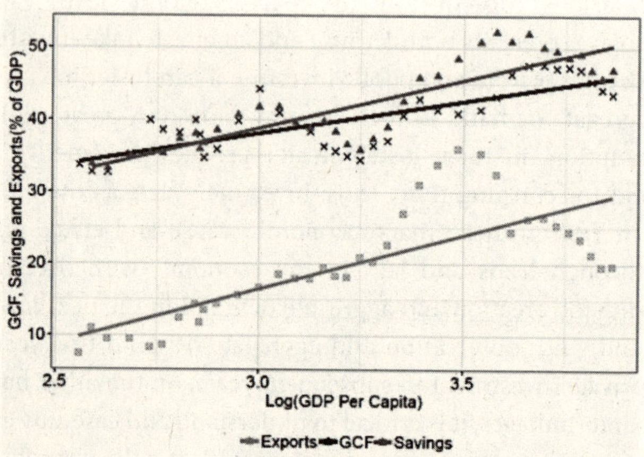

Figure 1: Share of GCF, savings and exports in GDP vs log (GDP per capita) in constant 2010 US$: China

Source: Economic Survey 2018–19

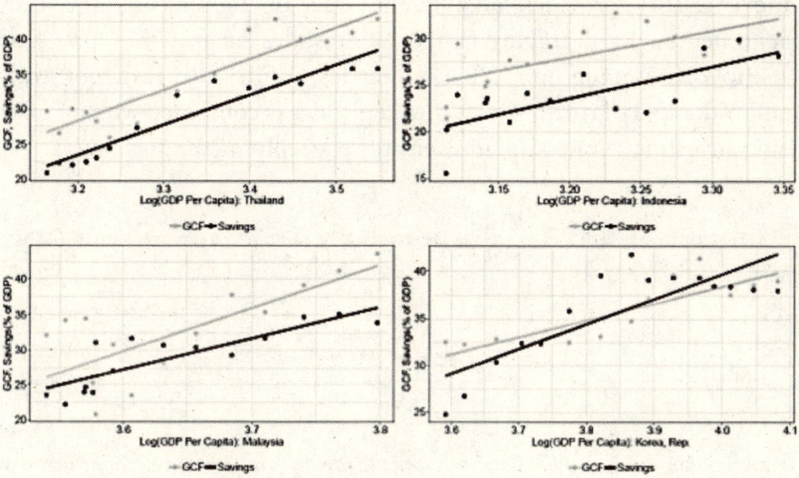

Figure 2: Share of GCF and savings in GDP vs log (GDP per capita) in constant 2010 US$: high-growth East Asian economies ex China

Source: Economic Survey 2018–19

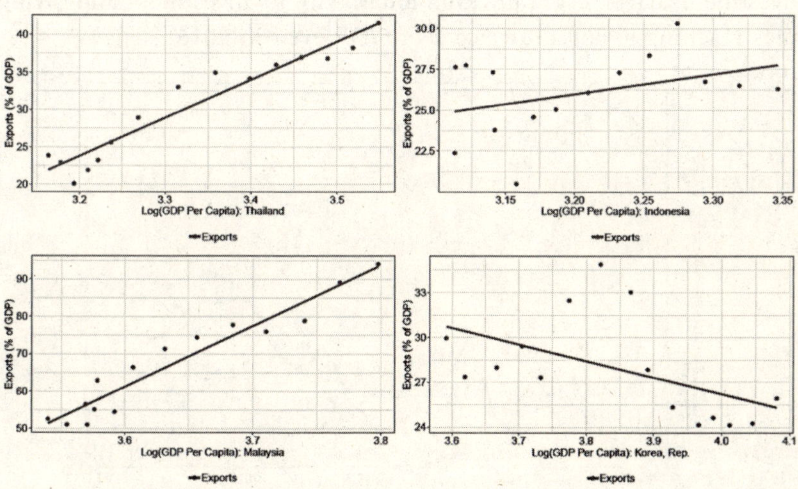

Figure 3: Share of exports in GDP (%) vs log (GDP per capita) in constant 2010 US$: high-growth East Asian economies ex China

Source: Economic Survey 2018–19

Sandri (2014) provides a different way of looking at the same phenomenon. By averaging across 62 episodes of growth spurts from 1960 to 2011 among non-OECD countries, Sandri (2014) demonstrates that productivity growth across these episodes is combined with a rapidly rising investment rate and an even more steeply increasing savings rate (Figure 4).

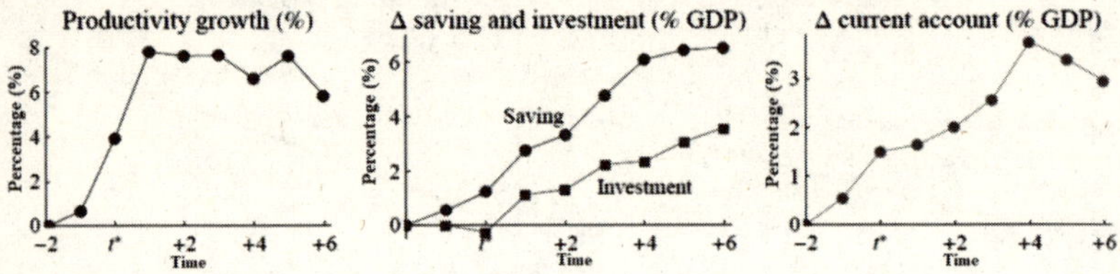

Figure 4: Changes in productivity, investment, savings and current account across 62 episodes of growth accelerations in non-OECD countries

Source: Economic Survey 2018–19

China has relied primarily on savings and investment, with consumption decreasing significantly as a share of GDP (Figure 5). It remains an investment-driven economy even today, with its investment and savings rates reaching about 45 per cent of GDP even in 2016.

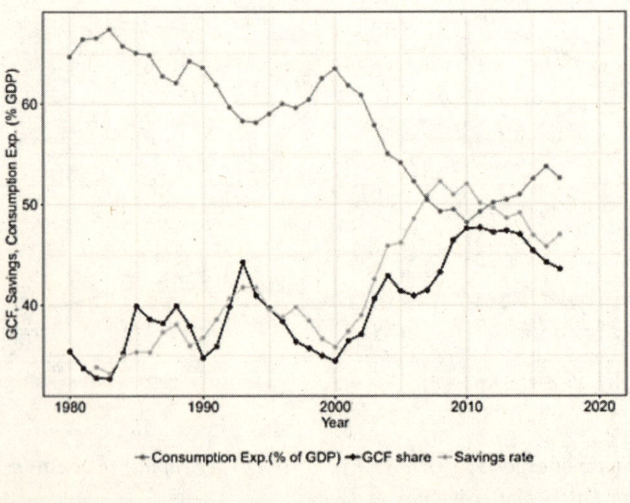

Figure 5: Consumption, GCF and savings to GDP for China

Source: Economic Survey 2018–19

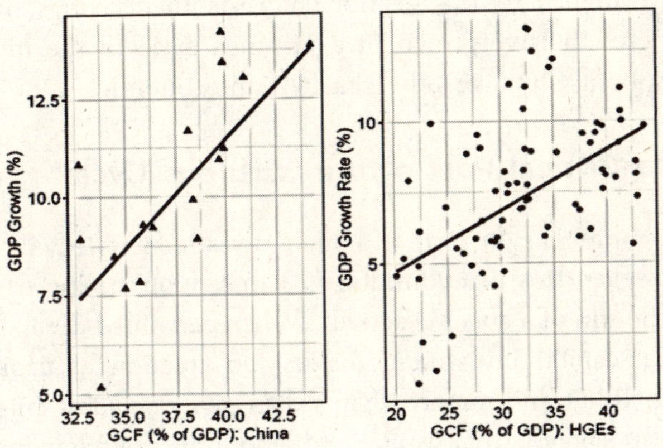

Figure 6: GDP growth vs GCF to GDP for China and high-growth East Asian economies ex China

Source: Economic Survey 2018–19

For China and other East Asian economies, Figure 6 shows the strong correlation between investment as measured by the GCF and GDP growth, while Figure 7 shows an equally stronger correlation between investment and savings.

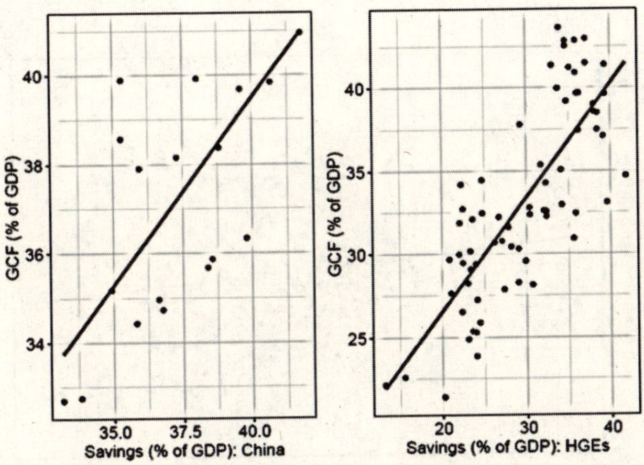

Figure 7: GCF to GDP vs savings rate for China and high-growth East Asian economies ex China

Source: Economic Survey 2018–19

Thus, the evidence in this section suggests that savings, investment and GDP growth have grown in a virtuous cycle in the high-growth economies, be it China or other East Asian economies.

Jobs as a Critical Part of the 'Virtuous Cycle'

A general apprehension is that a high investment rate will substitute labour. However, this is a common misconception arising from a view buried in the silo of a specific activity. When examined across the entire value chain, capital investment fosters job creation as capital goods production, R&D and supply chains also generate jobs. International evidence also suggests that capital and labour are complementary when high investment rate drives growth. For instance, Lin (2011) shows that the introduction of software and computers, while having replaced some white-collar jobs, has also generated new labour-centric tasks related to software and application development, computer security, as well as specialized tasks for loan application analysts and medical equipment technicians, etc. The success story of Township and Village Enterprises (TVEs) in China becoming the engines of its spectacular growth shows how labour-intensive manufacturing investment can simultaneously boost productivity, job creation and exports (Wei and Balasubramanyam

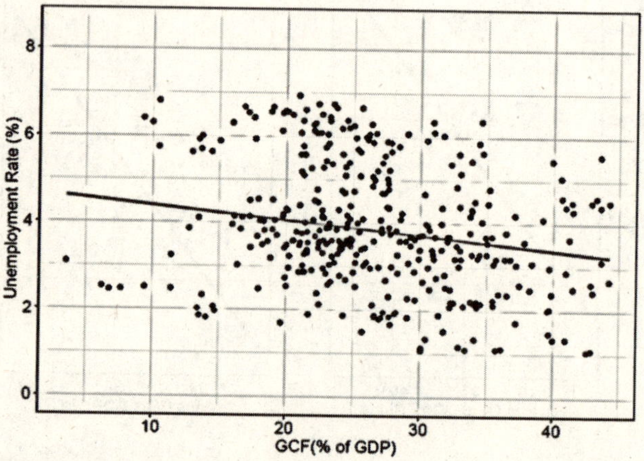

Figure 8: Unemployment rate vs GCF to GDP for East Asia and Pacific
Source: Economic Survey 2018–19

2015). While in 1980, there were about 1.4 million TVEs with 30 million employees, by 1996, there were 23.4 million TVEs with 135 million workers contributing nearly 30 per cent of China's GDP and 50 per cent of the industrial output (Perotti et al. 1999). By 1999, TVE exports accounted for 48 per cent of China's total exports and much of these were labour-intensive products involving simple production techniques (Fu and Balasubramanyam 2005). Figure 8 shows how unemployment rates decrease with greater GCF in East Asia and the Pacific, thereby providing additional evidence that labour and investment complement each other. Therefore, job creation can indeed be fostered by encouraging investment.

Exports as a Key Component of the 'Virtuous Cycle'

With the share of consumption in GDP constrained by the high level of savings, domestic consumption can, at best, act as a force multiplier when high income growth feeds consumption. So, where would the final demand for the large capacities created by high investment come from? The answer is exports. This is why an aggressive export strategy must be a part of any investment-driven growth model. Figure 9 shows the strong correlation between growth in exports and GDP growth for East Asian economies.

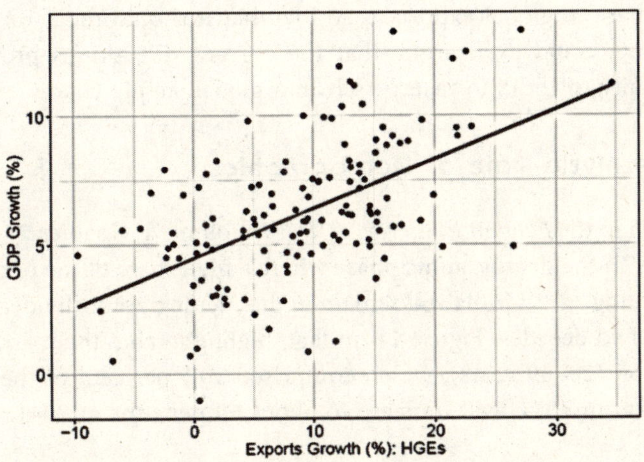

Figure 9: GDP growth vs growth in exports for East Asian economies

Source: Economic Survey 2018–19

The global market is extremely competitive, with the firms that are able to produce at the lowest costs having the ability to gain market share in exports. So, average productivity of firms in the economy becomes crucial to export competitiveness. As seen in Figure 10, capital investment enhances total factor productivity, which in turn enhances export performance. Therefore, investment becomes crucial to enhancing export performance.

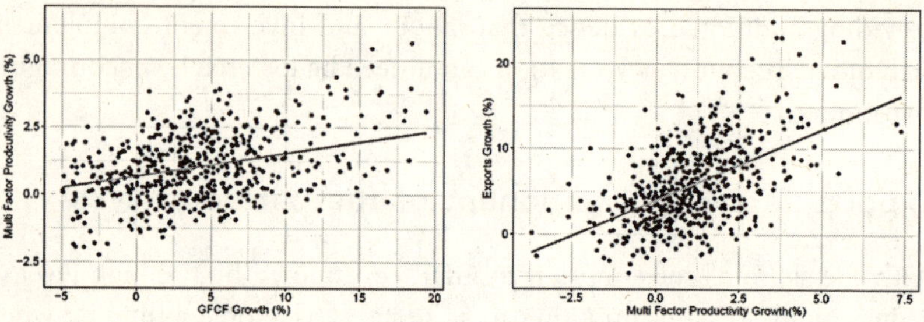

Figure 10: Effect of GFCF growth on productivity and in turn on exports for OECD countries

Source: Economic Survey 2018–19

While it is true that world trade is currently facing some disruptions, India's share in global exports is so low that it should focus on market share. One could even argue that the current disruptions provide an opportunity to India to insert itself into global supply chains.

The Catalytic Role of Demographics

As shown in the *Economic Survey 2018–19* (Volume 1, Chapter 7), India is currently in the demographic phase where a high share of the population is of working age.[111] India will remain in this 'demographic dividend' zone for over two decades. Figure 11, in fact, highlights that the working-age population (20–59 years), which comprised 50.5 per cent of the overall population in 2011, will increase to about 60 per cent in 2041.

[111]Ibid.

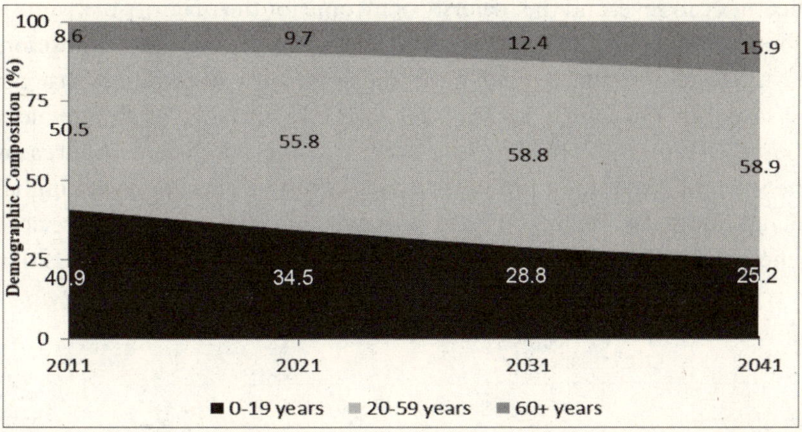

Figure 11: Demographic composition of India (2011–41)
Source: Economic Survey 2018–19

Change in demographics, especially the age structure of the population, has been shown to have had a significant effect on economic growth throughout Asia between 1960 and 1990 (Bloom and Williamson 1998). A rise in the share of the working-age population, brought about by a decline in the fertility rate, increases income per capita as output per worker remains unchanged but the number of youth dependents declines. The rise in the working-age share in Asia created this accounting effect, but it also brought with it behavioural changes. Savings increased as life expectancy increased (Lee, Mason and Miller 2000; Bloom et al. 2007), and consequently, investment increased. In fact, changes in growth of labour force per capita, changes in the savings rate and changes in the investment rate are three plausible mechanisms by which demographics affect economic growth (Higgins and Williamson 1997; Bloom and Williamson 1998).

Figure 12 shows how savings rate in China and other high-growth East Asian economies was driven significantly by change in its demographics from a predominantly young to an older population. While the top panels show the change in the demographics, the bottom panels illustrate how closely the household savings rate and the working-age proportion of the population move together in China and other East Asian economies. This makes sense because only people who are earning incomes can save, and the majority of income for the majority of people is labour income. But, in addition to this effect of demographic composition, having fewer 'mouths to feed' raises the availability of resources that can be saved for the future. Second, due to the importance of children as a source of retirement income, the decline in the number of children by the working generation promotes savings as the working generation has to rely more on savings for retirement in comparison to the previous generations. Finally, savings also increase as a result of a composition effect—a significant amount of savings takes place between the ages of 40 and 65 as people set aside funds for retirement.

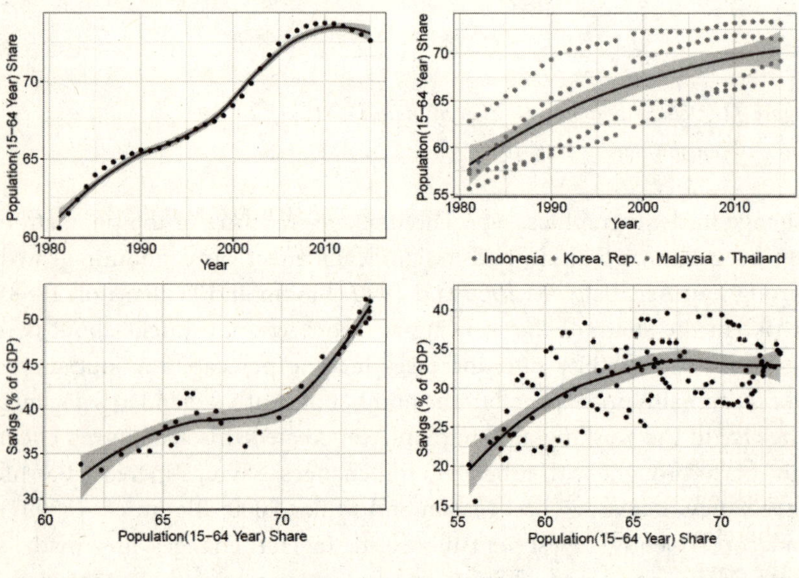

Figure 12: Impact of demographics on savings for China and other high-growth East Asian economies

Source: World Bank data

Note: Time period taken is 1980–2015 and high-growth economies pertain to Indonesia, Malaysia, Republic of Korea and Thailand.

As Bosworth and Chodorow-Reich (2007) show for Asia, both savings and investment rise with the proportion of the working population (Figure 13). Notice that this figure shows the coefficient of the effect of proportion of each age group in the population on investment and savings. A positive coefficient indicates that the effect of the age group is to increase savings/investment, while a negative coefficient indicates that this effect decreases savings/investment. Investment rises significantly with an increase in each of the age cohorts till age 50, while savings rises significantly with an increase in each of the age cohorts till age 60.

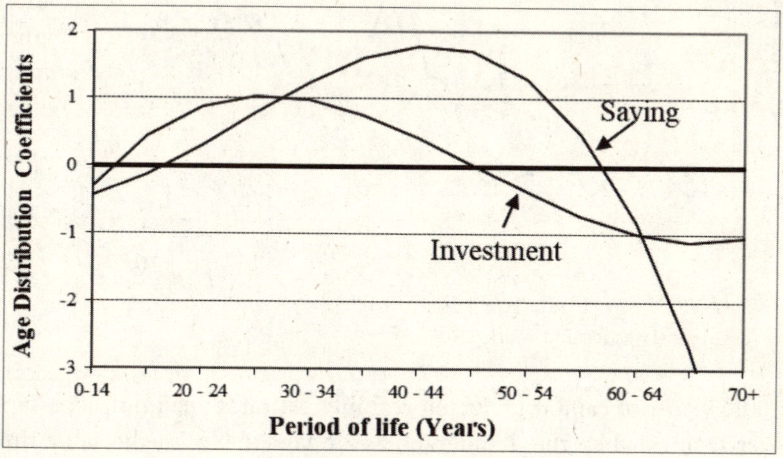

Figure 13: Impact of composition of demographics on savings in Asia
Source: Bosworth and Chodorow-Reich (2007)

Figure 14 shows how wages affected China's savings rate. This relationship is crucial to note because without an increase in the earnings of the working population, neither consumption nor savings can increase. Therefore, jobs that pay meaningful wages become crucial in driving the savings rate in the economy. The virtuous cycle that we describe fosters job creation by exploiting the complementarity between capital and labour on one hand, and by an increase in the overall productivity and labour productivity on the other.

Thus, our analysis shows that savings is driven primarily by demographics and income growth. Therefore, there is no point keeping domestic interest rates high in order to encourage savings behaviour; a mildly positive real rate is good enough. As demographics and wages are the major factors that drive savings, policymakers obtain a key degree of freedom. Specifically, the two parts of the financial system, the savers and the borrowers, can be disentangled. As investment depends crucially

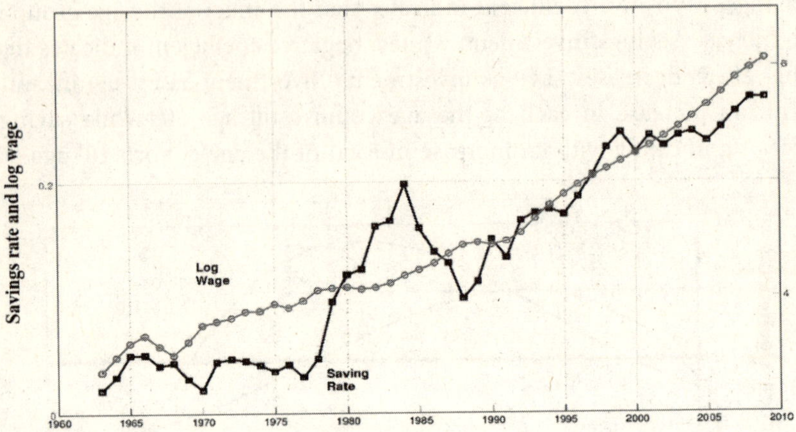

Figure 14: Impact of wages on savings in China

Source: Curtis, Lugauer and Mark (2011)

on a low cost of capital, reducing real interest rates need not necessarily lower savings when the demographics are favourable. At the same time, the reduction in real interest rates can foster investment and thereby set in motion the virtuous cycle of investment, growth, exports and jobs.

24

MAKE IN INDIA

Driving Virtuous Cycle in High Gear

Think of the delivery boy who delivers the food that you ordered on Swiggy, the pizza you wanted from Domino's, or the groceries you ordered from Amazon. These delivery boys work 10 hours a day to earn, on average, ₹17,000 a month.[112] If these delivery boys could work in a manufacturing factory, they would work only eight hours a day and earn, on average, ₹24,000 a month.[113] This example captures how important the growth of manufacturing is for India to overcome its biggest challenge—creating good-quality jobs for our young population.

Software, business process outsourcing (BPO) and the financial services sector employ well-qualified professionals with undergraduate and graduate degrees. However, these service sectors do not create the jobs required for a large proportion of our youth, who do not come from privileged backgrounds and cannot obtain higher qualifications. In this chapter, I make a strong case for India to grow its manufacturing sector to provide meaningful jobs to its youth. The manufacturing sector is 'special' because it is like an escalator: once a country starts manufacturing things, productivity goes up quickly, thereby helping the country catch up with high-income countries while creating meaningful jobs. After making the case for India to continue its focus on Make in India, I examine the concerns that various commentators pose about the focus on manufacturing. In essence, I highlight that policy failures that did not reform the factor markets prevented India from utilizing its comparative advantage of cheap labour. Given the emphasis of the Modi government on addressing these policy failures, India can certainly

---

[112]'How to Join Swiggy Delivery Boy? Salary and Shift Hours', *Job Hai*, 6 December 2022, http://tinyurl.com/4drpxax9. Accessed on 19 January 2024.

[113]'Factory Worker Salary in India', *Economic Research Institute*, http://tinyurl.com/ms27tab5. Accessed on 19 January 2024.

grow its manufacturing sector and thereby create the jobs necessary to avail its demographic dividend.

The Importance of a Large Middle Class

Those of us who grew up in middle-class India recognize the values that a middle-class upbringing gave us. Through their own examples, our parents taught us the importance of hard work and education and exemplified the patient acquisition of skills or knowledge needed to pursue long-term goals. Our personal experience, thus, teaches us the importance of a burgeoning middle-class for sustained, equitable economic development.

The middle class is crucial for maintaining sufficient consumption levels needed for new investments. The idea is straightforward: if people have enough money to spend, businesses will invest in producing more, driving economic growth. Nobel Laureate Milton Friedman postulated this idea as the PIH, which states that consumption by a household depends primarily on the permanent component of future income that a household anticipates.[114]

Manufacturing Helps to Create a Large Middle Class

Manufacturing plays a crucial role in fostering a strong middle class by creating meaningful jobs. Analysis by the Joint Economic Committee (JEC) of the US Senate shows that each manufacturing job supports an additional 1.6 jobs, and each advanced manufacturing job supports as many as 4.9 other jobs.[115] This larger 'job multiplier' for manufacturing is partly explained by manufacturing supply chains and the large number of supplier jobs that depend on the sector.

Manufacturing jobs typically offer greater job security compared to service sector jobs due to longer production cycles and reduced susceptibility to short-term economic fluctuations. After accounting

---

[114]Friedman, Milton, 'The Permanent Income Hypothesis', *A Theory of the Consumption Function*, Princeton University Press, 1957, http://tinyurl.com/4z4x36fb. Accessed on 19 January 2024.

[115]Joint Economic Committee | Democrats, *Manufacturing Jobs for the Future*, December 2013, http://tinyurl.com/4c4pzd2t. Accessed on 19 January 2024.

for the effect of workers' qualifications, manufacturing jobs pay 10–15 per cent more on average than service-sector jobs. Additionally, manufacturing jobs are more likely to provide essential benefits, such as healthcare and retirement plans, thus enhancing the quality of life for workers. In contrast, many service-sector jobs, such as those in retail and food service, offer minimum wages and lack benefits, making it challenging for workers to establish a stable financial future. Applying Friedman's PIH, the higher wages and the lower uncertainty together help to increase aggregate consumption more than service sector jobs.

Without a vibrant manufacturing base, societies risk division between those with access to stable, well-paying jobs and those facing job insecurity and precarious lives. Manufacturing emerges as a central force in achieving both high economic growth at the macroeconomic level and social and economic inclusion at the microeconomic level.

Kaldor's Laws on the Special Importance of Manufacturing

In the 1960s, British economist Nicholas Kaldor wrote on the special importance of manufacturing for economic growth. Several studies have found evidence consistent with Kaldor's thesis in recent times—both for advanced economies and developing ones. Evidence in the Indian context also supports Kaldor's thesis, making it essential to comprehend it specifically for India (Chakravarty and Mitra 2009; Kathuria and Natarajan 2013).[116]

According to Kaldor, the manufacturing sector is the best engine of growth because it can trigger the 'virtuous cycle' as discussed in Chapter 23. The manufacturing sector's contribution to the virtuous cycle stems from static and dynamic returns to scale. Specifically, both forward and backward linkages are quite strong in manufacturing when compared to agriculture and services. Therefore, the size of manufacturing operations at which the business becomes profitable is not small. As

[116]Chakravarty and Mitra (2009) covering the period 1973–2004 find that manufacturing is one of the drivers of growth, together with construction and services. Kathuria and Natarajan (2013) tested the hypothesis for all 15 states of India in the period from 1994–95 to 2005–06, and concluded that manufacturing had indeed acted as an engine of growth in India, despite its declining share in GDP.

manufacturing requires capital investment, it can be profitable only when the scale of operations is higher than the minimum threshold size. Beyond the threshold size, average cost per unit declines as fixed costs per unit decline, generating static returns to scale. The dynamic returns to scale manifest from learning by doing, which reduces the costs, potential errors, and coordination problems across different activities. Unlike services or agriculture, this combination of static and dynamic returns to scale makes manufacturing an increasing-returns-to-scale activity. In other words, as productivity increases in manufacturing operations, it encourages bigger scale of operations leading to higher output and employment. The higher scale, in turn, feeds back into higher productivity. These ideas lead to Kaldor's three laws of growth:

1. The speed at which the GDP grows is directly proportional to the extent to which manufacturing outpaces overall GDP growth. In other words, GDP growth is faster when the share of manufacturing in GDP rises.
2. As the manufacturing sector grows in size, its productivity increases, thereby generating a symbiotic relationship between productivity and size of the manufacturing sector.

The third law of Kaldor, which is less intuitive, states that:

3. As the manufacturing sector grows, the productivity of the non-manufacturing sector also increases. Unlike manufacturing, non-manufacturing sectors exhibit diminishing returns to scale. As labour moves into manufacturing from non-manufacturing sectors, the scale of operations of the non-manufacturing sectors decreases. Because of the diminishing returns to scale, a decline in the scale of operations makes the non-manufacturing sector more productive.

As with Keynes, the founder of the field called 'Keynesian economics' within macroeconomics, Kaldor attached considerable importance to demand-side factors. In the last several years, demand for phones and other electronic items has increased significantly in India. As the income of a household rises, the demand for manufactured products—two-wheelers, air-conditioners, refrigerators, microwave ovens, cars, textiles, home furniture, etc.—will increase. This will occur progressively at lower and lower levels of the income pyramid. For instance, a household that earns ₹5 lakh per annum now would look to graduate to a car from a two-wheeler while a household that earns ₹1 lakh per annum now would want to graduate to a two-wheeler. As the economy grows, household incomes will rise progressively and domestic demand for manufactured goods will continue to remain strong even in 2047. This is because when the household with ₹5 lakh per annum graduates to a car now, the household earning ₹2 lakh per annum will do so in a decade when their income rises to a similar level. With a domestic population of 140 crore and growing, the households that will graduate into higher income levels will not cease.

Why Is Manufacturing 'Special' for Catch-Up?

Research by Harvard economist Dani Rodrik is quite important to understand why manufacturing is essential for India to catch up with the advanced economies in per capita GDP. To understand Rodrik's work, first, we must understand the concept of 'convergence'. Theoretically, developing nations can utilize the technologies developed by advanced economies and attract capital from them to grow much faster than them. This thesis captures the concept of convergence. But convergence has not happened in reality.

Figure 1 illustrates this lack of convergence, or 'conditional convergence' as the economic literature jargonizes. In the left panel, the growth of GDP per worker is plotted against the initial level of real GDP per worker. Each observation in the chart corresponds to the growth of GDP per worker in a (country, decade) pair. To remove the effect of secular time-trends that can affect global economic prospects, the residuals after removing the fixed effects of each decade are plotted; these residuals are called the 'orthogonal part'. We find that there is no correlation between the initial level of GDP per worker and the subsequent growth in GDP per worker. As seen in the right panel in Figure 1, once the effect of time-invariant country characteristics is removed by plotting residuals that removed both time and country fixed effects, the convergence is very strong. Hence, when accounting for factors that remain constant over time, such as the quality of a nation's institutions, the extent to which the rule of law is enforced, the level of industriousness displayed by its citizens, and other similar aspects, there is a significant tendency towards convergence.

While the right chart is useful to understand the phenomenon of convergence, or the lack of it, it essentially throws the baby out with the bathwater. This is because a policymaker wants to know the policy apparatus that will enable a developing country to catch up with the advanced economies. But, by removing this interesting variation, the demonstration of convergence is of little value from a policy standpoint.

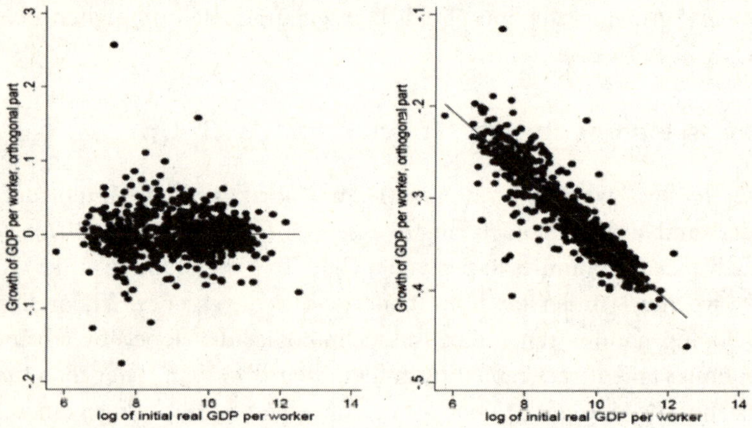

Figure 1: Lack of convergence in income levels across countries
Source: Rodrik (2011b)

Figure 2 replicates the same exercise as above for specific manufacturing industries—mostly the formal, organized ones—instead of the aggregate economy. The left panel plots the residuals after removing the fixed effects of each industry and each decade. The results in the left panel in Figure 2 are important for India as they reveal 'unconditional convergence'. Why unconditional? Because the convergence—the fact that manufacturing industries whose productivity is lower grow their productivity much faster than those manufacturing industries with higher productivity—does not depend on the characteristics of the country. Regardless of any country characteristics, be it geographic location, or other socio-economic features, labour productivity in manufacturing converges.

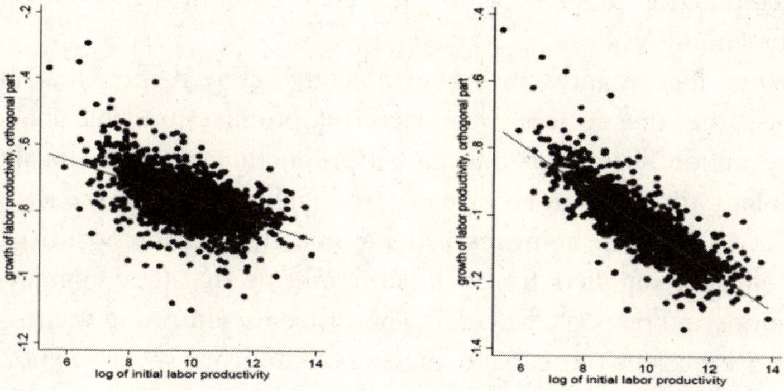

GDP growth per worker in manufacturing after removing industry and time fixed effects

GDP growth per worker in manufacturing after removing industry, time and country fixed effects

Figure 2: Unconditional convergence of productivity in manufacturing

Source: Rodrik (2011a)

The rate of convergence is quite large, equal to 4.1–7.8 per cent per annum, with the annual rate of convergence being higher over a five-year period than over a 10-year period (see Figure 3).

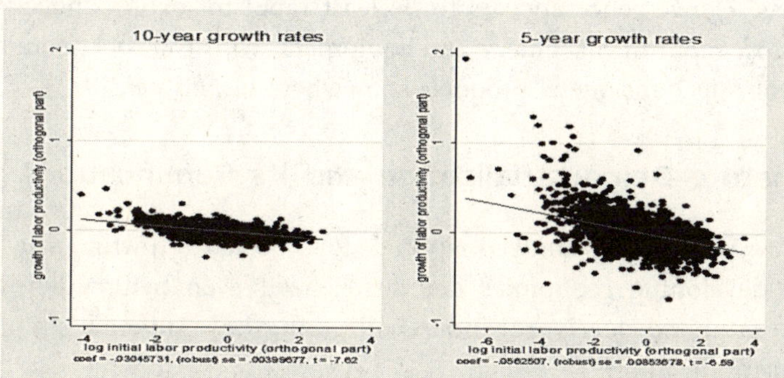

Figure 3: Rate of convergence of productivity in manufacturing

Source: Rodrik (2011a)

Crucially, unlike the convergence in GDP per capita or GDP per worker, convergence via manufacturing manifests as a robust phenomenon. Thus, the manufacturing sector relative to other sectors has a higher potential for technological progress, as its progress does not depend on country-specific conditions.

Why does manufacturing exhibit the convergence that is not witnessed in other sectors? Manufacturing produces tradable goods that can be rapidly integrated into global production networks, facilitating technology transfer and absorption. Crucially, even when the goods are produced just for the home market, they operate under competitive threat from efficient suppliers from abroad, requiring that they upgrade their operations and remain efficient. In contrast, agriculture and non-tradable services, especially those that operate in the informal sector, do not share these characteristics.

When the insights provided by Dani Rodrik's work are combined with those of Kaldor, we infer that developing manufacturing in India will accelerate the rate of technological progress of the economy, not just in manufacturing but also in the non-manufacturing sectors. Therefore, once India gets a toehold in a particular manufacturing sector—electronics recently and automobiles in the 1980s—productivity in such industries is likely to converge to the frontier. In fact, other research in convergence via manufacturing demonstrates that the rate of convergence in manufacturing is even stronger in the sectors that start exporting to the international markets. Convergence appears to be least rapid in textiles and clothing and most rapid in machinery and equipment, with transport equipment and iron, steel and metal products somewhere in between.

Premature Deindustrialization and Its Ramifications

If manufacturing is indeed special for job-led growth, why have many developing economies deindustrialized even before they could reach saturated levels of industrialization, i.e., suffered premature deindustrialization?

Three features of premature deindustrialization must be noted. First, advanced economies, which had previously achieved saturated levels of industrialization, have lost considerable employment in the manufacturing sectors with the effects being particularly salient in manufacturing jobs that require low levels of skill. However, the manufacturing sector's contribution to overall output has remained steady in the advanced economies.

Second, developing economies in Latin America and Africa seem to be running out of opportunities to industrialize their economies much sooner and at much lower levels of income than the advanced economies. These economies opened trade in manufacturing to integrate completely with the advanced economies. Moreover, unlike advanced economies, in these developing economies, the share of manufacturing has declined both in employment and in output.

Finally, Asian countries have not experienced deindustrialization in either output or employment. Asia has not only bucked the global trend in manufacturing employment, but it has also managed to maintain stronger manufacturing performance.

What explains these differing trends? Rodrik studies these patterns and attributes the deindustrialization in the advanced economies to technological improvements and that in the Latin American and African economies to globalization without possessing comparative advantage in manufacturing. In advanced economies, technology that replaced low-skilled labour with capital led to reduced use of labour in manufacturing without affecting output significantly. Technological advances in the advanced economies decreased the cost of production in manufacturing, thereby reducing the price of manufactured goods relative to non-manufactured goods. As the demand for manufactured goods is relatively inelastic, this demand did not increase much despite the decline in prices. Without a rise in demand, firms maintained the same level of output but with lower number of workers. Therefore, technology-led deindustrialization in advanced economies reduced employment in manufacturing but did not reduce output.

Latin American and African countries, which opened their trade in manufacturing and became completely integrated with the advanced economies, 'imported' the deindustrialization from the advanced countries. Most Latin American countries undertook significant trade liberalizations in the second half of the 1980s and early 1990s, transforming themselves into open economies. Many countries in sub-Saharan Africa experienced trade opening as well around the same time. But as the manufacturing output of these countries was relatively small as compared to that of the advanced economies, these open economies were also price-takers in the global market. This is unlike China and the rest of the Asian economies that were able to influence the price by significantly contributing to the global supply of manufactured goods. Given the integration with advanced economies even while they remained price-takers, Latin America and Africa required productivity growth in their manufacturing that was faster than in the advanced economies to offset the impact of technology depressing the relative price of manufacturing globally. Not only did such improvement in productivity not happen, increases in productivity in primary sectors reduced manufacturing attractiveness, thereby leading to decline in output and employment in manufacturing.

In contrast to the Latin American and African countries, Asian economies utilized their considerable comparative advantage to participate in the GVCs, and thereby enhanced their presence in manufacturing. Multinational corporations relocated production facilities to these developing countries due to the availability of cheap labour and their business-friendly regulatory regimes. These GVCs combined high-tech production techniques and know-how from the advanced economies, which resulted from technological shifts, with low-wage labour in Asian countries. This high-tech/low-wage combination is more competitive than high-tech/high-wage production in the advanced economies, as well as low-tech/low-wage production in Latin American and African countries.

Policy Failures Have Inhibited Manufacturing Growth

Despite its cheap labour, India has not been able to build a strong manufacturing sector primarily because of policy failures. Despite liberalizing product markets in 1991, India did not reform its 'factor markets', which refer to the markets for factors of production such as land, labour, power, transport, etc. As a result, domestic manufacturing firms have faced significantly higher costs of production compared to their global peers.

First, India's labour regime comprising 47 central laws and 200 state laws made the labour market rigid, inflexible and archaic, thereby impeding the growth of the manufacturing sector. Relatedly, multi-tier regulatory framework and complex procedures, prevailing at the central, state and local levels, increased the burden on investors and deterred them from venturing into capital-intensive projects. The procedures and costs for starting and especially closing of a manufacturing business remained cumbersome. Multiple land-acquisition policies as well as discretionary and ad hoc application of rules on how land can be acquired added to the complexity of doing business in the manufacturing sector. Securing environmental clearances for new projects also remained a key roadblock for investors in the past due to long delays and social hurdles.

Second, inadequate development of physical infrastructure—including the poor quality of power supply, road and railways network, as well as ports and airports—became critical stumbling blocks for the growth of the manufacturing sector. Specifically, as Ajay Chhibber highlights, India's rail freight charges are thrice of that in China and are among the highest in the world, while petrol and diesel prices, which contribute to the costs of transportation, are 50 per cent and 20 per cent higher than those in China. Further, our electricity prices are 30 to 40 per cent higher than those in China and other competitors.[117] Poor logistics caused delays and raised inventory costs, while high prices for power and credit inflated operating expenses. Credit constraints and higher costs of capital due to weaknesses in the financial sector have held back small- and medium-sized firms from expanding.

Recent Reforms Addressing Policy Failures

In 2020, three labour law bills passed in Parliament compressed 29 labour laws into four codes pertaining to (i) wages; (ii) industrial relations; (iii) social security; and (iv) occupational safety, health and working conditions. As a result, the number of sections in the labour laws has declined by 60 per cent from 1,232 to 480, with only one registration needed instead of six and only one license instead of four. Moreover, several (though not all) offences have been de-criminalized. Several firm-size thresholds have been raised to ease the compliance burden: from 10 to 20 to be called a factory, from 20 to 50 for contract worker laws to apply and from 100 to 300 for standing orders including those pertaining to layoffs.[118] As the subordinate legislation, i.e., rules for these laws need to be coordinated across all the major states, they have been delayed. Currently, 31 states have published draft rules under the Code

---

[117]Chhibber, Ajay, 'Manufacture or Service: Must We Choose?', *Business Standard*, 8 February 2024, http://tinyurl.com/29ps6h7h. Accessed on 15 February 2024.

[118]Arora, Aakanksha, Mahima and Aasheerwad Dwivedi, 'View: New Labour Laws Will Improve India's Ease of Doing Business Ranking', *The Economic Times*, 20 January 2021, http://tinyurl.com/5duphmr4. Accessed on 19 January 2024.

on Wages, while 26 states have come out with draft rules on the code on occupational safety. On the code on industrial relations and code on social security, preliminary processes have been completed by 28 states.[119] Once the rules are framed, these laws will come into force and thereby mark a crucial change in the labour market in India.

Along with this law change, there have been significant improvements in physical infrastructure (Figure 4) and efficiency of logistics (Figure 5), which have helped the rate of growth of merchandise exports and manufacturing exports exceed the growth rate of China for the first time (Figure 6). Furthermore, real-time vehicle tracking has reduced fleet turnaround time by 50 to 70 per cent, and digitizing supply chains has cut inventory by up to 20 per cent.

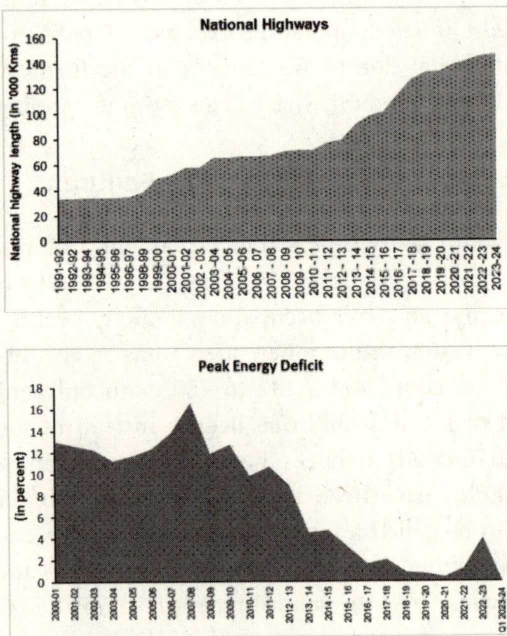

Figure 4: Strengthening of physical infrastructure

Source: Ministry of Road Transport and Highways, GoI; Ministry of Power, GoI

[119]Haq, Zia, 'Implementation of 4 Labour Codes Stalled', *Hindustan Time*, 8 May 2023, http://tinyurl.com/4ee75teu. Accessed on 19 January 2024.

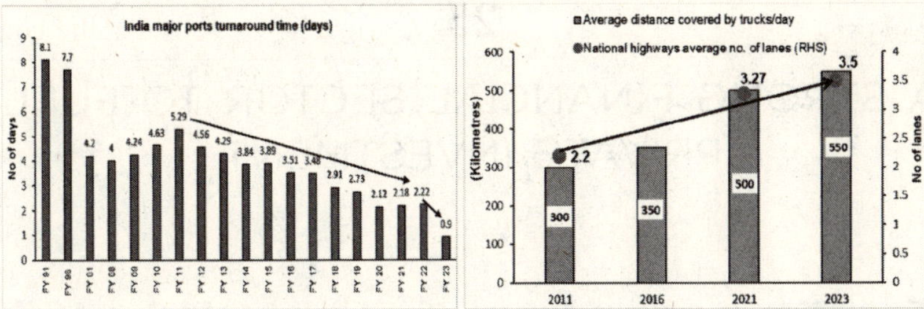

Figure 5: Significant improvement in efficiency of logistics

Source: Ministry of Ports, Shipping & Waterways, GoI; Ministry of Road Transport and Highways, GoI; NITI Aayog, GoI

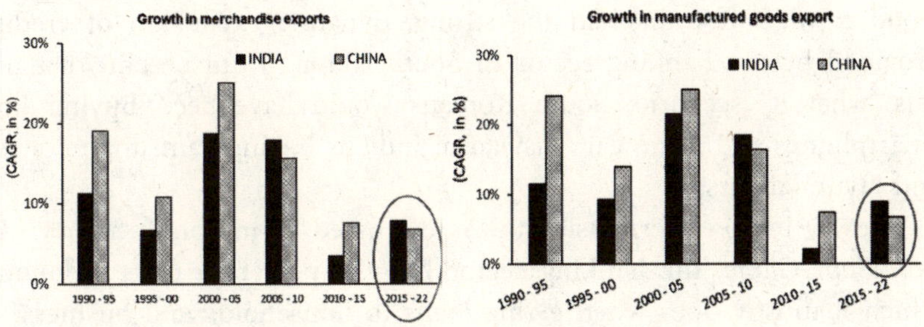

Figure 6: India's manufacturing exports showing encouraging signs over 2015–22

Source: The World Bank

◆

Given these improvements, India is poised to improve the productivity of its manufacturing. This is critical as Asian countries that avoided deindustrialization achieved it by combining their comparative advantage of cheap labour with favourable policies that enabled them to utilize this advantage.

25

A STRONG FINANCIAL SECTOR TO FUEL PRIVATE INVESTMENT

What is common between a Samsung smartphone, an LG air conditioner and a Hyundai car? Many of you will respond that they are South Korean companies. As a financial economist and a patriotic Indian at heart, the common thing for me is that these South Korean products remind me of the power of the banking sector to power manufacturing and exports. These commonalities make me wonder: what if India had the strong, dynamic expansion of credit provided by the banking sector in South Korea? I am certain that in this 'what if' scenario, South Koreans would have been buying Jio smartphones and Nano cars instead of Indians buying Samsung phones and Hyundai cars.

Power bestows responsibility. As discussed in my book *Money: A Zero-Sum Game*, the banking sector has the power to create money, which it mostly does when giving loans to households and businesses (Vaidyanathan and Subramanian 2022). The South Korean experience is one in which money was directed to investment in manufacturing and exports. Their comparative growth compared to us is a lesson in history that India must learn, at least now! Public-sector banks and the Indian banking sector in general need to do an honest assessment of their performance if they wish to earnestly contribute—commensurate with their special powers—to the developmental needs of the nation. As demonstrated in the economic surveys of 2019–20 and 2020–21, credit cycles in the banking sector—led by the PSBs—have broadly manifested as follows. First, banks over-lend to nefarious promoters while ignoring the genuinely creditworthy. Second, when such bad lending leads to huge loan losses, inadequate corporate governance in the banks ensures that these problems are rarely diagnosed, acknowledged and remedied in time. Instead, banks evergreen the bad loans so that they do not have to recognize on their books the losses that have already manifested in reality. Boards of banks and the senior management remain complicit in this, with the banking sector regulator often unable to detect such cases of evergreening before it is too late. Third, as a result of the evergreening, banks continue lending to 'zombies', i.e., firms that are dead in reality but kept on life-support by the banks to avoid declaring these firms as dead. Fourth, this combination of evergreening and zombie lending severely depletes bank capital by the time these issues are identified by the regulator. This is akin to a patient who requires a bypass operation, but the doctor fails to diagnose the condition in time. The loss of precious time then lands the patient in the emergency ward, requiring a quadruple bypass instead of a single bypass. Fifth, in their efforts to hold the guilty party that started this phenomenon with their corruption-laced lending to nefarious promoters, the regulators, courts and anti-corruption agencies round up a few bank officials and initiate criminal proceedings against them. In their over-zealous efforts to clean up the Augean stables after the horses have bolted, these agencies sometimes round up the innocent as well, even justifying the same sometimes as 'collateral damage'. Sixth, bankers respond to these punitive actions by becoming excessively risk-averse, thereby shrinking lending even to the genuinely creditworthy. As Spanish philosopher George Santayana declared, 'Those who do not learn from history are doomed to repeat it.' And India can ill afford to repeat such credit cycles resulting from past inefficiencies in the banking sector.

To avoid repeating previous mistakes, I highlight the critical importance of good 'lending infrastructure'. This is a catch-all phrase that captures the data, technological, personnel and organizational investments that globally advanced banks make to ensure that they screen borrowers with minimal error at the time of lending and then diligently monitor these borrowers to ensure that loan defaults—both wilful and distressed—are minimized. I show that this good lending infrastructure forms the critical element that can ensure equitable, yet sustained, high growth.

To demonstrate the tremendous impact of bank credit on economic growth, I provide evidence comparing India with other peer economies. While countries such as Malaysia, South Korea, Australia and Canada witnessed high economic growth led by a greater degree of credit penetration, India lagged on account of limited permeation of credit. I undertake a comparative analysis of the contrasting growth trajectories of these peer nations based on similar levels of private credit to GDP and GDP per capita in 1960.

Credit penetration in the economy is measured by the ratio of private credit outlays as a proportion of GDP. In 1960, the private-credit-to-GDP ratio ranged approximately between 5 per cent and 20 per cent for all these peer economies. While this ratio increased drastically for Malaysia, South Korea, Australia and Canada over the next 60 years, it recorded mediocre growth in India. India today remains at the bottom of these peer economies as far as credit penetration is concerned. As a result, despite having similar levels of per capita income in 1960, India lagged behind these economies in economic development as a strong, dynamic banking sector powered high economic growth in these countries while India was left behind.

Sluggishness of the Indian Banking Sector

I benchmark the performance of the Indian banking sector with that of other economies to assess the impact of the banking sector in an economy. Therefore, in this section, I employ a variety of cross-country comparisons to answer the counterfactual question—what could have been possible? I undertake two complementary sets of comparisons: one set comparing India with the rest of the world and the other set comparing India with OECD economies. This comparison has multiple advantages. First, averaging over all the countries in the world or all the OECD countries ensures that the comparison is across a broad number of countries. Second, and more crucially, an India that aspires to be a global economic power needs to look up for inspiration; comparison with the OECD economies is therefore the correct benchmark for India to look up for inspiration. Recognizing that the comparison between India and the world or India and the OECD economies indeed suffers from several differences, I undertake another set of country-by-country comparisons, in which I select countries whose banking sectors were almost at an identical level of penetration as India in 1960. Such a comparison over time provides the best possible apples-to-apples comparison.

I start by comparing India and South Korea. As seen from Figure 1, the level of private credit to GDP in South Korea and India were almost identical in 1960. Yet, today the level of private credit to GDP in South

Korea is more than three times that of India. The dotted lines in the figure show the respective trends.

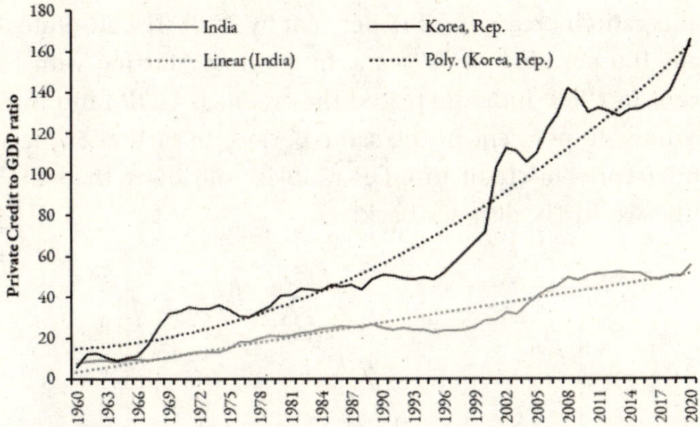

Figure 1: Private credit to GDP: India vis-à-vis South Korea

Source: The World Bank and IMF

Similarly, I compare India with another Asian country, Malaysia. As Figure 2 shows, India and Malaysia had almost the same level of penetration of private credit as a proportion of GDP in 1960. Malaysia now is way ahead at two-and-a-half times India's level. The dotted lines in the figure show the respective linear trends.

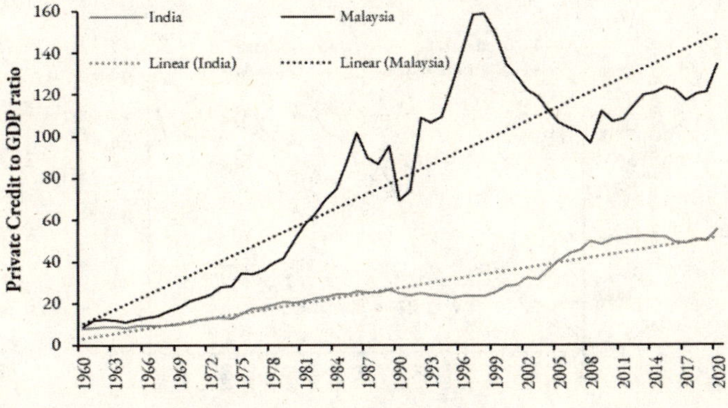

Figure 2: Private credit to GDP: India vis-à-vis Malaysia

Source: The World Bank and IMF

Next, I compare India and the world as shown in Figure 3. While the credit-to-GDP ratio for the world was 56 per cent—in 1962, the year from which reliable data for the world is available from the World Bank—this ratio increased to 147 per cent by 2020. The absolute increase was about 100 per cent in 60 years. In contrast, starting with less than 10 per cent in 1960, India increased the credit-to-GDP ratio in absolute levels by only 40 per cent in the same period. In fact, at 55 per cent in 2020, India's private-credit-to-GDP ratio is still lower than the 56 per cent of the world six decades back!

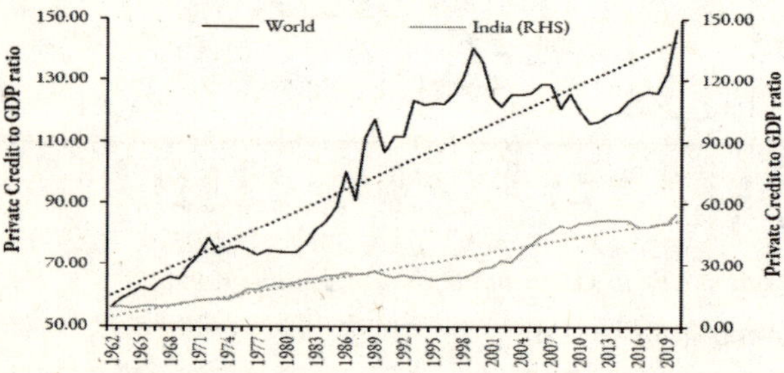

Figure 3: Private credit to GDP: India vis-à-vis the rest of the world
Source: The World Bank and IMF

A similar story is revealed in Figure 4, which compares India with the average for the OECD economies. The dotted lines in the figure show the respective linear trends.

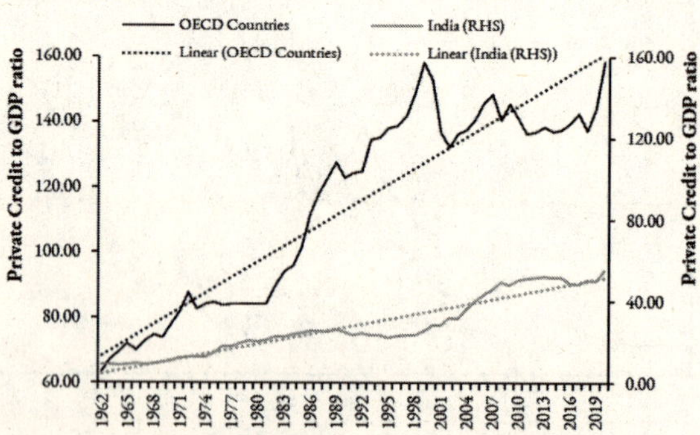

Figure 4: Private credit to GDP: India vis-à-vis the OECD economies
Source: The World Bank and IMF

The inseparable theorem of banking states that the primary business of banks is to supply credit. Unfortunately, India's banking sector has been sluggish in performing this primary duty whether in comparison to OECD countries or the rest of the world.

Palpable Inequity in Credit Allocation

The Indian banking sector has provided loans to rich promoters despite their questionable credit history, while simultaneously failing to increase the provision of credit to many segments of the population that remain starved of credit. For instance, according to CIBIL data, as of April 2022, of the 814 million citizens that are eligible for credit, more than 70 per cent are either unserved or under-served by credit markets in India.[120]

Figure 5 demonstrates the huge gaping inequalities in the distribution of credit in India. First, the figure shows the vast gap between urban and rural credit per capita. In 1991, urban credit per capita was ₹4,246 while rural credit per capita was 10-and-a-half times lower, at a mere ₹403; this was the performance more than two decades after banks were nationalized in 1969. Three decades after liberalization, in 2020, urban credit per capita was ₹1,98,362, while rural credit per capita was 18-and-a-half times lower at ₹10,670. From being about 10 times lower in 1991, now rural credit per capita is about 20 times lower than urban credit per capita.

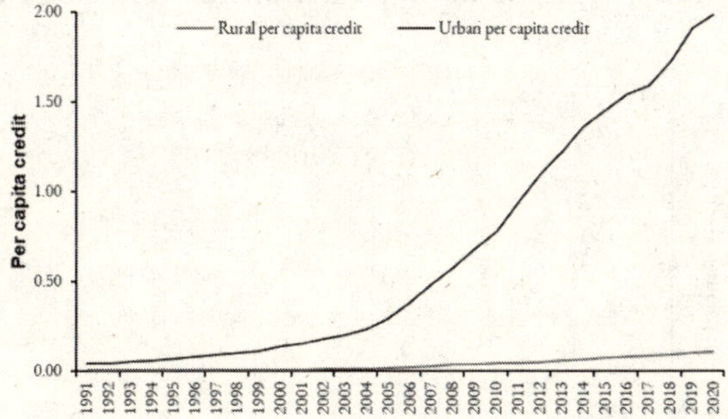

Figure 5: Per capita credit: Rural vis-à-vis urban

Source: RBI

[120] 'More than 160 Million Indians Are Credit Underserved', *TransUnion CIBIL*, 25 April 2022, http://tinyurl.com/4rpxchck. Accessed on 13 January 2024.

This enormous difference cannot be attributed to fewer bank branches in rural areas than in urban areas, as shown in Figure 6. In fact, the number of rural branches per lakh population in 1991 was 5.3, while that of urban branches per lakh population was 3.5. Yet, credit per capita was 10 times lower in rural areas than in urban areas. After a consistent decline since 1991, they became equal in 2006. Since then, branches per lakh population have grown similarly in both urban and rural areas. In fact, in 2020, rural branches were slightly higher than urban branches.

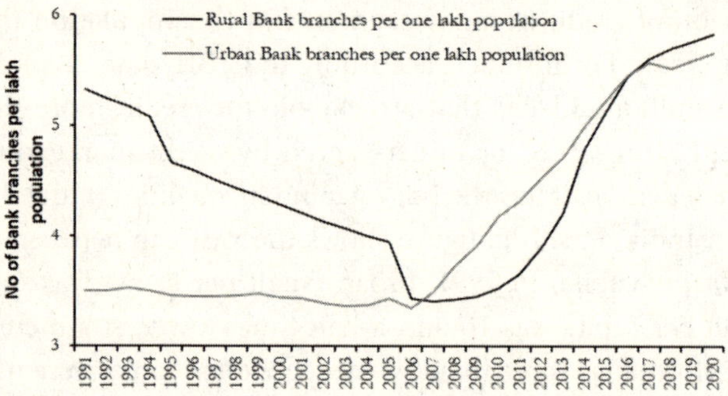

Figure 6: Bank branches per lakh population: Rural vis-à-vis urban

Source: RBI

As Figure 7 shows, even the number of branches for PSBs closely follows this trend.

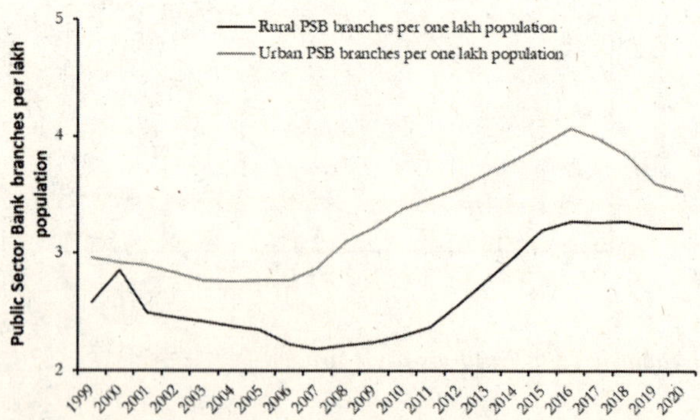

Figure 7: PSB branches per lakh population: Rural vis-à-vis urban

Source: RBI

If the number of branches in urban and rural areas does not explain this difference, do the differences in per capita income explain such vast differences in credit per capita? In 2020, per capita income was ₹98,435 in urban areas and ₹40,925 in rural areas. While per capita income in rural areas was about half of that in urban areas, credit per capita in rural areas was about 20 times lower than that in urban areas. While banks can possibly claim that the demand for credit is affected by income, these enormous differences may not simply be due to the differences in per capita income. A large literature in financial economics—that I discuss later in this chapter—shows that credit causes economic growth and reduces poverty. Therefore, even while the banking sector claims that the demand for credit is affected by income, the lower per capita income in rural areas may be, at least partly, due to the significantly lower credit provision to the rural areas by the PSBs over the years.

The disparity in credit allocation across different regions of the country becomes palpable when we contrast the per capita credit provided to the northeastern region of the country with the rest of the country. As shown in Figure 8, in 2006, from when these data are available, we see that the credit per capita for the Northeast was ₹3,227, while the rest of the country received a 25 times greater credit per capita at ₹81,210. This gap has only widened further in the last 15 years. In 2020, the credit per capita rose to ₹21,956 in the Northeast, while in the rest of the country it increased to ₹4,82,889.

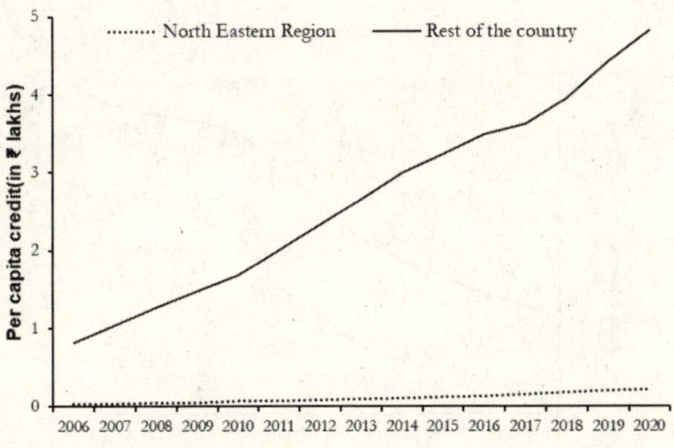

Figure 8: Per capita credit: Northeast vis-à-vis the rest of India (in ₹lakhs)

Source: RBI

The disparity in credit allocation remains as sharp even when we compare the entire eastern region with the rest of the country as shown in Figure 9.

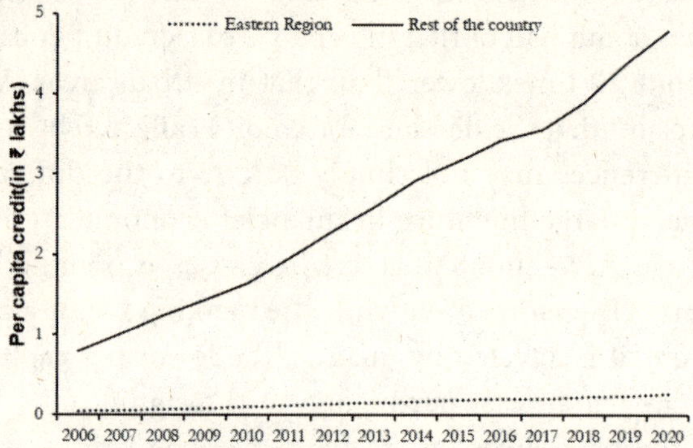

Figure 9: Credit allocation: East vis-à-vis rest of India (in ₹lakhs)
Source: RBI

Notwithstanding these regional disparities, the absence of bank branches cannot explain the banking sector's inability to use the power it is bestowed with in providing credit, thereby making distributional choices more equitably. As seen in Figure 10 and Figure 11, the number of bank branches per one lakh population is of a similar order of magnitude in the northeastern and eastern regions when compared with the rest of the country.

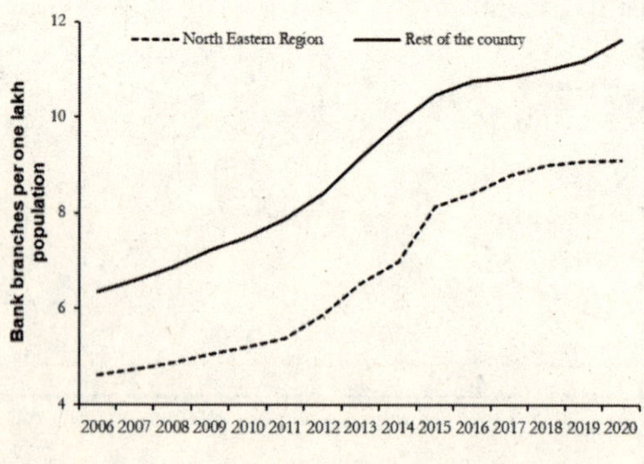

Figure 10: Bank branches per one lakh population: Northeast vis-à-vis the rest of India
Source: RBI

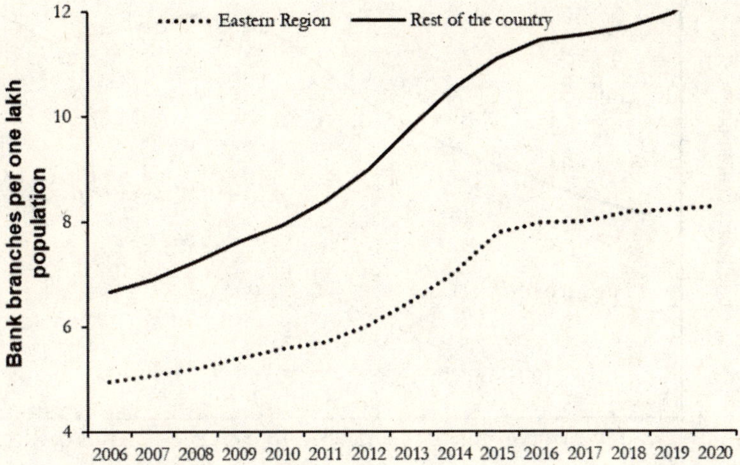

Figure 11: Bank branches per one lakh population: East vis-à-vis the rest of India

Source: RBI

Even branches of PSBs per one lakh population are of a similar order of magnitude in the northeastern (Figure 12) and eastern regions (Figure 13) when compared with the rest of the country.

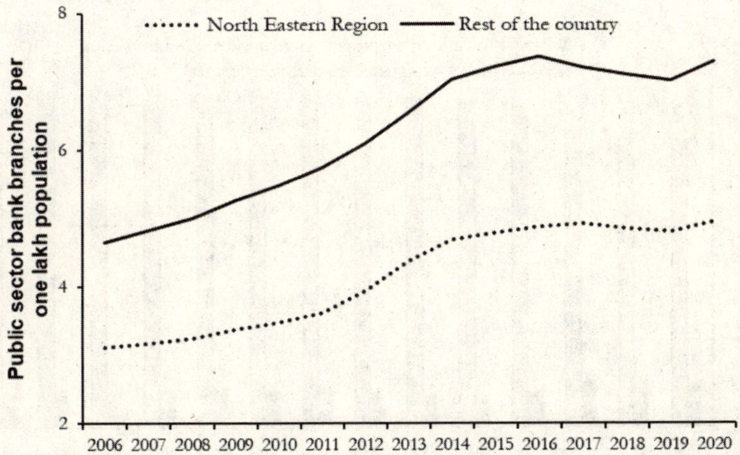

Figure 12: PSB branches per one lakh population: Northeast vis-à-vis rest of India

Source: RBI

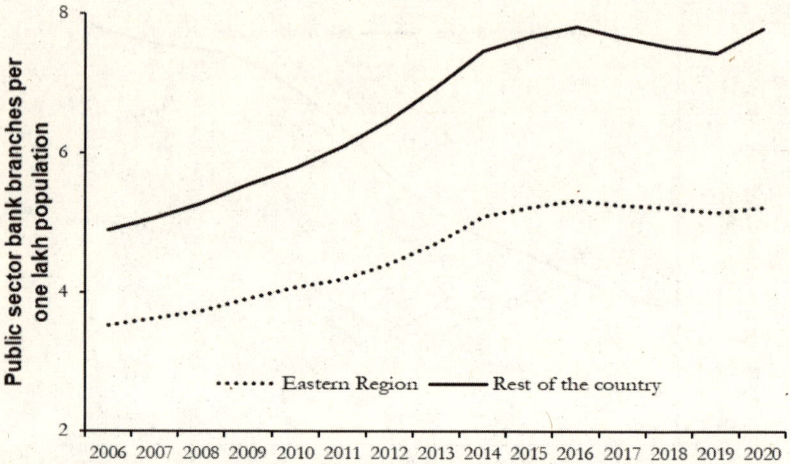

Figure 13: Bank branches per one lakh population: East vis-à-vis rest of India

Source: RBI

Even when we examine the proportion of industry credit that goes to smaller firms in the economy, this proportion is not only minuscule at 13–15 per cent, but the proportion has also fallen from 16 per cent in 2008–09 to 13 per cent in 2020 as shown in Figure 14.

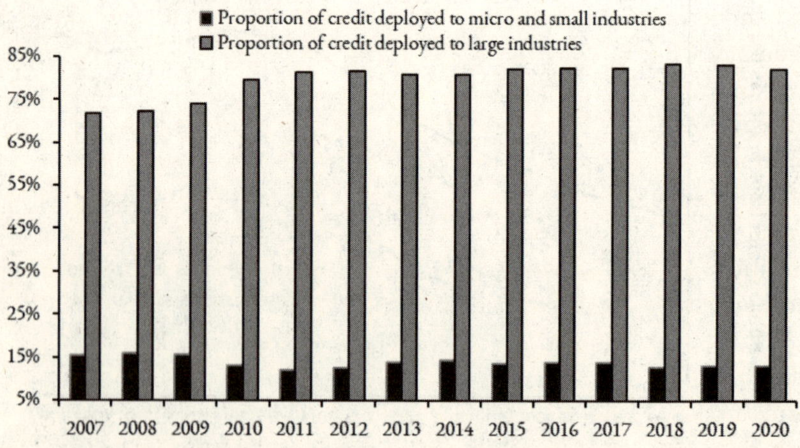

Figure 14: Proportion of credit to micro and small industries vis-à-vis large industries

Source: RBI

Power to Catalyse and Create a Virtuous Cycle

I use a toy economic model to show how credit supply by the banking sector can bring about economic growth. Since a shift in demand and supply of credit happens when interest rates remain unchanged, I abstract out interest rates in the example. In order to avoid any influence from existing institutions, I have used the example of a hypothetical economy. This will ensure that my exposition is without any preconceived biases.

Consider a hypothetical 'banana' republic, where 100 bananas are produced in a year (Q = 100) and the unit of account in this republic is the Indian rupee (₹). The money supplied (M) in the republic is ₹100 and the price (P) of each banana is ₹1. We assume that a bank in the banana republic *chooses* to give a new loan of ₹50 to a promising entrepreneur who has the technology to double the production of bananas. As loans increase deposits and deposits form part of the broad money supply in the economy, the money supply increases to ₹150 from the initial level of ₹100.[121] The loan given by the bank provides the necessary capital required to increase the production of bananas from 100 to 200. This causes the price of bananas to fall to ₹0.75, i.e., a deflation of 25 per cent even after the money supply (monetary inflation) in the economy has increased by 50 per cent. This is because while output has doubled, money supply has increased by a factor of only 1.5.

In contrast, suppose the bank provides this loan to a dubious promoter who does not have such a technology but is able to pull wool over the bank's eyes to demonstrate that he indeed has such a technology. In other words, the bank is unable to screen the borrower properly and separate the genuine borrower from the spurious one. In this case, output of bananas remains at 100 but money supply increases to ₹150 from the initial level of ₹100. This causes the price of bananas to rise to ₹1.5, i.e., an inflation of 50 per cent. This is because while output has remained unchanged, money supply has increased by a factor of only 1.5.

It is worth noting that the investment of ₹50 by the entrepreneur is due to the loan given by the bank. Banks lend—or do not lend—to the firms and sectors of their choice. If banks appropriately lend to productive firms and sectors in the economy, economic output increases. If they

---

[121]See *Money: A Zero-Sum Game* for the conceptual details.

tactlessly lend to unproductive firms and sectors, i.e., economic zombies, only monetary inflation increases without any significant increase in real output. Recall that economic output (GDP) is measured in real terms, i.e., sans price inflation.

Bank credit is an essential ingredient in promoting economic growth because the banking sector chooses the firms and sectors to lend. The choice is not just about whether the sector is productive or unproductive. The banking sector does backseat driving and influences, to a large extent, what gets produced in the economy. If it provides more credit capital to one sector vis-à-vis others, the output of that sector will increase relative to the rest.

An efficient flow of bank credit to all players constitutes an important component of the overall financial development of a nation, which plays a vital role in long-term economic growth. The banking sector assists and promotes entrepreneurial activities that contribute to higher productivity, for instance by providing credit capital to promising business ventures.

Bank Credit and Economic Activity

Bank credit can also help increase demand—household consumption of goods and services—in the economy. It increases the monetary income of households, which in turn boosts the demand for goods and services produced by businesses. Firms would look to increase their supply to fulfil this increased demand. Thus, as aggregate demand increases, businesses seek credit from the banking sector to expand their business. Thus, both credit supply and the demand for bank credit increase. Jobs increase because people need to be employed to increase production, and people's income increases, increasing their demand for goods and services.

If the economy is doing well, businesses would want to invest and expand. Investment in real activity such as capital expenditure by businesses has a stimulative effect on the economy, which again increases the demand for loans. This explains the causality from economic activity to demand for credit.

Taking a cue from the improving economic prospects, the banking sector would supply a greater amount of credit to the economy. Businesses will consequently increase their spending on investments. This creates a chain reaction that provides companies with easier and cheaper access to operating capital from the banking sector. Greater credit supply from banks helps businesses to continue production, increase employment opportunities and boost consumer spending. Thus, better economic prospects and increased output can lead to an increase in both demand and supply of bank credit, thereby creating a virtuous cycle. The banking sector has the power to catalyse and create this virtuous cycle.

The *Economic Survey 2019–20* shows detailed evidence that a slowdown of this virtuous cycle, starting from the slowdown in credit stemming from the overhang created by the crony lending until 2013–14, led to the slowdown in the economy in 2019–20.[122] Gupta and Tyagi (2022) also find evidence for a similar phenomenon leading to the slowdown in 2019–20. In fact, we can observe this in Figure 15. Credit growth from 2015 to 2021 has been a mere 9.02 per cent. In contrast, the average credit growth from 2005 to 2014 was an unprecedented 21.92 per cent. The dotted line in the figure shows the linear downward trend.

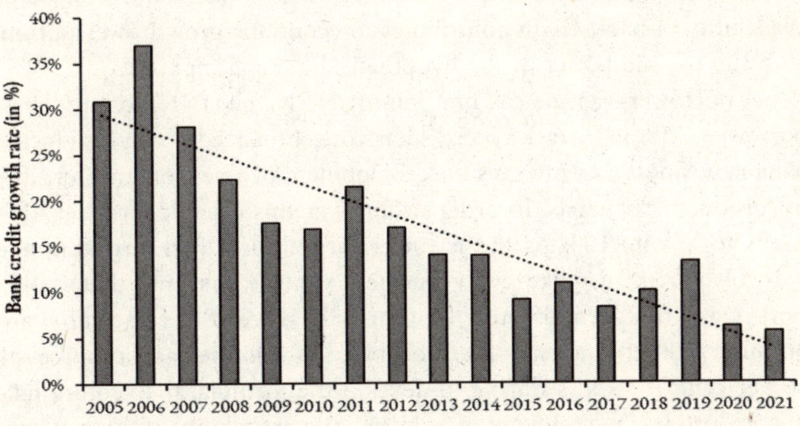

Figure 15: Bank credit growth rates in India in recent years
Source: RBI

Crony lending in India until 2013 increased money supply but scarcely increased output as the lending was made primarily to dubious projects. In fact, the unprecedented inflation in India until 2014 traces back to the sins of the banking sector in expanding money supply through dubious

[122]Ministry of Finance, GoI, *Economic Survey 2019–20: Volume 2*, January 2020, pp. 20–7, http://tinyurl.com/5yx738a3. Accessed on 27 December 2023.

lending without a concomitant increase in the output in the economy. The slowdown of lending leading to the economic slowdown starting from 2017 and the high inflation before 2014 clearly demonstrate the importance of the virtuous cycle of credit in influencing output and inflation in India.

Effect of the Banking Sector on GDP

Globally, a strong positive relationship exists between domestic credit outlays by banks as a percentage of GDP and economic growth. Since the 1990s, a large amount of literature has emerged in financial economics clearly demonstrating that credit causes economic growth. This literature comprises both theoretical studies that conceptually demonstrate the mechanisms through which credit fosters economic growth as well as empirical studies that explore a plethora of different settings to provide evidence of this phenomenon. To conceptually understand how better availability of bank credit contributes to economic growth, we continue with the toy model set in the hypothetical banana republic.

A borrower—let me call him Johnny No Name (JNN) to represent a borrower without a track record—has conceptualized a very productive banana business that involves the development of a new organic fertilizer for producing bananas. In order to uncover this organic fertilizer, JNN needs to invest ₹100. As the fertilizer formula is a path-breaking one, it involves risk just like every business venture. Assume that if JNN can create the formula, the venture will succeed spectacularly and produce ₹300 after a year. The probability of this spectacular success is 80 per cent. If JNN is unable to develop the formula, the venture fails, thereby producing cashflows of only ₹50; the probability of this outcome is 20 per cent.

Note that even allowing for the possibility that money a year later is less valuable than money today, the venture is outstanding as the expected cash flow is ₹250 (80%×₹300 + 20%×₹50), while the investment required is only ₹100.

The problem that JNN faces is that he does not have ₹100 to invest in this productive venture. He approaches a bank for a loan. The bank faces several uncertainties in lending to JNN. First, the bank cannot be sure that the venture will succeed with a probability of 80 per cent. The bank might perceive JNN as overly optimistic about his chances of success, which is a common trait among many entrepreneurs. Even worse, it is possible that JNN is aware that the chances of success are only 50 per cent but is exaggerating it to 80 per cent. Second, JNN may be lying about the cash flows from the venture if it fails. Instead of getting ₹50, as JNN claims, the true cash flow may be ₹0. Third, JNN may be a fraudster who falsely claims to be researching this path-breaking formula. In reality, JNN may have window-dressed such 'paraphernalia' to hoodwink the bank about researching such a formula but plans to run away with the ₹100 that he claims to need for investment. Fourth, even if the venture is indeed as path-breaking as promised by JNN, he may be able to 'hide' the cash flows from the bank after the venture succeeds, which is identical to JNN running away with the bank loan of ₹100. Fifth, the actual venture may be one-tenth in size, i.e., requiring an investment of ₹10 and generating cash flows of ₹30 if it succeeds and ₹5 if it fails. But JNN may gold-plate it and claim that the venture is 10 times in size. Economists call these real-world uncertainties that banks face as problems stemming from 'asymmetric information'.

To capture these problems involved in bank lending, let us call the genuine but unknown borrower 'JNN-Honest' and the fraudulent and unknown borrower 'JNN-Liar'. JNN-Honest truly seeks a bank loan to invest in the venture as described: ₹100 of investment yielding ₹300 with a probability of 80 per cent and ₹50 with a probability of 20 per cent.

Table 1

JNN-Honest	*Venture succeeds*	*Venture fails*
Cash flow	₹300	₹50
Probability	80%	20%

If the banking sector charges an interest rate of 15 per cent on average on their loans, then the return for the banking sector is 15 per cent when the venture succeeds. When the venture fails, the bank recovers only ₹50 of the loan principal of ₹100, i.e., the recovery rate (RR)[123] on

[123]Recovery rate (RR) is the extent to which principal on defaulted debt can be recovered, expressed as a percentage of face value.

the loan is 50 per cent. In other words, the loss given default (LGD)[124] on the loan is 50 per cent. Consequently, the return for the bank on the loan when the venture fails is −50 per cent, which happens with a probability of 20 per cent, i.e., the probability of default (PD) on the loan is 20 per cent. The PD is egregiously high[125] in our setup since we choose this characterization for ease of exposition and to develop insights into the effect of the banking sector's lending infrastructure. The breakeven rate for the bank on the loan is 12.50 per cent, i.e., with zero expected ROA (ROA=0). We note that the banking sector charges a loan interest rate of 15 per cent, i.e., higher than the breakeven rate. Consequently, the expected ROA for the banking sector from such loans is 2 per cent (80%×15% + 20%×−50%).

Table 2

ROA for the banking sector	*Venture succeeds*	*Venture fails*
Return on the loan	15%	−50% (LGD)
Probability	80%	20% (PD)

In contrast to JNN-Honest, JNN-Liar's investment of ₹100 yields ₹150 with a probability of 50 per cent and ₹0 with a probability of 50 per cent. Note that the venture is a bad one as the expected cashflow is ₹75 (50%×₹150 + 50%×₹0) while the investment required is ₹100.

Table 3

JNN-Liar	*Venture succeeds*	*Venture fails*
Cash flow	₹150	₹0
Probability	50%	50%

[124]Loss given default (LGD) is the loss incurred by a bank when the borrower defaults (does not pay back) on the loan, expressed as a percentage of face value. LGD=(1−RR).

[125]For the sake of rigorousness, we highlight that all the probabilities in this chapter are in a risk-neutral world. Mathematically, the Radon–Nikodym theorem (a result in measure theory) uniquely maps risk-neutral probabilities (where there is no compensation for risk) to real-world probabilities in the risk-averse world (where there is compensation for risk).

In this simple example, banks only lend to those borrowers that they identify as being of JNN-Honest type. So, banks charge the same interest rate for all borrowers, i.e., the banking sector charges a loan interest rate of 15 per cent to JNN-Liar too. The expected ROA for the bank from the loan to JNN-Liar is –42.50 per cent (50%×15% + 50%×–100%).

Table 4

ROA for the banking sector	*Venture succeeds*	*Venture fails*
Return on the loan	15%	–100% (LGD)
Probability	50%	50% (PD)

Note here that no bank would be willing to give a loan to the JNN-Liar type as the bank loses all its loan amount with a 50 per cent probability of failure (PD = 50%). Even if the banking sector were to charge an exceedingly high interest rate on the loan (which would get paid only when the venture succeeds), it will not be able to break even and consequently generates a negative ROA of –42.50 per cent.

Investing in Lending Infrastructure

In advanced economies, banks have developed the necessary lending infrastructure to be able to overcome such problems from asymmetric information, i.e., to be able to distinguish JNN-Honest from JNN-Liar.

One should not get misled if bankers in India recoil at this characterization and claim that even globally advanced banks made bad loans during the GFC. They are attempting to obfuscate the issue by mixing statistical outliers with statistical averages. Globally advanced banks making bad loans during the GFC was an outlier that did not involve traditional lending; it involved exotic credit derivatives stemming from securitization of loans (Vaidyanathan 2014).[126] Bad lending during the GFC was an outlier also because it preceded five decades of high-quality lending that generated enormous economic growth in these countries.

Public-sector banks have not invested adequately in the development of lending infrastructure required to accurately differentiate between

---

[126]Refer to Vaidyanathan (2014) for a detailed account of the use of credit derivatives in the GFC.

JNN-Honest and JNN-Liar. In order to quantify the disparities in lending infrastructure effectiveness, let us assume that the banking sector with its inefficient lending infrastructure has a 30 per cent chance of making Type-I and Type-II errors. Type-I error refers to incorrectly identifying a JNN-Honest as JNN-Liar, while Type-II error refers to incorrectly identifying a JNN-Liar as JNN-Honest. Conversely, with an improved lending infrastructure, the probability of making Type-I and Type-II errors decreases to 10 per cent.

Table 5

Probability of getting a loan	*JNN-Honest*	*JNN-Liar*
Inefficient lending infrastructure	70%	30%
Efficient lending infrastructure	90%	10%

Assume that 90 per cent of borrowers are of the JNN-Honest type and 10 per cent are of the JNN-Liar type. The banking sector with an efficient lending infrastructure will correctly identify 90 per cent of JNN-Honest -type borrowers and thus lend to 81 per cent borrowers of this type (90% × 90%) and wrongly identify 10 per cent of JNN-Liar-type borrowers as JNN-Honest and lend to 1 per cent such borrowers (10% × 10%). In contrast, the banking sector with an inefficient lending infrastructure will correctly identify only 70 per cent of JNN-Honest-type borrowers and thus lend to 63 per cent borrowers of this type (90% × 70%), and wrongly identify 30 per cent of JNN-Liar-types as JNN-Honest and lend to 3 per cent of such borrowers (10% × 30%).

Table 6

Proportion of ventures getting bank loans	*JNN-Honest*	*JNN-Liar*
Inefficient lending infrastructure	90% × 70% = 63%	10% × 30% = 3%
Efficient lending infrastructure	90% × 90% = 81%	10% × 10% = 1%

Since the banking sector charges an average loan interest rate of 15 per cent across all categories of borrowers, the expected ROA from loans to JNN-Honest is 2 per cent while the expected ROA from loans to JNN-Liar is −42.50 per cent.

A banking sector with inefficient lending infrastructure will have an ROA of –42.50 per cent on the loans given to the 3 per cent JNN-Liar borrowers that they incorrectly identified as JNN-Honest. Also, it has an ROA of 2 per cent on the loans given to the 63 per cent JNN-Honest borrowers. So, with a 15 per cent interest on average on their loans across 66 per cent borrowers (63% JNN-Honest borrowers and 3% JNN-Liar borrowers) of all categories, the expected ROA on their loan assets for the banking sector with inefficient lending infrastructure is –0.015%.

In contrast, a banking sector with efficient lending infrastructure will have an ROA of –42.50 per cent from the 1 per cent JNN-Liar borrowers that they incorrectly identified as JNN-Honest. Also, the sector will have an ROA of 2 per cent on the loans given to the 81 per cent JNN-Honest borrowers. So, with a 15 per cent interest on average on their loans across 82 per cent borrowers (81% JNN-Honest borrowers and 1% JNN-Liar borrowers) of all categories, the expected return on their loan assets with inefficient lending infrastructure is 1.20 per cent [(81%×2%)+(1%×–42.50%)]. Thus, a banking sector with an efficient lending infrastructure has a positive expected ROA (1.20%), while a banking sector with an inefficient lending infrastructure has a negative expected ROA (–0.015%) even when the loan interest rate is the same across loans.

A banking sector with an inefficient lending infrastructure turns down 27 per cent of creditworthy borrowers (90% × 30%). The remaining 63 per cent of JNN-Honest borrowers (out of 90% of JNN-Honest borrowers) generate a cash flow of ₹250 in expectation, while 3 per cent of JNN-Liar borrowers generate a cash flow of ₹75 in expectation, yielding a total output of ₹159.75 [(63%×₹250)+(3%×₹75)].

In contrast, a banking sector with an efficient lending infrastructure turns down only 9 per cent of creditworthy borrowers (90% × 10%). So, 81 per cent of JNN-Honest borrowers generate a cash flow of ₹250 in expectation, while 1 per cent of JNN-Liar borrowers generate a cash flow of ₹75 in expectation, yielding a total output of ₹203.25 [(81%× ₹250)+(1%×₹75)]. Thus, we can see that because of the better lending infrastructure possessed by the banking sector, the economic output is much higher (27 per cent) than if the lending infrastructure is inefficient. When such differences in output get cumulated year on year through the power of compounding, the inefficient lending infrastructure possessed by the banking sector has a material impact on GDP growth and GDP per capita.

Adverse Selection and Its Impact on GDP

The above differences will be starker because of the problem of 'adverse selection' that infests credit markets. This problem manifests because the JNN-Honest- and JNN-Liar-type borrowers 'pool' together and the banking sector cannot separate them out perfectly; after all, even an efficient banking sector makes Type-I and Type-II errors with a 10 per cent probability. Every borrower of the JNN-Liar type will accept the interest rate of 15 per cent charged by the banking sector. However, the JNN-Honest type will find the interest rate to be a bit too high and may decide to not take the loan. Specifically, the JNN-Honest-type expects that the interest rate charged should be 12.50 per cent—the breakeven rate, which is the fair rate according to them—instead of 15 per cent, given its cash flows. So, adverse-quality borrowers are more likely to 'select' into the loan than good-quality borrowers. This problem is, therefore, called adverse selection in credit markets. If more JNN-Honest-type borrowers decide to not take the loan, then the ROA for the banking sector worsens due to adverse selection. Consequently, the GDP of the economy would also be lower. The problem of adverse selection is disproportionately high in an economy with inefficient lending infrastructure, which, in turn, lowers its GDP. In comparison, the problem of adverse selection is much lower in an economy with efficient lending infrastructure and as a result its GDP is higher.

Moreover, when the banking system does not possess the lending infrastructure to be able to efficiently distinguish the JNN-Honest from JNN-Liar, many JNN-Honest-type borrowers get the incentive to behave like the JNN-Liar. They believe that if someone else can get away with not repaying his obligations to the bank, why should they not be able to do the same. Economists call this phenomenon 'moral hazard', which corrupts the population of good borrowers by increasing the proportion of JNN-Liars. Difficulties in the enforcement of credit contracts, a situation that prevailed in India before the enforcement of the IBC, exacerbate this phenomenon of moral hazard.

To understand this better, let us assume now that the borrowers consist of 80 per cent JNN-Honest type and 20 per cent JNN-Liar type, instead of the 90:10 proportion. With this detrimental change in the 'borrowing culture', the banking sector with an inefficient lending infrastructure lends to only 56 per cent JNN-Honest-type borrowers (80% × 70%) but to twice as many (6 per cent) JNN-Liar-type borrowers (20% × 30%) compared to the 3 per cent earlier. So, the interest that the banking sector must charge to break even becomes higher. At this significantly higher rate, the problem of adverse selection becomes even more severe because the JNN-Honest type will find it unfair to pay such an exorbitant rate of interest that is much higher than the breakeven rate. Then fewer JNN-Honest-type borrowers borrow from the bank. As a result, the output in this highly unfavourable equilibrium is much lower. Because of the inefficiency of the lending infrastructure of the banking sector, which exacerbates the problems of adverse selection and moral hazard, the economic output with an efficient lending infrastructure is much higher than that of a banking sector with an inefficient lending infrastructure.

As mentioned earlier, such differences in output due to the inefficiency of the banking sector accumulate over time and thereby lead to stark differences in GDP per capita. At the same time, a tremendous amount of credit rationing happens in the economy where only a small proportion of the JNN-Honest-type borrowers receive a bank loan under an inefficient lending infrastructure, while a much greater proportion of JNN-Honest-type borrowers receive a bank loan under an efficient lending infrastructure. Thus, inefficient lending infrastructure by the banking sector not only decreases GDP per capita but also exacerbates inequality. This is because the haves can access the right networks to get credit while the genuinely creditworthy get deprived of it.

Bank Lending and Growth: India vis-à-vis Peers

From approximately 8 per cent in 1960, the private-credit-to-GDP ratio for Malaysia rose to 134 per cent in 2020, an increase of approximately 1,500 per cent over the 60 years. This enormous increase in the flow of credit to the private sector facilitated a steep increase in the per capita GDP of Malaysia, which increased enormously by 4,900 per cent during this period. In complete contrast, the private-credit-to-GDP ratio in India recorded minimal growth, from 7 per cent in 1960 to 55 per cent in 2020. With an almost negligible percentage gap in private-credit-to-GDP ratios between these two countries in 1960, the gap widened to 79 per cent in 2020. In 2020, the per capita GDP of Malaysia is more than five times that of India as shown in Figure 16.

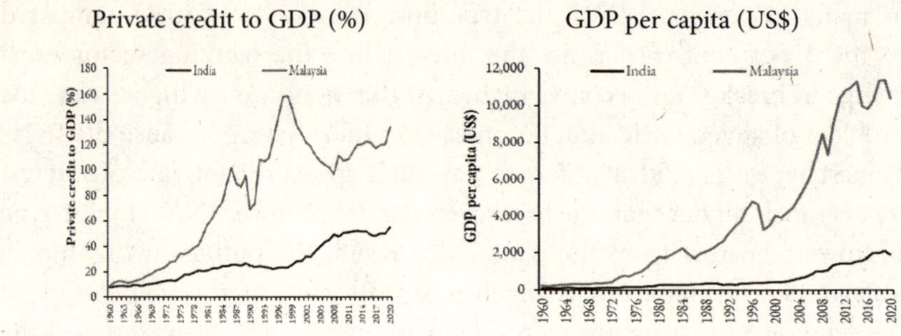

Figure 16: Credit penetration and economic growth: India vis-à-vis Malaysia

Source: The World Bank and IMF

The empirical evidence from Malaysia suggests the presence of a strong, direct causal relationship between bank lending and economic growth (Vaithilingam and Guru 2003). The periods of high private-credit-to-GDP ratios are associated with high levels of real GDP in Malaysia. The prospective reasons for the Malaysian economy's high degree of dependence on the banking sector as a source of finance are undeveloped capital markets much like in India.

Like Malaysia, South Korea also registered a drastic increase in the private-credit-to-GDP ratio—from approximately 5 per cent in 1960 to approximately 165 per cent in 2020—and, hence, greater economic growth than India over the past 60 years. As a result of this massive growth in credit penetration, the South Korean economy recorded much higher per capita GDP growth as compared to India. While South Korea (5.74 per cent) had two percentage points lower private-credit-to-GDP ratio than India (7.82 per cent) in 1960, it managed to outperform India over the last 60 years as shown in Figure 17. As of 2020, India lags behind South Korea in terms of private-credit-to-GDP ratio with a gap of approximately 110 per cent. As far as economic growth is concerned, while the two countries had similar levels of per capita GDP in 1960, presently, South Korean per capita GDP is almost 16 times that of India.

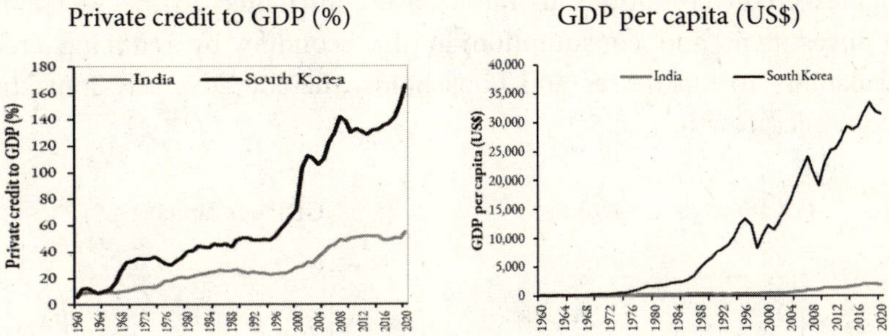

Figure 17: Credit penetration and economic growth: India vis-à-vis South Korea
Source: The World Bank and IMF

South Korea's economic success is attributed to its superior economic policy, especially its export-oriented strategy of development. A pivotal element supporting this export-oriented growth is the preferential credit allocation to channel capital to the traded-goods sector (Dornbusch and Park 1997). South Korea's credit policy, which favoured the export sector, helped in reinforcing its export-led growth strategy. Under the credit policy, financial resources were channelized to preferred industries at subsidized rates. Given that the export sector was given the bulk of the credit, it was this credit flow that facilitated the country's export-oriented economic growth.

In the case of Australia, the private-credit-to-GDP ratio increased from approximately 19 per cent in 1960 to approximately 141 per cent in 2020. Over the last 60 years, the gap between the corresponding ratios for India and Australia has grown tremendously as shown in Figure 18. From as low as 11 per cent in 1960, the gap has increased to 87 per cent in 2020. This stark contrast is also reflected in the per capita GDP of these two countries. Currently, the per capita GDP of Australia is more than 26 times that of India.

A higher degree of credit penetration has enabled greater economic growth in Australia; in contrast, the restricted credit permeation has resulted in low levels of economic growth in India. Empirical evidence suggests the presence of a strong positive relationship between credit supply and economic growth in Australia. A standard deviation negative shock to the supply of credit reduces the Australian GDP by approximately one-third of a percentage point after one year (Jacobs and Rayner 2012).

Tighter credit conditions in India have contributed to the weakening of investment and consumption in the economy by reducing credit availability to businesses and households, thereby adversely impacting economic growth.

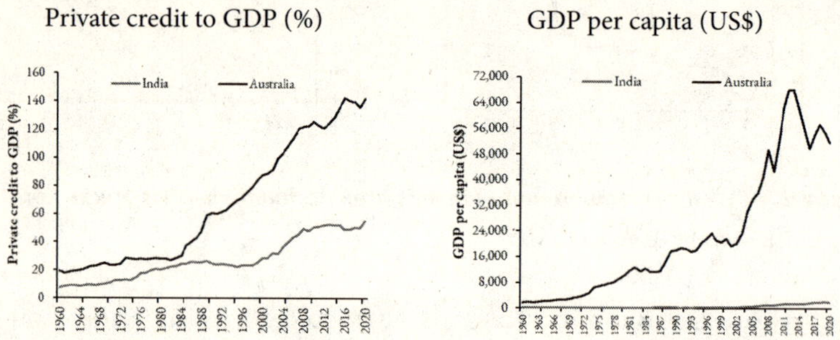

Figure 18: Credit penetration and economic growth: India vis-à-vis Australia
Source: The World Bank and IMF

The patterns for the Canadian economy for both private credit as a proportion of GDP and that of the per capita GDP are similar to those of Australia. From approximately 18 per cent in 1960, private credit as a proportion of GDP rose to approximately 124 per cent in 2008, with the corresponding ratio for India for 2008 standing at only 49 per cent. While this ratio remained under 20 per cent for both economies in 1960, Canada outperformed India in the subsequent years as shown in Figure 19. Consequently, while the Canadian economy experienced a credit-led growth in the last six decades, India has continued to lag on this front. The per capita GDP in Canada recorded a remarkable increase during the last 60 years. As of 2020, Canada's per capita GDP is approximately 22 times that of India's per capita GDP.

The contrasting growth trajectory of the Indian economy as compared to Malaysia, South Korea, Australia and Canada underlines the importance of credit supply by the banking sector. Empirical evidence thus clearly demonstrates that countries with greater credit penetration can achieve higher economic growth and that those with restricted credit dissemination limit their growth prospects.

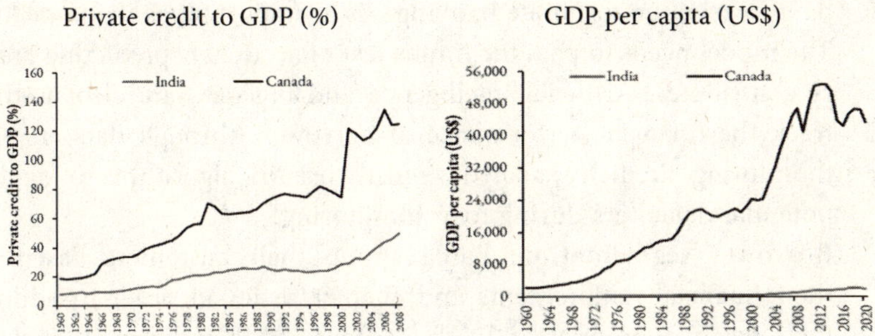

Figure 19: Credit penetration and economic growth: India vis-à-vis Canada
Source: The World Bank and IMF

Banking Infrastructure That India Needs to Create

Premier global banks use banking infrastructure that enables them to minimize their credit risk. As data science and AI are transforming the lending infrastructure of the banking industry, Indian banks must create banking infrastructure comprised of the following elements.

- **Data management:** With the large amount of data that the banking industry generates, efficient ways of collecting, processing and storing data have become extremely important. Big data tools today enable these processes to happen seamlessly. Thanks to data science, it is possible to curate these data into readily usable formats for downstream processes. Moreover, advances in NLP, machine learning (ML) and deep learning help handle 'unstructured data'. Unstructured data can be in the form of voice, text and images. Unstructured data analytics help the banking industry in credit risk modelling, which has not been possible until now.
- **Credit risk modelling**: Artificial intelligence and big data allow banks to better analyse the likelihood and manner in which loans will be repaid, by scientifically predicting the PD and LGD using data science, than basing lending decisions on subjective assessment. Building robust PD and LGD algorithms starts with feature engineering, which involves feature selection, feature construction and feature extraction. After modelling the different attributes of credit risk, such as PD and LGD, the model needs to be evaluated. Evaluation of credit risk algorithms—

be it in retail or corporate banking—is as important as its modelling. The model needs to pass the litmus test of accurately predicting credit risk attributes. Artificial intelligence and big data are also used to track the financial performance of borrowers through data-enabled monitoring. Predictive analytics mostly use ML algorithms to identify potential defaulters during loan monitoring.

- **Borrower segmentation**: Banks group their customers based on their financial requirements and characteristics in order to address their needs appropriately. In this scenario, ML techniques, such as classification and clustering, play a major role in determining potential customers as well as segmenting customers based on their financial information. Banks use unsupervised learning algorithms to segment borrowers based on their financial attributes in ways that were hitherto not possible. Data science also allows banks to assess how valuable a customer is. A common metric banks use is customer lifetime value (CLV). Customer segmentation helps in a better understanding of CLV, which in turn helps banks to fine-tune their credit risk strategies.
- **Fraud detection**: Traditionally, fraud detection has been a difficult task because frauds are rare, short-duration events with a high impact. With advances in ML, it has become easier for banks to detect frauds, such as in credit card transactions, by finding irregularities in transactional patterns. Fraud detection involves monitoring and analysis of the user activity to find any malicious pattern. With the increase in dependency on the Internet and e-commerce for transactions, the number of frauds in online transactions has increased significantly. Real-time analytics use rapid ML algorithms to run checks for possible frauds even as the transaction is being processed to prevent frauds in real time.
- **Customer support**: Data science and AI have automated customer support for the banking industry, thus lowering costs while making it highly efficient, personal and direct. For example, the use of chatbots in resolving customer queries has reduced customer waiting time and has increased customer interaction time. Similarly, virtual assistants can help customers operate many functions such as scheduling payments and reviewing past transactions though voice and text commands. With advances in NLP and voice analytics, customer support in the future is expected to be mostly AI-driven.

◆

As recommended in the *Economic Survey 2019–20*, India should implement the public-sector banking network. As the government owns all the PSBs, it also owns all the data that the PSBs generate. Therefore, the government has the legal standing to create an entity mirroring the Goods and Services Tax Network (GSTN), to bring together the massive amount of data generated by PSBs collectively and thereby utilize economies of scale to exploit this data using the methods described above. The transformative change in management of credit risk that this banking network would bring can enable India to grow credit in a sustained and equitable manner, thereby fostering high economic growth.

26

VITALITY AMPLIFIED

Nurturing India's Human Capital through Healthcare Excellence

Let us recall the scene from the popular 2009 Hindi film *3 Idiots*, where Rancho and Farhan are invited to Raju's house for dinner. Raju's mother describes how half her salary goes into the healthcare expenses of Raju's father. The scene depicted hilariously illustrates the plight of several poor and lower middle-class families in India where out-of-pocket healthcare expenses to take care of a sick family member can relegate the family to poverty.

Needless to say, the health of a nation critically depends on its citizens having access to an equitable, affordable and accountable healthcare system. Health affects domestic economic growth directly through labour productivity and the economic burden of illnesses (WHO 2001). Increasing life expectancy from 50 to 70 years (a 40 per cent increase) could raise the economic growth rate by 1.4 percentage points per year

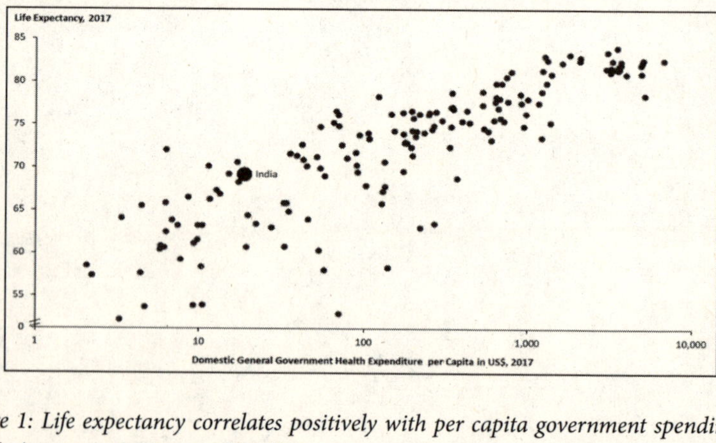

Figure 1: Life expectancy correlates positively with per capita government spending on health (centre and state combined)

Source: Economic Survey 2020–21

(WHO 2001). As Figure 1 shows, life expectancy in a country correlates positively with per capita public health expenditure. Figure 2 shows that maternal mortality correlates negatively with increase in per capita public health expenditure.

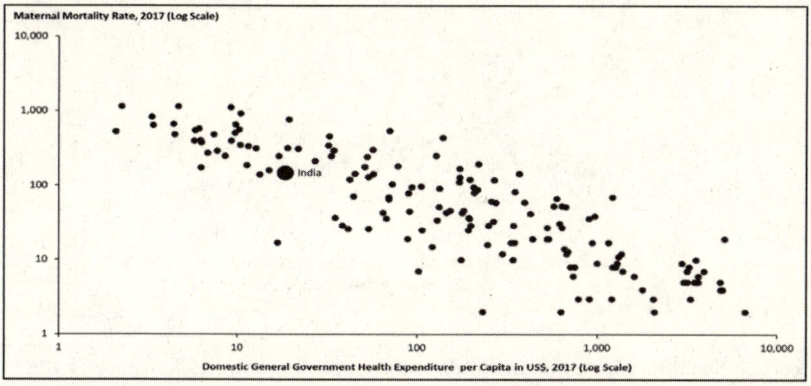

Figure 2: Maternal mortality correlates negatively with per capita government spending on health (centre and state combined)

Source: Economic Survey 2020–21

Increased prioritization of healthcare in central and state budgets is important, as it crucially impacts how much protection citizens get against financial hardships due to out-of-pocket (OOP) payments made for healthcare (WHO 2010). Out-of-pocket payments for health increase the risk of vulnerable groups slipping into poverty because of catastrophic health expenditures (O'Donnell et al. 2007; Berki 1986; van Doorslaer et al. 2006). Figure 3 shows that at low levels of public health expenditure, i.e., public healthcare expenditure as a per cent of GDP less than 3 per cent, out-of-pocket expenditure (OOPE) as a share of total health expenditure drops precipitously when public health expenditure increases. For instance, an increase in public health expenditure from the current levels in India to 3 per cent of GDP can reduce the OOPE from above 60 per cent currently to about 30 per cent.

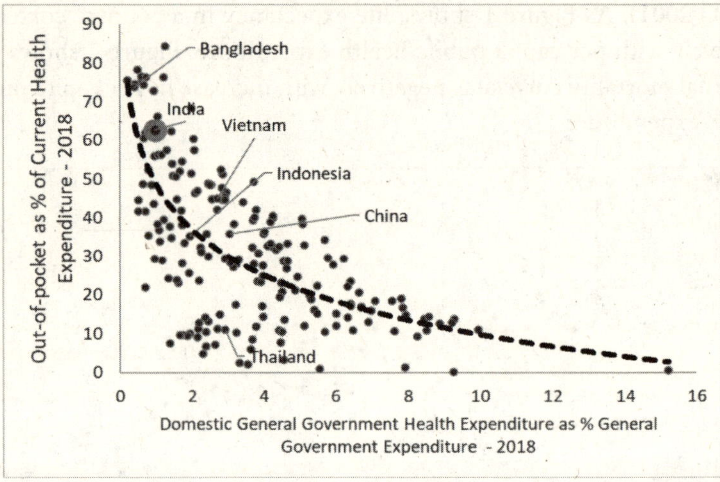

Figure 3: Small increase in public health expenditure can drastically reduce OOPE
Source: Economic Survey 2020–21

In fact, an increase in government healthcare spending over a decade in varied countries such as China, Indonesia, the Philippines, Pakistan and Thailand significantly decreased the OOPE of its citizens (Wagstaff, Eozenou and Smitz 2019).

Healthcare Needs Careful System Design

Healthcare systems do not self-organize using the force of free markets because of three key inherent and unchanging characteristics (Arrow 1963): (i) uncertainty/variability of demand; (ii) information asymmetry; and (iii) hyperbolic tendencies. Hence, any active system design of healthcare must be mindful of these inherent characteristics.

Uncertainty/Variability of Demand

The need for healthcare is often driven by factors that cannot be controlled or predicted. This is also coupled with the nature of demand, which is inelastic especially for emergency care. Given this uncertainty and variability at the individual level, pooling of healthcare expenditures via health insurance can help reduce healthcare risk at the macroeconomic level.

Information Asymmetry

Arrow (1963, 1951) explained that in healthcare markets, buyers of information (patients) rarely know the value of the information until after the purchase has been made and sometimes never at all. For example, when individuals avail of a healthcare service like dermatology (i.e., skin care), they may be able to readily evaluate the outcome. Therefore, for such services, low-quality providers have to reduce their price to remain competitive. In contrast, patients who must undergo open-heart surgery may find it very difficult to evaluate its quality and have to, therefore, rely on the reputation of the hospital/doctor as a proxy for the quality. For some services, such as preventive care and/or mental health, patients may never know for sure whether their provider did a good job.

This principal–agent relationship between the patient (as the principal) and the healthcare provider (as the agent) gets further complicated by factors that may influence this conflict of interest. For instance, altruism among doctors—a trait that is highly commended and looked for by patients—primarily serves to eliminate this conflict of interest. However, reimbursement rates pre-negotiated with insurance companies, advertising and private incentives for testing, etc., can exacerbate this conflict of interest. For instance, C-sections in pregnancies, which are more profitable for the hospital/physician, are overused (Guilmoto et al. 2019). Such non-price features of healthcare can lead to obfuscation of price and/or significant price dispersions for the same good/service.

Health insurance, which becomes desirable because of the uncertainty/variability in demand, creates another round of informational problems in healthcare markets. First, since health insurance covers (some of) the financial costs resulting from poor health behaviour, individuals may have less incentive to avoid them. This phenomenon is labelled '*ex-ante* moral hazard' (Ehrlich and Becker 1972). Pauly (1968) argued about the role of *ex-post* moral hazard in health insurance, which stems from the fact that the cost of an individual's excess usage of healthcare is spread over all other purchasers of insurance. This free-rider problem causes the individual to not restrain his usage of care. Given the *ex-ante* and *ex-post* moral hazard, incomplete insurance in healthcare is optimal. This prediction is consistent with the idea advocated by Holmstrom (1979) that optimal insurance contracts should be incomplete to strike a balance between reducing risk and maintaining incentives for the individual.

As Akerlof (1970) predicts, when little information is available on the quality of a product prior to purchase, and the quality of the product is uncertain, quality deteriorates to the lowest level in an unregulated market. While reputation can partially mitigate this market failure, the design of healthcare systems must account for it, which can otherwise lead to loss of consumer faith and resultant under-investment in healthcare.

Hyperbolic Tendencies

People tend to indulge in risky behaviour that may not be in their self-interest. Examples include smoking, eating unhealthy food, delaying seeking care, or, in the context of the pandemic, not wearing masks or not following social distancing protocols. Such individual behaviour may not only be sub-optimal for the individual but also creates negative externalities for the entire healthcare system through higher costs and poorer outcomes. Typically, consumers tend to demand primary care less than the economically optimal levels, as the price elasticity for this product/service is very high. For instance, among TB patients in Delhi who initially visited a qualified practitioner in 2012, the average length of time from when TB symptoms first appeared to when they reached a DOTS facility was 5.2 months (Kapoor et al. 2012). Similarly, India has a very low rate of screening for cancers among women in the age bracket of 15–49 years, at 22 per cent for cervical cancer, 10 per cent for breast cancer and 12 per cent for oral cancer, when compared to 62 per cent, 59 per cent and 16 per cent, respectively, in OECD countries (NFHS 4 and OECD Health Statistics 2015). In fact, the privately optimal preference for primary care may be so low that individuals may have to even be paid to use adequate primary care. Individuals also underestimate health risks and may, therefore, not purchase adequate health insurance.

System Design in Healthcare

Given these market failures, a free market where individual consumers purchase services from providers on their own while paying at the point of service leads to severely sub-optimal outcomes. These include demand that can be influenced and induced by suppliers, over-seeking of hospitalization and under-seeking of primary care/public health when compared to economically optimal levels, and catastrophic OOP spending in part due to the low preference for health insurance. Therefore, most well-functioning health systems are structured as oligopolies purchasing from oligopsonies instead of individual consumers purchasing from individual providers. The structure of the market has substantial implications for long-term trajectory of the health system. Countries with more fragmented health systems tend to have lower performance as reflected in higher costs, lower efficiency and poor quality. Therefore, in addition to providing healthcare services and financing healthcare, a key role for the government is to actively shape the structure of the healthcare market.

Present State of Indian Healthcare

Despite improvements in healthcare access and quality, India continues to underperform in comparison to other low- and lower middle-income countries. India was ranked 145th out of 180 countries (Global Burden of Disease Study 2016). Only few sub-Saharan countries, some Pacific Island nations, Nepal and Pakistan were ranked below India.

Poor Health Outcomes

As seen in Figure 4, despite improvements in maternal mortality ratio (MMR) and infant mortality rate (IMR), India still needs to improve significantly on these metrics. Countries such as China, Bangladesh, Bhutan, Cambodia, etc., have improved much more on these metrics than India.

Panel A Panel B

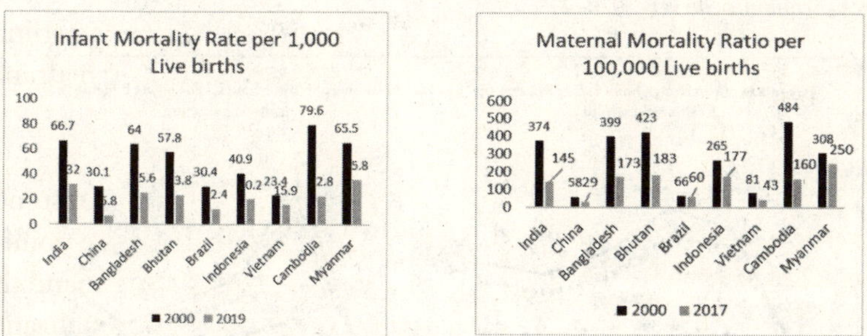

Figure 4: IMR and MMR in India and other countries

Source: Economic Survey 2020–21

Low Access and Utilization

At 3–4 per cent, the hospitalization rates in India are among the lowest in the world; the average for middle-income countries is 8–9 per cent and 13–17 per cent for OECD countries (OECD statistics). Given the increasing burden of non-communicable diseases (NCD), lower life expectancy, higher MMR and IMR and low hospitalization rates are unlikely to reflect a healthier population as compared to middle-income or OECD countries. In fact, they reflect lower access and utilization of healthcare in India.

High OOPE

As shown in Figure 3 and supported by Figure 5 below, India has one of the highest levels of OOPE in the world.

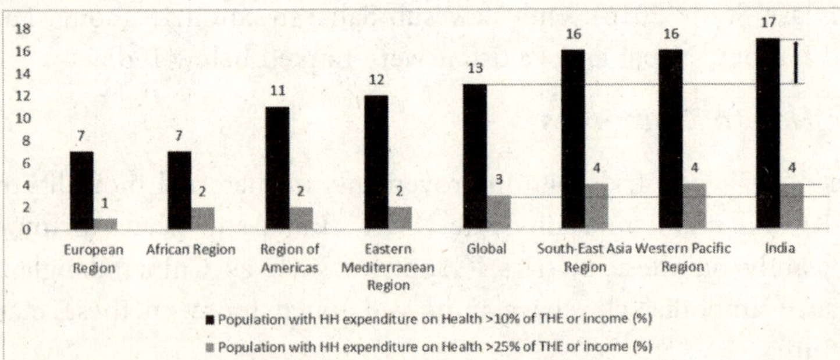

Figure 5: Comparison of health expenditure across different regions

Source: Economic Survey 2020–21

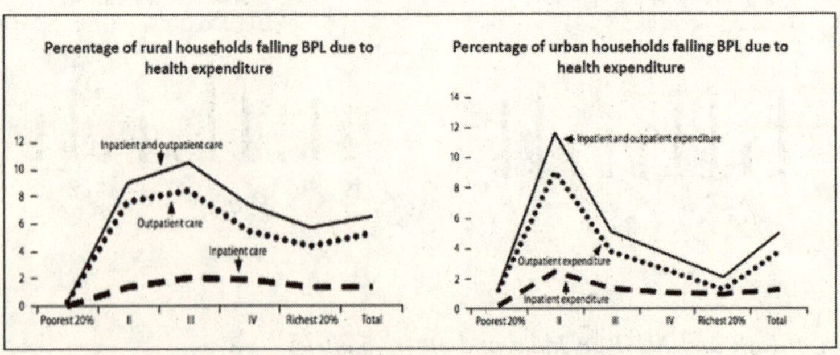

Figure 6: Households falling BPL due to health expenditure

Source: Economic Survey 2020–21

Though decreasing in recent years, inequity persists in availability of healthcare. However, recent data shows that the distribution of the public subsidy has improved in favour of the poor, more clearly in maternity and child healthcare. Earlier studies have argued that public-sector-based healthcare has been pro-rich (or aggressive) (Berman et al. 2017). This had resulted in poor households being disproportionately impacted by OOPE and pushed BPL (Figure 6). The percentage of the poorest utilizing prenatal care through public facilities has increased from 19.9 per cent to 24.7 per cent from 2004 to 2018, and there is a similar increase in the percentage of the poor accessing institutional delivery as well as postnatal care (Figure 7). The poorest utilizing inpatient care and outpatient care has increased from 12.7 per cent to 18.5 per cent and from 15.6 per cent to 18.3 per cent, respectively. At the same time, both inpatient and outpatient utilization among the richest dropped from 29.2 per cent to 26.4 per cent and 30.1 per cent to 26.9 per cent, respectively.

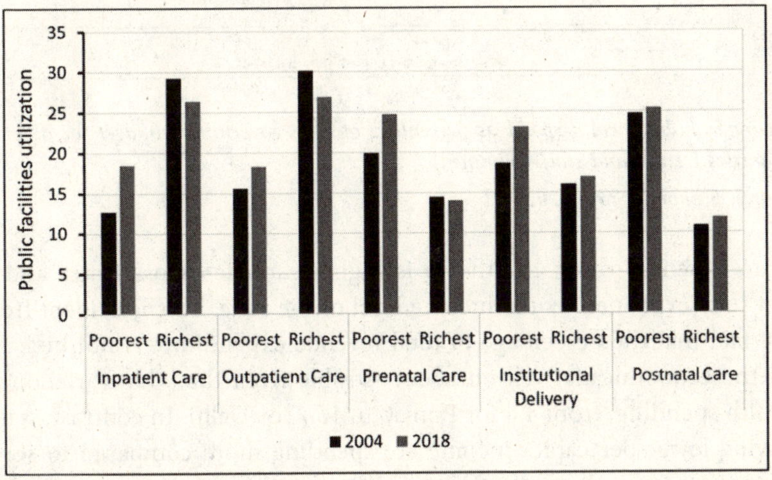

Figure 7: Increasing equity in healthcare (2004–18)
Source: Economic Survey 2020–21

Low Budget Allocations for Healthcare

As health is a state subject in India, spending on healthcare by states matters the most when examining government healthcare spending.

According to National Health Accounts (NHA) 2017, 66 per cent of spending on healthcare is done by the states. India ranks 179th out of 189 countries in prioritization accorded to health in its government budgets (consolidated union and state government). As Figure 8 shows, this prioritization of health in India is like donor-dependent countries, such as Haiti and Sudan, and well short of its peers in development.

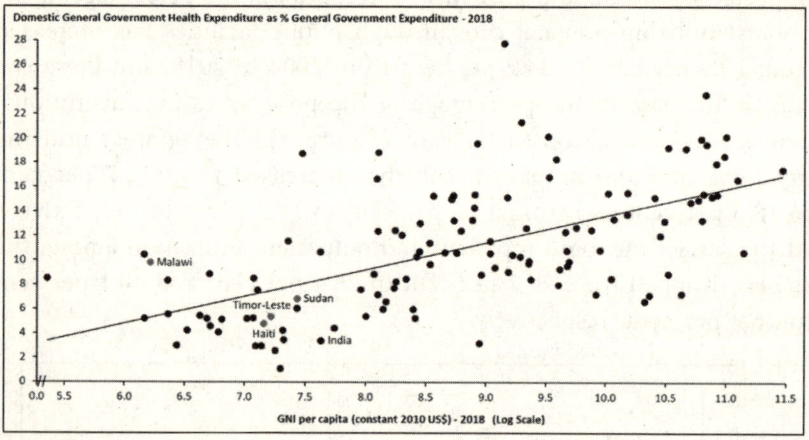

Figure 8: Public health spend as percentage of total government budget for different countries (centre and state combined)

Source: Economic Survey 2020–21

State expenditure on healthcare is highly variable across states and is not fully explained by the income level of the state. This is evident from the fact that the percentage of total revenue expenditure is not high for all the economically well-off states—visible from the wide variation in health spending, from 4.6 for Punjab to 16.7 for Delhi. In contrast, states having lower per capita income are spending more compared to some of the economically well-off states. Figure 9 illustrates the same: while healthcare spending per capita increases with the gross state domestic product (GSDP) per capita, healthcare spending as a per cent of GSDP decreases with the GSDP per capita. Thus, richer states are spending a lower proportion of their GSDP on healthcare.

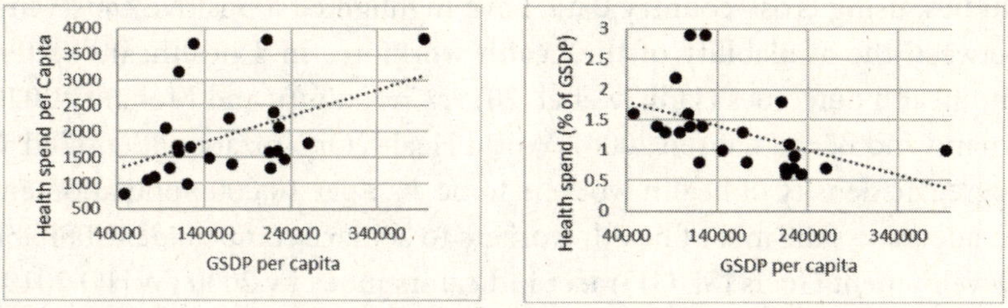

Figure 9: Healthcare spending across different Indian states

Source: Economic Survey 2020–21

States that have higher per capita spending have lower OOPE, which also holds true at the global level. Hence, there is need for higher public spending on healthcare to reduce OOPE. As the evidence in Figure 4 clearly demonstrates, an increase in public spending to 2.5–3 per cent can substantially reduce OOPE. Therefore, richer states should especially target increasing the healthcare spending as a per cent of GDP to 2.5–3 per cent (Figure 10).

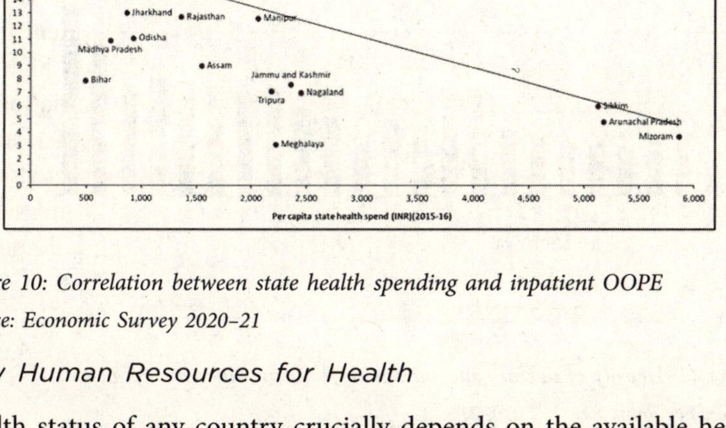

Figure 10: Correlation between state health spending and inpatient OOPE

Source: Economic Survey 2020–21

Low Human Resources for Health

Health status of any country crucially depends on the available health infrastructure in general and human resources for health. Several research studies, using cross-country data, have highlighted a positive causal link between the availability of the health workforce in a healthcare system and health outcomes (Jadhav et al. 2019; Choudhury and Mohanty 2020; Anand and Bärnighausen 2004). World Health Organization identified an aggregate density of health workers to be 44.5 per 10,000 population and an adequate skill-mix of health workers to achieve composite Sustainable Development Goals (SDG) tracer indicators index by 2030 (WHO 2019). The WHO also specified a lower range of 23 health workers per 10,000 population to achieve 80 per cent of births attended by skilled health professionals.

Although aggregate human resources for health density in India is close to the lower threshold of 23, there is a lopsided distribution of health workforce across states, and the skill-mix—as captured by the ratio of doctors to nurses and midwives—is far from adequate. State-level variations in the density of health workers and the skill-mix reflects that while Kerala and Jammu and Kashmir have a high density of doctors, states like Punjab, Himachal Pradesh and Chhattisgarh have a larger number of nurses and midwives but a very low density of doctors. Andhra Pradesh, Delhi and Tamil Nadu reflect a better balance of doctors and nurses and midwives (Figure 11 and 12).

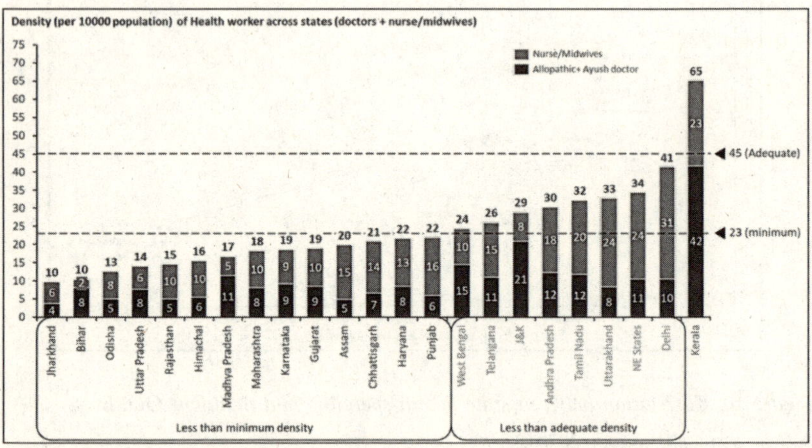

Figure 11: Density of doctors and nurses/midwives in different Indian states

Source: Economic Survey 2020–21

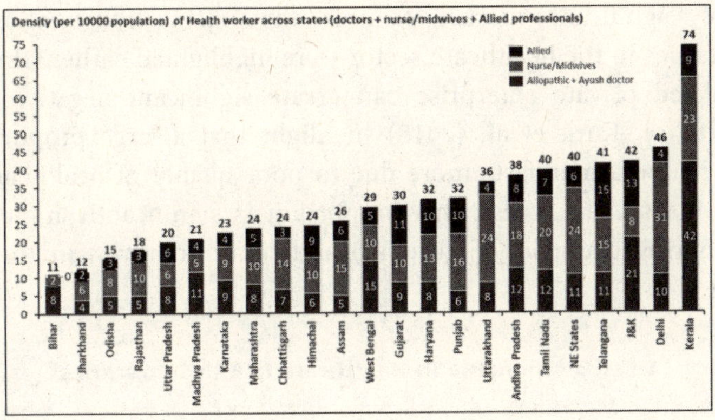

Figure 12: Density of doctors, nurses/midwives and allied professionals in different Indian states

Source: Economic Survey 2020–21

Need to Regulate Private Enterprise

While the share of public institutions has increased both in hospital and outpatient care, the private sector dominates in total healthcare provision in India. Around 74 per cent of outpatient care and 65 per cent of hospitalization care is provided through the private sector in urban India (Figure 13).

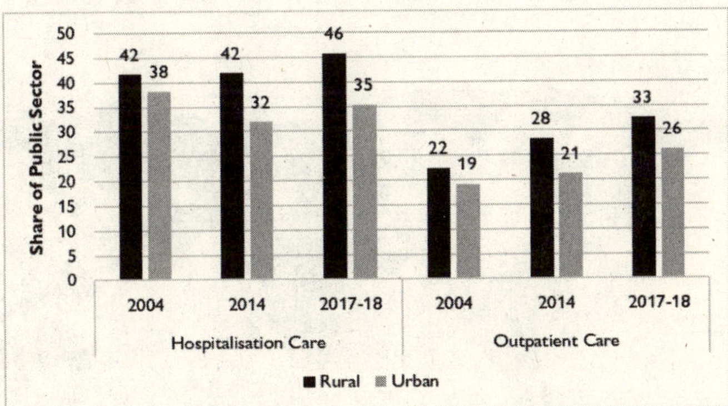

Figure 13: Share (percent) of public sector in total healthcare, hospitalization care and outpatient care

Source: Economic Survey 2020–21

The significant market failures that stem from information asymmetries in the healthcare sector were highlighted earlier. Therefore, unregulated private enterprise can create significant negative effects. For instance, Kurk et al. (2018) highlight that a large proportion of deaths in India manifests more due to poor quality of healthcare than due to insufficient access; this proportion is significantly higher than neighbouring countries (Figure 14) and other countries in the world (Figure 15).

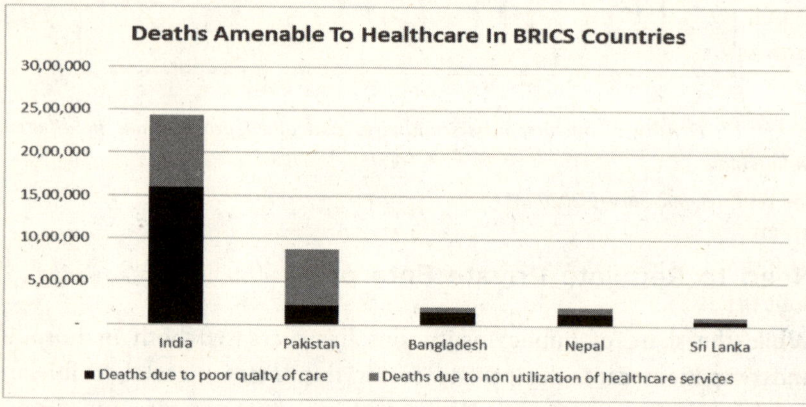

Figure 14: Poor care quality leads to more deaths than insufficient access to healthcare
Source: Economic Survey 2020–21

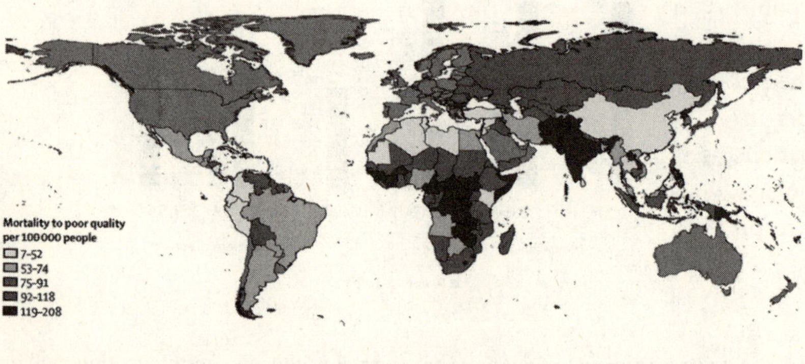

Figure 15: Mortality due to poor quality healthcare by country
Source: Economic Survey 2020–21

In fact, Kane and Calnan (2017) highlight the erosion of trust in the Indian healthcare sector. To understand the difference in quality between the public and private sector providers, we use data from Pradhan Mantri Jan Arogya Yojana (PMJAY). Among the most common metrics of quality in the hospital setting is unplanned readmissions (Mohpal et al. 2020). Readmissions typically impose a heavy burden on patients and their families and on health systems in general as a result of unnecessary care. In general, readmissions are costlier than original admissions. Data till November 2019 reveal that the average claim amount in a readmission case is ₹19,295 compared to ₹12,652 in the corresponding original case. The average length of stay is also higher during readmission—7.5 days versus 6.6 days. Crucially, the data shows that the mortality rate for neonatal procedures is much higher in private hospitals than in public hospitals—3.84 per cent and 0.61 per cent, respectively. Public-sector patients get readmitted to the same hospital 64 per cent of the time versus 70 per cent for private hospitals. About three-fourths of outpatient care and two-thirds of hospitalization care are provided through the private sector. So, the large proportion of deaths in India, manifesting due to poor quality of healthcare, is likely to reflect that the quality of treatment in the private sector may not be significantly better than that in the public sector (Base et al. 2012; Kumar and Prakash 2011; Coarasa et al. 2014; Russo 2015).

The problem of asymmetric information in healthcare is also reflected in the substantial variation in costs for treating the same disease between the public and private sector. Even though the quality of treatment in the private sector does not seem to be markedly better when compared to the public sector, yet, not only are the costs of treatment uniformly higher in the private sector, but also the differences are humongous for in-patient treatments of severe illnesses such as cancers (3.7×), cardio-vascular diseases (6.8×), injuries (5.9×), gastrointestinal diseases (6.2×) and respiratory diseases (5.2×) (NSSO data, Figure 16 and 17).

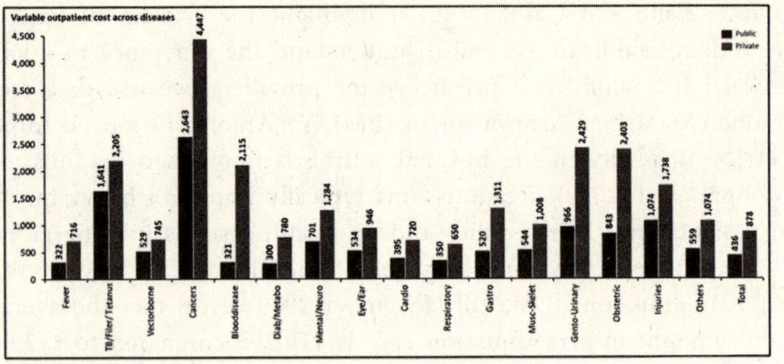

Figure 16: Substantial variation in costs for treating the same disease between public and private sector (outpatient care)

Source: Economic Survey 2020–21

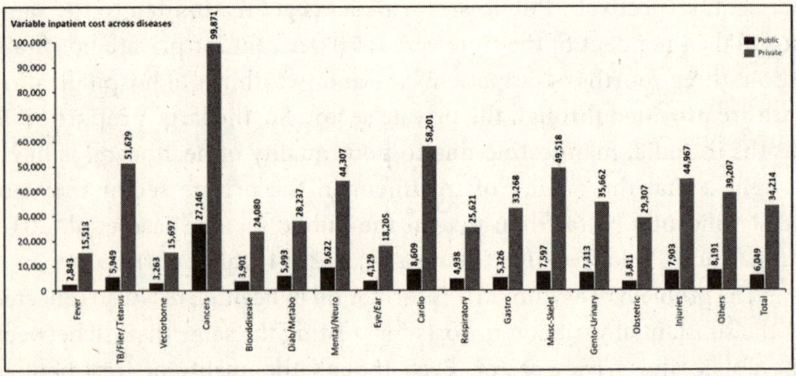

Figure 17: Substantial variation in costs for treating the same disease between public and private sector (inpatient care)

Source: Economic Survey 2020–21

Given the market failures stemming from significant asymmetric information, an unregulated private healthcare system is clearly sub-optimal compared to a system where policies mitigate the problem of asymmetric information. Parallels can be drawn from banking and financial intermediation—another industry that suffers from significant market failures due to asymmetric information—to design policies for mitigating these market failures.

Credit-rating agencies mitigate the information asymmetry faced by investors when investing in the debt of a firm. Specifically, credit-rating agencies assess the likelihood of the firm repaying the debt that it takes from investors, thereby the quality of the firm borrowing the money. Similarly, healthcare policymakers should consider creating agencies to assess the quality of healthcare providers—both doctors and hospitals. The Quality and Outcomes Framework (QOF) introduced by the National Health Service (NHS) in the UK in 2004 as well as other quality assessment practices introduced by the NHS provide a good example. The NHS quality assessment practices include national standards for major chronic diseases, annual appraisal of all doctors working in the NHS, and widespread use of clinical audits to compare practices, sometimes with public release of data. These should be evaluated carefully and considered for implementation.

Credit bureaus assess the quality of individual borrowers by assigning them credit scores, thereby mitigating the information asymmetry faced by a bank or financial institution in lending to the individual borrower. In the healthcare context, insurers as well as healthcare providers suffer from similar information asymmetry about the patient. As argued in Chapter 13 in Section 3 in this book, data from the NDHM can be utilized even within the framework of data privacy. By utilizing such data with the aid of AI and ML algorithms, the predictive aspects can be used to mitigate information asymmetry with respect to patients. Therefore, information utilities, à la the credit bureaus, should be evaluated and considered.

Finally, given the information asymmetries that make unregulated private enterprise sub-optimal in healthcare, regulation and supervision of the healthcare sector must be seriously considered. This is especially pertinent as regulation has grown in importance as a key lever for governments to affect the quantity, quality, safety and distribution of services in health systems (Clarke 2016).

Policy Suggestions

Covid-19 has highlighted the role of technology-enabled platforms as an alternate distribution channel for remote delivery of healthcare services. These platforms offer a promising new avenue to address India's last-mile healthcare access and delivery challenges. These technology platforms coupled with digitization and the promise of AI at-scale, have led to a drastic uptake in the utilization of telemedicine for primary care and mental health. Given India's unique last-mile challenges, such technology-enabled solutions need to be harnessed to the fullest. As we show, telemedicine depends crucially on Internet connectivity and health infrastructure. Therefore, both the central and state governments need to invest in telemedicine on a mission mode to complement the government's digital health mission, the NDHM, and thereby enable greater access to the masses.

The National Health Mission (NHM) has played a critical role in mitigating inequity in healthcare access. Similarly, the percentage of the poorest accessing institutional delivery increased from 18.6 per cent to 23.1 per cent and from 24.7 per cent to 25.4 per cent for postnatal care.

From a financial perspective, India has one of the highest levels of OOPE in the world, contributing directly to the high incidence of catastrophic expenditures and poverty. A negative correlation exists between the level of public spend and OOPE both across countries and states. An increase in public spend from 1 per cent to 2.5–3 per cent of GDP—as envisaged in the National Health Policy, 2017 (NHP 2017)—can decrease the OOPE from 65 per cent to 20 per cent of overall healthcare spend. In fact, PMJAY has been a marquee evolution in this direction, providing financial affordability to a large percentage of the Indian population.

A standardized system for quality reporting on healthcare for hospitals, physicians and insurance companies can start with basic input indicators to be reported mandatorily by every healthcare stakeholder. Over time, this can evolve to cover output and outcome indicators such as infection rates and re-admission rates. A start has been made in this direction by NITI Aayog through the Health Index at the state level. Finally, regulation and supervision of the healthcare sector must be seriously considered. This is especially pertinent as regulation has grown in importance as a key lever for governments to impact the quantity, quality, safety and distribution of services in health systems (WHO 2016).

27

KNOWLEDGE CATALYST

Empowering India's Human Capital through Education

As the chief economic advisor to the GoI, whenever I looked at the board containing the 16 names that preceded mine, I was reminded of the eternal gift of education that I received from my parents. Even though my father did not get the opportunity to attend university, he nevertheless gave me the precious gift of higher education. Having lost his father at the tender age of seven, my father finished school only because of the largesse of his elder brother and sister. Starting from the clerical grade in the Indian Railways, my father worked hard to pass departmental examinations and retired as a gazetted officer in the rank of assistant accounts officer. Some of the names that preceded mine stood in stark contrast as sons of IRS, IPS, ICS/IAS officers and other such sections of India's elite. This 'living the Indian dream' was made possible only through the unparalleled power of education in creating socio-economic mobility across generations.[127] There are countless such stories of kids from lower middle-class families in modern India finding advancement through the unique force of education.

Yet, these stories need to proliferate across the length and breadth of India and penetrate even less privileged sections of society for India@100 to be an economic powerhouse. After all, as Swami Vivekananda averred: 'How can there be any progress of the country without the spread of education, the dawning of knowledge?'

Of course, India has made rapid strides in enabling better education for its children. In the last decade, the number of universities has increased by 53 per cent from 723 in 2014 to 1,113 in 2023. More girls are now joining higher education than boys. The gross enrolment ratio (GER) for girls in higher education has more than doubled to 27.9 per cent in

[127]Sangeetha G., 'Living the Indian Dream', *The Asian Age*, 27 December 2018, http://tinyurl.com/2s4zb854. Accessed on 8 February 2024.

2020 vis-à-vis 12.7 per cent in 2010. Total enrolment in higher education, which was 3.4 crore in 2014, has gone up to 4.1 crore students in 2023.[128] Yet, to realize its demographic dividend, India needs to follow up on the New Education Policy (NEP), 2020, with several other measures to strengthen the quality of education.

Education: The Key to Unlock the Demographic Dividend

India's demographic advantage will persist till 2050 as seen in Figure 1. The age dependency ratio equals the sum of the young population (under age 15) and elderly population (age 65 and over) relative to the working-age population (ages 15 to 64). From 2018 to 2050, the dependent population will remain flat; it will start rising only from 2050.

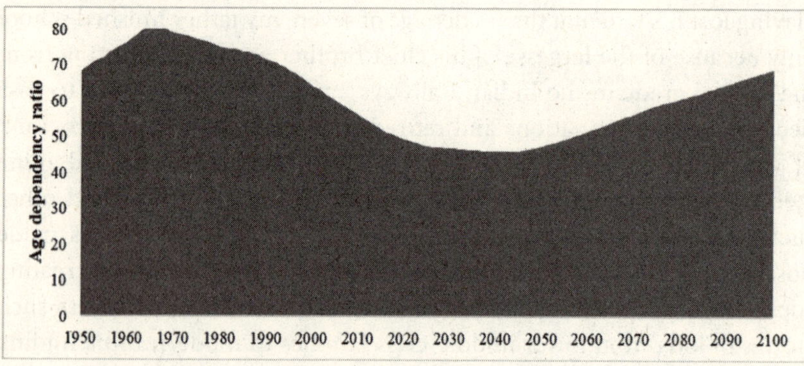

Figure 1: India's age dependency ratio from 1950 to 2100

Source: Our World in Data, University of Oxford

Note: Data is shown as the number of dependents per 100 working-age population. Projections to 2100 are based on the UN's medium population scenario.

Given this demographic dividend, education is critical for economic growth and social and economic inclusion. As shown in Figure 2, output increases the most in India with an increase in the quality of labour. The significance of education for economic growth has been widely

[128]Sarkar, Kanishka, 'Female Enrollment Ratio in Higher Education up Four Times in 20 Years: Indian Economy Report', *CNBCTV18*, 29 January 2024, http://tinyurl.com/nhb9fpnn. Accessed on 8 February 2024.

acknowledged since Gary S. Becker's ground-breaking research, which earned him the Nobel Prize. In fact, the historical evaluation of high-growth episodes in Chapter 5 showed clearly that every country improved its educational outcomes to further its economic growth. Among all factor inputs including capital, quality and quantity of labour, energy, material, and services, a 1 per cent increase in labour quality makes the greatest contribution—1.0–1.5 per cent—to growth over the three decades following liberalization. As the quality of labour depends significantly on education, this underlines the importance of education for India to reap its demographic dividend.

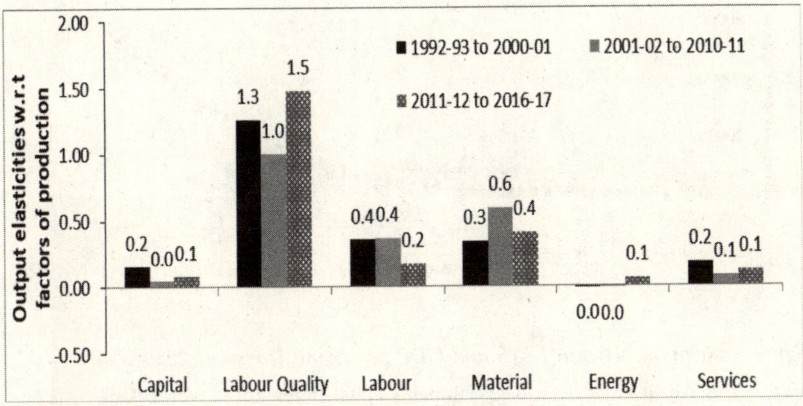

Figure 2: Output elasticities with respect to factors of production

Data: Estimated using KLEMS database; RBI

Note: Gross output at constant 2011–12 prices. In KLEMS data, human capital is measured in terms of labour quality, which takes into account changes in composition of age, sex and education of labour force.

Correlating the real GDP per capita with the World Bank's measure of learning-adjusted years of schooling (LAYS) shows that India is at a point where improvements in education can bring sharp enhancements in GDP per capita. The LAYS measure combines quantity as measured by the average years of schooling with quality as measured by test scores into a composite measure.

In Figure 3, we see that improvements in the LAYS index till about eight does not manifest in much enhancement in GDP per capita. However, after this threshold is reached, an increase in LAYS by one unit correlates with an increase in GDP per capita by about $10,000. The World Bank's World Development Report 2019 attributes about 10–30 per cent of cross-country differences in per capita GDP to differences in this measure.[129] As India's LAYS index is close to eight, improvements hereafter can significantly add to economic progress.

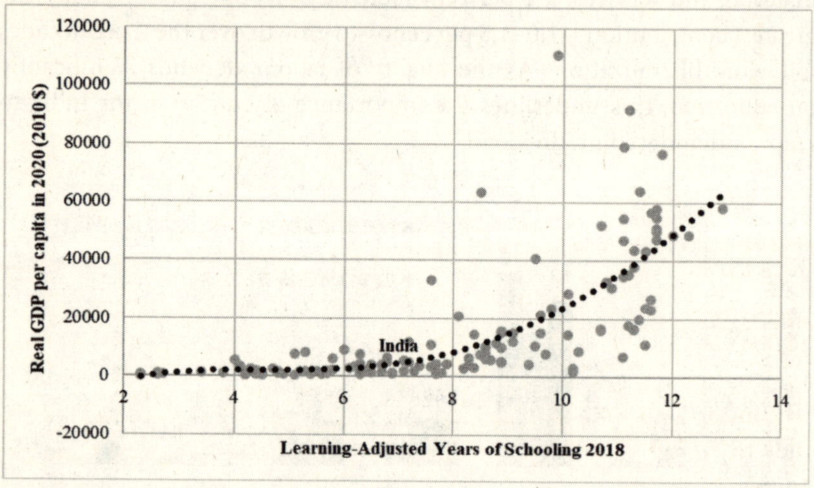

Figure 3: Relation between LAYS and GDP per capita (constant 2010 US$)
Source: The World Bank open data; Human Capital Index 2018, World Bank

In Figure 4, we find that secondary school education as measured by the GER in secondary school correlates negatively with intergenerational persistence, a metric that gauges lack of mobility in social strata across generations.

[129]The World Bank, *World Development Report 2019: The Changing Nature of Work*, 2019, http://tinyurl.com/hak3bphz. Accessed on 8 February 2024.

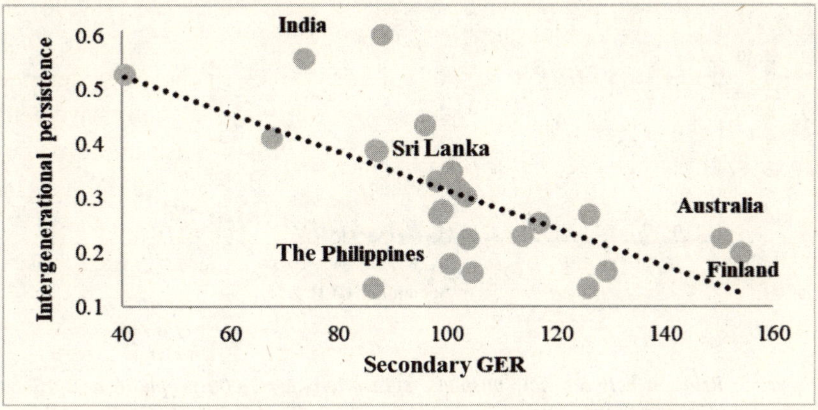

Figure 4: Intergenerational persistence and higher secondary school GER

Source: Author's calculations; data from Global Database on Intergenerational Mobility (GDIM), World Bank

The individuals who are educated and possess adequate knowledge will be able to enhance their wages and thereby lead to elimination of poverty; therefore, higher the level of education, lesser will be the number of poverty-stricken persons. The direct impact of education on reducing poverty is through increase in wages (Awan et al. 2011).

In Figure 5, we see an exponentially growing relationship between new business density, which is measured as new business registrations per 1,000 people in the ages 15–64, and secondary GER. We see that entrepreneurship starts increasing sharply once secondary GER exceeds 80 per cent. In fact, a World Bank study corroborates this finding. In their meta-analysis of empirical studies in this area, the study finds that an additional year of schooling in developing economies raises enterprise income by an average of 5.5 per cent.[130]

[130]Sluis, Justin van der, Mirjam van Praag and Wim Vijverberg, 'Entrepreneurship Selection and Performance: A Meta-Analysis of the Impact of Education in Developing Economies, *The World Bank Economic Review*, http://tinyurl.com/58w6tyaa. Accessed on 8 February 2024.

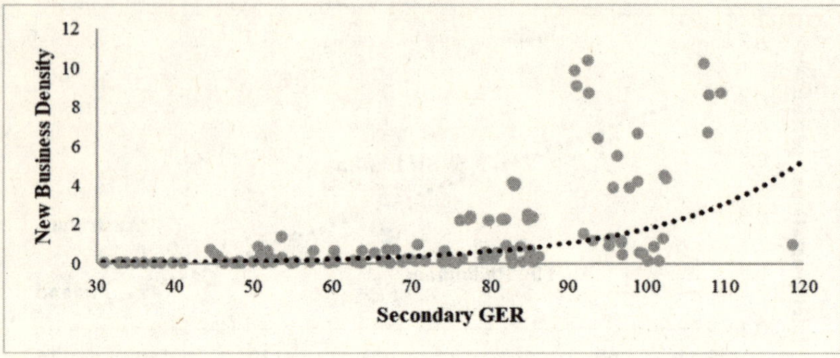

Figure 5: Relation between new business registrations per 1,000 people in ages 15–64 and secondary GER

Source: The World Bank open data (panel data till 2018)

Note: Countries included are Afghanistan, Bangladesh, Brazil, Bhutan, China, Indonesia, India, Japan, Sri Lanka, Maldives, Myanmar, Malaysia, Nepal, Pakistan, DPR Korea, Russian Federation, Singapore, Thailand, South Africa. Time period: 2006–16.

Education enhances innovative capability of the economy and increases the ability to generate new ideas and technologies. Further, countries having higher GER in secondary education also tend to have higher GII score (Figure 6).

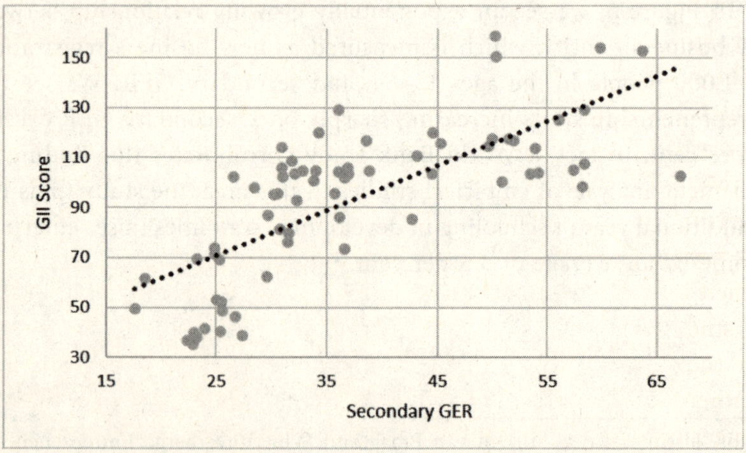

Figure 6: Relation between GII and secondary GER

Source: GII; World Bank open data

Complementing NEP: Identifying Areas for Improvement

The NEP brings important changes in India's education landscape:

1. Mother tongue or regional language will be used as the means of instruction till the primary grade. As I have explained earlier, this provision is meant to enhance students' comprehension and enable the flow of more effective communication with teachers.[131]
2. Schooling will begin from the age of 3 years with the age group of mandatory schooling changed from 6–14 years to 3–18 years. This new system will include 12 years of schooling with three years of Anganwadi or pre-primary education.
3. Mathematics and computational thinking will be given increased emphasis throughout the school years, with a focus on computer programming beginning in Class 6 onwards.
4. Interdisciplinary curriculum will bring together multiple disciplines to create a holistic learning experience that will enable students to become better problem solvers.
5. Introducing digital education in an online platform.
6. Teachers will be promoted or transferred based on a merit list.

Significant Learning Deficits that Increase from Classes 2–8

To realize the ambitions embedded in the NEP, it is important to address the significant deficits in learning as shown in Figures 7 and 8. Figure 7 shows that even in Class 8, the mathematical ability of many students is at the level of Class 2. The average deficit in mathematical ability increases with classes. While the average deficit in mathematical ability is two levels by the time students are in Class 5, it increases to four levels by the time students reach Class 8. Even more importantly, from the perspective of equity in educational outcomes, the dispersion in this deficit increases with class levels. In any given grade, the learning levels of students vary greatly, with some performing at the level expected for their grade, while others are significantly behind, struggling with mathematical abilities that are below their peers. This is particularly concerning given the objective of introducing computer programming

---

[131]Subramanian, Krishnamurthy, 'Their Bhasha, Their Future', *The Times of India*, 11 August 2023, http://tinyurl.com/3ytt26mf. Accessed on 8 February 2024.

from Class 6 and the ambition of introducing interdisciplinary learning. Learning computer programming becomes difficult without a strong foundation in mathematics. Similarly, problem solving becomes difficult without adequate understanding of mathematics. Therefore, addressing these learning deficits and the dispersion in the learning deficits is critical. Figure 8 shows a similar pattern for ability in language.

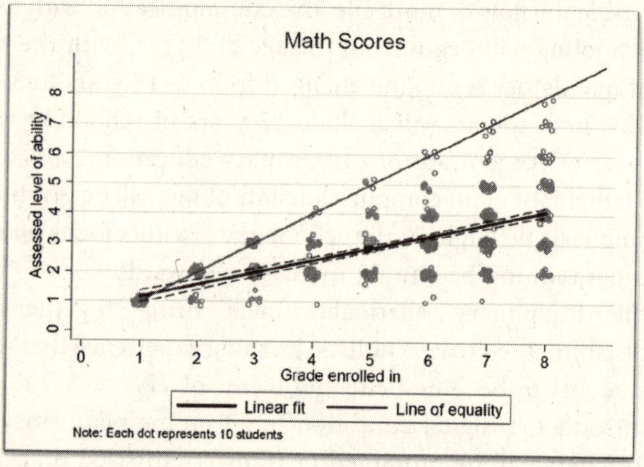

Figure 7: Level and dispersion in learning deficits in mathematics: Grades 1–8
Source: Muralidharan (2018)

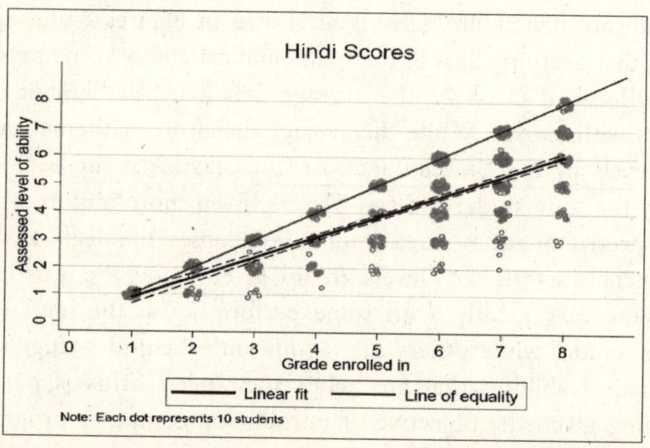

Figure 8: Level and dispersion in learning deficits in language: Grades 1–8
Source: Muralidharan (2018)

Findings from a foundational learning study (FLS) in 2022 of over 85,000 Class 3 students conducted by the Ministry of Education and the National Council of Educational Research and Training (NCERT) are pertinent here. In numeracy, between 31 to 77 per cent of Class 3 students did not meet the global minimum standards in tasks such as identification of numbers, addition and subtraction (Figure 9). In English and Hindi, 46 per cent and 54 per cent, respectively, of the sampled students were below the global minimum proficiency standards. In proficiency in regional languages, between 29 per cent and 80 per cent of students were below the global minimum standards (Figure 10).[132]

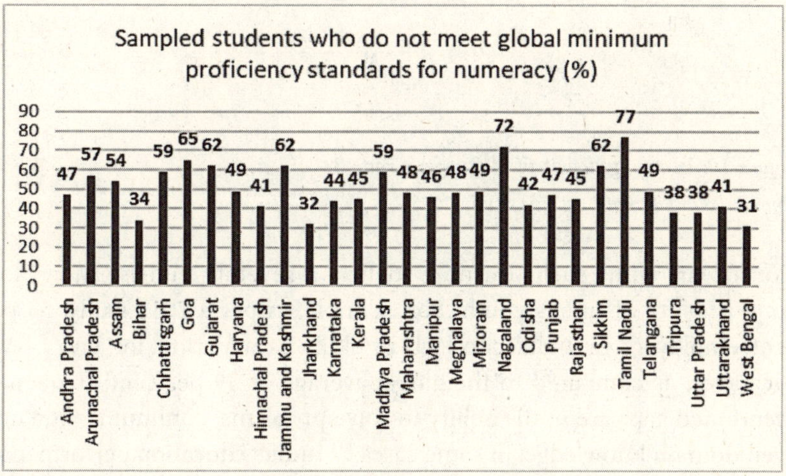

Figure 9: Learning deficit in numeracy: Grade 3

Source: Foundational Learning Study 2022

[132]Ministry of Education and National Council of Educational Research and Training (NCERT), *Foundational Learning Study 2022: National Report on Benchmarking for Oral Reading Fluency with Reading Comprehension and Numeracy,* September 2022, http://tinyurl.com/3e34cx77. Accessed on 15 February 2024.

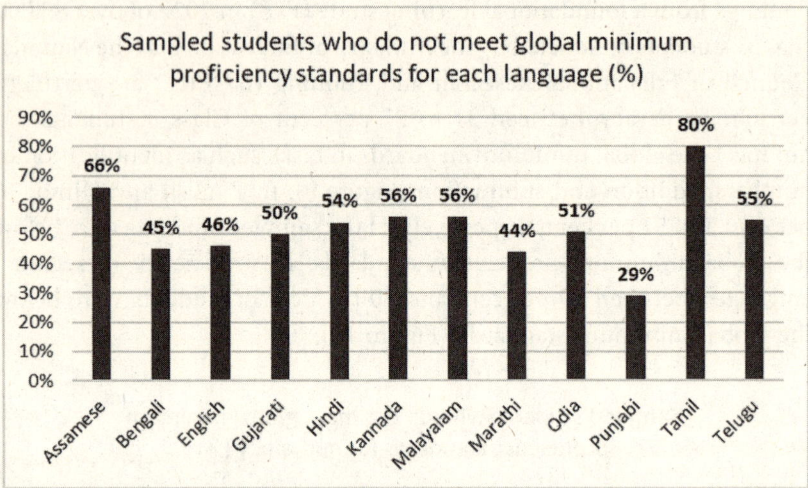

Figure 10: Learning deficit in language: Grade 3
Source: Foundational Learning Study 2022

Consistent with such learning deficits, several studies show low employability of India's youth. For example, as per a 2012 study, 53 per cent employers in India cite lack of skills as a reason for entry-level vacancies, as compared to the global average of 39 per cent; frequently mentioned gaps are in the ability to solve problems, communication and even domain knowledge, in some cases.[133] India's education performance, as measured by harmonized test scores in Figure 11 and LAYS in Figure 12, has not been at par with other countries with similar level of GDP per capita. In contrast, Vietnam does far better even after adjusting for its level of GDP per capita.

[133]Barton, Dominic, Diana Farrell and Mona Mourshed, 'Education to Employment: Designing a System That Works', *McKinsey & Company*, 1 January 2013, http://tinyurl.com/ykuxubzd. Accessed on 8 February 2024.

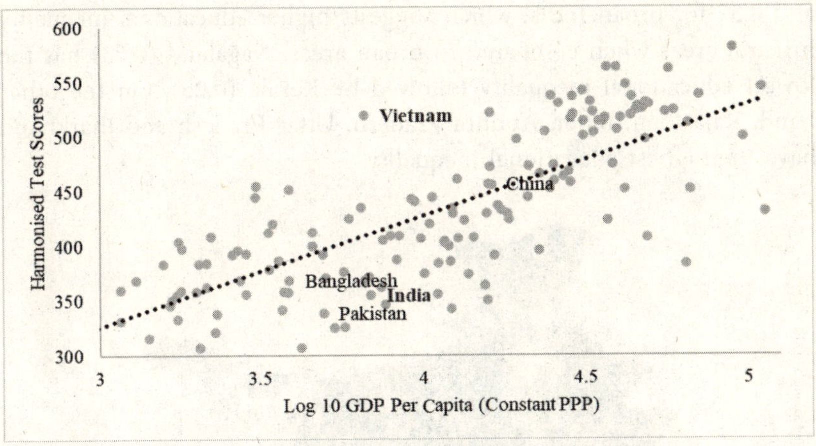

Figure 11: India's harmonized test scores compared to countries with similar GDP per capita

Source: The World Bank open data; Human Capital Index 2018, World Bank

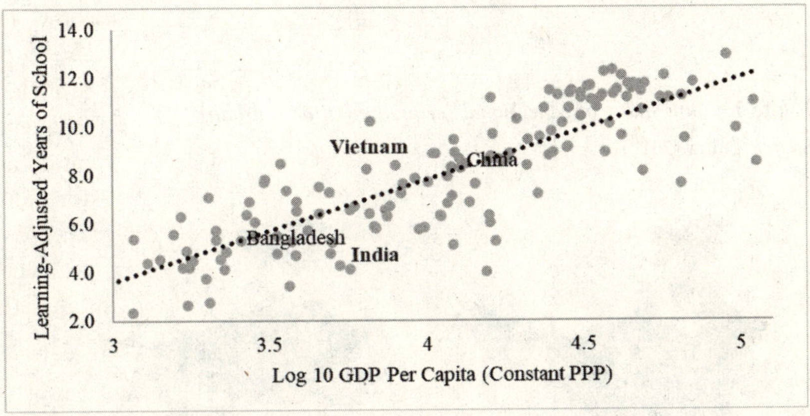

Figure 12: India's LAYS compared to countries with similar GDP per capita

Source: The World Bank open data; Human Capital Index 2018, World Bank

The dispersion in learning deficits that we see in Figures 7 and 8 also manifest as inequality in educational outcomes, as shown by the Gini index of educational inequality across major Indian states (Figures 13 and 14). The Gini index is 0.40 at the national level, 0.46 for rural India and 0.32 for urban India, which suggests higher educational inequality in rural areas when compared to urban areas. Nagaland (0.23) has the lowest educational inequality followed by Kerala (0.25). On the other hand, Rajasthan, Bihar, Andhra Pradesh, Uttar Pradesh and Jharkhand have the highest educational inequality.

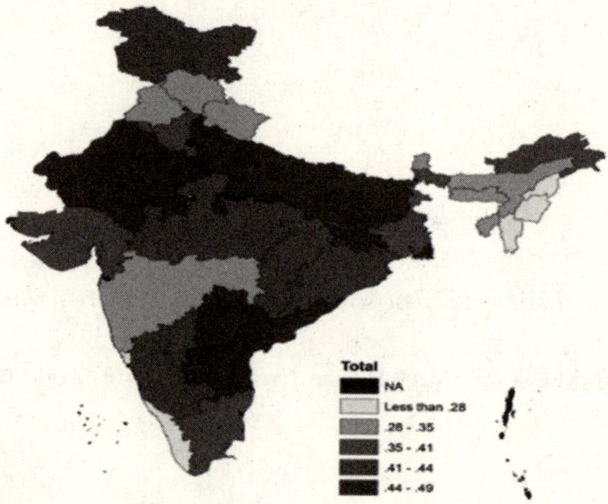

Figure 13: Gini Index of educational inequality (rural + urban)
Source: Dutta (2017)

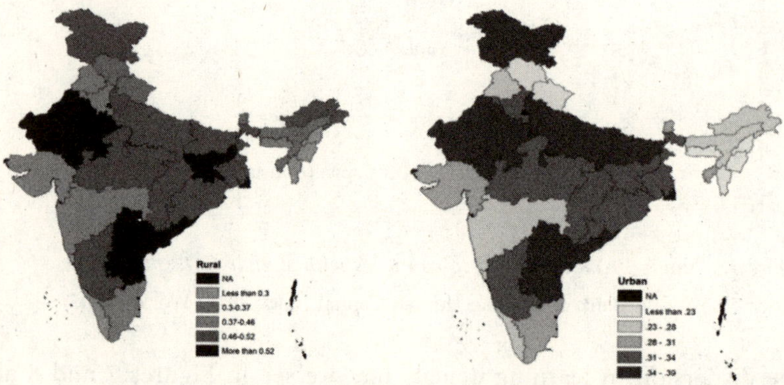

Figure 14: Gini Index of educational inequality separately for rural and urban areas
Source: Dutta (2017)

Spending More Doesn't Mean Learning More

Figure 15 shows that the difference in educational outcomes does not correlate much with differences in expenditure in education across states. In fact, as teachers' salaries, especially in government schools, comprise the largest component of education spending, policymakers need to keep in mind that numerous research studies indicate no discernible link between teachers' salaries and their ability to enhance learning outcomes.

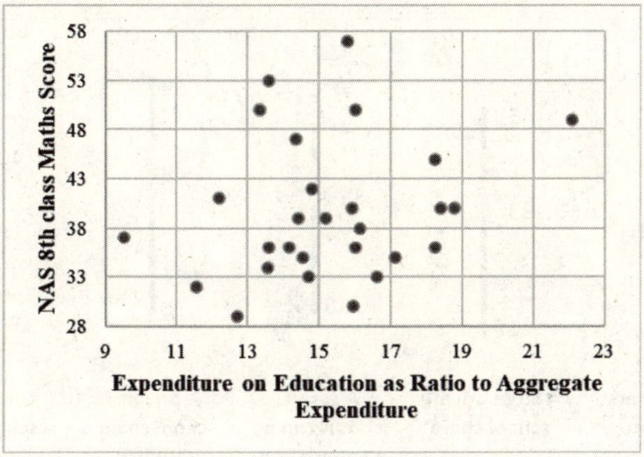

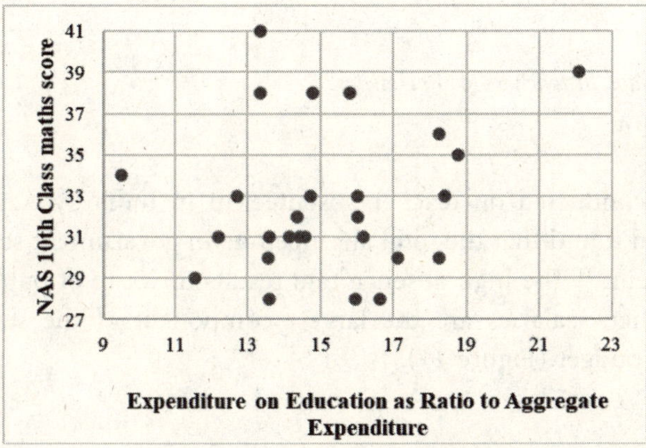

Figure 15: Correlation between expenditure on education and learning outcomes

Source: NCERT; RBI State Finances Report

Teacher Performance

Pan-India tests of teacher's competencies by the Centre for Teacher Accreditation (CENTA) shows that competencies are not significantly different across school types, but vary widely within schools of each category. Importantly, the analysis shows that teachers, conceptual understanding of the subject itself constitutes one of the biggest gaps (Figure 16).

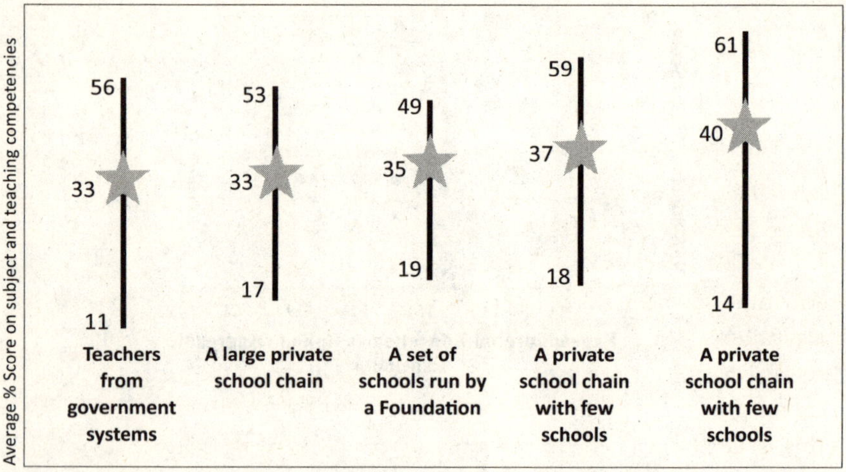

Figure 16: Gaps in teachers' competencies

Source: CENTA

A survey conducted on teacher absenteeism in India by Azim Premji Foundation found that the total absence rate in government schools was 18.9 per cent.[134] The high absence rate results in waste of public money since teachers' salaries are the largest component of the state school education budget (Figure 17).

[134]Azim Premji Foundation, *Teacher Absenteeism Study*, March 2017, http://tinyurl.com/3a8jy56r. Accessed on 8 February 2024.

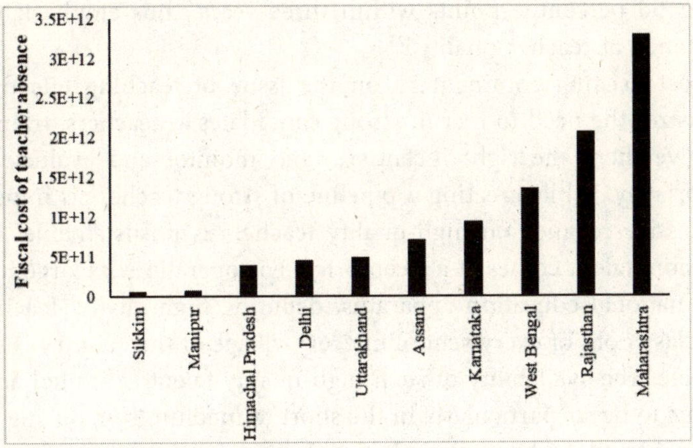

Figure 17: Fiscal cost of teacher absence
Source: MHRD

An important driver of the differences in teacher competencies is the aspiration associated with the teaching profession: there is no differential reward to teachers based on their competencies, which in turn limits career growth options. As mentioned earlier, the NEP seeks to address this issue through merit-based career paths for teachers, disallowing of non-teaching activities during school hours, and several changes to the pre-service teacher education system. A survey by CENTA of 12,690 teachers showed that 68 per cent of the teachers favoured merit-based career paths. Among these, the largest percentage (47 per cent) voted for teacher competencies as the primary parameter to determine merit as opposed to student learning outcomes, hours spent in training and other factors.

Improving Quality of Teaching, Not Just Teachers

Given that school infrastructure and expenditure on education do not seem to correlate strongly with learning outcomes of students, we need to focus on the actual process of teaching and learning as it happens inside a classroom. A seminal study on Tennessee students found that if two average eight-year-old students were placed under a high-performing and low-performing teacher, respectively, the students' performance differs by over 50 percentile points within three years, thus emphasizing the importance of teacher quality.[135]

Most existing commentary on the issue of teaching effectiveness emphasizes the need to recruit strong candidates as teachers, train them well, give them the right incentives, and monitor and evaluate them appropriately. While creating a pipeline of strong teachers is important, an excessive reliance on high-quality teachers is unsustainable. In any profession, talent comes at a steep price. For operations as large in scale as the national education apparatus, deputing high-quality teachers in every classroom of every school in every village of the country is simply infeasible. The availability of such high-quality talent is limited and will continue to be so, particularly in the short to medium run, during which there is bound to be a sizeable number of low- and average-quality teachers in the system. Moreover, it is not possible to monitor the qualitative aspects of teaching such as the relationships and atmosphere a teacher fosters in the classroom.

It is, therefore, desirable that the education policy focusses not just on the teacher alone but also other easily controllable aspects of the school system. Thus, improving teaching effectiveness must involve a two-fold strategy: improve the quality of teachers and enable high-quality teaching even without high-quality teachers. In other words, while recognizing that the quality of teachers cannot and should not be compromised, it is simultaneously important to address the fact that teachers will exhibit wide variations in the quality and style of teaching, not all of which can be monitored and corrected. Therefore, there should be in place strong systems and processes that ensure that even classrooms with average-quality teachers are not deprived of opportunities to learn well.

The idea is summarized in Table 1: a high-quality teacher is a sufficient condition for a child to learn well, but not a necessary one.

---

[135]Sanders, W.L., and J.C. Rivers, *Cumulative and Residual Effects of Teachers on Future Student Academic Achievement*, University of Tennessee Value-Added Research and Assessment Center, November 1996, http://tinyurl.com/97a56nsv. Accessed on 8 February 2024.

Table 1
Impact of teacher quality and teaching processes on learning

	Low-quality teacher	*High-quality teacher*
Low-quality systems	Poor learning	High-quality learning
High-quality systems	Medium- to high-quality learning	High-quality learning

Standardized Teaching Notes: Learning from Business Schools

At Harvard Business School, professors who teach the core curriculum in the first year of the MBA programme coordinate not just on the material that is to be taught to students but the pedagogical methods as well. If professors at Harvard Business School, who are, of course, high-quality teachers, find value in standardizing the learning process, then it is clear that there is a strong case for standardization of the learning process. This standardization of process to ensure high quality is a business model that is followed by several successful multinational firms, such as McDonald's, Subway, Starbucks, etc.

Inspired by these successful examples, the NEP must focus on developing standardized processes and manuals to address poor quality of instruction. This process/manual should be developed separately for each subject and for each class through a method that resembles the reviewing process in academic journals. For each combination of the triad—class, language of instruction and subject—an editorial team comprised of the senior-most teachers in that triad must be created. This editorial team will break up the syllabus in that subject into lessons. For each such lesson, the editors would seek submissions from the teachers. Each submission would be first filtered by the editorial team for passing a minimum level of quality; this would be a cursory examination that would decide if the submission is good enough to be sent for peer review. Each submission selected for peer review would then be submitted for the same. The editorial team would be required to create guidelines for peer review. Members of the editorial team would be paid 'overtime' and their teaching/administrative responsibilities would be minimal for the one-to-two-year period required to complete the standardization process. Submitters and peer reviewers would not get any reduction in their teaching/administrative responsibilities. However, both would be paid for their respective submissions if the manuscripts/peer reviews are accepted. The manuscripts that are accepted would receive a reward of ₹50,000, while each accepted review would receive a reward of ₹20,000. Each editor would be paid ₹20 lakh for the duration of the assignment.

As shown in Table 2, the budget required for generating this manual would be less than ₹2,000 crore.

Table 2
Budget for generating standardized teaching manuals across 12 major boards

	Number Required	*Per Unit Payment*	*Total Budget*
Editorial team (3 members)	12 classes × 12 major languages × 5 subjects = 720. Three editors for each = 2,160. Round off to approximately 2,000.	₹20 lakh per editor	₹40 crore
Successfully accepted submissions	Assuming 20 lessons in each triad of (class, lesson, subject), 720 × 20=14,400. Three best submissions accepted in each. So total of 43,200 successful submissions. Round off to 45,000 submissions.	₹1 lakh per successful submission	₹450 crore
Reviewers	Same as above	₹50,000 per review for a successful submission	₹225 crore
Testing Apparatus	National Testing Service to design tests that check the understanding of teachers on their conceptual understanding and the teaching manual.		₹1,285 crore
Total			₹2,000 crore

The peer reviews would be conducted anonymously to allow the reviewers to offer their honest feedback. Two sequential rounds of reviews would be conducted. In the first round, reviewers would either reject the submission or seek a revision in the manuscript. In the second round, the manuscripts would be resubmitted after incorporating the comments received from the reviewers. The revised manuscript would be sent to the same reviewer(s) for them to decide if the resubmission has adequately addressed the comments provided in the first round of review. If the resubmission is assessed to have not incorporated the comments, the manuscript can be rejected in the second round as well. The editor would assess using the peer-review report if the reviewer's comments are valid and decide on the status of the manuscript submission.

Periodic Teacher Evaluation

India can learn from the experience of Australia, which places teachers in one of four categories of competency: graduate, proficient, highly accomplished and lead. Each level comes with a detailed list of requirements and competencies that teachers must demonstrate to be awarded that qualification—they are assessed not just on their knowledge of the subject matter, but also on their pedagogical methods. Such a comprehensive list of competencies helps teachers understand their current level and set goals for each stage of their career. In this evaluation, the standardized learning plans described above can be used to test the teachers' proficiency in pedagogical methods. Each teacher in a class would be evaluated on their proficiency in the conceptual material necessary for that class subject as well as their understanding of the teaching manual.

Teacher Recruitment

There is a severe mismatch of demand and supply for teachers, with many schools facing an acute shortage of staff. The challenge in recruiting high-quality teachers is evident in the fact that less than 10 per cent of teachers and teacher aspirants pass the Teacher Eligibility Test (TET), a mandatory requirement to teach in public schools.[136] To achieve the balance between demand and supply of teachers in India, it is crucial to increase the number of teachers. This would need improvements

---

[136]KPMG and CII, *Improving Learning Outcomes by Raising In-Class Teacher Effectiveness*, December 2017, http://tinyurl.com/4mkj48cw. Accessed on 8 January 2024.

in the quality of candidates who enrol for teacher training and write the TET, which, in turn, would require improvements in the education system that produces these aspiring teacher candidates in the first place. Put differently, India needs to get out of this chicken-and-egg situation wherein poor learning outcomes create poor teachers who then create poor learning outcomes for the next generation of students, and so on.

India can learn from the experience of the world's top-performing education systems—Singapore, Finland and South Korea—which, not coincidentally, have also succeeded in attracting and retaining highly talented candidates for teachers. A McKinsey study examines what these countries do differently and highlights the following.[137] First, they make admission to teacher training programmes highly selective. Second, they pay for candidates' tuition and/or offer a living stipend for the duration of study. These initiatives make teaching an aspirational profession, as the entry requirements to any profession determine the prestige associated with it. A profession's prestige, in turn, attracts talent.

Teacher Training

Teacher training programmes in India often follow a one-size-fits-all approach. An NCERT study finds that teacher feedback is seldom incorporated systematically into designing in-service trainings, and training content is seldom tailored to local needs or issues. Only 35 per cent of teachers nationwide received in-service training, and only about half of these teachers found the trainings relevant.[138] In fact, teachers often complain that the same subject or topic is repeated in successive trainings over the years, adding little value to a teacher's repertoire of skills.

The model of teacher training itself needs revision. First, as research by Karthik Muralidharan demonstrates, a content-analysis examination of even the more advanced teacher training programmes reveals a predominant emphasis on subjects such as history, theory, sociology,

---

[137]Auguste, Byron, Paul Kihn, and Matt Miller, *Closing the Talent Gap: Attracting and Retaining Top-Third Graduates to Careers in Teaching*, McKinsey & Company, September 2010, http://tinyurl.com/696jka52. Accessed on 8 February 2024.

[138]Dhawan, Ashish, 'Restoring Dignity to the Teaching Profession in India', *Ideas for India*, 7 February 2014, http://tinyurl.com/bdhfzcdw. Accessed on 8 February 2024.

and philosophy of education, with minimal attention given to pedagogy and practical training.[139] In contrast, international evidence suggests that the most successful professional role-training incorporates substantial investment in the theory underlying the subject as well as practical experience and on-the-job learning. Second, the training curriculum is developed at the state level with experts training 'master trainers' at the same level. These master trainers then pass on the training to smaller resource groups at the district and block levels. Finally, these resource groups impart the training to elementary school teachers every year. Such a cascading model hinders the flow of feedback from the bottom-most level (teachers) to the top (state). Also, it dilutes quality of training as it trickles down from the top to the bottom. In contrast, tailoring teacher training to achieving proficiency in the teaching manuals described earlier can make teacher training effective. As teacher evaluation tests use these teaching manuals, teachers would also have the incentive to take these training programmes seriously. Setting up of a few apex teacher training institutes in each state in highly reputable institutes could also contribute significantly to training high-quality teachers.

Prahar: Ensuring Age-Appropriate Proficiency to Read, Write and Do Math

Given the learning deficits in reading, writing and mathematics, which we discussed earlier, ensuring age-appropriate proficiency of children in their mother tongue or regional language as well as in mathematical skills is critical. The effort should be continuous to ensure that this proficiency is developed even for the students that are lagging the most. To ensure this, the following steps for this initiative called Prahar must become part of the regular learning process:

1. Formative assessment: Using a standardized test along the lines of the *Foundational Learning Study 2022*, conduct a formative assessment every year of all enrolled students across all classes to ascertain functional ability to read and write. For this purpose,

[139]Muralidharan, Karthik, 'Reforming the Indian School Education System', *What the Economy Needs Now*, Abhijit Banerjee, Gita Gopinath, Raghuram Rajan, and Mihir Sharma (eds), Juggernaut, 2019.

create a national school-testing agency as an independent joint-venture between National Testing Service-India (NTS-I) and one or more private entities focussed on school education such as ConveGenius. The national school-testing agency would be entrusted with the responsibility to create and administer the tests.

2. Assign each student an initial Prahar-RW for competence in reading and writing and Prahar-M score for competence in mathematics. These scores would capture the assessment of foundational proficiency.
3. For those students whose competence is not up to the age-appropriate level, create four different categories in decreasing level of competence as measured in Step 3. Category 4 corresponds to the highest level of focus required, while Category 1 corresponds to the lowest level of attention and effort required.
4. Prahar: Initiate a 100-day intensive programme aimed at enhancing functional ability in mathematics and achieving age-appropriate reading and writing skills. This 100-day focussed teaching session will be conducted during the summer and Dussehra/Diwali vacations to bridge the gap before students go into the next class.
5. Re-assessment: Students will be moved across Prahar levels based on re-assessment every fortnight or month during the 100-day intensive programme.
6. Assign a class to older, previously unenrolled students: Older students who were previously not enrolled in schools may be assigned a suitable class based on their proficiency on the hundredth day of Prahar, allowing them to integrate into formal education.
7. Repeat the exercise every year during the summer break to effectively bridge learning deficits and provide opportunity for re-entry into formal schooling.
8. In order to assess learning progress, formative assessments will be undertaken annually by the national school-testing agency in a representative sample of all children.
9. Incentives that recognize and reward high performance at various levels—including state, district and school—and individual teacher achievements must be built-in.

Apart from the above, the objective of regular exams must evolve alongside the changing competence that students need to acquire. Today, factual information is easily available on the Internet via smartphones that are quite commonly owned even by the poorer sections of society. So, the need for memorization and regurgitation of facts/information in exams has drastically reduced. In contrast, among quantitative disciplines, the crucial skill lies in analysing problems by breaking them down into smaller components that align with previously learned concepts. This process involves applying the learned concept to that smaller piece of the problem, and subsequently synthesizing these smaller concepts to address the original problem. Acquiring this ability has become paramount for students in their learning journey. Therefore, exams should emphasize the ability to understand concepts, connect concepts across topics, and apply them creatively to solving newer problems in quantitative disciplines. Similarly, in qualitative disciplines, being able to understand different opinions on social/historical phenomena and then assess the merits and demerits of those opinions has become important. Therefore, exams should focus on the ability to critically evaluate diverse viewpoints on historical/social phenomena.

◆

As shown in Chapter 4, every country that has experienced high growth over a sustained period of time has achieved this by prioritizing education to develop a well-trained workforce. Therefore, India needs to place strong emphasis on high-quality education for its children and youth. As capital, labour and productivity together create economic growth, India's growth since the 1990s has manifested more from growth in capital and productivity, with labour contributing very little. Such a growth pattern exacerbates inequality in society and creates fault lines. In contrast, growth that also includes labour growth leads to sustained and equitably distributed prosperity. As education is critical to growth in which labour derives a significant share, high-quality education must remain a priority. While the NEP constitutes an important step in this direction, other policy steps must complement this important initiative.

ACKNOWLEDGEMENTS

Writing a book is never a solitary endeavour; it's a culmination of support, inspiration and collaboration from various corners. *India@100* has been a labour of love, made possible by the invaluable contributions and encouragement of many individuals. The idea for this book germinated while I was working on the Economic Surveys for the Government of India. So, my first share of gratitude goes to the outstanding team of young Indian Economic Service Officers that formed *TeamCEA* at the Ministry of Finance—Surbhi (who ably led the team), Sanjana, Tulsipriya, Amit, Aakansha, Kapil, Shreya, Gurwinder, Sonali, Rahul, Deekhsa, Neha, Abinash, Abhishek, Anshuman, Bharadwaj and Ritika. Thanks also goes to my colleagues Sanjeev Sanjal, A. Srija, Rajiv Mishra and Chandni Raina for their important contributions.

My brother Prof. Krishnamurthy Vaidyanathan (Indian School of Business [ISB]) has been the constant contributor to my intellectual journey. During the writing of the Economic Surveys, he was my first port of call at every stage—brainstorming, ideation, research, writing and proofreading. I always feel confident to take on the entire world once I have convinced him about an idea or its execution because while he's a well-wisher, he is also a strong critic.

My wife Kavita, who is my biggest fan and staunchest critic rolled into one, endured long periods of solitariness as her price for supporting this labour of love. I was privileged to have my wife as the taskmaster who pushed me to skip that weekend Bollywood movie to work on the next chapter of the book.

My Amma is my source of self-confidence. When she utters the magical words, 'Of course, you can do it!', then all the naysayers in the world become irrelevant. The boundless love and infectious enthusiasm of my beloved children, Ramya and Rishabh, always remains my best tonic, a reminder of what truly matters in life amidst the demands of writing.

I am deeply grateful to my intellectual home, the esteemed ISB, where I have had the privilege of serving as a professor. Its vibrant academic community, innovative spirit and commitment to excellence have been instrumental in shaping my scholarly journey. My thanks particularly to Dean Madan for his constant support, and my colleagues Professors Prasanna, Shashwat, Bhagwan, Shiv, Deepa and Anand for the stimulating discussions. I cannot thank my extremely able research associates, Tushar and Naina, enough for all their research support.

To several of my dear friends—both from IIT Kanpur and IIM Calcutta—and my colleagues, my loving thanks for patiently responding to my ideas and providing valuable feedback.

I am grateful to the team at Rupa, especially Yamini Chowdhury, Aditi Mehrotra, Kapish Mehra and Harshita Sabharwal, whose professionalism, expertise and dedication have been indispensable in bringing this project to fruition.

Last, but not least, I express my deepest appreciation to the readers of *India@100*. I sincerely hope that this book sparks conversations, ignites imaginations and contributes to a deeper understanding of India's exciting future. Hope you enjoy reading the book as much as I enjoyed penning it.

Thank you, one and all, for being a part of this enriching journey.

NOTES

Chapter 1: Tomorrow's Economic Powerhouse

Asea, Patrick K. and W. Max Corden. 1994. 'The Balassa–Samuelson Model: An Overview.' *Review of International Economics* 2, no. 3: 191–200.

Balassa, Bela. 1964. 'The Purchasing-Power Parity Doctrine: A Reappraisal.' *The Journal of Political Economy* 72: 584–96.

Bordo, Michael D., et al. 2017. 'The Real Exchange Rate in the Long Run: Balassa–Samuelson Effects Reconsidered.' *Journal of International Money and Finance* 75: 69–92.

Choudhri, Ehsan U., and Mohsin S. Khan. 2005. 'Real Exchange Rates in Developing Countries: Are Balassa–Samuelson Effects Present?' *IMF Staff Papers* 52, no. 3: 387–409.

Economic Survey 2018–19. Volume 1, Chapter 2. Government of India; Ministry of Finance. July 2019.

Economic Survey 2018–19. Volume 1, Chapter 7. Government of India; Ministry of Finance. July 2019.

Ernst-Young (EY). 2023. *India@100 Report: Realizing the Potential of a US$ 26 Trillion Economy*. http://tinyurl.com/42zdb5ky. Accessed on 30 January 2024.

Gente, Karine. 2006. 'The Balassa–Samuelson Effect in a Developing Country.' *Review of Development Economics* 10, no. 4: 683–99.

Goldman Sachs. 2022. 'The Global Economy in 2075: Growth Slows as Asia Rises.' http://tinyurl.com/22busc3e. Accessed on 30 January 2024.

Harberger, Arnold C. 2003. 'Economic Growth and the Real Exchange Rate: Revisiting the Balassa–Samuelson Effect.' Paper presented at a conference organized by the Higher School of Economics, Moscow.

Hassan, Fadi. 2016. 'The Price of Development: The Penn–Balassa–Samuelson Effect Revisited.' *Journal of International Economics* 102: 291–309.

Samuelson, Paul A. 'Facets of Balassa–Samuelson Thirty Years Later.' *Review of International Economics* 2, no. 3 (1994): 201–26.

Samuelson, Paul A. 1964. 'Theoretical Notes on Trade Problems.' *The Review of Economics and Statistics*: 145–54.

UNDP World Population Prospects 2022. United Nations; Department of Economic and Social Affairs. http://tinyurl.com/s98pbzsj. Accessed on 30 January 2024.

Chapter 2: Unleashing Economic Potential

C. Rangarajan, and D.K. Srivastava. 2017. 'Underlying Drivers of India's Potential Growth.' *EPW* 52, no. 25–6.

Domar, E. [1946] 1957a. 'Capital Expansion, Rate of Growth, and Employment.' *Econometrica* 14: 137–47. As reproduced in Domar, pp. 70–82.

Economic Survey 2018–19. Volume 1, Chapter 7. Government of India; Ministry of Finance. July 2019. http://tinyurl.com/5ccw6unz. Accessed on 1 February 2024.

Jorgenson, Dale W. 1991. 'Productivity and Economic Growth.' *Fifty Years of Economic Measurement: The Jubilee of the Conference on Research in Income and Wealth*, edited by Ernst R. Berndt and Jack E. Triplett. University of Chicago Press. http://tinyurl.com/2spm24wa. Accessed on 1 February 2024.

K. Vaidyanathan, and K.V. Subramanian. 2022. *Money: A Zero-Sum Game*. Krishnamurthy Vaidyanathan.

Chapter 3: Four Pillars of Progress

'Watershed Moment.' *The Hindu Businessline*. 11 February 2021. http://tinyurl.com/5ffchwtw. Accessed on 9 January 2024.

Economic Survey 2018–19. Volume 1, Chapter 1. Government of India; Ministry of Finance. July 2019.

Forrester, Jay. 2013. 'Economic Theory for the New Millennium.' *System Dynamics Review* 29: 26–41. doi: 10.1002/sdr.1490.

Li, David Daokui, and Eric S. Maskin. 2021. 'Government and Economics: An Emerging Field of Study.' *Journal of Government and Economics* 1: 100005.

Lin, Justin Yifu. 2011. 'New Structural Economics: A Framework for Rethinking Development.' *The World Bank Research Observer* 26, no. 2: 193–221.

Lin, Justin Yifu. 2021. 'New Structural Economics: A Framework of Studying Government and Economics.' *Journal of Government and Economics* 2: 100014.

Prime Minister Narendra Modi. 2021. 'Reply on Motion of Thanks to the President's Address.' 10 February 2021. http://tinyurl.com/3bkj6639. Accessed on 9 January 2024.

Chapter 4: Beyond Copy-Paste

Bose, Sukanya, and N.R. Bhanumurthy. 2013. 'Fiscal Multipliers of India.' Working paper 2013–125, NIPFP.

Economic Survey 2019–20. Volume 1, Chapter 1. Government of India; Ministry of Finance. July 2019.

Economic Survey 2020–21. Volume 1, Chapter 1. Government of India; Ministry of Finance. July 2020.

Economic Survey 2020–21. Volume 1, Chapter 3. Government of India; Ministry of Finance. July 2020.

Friedman, Milton. 1957. *A Theory of the Consumption Function*. Princeton University Press.

Goyal, Ashima, and Bhavya Sharma. 2018. 'Government Expenditure in India: Composition and Multipliers.' *Journal of Quantitative Economics* 16, no. 1: 47–85.

Kapoor, Amit, and Richard Dasher. 2023. 'Healing the Economy: Estimating the Economic Impact of India's Vaccination and Related Measures.' Working paper, IFC.

SBI Research. 2022. 'Executive Summary: How ECLGS Scheme Saved MSME Sector.' *The ECLGS that Saved 13.5 Lakh MSME Units, 1.5 Crore Jobs & 14% of Outstanding MSME Loans Turning into NPA*. p. 1.

World Bank. National Accounts data and World Development Indicators database; Emerging & developing Asia as defined in World Economic Outlook.

Chapter 5: The Middle-Income Trap Is Not Destiny

'Nourishing Dwarfs to Become Giants: Reorienting Policies for MSME Growth.' *Economic Survey 2018–19*. Volume 1, Chapter 3. Government of India; Ministry of Finance. July 2019.

Aiyar, Shekhar, et al. 2013. 'Growth Slowdowns and the Middle-Income Trap.' IMF Working Paper 13/71, Asia and Pacific Department.

Bulman, David, Maya Eden and Ha Nguyen. 2014. 'Transitioning from Low-Income Growth to High-Income Growth: Is There a Middle-Income Trap?' World Bank Policy Research Working Paper No. 7104.

Eichengreen, Barry, Park Donghyun and Shin Kwanho. 2013. 'Growth Slowdowns Redux: New Evidence on the Middle-Income Trap.' NBER Working Paper 18673.

Eichengreen, Barry. 2011. 'Escaping the Middle-Income Trap.' *Achieving Maximum Long-Run Growth*. Kansas: Federal Reserve Bank of Kansas City, pp. 409–19.

Engel, Jakob, and Daria Taglioni. 2017. 'The Middle-Income Trap and Upgrading along Global Value Chains.' WTO Working Paper.

Federal Reserve Economic Data on GDP per capita of Latin American economies.

Gill, Indermit S., and Homi Kharas. 2015. 'The Middle-Income Trap Turns Ten.' World Bank Policy Research Paper 7403.

Kim B. 2023. 'How to Escape the Middle-Income Trap: Lessons for the ODA Policy.' *Journal of Policy Studies* 38, no. 1: 45–58.

World Bank data on average growth rate in GDP per capita across various economies.

Zhou SJ, and Hu AG. 2021. 'What Is the "Middle Income Trap"?' *China: Surpassing the 'Middle Income Trap'*. Singapore: Palgrave Macmillan, pp. 1–32.

Chapter 6: Inequality and Growth

Agrawal, Pradeep. 2015. 'Reducing Poverty in India: The Role of Economic Growth.' IEG Working Paper No. 349.

Brady, David. 2003. 'Rethinking the Sociological Measurement of Poverty.' *Social Forces* 81: 715–52.

Cervone, Carmen, and Andrea Scatolon. 2019. 'Fair Enough? The Inequality Paradox, Inequality Awareness, and System Justification.' *The Inquisitive Mind* no. 41. https://tinyurl.com/23jmaktw. Accessed on 15 April 2024.

Curtis, J., and R. Andersen. 2015. 'How Social Class Shapes Attitudes on Economic Inequality: The Competing Forces of Self-Interest and Legitimation.' *International Review of Social Research* 5, no. 1: 4–19.

Engel, Jakob, and Daria Taglioni. 2017. 'The Middle-Income Trap and Upgrading along Global Value Chains.' WTO Working Paper.

Feldstein, Martin. 1999. 'Reducing Poverty, Not Inequality.' *The Public Interest*: 33–41.

Frohlich, Norman, Joe A. Oppenheimer and Cheryl L. Eavey. 1987. 'Laboratory Results on Rawls's Distributive Justice.' *British Journal of Political Science* 17: 1–21.

Henderson, David. 2018. 'Income Inequality Isn't the Problem.' *Hoover Institution*. https://tinyurl.com/5emenjev. Accessed on 15 April 2024.

Iceland, John. 2003. *Poverty in America*. Berkeley: University of California Press.

Jones, Charles I. 2015. 'The Economic Determinants of Top Income Inequality.' *Inequality & Economic Policy*, edited by Tom Church, Chris Miller and John B. Taylor. Hoover Institution, Stanford University.

Karadja, M., J. Mollerstrom and D. Seim. 2017. '(And Holier) Than Thou? The Effect of Relative Income Improvements on Demand for Redistribution.' *Review of Economics and Statistics* 99, no. 2: 201–12.

Kiatpongsan, S., and M. Norton. 2014. 'How Much (More) Should CEOs Make? A Universal Desire for More Equal Pay.' *Perspectives on Psychological Science* 9, no. 6: 587–93.

Kim B. 2023. 'How to Escape the Middle-Income Trap: Lessons for the ODA Policy.' *Journal of Policy Studies* 38, no. 1: 45–58.

Kraay, A. 2004. 'When Is Growth Pro-Poor? Cross-Country Evidence.' International Monetary Fund Working Paper WP/04/47.

Meyer, Bruce. 2014. 'When It Comes to Inequality Consumption Is What Matters.' *Income Inequality in America: Myths and Facts*. https://tinyurl.com/3udtfmpy. Accessed on 15 April 2024.

Miller, Matthew. 2003. *The Two Percent Solution*. New York: Public Affairs.

Mulligan, Casey B. 2015. 'The Effects of Redistribution Policies on Growth and Employment.' *Inequality & Economic Policy*, edited by Tom Church, Chris Miller and John B. Taylor. Hoover Institution, Stanford University.

Norton, M., and D. Ariely. 2011. 'Building a Better America—One Wealth Quintile at a

Time.' *Perspectives on Psychological Science* 6, no. 1. doi: 10.1177/174569161039352.

Picketty, Thomas. 2013. *Capital in the Twenty First Century*. MA: Harvard University Press.

Picketty, Thomas. 2020. *Capital and Ideology*. The Belknap Press of Harvard University Press.

Rawls, John. 1971. *A Theory of Justice*. Cambridge, MA: Harvard University Press.

Roemer, John E. 1998. *Equality of Opportunity*. Cambridge, MA: Harvard University Press.

Smith, Noah. 2014. 'What's Wrong with Ignoring Inequality.' *Bloomberg*. 2 October 2014. https://tinyurl.com/ycy8dmu6. Accessed on 15 April 2024.

Wilkinson, Richard G., and Kate E. Pickett. 2009. 'Income Inequality and Social Dysfunction.' *Annual Review of Sociology* 35: 493–511.

World Bank. 2000. *India Reducing Poverty, Accelerating Development. A World Bank Country Study*. Oxford University Press.

Zhou SJ, and Hu AG. 2021. 'What Is the "Middle Income Trap"?' *China: Surpassing the 'Middle Income Trap'*. Singapore: Palgrave Macmillan, pp. 1–32.

Chapter 7: Correlation vs Causation

Bajpai, N. 2011. 'Global Financial Crisis, Its Impact on India and the Policy Response.' Working Paper No. 5, Columbia Global Centers, South Asia, Columbia University.

Blanchard, Olivier. 2019. 'Public Debt and Low Interest Rates.' *American Economic Review* 109, no. 4: 1197–229.

Economic Survey 2020–21. Volume 1, Chapter 2. Government of India; Ministry of Finance. July 2020.

Herndon, Thomas, Michael Ash and Robert Pollin. 2013. 'Does High Public Debt Consistently Stifle Economic Growth? A Critique of Reinhart and Rogoff.' Working Paper No. 322, Political Economy Research Institute.

IMF and World Bank. Data for debt-GDP ratio across countries.

Panizza, Ugo, and Andrea F. Presbitero. 2012. 'Public Debt and Economic Growth: Is There a Causal Effect?' Working Paper No. 65, Money and Finance Research Group, 2012.

Pescatori, Andrea, Damiano Sandri and John Simon. 2014. 'Debt and Growth: Is There a Magic Threshold?' Working Paper No. 2014/034, IMF.

Reinhart, Carmen M., and Kenneth S. Rogoff. 2010. 'Growth in a Time of Debt.' *American Economic Review* 100, no. 2: 573–8.

Reinhart, Carmen M., Vincent R. Reinhart and Kenneth S. Rogoff. 2012. 'Public Debt Overhangs: Advanced-Economy Episodes since 1800.' *Journal of Economic Perspectives* 26, no. 3: 69–86.

Chapter 8: Reclaiming Justice

'Ending Matsyanyaya: How to Ramp up Capacity in the Lower Judiciary.' *Economic Survey 2018–19*. Volume 1, Chapter 9. Government of India; Ministry of Finance. July 2019.

Dutta, Pratik, et al. 2019. 'How to Modernise the Working of Courts and Tribunals in India.' Working Paper Series No. 258, NIPFP.

European Union. 2018. *European Judicial Systems: Efficiency and Quality of Justice*. CEPEJ Studies No. 26. Brussels: Council of Europe.

Kautilya. 1956. *Arthashastra*, translated by R. Shamasastry. Parimal Publications Pvt Ltd. http://tinyurl.com/25fw46xm. Accessed on 14 December 2023.

Supreme Court of India. 2018. *Indian Judiciary: Annual Report 2017–2018*. New Delhi.

Supreme Court of India. Court News. 2018. Data for High Courts and Subordinate Courts is from the National Judicial Data Grid (NJDG) and data for the Supreme Court of India is from its website.

Chapter 9: Revitalizing the Steel Frame

Administrative Reforms Commission, Government of India. n.d. 'Second Administrative Reforms Commission.' *Department of Administrative Reforms and Public Grievances*. https://tinyurl.com/3h299tcw. Accessed on 15 April 2024.

Administrative Reforms Commission, Government of India. 2008. *Second Administrative Reforms Commission: Refurbishing of Personnel Administration: Scaling New Heights*. 10th Report. Department of Public Grievances and Redressal. https://tinyurl.com/3eyrd9b8. Accessed on 15 April 2024.

Agarwal, O.P., and T.V. Somanathan. 2005. 'Public Policy Making in India: Issues and Remedies.' Occasional Paper, Centre for Policy Research, New Delhi.

Aiyar, Yamini, Ambrish Dongre and Vincy Davis. 2015. 'Education Reforms, Bureaucracy and the Puzzles of Implementation: A case study from Bihar.' Working Paper, International Growth Centre.

Aiyar, Yamini, and Mekhala Krishnamurthy. 2020. 'Lateral Entry, Biometric Attendance Won't Fix Modi's Bureaucracy Issue. Reinvest in the State.' *The Print*. https://tinyurl.com/4h635bc3. Accessed on 15 April 2024.

Aiyar, Yamini. 2020. 'Look beyond Rules to Reform the Bureaucracy.' *Hindustan Times*. https://tinyurl.com/ywv8t2s3. Accessed on 15 April 2024.

Ashraf, Nawa, and Oriana Bandiera. 2018. 'Social Incentives in Organizations.' *Annual Review of Economics* 10: 439–63.

Bandiera, Oriana, et al. 2020. 'The Allocation of Authority in Organizations: A Field Experiment with Bureaucrats.' NBER Working Papers 26733, National Bureau of Economic Research.

Banuri, Sheheryar, and Philip Keefer. 2013. 'Intrinsic Motivation, Effort and the Call to Public Service.' World Bank Policy Research Working Paper No. 6729. https://tinyurl.com/4yxpeyku. Accessed on 15 April 2024.

Bertrand, Marianne, et al. 2015. 'Determinants and Consequences of Bureaucrat Effectiveness: Evidence from the Indian Administrative Service.' https://tinyurl.com/bd6ym4en. Accessed on 15 April 2024.

Bertrand, Marianne, et al. 2020. 'The Glittering Prizes: Career Incentives and Bureaucrat Performance.' *The Review of Economic Studies* 87, no. 2: 626–55. doi: 10.1093/restud/rdz029.

Bó, Ernesto Dal, Frederico Finan and Martín A. Rossi. 2013. 'Strengthening State Capabilities: The Role of Financial Incentives in the Call to Public Service.' *The Quarterly Journal of Economics* 128, no. 3: 1169–218. https://www.jstor.org/stable/26372521. Accessed on 15 April 2024.

Business Standard. 2012. 'We Cannot Have a 100% Risk-Averse Bureaucracy: Edited Excerpt from Prime Minister Manmohan Singh's Speech on Civil Services Day on April 21 in New Delhi.' https://tinyurl.com/5365zfby. Accessed on 15 April 2024.

Dasgupta, A., and Devesh Kapur. 2020. 'The Political Economy of Bureaucratic Overload: Evidence from Rural Development Officials in India.' *American Political Science Review* 114, no. 4: 1316–34. doi: 10.1017/S0003055420000477.

Ghate, Prabhu. 1998. 'Reforming the Civil Service: Meeting Crucial Need for Expertise.' *Economic and Political Weekly* 33, no. 7: 359–65. https://tinyurl.com/mtu6jep7. Accessed on 15 April 2024.

Gupta, Akhil. 2012. *Red Tape: Bureaucracy, Structural Violence, and Poverty in India*. Duke University Press.

Hanna, Rema, and Wang Shing-Yi. 2017. 'Dishonesty and Selection into Public Service: Evidence from India.' *American Economic Journal: Economic Policy* 9 (3): 262–90. doi: 10.1257/pol.20150029.

Iyer, Lakshmi, and Anandi Mani. 2012. 'Traveling Agents: Political Change and Bureaucratic Turnover in India.' *Review of Economics and Statistics* 94 (3): 723–739. doi: 10.1162/rest_a_00183.

Kahneman, Daniel, and Amos Tversky. 1979. 'Prospect Theory: An Analysis of Decision Under Risk.' *Econometrica* 47: 263–91.

Kapur, Devesh, Pratap Bhanu Mehta and Milan Vaishnav (eds). 2018. *Rethinking Public Institutions in India*. Oxford University Press.

Kapur, Devesh. 2020. 'Why Does the Indian State Both Fail and Succeed?' *Journal of Economic Perspectives* 34, no. 1: 31–54.

Krishnan, K.P., and T.V. Somanathan. 2017. 'The Civil Service.' *Rethinking Public Institutions in India*. Oxford University Press. pp. 339–417.

Mathur, Kuldeep, and Navdeep Mathur. 2017. 'Assessing Administrative Reform in India.' *Chinese Political Science Review* 2: 40–55.

Merchant, Minhaz. 2012. 'Indian Asphyxiation Service (IAS).' *Economic Times Blog*. https://tinyurl.com/mpcse9hx. Accessed on 15 April 2024.

Muralidharan, Karthik. 2016. 'A New Approach to Public Sector Hiring in India for Improved Service Delivery.' *India Policy Forum, National Council of Applied Economic Research* 12, no. 1: 187–236.

Singh, Deepali, and Nafees A. Ansari. 2007. 'Administrative Reforms in India: An Overview.' *Indian Journal of Public Administration* 53, no. 3: 476–85.

Singh, Narinder. 2013. 'Civil Service Reforms in India: A Review.' *Journal of Politics and Governance* 2, no. 1, 2: 251–8.

Sneha, P., et al. 2021. 'Bureaucratic Indecision and Risk Aversion in India.' *Indian Public Policy Review* 2, no. 6 (Nov–Dec): 55–87.

Somanathan, T. V., and Gulzar Natarajan. 2022. *State Capability in India*. Oxford University Press.

Sumana, K. 2014. 'Administrative Reforms Committees in India-a Study.' *International Journal of Physical and Social Sciences* 4, no. 9: 455–64.

Tummala, Krishna K. 2002. 'Administrative reforms in India.' *Administrative Reforms in Developing Nations*. Westport: Praeger Publishers. pp. 29–48.

Vaishnav, Milan, and Saksham Khosla. 2016. *The Indian Administrative Service Meets Big Data*. Carnegie Endowment for International Peace. https://tinyurl.com/r24mztbp. Accessed on 11 May 2024.

Chapter 10: Efficiency Redefined

'Ease of Doing Business.' *Economic Survey 2019–20*. Volume 1, Chapter 6. Government of India; Ministry of Finance. July 2019.

Black, J. 2001. 'Managing Discretion.' Presented at Penalties: Policy, Principles and Practice in Government Regulation, Australia.

Braithwaite, J., T. Makkai and V.A. Braithwaite. 2007. 'Dimensions of Ritualism.' *Regulating Aged Care: Ritualism and the New Pyramid*. Cheltenham, UK: Edward Elgar. pp. 235–6.

Department of Commerce Report. 2019. *Logistics Ease across Different States (LEADS Index)*.

Department of Commerce Report. 2019. *Report of the High-Level Advisory Group (HLAG)*.

Economic Survey 2020–21. Volume 1, Chapter 6. Government of India; Ministry of Finance. July 2020.

Knight, F. H. 1921. *Risk, Uncertainty, and Profit*. Boston, MA: Hart, Schaffner & Marx; Houghton Mifflin Company.

Knight, Frank. 2013. 'Risk, Uncertainty and Profit.' Vernon Press.

Niti Aayog. 2017. *Ease of Doing Business: An Enterprise Survey of Indian States*.

Simon, Herbert A. 1991. 'Bounded Rationality and Organizational Learning.' *Organization Science* 2, no. 1: 125–34.

The 'World Rule of Law Index' published by the World Justice Project.

World Bank. 2020. *Doing Business*. The World Bank Group. https://tinyurl.com/2cvvu7c2. Accessed on 15 April 2024.

Chapter 11: Empowerment through Employment

Aiello, Chloe. 2018. 'Elon Musk Admits Humans Are Sometimes Superior to Robots, in a Tweet about Tesla delays.' *CNBC*.

Autor, David. 2017. 'Will Automation Take Away All Our Jobs?' *Ideas.Ted.Com*. http://tinyurl.com/yf3wck3j. Accessed on 15 February 2024.

Economic Survey 2018–19. Volume 1. Government of India; Ministry of Finance. July 2019.

Hauge, Jostein, and Christian Parschau. 2020. 'Is Automation Stealing Manufacturing Jobs? Evidence from South Africa's Apparel Industry.' *LSE Blogs*.

Hsieh Chang-Tai and Peter J. Klenow. 2014. 'The Life Cycle of Plants in India and Mexico.' *The Quarterly Journal of Economics* 129, no. 3: 1035–84.

Jadhav, Radheshyam. 2024. 'How Atmanirbhar Bharat Rozgar Yojana Helped Foster Employment During the Pandemic.' *The Hindu Businessline*. http://tinyurl.com/5bkwvkue. Accessed on 15 February 2024.

McKinsey Global Institute. 2017. *A Future That Works: Automation, Employment and Productivity*.

Pethokoukis, James. 2017. 'Will Technology Enable Workers or Replace Them? A Long-Read Q&A with Daron Acemoglu.' *AEIdeas*. http://tinyurl.com/47w44xye. Accessed on 15 February 2024.

Rodrik, Dani, and Stefanie Stantcheva. 2021. 'Fixing Capitalism's Good Jobs Problem.' *Oxford Review of Economic Policy* 37, no. 4.

United Nations Conference on Trade and Development (NCTAD). 2017. *Beyond Austerity: Towards A Global New Deal*.

World Bank Group. 2016. *World Development Report 2016: Digital Dividends*.

Chapter 12: Run after Learning to Walk

Artuc, Erhan, et al. 2019. 'Exports to Jobs: Boosting the Gains from Trade in South Asia.' *South Asia Development Forum*, ILO. p. 86.

Boffa, M., et al. 2016. *Overcoming the Middle-Income Trap: The Role of GVC Integration for Climbing-Up the Income Ladder*. https://tinyurl.com/mw4ephe8/. Accessed on 11 May 2024.

Grossman, G.M., and Rossi-Hansberg. 2008. 'Trading Tasks: A Simple Theory of Offshoring.' *American Economic Review* 98, no. 5: 1978–97.

Hummels, D., and P.J. Klenow. 2005. 'The Variety and Quality of a Nation's Exports.' *American Economic Review* 95, no. 3: 704–23.

Indiacensus.net. 2024. 'Population Density.' https://tinyurl.com/bdh5x9dp. Accessed on 15 April 2024.

PWC. 2023. *India Calling: Decoding the Country's Electronics Manufacturing Journey and the Way Forward.*

Reshoring Institute. 2022. 'Reshoring White Paper: Global Labor Rate Comparisons.' https://tinyurl.com/ynw26s23. Accessed on 15 April 2024.

Satia, J.K., and P.S. Thomas. 1989. 'Maruti Udyog Limited.' *Vikalpa: The Journal for Decision Makers* 14, no. 3 (July–September).

Taglioni, D., and D. Winkler. 2016. *Making Global Value Chains Work for Development.* World Bank Group. doi: 10.1596/978-1-4648-0157-0.

Veeramani, C., and Garima Dhir. 2019. 'Dynamics and Determinants of Fragmentation Trade: Asian Countries in Comparative and Long-Term Perspective.' IGIDR Working Paper No WP-2019-040, Mumbai. https://tinyurl.com/3rm7fkwx. Accessed on 22 January 2024.

Veeramani, C., Lakshmi Aerath and Prachi Gupta. 2018. 'Intensive and Extensive Margins of Exports: What Can India Learn from China.' *The World Economy* 41, no. 5.

Chapter 13: Digital Bridges

Ease My Trip. 2022. *From Humble Beginnings to Global Prominence: 2021–22 Annual Report.* https://tinyurl.com/48eke6sr. Accessed on 15 April 2024.

India Brand Equity Foundation. 2023. *Ecommerce Industry Report.* https://tinyurl.com/muhersck. Accessed on 15 April 2024.

Internet and Mobile Association of India (IAMAI), and ICUBE 2018 report on Internet users in India.

McKinsey Global Institute. 2019. *Digital India.* http://tinyurl.com/54vr9veb. Accessed on 24 January 2024.

Press Information Bureau. 2015. 'Pradhan Mantri Jan Dhan Yojana (PMJDY), Launched by the Prime Minister Shri Narendra Modi on 28th August 2014, Celebrates Its First Anniversary.' http://tinyurl.com/2thxmy7j. Accessed on 22 January 2024.

Press Information Bureau. 2023. 'Total Digital Payment Transactions Volume Increases from 2,071 Crore in FY 2017–18 to 13,462 Crore in FY 2022–23 at a CAGR of 45 per cent: MoS Finance.' https://tinyurl.com/59xuj9br. Accessed on 15 April 2024.

Chapter 14: The Unfair Climate Divide

Anderson, Jason, and Camilla Bausch. 2006. *Climate Change and Natural Disasters: Scientific Evidence of a Possible Relation between Recent Natural Disasters and Climate Change.* https://tinyurl.com/2h2dkuw8. Accessed on 11 May 2024.

Burgess, et al. 2017. *Weather, Climate Change and Death in India.* https://tinyurl.com/7evc2eu3. Accessed on 15

Emissions data from Our World in Data based on Global Carbon Project, UNWPP and disasters data from EM-DAT.

Government of India's Home Ministry. Disaster Score Index for vulnerability of various states and districts.

Grinsted, A. 2013. 'An Estimate of Global Glacier Volume.' *The Cryosphere* 7: 141–51. doi: 10.5194/tc-7-141-2013.

Indian Agricultural Research Institute. 2016–17. *Annual Report 2016–17*. Government of India. https://tinyurl.com/mvns5anz. Accessed on 15 May 2024.

International Disaster Database. 1960–2022. 'Access Data.' *Public EM-DAT*. https://tinyurl.com/yb5znd5d. Accessed

National Centers for Environmental Information (NCEI). n.d. 'The Global Anomalies and Index Data.' https://tinyurl.com/bdzxsnkp. Accessed on 15 April 2024.

OXFAM. 2020. *Climate Finance Shadow Report 2020*. https://tinyurl.com/bdeuafex. Accessed on 15 April 2024.

Press Information Bureau. 2021. '(Frequently Asked Questions (FAQs): National Action Plan on Climate Change (NAPCC)'. https://tinyurl.com/52ueuh9f. Accessed on 15 May 2024.

Ritchie, Hannah. 2019. 'Who Has Contributed Most to Global CO2 emissions?' *Our World in Data*. https://tinyurl.com/4unac49f. Accessed on 15 April 2024.

The Intergovernmental Panel on Climate Change (IPCC). 2014. *AR-5 Synthesis Report on Climate Change*. https://tinyurl.com/jc9y9nmv. Accessed on 15 April 2024.

Webster, P.J., et al. 2005. 'Changes in Tropical Cyclone Number, Duration, and Intensity in a Warming Environment.' *Science* 309, no. 5742: 1844–6.

Chapter 15: Agrarian Renaissance

Chatterjee, Shoumitro. 2023. 'Market Power and Spatial Competition in Rural India.' *The Quarterly Journal of Economics* 138, no. 3: 1649–711.

Committee on Doubling Farmers' Income. 2018. *Committee Report*. 14 Volumes. Government of India; Ministry of Agriculture. https://tinyurl.com/2aysw8hj. Accessed on 15 April 2024.

Dasgupta, Kunal, and Rao, Rahul. 2022. 'Land Misallocation and Industrial Development.' IIM Bangalore Research Paper No. 668.

Economic Survey 2019–20 . Volume 1. Government of India; Ministry of Finance. July 2019.

Economic Survey 2020–21. Volume 1. Government of India; Ministry of Finance. July 2020.

Ghosh, Pulak, and Nishant Vats. 2022. 'Safety Nets, Credit, and Investment: Evidence from a Guaranteed Income Program.' *SSRN*. doi: 10.2139/ssrn.4265112.

Mukherjee, Dilip. 2016. 'Moving Past the Mandis: A Revolution Waiting to Happen.' *Ideas for India*. https://tinyurl.com/y5kp4xnz. Accessed on 15 April 2024.

Sharma, Vijay, and Harsh Wardhan. 2017. 'Overview of Indian Wheat Economy: Production, Procurement, and Marketed Surplus.' *Marketed and Marketable Surplus of Major Food Grains in India*. New Delhi: Springer. doi: 10.1007/978-81-322-3708-2_4.

Sharma, Vijay, and Harsh Wardhan. 2017. 'Overview of Rice Economy: Production, Procurement, and Marketed Surplus.' *Marketed and Marketable Surplus of Major Food Grains in India*. New Delhi: Springer. doi: 10.1007/978-81-322-3708-2_3.

Sharma, Vijay, and Harsh Wardhan. 2017. 'Summary, Concluding Observations, and Policy Implications.' *Marketed and Marketable Surplus of Major Food Grains in India*. New Delhi: Springer. doi: 10. 1007/978-81-322-3708-2_9.

Standing Committee on Agriculture (2018–2019). 2019. *Sixty Second Report: Agriculture Marketing and Role of Weekly Gramin Haats*. Lok Sabha Secretariat, New Delhi.

Chapter 16: Manifesting Dreams from Data

Economic Survey 2019–20 . Volume 1. Government of India; Ministry of Finance. July 2019.

Economic Survey 2020–21. Volume 1. Government of India; Ministry of Finance. July 2020.

Jayaram, Anup. 'Economic Survey 2020: The Thali, India's Own Big Mac Index.' *Business Today*.

Chapter 17: Responsible Prosperity

Aristotle. 1962. *Nicomachean Ethics*, translated by Martin Ostwald. Indianapolis: Bobbs-Merrill.

Coase, Ronald. 1960. 'The Problem of Social Cost.' *Journal of Law and Economics* 3 (October): 1–44.

Confucius. 2007. *The Analects of Confucius*, translated by Burton Watson. New York: Columbia University Press.

Deodhar, Satish. 2018. 'Indian Antecedents to Modern Economic Thought.' Working Paper No. WP 2018-01-02, Indian Institute of Management Ahmedabad.

Gneezy, Uri, and Aldo Rustichini. 2000a. 'Pay Enough or Don't Pay at All.' *Quarterly Journal of Economics* 115 (3): 791–810.

Gneezy, Uri, and Aldo Rustichini. 2000b. 'A Fine Is a Price.' *Journal of Legal Studies* 29 (1): 1–18.

Gneezy, Uri, Stephan Meier and Pedro Rey-Biel. 2011. 'When and Why Incentives (Don't) Work to Modify Behavior.' *Journal of Economic Perspectives* 25, no. 4: 191–210.

Guiso, L., P. Sapienza and L. Zingales. 2004. 'The Role of Social Capital in Financial

Development.' *American Economic Review* 94: 526–56.

Hayek, Friedrich. 1944. *The Road to Serfdom*. University of Chicago.

Maddison, A. 2007. *Contours of the World Economy I-2030AD*. Oxford University Press.

Meier, Stephan. 2007a. 'Do Subsidies Increase Charitable Giving in the Long Run? Matching Donations in a Field Experiment.' *Journal of the European Economic Association* 5 (6): 1203–22.

Meier, Stephan. 2007b. 'A Survey of Economic Theories and Field Evidence on Pro-Social Behavior.' *Economics and Psychology: A Promising New Cross-Disciplinary Field*, edited by Bruno S. Frey and Alois Stutzer. Cambridge: MIT Press. pp. 51–88.

Olivelle, Patrick. 2013. *King, Governance, and Law in Ancient India: Kauṭilya's Arthaśāstra*. Oxford, UK: Oxford University Press.

Sanyal, S. 2016. *The Ocean of Churn*. Penguin.

Sapienza, Paola, and Luigi Zingales. 2012. 'A Trust Crisis.' *International Review of Finance* 12 (2): 23–131.

Shamasastry, R (trans.). 1956. *Kautilya's Arthashastra*. Mysore: Sri Raghuvir Printing Press, Mysore.

Shamasastry, R (trans.). 1956. *Kautilya's Arthashastra*. Parimal Publications Pvt Ltd. http://tinyurl.com/25fw46xm. Accessed on 14 December 2023.

Sihag, Balbir S. 2016. 'Kautilya's Arthashastra: A Recognizable Source of the Wealth of Nations.' *Theoretical Economics Letters* 6 (1): 59–67.

Spengler, J.J. 1971. *Indian Economic Thought*. Duke University Press. Durham.

Chapter 18: Liberating the Economy

Banerjee, A, and L. Iyer. 2005. 'History, Institutions, and Economic Performance: The Legacy of Colonial Land Tenure Systems in India.' *American Economic Review* 95 (4): 1190–213.

Cunningham, S. 2011. *Understanding Market Failures in an Economic Development Context*. Volume 4. Pretoria: Mesopartner Press.

Department of Financial Services. n.d. 'Debts Recovery Tribunals/Debts Recovery Appellate Tribunals.' *Ministry of Finance*. https://tinyurl.com/5yjbb3p4. Accessed on 30 November 2023.

Gulati, Ashok, Tirtha Chatterjee and Siraj Hussain. 2018. 'Supporting Indian Farmers: Price Support or Direct Income/Investment Support?' ICRIER WP 357.

Hayek, F.A. 1945. 'The Use of Knowledge in Society.' *The American Economic Review* 35 (4): 519–30.

Press Information Bureau. 2015. 'Recommendations of High Level Committee on restructuring of FCI.' https://tinyurl.com/mrym6wzk. Accessed on 15 May 2024.

Sahay, Arvind, and Saravana Jaikumar. 2016. 'Does Pharmaceutical Price Regulation Result in Greater Access to Essential Medicines? Study of the Impact of Drug

Price Control Order on Sales Volume of Drugs in India.' IIMA Working Papers WP2016-02-01, Indian Institute of Management Ahmedabad, Research and Publication Department.

Saini, Shweta, et al. 2017. 'Indian Food and Welfare Schemes: Scope for Digitization towards Cash Transfers.' ZEF-Discussion Papers on Development Policy No. 241. doi: 10.2139/ssrn.3019115.

The Competition Act, 2002. https://tinyurl.com/4s82mbzr. Accessed on 30 November 2023.

Chapter 19: Revolutionizing Success

B.S., Sunil. 2014. 'India's Stock Market Just Confirmed: It Really Pays to Have Political Connections.' *Quartz India*.

Bertrand, Marianne, Paras Mehta and Sendhil Mullainathan. 2002. 'Ferreting Out Tunneling: An Application to Indian Business Groups.' *The Quarterly Journal of Economics* 117 (1): 121–48.

Friedman, Milton. 1999. 'Policy Forum: "Milton Friedman on Business Suicide".' *CATO Institute*. https://tinyurl.com/mrxdmky3. Accessed on 15 April 2024.

IIFL Wealth. 2019. 'IIFL Wealth-Hurun India Rich List: Here Are India's Richest in 2019; Mukesh Ambani Tops Charts 8th Year in a Row.' *360 ONE Wealth*. https://tinyurl.com/3ajhch72. Accessed on 15 April 2024.

Kant, Krishna. 2016. '1991 to 2016: How the Sensex Has Transformed in 25 Years.' *Rediff.com*. https://tinyurl.com/2wu24xtj. Accessed on 5 November 2019.

Khanna, Tarun, and Yishay Yafeh. 2007. 'Business Groups in Emerging Markets: Paragons or Parasites.' *Journal of Economic Literature* 45, no. 2: 331–72.

Rajan, Raghuram. 2014. 'Saving Credit (Talk by Dr. Raghuram G. Rajan, Governor, Reserve Bank of India at the Third Dr. Verghese Kurien Memorial Lecture at IRMA, Anand on November 25, 2014).' *Reserve Bank of India*. https://tinyurl.com/2bmbsjwr. Accessed on 15 April 2024.

Romer, Paul M. 2000. 'Should the Government Subsidize Supply or Demand in the Market for Scientists and Engineers?' Working Paper 7723, NBER Working Paper Series, Cambridge, MA.

Chapter 20: Carpe Diem

Arora, A., et al. 2011. 'Private Investment in Human Capital and Industrial Development: The Case of the Indian Software Industry.' *Dimensions of Economic Theory and Policy: Essays for Anjan Mukherji*. New Delhi: Oxford University Press. pp. 301–16

Ghani, E., W. Kerr and S. O'Connell. 2011. 'Promoting Entrepreneurship, Growth, and Job Creation.' *Reshaping Tomorrow: Is South Asia Ready for the Big Leap?*, edited by Ejaz Ghani. Oxford University Press. pp. 168–201.

Chapter 21: Innovation Forge

Acharya, V.V., R.P. Baghai and K.V. Subramanian. 2014. 'Wrongful Discharge Laws and Innovation.' *Review of Financial Studies* 27, no. 1: 301–46.

Acharya, Viral V., and Krishnamurthy V. Subramanian. 2009. 'Bankruptcy Codes and Innovation.' *Review of Financial Studies* 22, no. 12: 4949–88.

Acharya, Viral V., Ramin P. Baghai and Krishnamurthy V. Subramanian. 2013. 'Labor Laws and Innovation.' *The Journal of Law and Economics* 56, no. 4: 997–1037.

Adak, Mehmet. 2015. 'Technological Progress, Innovation and Economic Growth; the Case of Turkey.' *Procedia—Social and Behavioral Sciences* 195: 776–782.

Chava, Sudheer, et al. 2013. 'Banking Deregulation and Innovation.' *Journal of Financial Economics* 109, no. 3: 759–74.

Donou-Adonsou, F., Sokchea Lim and Samuel Mathey. 2016. 'Technological Progress and Economic Growth in Sub-Saharan Africa: Evidence from Telecommunications Infrastructure.' *International Advances in Economic Research* 22, no. 1: 65–75.

Galindo, Miguel-Ángel, and M.T. Méndez. 2014. 'Entrepreneurship, Economic Growth, and Innovation: Are Feedback Effects at Work?' *Journal of Business Research* 67, no. 5: 825–9.

Saha, Sabyasachi, and Prativa Shaw. 2018. 'A Review of R&D and Sectoral Incentives in Manufacturing in Industrialised and Emerging Economies: Lessons for "Make in India".' RIS Discussion Paper 233, Research and Information System (RIS) for Developing Countries.

Sapra, H., A. Subramanian and K.V. Subramanian. 2014. 'Corporate Governance and Innovation: Theory and Evidence.' *Journal of Financial and Quantitative Analysis* 49: 957–1003.

Chapter 22: Private Prowess

Acharya, V.V., R.P. Baghai and K.V. Subramanian. 2014. 'Wrongful Discharge Laws and Innovation.' *Review of Financial Studies* 27, no. 1: 301–46.

Adak, Mehmet. 2015. 'Technological Progress, Innovation and Economic Growth; the Case of Turkey.' *Procedia—Social and Behavioral Sciences* 195: 776–82.

Affuso, L., A. Angeriz and M. Pollitt. 2009. 'The Impact of Privatization on the Efficiency of Train Operation in Britain.' CGR Working Paper No. 28, Centre for Globalization Research School of Business and Management, Queen Mary University of London.

Berkman, Henk, Rebel A. Cole and Jiang Lawrence Fu. 2012. 'Improving Corporate Governance Where the State is the Controlling Block Holder: Evidence from China.' *The European Journal of Finance* 20, no. 7–9: 752–77. doi: 10.1080/1351847X.2012.671784.

Borisova, Ginka, and William L. Megginson. 2011. 'Does Government Ownership

Affect the Cost of Debt? Evidence from Privatization.' *Review of Financial Studies* 24, no. 8: 2693–737.

Boubakri, Narjess, et al. 2018. 'The Market Value of Government Ownership.' *Journal of Corporate Finance* 50: 44–65.

Brown, David J., John S. Earle and Almos Telegdy. 2015. 'Where Does Privatization Work? Understanding the Heterogeneity in Estimated Firm Performance Effects.' *Journal of Corporate Finance* 41: 329–62.

Brown, J. David, John S. Earle and Almos Telegdy. 2006. 'The Productivity Effects of Privatization: Longitudinal Estimates from Hungary, Romania, Russia, and Ukraine.' *Journal of Political Economy* 114, no. 1: 61–99.

Chen, Gongmeng, et al. 2008. 'Control Transfers, Privatization, and Corporate Performance: Efficiency Gains in China's Listed.' *Journal of Financial and Quantitative Analysis* 43, no. 1: 161–90. doi: 10.1017/S0022109000002787.

Galindo, Miguel-Ángel, and M.T. Méndez. 2014. 'Entrepreneurship, Economic Growth, and Innovation: Are Feedback Effects at Work?' *Journal of Business Research* 67, no. 5: 825–9.

Gan Jie, Yan Guo and Chenggang Xu. 2014. 'Decentralized Privatization and Change of Control Rights in China.' *The Review of Financial Studies* 31, no. 10: 3854–94.

Ghosh, Saibal. 2011. 'R&D in Public Enterprises.' *Science, Technology and Society* 16, no. 2: 177–90.

Gupta, Nandini. 2005. 'Partial Privatization and Firm Performance.' *The Journal of Finance* 60, no. 2: 987–1015.

Li, Bo, et al. 2016. 'Do Share Issue Privatizations Really Improve Firm Performance in China?' *SSRN*. doi: 10.2139/ssrn.2684987.

Makhija, Anil K. 2006. 'Privatization in India.' *Economic and Political Weekly* 41, no. 20: 1947–51.

Megginson, William L. 2007. 'Introduction to the Special Issue on Privatization.' *International Review of Financial Analysis* 16, no. 4: 301–3.

Megginson, William L. 2010. 'Privatization and Finance.' *Annual Review of Financial Economics* 2, no. 1: 145–74.

Megginson, William L. 2017. 'Privatization, State Capitalism, and State Ownership of Business in the 21st Century.' *Foundations and Trends in Finance* 11, no. 1–2: 1–153.

Megginson, William L., and Jeffry M Netter. 2001. 'From State to Market: A Survey of Empirical Studies on Privatization.' *Journal of Economic Literature* 39, no. 2: 321–89.

Megginson, William L., et al. 2004. 'The Choice of Private versus Public Capital Markets: Evidence from Privatizations.' *The Journal of Finance* 59, no. 6: 2835–70.

Meher, Kishor, and Jana Samiran. 2012. 'Bottom Line of Divested PSEs in Post Privatization Scenario.' *4D International Journal of Management and Science* 9, no. 2: 28–54.

Chapter 23: Private Investment

Bloom, David E., and Jeffrey G. Williamson. 1998. 'Demographic Transitions and Economic Miracles in Emerging Asia.' *The World Bank Economic Review* 12, no. 3: 419–55.

Bloom, David E., et al. 2007. 'Demographic Change, Social Security Systems, and Savings.' *Journal of Monetary Economics* 54, no. 1: 92–114.

Bosworth, Barry, and Gabriel Chodorow-Reich. 2007. 'Saving and Demographic Change: The Global Dimension.' *SSRN*. doi: 10.2139/ssrn.1299702.

Chakrabarti, Rajesh, Krishnamurthy V. Subramanian and Sesha Meka. 2017. 'Localization of FDI Flows: Evidence on Infrastructure as a Critical Determinant of FDI.' *Journal of Law, Finance and Accounting* 2, no. 1: 205–46.

Curtis, Chadwick C., Steven Lugauer and Nelson C. Mark. 2011. 'Demographic Patterns and Household Saving in China.' *American Economic Journal: Macroeconomics* 7, no. 2: 58–94.

Curtis, Chadwick C., Steven Lugauer and Nelson C. Mark. 2017. 'Demographics and Aggregate Household Saving in Japan, China, and India.' *Journal of Macroeconomics* 51, no. C: 175–91.

Fu Xiaolan and V.N. Balasubramanyam. 2005. 'Exports, Foreign Direct Investment and Employment: The Case of China.' *World Economy* 28, no. 4: 607–25.

Higgins, Matthew, and Jeffrey G. Williamson. 1997. 'Age Structure Dynamics in Asia and Dependence on Foreign Capital.' *Population and Development Review* 23, no. 2: 261–93.

Lee, Ronald, Andrew Mason and Tim Miller. 2000. 'Life Cycle Saving and the Demographic Transition: The Case of Taiwan.' *Population and Development Review* 26: 194–219.

Lin Jeffrey. 2011. 'Technological Adaptation, to Overcome Loss Aversion: A Method for Improving Legislative Outcomes.' *Organizational Behavior and Human Decision Processes* 117, no. 1: 158–67.

Perotti, Enrico C., Laixiang Sun and Liang Zou. 1999. 'State-Owned versus Township and Village Enterprises in China.' *Comparative Economic Studies* 41: 1–20.

Ramos, Gabriela. 2017. 'We Need an Empowering Narrative.' *OECD Insights*. https://tinyurl.com/42r4z4vs. Accessed on 15 April 2024.

Rodrik, Dani. 2018. 'Second Thoughts on Economics Rules.' *Journal of Economic Methodology* 25, no. 3: 1–6.

Romer, Paul. 2015. 'Mathiness in the Theory of Economic Growth.' *American Economic Review* 105, no. 5: 89–93.

Sandri, Damiano. 2014. 'Growth and Capital Flows with Risky Entrepreneurship.' *American Economic Journal: Macroeconomics* 6, no. 3: 102–23.

Wei Yingqi and V.N. Balasubramanyam. 2015. 'A Comparative Analysis of China and India's Manufacturing Sectors.' Economics Working Paper Series 2015/003,

Lancaster University Management School. https://tinyurl.com/3vpt6sky. Accessed on 15 April 2024.

Chapter 24: Make in India

'Factory Worker Salary in India.' *Economic Research Institute*. http://tinyurl.com/ms27tab5. Accessed on 15 April 2024.

Arora, Aakanksha, Mahima and Aasheerwad Dwivedi. 2021 'View: New Labour Laws Will Improve India's Ease of Doing Business Ranking.' *The Economic Times*.

Chakravarty, S., and A. Mitra. 2009. 'Is Industry Still the Engine of Growth? An Econometric Study of the Organized Sector Employment in India.' *Journal of Policy Modeling* 31, no. 1: 22–35.

Friedman, Milton. 1957. *The Permanent Income Hypothesis*. Princeton University Press.

Haq, Zia. 2023. 'Implementation of 4 Labour Codes Stalled.' *Hindustan Times*.

Job Hai. 2022. 'How to Join Swiggy Delivery Boy? Salary and Shift Hours.'

Kathuria, V., and R.R. Natarajan. 2013. 'Is Manufacturing an Engine of Growth in India in the Post-Nineties?' *Journal of South Asian Development* 8, no. 3: 385–408.

Rodrik, Dani. 2011a. 'Unconditional Convergence.' NBER Working Paper No. 17546.

Rodrik, Dani. 2011b. 'The Future of Economic Convergence.' NBER Working Paper No. 17400.

Chapter 25: A Strong Financial Sector to Fuel Private Investment

Dornbusch, R., et al. 1987. 'Korean Growth Policy.' *Brookings Papers on Economic Activity*. https://tinyurl.com/5n76jhv3. Accessed on 15 April 2024.

Economic Survey 2019–20. Volume 2. Government of India; Ministry of Finance. January 2020. pp. 20–7.

Economic Survey 2020–21. Volume 1. Government of India; Ministry of Finance. January 2021.

Gupta, P., and A. Tyagi. 2022. 'Slowdown of the Indian Economy during 2019–20: An Enigma or an Anomaly.' NCAER Working Papers 137, National Council of Applied Economic Research.

Jacobs, D., and V. Rayner. 2012. 'The Role of Credit Supply in the Australian Economy.' Research Discussion Paper 2012-02, Reserve Bank of Australia.

K. Vaidyanathan, and K.V. Subramanian. 2022. *Money: A Zero-Sum Game*. Krishnamurthy Vaidyanathan.

K. Vaidyanathan. 2014. *Credit Derivatives*. McGrawHill Education.

Vaithilingam, S., B.K. Guru and B. Shanmugam. 2003. 'Bank Lending and Economic Growth in Malaysia.' *Journal of Asia-Pacific Business* 5, no. 1: 51–69. doi: 10.1300/j098v05n01_0.

Chapter 26: Vitality Amplified

Akerlof, G. 1970. 'The Market for 'Lemons': Quality Uncertainty and the Market Mechanism.' *The Quarterly Journal of Economics* 84, no. 3: 488–500.

Anand, S., and T. Bärnighausen. 2004. 'Human Resources and Health Outcomes: Cross-Country Econometric Study.' *Lancet* 364, no. 9445: 1603–9.

Arrow, K. 1963. 'Uncertainty and the Welfare Economics of Medical Care.' *American Economic Review* 53, no. 5: 941–73.

Basu, S., et al. 2012. 'Comparative Performance of Private and Public Healthcare Systems in Low- and Middle-Income Countries: A Systematic Review.' *PLoS Med* 9, no. 6: e1001244. doi: 10.1371/journal.pmed.1001244.

Berki, S.E. 1986. 'A Look at Catastrophic Medical Expenses and the Poor.' *Health Affairs* 5:138–45.

Berman, Peter, Manjiri Bhawalkar and Rajesh Jha. 2017. 'Government Financing of Health Care in India since 2005: What Was Achieved, What Was Not and Why.' *A Report of the Resource Tracking and Management Project. Harvard TH Chan School of Public Health*, Boston, MA.

Census of India. 2020. 'Population Projections for India—2018.' Registrar-General of India.

Choudhury, Mita, and Ranjan Kumar Mohanty. 2020. 'Role of National Health Mission in Health Spending of States: Achievements and Issues.' NIPFP Working Paper 317. https://tinyurl.com/2p98435n. Accessed on 15 April 2024.

Clarke, D. 2016. 'Law, Regulation and Strategizing for Health.' *Strategizing National Health in the 21st century: A Handbook*, edited by G. Schmets, D. Rajan and S. Kadandale. Geneva: World Health Organization.

Coarasa, Jorge, Jishnu Das and Jeffrey Hammer. 2014. 'Private vs. Public: In Many Countries the Debate Should Not Be about the Source of Primary Health Care but Its Quality.' *Finance and Development* 51, no. 4: 34–6.

Ehrlich, I., and G.S. Becker. 1972. 'Market Insurance, Self-Insurance, and Self-Protection.' *Journal of Political Economy* 80, no. 4: 623–48.

Guilmoto, C.Z., and A. Dumont. 2019. 'Trends, Regional Variations, and Socioeconomic Disparities in Cesarean Births in India, 2010–2016.' *JAMA Netw Open* 2, no. 3: e190526. doi: 10.1001/jamanetworkopen.2019.0526.

Hölmstrom, B. 1979. 'Moral Hazard and Observability.' *Bell Journal of Economics* 10, no. 1: 74–91.

Indian Council of Medical Research, Public Health Foundation of India, and Institute for Health Metrics and Evaluation. 2017. *India: Health of the Nation's States—The India State-Level Disease Burden Initiative.*' New Delhi, India.

Jadhav, Nitin, et al. 2019. 'A Report on Understanding Factors for Under-Spending of National Health Mission's Funds since Last 5 Years in Maharashtra.' *Research Gate*. doi: 10.13140/RG.2.2.34346.57284.

Kane, S., and M. Calnan. 2017. 'Erosion of Trust in the Medical Profession in India: Time for Doctors to Act.' *International Journal of Health Policy and Management* 6, no. 1: 5–8. doi: 10.15171/ijhpm.2016.143.

Kapoor, Sunil K., et al. 2012. 'How Did the TB Patients Reach DOTS Services in Delhi? A Study of Patient Treatment Seeking Behavior.' *PLoS One* 7, no. 8. doi: 10.1371/journal.pone.0042458.

Kruk, M., et al. 2018. 'Mortality Due to Low-Quality Health Systems in the Universal Health Coverage Era: A Systematic Analysis of Amenable Deaths in 137 Countries.' *Lancet* 392: 2203–12.

Kumar, C., and R. Prakash. 2011. 'Public-Private Dichotomy in Utilization of Health Care Services in India.' Consilience 5. doi: 10.7916/consilience.v0i5.4527.

Ministry of Statistics & Programme Implementation. 2019. *Periodic Labour Force Survey 2017–18*. Government of India, New Delhi. https://tinyurl.com/yc7xbxda. Accessed on 15 April 2024.

Mohpal, Aakash, Owen Smith and Sheena Chhabra. 2020. *Quality of Care in PM-JAY: A First Look at Unplanned Readmissions and Mortality*. PM-JAY Policy Brief 7. https://tinyurl.com/3vtr6yme. Accessed on 15 April 2024.

O'Donnell, O., et al. 2007. 'The Incidence of Public Spending on Healthcare: Comparative Evidence from Asia.' *World Bank Economic Review* 21: 93–123.

OECD. 2015. *Health at a Glance*. https://tinyurl.com/2s38mxkh. Accessed on 15 April 2024.

Pauly, M.V. 1968. 'The Economics of Moral Hazard: Comment.' *American Economic Review* 58, no. 3: 531–7.

Russo, Pierantonio. 2015. 'Cost Efficiency plus Quality Measures: Prescription for the Indian Healthcare Sector.' *ISBInsight*. https://tinyurl.com/2dw2k942. Accessed on 15 April 2024.

Schweppenstedde, et al. 2014. *Regulating Quality and Safety of health and Social Care: International Experiences*. Santa Monica, CA: RAND Corporation. https://tinyurl.com/3yub6kfx. Accessed on 15 April 2024.

Van Doorslaer, E., et al. 2006. 'Effects of Payments for Health Care on Poverty Estimates in 11 Countries in Asia: An Analysis of Household Survey Data.' *Lancet* 368: 1357–64.

Wagstaff, Adam, Patrick Eozenou and Marc Smitz. 2019. 'Out-of-Pocket Expenditures on Health: A Global Stocktake.' Policy Research Working Paper 8808, World Bank Group. https://tinyurl.com/mtc8ee52. Accessed on 15 May 2024.

WHO and The World Bank. 2020. *Global Monitoring Report on Financial Protection in Health 2019*. https://tinyurl.com/vsj2hx8v. Accessed on 15 April 2024.

WHO. 2001. 'Investing in Health for Economic Development.' https://tinyurl.com/ys6fdhat. Accessed on 15 April 2024.

WHO. 2010. *World Health Report 2010–Health Systems Financing: The Path to Universal Coverage*. https://tinyurl.com/kudycb8x. Accessed on 15 April 2024.

WHO. 2019. *Global Strategy on Human Resources for Health: Workforce 2030*. Geneva: World Health Organization.

Chapter 27: Knowledge Catalyst

Azim Premji Foundation. 2017. *Teacher Absenteeism Study: Field Studies in Education*.

CENTA. Insights on Teacher Competencies in India from 4 years of CENTA TPO-CENTA.

Dhawan, A. 2014. 'Restoring Dignity to the Teaching Profession in India.' *Ideas for India*. https://tinyurl.com/3sex94w7. Accessed on 11 May 2024.

Dutta, S. 2017. 'Educational Inequality in India: Evidence from 71st NSSO Round.' *Journal of Educational Planning and Administration* XXXI (1): 289–306.

KPMG and CII. 2017. *Improving learning Outcomes by Raising In-Class Teacher Effectiveness*.

Krishnamurthy Subramanian. 2023. 'Their Bhasha, Their Future.' *The Times of India*.

McKinsey & Company. 2010. *Closing the Talent Gap: Attracting and Retaining Top-Third Graduates to Careers in Teaching*.

McKinsey & Company. 2013. *Education to Employment: Designing a System that Works*.

Muralidharan, Karthik, Abhijeet Singh and Alejandro J. Ganimian. 2019. 'Disrupting Education? Experimental Evidence on Technology-Aided Instruction in India.' *American Economic Review* 109, no. 4: 1426–60.

Muralidharan, Karthik. 2019. 'Reforming the Indian School Education System.' *What the Economy Needs Now*, edited by Abhijit Banerjee, Gita Gopinath, Raghuram Rajan and Mihir Sharma. Juggernaut.

Sanders, W.L., and J.C. Rivers. 1996. *Cumulative and Residual Effects of Teachers on Future Student Academic Achievement*. Tennessee: University of Tennessee Value-Added Research and Assessment Center.

Sangeetha G. 2018. 'Living the Indian Dream.' *The Asian Age*.

Sarkar, Kanishka. 2024. 'Female Enrollment Ratio in Higher Education Up Four Times in 20 Years: Indian Economy Report.' *CNBCTV18*.

van der Sluis, Justin, Mirjam van Praag and Wim Vijverberg. 2005. 'Entrepreneurship Selection and Performance: A Meta-Analysis of the Impact of Education in Developing Economies.' *The World Bank Economic Review* 19, no. 2: 225–61.

World Bank Group. 2019. *World Development Report 2019: The Changing Nature of Work*.

INDEX